OZ CLARKE'S
WORLD OF WINE

OZ CLARKE'S
WORLD OF WINE

A GRAND TOUR OF THE GREAT WINE REGIONS

STERLING EPICURE
New York

An Imprint of Sterling Publishing Co., Inc.
1166 Avenue of the Americas
New York, NY 10036

Sterling Epicure and the distinctive
Sterling logo are registered trademarks
of Sterling Publishing Co., Inc.

Text © 2017 by Oz Clarke

All rights reserved. No part of this
publication may be reproduced, stored
in a retrieval system, or transmitted in
any form or by any means (including
electronic, mechanical, photocopying,
recording, or otherwise) without prior
written permission from the publisher.

ISBN 978-1-4549-2812-6

Distributed in Canada by Sterling
Publishing Co., Inc.
c/o Canadian Manda Group,
664 Annette Street
Toronto, Ontario, M6S 2C8, Canada

For information about custom editions,
special sales, and premium and
corporate purchases, please contact
Sterling Special Sales at 800-805-5489
or specialsales@sterlingpublishing.com

Manufactured in China

10 9 8 7 6 5 4 3 2 1

www.sterlingpublishing.com

A complete list of image credits
appears on page 320.

*Captions: Pages 2–3 View from Clayridge
Vineyard to Cloudy Bay Barracks Vineyard
in the Upper Omaka Valley, Marlborough,
New Zealand.
Pages 4–5 Sorting harvested Merlot
grapes in the vineyard of Château
Haut-Brion, Pessac-Léognan, Bordeaux,
France.*

For wine recommendations, special
offers, and news on Oz's upcoming
books and events, visit www.
ozclarke.com and sign up to the Oz
Clarke newsletter. Follow Oz on
Twitter @OzClarke

Contents

About Wine

Sometimes I stop and ask myself: When was the last time I had a glass of bad wine? Not wine that is out of condition, or corked wine, or wine that I've left hanging around in the kitchen for too long—but poor, stale, badly made, unattractive wine? Unless I've been extremely unlucky in the previous month or so, I won't be able to remember. The standard of basic winemaking is now so high that a wine drinker need never taste a wine that is not at very least clean, honest, and drinkable. It wasn't like that a generation ago. Then, I sometimes idly try to work out how many different grape varieties from how many different wine regions I've tried during a typical wine-taster's week. At a recent tasting, I counted the number of grape varieties contributing to an exciting array of wines. There were seventy different grape varieties from places as familiar as France, Italy, and Spain and as far flung as Tasmania, Brazil, New York, and Bolivia. It wasn't like that a generation ago, either.

For me, the thrilling thing about this modern world is that we now have choice—endless choice that gets bigger every year. With choice, comes excitement, challenge, but also confusion. But that's why this book is here to help you, so you can make sense of this cornucopia of flavors and delights that extends from the most famous and expensive wines of Bordeaux and Burgundy to the first nervous offerings of new vineyards from unsung valleys.

We, as wine drinkers, should take some credit for this transformation. If we were not prepared to try new things, to take some risk with unknown areas and unknown grapes, winemakers would neither bother to resurrect old areas and plant new ones nor bother to spread their activities beyond a few popular grape varieties. If we weren't prepared to be adventurous, wine companies would flood us with a sea of Chardonnay, Sauvignon Blanc, Cabernet, Merlot, and Shiraz/Syrah, gaudy labels and fantasy names bedecking wines that make no attempt to taste different or individual. But you and I would be missing out on so much.

We are in the midst of a revolution in wine that is bringing together the best of the new and the old. Traditionalists are realizing that maybe the old ways are not always the best, that they can learn something from the brash, younger generation. The modernists are quietly laying aside their reliance on cultured yeasts, scientific formulas, and refrigerated stainless steel tanks, and they're listening with respect to the old farmers with their gnarled vines and their quiet, unhurried ways of letting a wine make itself as it will. Yet, with all this hectic change, the eternal truths of what makes wine good and special have never been more evident. Every good winemaker knows that the final limiting factor on wine quality is the quality of the grapes. Every winemaker knows that some regions grow better grapes than others, some areas within those regions are more suitable, some small patches of the very same field are better than others, and some growers care more about their work and will always produce the finest fruit. I unashamedly admit that I am more excited by the vineyard, by nature's effect on the final flavor of wine, than I am by a winery, however full of state-of-the-art gadgets it may be.

If I'm in Côte-Rôtie, I want to climb to the highest point on the slope from whose grapes the juice always runs blackest and sweetest. I want to feel the poor stony soil crumble beneath my feet and touch the twisted, tortured trunk of the vine that each year struggles to survive on this barren slope and ripen its tiny crop. If I'm in Margaux, I want to tread the warm, well-drained gravel outcrops and then step off into the sullen clay swamps nearby, and, with this single step, I'll know why the gravel-grown grapes are precious and the clay-clogged ones are not. I want to see the Andes water gushing down into the fertile vineyards of Chile's Maipo Valley. I want to feel the howling mists chill me to the bone in California's Carneros and then feel the warm winds of New Zealand's Marlborough tugging at my hair. I want it all to make sense.

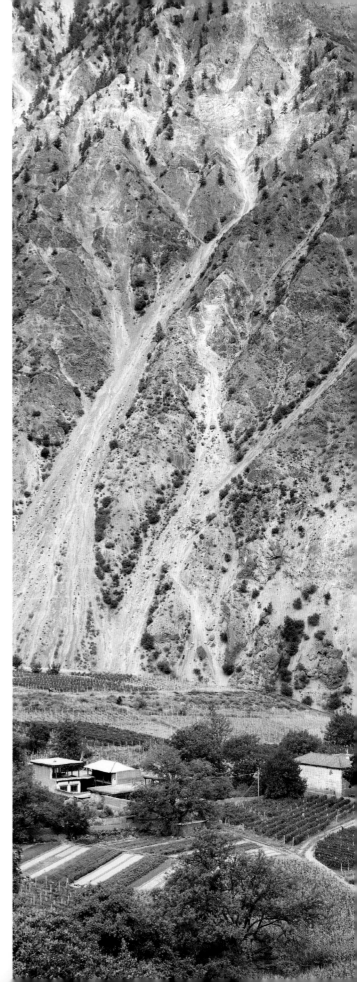

I want to take you to the oldest wine regions on the earth and the newest. I want to discuss the most common grape varieties and the rarest. I want to talk about styles of wine that have hardly changed for eight thousand years, and about styles that seem to have been invented only yesterday. Fashion does play a big part in wine. A generation ago, we lauded the rich, heady exotic Chardonnays of Australia's Hunter Valley or California's Napa. Now we crave the savory, lean offerings from Australia's Yarra Valley or California's Sonoma Coast. A generation ago we praised the light and often feeble attempts to ape Burgundy that marked the early Pinot Noirs of Oregon and New Zealand. Now we cheer their self-confident and definitely non-Burgundian Pinot Noirs with far greater conviction.

In this age, when change has come faster than ever before in the world of wine, it is certain that within the decade some vineyards now in decline will be fired by a new confidence and popularity; others now considered so chic will be struggling in the tough real world as their first flush of fame dissolves; and yet others, at this moment mere pastureland or rocky mountainside, will become flourishing vineyards producing wines whose flavors may be entirely different from anything yet achieved on this planet. All of these I want to share with you in this book.

China is now a serious wine-producing nation. These vineyards are near Ximangtong village in the LanCang River Valley, Yunnan Province. They are way up in the Himalayan foothills, and despite serious challenges with infrastructure, Yunnan could prove to be China's best vineyard region yet.

The Story of Wine

WINE IS AS OLD AS CIVILIZATION, probably older, while the vine itself is rooted deeply in prehistory. There was at least one species, *Vitis sezannesis*, growing in Tertiary time, just a mere sixty million years ago. I don't expect that *sezannesis* ever turned into wine—not on purpose, anyway—but aeons later its descendant *Vitis silvestris* surely did (and still does in Bosnia-Herzegovina, where it is called the Iosnica). By the Quaternary era, around 8000 BC, the European vine, *Vitis vinifera* (from which nearly all the world's wines are now made), had come on the scene.

The metamorphosis of grape into wine was almost certainly a happy accident. Imagine Stone Age people storing their harvest of hedge-growing wild grapes, *Vitis silvestris*, in a rocky hollow; some of the grapes squash, juice oozes out, and, in a flush of autumnal sunshine, begins to ferment. The result—however unpalatable to today's tutored taste—must have cheered the chill of cave-dwelling and provided a few much-needed laughs at the onset of pre-central heating winter. Similarly, in the houses of ancient Persia, Mesopotamia, Armenia, Babylon, the occasional jars of raisined grapes, ready for winter eating, surely began unexpectedly to bubble and froth and magic themselves into a sweet, heady drink. From such haphazard beginnings, wine evolved into an adjunct of civilization; the Georgians were probably at it around 6000 BC. Ancient paintings and sculptures show that both Egypt and China were making and drinking it around 3000 BC, but it was really the Greeks who first developed viticulture on a commercial scale and turned vinification into a craft. Their wines tended to be so richly concentrated that they were normally drunk diluted: two parts wine to five of water. They were syrupy sweet—yet with a sting of salt or a reek of resin, cadged from casks washed out in seawater or from amphoras lined with pitch pine. Through their trading travels, the Greeks spread their vine-and-wine knowledge around the Mediterranean and were particularly influential in Italy, to the benefit of the world's wine drinkers ever since.

A third-century AD mosaic from Roman Spain showing treading grapes in a shallow trough or lagar. *Some Spanish vineyards still use them.*

THE ROMANS

By the middle of the first century BC, vineyards criss-crossed the Italian landscape from southernmost Sicily to the Alpine foothills, and wine was both an everyday beverage and major export. More importantly, as the empire gained ground, so did the grape. In all their newly won territories, the Romans established vineyards—climate permitting (and even if it didn't look too promising they persevered, as in the Mosel, where they used straw fires, between the vines, to combat fall frosts). Today, Europe's traditional wine regions—Bordeaux and Burgundy, Rioja and Rhine, Loire and Languedoc—all can claim to have had Roman foundations.

Most of Rome's wine, whether made at home or in the provinces, was a somewhat plebeian tipple: tart and tough for quaffing young before it turned to vinegar. Often its taste was softened by the addition of honey, herbs, or spices, which also acted as preservatives. But not the top-notch wines. These, we must suppose, were noble creations, aged for a decade or more. The legendary Falernian—according to Pliny, so fiery it would catch light from a spark—reached its prime at twenty years yet happily would survive one hundred. The Romans' ability to age wine—primarily in earthenware amphoras (sealed with pitch or plaster) but later in barrels—represented a significant development in winemaking. But it was short-lived, doomed to disappear with the empire.

Because the art of amphora-making was lost and wine could no longer be matured—barrels were mostly for transport—quality suffered. But that aside, the Dark Ages were not as murky, in wine terms, as they might have been. In fact, the thrusting barbarians, ever thirsty, not only maintained existing vineyards but also extended them, as in Burgundy, where Germanic settlers cleared the forests and replanted them with vines. But throughout medieval times, the guardian of Western culture and civilization—Rome's legacy—was the Church; so, for one thousand years, monasteries largely nurtured Europe's wine heritage. They were expert agriculturalists able to study and develop vine and wine sciences; they were also powerful landowners, whose expansionist policies often involved acquiring established vineyards or planting new ones. The monks produced wine for sacramental purposes, for their own use—fairly frugal in most orders—but primarily for sale; along with other farm produce, it was a major source of income. In the absence of storage know-how, the wines themselves were mostly light and fresh—ripe for quick consumption. At that time, Burgundy was prized for drinking within the year and Bordeaux considered the better for being younger—the exact opposite of today.

WINE TIMELINE

6000 BC It looks as though the first wine was made in Georgia eight thousand years ago.

2000–146 BC Wine culture really got moving with the Greeks—and their wine god, Dionysus.

300 BC–AD 200 The Romans established most of Europe's greatest vineyard regions.

1100s–1200s Without the monasteries, wine culture might have died in the Dark Ages.

1154–1453 The birth of claret—England owned Aquitaine (Southwest France) for three houndred years and created Bordeaux's wine trade.

1500s–1600s The Germans developed the great Riesling grape during the sixteenth century.

1587 Sherry (Sack) became popular in England after Sir Francis Drake commandeered the king of Spain's barrels.

1632 You can't successfully transport or age wine in fragile glass. New "English" glass was strong.

1662 Christopher Merret in London first demonstrated how to make sparkling wine.

1681 Corkscrews—the first reference to a "steel worm" for extracting corks.

1716 The first legal attempts to delimit a wine area—in Chianti.

1740s The first airtight corks meant that wine now could be aged successfully in bottle.

1740s Modern wine bottles had straight sides so that they could be "laid down" to age.

1801 Chaptal, Napoleon's interior minister, first gave grape-growing and winemaking a scientific base in his famous *Traité*.

1843 Barolo is often thought of as Italy's greatest wine, but it only began being made in 1843.

1855 A classification of Bordeaux red and sweet wines and still in use today.

1855–1870s The concept of château—the development of the idea of single vineyards calling themselves "château," or "castle."

1857–1860s Louis Pasteur explained the roles of yeast in wine fermentation and of oxygen in wine spoilage.

1860 Wine labels—until 1860, wine bottles didn't have labels, because glue and suitable paper were not available.

1860 Murrieta and Riscal—the great Rioja wine region came to life with the establishment of these two companies.

1863 Phylloxera—a devastating infestation by an aphid that eventually attacked most of the world's vines.

1920–1933 Prohibition, the Great Experiment—actually the Great Failure—in trying to stop Americans from drinking alcohol.

1924 Bottling wine at the property was the only way to make sure it was genuine. Château Mouton-Rothschild was the first to do it.

1935 Appellation Contrôlée—France's commendable attempt to stop wine fraud by delimiting wine regions and their permitted grape varieties.

1936 The establishment of Cabernet Sauvignon as Napa Valley's great red wine variety by the Beaulieu winery.

A gradual progression from the bottle simply being a serving vessel (filled from the cask and taken to the table) to its modern, straight-sided manifestation (suitable for aging and for laying on its side).

CORKS AND BOTTLES

The role of the Church declined with the Reformation— at least in northern Europe—but this did not convulse the wine world half as much as the discovery of the usefulness of corks a century later. For the first time since the Roman era, wine could be stored and aged successfully. Throughout the Middle Ages, it had been kept in cask, which presented a dual handicap: first, too long in wood could rob a wine of all its fruit; secondly, once the cask was broached, the wine inevitably deteriorated unless drunk within a few days. The bottle, with its much smaller capacity, solved the former problem by providing a neutral, nonporous material that allowed for wine to age in a different, subtler way and removed the latter problem by providing sealed containers of a manageable size for a single session's drinking.

However, the cork-and-bottle revolution wasn't an instant success. Bottles back then were so bulbous they only stood upright, which meant the corks eventually dried out and let in air. But, by the mid-1700s, longer, flat-sided bottles were designed that would lie down, so contact with the wine kept their corks moist. Winemaking took on a new dimension. It became worthwhile for a winemaker to try to excel, wines from distinct plots of land could be compared for their qualities, and the most exciting could be classified and separated from the run-of-the-mill wines. Today's great names of Bordeaux, Burgundy, and the Rhine first began to be noticed.

In the early nineteenth century, Europe seemed one massive vineyard. In Italy, eight out of ten people were earning their living from wine, and in France vast plantings rolled southward from Paris. *Vitis vinifera* had emigrated—

thanks to explorers, colonists, and missionaries. It went to Latin America with the Spaniards, to South Africa with French Huguenots, and to Australia with the English. Could anything halt its triumphal progress?

Yes, phylloxera. Phylloxera is an aphid that feeds on and destroys *vinifera* roots. It came from North America in the 1860s and, by the turn of the century, had destroyed most of the world's vineyards. The solution, grafting *vinifera* on to American rootstocks—the phylloxera-resistant *Vitis riparia*—was expensive. The most immediate effect in Europe was that only the best sites were replanted, and the total area under vines shrank dramatically.

The end of the nineteenth century was a distressing time for wine. The phylloxera aphid was relentlessly continuing its devastation of the world's vineyards which continues to this day. This brought about chaos in Europe, where wine was an important part of the national economy of many countries. Fraud and counterfeiting of wine became almost universal, and this led in the 1930s to the establishment of France's appellation contrôlée laws. There had been efforts to delimit vineyard areas before—Chianti and Portugal's Douro had both done it—but the French laws have been followed and copied around the world in an attempt to guarantee authenticity. Our obsession with authenticity and provenance grew from the chaos of the first part of the twentieth century.

By now, science was making an enormous difference in the winery and in the vineyard. Louis Pasteur had unraveled the secret of yeasts in the 1860s as well as solved the problem of endemic spoilage in wine. Bordeaux, led by Château Mouton-Rothschild in 1924, had pioneered bottling wine at source to improve quality and to stop it from being adulterated. In Bordeaux in the

1950s, Émile Peynaud finally worked out the malolactic fermentation that causes wine to undergo a second fermentation. Wine schools were becoming professional centers, such as Montpellier in France and Geisenheim in Germany.

But the most important influence on wine in the second half of the twentieth century was the arrival of the Californians and Australians as major players. They had two highly influential wine schools, Davis in California and Roseworthy in Australia, both of which preached control at all stages of fermentation temperature, hygiene, and maturation conditions. Stainless steel tanks became widespread, and producers enthusiastically adopted the use of oak barrels for aging; indeed, the flavor of oak in wine is often more evident now than the flavor of the grape variety, more's the pity. But the New World believed in single-variety wines—especially Chardonnay and Cabernet Sauvignon—and began labeling their bottles accordingly, simplifying in one stroke the way wines were presented to the public. Californians and Australians also arrived in droves in Europe, partly to learn the secrets of the classic wine regions but also to import their New World philosophy. The "flying winemaker"—a New World winemaker employed to resuscitate moribund European vineyards and wineries—became a common sight, and transformed the quality of basic wine across Europe.

The result is that nowadays we need hardly ever drink sour, faulty wine. Admittedly, there has been an explosion of banal "branded" wines in the twenty-first century, but at least they are consistent, and for those who want something more exciting, there has never been a better moment than now to be a wine lover.

1949 Émile Peynaud ushers in the modern, science-based world of winemaking.

1951 The first vintage of Grange Hermitage, which became Australia's greatest and most famous wine.

1950–1960s The Bordeaux effect—the use of Bordeaux methods and Bordeaux grape varieties spread around the world.

1961 Ukrainian Konstantin Frank established *vinifera* grape varieties in New York State.

1963 A future without glass—alternative containers for wine. Tetra Briks and wine bag-in-boxes lead the way.

1964 Gallo's Hearty Burgundy was the first of the mass-market table wine brands—and it was good.

1966 Robert Mondavi founded the first new winery in the Napa Valley since Prohibition.

1968 Italy breaks the mold—Sassicaia Cabernet Sauvignon from Tuscany ushers in the modern era in Italy.

1960s–1970s The Burgundy effect—Burgundy's white grape, Chardonnay, spread around the world, followed more erratically by the red Pinot Noir.

1970s The development of mass-market wine brands worldwide.

1974 The first Beaujolais Nouveau race and the birth of the "new red wine" craze.

1975 White Zinfandel is pink, it's often called "blush," and it's a little sweet. It all began in 1975.

1976 The Judgment of Paris—the first time that New World wines beat French wines in a famous blind tasting.

1978 Parker Points—Robert M. Parker Jr. began his *Wine Advocate*, scoring wines out of one hundred.

1979 Opus One—the joint venture in California between Robert Mondavi and Philippe de Rothschild of Mouton-Rothschild.

1980s Varietal labeling—labeling a wine according to its grape variety dramatically simplified understanding wine for consumers.

1983 The first vintage I tasted of Montana Wines Marlborough Sauvignon Blanc. Its outrageous flavors blew me away.

1987 Flying winemakers—New World winemakers, usually Australian—who transformed the quality of Europe's basic wines.

1980s–1990s International consultants—nowadays most top wineries worldwide employ a consultant, and the top ones work on several continents. This is when it became popular.

1990s Cabernet conquers the world—it is now the most planted variety in the world. This is when it really took off.

1991 Canadian icewine—Canada made itself famous overnight with its extraordinary sweet icewines.

1998 Nyetimber from Sussex in England wins the trophy for the best sparkling wine in the world.

2000s Natural wine—the new century brings an increased interest in completely noninterventionist winemaking.

2000 Screw caps—The movement to stop cork-tainted wine by using screw caps kicks off in Australia and New Zealand.

2011 China becomes one of the most important wine-consuming and wine-producing countries in the world.

2014 Fraud and the trial of Rudy Kurniawan. The counterfeiting of old wine is finally exposed as a serious worldwide problem.

The Modern Picture

A COUPLE OF THOUSAND YEARS AGO, this map of the world of wine would have looked very different, with both winemaking and consumption being highest in the Middle East and the Eastern Mediterranean, and Greece and Italy not far behind. The rest of Western Europe hardly would have registered at all—and the New World hadn't yet been discovered. The adoption of Islam, with its ban on alcohol, by most Middle Eastern and North African countries has meant that, although vineyards still flourish there, hardly any produce wine grapes, and the center of wine production has shifted to Western Europe, mainly to Italy, France, and Spain. But the greatest growth today lies in the New World—in South America, South Africa, and Australasia—and most recently in China, which now has the second biggest vineyard area in the world. The vineyards outside Europe now account for 35 percent of the world's total grapes made into wine.

The question is, of course, who is going to drink the stuff? Consumption, which was generally falling in the mid-1990s, is creeping up again, generally outside Europe, but not yet fast enough to keep pace with production. Countries such as Argentina, South Africa, France, Italy, and Spain make far more wine than the locals will drink, and the current picture worldwide is that 10–20 percent more wine is made each year than is drunk. There are countries, such as Great Britain and Canada, that recorded significant year-on-year increases in wine consumption but have eased up; while America is now the biggest global consumer of wine, edging ahead of France and Italy, whose consumption continues to drop. It is the huge population of China that remains the big unknown. If this rapidly developing nation raised its per capita wine consumption to even one-tenth of that of America, then no one will to need worry about a global surplus. It's a changing world out there.

At the end of the twentieth century and into the present one, we saw steep declines in European vineyard acreage, often encouraged by national governments and the European Union. Those declines have now stabilized. Production is growing again—in spite of EU policies to control the situation. But let's look at the Spanish region of Castilla-La Mancha as an example of what is actually happening. The region's vineyards used to cover nearly 1,383,700 acres, around half of all Spain's vineyards. Now that figure is closer to 1,000,000 acres; but, if anything, the area now produces more wine, not less, and of a significantly higher quality. Partly, this is due to planting better grape varieties, but they still have 350,000 acres of the extremely neutral white Airén planted. Mostly, it is due to managing the vineyards more efficiently and introducing irrigation, which has been sort of legal here since 1996. The result is that some vineyards can quadruple their yields with no trouble at all. When irrigation becomes legal in southern France and southern Italy (as it surely will), yields will shoot up there, too. It is already being used on an ad hoc or experimental basis.

In the New World, there are no restrictions on planting, and the area under vine is growing fast to meet increasing export demands: Australia had 222,400 acres in 1997 and now has more than 333,600 acres. America has the best part of 1,000,000 acres. Chile's vineyard land, having steadily declined since the 1970s, is also on the increase again, thanks to successful exports. The decline of the huge vineyard area of Argentina has reversed, and South Africa's and New Zealand's vineyard areas are expanding slightly. Add to this the fact that none of the New World countries has regulations restricting irrigation and yields, unlike Europe, and you end up with large-scale production increases.

Indeed, if you look at where vineyard expansion and wine consumption have been most positive, it is in the New World and in the countries of Northern Europe, for whom the wine revolution that began in the 1980s is now a part of everyday life. (Their tiny vineyards have greatly expanded, too, with some decent results.)

The wine we are drinking is different. Some of the wines that are most popular now were of no great consequence a generation ago. Prosecco has become phenomenally popular worldwide as a sparkling style; English fizz is now sought instead of being thought of as a joke; Champagne is reacting to global warming by offering far more single-grower Champagnes now ripe enough to sell unblended. Rosé—and particularly, rosé de Provence—is no longer regarded as an expensive joke but as a category making up more than 10 percent of the world's wine. Sauvignon Blanc has become more popular, while Chardonnay has eased up, but this is largely because the flavor of oak that captivated us a generation ago, particularly when applied to Chardonnay, is now far less popular. Riesling is still not popular, but Pinot Grigio is especially popular, and Italian whites in general are trendy, whereas previously they were regarded as little more than mouthwash.

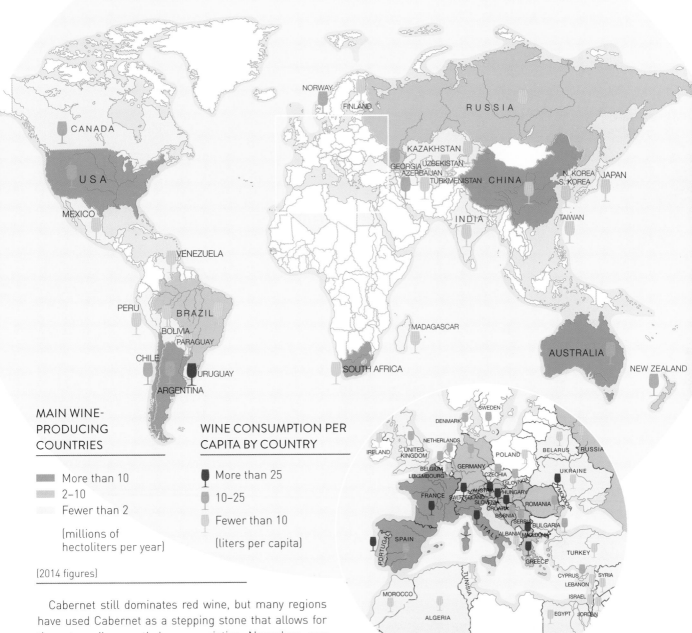

MAIN WINE-PRODUCING COUNTRIES

■ More than 10

■ 2–10

□ Fewer than 2

(millions of hectoliters per year)

(2014 figures)

WINE CONSUMPTION PER CAPITA BY COUNTRY

🍷 More than 25

🍷 10–25

🍷 Fewer than 10

(liters per capita)

Cabernet still dominates red wine, but many regions have used Cabernet as a stepping stone that allows for them to rediscover their own varieties. Nowadays, any country can offer wine made from its own particular grape varieties and find enough people to give it a try. Vineyard regions that had no reputation have developed good niche reputations by concentrating on their specialities: Virginia with its Viognier, New York with its Riesling, Brazil with its Moscatos and fizz, Uruguay with Tannat. Twenty years ago no one would have predicted the worldwide success story that is Argentine Malbec. Pinot Noir was still being talked of as a difficult variety that only Burgundy could grow. Now Chile, Australia, South Africa, Oregon, and Canada would dispute that, and California and New Zealand have half a dozen areas each making individualistic styles.

We have never been more technologically in charge, and understandably there has been a reaction toward natural yeasts, organic and biodynamic vineyards, and no-intervention wine styles epitomized by the "natural" and "orange" wine movements. As China finally steps into the wine ring, both as a producer and as a consumer, who knows what effect this will have in the next decade?

Grape Varieties

Most of the world's leading grapes end up with just one generally accepted name. However, the great Syrah or Shiraz grape has two names, Syrah being the French version and Shiraz the Australian one. Under either name, it makes some of the world's most richly flavored reds and the wines usually choose one name or the other, according to whether producers feel their style is restrained (Syrah) or rumbustious (Shiraz).

THERE ARE THOUSANDS AND THOUSANDS of grape varieties in the world. So why does it often feel as if you're being offered a choice of only Chardonnay or Cabernet Sauvignon when you buy a bottle of wine? How come those thousands sometimes seem to have been narrowed down to two? There are several answers. Most grape varieties are used for dessert grapes or raisins, or are rarely grown, or are the wrong species for winemaking. Of the thousand or so varieties that are at all significant for wine, only about thirty have international relevance, which leaves hundreds of obscure, but possibly excellent, local varieties to be discovered by the adventurous wine drinker.

Virtually all those one-thousand varieties are of the same species, *Vitis vinifera*, the species most people mean when they refer to wine vines. Yet *vinifera* is only one branch of the vine family; there are dozens of others growing in diverse climates all over the world, from the *Vitis amurensis* of Siberia to the *Vitis cariboa* of the tropics. They all produce grapes—indeed, America's first settlers made wines from the native *Vitis labrusca*, *Vitis riparia*, and *Vitis berlandieri*. The flavor of these wines has often been described as foxy, although a cross between hawthorn blossom and nail polish might be more accurate, which just sounds plain weird. You can still taste these wines in parts of North America, in Austria, and on the island of Madeira. Some are okay—but you can see why *vinifera* won the day.

It was only a few decades ago that Chardonnay was considered to be a Burgundian or Champagne grape; now it's grown in almost every wine region of the world with aspirations. Such movements of vines are not new—merely faster than they used to be. Vine cuttings have been transported vast distances over the centuries. Missionaries took cuttings from Spain to the Americas. The Syrah of the Rhône Valley and Australia (where it is called Shiraz) is believed to have come from Shiraz in Persia. Many of the vines we think of as Italian are, in fact, Greek in origin.

Why would people bother to take cuttings of a favorite grape variety to a country that probably already had plenty of its own vines? Because it has always been recognized that the crucial factor in the flavor of a wine is grape variety. Every grape has its own flavor, although most need specific climatic conditions to give their best. Thus, Cabernet Sauvignon grown in too cold a climate produces thin, grassy wine; in too hot a climate, the wine risks being baked and raisiny. But when the worldwide movement of vines creates a chance combination of right vine, right climate, and right soil, that's when classic wine styles are established.

TOP GRAPE PLANTINGS

GRAPE VARIETY
GLOBAL AREA 2014

 1. Cabernet Sauvignon
716,830 acres

 2. Merlot
660,188 acres

 3. Airén
623,605 acres

 4. Tempranillo
574,670 acres

 5. Chardonnay
491,228 acres

 6. Syrah
488,548 acres

 7. Grenache/Garnacha/Cannonau
456,490 acres

 8. Trebbiano Toscano
274,835 acres

 9. Sauvignon Blanc
272,157 acres

 10. Pinot Noir
214,146 acres

RED GRAPES

CABERNET FRANC

An underrated grape often overshadowed by Cabernet Sauvignon. Initially thought of as a blending partner in Bordeaux for Cabernet Sauvignon and Merlot, and as a varietal in the cool Loire Valley due to its ability to ripen early, it is now producing deep, raspberry-flavored wines in places as diverse as Argentina, Brazil, Canada, Chile, and Virginia.

CABERNET SAUVIGNON

The world's most famous and most widely planted grape variety. Its success is partly because it is Bordeaux's leading variety, and since Bordeaux is the world's leading wine area, new areas worldwide looked to Bordeaux for inspiration. It is also an adaptable grape, making wine that is recognizable through its black currant and black cherry flavors and serious tannic framework almost wherever you grow it. Blended in Bordeaux, it is frequently made as a single varietal elsewhere.

GRENACHE NOIR

Also known as Garnacha Tinta, this was until recently the world's most planted variety mostly because of its vast plantings in Spain. It is also important in southern France and, to a far lesser extent, in places such as Italy, North Africa, Australia, and California. Capable of especially high sugar levels in warm conditions, it is used mostly for blending, as in Châteauneuf-du-Pape.

MALBEC

This vine is now associated largely with Argentina, where it makes lush, plummy, violet-scented wines. Its homeland was Bordeaux, where its job was primarily to soften Cabernet Sauvignon. In Cahors, Malbec (here known as Cot or Auxerrois) can produce deep, damsony but tough wine. Chile and Australia do well with Malbec.

MERLOT

This red grape, with its rich, plummy fruit, its fondness for oak aging, and its tendency to mature in bottle relatively quickly, is a natural partner for Cabernet Sauvignon. On its own, it has become so fashionable simply because it's easy to drink: it is supple, luscious, low in tannin, and dark in color. With Cabernet Sauvignon, it forms the basis of the Bordeaux blend in Bordeaux and around the world. It can ripen too quickly in hot climates and give too much crop in fertile soil. Even so, on its own, it can be found almost everywhere.

Cabernet Sauvignon

NEBBIOLO

Nebbiolo is regarded as one of the great grapes of the world on very scant evidence—the small number of outstanding Barolo and Barbaresco wines made in Italy's Piedmont. This is a late-ripening grape, which rarely ripens before late October, when the fogs (*nebbie* in Italian) swirl through the vineyards. Even when ripe, the wines lack color and are generally particularly bitter, but the best do have marvelous dry fruit, tangy depth, and floral scent. Only Australia and Virginia have had much success outside Italy.

PINOT NOIR

This variety has the reputation of being the most fickle, the most demanding, yet ultimately the most rewarding of red wine grapes. Even in Burgundy, its homeland, successes are outnumbered by the mediocre. It needs cool conditions but buds and ripens early. Germany has had some success with it. In the New World, it was generally planted in unsuitable warm regions, yet slowly pockets of California, Oregon, Canada, South Africa, Chile, Australia, and New Zealand are making it work. It is also an important component in Champagne and other sparkling wines, including English wines.

Merlot

SANGIOVESE

Tuscany is Sangiovese's heartland, and it is the main grape of Chianti and Vino Nobile di Montepulciano and the sole grape of Brunello di Montalcino. With its thick skin and

Pinot Noir

Syrah/Shiraz

Chardonnay

Riesling

Sauvignon Blanc

numerous seeds it can make raw, lean wine if picked before it is fully ripe, and only the best vineyards regularly excel with it. Blended with Cabernet, it can make a fascinating, stylish bitter cherry-and-chocolate red wine. It is also important in Emilia-Romagna and elsewhere in Italy.

SYRAH/SHIRAZ

This grape was originally thought of as requiring hot conditions, but most of the finest Syrah wines are coming from areas that are merely warm. Indeed, its home base of the northern Rhône in France is not hot. In hot conditions, such as in Barossa Valley in Australia (where it is called Shiraz), the wines can be rich, dense, and succulent; but in cool areas, the flavors consist more of blackberry and raspberry scratched with pepper and scented with flowers. France and Australia are the main producers, but good wines also appear in Canada, California, Chile, Argentina, South Africa, New Zealand, and parts of Europe, from warm Spain and Italy to cool Switzerland.

TEMPRANILLO

Tempranillo dominates Spain's quality red wine production—to be frank, somewhat too much—and under a variety of names, such as Tinto Fino in Ribera del Duero, Ull de Llebre in Catalonia, and Cencibel in La Mancha and Valdepeñas. But it is most famous as the red wine grape in Rioja. In Portugal, it is called Aragonez or Tinto Roriz. It is also doing well in Australia and South America.

ZINFANDEL

America imported the first cuttings of this versatile red vine from Europe in the nineteenth century; they turned out to be the same as the Primitivo variety of southern Italy or Croatia's obscure Crljenak or Tribidrag. "Zin," however, has become a Californian speciality, used for every kind of wine. But its best expression is as a richly fruity red, full of blackberry or plum flavors. For this, it needs a fairly cool climate and not too much irrigation because yields can be high. Sugar levels can be high, too, giving a baked, portlike taste. The most intense

blackberry and pepper flavors come from old vines. It is not just confined to California; Mexico, Chile, South Africa, and Australia also make good Zinfandels.

WHITE GRAPES

CHARDONNAY

The world's favorite white grape is so adaptable it makes everything from light, dry sparkling wine to sweet, botrytized dessert wine, but its dry, oak-aged incarnation, based on the great wines of Burgundy's Côte d'Or, is the best-known style, found from Chile to China, and from California to New South Wales. The wine has such an affinity with new oak (which adds a rich, spicy butteriness) that it can be easy to forget what its varietal flavor is. Unoaked, cool-climate Chardonnay is pale, appley, and acidic; these flavors gradually soften toward melon and peach as the climate warms. It is an important component of Champagne and other sparkling wines. In Burgundy, Chardonnay can be a long-lived wine, but most examples should be drunk young.

CHENIN BLANC

In France's Loire Valley, this versatile grape can produce wines that are dry or sweet, still or sparkling. In both dry and sweet styles, all highly acidic when young, these wines can be put away for years. South Africa also makes a wide variety of Chenin wines, and a little is produced in New Zealand, Western Australia, and Argentina.

GEWÜRZTRAMINER

The name means "spicy Traminer," and that spice is a smell of roses, lychees, sometimes mangoes, often with a dab of face cream and a dusting of ginger. But Gewürztraminer can lack acidity, and it needs a cool climate to keep a tendency to high sugar levels in check. At its best in Alsace, followed by New Zealand and Italy's Alto Adige. The vine buds early and is susceptible to frosts. But if it survives these and is affected by noble rot in a warm fall, superb sweet wines are the result.

MUSCAT BLANC À PETITS GRAINS

The aristocrat of the Muscat family, this low yielder makes intensely grapey wines of more delicacy and fragrance than any of its cousins. It comes in all colors from white to brownish red, and it can make delicate scented whites right through to rich, exotic, fortified wines the color of burned toffee. It is grown throughout the Mediterranean, generally making scented sweet wines, but it also makes fizzy Asti in Italy and dry whites in Alto Adige and France's Alsace. It also makes some great fortified wines in Australia.

PINOT GRIS

Famous—or notorious—nowadays as Pinot Grigio, a light, mild, thirst quencher from northern Italy and Eastern Europe. However, as Pinot Gris in France's Alsace, it makes serious, honeyed golden wines of considerable power. New Zealand also makes some weighty Pinot Gris, but mostly the lighter style is followed in Romania, Slovenia, Hungary, England, and Germany as well as in British Columbia, Oregon, Washington, and (usually as Pinot Grigio) in California and Australia.

RIESLING

Cold-resistant, late-ripening grape that makes thrilling, delicate wines in Germany as fleeting as gossamer and as low as 7.5 percent alcohol, as well as some of the world's most intensely rich and sweet wines—and everything in between. Both the Mosel and Rhine valleys have numerous fabled vineyard sites. Elsewhere it is appreciated for its scent and citrus acidity, making excellent, generally dry wines in Australia, New Zealand, South Africa, New York, Canada, and France. Austria makes both sweet and dry versions.

SAUVIGNON BLANC

New Zealand has made this variety world famous with its wonderfully tangy, crunchy dry whites, but Sauvignon originates in Bordeaux and the Loire Valley in France. It is now grown in cool conditions all over the world, usually in an attempt to ape the New Zealand style, which only burst onto the world stage in the 1980s, but sometimes as an oak-aged wine more in the style of a top Bordeaux white. Spain and Italy both grow it, but it prefers cool conditions, such as those of Austria and Czechia. California and Australia are mostly a little warm, but South Africa and Chile have found cool spots, where it produces mouthwatering wines.

SÉMILLON

An important white grape in Bordeaux, both for dry whites and sweet Sauternes. It is normally blended with Sauvignon Blanc. The only other place to make a big success of it is Australia, especially in the Hunter Valley, where it makes a remarkable lemon zest, custard, and toast crust-flavored wine that demands aging.

VIOGNIER

Once hailed as the new Chardonnay, Viognier is no such thing. The wine is completely different—scented with apricot and ripe pear—and, unlike Chardonnay, it is difficult to grow. There used to be just several dozen acres in the world, centered on Condrieu in France's northern Rhône, but it has now spread, having most success in Virginia, California, Argentina, South Africa, and Australia. It is sometimes used to coferment with Syrah/Shiraz reds as is done traditionally in its homeland of Côte-Rôtie in the northern Rhône.

COMPOSITION OF A GRAPE

When it comes to imparting flavor to its wine, the juice of the grape rarely has much to offer. Muscat juice is sweet and perfumed—that's why we eat Muscat grapes as well as make wine from them—but most of the great wine grapes of the world are no fun at all to eat. At best, a ripe wine grape has a sugary, neutral-flavor, colorless pulp. Much of the character of a wine comes from its skin. As the grape ripens, the skin matures; its tannins become less aggressive, its color deepens, and all the perfume and flavor components build up. The trick is to try to ripen the grape so that sugar, acid, tannin, color, and flavor are all in balance at the time it is harvested. Both the seeds and the stems are bitter, which is why modern winemakers usually destem the grapes and avoid crushing the seeds.

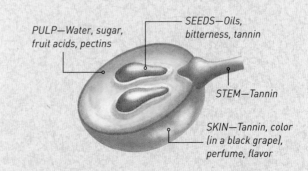

PULP—Water, sugar, fruit acids, pectins

SEEDS—Oils, bitterness, tannin

STEM—Tannin

SKIN—Tannin, color (in a black grape), perfume, flavor

In the Vineyard

ANYONE PLANTING GRAPES to make wine must ask two questions. What will the natural conditions (geography, geology, soil, climate) of my vineyard let me achieve? What do I, as a winemaker, want to achieve? Winemakers in the world's classic vineyard areas have developed their wine styles over the centuries by endlessly asking and answering these questions. Today, the world of wine is turbulent with change; yet these two questions are as important as ever.

A grape variety is chosen primarily for its ripening qualities: its ability to ripen at all in cool areas, such as Germany, or its ability to resist overripening in hot areas, such as the Mediterranean. The interaction of grape variety and climate produces a staggering spectrum of results. The Greeks might pick Liatiko grapes in July

Deep beds of gravel are warm and provide good drainage, which is vital in Bordeaux's damp maritime climate and can make all the difference between good and mediocre wine.

while the Germans spend time between Christmas and New Year bringing in their late, late Riesling for Eiswein.

Given that, genetically, the five-thousand or so grape varieties identified so far as being remotely connected with wine production are all different and react differently to soil and climate, let's look at these two basics and how they affect the siting of the vineyards.

SOIL

Many traditional producers consider soil the most important factor in the creation of great wine. Christian Moueix, who makes some of the world's most exclusive red wines in Pomerol in Bordeaux, reckons soil contributes 80 percent of the quality; others dismiss this view, particularly in places such as California, Australia, and New Zealand, where the link between soil and personality is not as yet proven by generations of experience. The truth is generally somewhere in between. There is no doubt that in certain remarkable vineyards the soil is unique and capable of shaping a wine's flavor. However, these chemical and mineral component parts defy analysis. In the Burgundy Grands Crus, great efforts have been made to explain variations in flavor from vines in different parts of the same vineyard—with no success.

On the other hand, the physical attributes of soil are more easily defined and are, in general, more significant. Most important of these is drainage. Well-drained soil— slate or gravel or chalk—encourages the vine roots down and down to find moisture. Furthermore, porous soil is generally poor—another reason for roots thrusting deep, this time in search of nourishment. The result is a stable environment way below the surface, which makes the vine itself less vulnerable to stress from drought and flood. Riesling likes slate, Cabernet likes gravel, Chardonnay likes limestone or chalk—all of them drain well.

A dry soil is also a warmer soil. This is crucial in cool-climate regions, where the stones that break up the soil and boost porosity also retain vital heat. Gravel in the Médoc and slate on the Mosel aid drainage and store heat for the chilly fall evenings. In Bordeaux, the late-ripening Cabernet Sauvignon—which thrives on the Médoc gravel—cannot ripen on the heavy cold clay of St-Émilion and Pomerol, where the quick-ripening Merlot rules supreme. However, for this reason, clay's coolness is useful in hot areas. Chardonnay, which grows well in Burgundy on only limestone, can grow well on clay in hotter areas. Light-colored soil, such as chalk and limestone, will reflect back heat.

CLIMATE

The second major influence is climate: water and warmth. Because wine, at its most basic, is rainwater sucked up and transformed by the vine (picking up some flavor from the soil on the way), too little water means not enough juice. Either you irrigate—a common practice in North America and the Southern Hemisphere (but largely forbidden in Europe except for "experimental" purposes)—or you choose a favorable site, somewhere with reliable rainfall, porous topsoil, and water-retentive subsoil underneath. Because such geological balance is rare and the weather generally unreliable, this perfect combination is seldom achieved. Too much water, however, is far worse than too little because all you can do is watch as your grapes swell and swell with excessive liquid. Just before harvest time, in particular, rainstorms, which dilute the character of the juice by swelling the grapes, can have a seriously bad effect on wine quality.

Obviously heat is essential to ripen grapes. But different varieties need different amounts, and although lack of sun is the chief problem in the traditional "classic" regions of Europe, in most other areas, such as Australia and South America, a surfeit of sun can make the grapes ripen too fast, before they have picked up enough character and flavor from the soil and before a good balance of grape sugar and acidity has been achieved.

SITING THE VINEYARD

In cool areas, you want to maximize warmth. Consequently, rows are planted ideally on a north-south axis to catch the midday sun. The best slopes may incline southeastward, as in Burgundy, for the morning sun to warm the vineyards; or southwestward, as in Germany's Rheingau, where morning mists shroud the vines and so late afternoon sun is all important. To conserve heat, the vines are planted close together and trained low; they are also aligned across the prevailing wind, so that precious warmth isn't blown out of the rows. Hot climates demand the opposite. Vineyards often face away from the sun and are trained high with a lot of foliage to shade the grapes; they are spaced further apart so that heat can disperse and what little water there is will not be divided among too many plants. The norm in "new" areas is about one-thousand vines to the hectare; in Burgundy it is ten thousand to the hectare. Somewhere between three thousand and five thousand is probably about right in most places.

ALTERNATIVE TECHNIQUES

Biodynamism: Biodynamic vineyards are loony fringe or at the heart of the ecological movement, depending on your viewpoint, but many of the world's finest winemakers have adopted their methods. These involve applying biodynamic preparations to the vines and carrying out specific tasks according to a biodynamic calendar influenced by earthly, solar, and celestial movements. Many of the wines are outstanding.

Organic: Organic methods primarily apply to the vineyard rather than the winery, and different countries have different regulations. "Organic" wine in America and Canada, for instance, cannot include sulfur, but it can in Europe. The crux of the movement is the decision not to use nonorganic fertilizers, herbicides, fungicides, or pesticides. The objective is a chemical-free vineyard and one without any GM material. Many vineyards operate on relatively organic lines, particularly in the fairly disease-free New World.

Natural wine: The biggest objection I have to the "natural" wine movement is the self-righteous way many supporters declaim that any wine not made their way is unnaturally and potentially toxic. This is nonsense. The world of wine is a broad church, in which natural wine is a welcome member. The objectives of natural wine are entirely laudable—a desire to return to the preindustrial, pretechnological, and chemical world. A little use of sulfur is sometimes tolerated. The result is some strikingly pure wines, some fascinatingly rustic wines, and some wines too dominated by wine faults to be attractive to anyone but the most obsessive devotee.

Orange wine: White wine is usually made from juice quickly pressed off the skins before fermentation. Orange wines are white wines made more like red, with the juice fermenting and aging together with the seeds, skins, and maybe stems. The result is wines of most unusual personality, chewy and bitter from the tannin in the seeds, skins, and stems, and with flavors more to do with sap and earth and dried-out fruits and herbs than the typical fresh modern whites. The color can be orange but doesn't have to be. Wines from Georgia produced like this in earthenware "Queri" pots have made such wines fashionable, and orange wines have been made in Friuli in northeast Italy since 1998. Many countries are trying the technique now, often with excellent results. But they're not like your average house white.

A YEAR IN THE VINEYARD

Whether your vineyard—planted with the right grapes in the right place—produces great wine depends on your year-long efforts and your luck with the endless vagaries of the weather. So let's look at a typical vineyard year in a temperate European area such as Bordeaux. The year starts straight after the grape harvest, in November; that's what growers call the beginning of winter.

WINTER

After the exhilaration and hyperactivity of the harvest, there's a hiatus. Winemaking becomes the priority. The vines relax, exhausted, as the temperature drops. At below 52°F, the vine gradually becomes dormant and will be relatively safe in this state down to a minimum of –18°F. Now is the time for lopping off the long branches—they make ideal fuel for grilling meat and fish next spring; for manuring; for plowing, especially in cold areas, where the soil is hilled up around the bottom of the vine for protection against frost; and, on steep slopes, for redistributing soil washed down by heavy rains. In some vineyards, December sees the start of pruning. If you prune severely, you will get far less fruit but far higher quality. Old or weak vines may require more lenient treatment, but the experienced pruner—with next year's vintage in mind—will assess each vine's capacity and cut accordingly.

January comes. The bone-chilling job of pruning back the vines continues. As February shuffles in, thoughts of springtime and the world alive again begin to get the better of the fierce damp winds.

The last job of winter is to take cuttings for grafting onto rootstocks. Especially in Europe, grafting is the only effective way of protecting *Vitis vinifera*—the vine species used for all serious winemaking. You have to do this because of the vine aphid *Phylloxera vastatrix* (wonderful name) that arrived from North America in the 1860s and proceeded to eat its way through all of Europe's vineyards and most of the rest of the world's as well. The sole remedy was—and still is—to graft European *vinifera* cuttings onto rootstocks of American varieties that can tolerate the nasty little beast because phylloxera has similar transatlantic origins. Without this grafting system, there would be no fine wine made in Europe today.

SPRING

March is when the vine wakes up, sap rises, and the pruned shoots drip with "tears." Pruning can be finished without coat and scarf, and the soil can at last be worked

Harvesting Cabernet Sauvignon in the Colchagua Valley, one of Chile's warmest regions and well suited to Cabernet.

again to give it a good airing and to uncover the bottom of the vines. Frosts in March aren't too much of a threat, but in April—when buds burst and shoots begin to emerge—they're far more menacing. You'll also have to start spraying against insects and disease because the vine isn't the only thing to wake up with the spring; its predators are on the move again—spiders, bugs, and beetles are out looking for food.

May brings hopes and fears in equal proportion. The shoots lengthen by the hour, leaves and tendrils sprout, and the first signs of the flower buds appear. Yet you must temper optimism with prudence. In a typical nonorganic vineyard, you must begin to spray against the two fungi, downy and powdery mildew (*peronospera* and *oidium*). From now on, you'll be spraying against one threat or another until fall. The weeds will be enjoying the spring sunshine, and you'll have to deal with those, too.

You'll be on the phone to the local weather office. Is there a risk of frost? The vine shoots can be killed outright by a late May frost, and the harvest will be devastated. In areas such as Chablis in Burgundy, the Rhine in Germany, and the Napa Valley in California, they use stoves, flame guns, torches, and great propellers to stop the frozen air from sliding into the hollows and murdering the young vines. In some places, they continually spray the vines with water, which freezes into ice around the buds and so keeps the temperature at zero. Uncomfortable for us but just about okay for a young vine.

SUMMER

Then it's summer. You want sun right through June because this is when the vine flowers. If it pours during this crucial ten-to-fourteen-day period, the flowers will not be fertilized; the bunches of grapes—and consequently the vintage—will be drastically reduced. Once flowering is over, you thin the shoots, keeping only the best, and tie them to wires to shape their growth. Throughout the long hundred-day haul from flowering to within striking distance of the harvest, spraying continues.

In July, you till the land again and also trim back excessive growth and vegetation so that you don't get too many grapes, which will dilute quality—unless you don't care, in which case you go on vacation.

Some vignerons never seem to go on vacation at all, but August is the most usual month to take time off. However, someone should be there, spraying and thinning the bunches. The grapes are changing color, softening, and gaining sugar. Yet hail can sweep up and ravage your vines without warning, while wet, warm weather can cause the onset of rot.

Sorting Pinot Noir at Helan Mountain, one of several boutique wineries in China making huge improvements in quality in recent years.

FALL

Harvest looms. It may be September, it may be October. In the winery, everyone is feverishly preparing equipment. Outdoors the temptation is to sit in the sun, chew the grapes, and dream of great things. But you must keep at it. Greatness is within your grasp. Make a last spray against rot, check daily for insect invasion, and keep the birds off—by nets, by scarecrows, by shotguns—but keep them off. It's your livelihood they're eating.

Then at last—the great day. Harvest starts. Out go the tractors, the troops of pickers, or maybe the giant harvesting machine to pluck the results of another year's labor. Hand-pickers cut the bunches off, then place them in boxes or baskets for collection. Depending on the height of the vines, the work is either backbreaking or knee-creasing and, depending on the time of day, cripplingly cold in the morning mist but happily hot in the afternoon sun. Mechanical harvesters, straddling the rows, knock the grapes off with fiberglass rods. As the grapes arrive at the winery, good will be separated from bad on the sorting tables or by optical lasers.

Whatever the method, as the grapes pile up, you are looking at your due reward or just desserts—nature's bounty or nature's revenge.

In the Winery

RED AND ROSÉ WINES

Wine is created by fermentation—yeasts turning grape sugar into alcohol. If you bought a few bunches of ripe grapes, squashed them, put the resulting goo into a bucket, and left it somewhere warm—well, a wine of some type would almost certainly be produced. It might taste more like vinegar, but technically it would be wine. This simple chemical reaction has been refined by hundreds of years of experience and, more recently, by high technology and microbiological know-how. It is difficult to generalize about winemaking styles and methods in countries and states as diverse as New Zealand and Texas, Argentina, and Tasmania. What France or Italy may regard as old hat, the wineries of Brazil or Mexico may barely have begun to think about. At every stage, even the most technocratic winemaker indulges in little personal adjustments—in all but the drabbest corporate winemaker lurks an artist's soul—each of which affect the final character of the wine. But some techniques are standard around the globe.

CRUSHING

The winemaking process begins when the grapes arrive. With the exception of Beaujolais and a few other wines using the whole-bunch method of fermentation (also called carbonic maceration), red grapes are put through a crusher to break their skins and release the juice. The crushing machine usually also removes the stems because these are bitter, but they can also have a delightful sappy flavor, and with some grapes, notably Syrah and Pinot Noir, a proportion is sometimes left on. The resulting must—the pulpy mush of flesh, juice and skins (which give red and rosé wines their color)—is pumped into a big vat, ready for fermentation.

FERMENTATION

Fermentation is caused by the action of yeasts on the sugars in the grape juice. Yeasts are naturally present in the vineyards and winery, but cultivated yeasts are generally used to ensure a controlled fermentation. At this stage, in the cool areas of Europe, if the sugar content of the grapes is too low, the addition of sugar is permitted to increase alcoholic strength, a process called chaptalization. Similarly, in hot regions, a little acid may be added if the grapes are very ripe.

For rosé wines, the fermenting juice is drawn off the skins after a day or so and the winemaking process then follows the same path as for white wines (page 24).

Fermentation lasts from a few days to a few weeks, depending on the yeast culture and cellar temperature. Temperature control is one of the most crucial tools available to the modern winemaker, and the introduction of stainless steel tanks and refrigeration in the 1950s were major breakthroughs in winemaking. Heat is needed to extract color from the skins, but excess heat destroys freshness and fruit flavor, and it can disrupt the fermentation process itself. Should the winemaker choose a cultured or a wild yeast? Modern cultured yeasts are controllable and produce specific results. Beneficial wild yeast strains have developed over centuries, and quality producers are increasingly favoring these.

Throughout the process, the grape skins surge upward, pushed by the stream of carbon dioxide released during fermentation. At the top, they form a thick "cap," which must be mixed back in continually by punching down or pumping the juice over the cap, so that the wine can extract maximum color and flavor and avoid air becoming trapped between the skins and the wine. Many red wines, including all those intended for long aging, are left to macerate on the skins for some days or weeks after fermentation is complete to extract all the flavor, color, and tannin from the skins and seeds; long maceration also softens the harsh tannins.

PRESSING

When red wine fermentation is finished—all the sugar having been converted to alcohol—the wine is drawn off the vat, and the residue of skins is pressed to produce a dark, tannic wine called "press wine." It may be used for blending and added to free-run wine to create a deeper, tougher style of wine, or it may be stored apart.

MALOLACTIC FERMENTATION

Technically, the wine is now made—but it is pretty raw stuff. To begin with, it probably has a sharp, green-apple acidity. This is reduced through malolactic fermentation, which converts tart malic acid into mild lactic acid.

Almost everywhere in the world where white wine is made the juice is fermented in large, refrigerated stainless steel tanks. These are at Château Haut-Brion in Bordeaux.

Almost all reds undergo this second fermentation, becoming softer and rounder. It occurs naturally when temperatures rise in spring, following the harvest, but it is often induced soon after the alcoholic fermentation by raising the temperature in the cellar and adding the appropriate bacteria.

BLENDING AND MATURING

The winemaker can alter the wine radically by blending the contents of two or more vats together. That could mean combining different grape varieties to add a whole new dimension of flavor. Some wines use only one variety but blend grapes from different vineyards. This may be done to achieve a consistent style or to balance the varying characteristics of the grapes.

The decision about whether to mature a wine in stainless steel or in oak is of enormous stylistic importance. Stainless steel (or concrete) is inert and amenable to accurate temperature control, which allows the fruit flavors free rein. Small oak barrels allow for controlled oxygenation and benign aging of what might otherwise be unduly aggressive wines, as well as add flavors of vanilla and toast.

If the wine is to be drunk young, it is put in large tanks of stainless steel or concrete to rest a short while before bottling. Almost all rosé is treated in this way. Red wine for aging, however, is stored—often in small oak barrels (*barriques*)—for anywhere from a few months to more than two years. If the *barriques* are new or used only once, they impart flavors of spice, herbs, perfume, and vanilla as well as add to the wine's tannic structure.

RACKING, FINING, AND FILTERING

During this prebottling period, dead yeast cells and other solids fall to the bottom of the tank or barrel. These are separated from the wine by racking—transferring the wine to clean barrels or tanks—which may take place several times before bottling. Racking naturally mixes oxygen with the wine, and this usually clears out any sulfuric or yeasty flavors.

With many top-quality wines, the last stage before bottling is fining, removing any particles held in suspension by means of a clarifying agent. The agent—typically egg white or bentonite—is spread over the surface and, as it falls down through the wine, it collects all impurities with it. Most other wines are also filtered; those for immediate drinking often receive a relatively fierce filtration to make sure no deposit forms in the bottle. Some of the best wines are filtered very lightly. Some top red wines are neither fined nor filtered and so develop a harmless deposit in the bottle. Wines with residual sweetness will be tightly sterile filtered.

BOTTLING

For best results, bottling should be cold and sterile, with an inert gas, such as nitrogen or carbon dioxide, introduced into the bottle ahead of the wine so that, when the cork goes in, there is no oxygen in the bottle. Some of the cheapest wines are either "hot-bottled" or pasteurized. Both treatments ensure the wine's stability but detract from its personality and make any further development impossible. Cork or screw cap may be the preferred closure.

WHITE WINES

The creation of any wine begins in the vineyard, but the winemaking process proper starts with the annual grape harvest. For white wines, this involves choices: pick early and make a snappily fresh wine for quick drinking; or pursue ripeness until the grapes fill with sugar; or, in some parts of the world, leave the grapes to overripen and hope for an attack of the sweetness-intensifying noble rot.

In warm wine regions, the sunshine that has ripened the grapes becomes the grapes' enemy as soon as they have been picked. White grapes are particularly vulnerable to oxidation. A common solution is to harvest at night or in the early morning, when the air is at its coolest. You can then pile your grapes into a refrigerated truck if the winery is a long way away, and you can sprinkle antioxidants, such as sulfur dioxide or ascorbic acid, over the bunches to keep them in good condition. Some producers crush the grapes immediately and chill the resulting must at the vineyard.

CRUSHING AND PRESSING

Grapes destined for white wines generally need more careful handling than those for reds. The grapes should be crushed without too much force and may then be left to steep for a while—juice, skin, pulp, seeds, and all— so that maximum grape flavor can be extracted from the skins, where all the varietal flavor and character lie. This skin contact may be as brief as an hour or as long as a day for white wine, and it will vary between grape varieties and also according to what will probably happen to the wine afterward—for example, whether it will go into a new oak barrel or a steel tank.

In general, contact between juice and skins isn't required, so pressing forms part of the same process as crushing. The best-quality juice emerges from the first gentle pressing. Further pressing will extract harsher elements from the skin as well as more juice—a bottled wine may be a blend of wines from different stages of pressing, according to the winemaker's requirements.

FERMENTATION

Once the juice has settled its solids or has been filtered or centrifuged to quicken the process (although filtration will invariably remove some potential flavor as well), it is pumped into a tank—generally of stainless steel, if the objective is to make a young fresh white. A suitable yeast culture is added to make sure the fermentation is both efficient and controlled and, in certain cases, to create

particular nuances of flavor. Alternatively, wild yeasts may be allowed to work.

Stainless steel tanks are the easiest to keep sterile and clean and in which to control temperature. The majority of white wines ferment at cool temperatures to give a fruitier, fresher style, at 60–64°F, with the temperature kept down by running cold water or a coolant through insulated jackets or through coils within the tanks. Top Rieslings and Sauvignons rarely see oak, but in general, for the finest white wines, the juice is fermented at up to 77°F in an oak barrel, which imparts a rich, mellow flavor even to a dry wine.

MALOLACTIC FERMENTATION

After the primary (alcoholic) fermentation, there is a second fermentation, the malolactic, in which green, appley malic acid is turned into soft, creamy lactic acid. Most classic whites undergo the malolactic, but because it reduces fresh-fruit character and tangy acidity, it is often prevented in modern, fruit-driven whites, such as Rieslings and Sauvignons, by the use of filtration, low temperature, or sulfur dioxide.

MATURING

Use of new oak *barriques* (225-liter barrels) is common not just for aging the best wines of Burgundy or Bordeaux, but also for the sturdier styles of white wine, particularly Chardonnay, from all over the world. The great Sauvignon-Sémillon dry whites of Pessac-Léognan as well as the luscious sweet wines of Sauternes are also generally fermented and aged in oak. New oak gives a toasty, vanilla taste to wine, and these days most bottles of good New World Chardonnay will have seen some oak during their fermentation and/or maturation. A final blend may consist of batches of wine that have spent time in new one-year-old and two-year-old oak barrels, as well as some that have stayed in stainless steel. If the barrels are new or fairly new, they give a strong, creamy, or spicy character to the wine. Older barrels merely soften and round out the wine due to the slight contact with oxygen. This maturation can take up to eighteen months, but, in general, six months is long enough for a white wine.

BOTTLING

A wine for drinking young is generally stored in a stainless steel tank, racked off its lees if necessary, fined, filtered, and then bottled—often at only six months or fewer—to maximize its fresh, fruity character. Ideally, the very best wines are hardly filtered at all.

SWEET WINES

The great sweet wines of France, Germany, Austria, and occasionally Australia, New Zealand, and America, are made from grapes that are left on the vine well after the normal harvest, so they are overripe and full of sugar; they also begin to shrivel, which concentrates the sugar. The best are attacked by a fungus called noble rot (*Botrytis cinerea*). It sucks out the water, concentrating the sugar even more. During fermentation, the sugar is converted by yeasts into alcohol; the more sugar in the grape juice, the higher the potential alcoholic strength. However, yeasts can work only in alcohol levels of up to about 15 percent. So when the yeasts stop, the rest of the grape sugar remains in the wine as sweetness—full of potential lusciousness.

Hungary's intensely sweet Tokaji is also made using botrytized grapes, which are added to a dry base wine. Another method of making wine sweet is traditional in parts of Italy (where it is known as *passito* or *recioto*) and in the Jura, France (for *vin de paille*). After picking, the grapes are laid on mats or in shallow trays, or the bunches are hung from rafters. They begin to dry out, losing water, which concentrates all the other constituents, especially the sugars.

Riddling, an important process in the Champagne method.

FORTIFIED WINES

Fortified wines have a neutral alcohol spirit added to them after partial or full fermentation to raise their alcohol level to between 16 and 24 percent. Yeasts cannot operate at more than 15 or 16 percent alcohol, so fermentation stops, and any remaining sugar stays in the wine as sweetness. Sherry can be sweet or dry, but most of the finest ones are dry, and the fortification is done when the fermentation is finished, serving to stablize the wine for what can be a lengthy maturing process.

Port is usually sweet. The high-strength spirit is added before the fermentation has finished, raising the alcohol level to about 19 percent and leaving a lot of sugar sweetness still in the wine. Wines are aged primarily in barrel or in bottle, depending on their style. Madeira can be sweet or dry. It gains its smoky, almost burned flavor through an aging process that includes warming the wine to imitate its traditional passage across the equator on sailing ships. France makes sweet fortified wines along the Mediterranean coast and in the Rhône Valley, and Australia makes mighty versions in northeast Victoria.

SPARKLING WINES

Carbon dioxide is given off during fermentation, and, if the fermenting wine is kept in a pressurized container, the gas is absorbed by the wine for as long as the pressure remains. This explains why, as soon as you open a bottle of sparkling wine, there is a whoosh of bubbles as the pressure is released. All the greatest sparklers are made by inducing a second fermentation in the final bottle. This is called the Champagne, traditional, or classic method. The still wine is bottled with a little sugar and yeast to restart the fermentation, tightly sealed (often with a crown cap), and stored in a cool cellar from a few months to several years. The second fermentation occurs, and the carbon dioxide bubbles dissolve in the wine, but the yeast cells die and are deposited as sludge on the inside of the bottle. So the bottle undergoes "riddling"—being twisted, tapped, and turned on their heads to move all the sludge to the bottle neck. The sludge is then disgorged—the neck of the bottle is frozen in brine, the stopper is removed, and the pellet of sludge pops out. The bottle is topped off—you can add a *dosage* of wine and sugar to adjust the sweetness—and put a proper cork in, wire it down, and you're done.

Cheaper fizz, such as Asti or Prosecco, is made by creating the second fermentation in a large tank—the "tank" or Charmat method.

What Does It Taste Like?

WHEN YOU BUY WINE, buy it for its flavor. Reputation, packaging, and price all vie to influence your choice, but they can't titillate your taste buds. The grape variety used is the most significant factor in determining the taste of a wine, but everything that happens to the grapes and their juice on the long journey from the vine to the glass in your hand contributes to that wine's unique identity. Read on and start getting the flavor you want.

GET THE FLAVOR YOU WANT

Your chances of walking into a wine shop and coming out with a wine that's enjoyable to drink, whatever the price level, are better now than ever before. The last quarter of the twentieth century saw a revolution in wine in terms of both style and quality, from which we are all now benefiting. All wines are cleaner and fresher-tasting than they were; reds are juicier, rounder, and softer; whites are snappier, zestier, more appetizing. There are more new oak barrels being used in expensive wines, which in terms of taste means nutty vanilla and buttered toast. But all wines don't taste alike. Indeed, there's never been a wider choice. Modern winemaking is rapidly eliminating faults—it's not eliminating individuality.

So how do you choose? How do you tell a wine that's just right for a summer lunch on the deck or patio from one that would be better suited to a winter evening in front of a log fire? Well, imagine if you could walk into a wine shop and just pick up a bottle from the "green, tangy white" shelf or go for a "spicy, warm-hearted red." That would make things pretty easy, wouldn't it?

You'll find that all those thousands of different flavors fall into the eighteen broad styles shown here. So, even if you don't yet know much about grape varieties and wine-producing regions, just choose a style that appeals and I'll point you in the right direction.

RED WINES

1. JUICY, FRUITY REDS

Refreshing, approachable, and delicious—tasty, refreshing reds are ideal for drinking with or without food, emphasizing bright fruit flavors and minimizing the gum-drying toughness of tannin.

This style had its birth in the New World, but it has spread right through Europe, overturning any lingering ideas that red wine must be aged. You don't age these wines. You buy them and you drink them. Chilean Merlot is the benchmark: young, well-balanced, and bursting with blackberry, black currant, and plum flavors. Spain produces a lot of inexpensive soft, supple reds in the same mold from La Mancha, Jumilla, Campo de Borja, and Calatayud. Try young Valpolicella and Teroldego from Italy and unoaked reds from Portugal's Douro region. California does young Merlots and Zinfandels and Argentina has smooth Tempranillo, ultrafruity Bonarda, and juicy Malbec. Beaujolais is famous for this style in France. Loire Valley reds have sharper but refreshing fruit, and Languedoc Merlot can be good.

2. SILKY, STRAWBERRY-ISH REDS

Mellow, perfumed reds with a gentle strawberry, raspberry, or cherry fruit fragrance and flavor. Good ones feel silky in your mouth.

Pinot Noir is the grape that produces the supreme examples of this style. Its home territory is Burgundy in France (Bourgogne in French). Virtually all red Burgundy is made from Pinot Noir. Beyond Burgundy, the best Pinot Noir comes from California—particularly Carneros, Sonoma Coast, Russian River, and Santa Barbara—and from Oregon, Chile, New Zealand, and occasionally Australia. Germany can nowadays hit the spot, too, and England is beginning to work it out. Cheap Pinot Noir is rarely good, but Chile's usually have loads of vibrant jellied fruit flavor. Red Rioja and Navarra, from Spain but made from different grapes, principally Tempranillo, can be soft and smooth with a fragrant strawberry-ish quality. This also appears in the lightest Côtes du Rhône-Villages from France.

3. INTENSE, BLACK-CURRANTY REDS

Full-flavored red wines with a distinctive black-currant flavor and those slightly bitter tannins from the grape skins that dry your mouth but make it water at the same time. They're made from Cabernet Sauvignon alone or blended with Merlot and other grapes to enrich the fruit flavors and soften the texture.

The Cabernet-base red wines of Bordeaux in France are the original black-curranty wines with, when at their best, a fragrance of cigar boxes and graphite. New World Cabernets have more black currant but also a vanilla flavor and sometimes mint. Cabernet Sauvignon is one of the most reliable wines you can get. It retains its characteristic flavors wherever it's from and at every price level—and that's rare in wine. Expensive ones should be ripe and rich with layers of intense flavor; while cheaper ones have simpler flavors that are more earthy, more jammy, or more green pepper lean. For budget Cabernets, look for Argentina, Chile, Australia, South Africa, and France's Pays d'Oc. Bordeaux, Chile, Argentina, South Africa, New Zealand, Australia, and California at the higher price level are outstanding. You'll also find these black-currant flavors in Spain's Ribera del Duero, from the Tempranillo grape, and a number of grapes, especially Touriga Nacional, give black fruit flavors in Portugal.

4. SPICY, WARM-HEARTED REDS

Dense, heartwarming, gloriously rich flavors of black-berry and loganberry, black pepper, and chocolate and mainly found in Syrah/Shiraz.

Australian Shiraz is the wine to try: often dense, rich, and chocolaty, sometimes fresher, with peppery, blackberry fruit, sometimes with a whiff of smoke or a slap of leather. In France's Rhône Valley, the same grape is called Syrah. Rhône Syrah tends to be a little more austere in style and smoky-minerally to Australia's rich spice, but the best have lush blackberry fruit. Look for the label Crozes-Hermitage or St-Joseph. For good value from France, try Pays d'Oc Syrah, Faugères, or Minervois. Portugal offers good value with a whole host of indigenous grape varieties. In Spain, try the weighty plums and vanilla flavors of Toro and the more expensive Montsant and Priorat. California Zinfandel and Petite Sirah are powerful, spicy, and rich. Argentina's heart-warming Malbecs and Chile's great big spicy-savory mouthfuls of Carménère are excellent value. Take a look at South Africa's smoky Pinotage, too.

5. MOUTHWATERING, HERBY REDS

Intriguing wines with a rasping herby bite and sweet-sour red fruit flavors—Italian reds do this better than any others.

There's a rasp of sourness in these reds that's intended to cut through steak or pasta sauce, not to be sipped as an apéritif. You'll find that same irresistible sour-cherry edge on wines made from all kinds of grapes—Dolcetto, Sangiovese, Barbera, Teroldego, Lagrein, and Refosco. Some may have a delicious raisiny taste, too. Even light, low-tannin Valpolicella has this flavor. Up in Piedmont, tough, tannic wines from Barolo and Barbaresco, made from the stern Nebbiolo grape, have a fascinating tar-and-roses flavor. A decent Langhe will give you the flavor for less money. Down in the South, grapes such as Negroamaro and Primitivo add round, pruny flavors to the sour-cherry bite. Sicilian reds, especially Nero d'Avola, are rich and mouth-filling.

6. EARTHY, SAVORY REDS

These are the classic food wines of Europe, the kind where fruit flavors often take a back seat to compatibility with food and the ability to cleanse the palate and stimulate the appetite.

France, especially Bordeaux, is the leader in this style. Even at the top end, most Bordeaux reds keep an earthy quality underpinning their richness. Even St-Émilion and

Pomerol generally blend attractive savoriness with lush fruit. Wines from Haut-Médoc, Médoc, Pessac-Léognan, and Graves on Bordeaux's Left Bank have stony or earthy flavors. Côtes de Bourg, Blaye, and basic Bordeaux and Bordeaux Supérieur are usually marked by earthy, savory qualities. You can find these flavors all over Southwest France, too.

Italy's main earthy, savory type is Chianti. Basic Sangiovese, Montepulciano, and Barbera wines throughout Italy often share this trait. Croatian, Romanian, and Hungarian Merlot are refreshingly earthy, Greek reds almost stony, and the more basic reds of northern Portugal and Spain follow this line. In the New World, fruit is riper and generally too rich for many of these styles, but some Cabernets and Merlots from places such as Canada, New York, Washington, New Zealand, South Africa, and even China may fit the bill.

ROSÉ WINES

7. DELICATE ROSÉS

Good rosé should be fragrant, refreshing, and deliciously dry—not sickly and sweet.

France is a good hunting ground for this style of wine. Attractive, slightly leafy-tasting Bordeaux rosé and Rosé de Loire are lovely dry wines. Elegant Pinot Noir rosés come from Sancerre in the eastern Loire and Marsannay at the northern end of the Côte de Nuits in Burgundy. The southern Rhône Valley produces plenty of dry but fruity rosés. Côtes de Provence is dry, beguilingly smooth, but often expensive. Bandol and Bellet are pricier still—but tastier, too. Northern Italy produces light, fresh pale rosato called chiaretto, from Bardolino high in the Dolomites from Lagrein. Garnacha rosado from Navarre and Rioja in northern Spain are tasty. English pinks are coming on nicely, too.

8. GUTSY ROSÉS

Dry, fruity rosé can be wonderful, with flavors of strawberries and maybe raspberries and rose hips, cherries, apples, and herbs, too. More color, more fruit flavor, more texture to roll around your mouth. Spain, Chile, Australia, and New Zealand do best.

Most countries make a dry rosé, and any red grape will do. Garnacha or Tempranillo from Spain is often excellent. Puglia and Sicily in southern Italy make mouth-filling rosatos, too. France has big, strong, dry rosés from Tavel and Lirac in the southern Rhône Valley. South America is a good bet for flavorsome, fruit-forward pink wines, as are fruity Australian Grenaches from the Barossa Valley or New Zealand pinks.

9. SWEET ROSÉS

Blush is the usual name, and most of it comes from California as Zinfandel. Anjou rosé is France's version.

Zinfandel from California, often described as "blush," is fairly sweet. Other sweetish rosés are Rosé d'Anjou from the Loire Valley and Portuguese rosados, such as Mateus and Lancers.

WHITE WINES

10. BONE-DRY, NEUTRAL WHITES

Crisp, refreshing whites whose flavors won't set the world alight—but chill them down and set them next to a plate of shellfish, and you've got the perfect combination.

In France, Muscadet from the Loire Valley and unoaked, minerally Chablis from Burgundy are spot on. In Italy, Soave, Orvieto, Verdicchio, Lugana, Fiano, Greco di Tufo, Grillo, and northern Pinot Bianco all fit the bill. Greek whites are often brushed with minerality and citrus without being fruity. Many of the "rediscovered" old white varieties in Europe make this style. You won't often find this style in the New World—winemakers here don't want neutrality in their wines.

11. GREEN, TANGY WHITES

Sharp, grapefruity, lime zesty Sauvignon Blanc from New Zealand, South Africa, and Chile lead the way.

Sauvignon Blanc from New Zealand—especially from Marlborough—has tangy, mouthwatering flavors by the bucketful. Chile and South Africa make similar, slightly softer wines, as does Spain with Rueda. Sancerre and Pouilly-Fumé from the Loire Valley in France are crisp and refreshing with lighter fruit flavors and a minerally or even smoky edge. Sauvignon de Touraine offers similar flavors at lower prices. Bordeaux Sauvignon is dry and fresh. The Loire also produces sharp-edged wines from Chenin Blanc, such as Vouvray and white Anjou. Riesling is the other grape to look for. Ideally, Rieslings are citrusy, minerally when young, with a streak of green apple and some high tensile acidity. The leanest, often with a touch of scented sweetness to balance the acidity, come from Germany's Mosel Valley; slightly richer ones come from the Rhine; drier, weightier ones from Austria and Alsace. Australian Rieslings, particularly from the Clare and Eden valleys, start bone dry and age to an irresistible lime-and-toast flavor.

12. INTENSE, NUTTY WHITES

Dry yet succulent whites with subtle nut and oatmeal flavors and sometimes the smell of struck matches. These wines are generally oak aged and have a soft edge with a backbone of absolute dryness. White Burgundy sets the style.

The best expression is oak-aged Chardonnay in the form of white Burgundy. This is the wine that earned Chardonnay its renown in the first place, and the style is sometimes matched in the best examples from the New World. Italian producers in Tuscany are trying it, too. Top-quality oak-aged Pessac-Léognans from Bordeaux are Sémillon blended with Sauvignon Blanc, giving a creamy, nutty wine with a hint of nectarines. Unoaked Australian Semillon from the Hunter Valley matures to become custardy and rich. The best white Rioja from Spain becomes nutty and lush with time.

13. RIPE, TOASTY WHITES

Upfront flavors of peaches, apricots, and tropical fruits with toasty oaky richness—the traditional flavor of Australian, Californian, and Chilean Chardonnay. Modern examples are generally showing more restraint.

This is the flavor of the Chardonnays that shocked and thrilled the world when California and then Australia began making them thirty years ago. They changed our view of what was possible in white wine flavor and style. Since then, we have begun to back off a little from such lush flavors, and the producers have throttled back a good deal. Many current Californian and Australian examples are relatively restrained. But the high-octane Chardies are still around if you yearn for one. If you ferment Viognier in new oak, it also gives toasty, exotic results. Sémillon in oak becomes mouth-filling and creamy, and barrel-fermented South African Chenin can be a real mouthful.

14. AROMATIC WHITES

Perfumy wines with exotic and floral fragrances— Gewürztraminer for scent, Viognier and Muscat for exotic fruit.

Gewurztraminer from Alsace is packed solid with roses and lychees, face cream, and a whole kitchen spice rack. No, it's not subtle, but with spicy food, especially Chinese, it can be wonderful. German versions are more floral, and the Italians make their Traminer more toned down. But Slovenia, Slovakia, Croatia, and Czechia are trying it, and New Zealand Gewürztraminer is a delight. Dry Muscat from Alsace is floral with a heady, hothouse grape scent. Southern France and Spain make less scented styles, and you can get delicate floral Muscats

in northern Italy. Viognier, at its apricots-and-spring flowers best in Condrieu, in the northern Rhône Valley, is planted in the south of France as well as California and Australia; and Godello from northwest Spain is also apricotty but crisper. Irsai Olivér from Hungary, Torrontés from Argentina, and Malagousia from Greece are heady and perfumed. Bacchus in England has a haunting aroma of fresh elderflower.

15. SPARKLING WINES

Bubbles are there to make you happy. Smile, you're drinking fun, not just wine. But good bubbly can have delicious flavors as well.

Champagne sets the standard. Good Champagne has a nutty, bready aroma, appley freshness, and fine bubbles. Sparkling wine from Australia, California, and New Zealand is made in the same way, and it's often just as good and usually cheaper. England is proving naturally suited to growing grapes for top-quality sparkling wine. Other good French fizzes are Crémant de Bourgogne, Crémant d'Alsace, sparkling Saumur, and Blanquette de Limoux from the south. Italian sparklers made from Chardonnay and Pinot Noir are in the Champagne style, but light, fruity

Prosecco and sweet, grapey Asti can be more fun. The best Lambrusco is red, snappy, and refreshingly sharp. Spanish Cava can be classy and good value. German Sekt, when made from Riesling, can be lean, sharp, and refreshing. Australian sparkling red wines are wild things all about fun and frolic instead of flavor.

16. RICH, SWEET WHITES

Luscious mouthfuls with intense flavors of peach, pineapple, and honey.

In France, the sweet wines of Bordeaux are at their gorgeous best in Sauternes and Barsac. These are rich and syrupy wines with intense flavors of peaches and pineapples, barley sugar, butterscotch, and honey, all balanced by acidity, and they can age for twenty years or more. Monbazillac, Cérons, Loupiac, and Ste-Croix-du-Mont are happy hunting grounds for cheaper, lighter versions. California, New Zealand, and Australia have a few intensely rich wines in this style, too. The Loire Valley produces honey- and quince-flavored sweet wines. Quarts de Chaume, Bonnezeaux, Coteaux du Layon, and Vouvray are the wines to look for. Only a few Vouvrays are sweet; they're labeled as *moelleux* or *liquoreux*. Alsace Sélection de Grains Nobles sweeties are rich and unctuous. The sweet wines of Germany have a language all their own. Beerenauslese and Trockenbeerenauslese are intensely sweet and extremely expensive. The best are made from Riesling; its piercing acidity keeps the sweetness from being overpowering. Austria's sweet wines are similar in style to Germany's but tend to be weightier. There's also a rarity called Eiswein, made from frozen grapes picked in the depths of winter. Canadian icewine is made in the same way, and China has made some. Hungary's Tokaji has a wonderful sweet-sour smoky flavor. Moscatel de Valencia from Spain is a simplehearted splash of rich, grapey fruit.

17. WARMING, FORTIFIED WINES

Sweet wines tasting of raisins and brown sugar, plum and blackberry syrup, able to take on board all kinds of other scents or flavors as they age—Port, Madeira, and sweet brown Sherry are the classics.

Port, the rich red fortified wine of Portugal's Douro Valley, is the classic dark sweet wine. The Portuguese island of Madeira produces some of the most fascinating warming fortifieds, with rich brown smoky flavors and a startling acid bite. Bual and Malmsey are the sweet ones to look for. Spain produces Oloroso dulce, a rare and delicious Sherry with stunning, concentrated flavors and black-brown intensely sweet Pedro Ximenez (or PX). Australian Rutherglen Muscat is astonishingly rich and dark. The fortified Marsala of Sicily and Moscato di Pantelleria are good wines, as rich as brown sugar, with a refreshing shiver of acidity.

18. TANGY, FORTIFIED WINES

Bone dry with startling, stark, almost sour and nutty flavors—this is the true, dry Sherry from Andalucia in southern Spain.

Fino is pale in color, very dry with a thrilling tang. Manzanilla can seem even drier and has a wonderful sourdough perfume and tingling acidity. Amontillado is dry, chestnut-colored, and nutty. Dry Oloroso adds deep, burned flavors. Montilla-Moriles is the neighboring region to Jerez and produces similar wines. The driest style of Madeira, Sercial, is tangy, steely, and savory; Verdelho is a little fuller and fatter. Australia and South Africa make excellent Sherry-style wines, although without the tang of top-class Spanish Fino or Manzanilla.

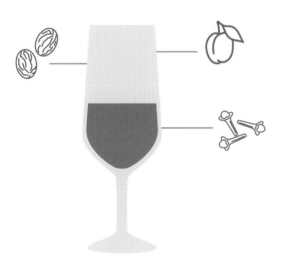

TASTE OF THE GRAPE

The taste of the wine is intimately bound up with the grape variety. Here are some of the classic flavors.

RED
» **Barbera** Snappy and refreshing.
» **Cabernet Franc** Medium, black currant, grassy.
» **Cabernet Sauvignon** Tannic, black currant, cedar, mint.
» **Carménère** Dark, black currant- and pepper-flavored.
» **Garnacha** Ripe strawberry and spice, often in a blend.
» **Malbec** Full, lush, plummy-scented.
» **Merlot** Juicy and plummy; part of the red Bordeaux blend. Black currant, honey, raisins, mint, plum.
» **Nebbiolo** Dark, very tannic and difficult to appreciate, prunes, raisins, tobacco, tar, game, chocolate.
» **Pinot Noir** Middleweight, fragrant, often delicate, strawberry, cherry, plum. Silky texture.
» **Pinotage** Love-hate sturdy, smoky, mulberry-and marshmallow-flavored red from South Africa.
» **Sangiovese** Medium to full, tobacco, cherry pit, herbs, sometimes vegetal, often chewy, raisins. The mainstay of Tuscan reds.
» **Syrah/Shiraz** Spicy and warm-hearted. Dark, tannic, savage sometimes, raspberry, black currant, blackberry, plum, herbs, pepper, chocolate, smoke.
» **Tempranillo** Light to medium, strawberry, vanilla, sometimes black currant, pepper.
» **Zinfandel** In California, spicy, dark, bramble and pepper flavors.

WHITE
» **Chardonnay** The classic all-purpose international grape. Dry white, from light, appley, and acid to full yeast, butter, cream, hazelnuts, oatmeal, toast.
» **Chenin Blanc** Very dry to sweet, green apples, lemon, nuts, chalk, to apricots, peach, honey, quince.
» **Gewürztraminer** Fairly dry to sweet, above all spice, tropical fruit, and cosmetic perfume. Best in Alsace.
» **Muscat** Dry to very sweet, above all grapes, peppery yeast, dessert apples to deep orange peel, molasses, raisins, and butterscotch.
» **Pinot Gris** Neutral in Italy (as in Pinot Grigio). Rich in Alsace, with a hint of honey, and pears in New Zealand.
» **Riesling** Very dry to very sweet, steely, slate, apple to lime, gasoline, raisins, even honey and tropical fruits.
» **Sauvignon Blanc** Very dry to sweet, green flavors, grapefruit, capsicum, nettles, gooseberry, asparagus, lime zest, and elderflower.
» **Viognier** Full dry, apricot, hawthorn blossom, sour cream.

Reading the Label

THE FRONT LABEL varies with the type of wine and from country to country, but it should tell you all the necessary information about the wine. There are now all kinds of labels around the world giving you all the information you need, far more than you need, or in some cases none at all. Here are a few fairly classic examples.

EUROPEAN WINE LABELS

The French appellation system is the most widely known system of quality control for wine in Europe. Other European countries have roughly equivalent gradings, although some have more categories. Quality within any of the levels is not consistent, and a good example of a simple wine will be better than a poorly made wine that has barely complied with the appellation rules.

BORDEAUX

1. **Classification** This tells you that the wine was included in the famous 1855 Classification of the red wines of Bordeaux.
2. **Traditional imagery** for a traditional Bordeaux producer. The vast majority of Bordeaux labels still feature a straightforward illustration of the château building. Any that do not are probably making a statement about their modern approach.
3. **Château name** Any wine estate in France, especially in Bordeaux, can take a château name, regardless of whether it has a grand building. Castello is the equivalent word in Italy, Castillo in Spain, and Schloss in Germany.
4. **Appellation** European wine regulations expect the appellation name to tell you all you need to know about the origin of the wine, its quality classification, and the grape varieties used. However, they often presume you have knowledge you don't possess. St-Estèphe in Bordeaux is best known for its slow-maturing, tannic red wines based on Cabernet Sauvignon.
5. **Vintage** The year the grapes were harvested. In most parts of the world, the year's weather influences the style of wine, its ripeness, alcohol level, and longevity. It's important to check the vintage to see whether the wine is ready to drink.

BURGUNDY

1. **Domaine bottling** This means that the wine was bottled on the estate. Anything not bottled "à la propriété" or "au domaine" will probably be a less distinguished offering from a large merchant or cooperative.
2. **Grand Cru** This is the top level of the Burgundy classification. Montrachet is the name of a famous Grand Cru and as such does not need to include the name of its village on the label.
3. **Name of the producer**, in this case a leading Burgundy estate. "Domaine" means wine estate and is commonly used in Burgundy instead of château.

WINE LABELS OUTSIDE EUROPE

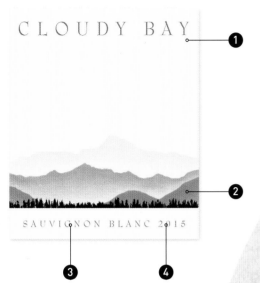

Labels from wine regions outside Europe are usually clearly laid out and easy to understand.

CLOUDY BAY

1. **Name of the wine producer** Wines produced out side the traditional appellation areas of Europe often promote the producer name over that of any region.
2. **Iconic design** A simple graphic image is commonly used for wine labels outside Europe in the same way as a European coat of arms. The Cloudy Bay brand has become instantly recognizable because of the strong image.
3. **Grape variety** The name of the grape is more important on this label than any region (Marlborough in New Zealand). Cloudy Bay has become such an iconic wine that you don't even need to include the name of the region. The grape variety is enough.
4. **Vintage** The year the grapes were harvested. Knowing how old the wine is will give you an idea of whether it will taste young or mature. Wines from the southern hemisphere go on sale in fall of the same year as the harvest.

ANATOMY OF A BOTTLE

1. **Closures** can be screw cap, as here (consistent and inert so the wine is reliable every time), or the more traditional cork, from the bark of cork trees chiefly found in Portugal and around the edges of the Mediterranean. It is the most efficient form of closure for wines requiring aging and the minute interchange of air which develops character. Plastic corks are okay for early-drinking wines.
2. **Capsule** used with a cork. Traditionally made of lead, but now tinfoil or plastic, it acts to keep the cork clean, stop insects, such as the cork weevil, from eating it, and helps maintain moisture, stopping the cork from drying out.
3. **Ullage** This is the gap between the closure and the wine. You want as small a gap as possible, because a large gap will show that the wine has begun to seep through the cork; because it will be replaced by air at a faster rate, decay will set in. Older wines have naturally more ullage because the cork will eventually shrink. In general, try to choose a wine with as little ullage as possible.
4. **Neck label** Some bottles have a neck label that usually shows the vintage date and maybe the shipper's name.
5. **Shoulder** This bottle has a typical Bordeaux shape with high shoulders. A Burgundy bottle should have sloping shoulders.
6. **Label** It should tell you all the necessary information concerning the wine. It varies with the type of wine and from country to country. There may also be a back label with additional information.
7. **Punt** This indentation in the bottom of the bottle is to catch sediment. Because few cheap wines have sediment, many of them are in bottles without punts.

The World of Wine

A sense of place may be the most precious, the most coveted character that a wine can possess. But can you smell it? Can you taste it? Can you feel it as you roll the wine across your tongue?

Sometimes you are sure that you can. Sometimes you are sure that the rich blackberry fruit you taste is streaked with a mineral fire and scratched with a smell of heat and hillside that could come only from the herb-strewn, sun-scorched vineyard you visited and where you bought the wine. Sometimes you are sure that the dancing acidity, the gossamer daintiness, and the cut of slate in a Mosel Riesling; or the dark, dry, imperious, gruff but not unfriendly fruit, rattled and rubbed by the undertow of stones and gravel, that you recognize in a brooding Bordeaux red—you are sure that these feel exactly "of their place." Other wines of less perfume, of less flavor, of less texture and presence still manage to tell you something of the grapes that gave them life. Not all vineyards are noble, beautiful, blessed by nature. Not all grape varieties are packed with personality, seductive or witty, cerebral, or swooning with scent. But if the winemakers are honest, if the grapes are grown well, and the wine is made with no attempt to be what it is not, then these wines also have a sense of place. We all have drunk a pitcher of basic red or pink or white that was just the perfect expression of the place where we were, the perfect flavor and texture. At that moment, with that meal, among those friends, it was the perfect wine. No other wine, no more sophisticated or expensive offering, could have given us such a sense of place.

Well, in this book I have tried to reveal the sense of place for as many wines as I can. I talk about wines great and small, about flavors memorable and fleeting. But, above all, I try to lead you into this wonderful world of wine that is my world of wine.

The village of Piesport huddles on the banks of the Mosel River, beneath a great south-facing wall of vines that manages to capture every last ray of summer sun to help the Riesling grapes ripen to perfection. You can understand at a glance why grapes can ripen here in such a northerly region—the vines are almost at the water's edge to benefit from the reflected light and heat from the river, and the forests on top of the hillside protect the vineyards from the winds. These wines can be fragile, pale, and an ethereal 7.5 percent alcohol, or dripping with honey and peach sweetness if picked very late in a warm year.

France

Nobody does it better—or do they? France has built her reputation on such wines as Champagne, from the cool, chalk hills east of Paris. But nowadays outside competition, particularly from countries with similar chalky soil, is forcing France to look to her laurels.

We've had our tiffs. I've stormed off and formed fleeting, flirtatious liaisons with other nations around the world, but I've always come back to France. When it comes to wine, no country can do so many things as well as France. My love of France, my respect for her natural genius in wine is deepened, not diminished, by contact with her rivals in Europe and elsewhere. The more I learn about wine in Chile, Australia, California, Italy, Spain, or New Zealand, the more I appreciate France.

But then, France is lucky. Her geographical situation is ideally suited to many of the grape varieties that make great wine, and her geological makeup has provided numerous sites perfectly suited to the measured ripening of these varieties. This combination provides a wide array of areas that achieve a precise balance between too much heat and too little, between too much rain and too little. The result is that the great varieties, such as Cabernet Sauvignon, Pinot Noir, Syrah, Chardonnay, and Sauvignon Blanc, will generally creep toward ripeness instead of rushing headlong. Just as with an apple, slowly ripened fruit gives the most delicious flavor, the balance among sugar, acidity, and perfume is most perfectly achieved. Nowadays, modern vineyard technology can mimic such conditions up to a point in warm areas, and perfect cool cellar and winemaking conditions can be created as easily at the equator as at the North Pole. However, such developments are only a generation old.

France's other priceless natural asset has always been her winemaking conditions. For two thousand years before the advent of refrigeration techniques, most major French wine areas were sufficiently cool by harvest time for the wines to ferment in a controlled way without artificial help, preserving the delicious but fragile balance of the fruit. Other great wine nations, such as Italy and Spain, America and Australia, had few areas that could rely on such luck. France also enjoyed her position at the crossroads of Europe, and she has a longer ongoing tradition of fashioning wines to suit the export markets than her competitors around the Mediterranean.

These days, it's true, newer countries and regions seem intent on stealing her thunder and proving that, whatever France can do, they can do better. We're in a fascinating period at the moment as France, with one eye on the New World, redefines her ideas of what makes a wine great and what makes her wines different from all others.

The Wine Regions of France

WE'RE STANDING ON THE BROW of the Montagne de Reims in the Champagne region of northern France. The pale spring sun hardly takes the edge off the damp westerly gale, scudding in over the soggy plains. We're just about at the northern limit beyond which the classic grape varieties will not ripen, but it feels as though we're way past it. Back in town, we descend windswept into the cool chalky cellars, dreaming of a good log fire and a hot toddy. No such luck. We have the "clear wines," the *vins clairs*, to taste. They cut our gums with the raw attack of a hacksaw slicing through a crab apple. Undrinkable. Yet once local magicians have been to work, this reedy, rasping liquid will transform into Champagne, the world's classic sparkling wine. No riper grapes, no less sour wine, no warmer, more protected slopes would do.

So let's flee to the other end of France to the parched terraces above the Mediterranean at Banyuls, just yards from the Spanish border. Let's go at harvest time and protect ourselves from the searing sun and scorching wind that shrivel Grenache grapes halfway to raisins on the vine. In the warmish cellars, we taste the thick, sweet juice of these ripened grapes, then try the wines a year old, then two years, five, ten, always getting deeper, more chocolate-rich, more molasses-like, more damson dark. This is Banyuls Grand Cru, the nearest thing in France to vintage Port. No less ripe grapes, no less luscious wine, no cooler, less sheltered sites would do.

These are the two extremes of France. In between, almost every conceivable type of wine is made, from the driest to the richest of whites, from rosés as ethereal as sweet pea's bloom to ones as ruddy as a butcher's cheeks, from carefree reds to toss back from the pitcher,

to reds as solemn as temples. All of these I'll try to show you in the following pages.

France's vineyards can be roughly divided into three areas. On the Atlantic coast, from the Loire Valley, down through Bordeaux, and on to the western Pyrenees, the climate is maritime. The Gulf Stream moderates the climate, but rain carried in by the westerly winds is a continual problem. In the Loire, mesoclimate and well-drained soil are crucial to decent wine. In Bordeaux, although the Landes pine forests draw off much rain, free-draining gravel beds are vital for the great Cabernet Sauvignon to ripen. This influence spreads up the Dordogne, Lot, Garonne, and Tarn rivers, lessening until the Mediterranean influence takes over east of Toulouse.

The grape varieties, the styles of wine, the food, the lifestyle, and the landscape all change. The vine grows naturally and easily right around the warm, inland Mediterranean. Summers are hot and dry; winters are mild. Close to the sea, breezes ameliorate the sun's heat but don't interfere with the ripening of the grapes.

CLASSIFICATIONS

France's wine classification system is slowly falling in line with general changes in the European Union wine industry, leading to four levels:

Vin is for generic wine at the bottom of the pile. It can indicate only the color of the wine, with no vintage or grapes used.

Vin de France is the first controlled basic category. It can show both grape variety and vintage on the label, covering both everyday wines and exciting nonmainstream innovations.

IGP (Indication Géographique Protégée/Protected Geographical Indication) replaces the middle-ranking Vin de Pays category. For instance, Vin de Pays d'Oc may now appear with Pays d'Oc IGP on the label. It'll taste exactly the same, but there'll be another gaggle of contented bureaucrats somewhere in Europe. The quality can range from ordinary to stunning. Most French single-variety wines bearing names such as "Chardonnay" and "Merlot" will be in this category.

AOP (Appellation d'Origine Protégée) is gradually replacing AOC (Appellation d'Origine Contrôlée). Guarantees origin and style of a wine but not its quality.

ENGLISH
CHANNEL

BELGIUM

LILLE

LUXEMBOURG

GERMANY

CHERBOURG

LE HAVRE

AMIENS

ROUEN

METZ

REIMS

CAEN

Seine

CHÂLONS-EN-
-CHAMPAGNE

ÉPERNAY

STRASBOURG

ALSACE

PARIS

CHAMPAGNE

Marne

Moselle

Rhin

BREST

Seine

Aube

Rhin

COLMAR

RENNES

Mayenne

Sarthe

Loir

VENDÔME

ORLÉANS

AUXERRE

TROYES

BAR-SUR-SEINE

TONNERRE

BAR-SUR-AUBE

Yonne

Saône

Doubs

MULHOUSE

VOSGES

SWITZERLAND

ANCENIS

ANGERS

TOURS

BLOIS

SANCERRE

POUILLY-SUR-LOIRE

DIJON

ST-NAZAIRE

Loire

L O I R E

BOURGES

BURGUNDY

BEAUNE

ARBOIS

NANTES

Sèvre Nantaise

SAUMUR

CHOLET

CHINON

REUILLY

Indre

Cher

BEAUNE

JURA

Lac Léman

GENÈVE

THOUARS

VIENNE

CHÂTEAUMEILLANT

CHALON-
SUR-SAÔNE

Ain

MÂCON

VILLEFRANCHE

SAVOIE

CHAMBÉRY

POITIERS

Vienne

Sioul

Allier

Loire

LYON

VIENNE

Isère

ALPS

ITALY

LA ROCHELLE

LIMOGES

CLERMONT-
FERRAND

ST-ÉTIENNE

Rhône

ATLANTIC
OCEAN

PÉRIGUEUX

Dordogne

l'Isle

VALENCE

Drôme

RHÔNE
VALLEY

Var

Gironde

BORDEAUX

LIBOURNE

BERGERAC

MASSIF
CENTRAL

Ardèche

BORDEAUX

Garonne

Lot

ORANGE

LANGON

CAHORS

Tarn

Gard

AVIGNON

NICE

AGEN

MONTAUBAN

NÎMES

Durance

CANNES

SOUTH-WEST

ALBI

AIX

PROVENCE

ST-TROPEZ

BAYONNE

AUCH

TOULOUSE

Hérault

BÉZIERS

MARSEILLE

TOULON

PAU

Garonne

Aude

CARCASSONNE

P Y R E N E E S

LANGUEDOC-
ROUSSILLON

PERPIGNAN

MEDITERRANEAN SEA

SPAIN

ANDORRA

BASTIA

C O R S E

AJACCIO

BONIFACIO

MAIN WINE REGIONS

- Bordeaux
- Loire Valley
- Champagne
- Alsace
- Jura
- Burgundy
- Savoie-Bugey
- Rhône Valley
- Provence
- Corsica
- Languedoc-Roussillon
- Southwest

IGP REGIONS

- --- Val de Loire
- --- Atlantique
- --- Comté Tolosan
- --- Pays d'Oc
- --- Méditerranée
- --- Comtés Rhodaniens

The great wines of St-Émilion and Pomerol on the right bank of Bordeaux are largely based on Merlot, and in the last decades of the twentieth century this grape rapidly became the wine drinker's darling, planted like fury all over the world.

Otherwise, the heat is tempered by regular westerly and northern winds and by planting vines up toward the mountain ranges that crowd in on the coastal plains. Vast amounts of ordinary wines are made out of grapes such as the red Carignan and Cinsaut and the white Macabeo and Ugni Blanc. When vines grow this easily, winemakers must tame their vigor if they want quality. Old vines and infertile stony soil reduce the yields, and then some magnificent wines ensue. The *vins doux naturels*, from Banyuls in the Pyrenees to Beaumes-de-Venise and Rasteau in the Rhône Valley, are heady and sweet. The Languedoc-Roussillon region is undergoing a revolution based on old, dark, savage reds from the varieties of the South, as well as bright, exciting, modern wines from international varieties led by Cabernet, Merlot, Syrah, and Chardonnay. Provence is still nervously nibbling at the revolution on her doorstep, but the reds and whites of the Rhône Valley are roaring and prancing with a self-belief in their stupendous qualities that is a joy to behold.

Above Lyon, the climate changes again, becoming more continental as the Mediterranean influence wanes. To the west, in the upper reaches of the Loire, the Atlantic influence flickers and dies. Winters become harsher, summers hotter. Vineyards stretch much further north on this eastern side of France, but grapes don't ripen that easily. Fall storms often herald the end of summer a crucial week or so before the harvest is ready, so mesoclimates are all-important here. In Burgundy, sheltered southeast-facing slopes, protected from the wet westerlies and angled to every ray of sun, are at a premium. The scattered mountain sites of Savoie and Jura hack out their small warm mesoclimates from forest and rock. Alsace squeezes up against the Vosges mountains, whose peaks to the west provide a rain shadow, making the region one of the sunniest and driest parts of France. Then there's Champagne: A few unlikely but ideal sites allow for Pinot and Chardonnay to ripen just enough to make the magical drink that is Champagne.

VIN DE FRANCE

In 2010, France's former Vin de Table category transformed into Vin de France. The classification encompasses mainly entry-level wines, sometimes made from multiregional blends, and many of these have not, as yet, lived up to my hopes that they would significantly improve the quality of the old Vin de Table. But, it is also being used by innovative, quality-driven producers who have generally chosen to opt out of the formal classification system in order to explore unusual blends, areas outside the traditional AOP or IGP classifications or unconventional vinification techniques. The Loire and Languedoc-Roussillon seem to be leading the way.

The vast area of the Languedoc is the largest wine-producing region of France and one of its most exciting, too.

Bordeaux

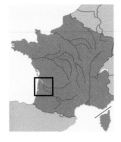

I CAN'T HELP IT. I love Bordeaux. It isn't the most friendly of wine regions. It isn't the most beautiful. Its wines can be pig-headed and difficult to understand when they are young, and some can be pretty harsh when they're still in barrel. Some never truly learn how to smile. But you know what they say about your first time.

Bordeaux was my first ever wine visit, my first ever vineyards. Bordeaux was my first wine-tasting. Bordeaux was my first great wine. First, first, first. I suppose it's not so strange for someone brought up in England. When I was in higher education at university, great wine was red, and great red wine was Bordeaux. Every wine-tasting session would always end up as a passionate discussion of the minutiae of different Bordeaux properties and vintages as we lapped up every scrap of knowledge we could. So it was only natural that one summer vacation I would optimistically jump into my bright yellow Mini and, armed with a precious introduction to the late Peter Sichel at Château d'Angludet in Margaux, head off to what I hoped would be wine drinkers' nirvana.

APPELLATIONS AND CLASSIFICATIONS

» **Red wines** At its most basic, the wine is simply labeled Bordeaux or Bordeaux Supérieur. Above this are the more specific AOCs covering subareas (such as the Haut-Médoc) and individual villages or communes (such as Pomerol, St-Émilion, or Margaux). Single-estate Crus Bourgeois from the Médoc are the next rung up on the quality ladder, followed by the Crus Classés (Classed Growths) of the Médoc, Graves, and St-Émilion. The famous classification of 1855 ranked the top red wines of the Médoc (plus one from Graves) into five tiers, from First to Fifth Growths (Crus); there has been only one change, in 1973, promoting Château Mouton-Rothschild to First Growth status. Since the 1950s, the Graves/Pessac-Léognan region has had its own classification for red and white wines. St-Émilion's classification (for only red wines) has been revised several times, the latest modification being in 2012; the possibility of regrading can help to maintain quality, as can the fear of getting relegated. Curiously, Pomerol, home of Châteaux Pétrus and Le Pin, two of the most famous red wines in the world, has no official pecking order.

» **White wines** The two largest dry white wine AOCs are Bordeaux Blanc and Entre-Deux-Mers, whose Sauvignon- and Sémillon-based whites are usually affordable and pleasant. There are plenty of good to excellent dry wines in the Graves and Pessac-Léognan regions; the Pessac-Léognan AOC contains all the dry white Classed Growths. The great sweet wines of Sauternes and Barsac were classified as First or Second Growths in 1855, at the same time as the reds, with Château d'Yquem designated "Superior" First Growth.

» **Second wines** Many top châteaux make "second wines" that are cheaper versions of their Grands Vins. These generally comprise wine from younger vines or barrels that didn't suit the blend of the main wine. Because they are far cheaper than the main label, they're usually worth trying.

» **Deluxe labels** Some properties with less prestigious appellations, such as Bordeaux Supérieur, make a "super-cuvée" to try to ape the wines of the top areas. These are generally oaky and heavy and more expensive—instead of more exciting and satisfying.

I had expected great rolling hills and dales all covered in vines. Jovial bucolic cellar masters and their swains ever eager to swap a tale and share a jar. Villages and towns bustling with the busy activities of wine. I should have gone anywhere but Bordeaux. At first I found no vineyards at all. Bordeaux was a splendid, haughtily magnificent place—well, the city center was; the rest was sprawling suburbia and industrial sites. As I drove out toward Margaux, the little villages seemed sullenly asleep and the land damp, low-browed, and devoid of vines. I did find the vines; of course, I did once I got to Margaux; I did find friendly if not exactly gregarious people, and across these broad, undulating acres, I did find some amazing châteaux—the grand houses at the center of many estates—but the Médoc, with the best will in the world,

isn't exactly a sylvan paradise. Once those vines start, that's all you get where the soil's at all suitable—vines. I found a few hills and dales around St-Émilion, but even there it is mostly just a carpet of vines. Graves isn't quite so wall-to-wall because many of its best vineyards are now buried under suburbia, the railroad marshaling yard, and an airport.

No great scenery, just vines, vines, vines. That is the key to why Bordeaux can claim the title of the world's greatest wine region. Although there are numerous places in France, the rest of Europe, North America, and the Southern Hemisphere that can boast great wines, most are produced in tiny quantities. Bordeaux has great swathes of land suited to different kinds of wine, and currently there are some 303,929 acres of vines.

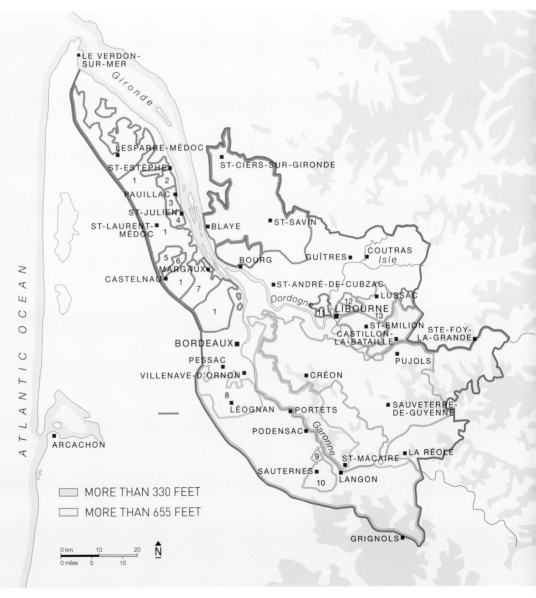

MAIN WINE APPELLATIONS

- — BORDEAUX
- — MÉDOC
  - **1.** Haut-Médoc
  - **2.** St-Estèphe
  - **3.** Pauillac
  - **4.** St-Julien
  - **5.** Listrac-Médoc
  - **6.** Moulis-en-Médoc
  - **7.** Margaux
- — GRAVES
  - **8.** Pessac-Léognan
- — SWEET WINES
  - **9.** Barsac
  - **10.** Sauternes
- — Bourg,
  Côtes de Bourg
- — Blaye,
  Côtes de Blaye
- — FRONSAC
  - **11.** Canon-Fronsac
- — POMEROL
  - **12.** Lalande de
  Pomerol
- — ST-ÉMILION
  - **13.** St-Émilion
  satellites
- — Castillon-Côtes
  de Bordeaux
- — Francs-Côtes
  de Bordeaux
- — Cadillac-Côtes
  de Bordeaux
- — Entre-Deux-Mers

MORE THAN 330 FEET
MORE THAN 655 FEET

0 km   10   20
0 miles   5   10

N

There are about 9,800 properties in all, with an average vineyard holding of 142 acres, which is high compared to many other parts of Europe. More than 40 percent of the producers bottle their own wine, the rest being sold in bulk; and cooperatives produce one-quarter of the wine. The region produces a staggering total of close to 900 billion bottles of wine. Every year.

In general terms, the vines to the west of the river Garonne and the Gironde estuary are called "Left Bank"; the Médoc and the Graves/Pessac-Léognan regions are the most important of these. "Right Bank" applies to the vineyards to the east of the Dordogne River and the Gironde. These are led by St-Émilion and Pomerol.

CLIMATE AND SOIL

Most of the Bordeaux region grows vines to a greater or lesser extent, but only certain favored localities regularly achieve exceptional quality. The sea to the west gives some clues. The Gulf Stream draws in warm tropical currents up this western shore of France, crucially ameliorating temperatures near the coast. Yet the Bay of Biscay is also notoriously stormy. Only the vast stretches of Landes pine forest to the west break the salt-laden westerly winds and suck down much of the rainfall that could otherwise ruin a vintage. The consequence is a pattern of generally hot summers and long, mild falls still only just warm enough to fully ripen the local grape varieties. But there's a fair amount of rainfall, too, and here's where the gravel and the limestone slopes come in.

The Garonne, the Dordogne, and the Isle rivers have, over the millennia, deposited deep gravel terraces in the broad ridges that characterize the Médoc and many parts of Pessac-Léognan and Pomerol. Gravel is virtually free-draining. When excess rain does fall, it drops straight through the gravel. The limestone slopes of St-Émilion, Bourg, Blaye, and Cadillac-Côtes de Bordeaux achieve this to a lesser degree.

Vines put down deep roots in gravel and limestone as they search for scant supplies of nutrients. In a climate only just warm enough to ripen the crop, an excess of water would bloat the grapes and fatally retard ripening. There are years when even the efficient draining gravel and limestone can't stop the crop being deluged, but the best vineyards—those that prune severely to restrict yield and have enough mature vines with deep roots in gravel or limestone—have an amazing record of producing good wines in years that should be write-offs. In years of drought, although clay soil holds water better, mature vines with roots stretching far into deep gravel beds will conserve enough water to survive the torrid heat and give a decent crop.

RED GRAPE VARIETIES

Bordeaux red wines can have up to six different varieties, and not many good properties use fewer than three. White wines come from five main grapes, and almost all properties use at least two.

The taste is only one part of the reason for planting several different varieties. Simple farming practicality is at least as important. Although the Gironde estuary and the Dordogne and Garonne rivers contribute stability of day and nighttime temperatures, spring frosts do occur. Though the Gulf Stream broadly acts as a warm water heater for the entire coastal region, maritime climates are very fickle, and June is often plagued with clouds and damp weather. Bordeaux generally enjoys the warm hazy falls typical of a mild maritime climate, but the Bay of Biscay can still send over torrential rainstorms in fall for several days at a time.

The Bordeaux varieties all bud, flower, and ripen at different times. A farmer might thus lose some of his crop, but not all. At harvest time, rain might catch the Merlot and Cabernet Franc crop, but afterward the sun often returns and can bring the slower maturing Cabernet Sauvignon or Petit Verdot to super-ripeness.

Each variety not only contributes its own flavor but also complements the flavors of the others. Each variety does more or less well on different types of soil. Part of the skill for a proprietor is knowing what land to plant with which variety and then working out how much of each will make up the best final blend. In an area such as the Haut-Médoc, where, in the best vineyards, the old timers say the soil "changes with every step," it all helps to explain why seemingly identical neighboring properties produce wines that are always fascinatingly different.

Cabernet Sauvignon is the most famous red variety, contributing a powerful color, a sinewy structure of tannin, and a dark, brooding fruit that takes years to open out to black currant, black cherry, cedar, and cigars. It doesn't like damp clay and performs best on deep, well-drained gravel in the Left Bank regions. It is the king of the Haut-Médoc's top vineyards, important in Pessac-Léognan, but much less important in the cool clay of St-Émilion and Pomerol on the Right Bank.

Merlot is the king in St-Émilion and Pomerol and indeed is the most widely planted variety in Bordeaux. It thrives in fertile but cool, damp clay. It gives high yields yet ripens early and produces succulent juicy wines of high alcohol and good color. In Pessac-Léognan and the Médoc, it is planted on less well-drained soil and softens and fattens the austere beauty of Cabernet Sauvignon.

The lesser red varieties are the perfumed yet lighter-bodied Cabernet Franc, used as a seasoning in the Médoc, but important in St-Émilion and Pomerol, particularly on limestone soil; Malbec, a juicy richly flavored grape, now in decline; and Petit Verdot, an excellent late ripener, full of perfume, color, and tannin but notoriously difficult to grow. Carménère, once considered extinct, is now making a cautious comeback.

WHITE GRAPE VARIETIES

Sémillon is the most important white variety, particularly in Graves and Sauternes. On its own, the wine can be relatively flat and waxy, but it gains marvelous complexity when blended with Sauvignon Blanc and aged for a year or two. In Sauternes, its susceptibility to noble rot makes it the favorite sweet wine grape.

Sauvignon Blanc is a trendy grape, but in Bordeaux, by itself, it rarely achieves the exciting flavors it can attain in the Loire or New Zealand. Blended with Sémillon, it adds a mouthwatering tang and an acid backbone that can work tremendously well. Muscadelle is an aromatic grape that can add a spiciness to dry whites and a grapey richness to sweet whites. Colombard adds a crucial green fruity zest to whites, especially in the Bourg and Blaye areas. Ugni Blanc is Cognac's distilling grape and, though still grown in Bordeaux, produces pretty thin stuff.

WINEMAKING IN BORDEAUX

The styles of wines the various grapes produce depend upon the amounts of each in the blend, the siting of the vineyard, and the ambitions and talents of the producer. Splendid sites are in a minority, as are ambitious producers. Only about 40 percent of growers bottle their own wine, the rest simply selling the grapes, the juice, or the wine to merchant houses or to the cooperatives.

Consequently, basic Bordeaux Rouge or Bordeaux Blanc will generally be a light, simple wine from the less-favored hinterland of Bordeaux. To be honest, such land is better suited to whites, which, when carefully made, are refreshing and appetizing. Red grapes rarely ripen fully in such soil, and basic Bordeaux Rouge is usually thin, often raw, and just occasionally appetizing. However, even in these lesser areas, an ambitious proprietor can do a great deal to improve his or her wine.

THE CHÂTEAU SYSTEM

The word "château" is a grand-sounding title. Its literal translation is "castle," and if you have visions of turrets, high fortified walls, and portcullis gates guarding the moat— well, that's all right. But there are few châteaux like that in Bordeaux. The idea of a château coming to represent a

BORDEAUX AOC

Bordeaux produces more famous red wines than any other region in the world. Yet these fabled and expensive wines comprise only a tiny part of what the region offers: red, rosé, dry, medium, and sweet white—and even fizz— from sixty different Appellations d'Origine Contrôlées spreading across the Gironde *département*. Most of the best wines are allowed specific district or commune AOCs (such as Margaux or Sauternes), but a vast amount of the wine—delicious, atrocious, and everything in between—is sold as Bordeaux AOC.

At its best, straight red Bordeaux is marked by bone-dry leafy fruit and an attractive earthy edge, and as global warming kicks in, raw, tannic examples are becoming less common. Good examples usually benefit from a year or so of aging. Bordeaux Blanc has joined the modern world with an increasing number of refreshing, pleasant wines. These may be labeled as Bordeaux Sauvignon. Drink them young. Bordeaux Clairet is a pale red wine, virtually rosé but with a little more substance. Bordeaux rosé is often pale, appetizing, and good value. Bordeaux Supérieur red covers the same area as the Bordeaux AOC, but the wines must have an extra 0.5 percent alcohol, a lower yield, and a longer period of maturation. The wines from many good small properties, or *petits châteaux,* are labeled Bordeaux Supérieur.

particular wine arose in the eighteenth century, when the wealthy businessmen and parliamentarians of Bordeaux began to hanker for magnificent estates at which to relax and indulge in some showing off. The Médoc was the area most of those grandees chose to explore, and the most impressive estates are generally found closer to the city of Bordeaux itself.

Almost all of these properties developed vineyards, too, and, by 1855, a hierarchy had sufficiently developed for a famous classification to be made that still largely holds today (page 50). What also began to happen was the adoption of the title "château" for an estate's wines, even when there was no imposing building deserving the name. In recent years, the use of the word "château" has spread throughout Bordeaux as a mark of supposed superiority and individuality. Any proprietor determined to improve his wine, and thus his selling price, will find that calling his estate "Château Something" is the first step in adding value to his wine, however uncastle-like his farmhouse may be.

The Left Bank/The Médoc and Haut-Médoc

RED GRAPES
Cabernet Sauvignon is the main variety, performing brilliantly on the warm gravelly Médoc soil. Lesser varieties are the softer perfumed Cabernet Franc, Merlot planted on cooler, less well-drained soil, Malbec (in the Bas-Médoc), and the late-ripening Petit Verdot. The old variety Carménère has begun to make a comeback.

CLIMATE
The soothing influence of the Gulf Stream sweeping along the Atlantic coast produces long, warm summers and cool, wet winters. The Landes pine forests act as a natural windbreak, sheltering the vineyards. Heavy rains can be a problem at harvest time.

SOIL
The topsoil is mostly free-draining gravel mixed with sand; the subsoil is gravel with sand plus some limestone and clay. The best vineyards are on the gravel outcrops.

GEOGRAPHY
Generally low-lying and flat with the main relief provided by gravel ridges and low plateaus, especially in the Haut-Médoc. Most of the top vineyards are on gentle rises facing east and southeast toward the Gironde estuary.

THE BEST PLACE to get a good look at the Médoc is from the middle of a traffic jam. I'd recommend about 9 a.m. or 5:30 p.m. on a nice bright spring day, sitting patiently on the lofty span of the Pont d'Aquitaine that sweeps across the Garonne River north of the city of Bordeaux.

Look north as far as the eye can see; out there are the great vineyards of Margaux and Cantenac. Further on—from this height they should still be visible—are St-Julien, Pauillac, and even St-Estèphe. Ah, bliss. Please God keep the traffic snarled up a little longer while you pause to dream.

I'm afraid dreams are your best bet. You are getting by far the best view of the land that is the Médoc, home to many of the greatest red wines in the world. But there's not much to see even from the bridge. There are the industrial sites, the sprawling suburbs, the scrubby-looking trees, and the mud flats glumly following the Garonne's shores around toward Macau and Margaux. But the vineyards? Don't great vineyards need slopes and hills and precious perfect exposures to the sun? It's difficult to believe that in this flat, marshy-looking pudding of a place these unique preconditions exist, but they do.

The highest spot in the Médoc—all 50 miles long of it—is only 141 feet above sea level. That's at the village of Listrac-Médoc, not even one of the best places. All the best vineyards are located between 13 feet above sea level (parts of Château Montrose in St-Estèphe and other good properties in Pauillac, St-Julien, and Margaux creep down this close to the slimy edge of the Gironde estuary) and 95 feet (Pauillac's Château Lynch-Moussas outstretches Château Pontet-Canet to reach these giddy heights). Amazingly, this pathetic 82-foot spread is enough to provide growing conditions for Cabernet Sauvignon, Cabernet Franc, Merlot, and Petit Verdot vines that the entire wine world envies and would give anything to possess.

Right. Let's get off this bridge if we can and head up toward Margaux. But keep your eyes peeled for two things: drainage ditches, or *jalles*, and those times when you suddenly realize that the land is almost imperceptibly rising up a yard or two. You might also look right to check whether you can see the glistening waters of the Gironde because the saying is that all the best vineyards in the Médoc are within sight of the estuary. Thinking about this, I realize that there's hardly a single top vineyard without a view of the water.

Those drainage ditches are critical because, before Dutch engineers arrived in the seventeenth century, the Médoc was a desolate, dangerous, flood-prone swamp. The Dutch, who are, I suppose, world experts on matters of drainage, dug the great channels that still slant east across the Médoc to the Gironde and created dry land where bog existed before. The slight rises in the land show where gravel ridges, washed down from the Massif Central and Pyrenees millennia ago, provide islands of warm free-draining soil rising out of the clay. Remember that the Médoc is not a particularly warm place and that the Cabernet Sauvignon, the main grape of the region, takes a long time to ripen. It needs these deep gravel beds that warm up quickly in spring if it is going to do well in most years. Indeed, in parts of Margaux, the fine gravel is mixed with white pebbles, which, they say, helps the ripening process by reflecting the light on to the grapes.

I'm taking the small D2 road up from Bordeaux because I never fail to get a thrill when the woodland sweeps aside and a broad, gentle slope to my right displays the excellent Château la Lagune. Almost immediately I plunge into more woods, but deep in a glade to my left is the fairytale keep of Château Cantemerle, whose gravel crest spreads out beyond the trees.

MARGAUX

A moment more and we're in the appellation area of Margaux, but not in its heart. There is a fair amount of sand and clay in many of the vineyards at Labarde and at Cantenac, but there are some fine properties, particularly on the southwest-facing slope around Château Brane-Cantenac. However, this is one of the thankfully few areas where the validity of the 1855 classification as a guide to the quality of the wines is questionable, although from about 1996 many of the underperforming properties began to get their act together. It's no good having lovely vineyards if you don't put heart and soul—and, I fear, bank balance—into the creation of great wine, and for most of the late twentieth century, châteaux around here with great potential seemed to lack the will to excel. A new generation taking over, some much-needed investment, and occasionally the purchase of the property by a well-funded outsider all can turn things around, and fine Cantenac properties, such as Brane-Cantenac, Cantenac-Brown, Kirwan, and du Tertre, are witness to this.

There is only one Classed Growth in the backwoods behind Cantenac: the Fifth Growth Château du Tertre, sitting on a knoll of gravelly soil just north of the little village of Arsac. With a little maturity du Tertre opens out into a delightful blend of black currant fruit and violet perfume far more consistently than do many of the properties with higher classifications and supposedly better sites nearer the Gironde estuary.

Châteaux Monbrison and d'Angludet aren't classified at all. Yet, due to the determination of their respective proprietors, the wines they produce, from supposedly inferior soil, can easily rival many Classed Growth Margaux wines. It is possible that Margaux has even more potentially great vineyard land than Pauillac or St-Julien to the north. Thank goodness for the new generation of proprietors and winemakers doing their best to prove this could be the case.

Altogether there are five villages in the Margaux appellation totalling 3,677 acres of vines and including a grand total of twenty-one Classed Growths, but the greatest Margaux vineyards begin around the village of Issan and continue on to the little town of Margaux itself. We're on a broad plateau here, gently sloping east to the river, and the ground seems white with pebbles and even the gravelly soil is frequently a pale sickly gray. But that's excellent for the vines. The soil offering few nutrients, the vines send their taproots deep below the surface. As a result, the wines of Margaux are rarely massive—although Châteaux Rauzan-Ségla and Margaux can be deep and chewy—yet they develop a haunting scent of violets and a pure perfume of black currants that is as dry as those sun-bleached pebbles yet seems as sweet as preserves.

The Margaux vineyards continue north to Soussans, yet they become darker, the clay more evident, and suddenly we dive into marshy woodland and they've gone. A matter of 16 feet or so difference in the height of the land, and we lose all that gravel and are left with damp cold clay. We're now in a kind of no-man's-land until we reach St-Julien about 8 miles ahead. There are vineyards here, around Lamarque and Cussac, the best being accorded the appellation Haut-Médoc, but they lack the brilliance of Margaux because the vineyards crucially lack the depth of gravel and the drainage but also because the owners haven't had the cash or the passion to invest.

MOULIS AND LISTRAC

There are, however, two small appellations just west of Arcins that do have gravel and can produce excellent wine: Moulis and Listrac-Médoc. Neither of these villages has any Classed Growth properties, but looking at the excellent vineyard sites of Moulis, in particular, you could be excused for thinking that the growers there were

KING CABERNET

Cabernet Sauvignon is the most famous red grape variety in the world, contributing a powerful color, a sinewy structure of tannin, and a dark, brooding fruit that takes ten to twenty years for the aggression to fade and the fruit to become as sweet and perfumed as fresh black currants and black cherries mingled magically with a fragrance of cedarwood and cigar boxes. It is this character that has made red Bordeaux famous for at least two centuries. Cabernet Sauvignon doesn't like damp clay and performs best on deep, well-drained gravel in the Left Bank regions, where it is blended with varying amounts of Merlot, Cabernet Franc, and sometimes Petit Verdot. It is the king of the Haut-Médoc's top vineyards, important in Pessac-Léognan just to the south, but is much less important in the cool clay of St-Émilion and Pomerol on the Right Bank.

a little unlucky. Above all, over near the railroad, around the village of Grand Poujeaux there are some splendid deep gravel ridges that would definitely have qualified for honors if they had been within the boundaries of such major villages as Margaux or St-Julien. Never mind; it allows us as wine drinkers that rare experience in Bordeaux: relatively bargain-priced wine of classic quality. The leader of this group of gravel-based wines is Château Chasse-Spleen—splendidly dark and sturdy but beautifully ripe at its core. Other high grade wines also come from such châteaux as Maucaillou and Poujeaux.

Moulis is the better of these appellations, with a fine ridge of gravel running through its midst. Listrac-Médoc has some gravel, too, but is a crucial mile or so further away from the mild influence of the Gironde, and is located another 65 feet higher. Higher vineyards are cooler vineyards, and in a marginal climate like the Médoc, even 65 feet makes a difference. Whereas the Moulis wines are generally marked by an attractive precociousness, a soft-centered fruit and smooth-edged structure, Listrac wines are always sterner, more jut-jawed, and less easy to love, although a greater percentage of Merlot in the

MÉDOC APPELLATIONS

» **Médoc AOC**   The Médoc peninsula, north of Bordeaux on the left bank of the Gironde estuary, produces a good fistful of the world's most famous reds. These are all situated in the Haut-Médoc, the southern, more gravelly half of the area. The Médoc AOC, for only reds, covers the northern part. The best vineyards are on gravel outcrops from the ever-present clay and, with a little help from climate change and improved grape-growing and winemaking methods, are producing increasingly attractive, earthy but juicy wines.

» **Haut-Médoc AOC**   The finest gravelly soil is here in the southern half of the Médoc peninsula; this AOC covers all the decent vineyard land not included in the six village AOCs (Margaux, Moulis, Listrac, St-Julien, Pauillac, and St-Estèphe). Wines vary in quality and style but often achieve a delightful balance beween black fruit, cedar scent, and a mild stony undertow.

» **Listrac-Médoc AOC**   Set back from the Gironde and away from the best Haut-Médoc gravel ridges, Listrac wines can be good but rarely thrilling and are marked by solid fruit, a slightly coarse tannin, and an earthy flavor. More Merlot and warmer vintages are now producing softer wines with more perfume and appeal.

» **Margaux AOC**   AOC centered on the village of Margaux but also including other villages, such as Cantenac and Labarde. The best wines are off deep gravel banks, most of which are based around the village of Margaux. The wines are rarely heavy and should have a divine perfume after seven to twelve years.

» **Moulis AOC**   Small AOC within the Haut-Médoc. Much of the wine is excellent—delicious at five to six years old, although good examples can age for ten to twenty years—and not overpriced.

» **Pauillac**   The deep gravel banks around the town of Pauillac in the Haut-Médoc are the heartland of Cabernet Sauvignon. For many wine lovers, the king of red wine grapes finds its ultimate expression in the three Pauillac First Growths (Latour, Lafite-Rothschild, and Mouton-Rothschild). The large AOC also contains fifteen other Classed Growths. The uniting characteristic of Pauillac wines is their intense black-currant fruit flavor, pencil-shavings perfume, and undertow of graphite. These are the longest-lived of Bordeaux's great red wines.

» **St-Estèphe AOC**   Large AOC north of Pauillac with five Classed Growths. St-Estèphe wines have high tannin levels, and many start out with relatively earthy textures, but given time (ten to twenty years) those sought-after flavors of black currant and cedarwood do peek out. More Merlot has been planted to soften the wines and make them more accessible at an earlier age. As vintages get drier and hotter, these wines are coming into their own.

» **St-Julien AOC**   Situated directly south of Pauillac. For many, St-Julien produces perfect claret, with an ideal balance between opulence and austerity and between the brashness of youth and the genius of maturity. It is the smallest of the communal Haut-Médoc AOCs, but almost all is first-rate vineyard land and quality is high. The most cedar-and-cigar-box -scented wines come from the riverfront properties.

Château Margaux is one of the grandest and most elegant châteaux in Bordeaux. Built in 1810, the château is now almost hidden from passers-by on the road by an avenue of tall, stately trees. The wine is frequently one of Bordeaux's finest reds, too.

blend is making them more supple these days. The quality is there all right, but the style is old-fashioned and reserved. Even a supremely well-equipped and well-financed property such as Château Clarke, which strains every sinew to make a spicy, ripe-fruited, oak-scented "modern" classic, is often ultimately defeated by nature, its wine demanding the traditional decade of aging that most Listracs have always needed in order to shine.

ST-JULIEN

Your car has to change gear when you cross the wet meadows and the drainage channel beneath Château Beychevelle and enter the St-Julien AOC. It can change down a gear to navigate the left turn and upward sweep of the road, as suddenly the vineyards surge into existence once again. But you change gear up in wine terms, up into the highest gear in the red wine world, because St-Julien and its neighbor Pauillac just to the north have more great age-worthy red wines packed tight within their boundaries than any other patch of land on the Earth.

The St-Julien appellation is only 2,270 acres, but it has eleven Classed Growths; Pauillac has 3,007 acres and eighteen Classed Growths, including three First Growths. Here, the Cabernet Sauvignon, aided and abetted by the Merlot and the Cabernet Franc (and, in some châteaux, the Petit Verdot), exploits the deep gravel banks and the mellow maritime climate to produce grapes of an intensity and, above all, a balance between fruit and tannin, perfume and acid, which you simply don't find elsewhere. Add to this some of the world's highest prices for wine, which in itself is no good thing—although when the profit is reinvested in an almost obsessive care of the vineyard, superior winery equipment, and row upon row of fragrant new oak barrels in which to age the wine, well, your pockets have to be deep. But you buy not only superb quality, you buy enviable consistency, too.

Château Beychevelle looks merely attractive from the roadway. Seen from the yards and lawns that run down toward the Gironde, it is a stunning piece of eighteenth-century architecture. The villages of Margaux, St-Julien, and Pauillac may consist largely of featureless vine monoculture, but the numerous enchanting and occasionally magnificent châteaux buildings do add a distinct air of romance and sophistication. I'm all for that because otherwise I'm afraid we're back to the same basics as in Margaux further south—drainage and gravel. The impoverished soil really makes the vine reach deep into the earth for nutrients, and, despite modern fertilizers and certain vine clones bred for high yield making their presence felt, such infertile soil naturally keeps the volume of the harvest down.

We're in a cool climate here, remember. Gravel is a warm, well-drained soil, and a small crop ripens more quickly when those fall rain clouds start to build up out in the Bay of Biscay.

That drainage channel we drove over close to Château Beychevelle is important because there is a whole ridge of vineyards running westward toward St-Laurent whose soil is a little heavier than is usual for St-Julien, and yet whose angle to the south and slope down toward the drainage channel help to produce excellent wines.

1855 CLASSIFICATION OF RED WINES

In 1855, the wine brokers of Bordeaux classified the leading châteaux of the Médoc into five levels and included with them one Graves property, Haut-Brion. They based their classification on the market prices of the wines. This is the original 1855 list brought up to date to take account of name changes and divisions of property as well as the promotion of Château Mouton-Rothschild to First Growth in 1973. Properties are listed in the order in which they were classified instead of being listed alphabetically. The commune name is in brackets.

» **First Growths (Premiers Crus)** Lafite-Rothschild (Pauillac); Margaux (Margaux); Latour (Pauillac); Haut-Brion (Pessac-Léognan); Mouton-Rothschild (Pauillac; since 1973).
» **Second Growths (Deuxièmes Crus)** Rauzan-Ségla (Margaux); Rauzan-Gassies (Margaux); Léoville-Las-Cases (St-Julien); Léoville-Poyferré (St-Julien); Léoville-Barton (St-Julien); Durfort-Vivens (Margaux); Gruaud-Larose (St-Julien); Lascombes (Margaux); Brane-Cantenac (Margaux); Pichon-Baron (Pauillac); Pichon-Longueville-Comtesse de Lalande (Pauillac); Ducru-Beaucaillou (St-Julien); Cos d'Estournel (St-Estèphe); Montrose (St-Estèphe).
» **Third Growths (Troisièmes Crus)** Kirwan (Margaux); d'Issan (Margaux); Lagrange (St-Julien); Langoa-Barton (St-Julien); Giscours (Margaux); Malescot-St-Exupéry (Margaux); Boyd-Cantenac (Margaux); Cantenac-Brown (Margaux); Palmer (Margaux); La Lagune (Haut-Médoc); Desmirail (Margaux); Calon-Ségur (St-Estèphe); Ferrière (Margaux); Marquis d'Alesme-Becker (Margaux).
» **Fourth Growths (Quatrièmes Crus)** St-Pierre (St-Julien); Talbot (St-Julien); Branaire-Ducru (St-Julien); Duhart-Milon (Pauillac); Pouget (Margaux); La Tour-Carnet (Haut-Médoc); Lafon-Rochet (St-Estèphe); Beychevelle (St-Julien); Prieuré-Lichine (Margaux); Marquis de Terme (Margaux).
» **Fifth Growths (Cinqièmes Crus)** Pontet-Canet (Pauillac); Batailley (Pauillac); Haut-Batailley (Pauillac); Grand-Puy-Lacoste (Pauillac); Grand-Puy-Ducasse (Pauillac); Lynch-Bages (Pauillac); Lynch-Moussas (Pauillac); Dauzac (Margaux); d'Armailhac (Pauillac); du Tertre (Margaux); Haut-Bages-Libéral (Pauillac); Pédesclaux (Pauillac); Belgrave (Haut-Médoc); Camensac (Haut-Médoc); Cos Labory (St-Estèphe); Clerc-Milon (Pauillac); Croizet-Bages (Pauillac); Cantemerle (Haut-Médoc).

Châteaux Gruaud-Larose and Branaire-Ducru are the most significant of the properties here. However, for the true genius of St-Julien—of wines of only middling weight that develop a haunting cigar, cedar, and black-currant fragrance as they age—we need to go back to the slopes near the Gironde, where three gravel outcrops push their way eastward and down toward the estuary. Château Ducru-Beaucaillou and the three Léoville properties occupy these slopes. Great wines all.

PAUILLAC

You can't tell where you leave St-Julien and enter Pauillac, the vines are so continuous. Well, yes you can—there's another little stream helping to drain famous vineyards such as Château Latour. Where the road crosses the stream, there's the boundary, and there is a change in wine style; Cabernet Sauvignon becomes even more dominant in Pauillac, the wines are darker and take longer to mature and yet have a more piercing black-currant fruit that mingles with the cedar-and-cigar-box fragrance. Certainly the extra percentage of Cabernet Sauvignon deepens the color of the wine, but that's possible only because Pauillac has the deepest gravel beds in the whole Médoc, stretched out across two broad plateaus to the south and north of the town of Pauillac. There's some iron in the gravel and a good deal of iron pan as subsoil. No one's ever proved it, but a lot of growers reckon iron in the soil gives extra depth to a red wine.

You certainly get your depth in Pauillac. Pauillac has eighteen Classed Growths in total and three of the 1855 Classification's five First Growths, each playing a different brilliant variation on the same black-currant and cedarwood theme, as well as a clutch of other excellent properties. Once again, the adage that the best vineyards have a view of the river holds sway because the buffeting of tides and currents that piled up those vital gravel banks has obviously left the deepest ridges close to the estuary. But the ridges go a long way back in Pauillac, and standing on tiptoe you can still just about see the river from properties such as Pontet-Canet and Grand-Puy-Lacoste. In fact, these two properties give some of the purest expressions of black-currant fruit and cedar perfume of any châteaux in Pauillac.

Every signpost in St-Julien and Pauillac bears yet another name dripping with the magic of memorable vintages and the promise of more to come. How much longer can this parade of excellence go on? Not much longer, I'm afraid. Cruising north past Château Lafite-Rothschild, past its unusually steep, well-drained vineyards, there's one more drainage stream ahead of us, and one long slope running along its north bank.

ST-ESTÈPHE

Here, we're in St-Estèphe, and despite the quality of these frontline vineyards, such as Cos d'Estournel, Cos Labory, and Château Lafon-Rochet, facing Pauillac over the Jalle du Breuil stream, from now on the gravel begins to fade, and there is more clay. We're further north, and ripening is slower here than in, say, Margaux. There's much more of the earlier-ripening Merlot planted to try to provide fleshy flavor from the clay soil. Despite the size of the appellation, at 3,000 acres only a whisker smaller than Pauillac, a mere five properties were classified in 1855. The best wines are very good—full, structured, and well-flavored and Montrose and Calon-Ségur on their patches of gravel and limestone can be among Bordeaux's best—but if you sometimes wonder whether they don't lack a little scent, whether they don't carry with them the vaguest hint of the clay beneath the vines, you're not wrong.

HAUT-MÉDOC

St-Estèphe marks the northern end of the great Médoc villages. Yet from the very gates of Bordeaux at Blanquefort, right up to St-Seurin-de-Cadourne, about a mile north of St-Estèphe, there are patches of land outside the main villages where a decent aspect, some good drainage, and sometimes some gravel occur. Often these vineyards are interspersed with woods, and almost all of these can use the Haut-Médoc AOC. There are even five Classed Growths within the AOC, which has 11,285 acres of vines, but, these apart, few wines exhibit the sheer excitement of the riverfront gravel-bed wines. Good proprietors make good wine, and climate change is helping.

MÉDOC

North of St-Seurin lies the Bas-Médoc (Lower Médoc), although its appellation is simply Médoc to spare the locals' egos. It's a flat but relaxing landscape covering 13,524 acres of vines, right up to the tip of the Médoc peninsula, although vineyards peter out north of Valeyrac. The whole area was a marsh before the Dutch started draining it in the eighteenth century. It's not ideal wine country, but there are a few gravel outcrops and some sandy clay, and on these there are an increasing number of well-financed, well run properties. Between them they produce a good deal of decent red wine and occasionally, as at Châteaux Potensac or Tour Haut-Caussan, something really good. With the gradual climate warming that has been evident in vintages such as 2003, '05, '09, and '15, we can expect more and more properties to deliver.

Graves and Pessac-Léognan

RED GRAPES
The main variety is Cabernet Sauvignon backed up by a relatively higher percentage of Merlot than in the Médoc further north, then Cabernet Franc and some Malbec.

WHITE GRAPES
Sémillon and Sauvignon Blanc dominate, with occasionally a little Muscadelle and Sauvignon Gris.

CLIMATE
These are the most southerly vineyards in Bordeaux and are slightly warmer and wetter than the Médoc, leading to earlier ripening for most varieties.

SOIL
In the north of the region, nearest Bordeaux, the top soil is typically gravelly.

GEOGRAPHY
Outside the vast urban sprawl of Bordeaux, the landscape is one of rolling low hills, forest, and numerous small valleys. It is generally higher than the Médoc, providing gentle slopes with good aspect to the sun.

I WONDER HOW MANY of the famous old Graves vineyards I've walked over and never knew it. How many have I driven over, how many have I taken the train through, spent the night in—even landed in an airplane in—and never known. Dozens, I reckon, because most of the famous Graves vineyards of a century or so ago have long since been eaten up by the sprawling expansion of the city of Bordeaux, and the development of the airport complex, which, romantically, has placed a few vines in the arrivals area. At the beginning of the twentieth century, there were 168 wine properties in the three major communes closest to the city of Bordeaux—Talence, Pessac, and Mérignac. Now there are only ten.

The Graves region was the center of fine wine production in Bordeaux for hundreds of years because it reached right to the very outskirts of the city. In the days when transport was both difficult and dangerous, this proximity to the town was of crucial importance. Bordeaux became rich and powerful partly by establishing itself as the chief supplier of French wine to Northern Europe and later to North America. So the city naturally grew bigger. Remove a few vineyards, build a few houses, cut down some more forest, plant some more vineyards. It was a natural progression.

What the city builders didn't know—or didn't care about—was that the unique gravelly soil that gives the Graves region its name doesn't stretch out to infinity. Talence and Pessac, closest to the heart of the city, have the best soil in Graves, but there's hardly room for a row of vines among the crowded rows of suburban villas. At Léognan, there are at last signs of some vineyards and more at Cadaujac and Martillac. A mere couple of miles further south, and the

GRAVES APPELLATIONS

» **Graves AOC** The large Graves region (8,650 acres) covers the area south of the city of Bordeaux to Langon, but the villages in the northern half broke away in 1987 to form the Pessac-Léognan AOC. In the southern Graves, a new wave of winemaking has produced plenty of clean, bone-dry white wines with a lot of snappy freshness, as well as more complex soft, nutty, barrel-aged whites, and some juicy, quick-drinking reds. Sweet white wines take the Graves Supérieures AOC; the best make a decent substitute for the more expensive Sauternes.

» **Pessac-Léognan AOC** AOC for the northern (best) part of the Graves and including all the Classed Growths. The supremely gravelly soil tends to favor red wines. Thanks to cool fermentation and the use of new oak barrels, this is also one of the most exciting areas of France for top-class white wines.

gravel starts to disintegrate into sand and clay. Good wines abound in these southern reaches of Graves, all the way down to Langon, but there aren't any great ones, and they don't have the Pessac-Léognan appellation.

The Graves region technically begins north of Bordeaux, at the Jalle de Blanquefort, the southern boundary of the Médoc. It then continues around and through the city for 35 miles, ending just south of Langon. Vines now cover about 8,650 acres, only around one-third of the more than 24,710 acres covered about one hundred years ago. Of these, 3,978 acres are in the Pessac-Léognan AOC, 833 acres are used for the production of the rare semi-sweet Graves Supérieures, and the remainder are AOC Graves. Since 1987, the traditional superiority of the soil immediately to the south and west of the city has been rewarded with a separate appellation, Pessac-Léognan, which covers ten communes and includes all sixteen Graves Classed Growths.

The excellent quality of the Pessac-Léognan reds is no new phenomenon; Pape-Clément was established as early as 1305, and Samuel Pepys was noting in his diary in 1663 that he had come across "a sort of French wine called Ho Bryan that hath a good and most particular taste that I ever met with." I'm not sure about the grammar, but the gist of this tasting note is that he'd found a wine called Haut-Brion that was an absolute smasher. Haut-Brion is still the leading Pessac-Léognan château and one of Bordeaux's greatest wines. In 1663, it provided the first example of a single property's name being recommended in the English language, and it is fair to assume it was the best (or the best marketed) Bordeaux wine being made then.

RED WINES

In those days, Graves wine would almost certainly have been red. The protective pine forests to the west, the warming Garonne River to the east, and the pale, well-drained gravel soil, as well as the fact that the Graves vineyards are the most southerly in Bordeaux—all these factors would have helped the grapes to ripen earlier than in the Médoc or in St-Émilion.

Most Bordeaux reds were pale and thin (until they were blended with something else), and vineyards that could produce ripe grapes were much prized. Even today, Pessac-Léognan has a reputation for producing good reds in worse years because of its ability to ripen Cabernet Sauvignon and Merlot grapes that little bit earlier, before the fall winds sweep in off the Bay of Biscay. For classic Graves flavors—a mellow earthiness, a soft-edged, yet cool plum and black-currant fruit, and, as the wine matures, a thrilling tobacco-cedar scent—cooler vintages such as 2004, '10, and '14 are the ones to seek.

WHITE WINES

Just over one-quarter of the vineyard area is planted with white grapes—Sémillon and Sauvignon Blanc and, here and there, a little Muscadelle to add a hint of exotic spice to the wine. With the exception of minute amounts of brilliant wine from properties such as Haut-Brion, Laville-Haut-Brion, and Domaine de Chevalier, white Graves was a byword for decades for flat, sulfurous, off-dry liquids. Even most of the Classed Growths produced dull, mediocre wine. However, the explosion of demand for good white during the 1980s and the consequent spiraling of price for such wines as white Burgundies and white Loire Sauvignons persuaded the more forward-looking growers to make some effort. After all, Sémillon and Sauvignon Blanc are both good grape varieties and complement each other wonderfully, and both the gravelly Pessac-Léognan soil and the sandier southern Graves soil are suitable for high-quality white wine production.

All that was needed was the will to improve, the know-how, and some investment, and during the 1980s and '90s, led by Domaine de Chevalier, Fieuzal, la Louvière, and Smith-Haut-Lafitte, almost all important properties modernized their wineries, using new oak to ferment and to age their wines. Although Graves and Pessac-Léognan are best known for their red wines, the modern white equivalents are easily of the same quality and are now without any doubt some of France's most exciting wines.

THE GRAVES CLASSIFICATION

The Classification first came out in 1953 but only for red wines. White wines were added in 1959. Châteaux are listed alphabetically, followed by their commune name in brackets. Some are classified for red wine (R), some for white (W), and a handful for both (RW). All the properties are in the Pessac-Léognan appellation.

Bouscaut (Cadaujac) ♟ ; Carbonnieux (Léognan)♟ ; Domaine de Chevalier (Léognan)♟ ; Couhins (Villenave-d'Ornon) ; Couhins-Lurton (Villenave-d'Ornon) ; de Fieuzal (Léognan)♟; Haut-Bailly (Léognan)♟; Haut-Brion (Pessac)♟; Latour-Martillac (Martillac)♟ ; Laville Haut-Brion (Talence) ; Malartic-Lagravière (Léognan)♟ ; La Mission Haut-Brion (Talence)♟; Olivier (Léognan)♟ ; Pape Clément (Pessac)♟; Smith-Haut-Lafitte (Martillac) R; La Tour Haut-Brion (Talence)♟.
Note: La Tour Haut-Brion was integrated into La Mission Haut-Brion in 2005. From 2009, Laville Haut-Brion has been called La Mission Haut-Brion Blanc.

The Right Bank

RED GRAPES
Merlot does best on the cool, heavier clay of St-Émilion and Pomerol, with greater or lesser amounts of Cabernet Franc and Cabernet Sauvignon on gravel outcrops. There is a small amount of Malbec.

CLIMATE
The maritime influence begins to moderate, producing warmer summers and cooler winters than in the Médoc.

SOIL
A complex pattern shows gravel deposits, sand, and clay mixed with limestone. The top vineyards are either on the limestone côtes around St-Émilion, the gravel outcrops of Pomerol/Figeac, or the heavy clay of Pomerol.

GEOGRAPHY
Generally flat, especially in Pomerol, the land rises steeply in the côtes south and southwest of St-Émilion. Elsewhere the slopes are at best moderately undulating.

WHAT A DIFFERENCE 19 miles make. I head east from Bordeaux on the N89 away from the prosperous, cosmopolitan city, and, by the time I cross the Dordogne River into the Libournais wine region, I am in a totally different world. The main town, Libourne on the Dordogne River, is a toy-town affair compared to the city of Bordeaux. Its narrow streets and folksy market square could be in any one of a hundred towns in France.

The Libournais is packed with vines; indeed, there's room for little else, so much so that in this region you get few of the copses and meadows that offer a welcome break from vineyards in the Médoc. But, unlike the Médoc, this is down-to-earth vine-growing, with nothing vainglorious or self-indulgent. St-Émilion has 13,750 acres of vines, yet these are divided among more than one thousand growers. Pomerol has a mere 2,009 acres, and the average

THE ST-ÉMILION CLASSIFICATIONS

This is the current St-Émilion classification, with 2012 promotions marked *:
» **Premiers Grands Crus Classés [A]** Angélus*, Ausone, Cheval Blanc, Pavie*
» **Premiers Grands Crus Classés [B]** Beau-Séjour Bécot, Beauséjour (Duffau-Lagarrosse), Belair-Monange, Canon, Canon-la-Gaffelière*, Clos Fourtet, Figeac, La Gaffelière, Larcis Ducasse*, La Mondotte*, Pavie-Macquin, Troplong-Mondot, Trottevieille, Valandraud*
» **Grands Crus Classés** L'Arrosée, Balestard-la-Tonnelle, Barde-Haut*, Bellefont-Belcier, Bellevue, Berliquet, Cadet-Bon, Ch. Cap de Mourlin, Le Chatelet*, Chauvin, Clos de Sarpe*, Clos des Jacobins, Clos La Madeleine*, Clos de l'Oratoire, Clos St-Martin, La Clotte, La Commanderie, Corbin, Côte de Baleau*, La Couspaude, Couvent des Jacobins, Dassault, Destieux, La Dominique, Faugères*, Faurie de Souchard, de Ferrand*, Fleur-Cardinale, La Fleur-Morange*, Fombrauge*, Fonplegade, Fonroque, Franc Mayne, Grand Corbin, Grand Corbin-Despagne, Grand Mayne, Les Grandes Murailles, Grand-Pontet, Guadet, Haut Sarpe, Jean Faure*, Laniote, Larmande, Laroque, Laroze, La Marzelle, Monbousquet, Moulin du Cadet, Pavie-Decesse, Péby Faugères*, Petit Faurie de Soutard, de Pressac, Le Prieuré, Quinault l'Enclos*, Ripeau, Rochebelle*, St-Georges-Côte Pavie, Sansonnet*, La Serre, Soutard, Tertre-Daugay (Quintus), La Tour Figeac, Villemaurine, Yon-Figeac.

holding is only 10 acres. A successful Médoc property will probably average 99 acres. With few exceptions, a sturdy no-nonsense farmhouse is all we'll get in the Libournais. Even the ultra-expensive, minuscule quantity "super-cuvées" that have become so fashionable have been sardonically termed *garagiste*, or "garage," wines with good reason.

But there are redeeming features in this region. Founded in the eleventh century (although originally settled in Roman times), the lovely town of St-Émilion is a jumble of old houses squeezed into a cleft in the limestone plateau looking out over the flat Dordogne Valley. The coarsely cobbled streets are narrow and steep, and the whole town has been declared an ancient monument to preserve it for posterity. Indeed, the whole St-Émilion appellation was proclaimed a World Heritage Site by UNESCO in 1999.

Then there are the flavors. I'm almost tempted to say "then there is the flavor" because the joy of so many of all the great wines of Pomerol and St-Émilion lies in the dominance of one grape—Merlot. Bordeaux reds are famous for their unapproachability in youth and their great longevity. That reputation has been built by the grandees of the Médoc, where Cabernet reigns supreme. Cabernet Sauvignon wines are tough and aggressive when young, but Merlot wines exhibit a juicy, almost jam-sweet richness just about from the moment the grapes hit the vat. Bordeaux without tears? You want Pomerol or St-Émilion. Their best wines will age just as long as the best Médocs, particularly when they are backed up with a judicious dose of the fragrant Cabernet Franc. They're so attractive young that most of them never get the chance.

The intensively farmed Libournais is an exclusively red wine region, although a few white wines are made over toward Bergerac, east of St-Émilion. There is some Cabernet Sauvignon planted here—perhaps 10 percent or so—but the lack of warm gravel soil in most of the Libournais means that it rarely ripens properly despite the climate being relatively warmer and more continental than in the Médoc. Château Figeac in St-Émilion and Vieux-Château-Certan in Pomerol are two exceptions that manage to ripen it well. In Pomerol and St-Émilion, the Cabernet Franc gives far better results than Cabernet Sauvignon, especially where there is a decent amount of limestone in the soil and subsoil; the great Château Cheval Blanc has almost 60 percent Cabernet Franc.

Although vines have grown here since Roman times, the emergence of St-Émilion as one of Bordeaux's star turns is fairly recent, and Pomerol's soaring reputation is more recent still. History and geography have conspired against both areas. The majority of Bordeaux's export trade has always been carried on from Bordeaux itself.

Those 19 miles may seem trivial now, but until the 1820s there were no bridges across the Garonne and Dordogne rivers between Bordeaux and Libourne. Few Bordeaux merchants felt the need to make the short but tiresome journey to the Libournais region when they had the Graves and the Médoc right on the city's doorstep. A band of Libourne merchants did ship their local wines, but they were generally regarded with disdain, and Libournais wines were accorded little respect and low prices.

When the Paris–Bordeaux railroad opened in 1853, with a station in Libourne, this freed local producers from the thrall of Bordeaux's merchants. Ever since, a mainstay of Libourne's trade has been the network of consumers in northern France, Belgium, and Holland, who happily soak up whatever wine is available, undeterred by the fact that not a single Libournais wine was included in Bordeaux's 1855 Classification.

CLASSIFICATIONS

St-Émilion is divided into two appellations: basic St-Émilion AOC and St-Émilion Grand Cru AOC. The latter now has its own classification system (see previous page), which includes a mechanism for promoting or demoting wines during an intended revision every decade, making it potentially one of the best systems of its kind. The classification has two categories: Premier Grand Cru Classé, divided into Groups A and B, and Grand Cru Classé. These revisions have worked reasonably well, but with every revision there are legal challenges. My view is always that most demoted châteaux deserved their fate and that those which are seriously run should put their shoulder to the wheel and aim for promotion next time. I prefer effort instead of lawsuits every time. Pomerol has no classification system and doesn't seem to need one because its wines are now the most expensive in Bordeaux. This is a remarkable achievement because Pomerol was only officially delimited as an AOC in 1928.

ST-ÉMILION

There aren't many vineyards where you can stumble upon well-preserved Roman archaeological remains, but it's more probable that you will in the *côtes* vineyards clinging to the steep slopes directly to the south of the beautiful town of St-Émilion. Much of St-Émilion's wine is still stored in caves dug into the limestone rock in Roman times. There is no doubt that wine was being made in St-Émilion by the Romans, and you can trace its modern history as far back as 1289, when Edward I, king of England and duke of Gascony, specified boundaries for St-Émilion, encompassing eight communes in all, which

The town of St-Émilion is the loveliest—and liveliest—wine town in Bordeaux, and the vineyards come right up to the town walls.

are virtually unchanged today. With the exception of a few planted on flat, alluvial-rich river land near Libourne, the St-Émilion vineyards still adhere to historic boundaries.

Although influenced by the nearness of the Bay of Biscay, St-Émilion's climate is more continental than the Médoc's across the Gironde to its northwest. There are more extreme temperature drops at night in St-Émilion, but warmer daytime temperatures and fewer summer-to-fall rains in most years mean an early harvest in most vintages.

The only areas of warm gravel soil in the region are the small St-Émilion *graves* zone next to Pomerol and some gravel residue down by the Dordogne. The lack of it elsewhere retards ripening and explains today's dominance of the Merlot grape in St-Émilion. Merlot is an early-ripener and relatively at home in cool, damp, fertile clay. Even where the soil is warmer and better-drained, Cabernet Franc is the preferred variety instead of Cabernet Sauvignon.

One major reason for the growers' enthusiasm for Cabernet Franc, or Bouchet as they call it locally, is the pervasive presence of limestone in many of the best St-Émilion vineyards. Just as Cabernet Franc thrives in the Loire Valley on very limey soil, so do Merlot and Cabernet Franc on the plateau that surrounds the town of St-Émilion and the steep slopes that fall away toward the Dordogne River plain. Nearly all the best wines come from these slopes of the plateau, directly south and southwest of the town of St-Émilion. The ground slowly drops away to the north and west of the town, and the unspectacular land produces attractively soft but not memorable wines. The soil here is called *sables anciens*, or "ancient sands." Vines grown in sand usually produce wines with loose-knit gentle flavors, and that's exactly what you get here.

But hold on. Just before we come to the border with the Pomerol AOC on the D245 road, there's a dip for a stream, after which the ground seems to rise in a series of waves toward the north. Just for a moment, the deep gravel topsoil that is so important in most of Bordeaux rears its head. This *graves* soil covers only around 150 acres out of the whole AOC, but two of the most magnificent of all St-Émilions—Château Figeac and Château Cheval Blanc—are here and pack these vineyards with more Cabernet Sauvignon and Cabernet Franc than Merlot. The results are stunning.

One additional source of stunning wines has been the "garagiste" phenomenon. Garagiste wines revolutionized Bordeaux's staid world in the 1990s by proving that small plots of almost unheralded land—almost always in St-Émilion and usually planted with Merlot—could make dense, rich red wines that sold for fabulous sums if you restricted yields, maximized ripeness, and soaked the wine in new oak flavors.

ST-ÉMILION SATELLITES

Four small appellations—Montagne, St-Georges (part of the commune of Montagne), Lussac, and Puisseguin—are based north of the Barbanne River, which acts as the northern boundary for St-Émilion and Pomerol. Their wines used to be sold as St-Émilion, but since 1936 they have been allowed only to hyphenate St-Émilion to their names. The wines are similar to St-Émilion—fairly soft although earthy sometimes—but they never quite gain the perfume and sheer hedonistic richness of a really good St-Émilion.

POMEROL

There isn't much to see in Pomerol apart from fields, vines, and a tall church spire. Bordeaux often seems determined to prove that the dullest-looking vineyards can produce the most memorable flavors. In which case Pomerol, only 8 miles square, squeezed into the virtually flat land to the north and east of Libourne, is a tour de force. But let's look below ground.

THE MERLOT STORY

The great wines of Pomerol and St-Émilion, on the right bank of the Dordogne, are largely based on Merlot and the best of these—for example, Château Pétrus, which is in effect 100 percent Merlot—can improve for twenty to thirty years, but with their spicy, exotic opulence and richness, they are shockingly easy to drink young. It is also the main variety in the right bank areas of Fronsac, Lalande de Pomerol, various satellites of St-Émilion, and in Castillon-Côtes de Bordeaux and Francs-Côtes de Bordeaux. All of these have shown themselves capable of making wine as good as Pomerol or St-Émilion, using primarily Merlot. Further up the Gironde, Blaye uses it for gentle, easy-going reds. In fact, there is more Merlot than Cabernet Sauvignon planted throughout Bordeaux, and I doubt if there is a single red wine property in all Bordeaux that does not have some growing because the variety ripens early, can cope with cool conditions and damp, clay soil, and is able to bear a heavy crop of fruit. In a cool, rainy area, such as Bordeaux, Cabernet Sauvignon cannot always ripen easily, so the soft, mellow character of Merlot is a fundamental component of the blend, even in the best Cabernet-dominated wines.

THE RIGHT BANK APPELLATIONS

» **St-Émilion AOC** The town of St-Émilion is the center of Bordeaux's most historic wine region and now accorded UNESCO Heritage Status. The finest vineyards are on the plateau and *côtes*, or steep slopes, around the town, although an area to the west, called the *graves*, contains two famous properties, Cheval Blanc and Figeac. It is a region of smallholdings, and the cooperative plays an important part. The dominant early-ripening Merlot grape gives wines with a come-hither softness and sweetness rare in red Bordeaux. St-Émilion is the basic AOC, with four "satellites" (Lussac, Montagne, Puisseguin, St-Georges) allowed to annex their name to it. The best producers are found in the more tightly controlled St-Émilion Grand Cru AOC.

» **St-Émilion Grand Cru AOC** St-Émilion's top-quality AOC, which includes the estates classified as Grand Cru Classé and Premier Grand Cru Classé (see below) as well as many others simply labeled St-Émilion Grand Cru. The classification is revised approximately every ten years, most recently in 2012. This AOC also includes many of the new wave of limited edition *vins de garage*, or "garage" wines.

» **St-Émilion Premier Grand Cru Classé AOC** The St-Émilion élite level, divided into two categories—A and B—with (since 2012) Angélus and Pavie joining Cheval Blanc and Ausone in category A (page 54).

» **St-Émilion satellites: (Lussac St-Émilion)** Much of the wine tastes like a lighter St-Émilion and is made by the first-rate local co-op. **(Montagne St-Émilion)** Rather good reds. The wines are normally ready to drink in four years but age well in their slightly earthy way. **(Puisseguin St-Émilion)** The wines are generally fairly solid but with an attractive chunky fruit, for drinking at three to five years. **(St-Georges-St-Émilion)** The smallest satellite, with lovely, soft wines that can nevertheless age for six to ten years.

» **Pomerol AOC** This AOC includes some of the world's most desirable red wines. Pomerol's unique quality lies in its deep clay (though gravel plays an important part in some vineyards) in which the Merlot grape flourishes. The result is seductively rich, almost creamy wine with wonderful mouth-filling fruit flavors: often plummy but with black currant, raisin, and chocolate, too, and mint and minerals to freshen it up.

» **Lalande-de-Pomerol AOC** To the north of its more famous neighbor Pomerol, this AOC produces ripe, plummy wines with an unmistakable mineral edge that are attractive at four to five years old but age reasonably well, too. They lack the concentration of top Pomerols but provide ripe, mouth-filling pleasure at a much lower price.

» **Fronsac AOC** Small area west of Pomerol making good-value Merlot-base wines. Top producers have taken note of the feeding frenzy in neighboring Pomerol and sharpened their act accordingly, with finely structured wines, occasionally perfumed, and better with at least five years of age.

» **Canon-Fronsac AOC** This AOC is the heart of the Fronsac region. The wines are relatively sturdy when young but can age for ten years or more.

» **Côtes de Bourg** Earthy but black-currenty reds from the right bank of the Gironde, which can age for six to ten years. A little dry but dull white.

» **Côtes de Bordeaux** Four new regional AOCs (see below) and a source of good-value reds.

» **Blaye-Côtes de Bordeaux AOC** Much improved AOC on the right bank of the Gironde. The fresh, Merlot-base reds are ready at two or three years but will age for more. Top red wines can be labeled under the quality-driven Blaye AOC. Good modern whites.

» **Cadillac-Côtes de Bordeaux AOC** Hilly region overlooking Graves and Sauternes across the Garonne with a lot of well-situated limestone slopes. For a long time best known for sweet wines, but the juicy reds have now forged ahead. Delicious at two or three years old but can last for five or six years.

» **Castillon-Côtes de Bordeaux AOC** Area east of St-Émilion that has surged in quality in recent years. The best wines are full and firm, yet have the lushness of St-Émilion without the high prices, although they are no longer cheap.

» **Francs-Côtes de Bordeaux AOC** Tiny area east of St-Émilion for reds and a little white; the top wines are good value. The Thienpont family (Ch. Puygueraud) is the driving force.

Luckily, in this very small area there is a surprising diversity of soil types, which contributes to the fascinating array of flavors the Pomerol wines offer. As for grapes, the juicy Merlot is king here. These are among the most luscious, heady, and sensuous red wines in the world, and, although Cabernet Franc and the odd few rows of Cabernet Sauvignon help out, Merlot bestrides Pomerol in brilliant braggart fashion. Every grape has its perfect vineyard site. For Merlot, it's Pomerol.

The easy equation is clay and Merlot. Merlot that has grown on clay gives the kind of structure that most of the Merlot grown worldwide does not attain, and there is a lot of clay in Pomerol. Given that the climate here is basically the same as that of St-Émilion—relatively warm in Bordeaux terms—the Merlot shoots to super-ripeness in most vintages.

At the heart of Pomerol lies the great Château Pétrus, with its thick clay soil, mixed up with some sand and a thick but broken crust of iron pan. Around it lies a plateau that is a mere 115 feet high—a mix of cloggy clay with gravel and chunks of rusty hardpan, stretching for nearly 1 mile from Château Trotanoy in the west to Château Cheval Blanc over the border in St-Émilion. Just about all the greatest Pomerols come from this tightly packed patch of land.

This is the center of the appellation, but there's more to Pomerol. Gravel now begins to play a bigger part than clay as the vineyards spread out from the center and the wines lose the richness of the greatest Pomerols, yet they continue to blow kisses of soft-centered pleasure across the stern brow of Bordeaux. When the vineyards reach the town of Libourne and stretch across its northern suburbs, the gravel becomes sandier, then sand and sandy clay take over. These vineyards produce nice wines still, usually lush and soft, but they are predictably enjoyable instead of swirling with exotic and unpredictable abandon.

LALANDE-DE-POMEROL

North of Pomerol, over the Barbanne River, is the appellation of Lalande-de-Pomerol, which has about 2,865 acres planted with vines. In general, the sandy gravel soil here produce attractive, slightly leaner versions of the Pomerol style, but the commune of Néac, whose wines used to be sold under its own name, has a plateau of good gravelly soil that reaches right down to the border with Pomerol, producing wine of a very decent flavor and weight that could often be mistaken for a full-blown Pomerol but at a significantly lower price.

FRONSAC AND CANON-FRONSAC

Fronsac is a delightful region of tumbling hills, bordered by the Dordogne and Isle rivers just to the west of Libourne. This rolling countryside comes as something of a relief after the flat monoculture of Pomerol and most of St-Émilion and rates as my top picnic spot in the Libournais. It's not surprising that the Libournais merchants built their weekend châteaux here rather than in the flat fields of Pomerol or St-Émilion. But the wines, which were more highly regarded than those of St-Émilion until the mid-nineteenth century, with a few exceptions, fail to shine. The vineyards are good, particularly the south-facing limestone bluffs of the Canon-Fronsac subdivision and those around the village of Saillans. There's been a lot of investment recently in the area, and Merlot, Cabernet Franc, and Malbec all suit the terrain. Although the wines have some of Pomerol's plummy richness, some of its mineral backbone, and develop some Médoc-like cedar perfume with maturity, many of them still struggle to overcome a tendency to rough tannins and a rusty metallic streak.

The 1982 vintage was a milestone for modern Bordeaux. It created the reputation of Robert Parker, the most influential wine critic of all time and by doing so indirectly changed the wine styles of areas all around the world. It also cemented the reputation of the top wines of the tiny area of Pomerol, of which Pétrus is the most famous.

Everyday Bordeaux Reds and Whites

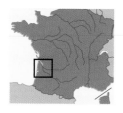

SOME OF THE OUTLYING vineyard areas on Bordeaux's Right Bank were famous centuries ago, when across the Gironde on the Left Bank the Médoc area was just a marsh. Indeed, the Romans were attracted to the limestone slopes of Blaye and Bourg but gave short shift to such modern-day luminaries as Margaux and Pauillac. Other areas, with little reputation so far, could be shining stars within a generation, given a little luck and a good deal of effort and investment.

GRAPES

Red wine sites are mostly Right Bank and inland with clay in the soil calling for a high proportion of Merlot. Cabernet Franc offers stolid support with some Cabernet Sauvignon (especially in Bourg) and Malbec sometimes added to the blend, too. Sauvignon Blanc is increasingly the grape of choice for white wines, but you will find plenty of Sémillon and some Muscadelle, too, with dwindling quantities of Merlot Blanc, Colombard, and Ugni Blanc.

CÔTES DE BORDEAUX

Bordeaux's famous wine regions—the Médoc, Graves, and Right Bank—are nicely self-contained, with identifiable styles of wines, a particular history, and an established status. But what about the five Côtes—Blaye, Bourg, Castillon, Francs, and Cadillac-Côtes de Bordeaux? What do they mean if anything? I shouldn't be joining all these areas up under one heading because they are all so different in their wine styles, and their present fortunes and future prospects are so mixed. Yet the Côtes areas have been loosely trying to market themselves as a grouping since the 1980s, albeit without much success. However, from 2009 four areas (except Bourg for the time being) decided to bind themselves up in a single new appellation—Côtes de Bordeaux—the slopes of Bordeaux—preceded by their regional name. I'm not really convinced it's the right idea for an appellation. Blaye is different from Bourg, and Castillon and Francs are very different from the first two, while the Cadillac-Côtes de Bordeaux slopes are on another river—the Garonne—and a different geological system entirely.

The Côtes de Bourg and Blaye-Côtes de Bordeaux (where the best reds can be labeled simply Blaye AOC) are directly across the Gironde from the celebrated communes of the Médoc, while the sun-drenched slopes of Francs-Côtes de Bordeaux and its neighbor Castillon-Côtes de Bordeaux extend inland from the more famous Right Bank appellations of St-Émilion and Pomerol. Money and expertise have piled into both Castillon and Francs, and the best properties share the characteristics of the St-Émilion Côtes wines. These appellations are all succeeding primarily with reds, and the top wines are good value. There is also a small amount of white wine. The Cadillac-Côtes de Bordeaux is away from the other Côtes—a hilly region overlooking Graves and Sauternes across the Garonne. It used to be better known for sweet wines. The juicy reds are now the stars here.

CÔTES DE BOURG

Bourg is a smaller area directly upstream of Blaye on the right bank of the Dordogne, where it flows into the Gironde. The steep limestone slopes and plateau with occasional patches of gravel are much more intensely cultivated with vines than the Blaye region just to the north, with 9,760 acres of red varieties and just 71 acres of white. Bourg reds could be splendid if the will and investment were there, and there are one or two star turns, such as the brilliant Château Roc de Cambes, showing the potential of the region.

ENTRE-DEUX-MERS

Entre-Deux-Mers is the large region between the two rivers, the Dordogne and the Garonne. The name means "Between two tides," and this is a charming rural area. The appellation covers about 3,700 acres of vines and is solely for dry whites, which are now some of the snappiest and best value in the whole of France. The region also produces much of the red, rosé, and white wine sold under the Bordeaux AOC. It contains a small enclave of reds at Graves de Vayres and subregions of supposedly higher quality at Ste-Foy, Haut-Benauge, and St-Macaire, but the best red wines from between the rivers take the new Cadillac-Côtes de Bordeaux appellation. Good dry whites are made here, too, but can claim only the basic Bordeaux AOC.

Bordeaux Sweet Whites

WHITE GRAPES
Sémillon, the variety most prone to noble rot, is blended with lesser amounts of Sauvignon Blanc and sometimes Muscadelle.

CLIMATE
The crucial factor is the combination of early morning autumnal mists rising off the Garonne and the Ciron rivers and plentiful sunshine later in the day.

SOIL
The common theme is clay with varying mixtures of gravel, sand, and limestone.

GEOGRAPHY
The landscape ranges from moderately hilly around Sauternes, Bommes, and Fargues to lower, more gentle slopes toward the river in Barsac and Preignac.

IT'S A FRUIT FARMER'S NIGHTMARE. Here I am, desperately trying to ripen my grapes in the supposedly warm days of an early fall in the southerly reaches of the Bordeaux area, and every morning this great cloud of mist rises off the surface of the local river and creeps up the slopes of my vineyard. How can my grapes ripen in the morning sun when they're shrouded in chilly mist? How can I keep them free of disease when they're blanketed with damp fog every morning? Well, at least by the end of the morning the sun has blazed its way through the mist and burned it all away. Heat now courses through my vineyards—but it's hardly an improvement because the hotter the day becomes, the more the humidity left over from the fog makes the air as clammy as a Turkish bath. Trying to avoid rot breaking out all over the vines is a virtual impossibility.

Which, in this case, is the whole point of the exercise. Here, I'm talking about the vineyards of Sauternes and Barsac. They make some of the world's greatest sweet wines. The only way they can get their grapes sufficiently full of sugar is to encourage them to rot on the vine. But this isn't any old kind of rot: it's a very particular version called noble rot, or *pourriture noble*—or botrytis if you like. Sauternes and Barsac are two of the few places in the world where it is a natural occurrence—all because of the little Ciron River that sneaks past Sauternes and Bommes, then turns to the northeast as its valley widens out and fills with vines, until it hits the major Garonne River between Barsac and Preignac. It is a fairly short, ice-cold river that rises from deep springs in the nearby

THE 1855 CLASSIFICATION OF BARSAC AND SAUTERNES

» **Superior First Growth (Premier Cru Supérieur)** d'Yquem (Sauternes).
» **First Growths (Premiers Crus)** La Tour Blanche (Sauternes); Lafaurie-Peyraguey (Sauternes); Clos Haut-Peyraguey (Sauternes); Rayne-Vigneau (Sauternes); Suduiraut (Sauternes); Coutet (Barsac); Climens (Barsac); Guiraud (Sauternes); Rieussec (Sauternes); Rabaud-Promis (Sauternes); Sigalas-Rabaud (Sauternes).
» **Second Growths (Deuxièmes Crus)** de Myrat (Barsac); Doisy-Daëne (Barsac); Doisy-Dubroca (Barsac); Doisy-Védrines (Barsac); d'Arche (Sauternes); Filhot (Sauternes); Broustet (Barsac); Nairac (Barsac); Caillou (Barsac); Suau (Barsac); de Malle (Sauternes); Romer du Hayot (Sauternes); Lamothe (Sauternes); Lamothe-Guignard (Sauternes).

SWEET WHITE WINE APPELLATIONS

Barsac AOC Lying close to the Garonne River and with the little Ciron River running along its eastern boundary, Barsac is the largest of the five communes in the Sauternes AOC; it also has its own AOC, which is used by most but not all of the top properties. The wines have less power and more finesse than Sauternes.

Sauternes AOC The name Sauternes is synonymous with the best sweet wines in the world. Sauternes and Barsac both lie on the banks of the little Ciron River and are two of the very few areas in France where noble rot occurs naturally. Production of these intense, sweet, luscious wines from botrytized grapes is a risk-laden and extremely expensive affair, and the wines are never cheap. From good producers, the wines are worth their high price. As well as 14 percent alcohol, they have a richness full of flavors of pineapple, peach, beeswax, barley sugar, and spice. Good vintages should age for five to ten years and can last two or three times as long.

LIGHTER, LESS LUSH WINES

» **Cadillac AOC** Sweet wine from the southern half of Cadillac-Côtes de Bordeaux. Styles vary from fresh, semisweet to richly botrytized wines. The wines have greatly improved in recent years. Drink young.

» **Cérons AOC** Sweet, soft, mildly honeyed wine from the Graves region of Bordeaux—not as sweet as Sauternes and not so well known, nor so highly priced. Most producers now make dry wine under the Graves AOC.

» **Loupiac AOC** A sweet wine area across the Garonne River from Barsac. The wines are attractively sweet without being gooey. Drink young in general, although the best can age.

» **Ste-Croix-du-Mont AOC** Best of the three sweet wine AOCs that gaze jealously at Sauternes and Barsac across the Garonne River (the others are Cadillac and Loupiac). The wine is mellow and sweet rather than splendidly rich. Top wines can age for at least a decade.

Landes. The Garonne is much warmer, especially by the end of the summer, and the collision of two water flows of different temperatures creates the mist, particularly in early morning, which drifts back up the Ciron Valley. However, this mist just by itself is no good. Barsac and Sauternes are so special because, by the time those mists become daily occurrences in fall, the Sémillon and Sauvignon Blanc (and occasionally Muscadelle) grapes should be fully ripe and turning plump and golden. If the grapes are unripe, noble rot won't develop, although the closely related black rot, sour rot, and gray rot will—and simply destroy the grapes.

NOBLE ROT

Noble rot is different. Instead of devouring the skin and souring the flesh inside, the spores latch onto the skin and gradually weaken it as the grape moves from ripeness to overripeness. The skin becomes a translucent browny gold, but the grape is still plump and handsome. Not for

A noble-rotted grape looks horrible—wizened and often coated with a furry fungus—but makes the world's finest sweet wine.

long. If the warm humid weather continues, the skin is so weakened by the noble rot that it begins to shrivel. The water content in the grape dramatically reduces while the sugar, glycerin, and acidity content is concentrated by dehydration. A noble-rotted grape looks horrible—wizened, maybe coated with furry fungus. It feels horrible, too. Pick one, and it will dissolve into a slimy mess between your fingers, the skin so weakened it can hardly contain the flesh. But persevere. Put that nasty gooey pulp into your mouth—it is intensely, memorably, syrupy sweet, sweeter than any grape left to ripen in the normal way. That's the magic of noble rot. This sugar level may be twice the level achieved through natural ripening. Infection by noble rot is the classic method to make quality sweet wine.

CHÂTEAU D'YQUEM

This is the best, most concentrated, most complex and long-lived Sauternes of all. It's also the most famous, acting as a symbol of supreme luxury across the globe. The medieval château stands at the highest point in the Sauternes vineyards, and the grapes are picked and the wine made with meticulous care; the pickers may be sent through the vines for up to eleven successive pickings in some years, and instructions are relayed to them from the press house even as they pick berry by berry as to the kind of grapes that are needed. In years when the noble rot—or botrytis—is most plentiful, word might even come through to pick more unbotrytized grapes to maintain the balance of the wine. Low yields mean each vine produces only a glass of wine. Compare that to the red wine First Growths of the Médoc, where each vine might be expected to yield a full bottle of wine. The grapes are fermented in new oak barrels and left to mature for thirty months before bottling. It is one of the world's most expensive wines and in constant demand because of its richness and exotic flavors.

Botrytized wines have been made here for generations, but nobody knows who first dared to ferment the juice of these rotten grapes and to taste the result. The 1810 cellar book at Yquem refers to *triage*, or successive selective pickings, but this was probably common practice long before that.

These days, Yquem is drunk with fruit desserts, with Roquefort cheese, or with foie gras (ambrosial combinations all), but according to nineteenth-century menus, it was then also served with fish. I'd drink it all by itself.

A dry white, Ygrec, is made in most years, too. It has great intensity and is expensive and rare.

In the famous 1855 classification of Bordeaux wines, Chateau d'Yquem was classified Superior First Growth above all other wines, and it is still the most famous—and many would say the greatest—sweet white wine in the world.

Burgundy

BURGUNDY. I LUXURIATE IN THAT name. I feel it roll around my mouth and my mind like an exotic mixed metaphor of glittering crusted jewels, ermine capes, the thunder of trumpets, and the perfumed velvet sensuality of rich red wine. It has been all those things because Burgundy is not just the name of a wine.

In the fourteenth and fifteenth centuries, Burgundy was a grand duchy, almost a kingdom, spreading up eastern France, through Belgium, to the North Sea. Its power and wealth rivaled that of the French throne. Burgundy *was* the pomp and circumstance of jewels and ermine and trumpet voluntaries, as well as the flowering of arts and architecture and the subtle but pervasive influence of some of France's greatest monastic establishments.

APPELLATIONS AND CLASSIFICATIONS

There are five basic levels of AOC in Burgundy.

» **General regional AOCs** "Bourgogne" is the basic AOC covering red, white, rosé, and sparkling wines that do not qualify for one of the higher AOCs. From a single estate, instead of a merchant, it can be Burgundy's best value. Coteaux Bourguignons is even more basic, including reclassified Beaujolais.

» **Specific regional AOCs** These are a halfway house between general regional appellations and single village AOCs—for example, Chablis or Beaujolais. Bourgogne-Côte d'Or is for declassified grapes from the Côte de Nuits and Côte de Beaune. The Bourgogne Hautes-Côtes de Nuits and Hautes-Côtes de Beaune AOCs apply to certain villages or communes in the hills to the west of the main Côte d'Or vineyards. Côte de Beaune-Villages and Côte de Nuits-Villages apply to villages in their respective parts of the Côte d'Or, and the wine can be blended across separate villages or not.

» **Village AOCs** These apply to wine of a single village or commune, and there is a growing move to include vineyard names on the label even if they're not top rank; for example, Meursault "le Cromin." The majority of village wines are still blends of several vineyards within the village. At village level, vineyard names in small letters on the label are called *lieux-dits*.

» **Premiers Crus (First Growths)** Despite the name, these are the second best vineyard sites in Burgundy. Even so, they include some of the region's finest wines and some that would be Grand Cru in any future reclassification. The village name on the label will be followed by the vineyard name; for example, Gevrey-Chambertin "Combe-aux-Moines."

» **Grands Crus (Great Growths)** These are Burgundy's top vineyards and account for only 1 percent of Burgundy's wine. They are found only in Chablis and the Côte d'Or. Their precise locations have been delineated and refined over the centuries. Some are walled and include 'Clos' in their title. The reds are mostly in the Côte de Nuits, and almost all the whites are in Chablis and the Côte de Beaune. Except in Chablis, a Grand Cru vineyard name will stand alone on the label without the village name; for example, Chambertin is from the village of Gevrey-Chambertin. Indeed, many of the Côte d'Or villages have hyphenated their own name to the name of their most famous vineyard. Grand Cru and Premier Cru classifications apply only to the vineyard and the potential for quality such a site posseses. The human element is not counted; while a good grower can maximize a site's potential, a bad grower or winemaker can ruin a PremierCru or Grand Cru through lazy viticulture or feeble winemaking.

MAIN WINE APPELLATIONS

— CHABLIS/
    GRAND AUXERROIS
    1. Chablis, Petit Chablis
    2. Chablis Grands Crus
— CÔTE DE NUITS
    3. Hautes-Côtes de Nuits
— CÔTE DE BEAUNE
    4. Hautes-Côtes de Beaune
— CÔTE CHALONNAISE
    5. Bouzeron
    6. Rully
    7. Mercurey
    8. Givry
    9. Montagny
— MÂCONNAIS
    10. Viré-Clessé
    11. St-Véran
    12. Pouilly-Fuissé
— BEAUJOLAIS
    13. Beaujolais Crus

See also
Côte de Nuits **page 71**
Côte de Beaune **page 75**

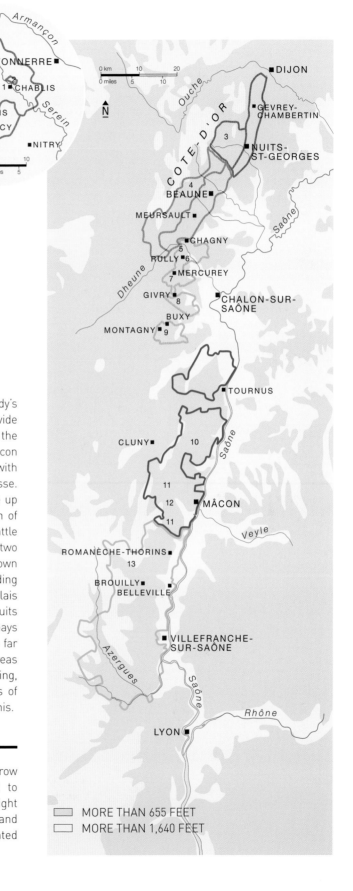

MORE THAN 655 FEET
MORE THAN 1,640 FEET

These may have faded, but one part of Burgundy's glorious history remains: its remarkable ability to provide great food and great wine. Look at the map (right), at the town of Mâcon, right in the center. To the east of Mâcon lie the rich farmlands of the Saône Valley packed with vegetables, fruit, and the famous chickens of Bresse. To the west of Mâcon, as the hills of the Morvan rise up toward the central plateau of France, the small town of Charolles has given its name to the local Charollais cattle that provide France's finest beef. Between these two extremes of mountain and plain, as the ridges slope down toward the flat valley floor, are the vineyards providing every kind of wine, from the gurgling reds of Beaujolais in the south to the intense giants of the Côte de Nuits reds in the north, from the round, supple Chardonnays of the southern Mâconnais to austere Chablis in the far north. The Mâconnais, Chalonnais, and Auxerrois areas also produce excellent fizz. Only sweet wines are lacking, although the black-currant liqueur Crème de Cassis of Nuits-St-Georges goes some way toward redeeming this.

GRAPE VARIETIES

Pinot Noir is a tantalizingly difficult grape to grow successfully, and its juice is tantalizingly difficult to ferment into wine and then mature to just the right age, but, ah, when it works, there's no grape like it, and the twenty-first century is unearthing more talented Burgundy exponents than ever before.

The Côte d'Or is its heartland, although some is grown in the Yonne and a fair amount in the Mâconnais and Chalonnais. It's a very ancient vine and prone to mutation. It buds early and ripens early but is an erratic yielder and is prone to rot. If this all sounds as if it's more trouble than it's worth, well, you'd be right—were it not capable of the most astonishing marriage of scent and succulence, savagery and charm when grown by an expert in one of Burgundy's best sites.

Of the other red varieties, Gamay makes deliciously juicy wines in Beaujolais, less good ones in the Mâconnais, and is a marginal producer in the Côte d'Or. César and Tressot are two old Yonne varieties, the latter now virtually extinct.

Chardonnay is grown with such success around the world that it is easy to forget that Burgundy is where it made its reputation. It can, in the right circumstances, still produce its greatest wine here, particularly on the limestone slopes of the Côte de Beaune. However, it performs reliably well all over Burgundy. It buds early, making it prone to frost in Chablis, but it ripens early, too, and is a consistent yielder of generally ripe grapes. This allows for it to produce lean but balanced wines in Chablis; marvelously full yet savory and refreshing wines in the Côte d'Or; chalkier yet attractive wines in the Côte Chalonnaise; and plumper, milder wines in the Mâconnais. Of the other white grapes, Aligoté is widely grown, especially in the northern Côte Chalonnaise, and produces a sharp lemony wine, sometimes with a soft smell of buttermilk. The owner of world-famous Domaine de la Romanée-Conti makes a good one. Pinot Blanc and Pinot Gris are occasionally found.

THE YONNE REGION

The Chablis or Yonne region is about 100 miles north of Beaune and used to be at the center of a vast vineyard area supplying Paris with basic *vin ordinaire*. The Yonne was one of several regions east of Paris that churned out oceans of thin, mean reds and whites to slake the capital's thirst. None of the areas was suitable for viticulture, and when the railroads came and made possible the transport of enormous amounts of cheap wine from the Mediterranean coast, demand for these raw northern brews disappeared.

Only the very best survived, and the most famous is Chablis, centered around the little town of the same name and a few surrounding villages, where suitable mesoclimates and limestone and clay soil let the Chardonnay grape creep to ripeness and create highly individual wine. Elsewhere in the Yonne, mainly southeast of Auxerre, several varieties, mostly red Pinot Noir and white Chardonnay and Aligoté, are increasingly grown but are accorded only the Bourgogne AOC, with the best of them, such as Chitry and Epineuil, also using their village name on the label. Many of their grapes now go to make very good Crémant de Bourgogne fizz. The village of St-Bris now has an appellation for its Sauvignon Blanc.

CÔTE D'OR

Dijon is at the northern end of the world-famous Côte d'Or, divided into the Côte de Nuits and Côte de Beaune, and from here, south to Lyon, there is an almost unbroken vista of vines, comprising the Burgundy region. Because we are fairly far north here, the southern warmth begins to dominate only around Mâcon, so vineyards facing the sun are crucial for ripening grapes.

The Côte d'Or—divided into the Côte de Nuits in the north, between Dijon and a point just south of Nuits-St-Georges, and the Côte de Beaune, which continues southward past Beaune to a point just west of Chagny—consists of east- to southeast-facing, well-drained slopes on alkaline ground, mixing rich marls and pebbly limestone for the best results. The hills stretch away to the west, and the tiny strip of vines hug the ridge; these hills provide crucial protection from the prevailing westerly wind as well as drawing off a lot of the moisture from the clouds before they reach the Côte d'Or. Pinot Noir dominates the Côte de Nuits, while the Côte de Beaune vineyards have a mixture of Pinot Noir and Chardonnay. Scattered vineyards just to the west of the Côte d'Or, in the area called the Hautes-Côtes, can make good, light wine in warm years and will surely be beneficiaries of global warming.

CÔTE CHALONNAISE

South of Chagny and west of Chalon-sur-Saône, the protective ridge of mountains breaks down somewhat, and this region, the Côte Chalonnaise, is more sparsely planted with vines, the vineyards generally nestling into south- and southeast-facing mesoclimates and leaving the more exposed land free for grazing and orchards. Chalonnais reds and whites can be good, but their less perfect vineyard conditions show in the wines' relative leanness. Traditionally, much of this wine was transformed into sparkling wine, Crémant de Bourgogne, but increased demand for still Pinot Noir and Chardonnay wines has encouraged producers to make more efforts to ripen their grapes and use them for still wine, while investment by some of the region's leading producers in new oak barrels for making the wine has also greatly improved standards.

The medieval tiled roof of the magnificent Hotel-Dieu in Beaune, the wine capital of Burgundy for many centuries.

MÂCONNAIS

Southwest of Tournus and west of Mâcon, the vineyards begin to spread out. This is the Mâconnais, increasingly a Chardonnay region, although Gamay and Pinot Noir are also grown for red wines. The best vineyards are still those closest to the ridge of hills in the west, and famous wines, such as Pouilly-Fuissé, depend on steep slopes and well-drained limestone soil for their quality. The flatter land that spreads out toward the Saône is mirrored by softer, less defined wines, usually selling as Mâcon Blanc or Mâcon Blanc-Villages. A new generation of growers is beginning to show what the area can achieve with more effort.

In the south of France, in Eastern Europe, and obviously in the New World, winemakers are producing excellent, tasty, fairly priced Chardonnays from land that supposedly lacks the advantage of Burgundian terroir. This throws down a direct challenge to the Mâconnais in particular. Luckily, the new wave of growers is beginning to realize that a Burgundian birthright is a big plus in the wine world but that the world does not owe them a living just because of it. Production today is still largely in the hands of highly efficient cooperative groups intent on supplying decent although not spectacular wine, but the new single domaine wines are set to revolutionize the region and redefine the quality potential.

BEAUJOLAIS

The soil, the architecture, and certainly the wine style change abruptly just south of Pouilly-Fuissé as we plunge into Beaujolais. Here, almost all the wines are red (there is just a little rosé and occasional Beaujolais Blanc from Chardonnay grapes), and the grape is Gamay. Once again, the western slopes play their part, providing good southerly and easterly aspects, protection from wind, and good drainage. The slopes to the northwest and west of Belleville are granite based and provide the generally unregarded Gamay grape with a rare chance to shine. These slopes harbor the ten Crus—the communes that produce the best Beaujolais wines, and use their own names on the label instead of Beaujolais. Intermingled with the Crus and spreading southward are the communes that make Beaujolais-Villages, while the broader, clay-dominated vineyards reaching down to Lyon provide simple quaffing Beaujolais in vast quantities.

MERCHANTS, GROWERS, AND COOPERATIVES

Burgundy's vineyards are some of the oldest in France, established by the Romans if not by the Gauls before them, nurtured through the centuries by the monasteries and subsequently by the Duchy of Burgundy. Once large homogeneous estates, Burgundian vineyard holdings are nowadays incredibly fragmented due to the Napoleonic laws, which decreed that every inheritance be equally divided among all offspring. To cope with an increasingly erratic supply, a merchant class arose, based primarily in the town of Beaune but also in Nuits-St-Georges, whose job was to seek out sufficient small parcels of the well-known vineyard names to make up into salable and marketable quantities. These merchants would buy from numerous growers and blend the wines and bottle them in their cellars. Honest merchants made good wines, dishonest merchants didn't. So there's no change here. But however good the blending, in a region like Burgundy, where nuance of flavor should be everything, those nuances were lost. In the Mâconnais and Beaujolais, smallholders were more likely to band together into cooperatives. These might well then sell their blends to merchants, but several in the Mâconnais, such as those at Clessé, Lugny, Viré, and Azé, have established strong reputations of their own, as has the excellent Buxy cooperative in the Côte Chalonnaise.

Burgundy's reputation for much of the twentieth century was created and maintained by these *négociants*, or merchant houses, and most of the Meursault, Beaune, or Nuits-St-Georges you find will be from a merchant. But always buy a grower's domaine wine if you can.

Chablis

WHITE GRAPES
Chardonnay is the only grape allowed for Chablis.

CLIMATE
The maritime influence lessens as you go east, and the winters become longer and colder, summers warmer and drier. Hail storms and spring frosts are the greatest hazards to vines in this northerly region.

SOIL
A mixture of marly limestone and clay with two main types: Kimmeridgian and Portlandian.

GEOGRAPHY
The exposure and angle of the slope are critical in this northern region. The best vineyard sites are on the southeast- and southwest-facing slopes of hills along the banks of the Serein.

IT'S SO COLD AS I SCRAMBLE UP the damp slopes of the Grand Cru vineyards looming above the little Serein River as the freezing air worms its way under my coat and seems to settle very precisely inside my joints. I stumble down the stairs to the producers' cellars and an eternal truth is revealed: if hot air rises, cold air descends. From the mist-wreathed woodland above the vineyard slopes to the gray charmless asphalt of the town streets, the cold finally tumbles down the stairwell like a cloud of invisible ice, into the cellars where the wine is fermented and matured. Ah, the rigors of Chablis in early spring.

This chill austerity in the climate, in the vineyards, in the little town, and its maturation cellars, too, gives Chablis its uniqueness. Its glinting, cold green mineral attack allows Chablis a special hauteur in a modern wine world caught in a feeding frenzy for the heady flavor of ripeness and warmth. This niche is one that the growers and producers of Chablis would do well not to desert in the face of those hot-blooded flavors of Chardonnay from warmer climes.

Chablis' vineyards are right at the limit beyond which the Chardonnay grape will not ripen. The Kimmeridgian limestone clay—a soil with fossilized oyster shells—is present in all the traditional Chablis vineyard sites and gives a very particular character to the wines. Because of global warming, modern moves to increase Chablis' vineyard area onto soil with a different limestone character and to increase yields in the vineyards have actually been fairly successful. Indeed, the least favored Petit Chablis vineyards nowadays generally give a very attractive, sharp, minerally wine—at a lower price.

Let's look at the heart of Chablis to see why it became famous in the first place. It is the first vineyard area you come across as you roar down the Autoroute du Soleil from Paris. It consists of a small, chilly, isolated jumble of vineyards in the frost-prone valley of the Serein River about 100 miles north of Beaune, the wine capital of Burgundy's Côte d'Or.

This northern outpost of the Burgundy region is virtually all that is left of the extensive Yonne vineyards that used to supply the bulk of Paris's everyday wine, but Chablis survived—*just*—because the grape it grows is the great Chardonnay of white Burgundy fame. Huddled along the banks of the tiny

---

CHABLIS GRANDS CRUS AND MAIN PREMIERS CRUS

» **Grands Crus** Blanchot, Bougros, Les Clos, Grenouilles, Preuses, Valmur, Vaudésir.
» **Main Premiers Crus** Beauroy, Côte de Léchet, Fourchaume, Mont de Milieu, Montmains, Montée de Tonnerre, Vaillons, Vau Ligneau, Vau de Vey, Vaucoupin, Vosgros.

Top Chablis' wines come from the Grand Cru vineyards planted on a single sweep of hill directly north and east of the town of Chablis.

Serein River, angled toward the southwest, and protected from the harsh winds of this semi-continental climate, a few slopes of Kimmeridgian limestone can, in a good summer, produce sublime dry white wine.

There has been considerable expansion recently, and Chablis now has about 13,435 acres of vines. This is more than a tenfold increase since the 1950s, when Chablis was at its nadir. Much of this increase has merely been the return of good vineyard to production, but some of the new plantings are on barely suitable soil.

GRANDS CRUS AND PREMIERS CRUS

Despite the general expansion, the Grands Crus have remained virtually unchanged and command a long, steep, southwest-facing slope of vines rising up at between 490 and 820 feet from the Serein River opposite the town of Chablis. The mesoclimates created by aspect to the sun and the warming influences of the river and the town are all-important. Frost has always been a far greater problem in Chablis than elsewhere in Burgundy, and the Grands Crus were always the worst hit, for the narrow Serein Valley tends to trap cold air masses. Various protection methods now combat the worst effects of the frost. Seven different Grand Cru vineyard sites cover about 250 acres, all contiguous but all subtly different. Their true characters become evident only with a judicious marriage of low yields in the vineyards and a few years of bottle aging. The modern tendency to use new oak barrels for both fermenting and aging can produce delicious results but usually blurs the distinctions between each site. A newly established Grand Cru Syndicate looks determined to preserve these distinctions. There has been a massive expansion of Premier Cru sites, with the result that the words "Premier Cru" on a Chablis label no longer guarantee a wine much superior to a basic Chablis. However, there are some excellent traditional Premier Cru sites, usually not as steep as the Grands Crus and often with a more south to southeast aspect, thereby missing some of the warm afternoon sun. Those on the Serein's east bank are best, although there are other fine ones directly southwest of the town.

CHABLIS AND PETIT CHABLIS

Simple Chablis is made further away from the town of Chablis itself, its quality depending upon the mesoclimate and the determination of the grower. Petit Chablis—the lowest form of Chablis from the least suitable sites—is being systematically upgraded to Chablis, but what is left as Petit Chablis can be sharp and tasty.

Côte de Nuits

RED GRAPES
Pinot Noir is the only grape except in the most basic wines.

WHITE GRAPES
Among the few Côte de Nuits whites, Chardonnay is the main grape, although some of the best examples use a white mutation of Pinot Noir.

CLIMATE
It is sunnier here in the growing season than in Bordeaux, but the falls are cool and the winters long and cold. Spring frosts and hail can cause problems. The Hautes-Côtes are less protected from the prevailing westerly winds and can get heavy rain.

SOIL
The Côte d'Or is basically a limestone ridge. The middle slopes provide the best drainage for the vines.

GEOGRAPHY
The top vineyards are on the middle slopes from 820 to 985 feet, where the steeper gradients as well as the soil structure facilitate drainage. The south- or southeast-facing aspect of the best sites also enhances exposure to the sun and therefore ripening.

MY FAVORITE PLACE in the Côte de Nuits, one of the world's greatest vineyard regions, isn't the most famous. It's in the village of Prémeaux, just to the south of the town of Nuits St-Georges. Here, you can step off the N74 road into the vines right below the marvelous Clos Arlot vineyard. At this point, the Côte de Nuits is little more than 295 feet across, one side to the other. Admittedly, this is the narrowest part, but the point is that the Côte de Nuits, which includes many of the most famous red wine names in the world, is a mere sliver of land snaking its way in and out of an east-facing escarpment

CÔTE DE NUITS VILLAGES AND TOP VINEYARDS
(from north to south)

» Marsannay
» **Fixin Main Premiers Crus:** Clos du Chapitre, La Perrière, Les Hervelets.
» **Gevrey-Chambertin Grands Crus:** Chambertin, Chambertin-Clos de Bèze, Chapelle-Chambertin, Charmes-Chambertin, Mazoyères-Chambertin, Griotte-Chambertin, Latricières-Chambertin, Mazis-Chambertin, Ruchottes-Chambertin. **Main Premiers Crus:** Les Cazetiers, Clos St-Jacques, Clos des Varoilles, Combe aux Moines, Aux Combottes, Estournelles St-Jacques, Lavaut St-Jacques.
» **Morey-St-Denis Grands Crus:** Bonnes-Mares (part), Clos des Lambrays, Clos de la Roche, Clos St-Denis, Clos de Tart. **Main Premiers Crus:** La Bussière, Clos des Ormes, Les Milandes, Les Monts Luisants, Les Ruchots.
» **Chambolle-Musigny Grands Crus:** Bonnes-Mares (part), Musigny. **Main Premiers Crus:** Les Amoureuses, Les Baudes, Les Charmes, Les Cras, Les Fuées, Les Sentiers.
» **Vougeot Grand Cru:** Clos de Vougeot.
» **Vosne-Romanée Grands Crus:** Grande-Rue, Richebourg, La Romanée, La Romanée-Conti, Romanée-St-Vivant, La Tâche, and (in the commune of Flagey-Échézeaux) Échézeaux, Grands-Échézeaux. **Main Premiers Crus:** Les Beaux Monts, Aux Brûlées, Les Chaumes, Clos des Réas, Cros Parantoux, Aux Malconsorts, Les Suchots.
» **Nuits-St-Georges Main Premiers Crus:** Aux Boudots, Aux Bousselots, les Cailles, aux Chaignots, Clos des Argillières, Clos Arlot, Clos des Corvées, Clos des Forêts-St-Georges, Clos de la Maréchale, Clos des Porrets-St-Georges, Les Damodes, Aux Murgers, Aux Perdrix, Les Porrets-St-Georges, Les Pruliers, La Richemone, Roncière, Les St-Georges, Aux Thorey, les Vaucrains, Aux Vignes Rondes.

that marks the eastern edge of the Morvan hills. The Côte lies between about 820 and 1,150 feet above sea level. The escarpment is limestone, which continues down the slope to the plain. On this slope, over the millennia, soil has been created through a mixture of eroded limestone, pebbles, and clay. An outcrop of rich dark marlstone is particularly in evidence in the middle of the slope at around the 900-foot mark. All the greatest vineyards are situated within 80 feet, more or less, of this height and face mainly east or southeast.

PINOT NOIR'S HOMELAND

The top vineyards are planted with Pinot Noir. Indeed, the whole Côte de Nuits is overwhelmingly a red wine slope with just a little rosé being made at Marsannay in the north and a few bottles of rare white being made at Morey-St-Denis, Nuits-St-Georges, Vougeot and, most famously, Musigny at Chambolle-Musigny. Otherwise Pinot Noir rules. White grapes prefer impoverished, easy-draining limestone soil, and in the Côte de Beaune to the south there are various instances of limestone dominating the slopes. But here in the Côte de Nuits, limestone merely seems to temper the rich marl soil and reduce its fertility. Overfertile soil never produces great wine, but this mixture seems just right.

CÔTE DE NUITS CLASSIFICATIONS

The great vineyards start in the north at the village of Gevrey-Chambertin and form an almost unbroken line through Morey-St-Denis, Chambolle-Musigny and Vougeot to Vosne-Romanée. Many of the Nuits-St-Georges vineyards are also very good, although none

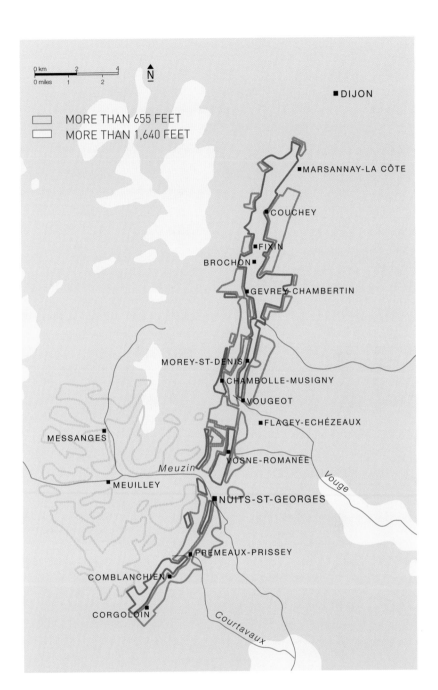

MAIN WINE APPELLATIONS

— Regional Bourgogne appellations and Côte de Nuits-Villages
— Hautes-Côtes de Nuits
— Village AOC boundary
— Premier Cru
— Grand Cru

CLOS DE VOUGEOT

I've always had a soft spot for the wine of Clos de Vougeot because at its best it possesses a lush, mellow, hedonistic quality—soft, scented, and soothing, indulgent and irresistible. Which, I am sure, was not at all the intention of the Cistercians who created this great walled vineyard and its grand château buildings in the fourteenth century. The Cistercians were a monastic order founded to combat the fleshy worldliness of the Benedictines. Austerity and self-deprivation were their watchwords.

But they knew the value of wine. The greatest vineyards of Burgundy—the Grands Crus—were painstakingly worked out and mapped, literally vine row by vine row, by the Cistercian monks according to their soil type, drainage, aspect to the sun, or exposure to cold winds. The Burgundian Grand Cru system is the supreme example of the French wine philosophy based on the terroir, the precise place of the vines. The delineation and enclosure of the large 125-acre vineyard of Clos de Vougeot is their greatest legacy. One can argue that other Grands Crus make even finer wines than Clos de Vougeot, and the elegant monastic buildings are now largely used for promotional purposes by the Burgundy wine trade, but the delineation and enclosure of the vineyard at Clos de Vougeot is living testimony to where Burgundy's greatness was born. The Clos is now divided among eighty-plus owners, so the results can be mixed. Better wine should come from the middle and upper slopes, but the best results come from producers who know what they are doing, regardless of site.

are classified as Grand Cru. Over the centuries, vines in the best sites have consistently ripened earlier than those too high up the slope or on flatter ground at the bottom. So a minutely accurate system of vineyard classification has evolved. The Grands Crus are so carefully and jealously delineated that every single row of vines is separately assessed. The same goes for the second rank of vineyards, the Premiers Crus.

There are numerous instances of certain rows of vines being excluded from the higher appellation and condemned to the third tier—the village appellation. Even so, the village AOC is still applied to only decent land, which almost always lies between the N74 and the escarpment to the west. Some vineyards, in the north at Brochon and Fixin, and in the south between Prémeaux-Prissey and Corgoloin, use the collective appellation Côte de Nuits-Villages. Less suitable land, such as the flatter vineyards to the east of the N74 (better suited to cattle and vegetables), is relegated to regional or generic appellations— Aligoté, Bourgogne, Bourgogne Passe-Tout-Grains, and Coteaux Bourguignons (a controversial new appellation that includes Beaujolais).

The good Côte de Nuits Burgundies are very grand indeed. Red wines from a cool area, such as Burgundy, should be delicate, not monumental, but that relatively rich soil, sloped east and southeast, can, when the summer is warm and the grape grower careful to limit his yield, produce wines of disturbing, heady brilliance. These can often be dark and brooding when young, especially those from Gevrey-Chambertin, but may break out into glorious exotic scents as they age, in particular at Vosne-Romanée and Chambolle-Musigny, finally maturing into a state of delectable decay, when all the savagery, sweetness, and scent melds into a dark, ripe autumnal richness of astonishing beauty. From the best growers, the nuances of flavor detectable in wines from vines only yards apart offer a marriage between the hedonistic and the intellectual that hardly any other wines ever manage. From a bad grower or merchant, there are few bigger nor more expensive disappointments than a thin, lifeless wine masquerading under these great names.

VILLAGES OF THE CÔTE DE NUITS

Marsannay is the first serious wine village as you head south from Dijon. It used to be famous for rosé but is now an increasingly useful supplier of good, perfumed, although lightweight reds and some pleasant whites. The slopes at Couchey, Fixin, and Brochon might look pretty suitable for vines; they grow Pinot Noir, but little of great excitement ever comes to light. Fixin's heavy clay soil can give good sturdy reds in a hot year.

The real fireworks start at Gevrey-Chambertin. Here, the rich marl soil comes properly into play with red clay peppered with stones and outbreaks of rich subsoil through a thin layer of topsoil on the higher sites. The narrow east- and southeast-facing slope under its protective forest brow continues almost unbroken between Gevrey-Chambertin and Nuits-St-Georges. Here, Pinot Noir really shows what it can do.

Those village names, by the way. Over the centuries, the best Côte d'Or villages found that they had one vineyard above all whose wines people sought. The village of Gevrey had Chambertin, the village of Chambolle had Musigny, and so on. So, to grab a little reflected glory from their greatest vineyard—and a little more profit from allying their less exciting wine with that of the star performer—wine producers hyphenated the vineyard name to that of the village for their wines.

But back to Gevrey-Chambertin. This village distinguishes itself with nine Grands Crus—the most of any Côte d'Or commune—safely protected from the wet westerlies by the Montagne de la Combe Grizard. The lesser vineyards spread down to and, unusually, across the N74, where a pebbly subsoil is supposed to provide enough drainage. Maybe. The potential for riches at every level in Gevrey is high, but the variation among producers is dramatic. It's a problem of popularity. Chambertin, which can be so sensuously savage at its best, is one of France's most famous reds. Wines with Chambertin in their title are not difficult to sell.

Morey-St-Denis is a good deal less famous, but the vineyards are just as good. There are five Grands Crus, on slightly steeper slopes with a little more limestone in evidence and, indeed, one steep, infertile site—Monts Luisants—that is famous for a beefy white. The reds, led by Clos de la Roche, have a sweet, ripe, fruity depth and a chocolaty softness.

Chambolle-Musigny is set into a little gully in the hillside, so there is a brief loss of protection for the vines, and the Grand Cru, Bonnes-Mares, ends abruptly north of the village. The other Grand Cru, Musigny, doesn't commence until the southeast-facing slope begins again near Vougeot. At its best, Chambolle-Musigny can be hauntingly perfumed.

Vougeot's most important vineyard is the 125-acre walled Grand Cru, Clos de Vougeot. This runs right down to the N74, onto considerably lower and more alluvial soil than any other Grand Cru. Add to this eighty different owners all eager to exploit the famous name, and you have a recipe for some decidedly rum bottles of Clos de Vougeot. At its best, though, it is fleshy and rich, and some of Burgundy's best red producers have vines here.

Directly above the fine, higher vines of Vougeot are those of Grands Crus Échézeaux and Grands-Échézeaux. Their parent village, Flagey, is down in the plain, and they are considered to be part of Vosne-Romanée. Lucky them because the other six Vosne Grands Crus, especially La Tâche and La Romanée-Conti, are the most famous and expensive of all Burgundies. Intoxicating in their spice and heady scent, thrilling in their depth of dark fruit, they really do lead the way. The red clay spattered with pebbles undoubtedly puts the other Vosne Grands Crus and Premiers Crus on a special level.

At the southern end of the Côte de Nuits, Nuits-St-Georges might seem unlikely to be Vosne's neighbor—it has no Grands Crus at all. Instead it has thirty-eight Premiers Crus, but many of these are very good. In the valley to the west, the protective curtain is broken, and many of the vineyards are on flat alluvial soil. But south of Nuits down to Prémeaux, the slopes steepen, narrow, and veer back toward the southeast. Here, great wines are made, Grands Crus in all but name.

THE HAUTES-CÔTES DE NUITS

Up in the hills behind the Côte de Nuits slopes, planted in carefully selected sites, are the vines of the Hautes-Côtes de Nuits appellation. In warm years, the Hautes-Côtes de Nuits vineyards with the best aspect and drainage can make light, pleasant, mostly red wine from Pinot Noir. But the word "Hautes," or "high," is important. We're far north here for a major red wine area. Red grapes usually need more heat to ripen than white—and the higher you get above sea level, the cooler the sun's rays become and the more exposed you are to wind and rain. That makes for thin wine most years.

Côte de Beaune

RED GRAPES
*Pinot Noir is the only grape
except in the most basic wines.*

WHITE GRAPES
*Chardonnay is the official grape,
although there may still be some
Pinot Blanc and Pinot Gris.*

CLIMATE
*The slopes are gentler here,
providing less shelter from the
westerly winds, so rainfall is
higher than further north and
heavy rain can be a problem. The
temperatures are marginally
milder than in the Côte de Nuits.*

SOIL
*The soil structure is basically
similar to the Côte de Nuits but
with limestone outcrops more
in evidence, and these are often
where the best vineyards, such
as le Montrachet, are sited.*

GEOGRAPHY
*There are some lower slopes
and more gentle gradients than
in the Côte de Nuits, but the
south- to southeast-facing aspect
of many vineyards is even more
critical here.*

I'M NOT A GREAT RESPECTER of traditions and reputations just for the sake of them. In the world of wine, I think that often there are more ill-deserved reputations and baseless traditions than the other way around. But I have to say, the first time I trekked up the narrow lane from the main road (the N6) at the village of Chassagne-Montrachet, patted the crumbling stone wall on the left somewhat gingerly with my hand, and then sneaked into the vineyard of le Montrachet, my heart was thumping with excitement.

Le Montrachet is possibly the greatest white wine vineyard in the world. But why? I tasted the grapes from its vines, then crossed the lane to taste the grapes of Bâtard-Montrachet—another of the great Grand Cru vineyards—only 30 feet lower down. They were different. Le Montrachet's grapes seemed to have more intensity, more vibrant personality before they'd even been picked off the vine. I clambered over the wall above Le Montrachet to the adjacent Chevalier-Montrachet vineyard. It's a matter of a couple of yards, but the stony soil of Chevalier gives more austere grapes, which in turn gives leaner, haughtier, yet still superlative wine.

Since then, on other occasions I've scratched away at the soil of Le Montrachet and know that it is stonier and less rich than that of its neighbors, except for the ultra-stony Chevalier-Montrachet. The slope is just that little bit steeper as it gently changes angle from an easterly to a southeasterly aspect. I've felt my face warmed by early morning sun in the midst of its vines. I've sweltered under blazing midday sun; and in high summer, late into the evening, as the surrounding vineyards are cooling in the shade, I've felt the sun's rays still streaking toward me across Le Montrachet's tiny clump of vines as it sinks into a dip in the hills.

Mesoclimate. The perfect conjunction of soil, angle of slope, and aspect to the sun, providing just that bit more chance for these northern grapes to ripen to perfection. In every commune on the Côte d'Or, the endlessly changing geological and climatic conditions create little plots of vineyard, some only a couple of acres broad, which give wines of more power, personality, or finesse than those of their neighbors. This is what makes the Côte d'Or so fascinating, yet so exhausting a region to get to know.

Whereas the most famous wines of the Côte de Nuits, directly to the north of the Côte de Beaune, are all red, most of the world-renowned wines of the Côte de Beaune are white, and that's due to those mesoclimates again. In fact, 75 percent of Côte de Beaune wines are red. The fertile, red-tinged soil and, periodically, the marl that is such a feature of the Côte de Nuits occupy the majority of the slopes, and in these cases Pinot Noir predominates. But the slopes here are less extreme, and the red Côte de Beaune wines, even from the one red Grand Cru vineyard of Corton, right next to the Côte de Nuits, have a rounder charm and less savage power than those of the Côte de Nuits itself. Wines from Aloxe-Corton, Beaune, Volnay, and, in a rougher way, Pommard, are all marked by perfume rather than by power. The whites at their best, however—from Chardonnay grapes planted where limestone dominates the darker clay—are marked by virtually every characteristic you could ask of a dry white wine. I say dry because there is no sugar left in wines like

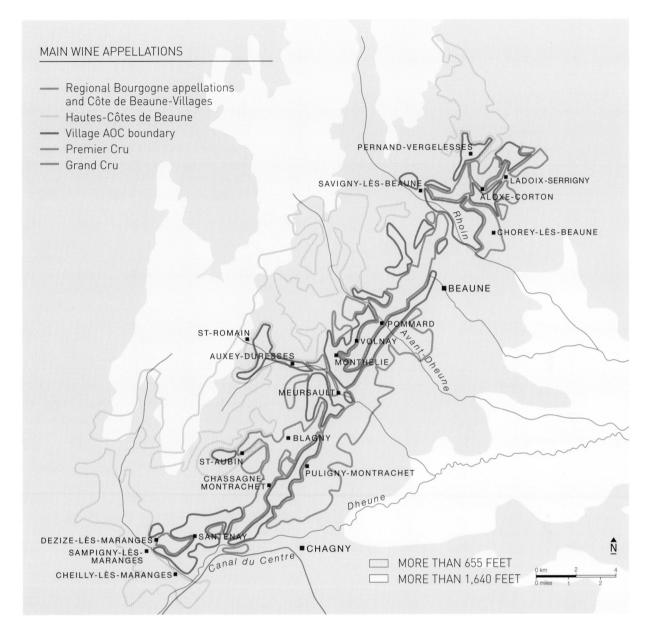

MAIN WINE APPELLATIONS

— Regional Bourgogne appellations
and Côte de Beaune-Villages
— Hautes-Côtes de Beaune
— Village AOC boundary
— Premier Cru
— Grand Cru

PERNAND-VERGELESSES

SAVIGNY-LÈS-BEAUNE
LADOIX-SERRIGNY
ALOXE-CORTON

Rhoin

CHOREY-LÈS-BEAUNE

BEAUNE

POMMARD

ST-ROMAIN
VOLNAY
Avant-Dheune

AUXEY-DURESSES
MONTHÉLIE

MEURSAULT

BLAGNY

ST-AUBIN
PULIGNY-MONTRACHET
CHASSAGNE-
MONTRACHET

Dheune

DEZIZE-LÈS-MARANGES
SANTENAY
SAMPIGNY-LÈS-
MARANGES
CHAGNY
CHEILLY-LÈS-MARANGES
Canal du Centre

N

☐ MORE THAN 655 FEET
☐ MORE THAN 1,640 FEET

0 km   2   4
0 miles   1   2

Corton-Charlemagne, Meursault, Puligny-Montrachet, Chassagne-Montrachet, or the host of others that the different villages make. Yet the honey and butter lusciousness, the cream, the wafted scent of grilled nuts still warm from the fire, the cinnamon and nutmeg spice that ripples through the orchard fruits—all these flavors, plus the taut backbone of mineral, of herb, of smoke from a forest glade, are there. I can remember bottles like these drunk twenty years ago as clearly as if my glass were being refilled in front of me this very minute.

What is equally exciting is that, if you seek out good producers, you really can taste the difference in wines that come from neighboring patches of vines. The Burgundian system of delineating each vineyard plot with distinctive characteristics is the most comprehensive in

the world. Meursault-Perrières does have stonier soil than its neighbor Meursault-Charmes; the wine is tauter, it promises more, and will perhaps give more sublime satisfaction in time. That's how it should be, and fairly frequently that's how it is.

CÔTE DE BEAUNE CLASSIFICATIONS

As in the Côte de Nuits, the top vineyard sites are given the status of Grand Cru, but the procession of Grands Crus at around the 900-foot mark isn't repeated in the Côte de Beaune, and there are only two groups of Grands Crus: one in the north, with the great hill of Corton at Aloxe-Corton, and one in the south with Montrachet and its siblings straddling Puligny-Montrachet and

CÔTE DE BEAUNE VILLAGES AND TOP VINEYARDS (from north to south)

- » **Ladoix Grands Crus:** Corton (part), Corton-Charlemagne (part).
- » **Pernand-Vergelesses Grands Crus:** Corton (part), Corton-Charlemagne (part). **Main Premiers Crus:** Ile des Vergelesses, Les Vergelesses.
- » **Aloxe-Corton Grands Crus:** Corton (part), Corton-Charlemagne (part). **Main Premiers Crus:** Les Chaillots, Les Maréchaudes, Les Valozières.
- » **Chorey-lès-Beaune**
- » **Savigny-lès-Beaune Main Premiers Crus:** Aux Guettes, Les Lavières, Aux Serpentières, Les Vergelesses.
- » **Beaune Main Premiers Crus:** Les Avaux, Les Boucherottes, Les Bressandes, Les Cents Vignes, Champs Pimont, Le Clos des Mouches, Le Clos de la Mousse, Clos du Roi, Les Cras, Les Epenotes, Les Fèves, Les Grèves, Les Marconnets, Les Teurons, Les Toussaints, Les Vignes Franches.
- » **Pommard Main Premiers Crus:** Les Arvelets, Les Boucherottes, Clos Blanc, Clos de la Commaraine, Clos des Epeneaux, Les Grands Epenots, Les Petits Epenots, Les Pézerolles, Les Rugiens-Bas, Les Rugiens-Hauts.
- » **Volnay Main Premiers Crus:** Les Angles, Clos de la Bousse d'Or, Les Caillerets, Champans, Clos des Chênes, Clos des Ducs, Les Santenots, Taille Pieds.
- » **Monthelie Main Premiers Crus:** Les Champs Fulliot, Les Duresses, Sur la Velle.
- » **Meursault Main Premiers Crus:** Les Charmes, Les Perrières, Les Genevrières, Les Gouttes d'Or, Le Porusot. Certain red wines can also be sold as Volnay or Blagny.
- » **Auxey-Duresses Main Premiers Crus:** Climat du Val, Clos du Val, Les Duresses.
- » **St-Romain**
- » **Puligny-Montrachet Grands Crus:** Bâtard-Montrachet (part), Bienvenues-Bâtard-Montrachet, Chevalier-Montrachet, Le Montrachet (part). **Main Premiers Crus:** Le Cailleret, Le Champ Canet, Clavaillon, Les Combettes, Les Demoiselles, Les Folatières, La Garenne, Les Pucelles, Les Referts, La Truffière.
- » **St-Aubin Main Premiers Crus:** Le Charmois, La Chatenière, En Rémilly.
- » **Chassagne-Montrachet Grands Crus:** Bâtard-Montrachet (part), Criots-Bâtard-Montrachet, Le Montrachet (part). **Main Premiers Crus:** Les Baudines, La Boudriotte, Cailleret, Les Champs Gains, Les Chaumées, Les Chenevottes, Clos St-Jean, Les Embasées, La Grande Montagne, Les Grandes Ruchottes, Les Macherelles, La Maltroie, Morgeot, La Romanée, Les Vergers.
- » **Santenay Main Premiers Crus:** Beauregard, Le Clos des Mouches, Le Clos de Tavannes, La Comme, Grand Clos Rousseau, Les Gravières, La Maladière, Passetemps.
- » **Maranges**

Chassagne-Montrachet. Apart from these two, the best vineyards for both red and white wines are Premiers Crus. The same detailed examination of the vines, row by row, took place to determine the status of a plot of land because, in this cool area, the slightest nuance can make the difference between great and merely good wine. An almost imperceptible dip in the field, a scarcely registered change in slope angle or exposure to the sun, a brief streak of clay running across a limestone ridge—all these tiny details combine to form the great imponderable the French call terroir. Of all the French areas to take terroir seriously, the Côte d'Or, with its obsessive classification, is the most passionate. Below these levels are the village appellations, and although many of these are on flatter, alluvial land, the quality is still pretty good. Sixteen villages can use the title Côte de Beaune-Villages for their reds instead of their own village name, but these days this option is rarely exercised except by merchants eager to make up a blend. Côte de Beaune is a tiny red and white appellation from a slope west of Beaune. The least good vineyards qualify only for the Bourgogne, Bourgogne Passe-Touts-Grains, or Coteaux Bourguignons appellations.

VILLAGES OF THE CÔTE DE BEAUNE

The Côte de Beaune really begins with the great hill of Corton, and three villages share its slopes: Ladoix,

Aloxe-Corton and Pernand-Vergelesses. This impressive, proud crescent of vines swings right around from east to west with the pale, weathered limestone soil of Corton and Corton-Charlemagne producing white wine right up to the forest fringe at about 1,150 feet. The lower slopes produce round, succulent red Corton; in general the east-facing slopes are best for red, the west-facing for white.

Savigny is tucked into the valley just northwest of Beaune with less protected and, indeed, some north-facing vineyards, but its reds and whites are generally good. Beaune is more famous, and the style of its wine is more traditionally soft and mellow; excellent red and white Premiers Crus reach down toward the town itself. Pommard and Volnay have steep, uneven slopes climbing up into the scrub-covered hills. They jig in and out, creating numerous different aspects to the sun, affording erratic protection for the vines. This means that the mesoclimate becomes particularly important, especially for the demanding Pinot Noir, which dominates Pommard and Volnay. These are often delimited by wall enclosures found throughout the Côte de Beaune and Côte de Nuits.

The heart of the Côte de Beaune runs from Meursault to Puligny-Montrachet and Chassagne-Montrachet. Here, between about 790 and 985 feet, with a few fine vineyards as high as about 1,150 feet around the hamlet of Blagny, the Chardonnay revels in the spare stony soil and the limestone outcrops jutting to within inches of the surface, delights in the dips and curves of the east- to southeast-facing slopes, and produces a fascinating array of wonderful flavors. All are minutely but recognizably different, and every one, when created by a serious producer, is a triumphant vindication of the notion of terroir. At Chassagne-Montrachet the soil becomes heavier again, spreading southwest to Santenay and then trailing away further west to Maranges, and more red than white is grown once again.

HAUTES-CÔTES DE BEAUNE

You can see numerous vineyards in the hills behind the Côte de Beaune. These are included in the appellation Hautes-Côtes de Beaune. It's a heavenly part of Burgundy, with twisting country lanes, ancient avenues of trees, and a peaceful tranquillity. But these slopes are at a slightly higher altitude—a crucial 165–330 feet or so—than those of the Côte de Beaune and are less perfectly angled to the sun and less protected from the prevailing wind and the rain. In a warm year, they produce pleasant light reds and whites—just right for a picnic in one of the high meadows.

The famous vineyard of Le Montrachet sits along the aptly named Côte d'Or, or "Golden Slope," running north to south of Beaune.

Côte Chalonnaise

RED GRAPES
Pinot Noir is the main permitted grape.

WHITE GRAPES
The main grape is Chardonnay with some Aligoté at Bouzeron.

CLIMATE
It is less sheltered from westerly winds here than in the Côte d'Or, but although it is cooler, the Côte Chalonnaise can also be drier. Getting enough sun to ripen the grapes is the main problem.

SOIL
The soil here is based on limestone or a mixture of limestone and clay.

GEOGRAPHY
In this scattering of low hills, a good aspect is vital for ripening, and the best sites are on south-, southeast-, and east-facing slopes at about 720–1,150 feet.

I KNOW ALL ABOUT the prevailing westerly winds in the Côte Chalonnaise. A few years ago, in high summer, I was nosing about the Burgundian vineyards, trying to work out what was what, and ended up at dusk with no hotel booking. *How exciting*, I thought. A night under the stars, warmed by the balmy August zephyrs. I hardly bothered with a blanket but plonked myself down on the broad ridge of vineyards just south of the village of Bouzeron and drifted off to sleep with a little smile of contentment playing on my lips. Then the wind started. Wow. Balmy August zephyrs? Atlantic gale more like, as I stumbled freezing back to the car and spent a miserable rest of the night waiting for an early, and chilly dawn.

It made me appreciate just what a crucial job Burgundy's high hills do in protecting their vineyards against the prevailing westerlies. In the Côte d'Or, the range of hills is relatively unbroken from Dijon in the north to Santenay in the south. But then they trail unconvincingly away to the west, and what takes their place around the town of Chagny is a hodgepodge of disjointed hillocks offering rare shelter from the wind and occasional sloping land angled toward the sun. This is the Côte Chalonnaise. A jumbled collection of mesoclimates growing the same grapes as the Côte d'Or to the north, occasionally making wines of similar quality, but rarely with their richness, roundness, or perfume. A poor relation? Yes. But what are are they a poor relation to? The greatest Pinot Noir and Chardonnay vineyards in France, possibly in the world. A poor relation to these isn't so bad.

Even so, you have to choose your sites carefully here. The best are on limestone-dominated slopes, slanted, sometimes steeply, to between southeast and southwest to catch every available ray of sun. Most vines are planted at between about 720 and 1,150 feet above sea level—much the same as in

Picking Pinot Noir grapes above the village of Rully.

the Côte d'Or—but, with the shining exception of the top section of the famous Corton hill, no exciting Côte d'Or vineyards are set above 985 feet. The leanness that characterizes many Chalonnais wines is easily explained by this relatively high altitude, less-than-perfect wind protection, and the lack of gently angled, continuously southeast-facing slopes.

BOUZERON

The leanness doesn't matter at Bouzeron, the most northerly Chalonnais appellation, because Bouzeron has made its reputation with a lemon-sharp, peppery, yet buttermilk-scented dry white from the Aligoté grape. There is some Chardonnay and Pinot Noir sold simply as Bourgogne, but Aligoté is the main wine here. Wine from old vines, marked *vieilles vignes*, generally has a little more Chardonnay-like richness to it.

RULLY

Rully has traditionally been seen as a sparkling wine area, but now it deserves better. The light, lean wines from some steepish limestone slopes have the delicacy and acidity much prized by fizz makers, but a better understanding of vineyard practice and winemaking and some self-confidence have been injected into the area by merchant houses, such as Rodet, and some young growers. Add to this the warming effect of climate change, and there are now significant amounts of good Rully—both the light but cherry-scented Pinot Noir reds and lean-limbed but tasty Chardonnays, especially with oak barrel aging. Some of the better vineyards have Premier Cru status, but it doesn't mean that much.

MERCUREY

Mercurey to the south is the largest Chalonnais village appellation, with just under 90 percent of production being red wine from Pinot Noir. Again, we're not talking about really big-boned wines here—the leanness still comes through—but there is a considerable difference in perfume and style between the lighter wines from the limestone slopes and the chunkier ones from the clay vineyards. The whites have rarely been special, but, as in Rully, efforts by leading growers, as well as the main merchant houses, such as Faiveley and Rodet, have greatly improved the whites and added more flesh to the reds, which may be lean but often have a most attractive strawberry fruit. There is a fair number of Premier Cru vineyards, the best south-facing slopes being located to the north of the town.

GIVRY

Givry has an impressive ring of southeast-facing vines rising to the west of the town. The best sites give a red wine of reasonable depth and considerable flavor in warm years. After a few years of aging, it can develop an almost sweet strawberry and cherry fruit. There is some white from Chardonnay, but little of it is that exciting.

MONTAGNY

Several miles south, again on steep slopes and in the clefts of little valleys, the all-white Montagny appellation is at last producing interesting, dry, yet softly toasty Chardonnay wines from what is clearly excellent vineyard land. The most important producer is the go-ahead cooperative at Buxy, La Cave des Vignerons de Buxy, which has transformed the quality of basic Chalonnais reds and whites. The southern Chalonnais continues to develop and will produce exciting wines in the future, but it still lacks the prerequisite for real progress—the emergence of a bevy of good individual estates. The Mâconnais, to the south, is developing precisely that.

CRÉMANT DE BOURGOGNE

The prime objective of the vineyards of Burgundy is the production of still wines—some of the world's most perfumed reds and some of the most complex whites from the best vineyards in the center and north, and pleasantly rounded, fruity reds and gentle whites from the southern vineyards. But Burgundy is a marginal vine-growing area, particularly in the northerly Yonne region, where the southernmost Champagne vineyards are not that far away from those of Chablis. The weather is unpredictable, and frequently the wine produced is too thin and unripe to make enjoyable drinking on its own. In which case, it's just fine as a sparkling wine base.

The Côte Chalonnaise, especially Rully with its exposed limestone slopes, used to be the center for Crémant de Bourgogne, and, further north, Nuits-St-Georges even boasted several well-known brands. But the best producers are now in the Auxerrois zone of the Yonne region, where excellent white and rosé is produced, particularly at the Caves de Bailly, and in the Mâconnais, where co-ops such as Lugny and Viré use much of their Chardonnay and Pinot Noir grapes to produce excellent Champagne-method sparkling wine. Gamay, Aligoté, Pinot Blanc, Pinot Gris, Melon de Bourgogne, and Sacy are also allowed in small measure.

The Mâconnais

RED GRAPES
Gamay is the main variety, followed by Pinot Noir.

WHITE GRAPES
Chardonnay is the main grape, with small amounts of Aligoté.

CLIMATE
The Mediterranean influence begins with higher temperatures and occasional storms. Overall, annual rainfall is higher than in the Côte d'Or to the north. Spring frosts can be a problem.

SOIL
There are two basic types of soil: limestone, favored by the white vines, and a mix of clay and sand, favored by the reds.

GEOGRAPHY
This is a region of low hills cut by a series of transverse valleys, which usefully create south-, southeast-, and southwest-facing slopes with good exposure to the sun.

YOU CAN APPROACH the Mâconnais at about 170 miles per hour on the TGV train from Paris that drops its dazed travelers at Mâcon station before surging onward to Lyon and the Mediterranean. You can approach the Mâconnais at half the speed—or slightly less if you're a law-abiding citizen—on the Autoroute du Soleil. You can approach it at whatever ambling, easy-going pace that the farmers' droning tractors, the smallholders' wheezing Deux Chevaux, and the odd roaming sheep, cow, and goat will let you—by the country roads that twist and turn through the charming rural backwaters at the southern end of the Côte Chalonnaise, gradually dropping down to the blander, broader spaces of the Mâconnais.

I'd take the time to meander if I were you. The Mâconnais stretches north to south for about 30 miles, from the southernmost tip of the Côte Chalonnaise to the border with the Beaujolais region at St-Vérand. It is mainly a vista of gently rolling hills and dales, vines sharing the land with other crops and with Charollais cattle.

The air that can seem so damp and chilly across northern France and most poignantly so in Burgundy's Côte d'Or, seems warmer here, friendlier, more benign. The sun spreads itself more broadly in a sky that is wider and colored increasingly with the azure of the South stretching into infinity. The houses—these are what finally tell you you're leaving the North of France behind. The angular, defensive rooftops and storm-colored slates give way to the warm, rounded terracotta tiles found in Provence. The roofs become almost flat, and open porches face southward toward the sun. The heart-warming South begins here in the Mâconnais.

Until relatively recently, most of the approximately 16,060 acres of Mâconnais vineyards produced red wine, mainly from Gamay but with some Pinot Noir being grown, too. Most of the Gamay wines are earthy and rough, acidity dominating their meager fruit. Much of the Pinot Noir is used to make sparkling Crémant de Bourgogne, and now fewer than 9 percent of the Mâconnais vines are red. Most of the still red Mâcon wine is sold as Mâcon Supérieur, which has a slightly higher minimum alcohol level than straight Mâcon.

Not surprisingly, and reflecting the explosion of worldwide interest, the Chardonnay grape now occupies 90 percent of the Mâconnais vineyards. (There is just a little Aligoté, too.) Indeed, there is a village called Chardonnay here, near Tournus in the north of the region, which tradition claims as the birthplace of the Chardonnay vine. There is no reason why this shouldn't be true because Chardonnay is the traditional white grape here. But the locals have taken an awfully long time to show any great pride in their famous offspring, and the wines were rarely exciting. Until recently, a Mâcon Blanc or Mâcon Blanc Villages from a merchant or a cooperative was always the cheapest Burgundy white on any wine list and was usually listless and drab. But the cooperatives, one by one, have upped their game, and now we are seeing a gentle flowering of single estates showing just how good Mâconnais Chardonnay can be.

THE POUILLY APPELLATIONS

Certainly the Pouilly-Fuissé vineyards are some of the best Chardonnay ones in France. This wine, however, became too famous for its own good—primarily because of its phenomenal success on the American market—and this had the usual consequences of overproduction with a lowering of quality and scary price hikes.

Yet the beautifully angled vineyards that carpet the lower slopes of the magnificent rock of Solutré and its near twin, the rock of Vergisson, are of a superb quality. An increasing number of growers here produces delectable examples of Chardonnay under the Pouilly-Fuissé banner, with the round, oatmealy softness of a Meursault fattened out and honeyed by the warmer Mâconnais sun. But most Pouilly-Fuissé is still made by cooperatives and sold under merchants' labels. Despite the improvement in some merchants' offerings, too many of these are simply pleasant dry Chardonnay at a far from simply pleasant price. The emergence of an increasing number of independent growers is at last raising standards all round.

Pouilly-Fuissé comes from five villages—Chaintré (generally regarded as the least good), Solutré, Vergisson, Pouilly, and Fuissé. The nearby villages of Loché and Vinzelles, between Pouilly-Fuissé and Mâcon, have attached Pouilly to their names to share some of the glory, but, although their wines can be pleasant, the vineyards are flatter and more fertile and thus are less capable of growing the best Chardonnay grapes.

ST-VÉRAN

A more recent Mâcon appellation is St-Véran, which lies right on the border with the Beaujolais region. Vineyards in the southern part of the appellation around the villages of St-Vérand (note the "d" in the village name and not the appellation name), Chânes, Chasselas, Leynes, and St-Amour-Bellevue can produce either white St-Véran, which has mopped up most of what used to be called Beaujolais Blanc, or red St-Amour, one of the top Beaujolais Crus, and it is not uncommon to find producers here who make both wines. Wines from here are usually relatively stony in character.

There is another section of St-Véran vineyards north of Pouilly-Fuissé, on the outskirts of the villages of Davayé and Prissé, and these wines are much fuller and fatter. The quality of St-Véran is fairly good—the wine is light and dry, rarely made with any oak, and often has a hint of muskiness common in the southern Mâconnais. If you want to check the discreet charm of the Mâconnais at a fair price, St-Véran is a good place to start.

MÂCON-VILLAGES AND MÂCON-BLANC

Although there is a simple Mâcon Blanc appellation, the most common white wine is Mâcon-Villages. The best twenty-six villages can add their own name to the appellation—as in Mâcon-Lugny. Two of the best villages now have their own appellation, Viré-Clessé. Other good villages include Bussières, Chaintré, Chardonnay, Charnay, Clessé, Cruzille, Davayé, Igé, Lugny, Prissé, la Roche Vineuse, Uchizy, and Verzy. Production is dominated by one of France's most efficient networks of cooperatives. Their organizational clout has brought about much of the region's prosperity. The standard of wine produced is generally now decent to good, and the cooperatives also produce Crémant de Bourgogne, some of France's best sparkling wine. But to really understand the potential of these pleasant rural vineyards, you must buy from the growing band of individual growers. Fiercely committed to raising standards, they vehemently oppose high yields and machine harvesting, and their Chardonnay wines show just how good the Mâconnais region could be.

Vineyards nestle on the lower slopes of the spectacular rock of Solutré, which rears from the landscape around Pouilly-Fuissé.

Beaujolais

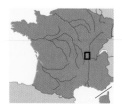

RED GRAPES
Gamay is the only variety allowed for Beaujolais, accounting for 98 percent of the Beaujolais vineyards.

WHITE GRAPES
A tiny amount of Chardonnay is planted for white Beaujolais (2 percent of the vineyards).

CLIMATE
Warmer and sunnier than northern Burgundy, the region is partly protected from prevailing westerly winds by the Monts du Beaujolais.

SOIL
The most important aspect is the granite subsoil, which influences the northern zone, where the best vineyards are situated and on which Gamay thrives. Further south, nearer Lyon, the soil is richer, primarily clay and limestone, and is less suited to Gamay.

GEOGRAPHY
The vineyards lie between about 500 and 1,640 feet and face all directions, although many of the best face southeast.

IN MY MIND, BEAUJOLAIS is a magical haven of hills, of a bucolic way of life far removed from the drab conformity of city life. But it isn't. Perhaps it never was. In the days immortalized by Chevallier in his famous novel *Clochemerle*, Beaujolais was a beautiful but poverty-stricken region. Its job was to provide the basic table wine of Lyon, France's second city. The Lyonnais had monumental thirsts but were used to paying little for their tipple.

BEAUJOLAIS NOUVEAU

That all changed with the advent of Beaujolais Nouveau, or Beaujolais Primeur, the wine of the new vintage. What a stroke of genius. Beaujolais has been drunk as young as possible in Lyon since the vineyards were first planted. Then in the 1950s, the Parisians caught onto the idea, then the British in the 1970s, followed by the Americans and the Japanese. There used to be a lot of razzmatazz attached to the race to get the first bottles to London on the third Thursday in November, with cars, airplanes, and motorcyles leaving speed limits in shreds behind them. Well, that's a thing of the past, and now that the first wines of each year arrive in Northern Europe from Australia or Chile some time in the summer, even the thrill of drinking the first of the new vintage has lost its gloss. Hardly anyone now notices the arrival of the first Beaujolais Nouveau, which is a shame because when it's good it's just the thing to ward off the gloom of a dank November day. Quality is generally reasonable, and the wine can be delicious until Christmas and the New Year. Even then, the better ones gain depth and richness for another few months and make good picnic wines in summer.

Administratively, Beaujolais is considered part of Burgundy or La Grande Bourgogne, but as far as wine goes, the two regions are completely different. The dominant grape in Beaujolais and the only one used for Beaujolais is Gamay, barred from all but the most basic wines in the rest of Burgundy because of the raw, rough flavors it tends to produce on alkaline soil. But in Beaujolais the soil is different, and here the Gamay can produce bright, juicy-ripe glugging wine difficult to beat for sheer uncomplicated pleasure. This should be particularly so in the gently rolling, southerly vineyards nearest Lyon, where rich clay and limestone soil grow the light, easy reds sold simply as Beaujolais or Beaujolais Nouveau. But yields are far higher than they used to be, and so many of the wines lack the fruit and perfume that made Beaujolais famous in the first place.

BEAUJOLAIS OR WHOLE-GRAPE METHOD OF FERMENTATION

The release of the first wine of the vintage has always been a cause for merrymaking throughout wine regions the world over. Far from being a modern phenomenon, the Nouveau celebrations take us right back to the heart of tradition. Luckily Beaujolais' Gamay grape naturally has a bright strawberry and peach flavor that is accentuated when vinified by the Beaujolais or whole-grape method of fermentation or carbonic maceration, which is used with varying success all around the world by people wanting to create reds to drink very young. Many of the fresh juicy reds from grapes such as Carignan in the South of France are made this way, and the juicy, gluggable, young Riojas known as "Joven" or "Bodeguero" also use this method.

THE BEAUJOLAIS CRUS

The northern part of the Beaujolais region contains the potentially superior vineyards. The most important of these are the ten Beaujolais Crus, or "growths," which account for 25 percent of all Beaujolais production; each Cru has its own appellation d'origine contrôlée. The Cru vineyards produce wine with an identifiable character, and most have a granite subsoil, which is rarely associated with fine wine—Hermitage in the Rhône Valley, south of Lyon, being a notable exception.

St-Amour is the most northerly commune, sharing its vineyards with the Mâconnais St-Véran appellation. Traveling south come Juliénas, Chénas, and Moulin-à-Vent, all capable of producing well-structured wines. The perfumed wines of Fleurie and Chiroubles come next, followed by Morgon, whose best wines develop a delightful cherry perfume. Régnié, with its sandy soil, is the newest Cru, although so far it has not really justified its right to be a Cru, and farthest south are Brouilly, the largest Beaujolais Cru, and Côte de Brouilly, both of which can produce delightful gluggable wines.

BEAUJOLAIS-VILLAGES

Thirty-eight other communes, mostly in the north of the region between Vaux-en-Beaujolais and St-Amour-Bellevue on the border with the Mâconnais region, qualify for Beaujolais-Villages status. This appellation is for wines that are better than basic Beaujolais but supposedly less fine than Crus. But what does the word "fine" mean?

Frankly, we're not after the longevity and complexity that may characterize the greatest red wines from Bordeaux, Burgundy, or the Rhône. What we want of the best ordinary Beaujolais is the uncomplicated cherub-cheeked, red-fruit ripeness and spicy blossom perfumes. But we want those fruits to be riper, those perfumes more heady, and the wine's soft-centered, smooth consistency to leave lingering trails in the memory long after the flavor fades. These are the blessings of youth.

There is hardly a Brouilly, a St-Amour, or a Chiroubles that should be aged for even as long as a couple of years. An occasional bottle of Morgon, Juliénas, Fleurie, or particularly Moulin-à-Vent does begin to resemble a charming, mild-mannered Côte de Beaune Burgundy after five to ten years of aging, but these are the exceptions. As in the rest of Beaujolais, vineyard yields are generally too high even in these top Cru vineyards, and a grape such as Gamay can aspire to class only if yields are kept low.

BEAUJOLAIS CRUS

The northern part of the Beaujolais region contains potentially the best vineyards, called Crus. Heading from north to south the ten Crus are:

» **St-Amour** The wine is much in demand through the romantic connotation of its name. Wines with great intensity of color and benefiting from a few months to soften.
» **Juliénas** Attractive, "serious" Beaujolais that can be big and tannic enough to develop further in bottle.
» **Chénas** Usually fairly austere and needing time to develop Burgundian tones.
» **Moulin-à-Vent** Dark and powerful wines.
» **Fleurie** The best known Cru. Wines can have a delightful juicy fruit, but high demand means that many are overpriced and dull.
» **Chiroubles** Light, fragrant delicious wine from the Cru with the highest vineyards.
» **Morgon** At their best, the wines have marvelous potential to age. Many commercial wines are no more than pleasant, for early drinking, and pricey.
» **Regnié** In the best years, the wines can be light, aromatic, and enjoyable.
» **Côte de Brouilly** More intense and deeper in color than its neighbor, Brouilly.
» **Brouilly** Soft, fruity wine for drinking young.

Champagne

RED GRAPES
Pinot Noir and Pinot Meunier account for 70 percent of all Champagne grapes.

WHITE GRAPES
Chardonnay accounts for 30 percent of the plantings.

CLIMATE
Cold, wet, continental climate, but the northerly latitude gives more daylight hours in the growing season than Provence. Rain and late spring frosts are the main enemies.

SOIL
Shallow topsoil as little as 6 inches in places covering subsoil largely of chalk up to about 655 feet thick.

GEOGRAPHY
Mainly east- and southeast-facing vineyards, which lie between about 330 and 655 feet high, and are protected by thickly wooded hilltops.

THEY WEREN'T PAYING THE AREA around Reims and Épernay northeast of Paris any compliments when they called it Champagne. They weren't thinking of glittering first night parties, of dandies and dancing girls, the hectic celebrations of a Grand Prix winner, or the tingling joyful tension of a lover with warm words in his mind and brave deeds in his heart.

The word "Champagne" comes from the Latin *campania*, meaning "open, flat countryside," and I sometimes feel this is an incredible understatement as I urge the car onward. Driving through the pale, lonely plains to the east of Reims, the sea of corn enlivened by an occasional steepling grain silo, I feel more as if I were in the depths of the Oklahoma prairie than trying to make a dinner date in the heart of one of the world's greatest wine regions. As I plow through the flat sugar-beet fields of the Pas de Calais, still saturated

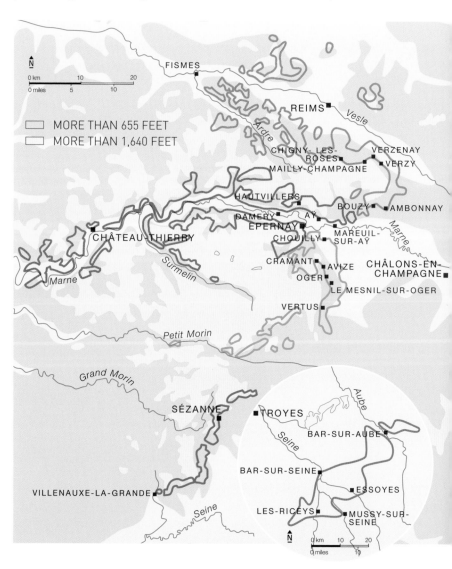

CHAMPAGNE DISTRICTS

— Montagne de Reims
— Vallée de la Marne
— Côte des Blancs
— Côte de Sézanne
— Côte des Bar

by squalls from the English Channel, past the giant slag piles of long-dead coal mines and once again out onto the chalky windswept plains to the north of Reims, I don't scent the slightest possibility of any vines ever ripening under such inhospitable conditions. It is simply too cold, too windy, too rainy for growing grapes.

This whole expanse of northeastern France is a desolate, underpopulated province of broad cornfields and dark forests, which experienced some of the fiercest fighting in World War I and II, even in and around the Champagne vineyards. In what many historians reckon may have been the bloodiest battle ever to take place, Attila the Hun was finally turned back east of Reims near Châlons-en-Champagne.

CLIMATE AND SOIL

But in this flat landscape there is one brief eruption of low hills—a grouping of cliffs, slopes, and valleys of ancient chalk. These hills provide just the amount of protection and privileged mesoclimate that the grape vine needs. The Montagne de Reims and the Côte des Blancs are two of these ridges. The cleft where the Marne River pushes its way westward toward Paris is a third. Little pockets, such as the Côte de Sézanne and the Côte des Bar further south, can also provide suitable conditions for ripening the vine. Just.

Yet this knife-edge between ripeness and unripeness is what gives the wine of Champagne its peculiar suitability to form the base for a sparkling wine. The cold falls and icy winters that grip the whole region in a joyless embrace are what, by chance, created the now famous bubbles in the first place.

High acidity is crucial in the base wine for a good fizz. If you can lengthen the ripening time of the fruit as much as possible so that it creeps to maturity only in the golden days of fall, you will be able to retain high acidity yet have physically mature grapes. The flavors that these give are infinitely superior to those obtained from grapes grown in warmer climates simply picked early. All you get then is green, raw unripeness. You can't make great wine out of that.

Champagne's days are cooled by the damp Atlantic breezes that sweep in unhindered from the west. Those winds often bring rain—and at the wrong time, too. Although the total annual rainfall is lower than in regions such as Bordeaux, Burgundy, and the Loire, nearly 60 percent of it falls in the summer and early fall, with July and August being particularly hard hit when the rain causes mildew and rot among the ripening grapes. But this is where the importance of the right soil comes in. With the exception of the southerly Côte des Bar, Champagne's vines are planted on a thick chalk subsoil that frequently keeps breaking through the topsoil.

ALL THAT CHALK

A thick, billowing seam of chalk runs across northern France to Calais and across southern England. This is the subsoil for the Champagne vineyards. Chalk has a perfect balance between porosity and water retention and is able to nourish vines equally well in dry or wet years. Its brilliant whiteness helps the soil's ability to reflect sunlight back onto the vines, and chalk retains heat well, all vital factors in such a northerly vineyard region. Chalk is also alkaline, which in turn produces grapes with high acid levels—perfect for sparkling wine. In addition, the region's *caves*, or cellars, dug deep into the chalk, mainly in the towns of Reims and Épernay, are cold and damp, providing an ideal environment for storing bottles while the Champagne inside undergoes its second fermentation. This is because the slower the yeasts set to work, the smaller the bubble and the more persistent the fizz in the finished wine. Champagne produces the world's finest sparkling wine. It increasingly looks as though the same soil in southern England will produce bubbles to equal them. May battle commence.

The chalk is porous and fissured, holding enough water to nourish the vine but not drown it. The vine roots burrow into the soft, almost spongy stone, thus anchoring the plant against climatic extremes above ground. Because the chalk is so close to the surface, it is relatively warm and may even reflect sunlight back onto the vine, aiding the grapes' final struggle for ripeness as fall drifts toward winter.

FROM STILL WINE TO SPARKLING

This somber scenario means that wines with truly ripe, sun-filled flavors simply aren't part of the Champagne repertoire, although historically the region's reputation was based on still red wines. But highly acidic grapes, picked just as winter set in, would have fermented slowly and inefficiently. As the freezing winter air filled the wine cellars, the yeasts would simply have become too cold to go on with their job; they'd have packed up and gone into hibernation. In the days before central heating, they'd have lain dormant until the following spring had warmed the cellars up and—hey presto—they'd have finished off their fermentation with a final brisk burst of bubbles to emerge as still wines.

The English and the Parisians used to buy a lot of Champagne wine. Because until modern times young wine was prized more than old, it would be shipped to them in barrel during the winter. Once the spring came, it would begin bubbling again.

Traditionally, much effort was put into ridding the wines of their bubble, but in England, in the carefree period after Charles II's restoration in 1660, and in the pleasure-mad days in France that followed the death of Louis XIV in 1715, a vogue developed for frivolous sparkling wines that may have upset connoisseurs of those times but which has ensured Champagne's fame ever since. No one then understood exactly why the fizziness came and went, although Christopher Merret, an Englishman, seems to have worked it out in 1662. The English also managed to preserve the bubbles into the summer because they had developed particularly strong glass bottles and they used cork instead of rags soaked in oil as stoppers.

MAKING CHAMPAGNE

The essence of the Champagne method, or *méthode champenoise*, of making sparkling wine is that a second fermentation of the wine takes place in the final bottle. The carbon dioxide given off during this fermentation can't escape, so it stays dissolved in the wine under pressure, ready to froth up as soon as the cork is released.

The still wine is bottled. At the time of bottling, a solution of sugar, wine, and a little yeast, the *liqueur de tirage*, is added, and the bottle is resealed (with a cork or a crown top) and stashed away in a cool, dark cellar while the wine begins its second fermentation. This lasts between ten days and three months. The wine is then left alone, ideally for several years, because aging it on its lees—the dead yeasts from the fermentation—will enable it to develop a wonderfully rich, cookielike flavor.

But, of course, the lees can't stay there forever and decanting is hardly the answer; the bubbles would disappear along with the lees. It was Champagne's most famous widow, La Veuve Clicquot—or, to be strictly accurate, her cellarmaster, Antoine Muller—who came up with the technique of riddling. It involves placing the bottles in racks (*pupitres*) in which they can be progressively turned and upended, thus coaxing the lees onto the cork. Riddling, if done by hand, is a very labor-intensive and skilled affair. Every bottle must be twisted and turned each day, and riddlers do it at tremendous speed. But not as fast as machines, which is why almost all Champagne houses now use automatic riddlers, in which great crates of bottles are mechanically turned fraction by fraction.

At the end of the process, the bottles are vertical, upside down, and there is a small pale mound of sludge piled on each cork. In order to get it out, the bottles are placed with their necks in a bath of freezing brine; it freezes the wine in the neck of the bottle just enough for the cork or crown top to be whipped out, along with its load of sediment, and another closure inserted. This process is known as disgorging (*dégorgement*). Some wine will also escape with the lees—so before the final cork is inserted the bottles are topped off. Because most people don't like absolutely dry Champagne, a little sweetening is added at the same time. Not a lot, however. Brut Champagne still tastes dry and contains only up to 12 grams (about a tablespoon) of sugar per liter but usually a lot less. Extra dry, confusingly, is a little sweeter, and sec, which means dry, is sweeter again. But they still taste only a little off-dry. Demi-sec is medium, and doux or rich Champagnes are sweet. The only thing the wine has to do now is age some more: about three years is ideal for nonvintage, and twice as long for vintage Champagne.

Bottles would still burst, but not half as often as did the weaker French bottles. Gradually, in the latter part of the seventeenth century, the English, and the French—led by Dom Pérignon, who was in charge of the cellars at Hautvillers Abbey between 1670 and 1715—developed methods to create a reliably fizzy wine by inducing a second fermentation in the bottle.

The reputation of Champagne is based on this last achievement. By adding a little yeast and sugar to a still wine and then corking the bottle tightly, the wine referments in the bottle, and the bubbles dissolve, waiting to burst forth when the bottle is opened. This is the traditional Champagne method of making sparkling wine, and is used across the world for top-class bubbly. Others have since improved upon Dom Pérignon's methods for creating a reliable sparkling wine, but he was perhaps more important for formulating other principles now accepted as fundamental to quality in Champagne. Above all, he saw the need to restrict yields to achieve ripeness and to blend together the wines of different vineyards and communes to produce the best end result.

THE CLASSIFICATION OF CHAMPAGNE VINEYARDS

In the marginal climate of Champagne, limited vineyard sites can produce an attractive, multifaceted wine in most years. However, the three grape varieties used for Champagne, each grown on different sites, can contribute a more rounded flavor to a final blend. Older "reserve" wines held back from the previous year may also be added for extra flavor. As a result, Champagne is usually a blend of different wines, often from all over the region, most of it is sold as nonvintage. A vintage is "declared" in the best years and with warmer conditions. This means more years than not. The so-called "de luxe" cuvées are also blends from different vineyards, unless they come from a single grower.

Merchant houses—the most important are in Reims, Épernay, and Ay—and cooperatives handle most Champagne production, buying grapes from the growers based on a guideline price per kilogram, determined by a tribunal of officials, growers, and producers and renegotiated every three or four years. Prices are fixed by a system known as the *échelle des crus*, or "ladder of growths," whereby villages, not individual vineyards, are classified according to quality on a scale ranging from 100 percent down to 80 percent. There are villages accorded the title Grand Cru, and these receive 100 percent of the agreed grape price per kilogram. The forty-one villages with Premier Cru status receive between 90 and 99 percent. All the other less-favored villages receive between 80 and 89 percent.

CHAMPAGNE STYLES

» **Nonvintage (NV)** Most Champagne is a blend of two or more vintages. Quality varies enormously, depending on who has made the wine, how long it has aged, and how much so-called Reserve wine (from an older vintage) is used in the blend. Brut is a dry but rarely bone-dry style. More completely dry styles—called Brut Nature or Zéro Dosage—are appearing and tasting good primarily because climate change is providing riper grapes that don't need sugar to hide their rawness. Somewhat confusingly, Extra Dry denotes a style less dry than Brut.
» **Vintage** denotes Champagne made with grapes from a single harvest. As a rule, it is made only in the best years, but nowadays you'll find some vintage releases in all but the worst years.
» **Blanc de Blancs** A lighter and at best supremely elegant style of Champagne made solely from the Chardonnay grape. Delightful young, it ages well.
» **Blanc de Noirs** White Champagne, fuller in style, made entirely from black grapes, either Pinot Noir, Pinot Meunier, or a combination of the two. Best with some age.
» **Rosé** Pink Champagne made either from black grapes or (more usually) by mixing a little still red wine into white Champagne. Good pink champagne—usually a little weightier than white—can have a delicious fragrance of cherries and raspberries. Usually drunk young, the best will age.
» **De luxe cuvée** In theory, the finest Champagne and certainly always the most expensive, residing in the fanciest bottles. Don't drink too young if you get the chance and the choice.
» **RD, or *récemment dégorgé*** A style pioneered by Bollinger. The wine is left to age for longer than usual on its sediment—this may be just a few years or up to twenty or more. The wine is then disgorged and immediately shipped to market, and the result is a thrilling blend of maturity and exhilarating freshness.

GRAPE VARIETIES

Not only are some vineyards better than others, but they are also better suited to particular grape varieties. Three main varieties are grown in Champagne: two red varieties, Pinot Noir and Pinot Meunier, and one white, Chardonnay.

Just south of Reims is the Montagne de Reims with vineyards on its northern, eastern, and southern slopes. Pinot Noir dominates these vineyards, especially those in the Grand Cru villages, and much of the backbone for the Champagne blends comes from these grapes and from those grown in the Côte des Bar region over about 60 miles. Pinot Noir is also used for the rare still wines of Champagne, such as Bouzy Rouge, which is light but perfumed with strawberry fruit. Chardonnay dominates the chalky, east-facing slopes of the Côte des Blancs south of Épernay. The other particularly successful areas for Chardonnay are the village of Villers-Marmery at the eastern end of the Montagne de Reims and the chalky Côte de Sézanne to the south. Chardonnay from the northern sites adds zest and lively, lean fruit to the Champagne blend, while that from the Côte de Sézanne will probably add a creamy, honeyed roundness. Blanc de Blancs Champagne is from 100 percent Chardonnay.

Pinot Meunier is the Champagne workhorse. Most villages grow some, with the exception of the top Côte des Blancs communes and Bouzy in the Montagne de Reims. Growers like it because it buds late, avoiding spring frosts, yet ripens more quickly than Pinot Noir as fall closes in. Blended with the other two varieties, it can add a pleasant, mildly perfumed quality that softens the more austere, slow-developing characteristics of Pinot Noir and Chardonnay.

BOTTLE SIZES

There are myriad different bottle sizes used for Champagne, although the ones at the larger end of the scale are rarely made nowadays. A standard Champagne bottle contains 750 milliliters (25 ounces). Large bottles are named after biblical figures and are filled with Champagne fermented in standard bottles or magnums (two bottles).

The most common names and sizes are: Magnum (two bottles); Jeroboam (four bottles); Methuselah (eight bottles); Salmanazar (twelve bottles); Balthazar (sixteen bottles); and Nebuchadnezzar (twenty bottles). There are other sizes, from Melchior (twenty-four bottles) up to Melchizedek (thirty bottles), but I've never seen them.

Shown left are the smallest size (the quarter bottle), the Nebuchadnezzar (twenty bottles), and the standard bottle (750 ml).

Alsace

RED GRAPES
Pinot Noir is the only red grape, occupying 10 percent of the plantings.

WHITE GRAPES
Riesling and Pinot Blanc are at 21 percent each, followed closely by Gewurztraminer and then Pinot Gris. There are smaller amounts of Sylvaner and the two Muscat varieties.

CLIMATE
Despite the northerly latitude, the region benefits from plentiful sun and low rainfall caused by its location in the rain shadow created by the Vosges mountains.

SOIL
The region divides into three main zones: mountain, mid-slopes, and foothills and plains. The best sites are on the middle slopes, which are limestone based with marly clay and sandstone topsoil.

GEOGRAPHY
The vineyards are sited between about 560 and 1,380 feet, with the best sites on the well-drained, sheltered, steep, middle slopes.

YOU ONLY HAVE TO STAND in the middle of the steeply sloping vineyards to the west of Colmar to realize there's something special about Alsace. Over to the west, dark clouds pile ominously above the mountains; yet here, where the Riesling and Gewurztraminer vines climb gamely up toward the wooded brows of the Vosges eastern foothills, the sky is as clear and blue as dreams, the sunshine is warm and mellow, the air is pure and sweet with the perfume of flowers and alive with the twittering chatter of insects. In these vineyards, grapes for some of the most heady and exotic wines in Europe ripen in the summer sun.

The vineyards of Alsace sit in a rain shadow created by the Vosges mountains that rise high above the Rhine Valley. Most of the rain brought by the westerly winds falls over these mountains and forests. By the time the clouds reach the vineyards, they have just enough rain left to cast a few refreshing showers on the vines and then evaporate into the warm air. Alsace is almost as far north as vineyards can go in France—only Champagne is marginally further north. Yet that rain shadow allows Colmar to be the second driest spot in France, beaten only by Perpignan, down on the Spanish border. Perpignan cooks under torrid skies. Not so Alsace. Perpignan produces rough-and-ready hot-climate reds; Alsace, because of cool northern temperatures, allied to day after day of

APPELLATIONS AND CLASSIFICATIONS

» **Alsace AOC** The general AOC covering the whole region. It appears on all labels. Any of the permitted grape varieties may be used. Currently, there is no intermediate level between AOC and Grand Cru, but work is being done on a Premier Cru, and there's talk of a Villages level, too.
» **Alsace Grand Cru AOC** This AOC covers certain special vineyards and, with one exception, Zotzenberg for its Sylvaner, is allowed only for wines made from Gewurztraminer, Muscat, Pinot Gris, and Riesling.
» **Crémant d'Alsace AOC** This AOC is for sparkling wine produced over the whole region and made in the traditional method, usually from Pinot Blanc or Riesling.
» **Vendange Tardive** Late-harvested wine made from very ripe Gewurztraminer, Riesling, Pinot Gris, and occasionally Muscat. Usually fairly sweet.
» **Séléction de Grains Nobles** A higher category than Vendange Tardive made from even riper grapes of the same varieties, often affected by sugar-intensifying noble rot. These are usually sweet and impressive, although the varietal flavors will be subdued.

clear skies, can provide the ripeness—and therefore the higher alcoholic strength—of the warm south but also the perfume and fragrance of the cool north.

Politically, Alsace has been caught between two inimical philosophies. The Rhine is southern Germany's great waterway. Nowadays, it forms a natural frontier as it runs northward from Basel on the Swiss border but, in less peaceful times, the river and the flat farmland on both its banks formed an obvious battleground whenever the French and Germans went to war. The frontier between the two then was seen as the Vosges mountains to the west, on whose eastern foothills all Alsace's vineyards are planted. Prussia gained control of Alsace in 1870, France won the region back in 1918; by 1940, Alsace was again under German occupation, before finally reverting to France in 1945.

After several generations of confused national identity, the region has settled into a reasonably contented dual personality. The Alsatian people maintain proudly, even ferociously, that they are as French as any French person can be. Yet most of the names of their villages are German (for example, Riquewihr and Westhalten), and the villages themselves with their tall, half-timber houses look as though they've stepped off the set of some German operetta; most family surnames are German (although Christian names are usually French), and the local Alsace dialect has far more in common with German than French.

GRAPE VARIETIES AND WINE STYLES

The grape varieties that make Alsatian wine are, for the large part, not typical in the rest of France. The region's two most famous grapes, Riesling and Gewurztraminer, although enthusiastically planted in Germany and much of Central Europe, are conspicuous by their absence elsewhere in France. Sylvaner doesn't appear elsewhere in France and is on the decline in Alsace; Pinot Gris and Pinot Blanc are tolerated at best in a very subordinate role in Burgundy. Only Pinot Noir, Burgundy's best red grape, and the white Muscat, planted in the fortified wine appellations around the Mediterranean, have genuine legitimacy in France.

The dual personality of Alsace is reflected by the wines, too. Alsace's French grape varieties take on a Germanic perfume, while the German grapes proudly distance themselves from the flavors one would find over the border in Germany itself.

Traditionally the difference has been more marked with Riesling because nearly all Germany's great Rieslings were sweet, whereas all those of Alsace were dry. Nowadays, Germany makes increasing amounts of dry

Rieslings, many very good, but they are generally taut and lean as well as subtly scented. Alsace's best Rieslings, on the other hand, are fat and round in the mouth yet marvelously dry, streaked with cold lime-pith acidity yet thick with glycerin ripeness. The two countries' other wines are also distinctive. Germany's Gewürztraminer is generally made with a certain fat sweetness and perfume. Alsace goes for the perfume of freshly plucked tea roses and the ripeness of lychee and mango. Gewurztraminer needs a long, ripening season and loves Alsace's sunny, dry weather that continues well into fall. In Germany, Pinot Gris is traditionally called Ruländer and is attractively honeyed and sweetish, although it is also appearing in a full oaky style under the Grauburgunder label, whereas Alsace Pinot Gris revels in spicy, musky, honeyed, and exotic flavors. Most Alsace Pinot Noir is pale and floral, despite some efforts to darken it up and make it more muscular, whereas Germany is making a number of Spätburgunders with impressive Burgundian depth. Alsace Muscats have a light, dry grapey perfume instead of the heady but weighty hothouse flavors preferred in the Muscats from France's far south.

Virtually all the finest wines come from a central section of vineyards in the Haut-Rhin *département* west of Colmar, a miraculously preserved medieval market town rightly called the Wine Capital of Alsace. Good wines are made in the north of Alsace, in the Bas-Rhin *département*, but they rarely have the ripeness or intensity of those from the vineyards of the Haut-Rhin, which lie further south. The vineyards that twist in and out of the folds in the Vosges eastern foothills are dotted with magical little villages, but those tilting gabled houses are inhabited by the people who tend the vines and make the wine; those rickety wooden doors do lead down to cellars that have housed the vats and barrels for hundreds of years.

The vineyards date back to the second century, when the Romans planted most of the lower foothills with vines. There are specific vineyards, such as Goldert in the village of Gueberschwihr and Mambourg in Sigolsheim, whose documented reputation stretches back to the eighth century, when Alsace was ruled by the Franks, and these ancient vineyards now form the core of the present Grand Cru system of wine classification in Alsace.

After World War II, when Alsace finally reverted to France, the winemakers determinedly set out to achieve appellation d'origine contrôlée status for their region and decided to do so by concentrating their efforts on the single appellation—that of Alsace, which was finally granted only in 1962—but with the different grape names prominently displayed on the best wines to indicate what flavors the drinker should expect. This labeling by grape variety may seem commonplace now because of the influence of New World wines, but it was novel in France, where more and more precise delineation of the origin of a wine was at the heart of the appellation system. Grand Cru means "great growth" and is intended to apply to particular patches of land that have traditionally produced the finest grapes, and it wasn't until 1983 that a provisional list of Grand Cru sites was produced.

The people with the power to market and promote Alsace as a wine region of quality were the big merchant houses, but their objective was to produce large quantities of wine at various but consistent levels of quality, so they needed to blend from numerous different vineyards and hardly ever named the actual vineyard site, preferring to promote their own names as brands. Despite owning large tracts of Grand Cru vineyards, the leading merchant houses are mostly unwilling even now to put vineyard names on their wines and, indeed, prefer to emphasize their companies' reputations instead. Their position is understandable and not solely self-interested. However, the concept of superior vineyard sites is crucial in marginal vineyard regions where only the most favorable mesoclimates can truly excel.

At present there are fifty-one Grand Cru sites covering 8 percent of Alsace vineyards, but they represent only 4 percent of Alsace's total wine production. Basic maximum yields are lower than for simple Alsace wines.

The current law states that only four "noble" grapes planted in these sites are entitled to the Grand Cru appellation—Gewurztraminer, Riesling, Pinot Gris, and Muscat—apart from the Grand Cru Zotzenberg for Sylvaner; but in the future each local area may be allowed to nominate other varieties that perform particularly well in a given site. There is no doubt that many of the best sites, exploited by the best growers, do produce unique personalities in the wine that dominate varietal character, especially in Rieslings. But there are still numerous wines sporting Grand Cru labels that offer nothing special. Currently, there is no intermediate level of quality between the great Grand Cru vineyards and the simple Alsace AOC, but it is possible to add a vineyard name to your label even if it isn't a Grand Cru. There is talk of creating a Premier Cru classification, and thirteen villages can now add their name to the all-embracing Alsace appellation. Things are on the move.

THE CLIMATE OF ALSACE

Alsace can muster enough sunshine to ripen grapes because of the Vosges mountains that run from north to south for about 40 miles in the west of the region. These mountains create a narrow but beneficial rain shadow over the vineyards in their lee. The prevailing westerly winds bring moisture-laden air in from the Atlantic. The Vosges are the first major obstacle that the air reaches, and as it rises to pass over the mountains, it cools and the moisture condenses and falls as rain, leaving the eastern slopes dry and sunny.

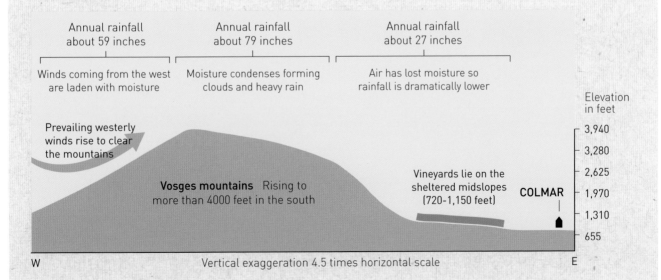

The Loire Valley

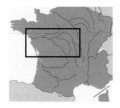

RED GRAPES
The most important grape is Cabernet Franc. Other varieties include Cabernet Sauvignon, Gamay, and Cot or Malbec. Pinot Noir is used for Sancerre reds and rosés.

WHITE GRAPES
Chenin Blanc is the main grape in Anjou and Touraine, with increasing amounts of Chardonnay and Sauvignon Blanc. Sauvignon Blanc is the grape of Sancerre and Pouilly-Fumé.

CLIMATE
A mild maritime climate moderated by the influence of the Gulf Stream produces warm summers and mild falls and winters. Ripening can be a problem. Further inland in Sancerre and Pouilly, the summers are longer and drier.

SOIL
The river is the dominating factor with the flatlands near the river mostly alluvial. Slopes and plateaus away from the river are mainly limestone. Much of Saumur is limestone. In Sancerre and Pouilly, the best vineyards are on limestone with some flint.

GEOGRAPHY
In this area of low hills, specific aspect to the sun is vital for ripening. The best sites are on the steeper slopes and face southwest, south, or southeast.

I SOMETIMES WONDER WHETHER the Loire River is just too long for its own good. It starts brightly enough, cascading and splashing out of the Ardèche gorges only about 30 miles west of the Rhône at Valence, full of purpose and vivacity. But by the time the river gets to Pouilly and Sancerre, sites of its first world-famous wines, the initial breezy seaward flow has slowed to a walk. As the river makes its great arc northward to Orléans, past the haunting Sologne marshes, and then loops wearily south and west, through Blois, Tours, Angers, Nantes, and finally to the Atlantic at St-Nazaire, the walk slows to an amble, the motion of the water so listless that the valley seems caught in a reverie, completely unconcerned about reaching its destination on the turbulent shores of the Bay of Biscay. Great gravel banks push through the river's surface, children paddle in the shallows, parents picnic and gossip on the warm pebbles. It doesn't seem as though the lazy summer Loire has the character to be a great wine river, home of some of the most thrilling and individual wines in France.

GRAPE VARIETIES

The Loire is predominantly a white grape region, producing enormous quantities of wine from Melon de Bourgogne—one of the world's most neutral white grape varieties and better known as Muscadet. Its virtue, when grown in the maritime climate near Nantes, is that it retains freshness, which makes it an exceptionally good partner to the local seafood.

Sauvignon Blanc needs a relatively cool climate to express its trademark pungency, its bright green, grassy, gooseberry freshness and slightly smoky perfume. In Sancerre and Pouilly, in the hands of a good winemaker, Sauvignon Blanc excels at such mouth-tingling crispness. Touraine produces Sauvignon

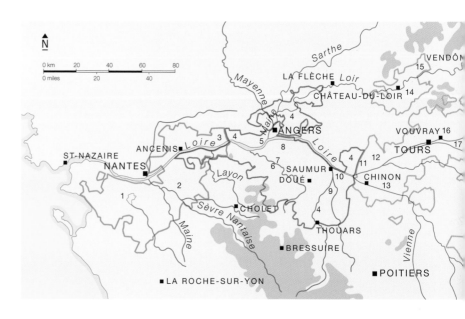

with an even fresher zesty green flavor, at a lower price. This is perhaps the purest expression of Sauvignon Blanc's personality in France, and its pleasure lies in marrying the greenness with proper ripeness.

Chenin Blanc needs warmth to thrive. Its flavors are raw and harsh when it fails to ripen fully. Few other places in the world take Chenin Blanc seriously, but here in the Loire Valley it can reach heights undreamed of elsewhere. The tufa soil (a type of chalky limestone) keeps the acidity levels high, enabling the greatest dry and sweet Chenin wines to last for decades, when they mature to a honeyed, minerally richness. Chenin is used here for everything from sparkling wines to dry wines to botrytized sweet ones.

Cabernet Franc, used largely as a seasoning grape in Bordeaux, is the main red wine grape grown in the Loire. In Bourgueil, St-Nicolas-de-Bourgueil, and Chinon, its mouthwatering perfume and smooth texture make some of France's most lovely red wines. At its best, Cabernet Franc has an unmistakable and hugely appealing raspberry fruit and a summery tang of black currant leaves. Delicious young, its wines can also be very long-lived. It is used for rosés, too.

Pinot Noir, the great grape of Burgundy, is grown in the Loire in Sancerre and Menetou-Salon, where in ripe years, it makes wines with good fruit and structure. Most red Sancerre, however, is made to be drunk young. Some Pinot Noir goes into rosé production.

Gamay makes fresh, juicy Beaujolais-like reds and rosé wines designed to be drunk young. The Teinturier Gamay (red-fleshed, as opposed to the Gamay Noir à Jus Blanc) is also grown in Touraine, but its wines are robust, solid, and unaromatic.

SPARKLING WINES

It would be easy to look upon the Loire Valley sparkling wine industry simply as a mechanism for soaking up large amounts of otherwise undrinkable local wines because most of the best sparklers are made from a very acid base wine. But this wouldn't be fair. Although in a warm year the late-ripening Chenin Blanc can make excellent still wines, in the all-too-frequent cool years of this region this high acid variety simply doesn't get ripe enough. So a cool year provides the perfect material for sparkling wines.

The best sparkling wines are made by the traditional method (as used in Champagne)—that is, with a second fermentation in the bottle—and tend to come from cool vineyards of limestone-dominated soil and subsoil. Both Saumur and Vouvray, which produce the two most important sparkling wine appellations in the region, are predominantly limestone areas. Vouvray and its neighboring appellation of Montlouis use only Chenin Blanc for their fizz, and, if you give the bottles a few years to soften, they attain a delicious nutty, honeyed quality yet retain the zing of Chenin acidity. Saumur Mousseux is usually based on Chenin but may include other varieties, such as Chardonnay, Sauvignon, and Cabernet Franc, which bring a welcome softness. Crémant de Loire, covering Anjou and Touraine, is generally softer still.

MAIN WINE APPELLATIONS

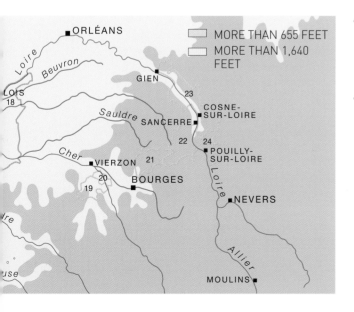

— NANTAIS
1. Gros Plant du Pays Nantais
2. Muscadet
3. Coteaux d'Ancenis
— ANJOU-SAUMUR
4. Anjou-Coteaux de la Loire
5. Savennières
6. Anjou-Villages
7. Coteaux du Layon
8. Coteaux de l'Aubance
9. Saumur
10. Saumur-Champigny

— TOURAINE
11. St-Nicolas-de-Bourgueil
12. Bourgueil
13. Chinon
14. Coteaux du Loir
15. Jasnières
16. Vouvray
17. Montlouis
18. Cheverny, Cour Cheverny
— CENTRAL LOIRE
19. Reuilly
20. Quincy
21. Menetou-Salon
22. Sancerre
23. Coteaux du Giennois
24. Pouilly-Fumé, Pouilly-sur-Loire

PAYS NANTAIS

These wines of the Pays Nantais are some of the most famous, for this is the home of Muscadet and the four Muscadet appellations, which between them make up one of the highest volume wines of French wine production. At best it has a quenching freshness, a hint of lemon and pepper, a hint of apricot, and if you're lucky, a hint of cream. But we're talking about hints here—the one thing Muscadet never does is taste a good deal of anything. That is the basis for its success.

Because Melon de Bourgogne, aka Muscadet, was the only variety in the Nantes region to survive the devastating frosts of 1709–10, it was enthusiastically adopted by local growers. For more than two centuries Muscadet and its more acidic neighbor, the Gros Plant, did an excellent job of providing cheap, light white wine to accompany the local seafood. But Parisians eat seafood, too, and they adopted Muscadet as their seafood wine. Then, during the 1970s and '80s, the export markets started drinking Muscadet as a kind of first-step French dry white.

Good Muscadet, especially from the Sèvre-et-Maine area southeast of Nantes, can be an absolute charmer—relatively neutral in taste but with a streak of grapefruit and pepper assertiveness and a mild creaminess, too.

Because of the innate neutrality of the grape, the best examples are left on their yeast lees and are undisturbed before being bottled directly off the lees—thereby capturing a little of the yeasty creaminess and also some of the natural carbon dioxide in the wine. These wines are labeled *sur lie*, and their blend of freshness, neutrality, and soft texture make them perfect seafood wine. The tangy, acid Gros Plant du Pays Nantais, from the flat vineyards whipped by the salty ocean gales to the southwest of Nantes, can equal Muscadet as the perfect accompaniment to seafood.

ANJOU-SAUMUR

We now head upstream to Anjou, with its plantations of the thoroughly difficult, exasperating, but sometimes majestically rewarding Chenin Blanc grape variety and its frequently rustic but sometimes delightful reds.

Much of Anjou isn't ideal for the vine—remember that the Loire Valley is as far north as the vine can ripen on the west coast of France, and most of Anjou is planted with cereal crops and vegetables able to withstand the wind and rain better than any grape vines can. Those vines planted away from the various river valleys on exposed land are unlikely to produce anything but the most basic wine, generally the palest of pale whites or a pale pink from various struggling reds.

But there are sheltered vineyards, usually facing southwest, ideally planted on limestone or slate soil, which can produce some absolute stunners. Most brilliant of these and most unexpected are the sweet Chenin wines that emerge from the folds of the river banks along the Layon Valley and to a lesser extent the Aubance Valley, both formed by southern tributaries of the Loire River.

Generally, however, the Chenin Blanc makes medium or dry wines in Anjou. The most famous of these whites is the dry Savennières, perched on the north side of the Loire, just to the west of Angers, a gaunt, austere wine with the distant beauty of an ice maiden. Most of the rest of Anjou's whites come from vineyards south of the Loire.

But for those grapes that fail to ripen properly, there is still a haven. In the eastern part of Anjou, bordering on Touraine, is Saumur, one of France's chief production centers for sparkling wine. The soil around Saumur is more chalky than in the rest of Anjou, which encourages a certain leanness in the wines. This, combined with cool ripening conditions, often produces just the kind of acid base wine that sparkling wine manufacturers like.

Red wines are less successful in most of Anjou, but there are pockets of decent Gamay and Cabernet Franc—the best of these Cabernet Franc vineyards claiming an Anjou-Villages appellation—while the Saumur-Champigny vineyards to the southeast of the town can make delightful fragrant reds of varying weights.

SWEET WINES OF THE LAYON VALLEY

Across from Savennières the Layon River joins the Loire, and along the Layon's northern banks the Chenin grape produces some of the finest sweet wines in France. Even so, it is often a long wait to achieve the necessary overripeness, but good sites allied to meticulous producers can manage it on a regular basis.

Most great sweet wines are made when the grapes are attacked by the noble rot fungus called botrytis. For the last few miles before the two rivers join, the influence of both causes morning mists to form along the Layon and its little tributaries. This humidity rising from the streams in warm autumns provides perfect conditions for the development of noble rot, which, as in Sauternes (page 61), helps to concentrate the grapes' sweetness to a remarkable degree. A combination of climate, the Chenin Blanc grape, and those growers with nerves of steel means that sweet wines can be made here even in the most difficult years. These luscious wines can be utterly magical.

In particular at Chaume, Quarts de Chaume, and Bonnezeaux, a perfect sheltered south to southwest exposure allows grapes every chance to ripen then rot, hopefully to form the welcome fungus.

Coteaux du Layon covers twenty-five communes in the Layon Valley. Coteaux du Layon-Villages covers six of the best seven villages between Faye d'Anjou and St-Aubin de Luigné, and the seventh, Chaume, has recently been promoted to its own appellation, joining those of Quarts de Chaume and Bonnezeaux with their perfect conditions and slopes for when the fall weather holds. Both the Coteaux de l'Aubance and the Coteaux de la Loire make reasonable sweetish white wines.

TOURAINE

The best Loire reds come from Touraine, a few miles to the east where the breezes seem to soften and the air to mellow. Touraine appellations St-Nicolas-de-Bourgueil, Bourgueil, and Chinon use the Cabernet Franc grape to create gorgeously refreshing, tangy reds—wonderful young but also capable of staying fresh for decades.

The other famous wine in Touraine is Vouvray. From a good producer the dry, medium, sweet, or fizzy white wines of Vouvray can be a revelation, each of them fit for sipping on the balustrades of some of the most grandiose of Touraine's châteaux.

CENTRAL VINEYARDS

As we turn south from Orléans up the Loire, past the minor wine towns of Gien and Cosne, we come to the mainstream appellations of Sancerre and Pouilly-Fumé—regarded by many as the quintessential Sauvignon Blanc styles. Most of Pouilly makes high-quality, high-priced Sauvignon Blanc, and Sancerre across the river also concentrates on Sauvignon whites. Recently, however, top Sancerre producers have been paying more attention to Pinot Noir, a traditional variety in the area. By reducing yields, they have produced some remarkably full-bodied reds, showing how dilute most other red Sancerres are.

Menetou-Salon adjoins Sancerre and makes delicious Sancerre lookalikes (white, rosé, and red) but a little cheaper. Going further west still, past the historic town of Bourges, brings us to Reuilly with its light reds and rosés. But Reuilly and its neighbor Quincy are much better at making good, snappy Sauvignon whites filled with the aroma of gooseberries and green grass.

UPPER LOIRE

We could continue up the river, eyes peeled for any signs of life beneath its placid surface, for another 100 miles and more until, past Roanne in the Loire gorge, it finally shows fitful signs of life. But if we do, we won't find too many vines trailing down to the water's edge. There's little wine of consequence between Pouilly and Roanne, except for some made around St-Pourçain close to the Allier, a tributary of the Loire. Finally, we reach the Côte Roannaise and the Côtes du Forez regions, which are best known for Gamay reds and which, at their juicy, crunchy best, give Beaujolais a run for its money.

THE ORIGINAL SAUVIGNON BLANC

If you look for some ancient tradition of fine Sauvignon Blanc wine, you won't find it. Indeed, most people think that this bright, vivacious, mouthwatering white wine was invented in New Zealand during the 1980s. Well, the crisp, green-tinged wine we think of as Sauvignon isn't such a recent creation, and it's not really from New Zealand. Sauvignon Blanc is one of the Loire Valley's main white grapes. But it wasn't given any respect until the 1950s. It is the white mainstay of the villages of Sancerre and Pouilly, two limestone outcrops on the banks of the Loire, but was traditionally dismissed as a simple country wine. Then the Parisians discovered it and decided it was the perfect fresh, fun dry white when such wines were virtually nonexistent amid a sea of fruitless, sulfurous muck. Sauvignon wines from Sancerre and Pouilly became chic in Paris and then throughout the world. I'm not sure that New Zealand Sauvignon Blanc owes its character to anyone else, but if it did, it would be to these tangy dry whites.

The Rhône Valley

RED GRAPES
In the northern Rhône, Syrah is the only grape. Grenache is the main grape in the southern Rhône with many other supporting varieties.

WHITE GRAPES
In the northern Rhône, Viognier is the main grape with some Marsanne and Roussanne. In the southern Rhône, whites are less important than reds, and there are many minor varieties.

CLIMATE
In the northern Rhône, the climate is continental with some Mediterranean influence, such as burning summer sun. The southern Rhône has a true Mediterranean climate: hot, dry summers and warm, wet winters.

SOIL
In the northern Rhône, the slopes overlooking the river are steep and rocky. The southern Rhône covers a huge area with a wide variety of soil types, from the heavy clay of the upper slopes of Gigondas to the stony alluvial deposits of the plains around Châteauneuf-du-Pape.

GEOGRAPHY
In the northern Rhône, between the towns of Vienne and Valence, steep, well-drained terraces are etched into the hillsides overlooking the river. In the southern Rhône, ripening the grapes this far south is not a problem, and many of the best vineyards are on the flat land of the valley floor.

ONE OF MY FAVORITE PLACES in France is directly after the cacophonous, frightening, fume-filled tunnel that burrows through the center of Lyon and emerges in a tumult of overheated, angry drivers and conflicting road signs next to the main railroad station. It's a seedy, grubby, mistrustful part of town. I like it because here I turn right, down the Rhône Valley. This is where I turn my back on the last of the glum North and travel toward the broad open skies, the balmy evening air, and the glittering Mediterranean. For me, this urban wasteland is the divide, after which I head into the sweet embrace of the South.

The Rhône Valley is the artery running down the center of France, a surging flood sweeping us toward all the pleasures of the South. Anyone who spends long winter hours wrapped up tight against the chilly damp, anyone who searches the leaden summer skies longingly for a glimpse of golden sunshine will know what I mean.

The Rhône River powers its way through Lyon with the urgency of an express train, churning through the deep channels it has cut itself against the eastern crust of the Massif Central, south of Vienne, before it sweeps out into the parched open spaces south of the hill of Hermitage at Tain. Taking a more languid course, it still gathers awesome power, only half-controlled by the engineering skills of man, and spreads itself across the increasingly arid red landscape past Avignon. It finally ripples out like a fan, its eastern estuary beckoning me past Marseille and Toulon to Provence. Its numerous western streams create a haunting delta of marshes and lagoons backed by the wild hills and valleys of Languedoc, Minervois, and Corbières and the distant Pyrenees. The Rhône, with its great peacock tail of Provence and Languedoc, is one of the parts of France that I came to love late but I've come to love well.

The Rhône rises way up in the Swiss Alps, and vines are grown along its banks almost continuously from here down to the confluence with the Durance River, just north of the marshy Rhône delta on the borders of Provence and Languedoc. Along its upper reaches, the Rhône spawns some of the most featherlight, wispy white wines of Europe, as well as some surprisingly beefy reds and whites on the steep, sun-trapping slopes of the Valais. But after melting into the broad, calm waters of Lake Geneva, it reemerges on the other side of the French border, ready for the dash to the Mediterranean. Its first wines on this side, still Alpine and snow-white in character, are those from the Savoie and Bugey regions. Some of the best whites are made from Altesse (often called Roussette) from Chignin, near Chambéry (page 102). The reds are led by the peppery, robust Mondeuse grape.

NORTHERN RHÔNE

Some 30 miles of industrial suburbs sprawl to the south of the city of Lyon, and little to tax the wine drinkers' taste buds occurs until after the town of Vienne. The exit off the autoroute marked Ampuis should quicken your pulse.

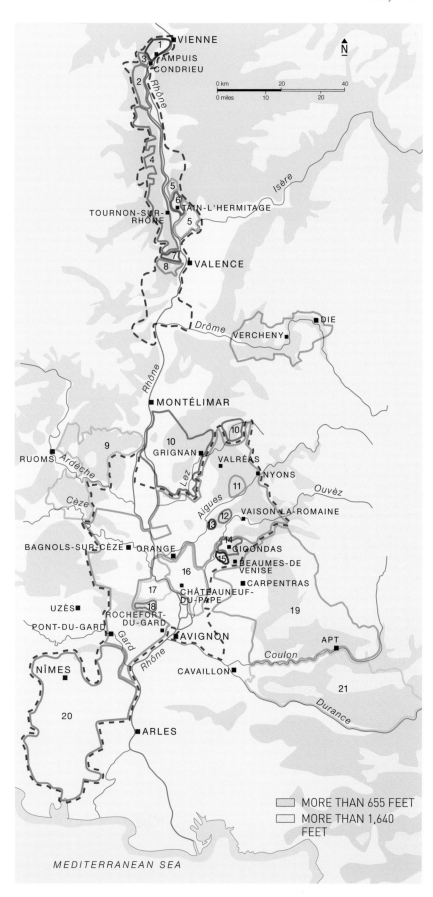

MAIN WINE APPELLATIONS

- - - - Côtes du Rhône
──── Côtes du Rhône-Villages
──── Clairette de Die

1. Côte-Rôtie
2. Condrieu
3. Château-Grillet
4. St-Joseph
5. Crozes-Hermitage
6. Hermitage
7. Cornas
8. St-Pèray
9. Côtes du Vivarais
10. Grignan-les-Adhémar
11. Vinsobres
12. Rasteau
13. Cairanne
14. Gigondas
15. Vacqueyras
16. Châteauneuf-du-Pape
17. Lirac
18. Tavel
19. Ventoux
20. Costières de Nîmes
21. Lubéron

MORE THAN 655 FEET
MORE THAN 1,640 FEET

Take a look down the river toward the vines of Côte-Rôtie. The east-facing slopes you'll see are as steep as any in the wine world, and they sport a patchwork of vines that looks as though they must be tacked or glued to the rock. Surely no human being could work this almost cliff face. Surely no vines could establish a toehold on the scree and slate that shift and slither on these scarps. But a growing band of dedicated winemakers does tend such vertiginous slopes as these, and the vines that manage to establish a root system produce wines that are as great as any in France.

SYRAH OR SHIRAZ?

Syrah is now one of the most fashionable grape varieties in the world, fueling the imagination of ambitious winemakers from Canada to New Zealand, from the Americas to Australia, and without Australia, Syrah wouldn't be anything like the global superstar it is.

Yet in Australia, Syrah isn't even called Syrah. They call it Shiraz—a perfectly valid name because one of the great legends about the variety is that it originated in the ancient Persian city of Shiraz. Scientists think otherwise, but I like the romance of a grape variety being carried through the Middle East and Europe for hundreds of years and finally ending up on the mighty hill of Hermitage in the northern Rhône Valley, where the French call it Syrah. It flourished here in relative obscurity until the 1980s, making small amounts of one of France's most impressive reds, Hermitage. The fact that hardly anyone knew of this wine would explain why it was not initially chosen by the New World pioneers of the twentieth century to challenge the primacy of Europe. They chose, above all, the red grapes of Bordeaux led by Cabernet Sauvignon and the grape of white Burgundy, Chardonnay. The discovery of Hermitage and Côte-Rôtie by American wine critics in the 1980s transformed the northern Rhône and its Syrah reds into a goldmine. But Australia had been growing Syrah since the 1840s. No one took any notice elsewhere in the world, and in any case most of the grapes were turned into sweet "Port." But then along came Grange Hermitage and Hunter Valley Shiraz, a new generation of wine enthusiasts and the arrival—again—of American wine critics. Suddenly Shiraz was more famous than Syrah.

Nowadays, both names are used around the world. Syrah implies a drier, more scented style, Shiraz a richer, burlier, more chocolaty style. But Syrah and Shiraz are the same grape.

These steep slopes are the heart and soul of what we call the northern Rhône, a stretch of the river between the towns of Vienne and Valence, whose great vineyard sites are all characterized by the steepness of their crystalline, rocky hillsides and by the particular grape varieties planted here. Life as a *vigneron* isn't easy, and the struggle and commitment required by the grape grower to make great wine are mirrored in the passionate flavor of the reds and the wild, heady perfumes of the whites.

Above all, the Syrah grape finds perfect expression here. Syrah vines may have been planted in the region as long ago as 600 BC if local traditions concerning the hill of Hermitage are to be believed. If so, the savagery of the Syrah's wines, allied to perfumes that seem to have their beginnings in an altogether different, less predictable time, are a fitting and impressive testament. Côte-Rôtie also claims Roman roots. The slopes here are as steep as 55 degrees and the Syrah vines are tethered to a quartet of posts to try to establish themselves on the crumbly clifflike slopes. Côte-Rôtie's wines are more fragrant than those of Hermitage, while the wines of Cornas to the south are more sturdy and foursquare. In between, St-Joseph and Crozes-Hermitage are also capable of fine, fruit-filled wines.

The most immediately thrilling of northern Rhône whites are those of the Viognier grape from the rocky terraces of Condrieu and Château-Grillet. At their best, these wines are as overwhelmingly perfumed as a hothouse in summer, but a breathtaking freshness as open and welcome as hawthorn blossom wafting on a spring day's breeze breaks through the aroma of peach and apricot. The Viognier, with its low and unpredictable yields, used to be one of the world's rarest grapes. Now it is the height of fashion. Reclaimed vineyard plantations in Condrieu and large-scale new plantings in Languedoc and overseas in America, Australia, Chile, and Argentina have almost (but not quite) made it commonplace as a variety. But despite its worldwide spread, few of these growers achieve the glories of the best Condrieu wines.

The Marsanne and Roussanne grapes are not such eye-catching performers, but they are the varieties behind the white wines of Hermitage, Crozes-Hermitage, St-Joseph, and St-Péray. Usually a little flat to start, they can develop impressive layers of rich, viscous flavors if you have the patience to wait. St-Péray marks a natural break in the Rhône Valley. Until this point, most of the fine wine has been produced on east- and south-facing slopes of granite marking the eastern edge of the Massif Central. From now on, as the Rhône Valley spreads broad and wide, the emphasis changes.

THE GREAT HILL OF HERMITAGE

No one's absolutely sure, but as you stand at the base of the hill of Hermitage, wedged in between the railroad line and the rapidly ascending vineyard slopes in front of you, you just may be gazing up at the oldest vineyard in the Rhône Valley. There is a strong local belief that the Phocaeans, travelers from southern Greece in ancient times, worked their way up the Rhône from Marseille and were carrying vines with them. The scientist in me says the vines couldn't have been Syrah, but the romantic in me says perhaps they were. The towering hill of Hermitage clearly impressed the newcomers, and the locals say that sometime after 600 BC a few Phocaeans stopped and planted a vineyard there. Which would make Hermitage not only the oldest vineyard in the Rhône Valley but probably the oldest vineyard in France.

I hope the story's true because Hermitage deserves the accolade. It's a magnificent vineyard site. When Virgil wrote a couple of thousand years ago that "vines love an open hill," he couldn't have found a better one than the hill of Hermitage. It is capable of producing majestic reds and intriguing whites, able to stand the test of time as well as any other French wines. The red wines manage to combine a rough-hewn, animal power with a sweetness of fruit and wildness of perfume. This may be less academically correct than great Bordeaux and less sensually explicit than great Burgundy, but it catches you unawares and spins you in a dizzy pirouette in a way that no other red wine can.

White Hermitage lacks the immediate charm and fragrance of France's other great white wines and may seem fat and sulky almost before it's bottled. Its pudgy sullenness is surely no candidate for making old bones. I don't think many Rhône winemakers can explain it either, but good white Hermitage, often made solely from the Marsanne grape but generally with a little Roussanne added, appears to get a second, third, and even a fourth wind and seems to get younger as its red brother gets older. It can develop a leaner, fresher, flinty mineral tone, but it never loses its rich, ripe core of honey, nuts, and rolls streaked with spice and topped with crystal sugar.

The Hermitage hill has only about 335 acres of vines, and in the photograph below you can see how wonderfully exposed to the sun these are. The locals say the sun always sets last on these granite slopes of Hermitage, but it's obvious that the sun rises there first as well. The generally granite soil and the numerous terrace walls heat up in the warmth of the sun's rays and help promote the ripening of the grapes. The drainage is clearly excellent, and the Mistral wind that blows down the valley will blow away any excess moisture in any case—yes, Virgil would have liked Hermitage. More than two-thirds of the Hermitage vines are red Syrah. The burliest, most virile red wines come from the most forbidding granite plots, Les Bessards and Le Méal. If you're after something with less muscle and more aroma, the high L'Ermite and the lower Les Greffieux do the trick.

The hill of Hermitage looms above the town of Tain l'Hermitage and the Rhône and produces some of the most powerful red wines in France.

SOUTHERN RHÔNE

In the southern Rhône, the eastern bank of the river hosts all the fine wines, and, with the exception of Châteauneuf-du-Pape, all the truly exciting flavors come from the vineyards in the lee of Mont Ventoux and the Dentelles de Montmirail.

But the natural break isn't just in the wines: it's in the air you breathe, the scorched feel of the soil under your feet, and in the stark difference in vegetation as pear, apricot, and cherry orchards and vegetable gardens give way to olive and peach groves, lavender, and melon fields and herb-strewn outcrops of rock bleached as white as a desert corpse's bones.

The sun doesn't necessarily shine for longer periods here, but the whole character of this wide river basin is open and exposed. Once the Mistral starts, the word "exposed" takes on an entirely new meaning. The Mistral is the fierce northwesterly gale that rakes the people and the crops of the southern Rhône for up to three hundred days a year. On the remaining days, don't be surprised to find the Sirocco blowing from the south. The vines are mostly trained close to the ground as little bushes to defend them against the wind and also to soak up extra warmth from the stony soil. The Mistral is reckoned to send a fair number of people mad each year, but in compensation it does wonders in drying out the crops after a rainfall; rot is rarely a problem down here.

While the northern Rhône specializes in small amounts of high-quality reds and whites, the southern Rhône's chief job is to churn out vast quantities of predominantly red Côtes du Rhône. The Rhône region is, along with Bordeaux and Burgundy, one of three major producers of French appellation wine, and 85 percent of this is basic Côtes du Rhône, almost all of it from the south between the towns of Montélimar and Avignon. In the last ten years, the quality in general has risen, and many smaller domaines truly shine despite their humble Côtes du Rhône AOC. There are other highlights, too. The little appellation of Clairette de Die, way up the Drôme tributary, makes delightful fizz. There are some unctuously sweet fortified wines, led by Muscat de Beaumes-de-Venise, and there are some truly grand table wines, headed by the fabulous reds of Châteauneuf-du-Pape. These are followed by the

VILLAGE NAMES TO CHECK OUT

The Côtes du Rhône-Villages is a vast AOC covering about 8,350 acres of vineyards over ninety-five communes in the departments of Ardèche, Drôme, Gard, and Vaucluse in the southern Rhône. Seventeen of these villages that have traditionally made better wine have the right to add their names on the AOC label:
Four villages in the Drôme: Rochegude, Rousset les Vignes, St-Maurice, and St-Pantaléon les Vignes.
Nine villages in the Vaucluse: Gadagne, Massif d'Uchaux, Plan de Dieu, Puyméras, Roaix, Sablet, Séguret, Valréas, and Visan.
Four villages in the Gard: Chusclan, Laudun, St-Gervais, and Signargues.
The best Côtes du Rhône-Villages can apply for promotion to Cru status, allowing them to label their wine solely with their village names. Cairanne, Vacqueyras, and Vinsobres are notable promotions so far.

VINS DOUX NATURELS

Rasteau and Beaumes-de-Venise are top red wine communes in the southern Rhône, but if you're after a slug of gutsy, dry red wine, check that label closely. Beaumes-de-Venise is actually more famous for its golden sweet wine than for its red, and Rasteau is also a fortified wine, with both red, rosé, white, and *rancio* versions. These oddballs are called *vins doux naturels*, or natural sweet wines. Unnatural is more like it because they are made by whacking in a hefty dose of almost 100 percent alcohol spirit when the fermentation is only partly completed. This stops the fermentation, and all the remaining unfermented grape sugar is left in the wine as sweetness.

At Rasteau, they use the red grape Grenache and although the wine—either in its peppery, jammy, but relatively fruity young style or its copper-colored, oxidized *rancio* style—seems to be a throwback to some antediluvian wine culture, fortified Rasteau has been made only since 1934. It has never achieved a more than strictly local following. Muscat de Beaumes-de-Venise is made from the excellent Muscat à Petits Grains grape. This rich, syrupy fruit has a heady orchard and floral aroma, and as an apéritif or dessert wine, in a sorbet or served with one, it is a delight.

reds of Gigondas, Vacqueyras, Cairanne, Rasteau, Lirac, Beaumes-de-Venise, and the best Côtes du Rhône-Villages (such as Valréas and Visan) and sometimes supported by decent rosé in Tavel and Lirac and whites in Châteauneuf-du-Pape. Costières de Nîmes does all three colors well. The dominant grape is the fleshy, alcoholic red Grenache that thrives in hot, dry climates, such as that of the southern Rhône. However, most wines produced here are blends. Châteauneuf-du-Pape allows no fewer than thirteen different varieties, and most southern Rhône reds will include at least Syrah, Cinsaut, or Mourvèdre in their blends. Grenache Blanc, Clairette, Bourboulenc, and Roussanne are the most important white varieties planted and usually blended, too.

CHÂTEAUNEUF-DU-PAPE AND APPELLATION CONTRÔLÉE

In the 1920s French wine—indeed, the wine of all Europe—was in a parlous state. The late nineteenth century had seen a series of disastrous diseases and pest infestations, and producers were still licking their wounds. Adulterated and fraudulent wine was widespread. So in 1923, Baron Le Roy of Château Fortia in Châteauneuf-du-Pape set down six articles designed to protect the integrity of the vineyard and its wines. They stated the criteria that had to be followed for Châteauneuf-du-Pape. A delineated area, specific grape varieties, pruning and training methods for the vine, a minimum alcohol level, a discarding of 5 percent of the crop at harvest, no rosé wine, and a tasting test were among the rules. These still stand today, but more importantly, they were taken as the starting point for the entire French appellation d'origine contrôlée system that came into being in 1935. One more thing. Châteauneuf-du-Pape was the first AOC to forbid the landing of flying saucers inside the commune boundaries. That seems eminently sensible. But quirky as it may seem, this ruling was tacked onto the six articles in 1954, and as far as I know, it's still there.

The ruined papal château of Châteauneuf-du-Pape bakes in the high summer sun. The large, smooth stones, or galets, *by reflecting the heat and preserving it after sundown, make these vineyards some of the hottest in France.*

Jura, Savoie, and Bugey

RED GRAPES
Poulsard is the main Jura grape, with Pinot Noir and Trousseau increasing slowly. Gamay is the most extensively planted red variety in Savoie, with the more interesting Mondeuse following behind. Some Pinot Noir is also grown.

WHITE GRAPES
Chardonnay is the most planted Jura grape, followed by Savagnin, the only permitted variety for vin jaune. More than half the total plantings in Savoie are of Jacquère, followed by Altesse.

CLIMATE
This is basically a continental climate, although with high rainfall, and temperatures that decrease sharply with altitude. The severity in Savoie is moderated by the main lakes.

SOIL
In the Côtes du Jura, the soil is mostly dark marly clay on the lower slopes, with limestone on the higher ones. In Bugey, limestone and marly limestone predominate. Savoie vines are grown mostly on limestone-rich soil that is alluvial in origin.

GEOGRAPHY
In the Jura, the vines are grown on south- or southwest-facing sites at an altitude of between about 820 and 1,310 feet, not dissimilar to Burgundy's Côte d'Or. In Bugey, vineyards are widely scattered on low hillsides. The vineyards in Savoie are also scattered but may go as high as about 2,000 feet in the foothills of the Alps and are often south- or southeast-facing with a good aspect to the sun.

MOUNTAIN PEOPLE ARE DIFFERENT. Isolation and a hostile, unpredictable environment, where life is a continual battle, breeds individuality. Both the Jura and Savoie reflect this individuality but in different ways.

JURA

The Jura mountains run up the eastern side of France and act as a natural border with Switzerland. On the Swiss side, the thickly wooded slopes fall dramatically down to the calm prosperity encircling Lake Geneva. The French side, staring balefully out west across the Saône Valley to Burgundy, is a mixture of high meadowland, dense forest, astonishing gorges, and sudden splashes of tranquil vineyard. But few of the wines are tranquil.

The native Jura grapes are the beefy red Trousseau; the pallid semi-red Poulsard making a pale, scented red and a pink Crémant du Jura fizz; and the unnerving yet fascinating white Savagnin, used to make the flor-aged *vin jaune*. This yellow wine is a freakish oddball. It has to be aged for six years in cask without topping off the evaporated wine. During this time, a yeast film develops on the wine in the same way as in Jerez's Fino Sherry. The result is a wine with a raging, sour woody brilliance. Château-Chalon makes the most famous and most expensive *vin jaune*, although it is made all over the Jura in small quantities. But there are signs of Burgundian influence from across the valley: Pinot Noir is the second most planted red grape and produces an attractive pale red. Chardonnay makes light dry whites as long as it's not made in casks that have held Savagnin, and the sparkling Crémant du Jura, which accounts for one-quarter of the region's production, is particularly good. From a blend of typically Chardonnay, Savagnin, and the red Poulsard, production of the curious sweet wine *vin de paille* is also increasing. Like *vin jaune*, these wines can age for decades.

SAVOIE AND BUGEY

The Savoie vineyards are scattered in distinct plots over a wide area but mostly in sight of the Alps. Like Jura, Savoie has a range of native grapes, but the character of their wines couldn't be more different. Chasselas wine, from near Lake Geneva, is so ethereal as to be almost transparent, often in flavor as well as looks. The ubiquitous Jacquère variety makes wine that is also almost water-white but packs a tangy angelica and grapefruit pith punch. But the best sites are reserved either for the dark, loganberry-scented Mondeuse or for the white Altesse (often called Roussette) and in Chignin, near Chambéry, for Roussanne (locally called Bergeron). All three are capable of producing exceptional wines. The vines are restricted mainly to the southerly lower mountain slopes before they become too steep for any *vigneron* to work.

The tiny Savoie Cru Crépy produces featherlight Chasselas white from vineyards near Lake Geneva; the nearby Crus of Ripaille and Marin are often a touch weightier. The vineyards of the slightly larger Seyssel appellation overlook the Rhône and produce a fine still Roussette and a good-value

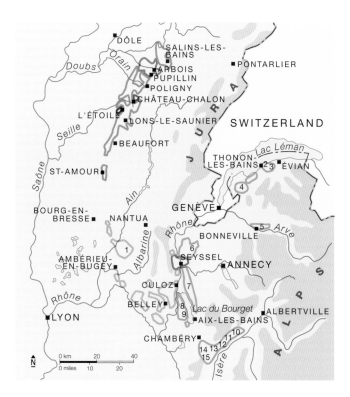

MAIN WINE APPELLATIONS

JURA
— Côtes du Jura
— Arbois
— Château-Chalon
— L'Étoile
BUGEY
— Bugey, Roussette
  du Bugey
  MAIN CRU
1. Bugey Cerdon
SAVOIE
— Savoie, Roussette
  de Savoie
  MAIN CRUS
2. Ripaille
3. Marin
4. Crépy
5. Ayze

6. Roussette de
   Savoie Frangy
7. Chautagne
8. Roussette de
   Savoie Marestel
9. Jongieux
10. St-Jean de la
    Porte
11. Cruet
12. Arbin
13. Chignin, Chignin-
    Bergeron
14. Apremont
15. Abymes
— Seyssel

▢ MORE THAN 1,640 FEET
▨ MORE THAN 3,280 FEET

View over the vineyards and town of Arbois, wine capital of the Jura region.

traditional-method fizz from Roussette blended with the obscure variety, Molette. Toward Lake Bourget, Gamay, Chardonnay, and Pinot Noir do well, while in Jongieux, Roussette is king, especially in the tiny Cru of Marestel, where it produces an almost rich, dry white with peach and apricot flavors, developing nuttiness after a few years.

But for me, the core of the Savoie vineyards is further south, near Chambéry, where the high peaks of the Alps jut out rudely into the valley and then swing around to follow the Isère Valley up toward the skiing center of Albertville. The Crus of Apremont and Abymes produce fresh dry whites from Jacquère. Jacquère also does well in Chignin, but here Roussanne is revered to make sumptuously floral and peachy Chignin-Bergeron. From around Chignin and northeast toward Albertville in the Combe de Savoie, growers are giving increasing space to Mondeuse, a rich grape with formidable dark loganberry and woodsmoke flavors seasoned with the crunch of black peppercorns, which, with low yields, makes a wine with enough intensity to partner a rich meat stew.

To the west of Lake Bourget is the Bugey region, which has become trendy for the semisweet pink fizz Cerdon. Scattered patches of vines among woods and hills now total 1,235 acres. All the Savoie and some Jura grape varieties are grown here, but the pale yet surprisingly intense Chardonnay works best.

Provence

RED GRAPES
Typical southern varieties, such as Grenache, Carignan, and Cinsaut, are most important, with significant amounts of Mourvèdre, Syrah, and Cabernet Sauvignon.

WHITE GRAPES
The main grapes are Ugni Blanc and Clairette, followed by Sémillon, Grenache Blanc, Sauvignon Blanc, Rolle, and Bourboulenc among others.

CLIMATE
The climate is classic Mediterranean—hot dry summers, warm wet winters, with blasts from the Mistral helping to dry the grapes after the occasional deluge.

SOIL
A complex soil pattern includes stony limestone, sandstone, clay, shale, and gravel underlying the plantings in different areas.

GEOGRAPHY
A diverse terrain has vines growing on slopes, foothills, and lowland, especially where sheltered to the north by ridges and plateaus.

THE ANCIENT GREEKS PLANTED VINES HERE in the sixth century BC and the Romans produced wine supposedly fine enough to ship to Rome. But this exotic, irresistible corner of France, stretching from the swooping slopes of the Montagne du Lubéron east of Avignon, through forests and gorges full of pine trees, herbs, and olive groves, down to the azure sea—if the inhabitants of this enchanted land thought that wine quality mattered, wouldn't they have done something about it by now?

Well, some people are doing something and increasingly so, prompted by a new generation or a change in ownership, often bringing foreign investment to the region. Single estates are sprouting in les Baux-de-Provence, around Aix-en-Provence, and in the large Côtes de Provence appellation, often hewn from scratch out of rock and *garrigue* to create new and fascinating flavors. The established appellations of Bellet, Bandol, Cassis, and Palette represent tiny enclaves of individuality amid swathes of vineyards churning out shabby rosés, fruitless whites, and scorched reds. An easy-going vacation market makes it easy for producers to forego the sacrifice and commitment needed to produce the great wine that is certainly possible here. Vines are crucially important in Provence because most of the land won't support much else. Almost half the cultivated land in Provence is vines, with those other hardy performers, olives and almonds, also being important. So, accepting that a large amount of Provençal wine is simply overpriced vacation hooch, let's see where things are better than this.

GRAPE VARIETIES

In general, pinks and reds come from the usual southern varieties of Grenache, Cinsaut, and Carignan. Mourvèdre makes a big contribution at Bandol. Syrah and Cabernet Sauvignon are vital further inland, especially around Aix, while strange ancient grapes, such as Fuella in Bellet, Tibouren around St-Tropez, and Manosquen in Palette, add a certain spice.

The whites are dominated by the southern varieties, Grenache Blanc, Clairette, and Bourboulenc, with a growing amount of Rolle. There are patches of Sémillon, Sauvignon Blanc, Roussanne, and Chardonnay, too.

In general, the soil is poor and infertile. However, Cassis and Bandol have a good deal of clay and limestone, and Bandol has gravel, too. In the west, the desolate moonscape of les Baux-de-Provence has vineyards planted amid the rubble of bauxite, and only a substructure of water-retentive limestone allows the vine to survive.

The climate differs, too, but sun and wind are everywhere. Although the Mistral barely troubles Bellet in the east, it whips through the low bush vines of Bandol and Cassis, and at les Baux-de-Provence the vines are trained north to south to minimize its force, while Palette rings its north-facing vineyard with pines. Yet, with the fierce southern sun, the Mistral is crucial for cooling the grapes; at Bandol it is abetted by sea breezes, and both these winds keep the vines remarkably free of rot. With grapes near full ripeness, a good gust of warm dry wind does wonders in keeping disease at bay.

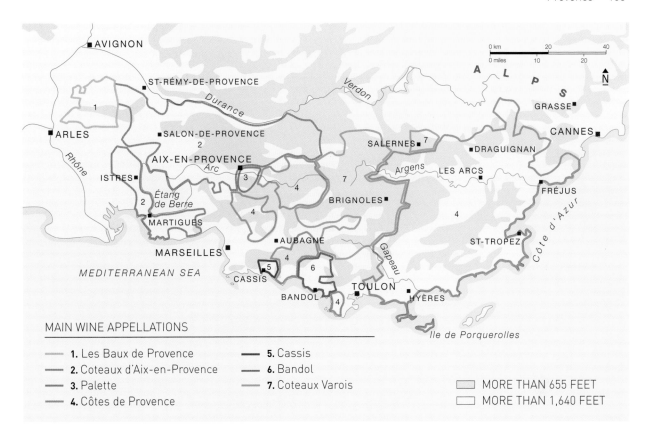

MAIN WINE APPELLATIONS

1. Les Baux de Provence
2. Coteaux d'Aix-en-Provence
3. Palette
4. Côtes de Provence
5. Cassis
6. Bandol
7. Coteaux Varois

MORE THAN 655 FEET
MORE THAN 1,640 FEET

It isn't surprising that in such torrid conditions, red wines perform best. Les Baux-de-Provence has concentrated on reds based on Syrah and Cabernet Sauvignon, sometimes with a little Grenache. That would be thought of as an Australian combination today, but the idea came from a Dr. Guyot, one of France's top wine experts in the 1860s, who said he thought such a combination would thrive around Aix. But Domaine de Trévallon in Les Baux-de-Provence took the plunge. Coteaux d'Aix-en-Provence has a considerable reputation for red wines but is dominated by under-achievers, and many of its best wines are rosés. I prefer the strange, pine-needle gauntness of Palette or the fascinating herbs and animal power of Bandol. Based largely on the Mourvèdre grape, Bandol is a prospering appellation whose wines seem to improve every year as the vines age and Mourvèdre increases its domination. There are good Côtes de Provence reds, usually from estates that have reduced the percentage of Carignan in favor of Syrah and Cabernet, and the Coteaux Varois is producing a growing number of good red wines.

Les Baux-de-Provence and Bandol produce the best rosés and Cassis and Palette, in their very different ways, the best white wines. There is some good Côtes de Provence from Rolle, Bourboulenc, and Sémillon grapes. But I don't know—as the sun rises higher in the sky and the shade of the restaurant beckons, so long as the wine is ice cold, just about anything will do.

CORSICA: THE BEAUTIFUL ISLAND

The ancient Greeks called Corsica the "Beautiful Island," and in wine terms it certainly is a heavenly place. The climate is perfect, with mountains and sea moderating the blazing heat. But for many years, the wines were not so special. Things are improving, however, both in the traditional vineyards of the north, west, and south, where yields are low and conditions difficult, and in the large, mechanized plantings on the flat prairie land in the east. Today, these eastern vineyards are making good varietal wines from Chardonnay, Syrah, and Cabernet.

However, Corsica's tradition is based on the local red Nielluccio, the red Sciacarello, and the white Vermentino, all Italian varieties. Patrimonio in the north produces full-bodied herb-scented reds as well as some rich Muscat du Cap Corse and fragrant Vermentino. Ajaccio to the west suits the Sciacarello. The overall AOC is Vin de Corse with five subregions: Calvi, Coteaux du Cap Corse, Figari, Porto Vecchio, and Sartène. A new generation of winemakers is beginning to make its mark, with the gradual replanting of the vineyards with traditional Corsican varieties and a marked improvement in wine-making techniques to achieve some good modern, yet authentically Corsican wines.

Languedoc-Roussillon

RED GRAPES
There is a huge variety of grapes: traditional (such as Carignan, Grenache, Cinsaut, Syrah) and international (Cabernet, Merlot).

WHITE GRAPES
Whites are less important but include Grenache Blanc, Mauzac, Clairette, Muscat, Bourboulenc, Chardonnay, Viognier, and Sauvignon Blanc.

CLIMATE
The summers are hot and dry, winters cool and wet, with temperatures decreasing with increasing altitude. The chilly Mistral from the north and mild sea breezes help cool the vines.

SOIL
This huge area displays a great diversity of soil types, some highly localized. Broadly, they encompass the shale and marly limestone of the hills overlaid with clay in the best sites, red pebbly lateritic soil, and gravelly alluvial terraces among others.

GEOGRAPHY
The rugged landscape provides numerous and varied sites for vines, the broadly west-east orientation of the valleys combining protection from the north with good southern aspects.

LANGUEDOC-ROUSSILLON IS THE MOST COMPLETE wine region in France. It is France's largest by a long way, comprising more than one-third of France's total vineyard acreage, and yet it does not have one single world-famous wine style to show for it. It is one of the most old-fashioned, hidebound, reactionary parts of the French wine scene, and at the same time it is France's most exuberantly modern, most outward-looking, most international. Contradictions are at the heart of Languedoc-Roussillon. Let's look at a few of them.

Every year sees more passionate, imaginative winemakers arrive in the South of France determined to create great wine their own way, outside the traditional strictures of the grand appellations, where innovation is generally stifled and rules are strictly to be obeyed. Most of these innovators are French, many of them refugees from such traditional and hidebound regions as Bordeaux and Burgundy, where types of vine variety and methods of growing grapes are strictly circumscribed. But people come from much further afield, from as far as California and Australia, seeking to put their New World ways to work in an Old World setting. In France, the Languedoc is the only alternative.

If we head southwest from Montpellier across the country, every second village will have a cooperative winery. If we find one in five where the wine is not stale and flat, I should be surprised, but thirty years ago we would not have found one in fifty. Altogether there are about three hundred wine cooperatives in the Languedoc, but there used to be many more, and in a number of those villages the looming cooperative buildings are now empty, their old concrete vats drained of wine. This isn't a bad thing because there really is no place for dull, dirty wine today. Why should we buy it? Why should we drink it when we have so many alternatives? Well, we don't, so a fair number of these cooperatives have amalgamated in an attempt to modernize production and gain a critical mass of volume that they might actually be able to market and make some money from. If they're looking for an example to follow, they could do worse than to copy the methods of the master of decent, cheap wine—Australia. Indeed, Australian "flying winemakers" were the first to see the potential of the Languedoc to be the New World of Europe. But it shows how slowly Europe moves. That was more than thirty years ago.

The laissez-faire attitude that characterizes the non-AOC areas of Languedoc-Roussillon mirrors Australia. So does the hot sun, the dry earth, and a reputation that owes nothing to the past but everything to the present and the future. Under such circumstances, it made absolute sense to rip out the old, largely mediocre local vines and plant the international stars—Cabernet Sauvignon, Merlot, Syrah, Chardonnay, Sauvignon Blanc, and Viognier. This is one side of what is so exciting in Languedoc-Roussillon. Innovation, excitement, lack of restrictions when transforming lead into gold. But there is another side. The side of some of the most ancient wines in France, some of the most ancient and distinctive styles, relying on ancient grape varieties such as Carignan, Grenache, Syrah, or Mauzac rather than Cabernet Sauvignon or Chardonnay.

If we go north from Béziers to Faugères, the road rises away from the plain toward the gaunt mountains of the Cévennes. The land is bleak but beautiful as we cut across through empty, twisting country lanes curling around the

MAIN WINE APPELLATIONS

- **1.** Languedoc Pic St-Loup
- **2.** Languedoc Grés de Montpellier
- **3.** Muscat de Frontignan
- **4.** Terrasses du Larzac
- **5.** Picpoul de Pinet
- **6.** Clairette du Languedoc
- **7.** Faugères
- **8.** St-Chinian
- **9.** Minervois
- **10.** Cabardès
- **11.** La Clape
- **12.** Corbières
- **13.** Malepère
- **14.** Limoux
- **15.** Fitou
- **16.** Tautavel, Latour de France
- **17.** Maury
- **18.** Côtes du Roussillon-Villages
- **19.** Côtes du Roussillon
- **20.** Collioure, Banyuls
- - - - Rivesaltes

MORE THAN 655 FEET
MORE THAN 1,640 FEET

low slopes of the mountain range; the soil is barren, smothered in rock and stone, and only olive trees and vines survive. But there are vineyards that go back to the ninth century at least, when monasteries planted these hills with vines knowing that only poor soil gives great wine. Good soil gives good fruit and vegetables. At Faugères, at St-Chinian, cross the base of the towering Montagne Noire to Minerve—capital of the Minervois where the heretic Cathars were besieged during the Albigensian Crusade in 1210 but where vineyards had been established for more than one thousand years before by the Romans—on across the wide Aude Valley into the mountain passes of the Corbières, last holdout of the Cathars, but planted with vines by the Romans, too. These vineyards have suffered centuries of neglect, but that may justly be thought of as the true cradle of French viticulture, along with those of Hermitage.

Nowadays, there is a ferocious, proud revival going on in these upland vineyards, in many other parts of Minervois, and in Coteaux du Languedoc zones such as la Clape, the rocky scrub-strewn mountain south of Narbonne that used to guard its harbor mouth in the days when Narbonne was the first city of Roman Gaul and which is one of the coolest growing zones in the Midi. The

wines are generally red, often still based on the Carignan grape, but old Carignan vines in poor stony soil can give excellent wine, especially when the blend is abetted by Grenache, Syrah, Cinsaut, and Mourvèdre.

There are other great historic wines, too. Limoux, high up in the Aude Valley southwest of Carcassonne, claims that its sparkling wine, Blanquette de Limoux or Crémant de Limoux—based on the Mauzac grape that gives it its striking "green-apple skin" flavor—is the oldest sparkling wine in the world, supposedly dating from 1531, more than a century before Champagne claims to have discovered how to make wines sparkle.

FORTIFIED WINES

Frontignan, on the shores of the salt lagoons near Montpellier, was known for its sweet Muscat wine in Pliny the Younger's time, and Arnaud de Villeneuve, a doctor at Montpellier, discovered how to make fortified wine here in the late thirteenth century. This discovery spread around Languedoc-Roussillon to Rivesaltes and on down to the foothills of the Pyrenees at Banyuls, where they applied it to the Grenache grape, baked to super-ripeness on the terraced hillsides overlooking the Mediterranean.

At Banyuls they don't just fortify this heady purple juice; they age it and purposely oxidize it in large old oak barrels or sometimes in smaller barrels left out exposed to the elements for at least thirty months. The result is a strange, exotic, dark, molasses-chocolate wine. Proof that Languedoc-Roussillon makes every conceivable kind of wine, and it makes them all increasingly well.

WINE AREAS

It's understandable that such a large region has so many different climatic and geological conditions suitable for very different kinds of wine. It was the sheer ease of cultivation and reliability of weather that caused the great plain stretching from Montpellier to Narbonne to become the provider of France's cheap wine from the early 1800s onward. This reliable weather and ease of cultivation now makes these plains the heartland of the Pays d'Oc movement, which is making varietal wines such a force in French wine. Their most important contribution is to show that modern vineyard and winery methods can make delicious white wines here—something never before achieved.

Yet this is not just prairie; the land dips and rises endlessly, providing myriad different soil and meso-climates. Now their potential is being explored, and there is a number of increasingly good appellations d'origine contrôlée. The best are for red wines—several of the top Languedoc Crus, such as La Clape, Pic St-Loup, Terrasses du Larzac, Grès de Montpellier, and Montpeyroux, as well as Minervois and Corbières. There is a group of good fortified vins doux naturels AOCs led by Muscat de Frontignan and one or two lonely but delightfully zingy white appellations such as Picpoul de Pinet. The sun is never a problem, and the ever-present wind moderates the heat, the sea breezes being fairly humid and mild, the north winds, which sweep over the Montagne Noire, hard and dry. As we rise up toward this impressive southern bulwark of the Massif Central, the protected sites and the impoverished soil roast the red grapes to a dark, but sweet-hearted super-ripeness that, mixed in with the ever-present wild aromas of the hills, makes good modern wines from the appellations of St-Chinian, Faugères, or Minervois (especially the subzone entitled to its own appellation, Minervois-La Livinière).

Corbières and Fitou are sheltered by their mountain range as the foothills of the Pyrenees south of the Aude slowly rise to lofty peaks on the Spanish border. Near the Mediterranean, the general effect is hot, but once past Carcassonne to the west, as the Mediterranean influence gives way to the Atlantic, increasingly cool conditions produce truly delicate reds and whites from grapes such as Chardonnay, Sauvignon Blanc, Cabernet, and Merlot.

The last great plain before Spain is that of the Agly River. The sun is that bit hotter here, and the relentless Tramontane wind sears the vines. The late-ripening Carignan—helped by the widespread use of carbonic maceration to extract color and flavor but not tannin from the grapes and by a leavening of Cinsaut, Syrah, and Grenache—produces sturdy Côtes du Roussillon and, largely in the southern foothills of Corbières, Côtes du Roussillon-Villages. Rivesaltes makes good Grenache *vin doux naturel*, but better Muscat, while way down on the Spanish border overlooking the Mediterranean, Grenache makes the sweet fortified wine of Banyuls. The tiny fishing port of Collioure has its own appellation, which uses the usual southern red grapes, but it is finding that low-yielding, sun-soaked terraces, with their awesome sea view and brow-cooling breeze, could be one of the great sites for that most difficult but tempestuous of all the southern French varieties—Mourvèdre, which is said to like its face in the hot sun and its feet in the water—exactly what it gets in Collioure.

VINS DOUX NATURELS

Here's a misnomer if ever there was one. These wines are no more naturally sweet than any other fortified wine; they're sweet because the fermentation is stopped by the addition of brandy. There are two main styles of *vins doux naturels*: the whites based on Muscat à Petits Grains or Muscat of Alexandria and the reds based on Grenache. Each of these naturally achieves very high sugar levels in the hot Mediterranean sun. But the object with Muscat wines is to preserve their aroma and fruit, so they are sometimes given skin contact before a cool partial fermentation and ideally an early bottling and youthful drinking. Frontignan is the most famous, Mireval and Lunel fairly obscure, St-Jean-de-Minervois rare but good, and Muscat de Rivesaltes the most up-to-date and attractive. Beaumes-de-Venise in the Rhône Valley also makes a fragrant version (page 100).

To make the Grenache wines of Rivesaltes, Maury, and Banyuls (and Rasteau in the Rhône Valley, page 100), alcohol to "mute" the wines is added either to free-run juice or to the skins and wine together, and the wines are then kept for between two and ten or more years in casks or vats, sometimes parked outside exposed to the air and the hot daytime temperatures, sometimes left not quite full if the traditional oxidized *rancio* style is being sought. Young, fresh aromas are not the point here; deep, dark, disturbing richness is.

Southwest France

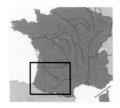

RED GRAPES
The main grapes are the Bordeaux varieties: Cabernets Sauvignon and Franc, Merlot, and Malbec, with local specials, notably Tannat and Negrette.

WHITE GRAPES
Sémillon and Sauvignon Blanc predominate in the north, with Petit Manseng, Gros Manseng, and other local varieties in the south.

CLIMATE
The climate is similar to Bordeaux, with strong Atlantic influences, although with slightly higher temperatures and lower rainfall.

SOIL
The great variety of soil includes the sandstone and marly limestone of the Bergerac and Tarn regions, Kimmeridgian limestone in Cahors. Alluvial sand and gravel are common in the Southwest.

GEOGRAPHY
Protection from Atlantic gusts can be important here, favoring south-, east,- and southeast-facing sites.

THE SOUTHWEST OF FRANCE looks so easy to understand. There you have the great king Bordeaux lording over the whole region, its robes spilling outward from the Gironde. Vassal states such as Bergerac, Côtes de Duras, Côtes du Marmandais, and Buzet kneel at the hem, imitating Bordeaux's styles, using the same grapes, and generally making good wines but not so good that they'll disturb the equanimity of Bordeaux. That's how it seems, but it's much more complicated than that. Not only do areas such as Bergerac and the Marmandais have their own interesting features, but Buzet overlaps with an entirely different culture in the region of Armagnac. Cahors may base its wines on the Bordeaux grape Malbec—but as though in defiance of its long isolation up the winding Lot River, Cahors crafts from it a most un-Bordeaux-like wine. As the hills and valleys roll away from Bordeaux, the Atlantic influence starts to be matched by that of the Mediterranean, and we enter a fascinating world of ancient vineyards, ancient grape varieties, and thrilling wine styles.

BERGERAC AND THE DORDOGNE

You wouldn't even know you'd left the Bordeaux region as you take the D936 through the Bordeaux town of Castillon-la-Bataille. The prosperous flat valley of the Dordogne is still a benign rural marriage of corn, meadow, and vines. But although Cabernet and Merlot, Sauvignon and Sémillon are grown in virtually identical conditions, you've crossed the border between Gironde and Dordogne, and the wines aren't AOC Bordeaux, but instead AOC Bergerac or AOC Montravel. You wouldn't really know you'd left Bordeaux when you taste most Dordogne wines either. The soil is similar, generally tending toward the sandy clay type with some limestone outcrops. Sunshine and heat are similar, although rainfall is usually lower.

The appellations can easily get confusing, but most of the dry reds and whites will end up calling themselves Bergerac or Côtes de Bergerac, and, at the western end, on the north bank of the Dordogne, the dry whites can call themselves Montravel, and the semisweets and fairly sweets, Côtes de Montravel and Haut-Montravel respectively. Southeast of Ste-Foy-la-Grande, sweet wines can be called Saussignac but are generally called Côtes de Bergerac Moelleux, and, northwest of the town of Bergerac, Rosette semisweet whites hardly ever appear under their own name. The Bergerac appellation wines are mostly virtually indistinguishable from their Bordeaux counterparts.

Two subregions that outshine the rest and do usually use their own names are Pécharmant and Monbazillac. Pécharmant's vineyards are on a plateau mostly tilted toward the south, where a mixture of chalky and gravelly clay sits above an impermeable iron hardpan. These reds are often Bergerac's best: deep, dark, but full of fruit and capable of aging. Monbazillac's vineyards frequently face north, sloping down to the river valley, losing heat, but gaining river mists that encourage noble rot and the production of sweet white wine. Most Monbazillac is mildly sweet, but more and more growers are prepared to let their grapes overripen sufficiently to make truly sweet wine.

GARONNE AND TARN WINES

Next to Bergerac lies the Côtes de Duras appellation and, straddling the Garonne Valley further south, the Côtes du Marmandais. These wines are basically Bordeaux in all but name, although in the latter, the local grape Abouriou, in small amounts along with Fer Servadou, Gamay, and Syrah, can add something to the red. Buzet, too, on the south banks of the Garonne and intertwined with the Armagnac brandy region, uses Bordeaux grapes effectively for both reds and whites.

Along the Tarn River, the Côtes du Frontonnais has its marvelous Negrette grape. The vines love the hot Toulouse weather and deep gravel beds and make a succulent, soft-centered red, velvet smooth and darkly sweet with licorice and strawberries. Negrette is often blended with Malbec, Cabernet, and Syrah, but I like as much Negrette as I can get. Gaillac, a large area further up the Tarn, is dominated by giant cooperatives but has tremendous potential. Six white grape varieties are used for a broad swathe of styles, from dry to sweet, from still to hinting at bubbles to fully foaming. Eight different red varieties contribute to wines that are often at their brisk best when peppery and young but are sometimes made to age impressively.

THE LOT RIVER

The Cahors AOC, about 50 miles northwest of Gaillac, concentrates on a single wine—a fascinating, tobacco-scented, green apple–streaked, yet plum and prune-rich red made largely from the Malbec grape, here called Cot or Auxerrois. The region was famous for "black wine" much in demand for blending with pale Bordeaux reds during the years of English supremacy in Aquitaine, but it was not until the 1970s that a band of local growers, along with a good cooperative, rediscovered its former glories. Now, with vineyards planted on the high stony limestone plateau, or *causses*, and the sand and gravel alluvial terraces lower down in the Lot Valley, with a climate caught between the influences of the Atlantic and the Mediterranean, and with the Lot twisting and turning like a demented serpent to create endless mesoclimates, Cahors is producing some of the most individual wines in the Southwest.

Further along the Lot are three obscure wine areas. Marcillac, with its strong, dry reds, produced mainly from the Fer Servadou, is the best known.

THE PYRENEAN FOOTHILLS

Traveling south from Agen into the foothills of the Pyrenees, we come to Madiran. The chief variety is Tannat, its tough, rugged style needing a while to come into focus. However, modern winemaking and new oak barrels have helped smooth some of its rougher edges. A little white called Pacherenc du Vic-Bilh is made from a blend of four Southwest grapes with the emphasis on the flinty, pear-skin-scented Ruffiac. Just to the north of Madiran, Côtes de St-Mont uses the same grape varieties to make attractive snappy reds and pleasant whites. The Tursan AOC makes wines similar to Côtes de St-Mont.

Further up into the Pyrenees foothills are Béarn, an uninspiring region, and Jurançon, which uses Petit Manseng, Gros Manseng, and Petit Courbu to make

The fourteenth-century bridge over the Lot River at Cahors was built when the English ruled Aquitaine.

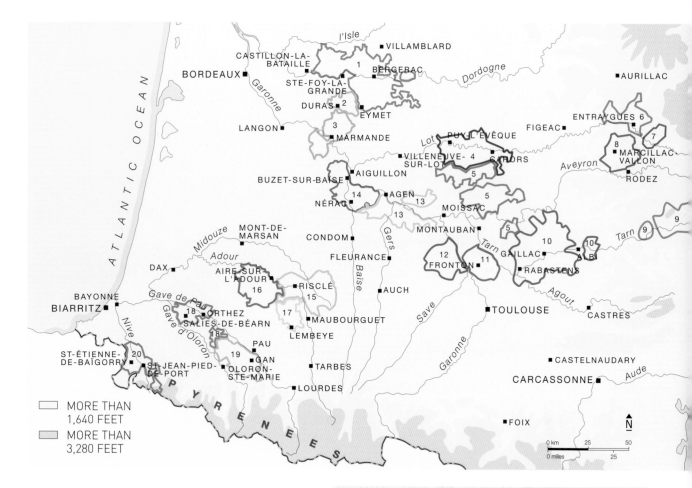

MAIN WINE APPELLATIONS

- **1.** Bergerac, Côtes de Bergerac
- **2.** Côtes de Duras
- **3.** Côtes du Marmandais
- **4.** Cahors
- **5.** Coteaux du Quercy
- **6.** Entraygues-Le-Fel
- **7.** Estaing
- **8.** Marcillac
- **9.** Côtes de Millau
- **10.** Gaillac
- **11.** Fronton
- **12.** St-Sardos
- **13.** Brulhois
- **14.** Buzet
- **15.** St-Mont
- **16.** Tursan
- **17.** Madiran, Pacherenc du Vic-Bilh
- **18.** Béarn
- **19.** Jurançon
- **20.** Irouléguy

mostly dry white wines. But the many sheltered valley sites, where the vineyards lie at an average altitude of 985 feet, let the grapes bake in the sun. The low-yielding Petit Manseng often shrivels on the vines, concentrating its juice to make sweet wines dripping with honey and nuts, cinnamon and ginger, but always refreshingly cut with a slash of lemon acidity. If you continue into the chilly mountain valleys to the border of Spain, you'll find the tiny outpost of Irouléguy, whose strange gritty mountain red marks a final, defiant flourish of French tradition before the entirely different world of the Iberian peninsula takes over on the far side of the snowy peaks.

COGNAC AND ARMAGNAC

Oh, the good life. You have just finished dinner, and your host suggests a Cognac or Armagnac. But what is the difference? Both these brandies come from the West of France—Cognac from north of Bordeaux and Armagnac from the Gascony region 100 miles south—but the grapes used, the distillation, blending, and aging methods and tastes and flavors are different. To sum up, Armagnac has a fierier character and greater depth partly from its distillation method. Cognac is distilled twice, in pot stills; most Armagnac goes just once through a continuous still. The single distillation of Armagnac leaves more flavor compounds in the spirit; it is less pure, therefore, but also richer. Cognac is more delicate, more complex and more subtle. Most Cognac and Armagnac are sold relatively young (both can be as young as two years), and there are various categories for older brandies.

» **For Armagnac:** 3 Étoiles (3 stars): at least two years old. VSOP or Réserve: at least five years old. Napoléon, Vieille Réserve or XO: six years old. Hors d'âge: ten years old.

» **For Cognac:** VS (Very Special, or 3 star): at least two years old. VSOP (Very Superior Old Pale): at least four years old. XO (Extra Old): at least six years old.

Italy

Italy is a land of immense geographical contrasts. The landscape around Gaiole in Chianti in Tuscany is one of the most typically Italian, with rows of cypresses and gentle slopes dotted with vines and olive trees and hills rolling away into the distance.

Despite my best efforts to succumb to Italy's charms, I still find it an exasperating country. No other nation can so easily fill my eyes with tears at the sheer beauty of its human achievements, yet no other country makes me want to weep as I wonder how it manages to function at all. I look at the positively unjust showering of natural gifts on Italy, particularly in its beautiful, memorable vineyards, and ask—why do I have to wade through so much dross? Ah, but then come the jewels unlike any others, and, well, is it possible to have it any other way? There are countries where you can easily understand the potential and range of their wines, good or bad. Reliable, conformist, unlikely to let you down. Unlikely to thrill you either. Italy's not like that. Would you want it to be? Some of her most famous vineyards produce some of her worst wines. Some of her greatest wines had no legal standing at all until 1995. The DOC system, set up in 1963 to make sense of the anarchy that was Italian wine, has spent as much time enshrining mediocrity and protecting incompetence as it has promoting and preserving quality and regional character. In an area such as Tuscany, where great wine names such as Chianti had come to be meaningless, the region's innovative, quality-conscious producers were forced to go outside the law rather than submit to regulations that had nothing to do with excellence and everything to do with political expediency.

And yet, and yet. From the northern terraces in the snowy embrace of the Tyrolean Alps to the southern islands that are mere specks on the horizon within hailing distance of Africa, Italy has more continuous vineyard land than any other country. The Apennine backbone running down the center of the country means that increasing sunshine can almost always be countered with altitude. The surrounding seas provide calm, soothing maritime influences to all the wine regions except those of the far north. Most of the grape varieties are Italian originals. Italy, at last, swarms with enthusiastic, talented young growers and winemakers passionate to test just how good her wines can be. The timing is perfect. The new wave of wines across the world has been based largely on French role models and French grape varieties. But the twenty-first century has brought with it a hunger for new directions and new flavors. Italy, with her maverick mentality, her challenging wine styles, and her jungle of grape varieties, is ready to take on the role of leadership she has avoided for so long. From the Dolomites in the far north to Sicily in the broiling south, Italy has finally woken up.

The Wine Regions of Italy

VINES AND ITALY DO GO TOGETHER. Indeed, given the amount of wine that Italy produces, first-time visitors to the country might expect every imaginable nook and cranny to be planted with vineyards. But they'd be wrong. There are vast tracts of vines in Italy, but these tend to be concentrated in a few regions: Piedmont in the northwest; Veneto and Friuli in the northeast; Tuscany and Emilia-Romagna in west central Italy; Marche and Abruzzo in the center-east; Puglia in the south; and the islands of Sicily and Sardinia. In between you often don't see a vine. Even

so, more vines are growing in Italy than in almost any other country on Earth. (Only Spain, China, and France have more.) When you remember how long Italy is, it's obvious that there will be enormous differences of wine styles. In the Alpine valleys of the Aosta Valley, you are far closer to London than you are to the tiny island of Pantelleria, which almost touches the African shores of Tunisia. From the Alps to Sicily runs the great spine of the Apennines. Indeed 80 percent of the country is hilly or mountainous, and the endless twists and turns provide a vast array of beautifully exposed slopes on which the vine can bask. Their altitude is important, too. The northern

CLASSIFICATIONS

Introduced in 1963 and updated in 1992, the Italian classification system was overhauled in 2010, leading to four levels:

» **Vino** (generic wine) is at the bottom of the wine pyramid; it may be produced anywhere in the European Union, and must not show indication of origin, nor vintage, nor the grapes used, but only the color of the wine.

» **Varietali** (varietal wines) are made from at least 85 percent of one authorized international grape (Cabernet, Chardonnay, Merlot, Sauvignon Blanc, Syrah), or a blend of two or more of them; grape(s) and vintage may be shown on the label.

» **IGP** (Indicazione Geografica Protetta/Protected Geographical Indication), replacing IGT, refers to the production of wine from a specific territory (of which there are 118), and following regulations on viticultural and vinification practices.

» **DOP** (Denominazione di Origine Protetta/Protected Designation of Origin) comprises two quality subcategories—**DOC** and **DOCG**—from smaller zones (within an IGP area) with notable climatic

and geological characteristics and a tradition of quality winemaking. At the time of writing, there are 333 DOCs (Denominazione di Origine Controllata/Controlled Designation of Origin). The top-quality level is DOCG (Denominazione di Origine Controllata e Garantita/Controlled and Guaranteed Designation of Origin), which must be assessed by a panel of tasters to guarantee its authenticity and quality. There are currently seventy-four DOCGs.

» The term **"Classico"** applies to wines from an historic area; **"Superiore"** wines have 0.5 percent more alcohol than the regular DOP wine, ideally due to lower yields; **"Riserva"** wines have extended aging. No hierarchical classification yet exists in Italy, but from the Barbaresco vintage of 2006 and the Barolo vintage of 2010, the *menzioni geografiche aggiuntive*, or subzone delimitation of vineyards, was officially introduced in the Langhe; mention of a single vineyard/subzone on a Barbaresco or Barolo guarantees that at least 85 percent of the fruit comes from that vineyard.

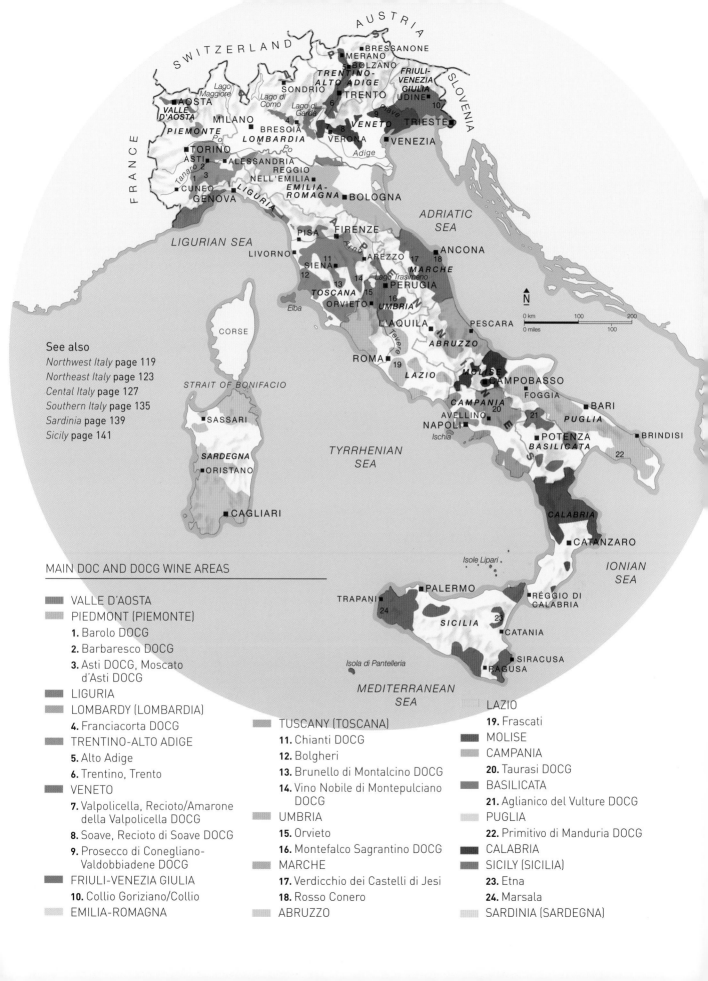

SWITZERLAND
AUSTRIA
SLOVENIA
FRANCE

BRESSANONE
MERANO
BOLZANO
TRENTINO-ALTO ADIGE
FRIULI-VENEZIA GIULIA
TRENTO
UDINE
SONDRIO
Lago Maggiore
Lago di Como
Lago di Garda
AOSTA
VALLE D'AOSTA
MILANO
BRESCIA
VENETO
VERONA
TRIESTE
PIEMONTE
LOMBARDIA
Po
Po
VENEZIA
TORINO
Adige
ASTI
ALESSANDRIA
REGGIO NELL'EMILIA
Tanaro
1
2
3
CUNEO
EMILIA-ROMAGNA
LIGURIA
GENOVA
BOLOGNA
ADRIATIC SEA
LIGURIAN SEA
PISA
FIRENZE
Arno
ANCONA
LIVORNO
AREZZO
17
18
MARCHE
SIENA
11
12
13
14
Lago Trasimeno
PERUGIA
TOSCANA
15
ORVIETO
16
UMBRIA
Elba
L'AQUILA
PESCARA
Tevere
ABRUZZO
ROMA
19
LAZIO
MOLISE
CAMPOBASSO
FOGGIA
CAMPANIA
20
21
BARI
AVELLINO
PUGLIA
NAPOLI
Ischia
POTENZA
BASILICATA
BRINDISI
22
CORSE
STRAIT OF BONIFACIO
SASSARI
SARDEGNA
ORISTANO
TYRRHENIAN SEA
CAGLIARI
CALABRIA
CATANZARO
Isole Lipari
IONIAN SEA
RÉGGIO DI CALABRIA
PALERMO
TRAPANI
24
SICILIA
23
CATANIA
SIRACUSA
RAGUSA
Isola di Pantelleria
MEDITERRANEAN SEA

N
0 km   100   200
0 miles   100

See also
Northwest Italy page 119
Northeast Italy page 123
Cental Italy page 127
Southern Italy page 135
Sardinia page 139
Sicily page 141

MAIN DOC AND DOCG WINE AREAS

VALLE D'AOSTA
PIEDMONT (PIEMONTE)
  1. Barolo DOCG
  2. Barbaresco DOCG
  3. Asti DOCG, Moscato d'Asti DOCG
LIGURIA
LOMBARDY (LOMBARDIA)
  4. Franciacorta DOCG
TRENTINO-ALTO ADIGE
  5. Alto Adige
  6. Trentino, Trento
VENETO
  7. Valpolicella, Recioto/Amarone della Valpolicella DOCG
  8. Soave, Recioto di Soave DOCG
  9. Prosecco di Conegliano-Valdobbiadene DOCG
FRIULI-VENEZIA GIULIA
  10. Collio Goriziano/Collio
EMILIA-ROMAGNA

TUSCANY (TOSCANA)
  11. Chianti DOCG
  12. Bolgheri
  13. Brunello di Montalcino DOCG
  14. Vino Nobile di Montepulciano DOCG
UMBRIA
  15. Orvieto
  16. Montefalco Sagrantino DOCG
MARCHE
  17. Verdicchio dei Castelli di Jesi
  18. Rosso Conero
ABRUZZO

LAZIO
  19. Frascati
MOLISE
CAMPANIA
  20. Taurasi DOCG
BASILICATA
  21. Aglianico del Vulture DOCG
PUGLIA
  22. Primitivo di Manduria DOCG
CALABRIA
SICILY (SICILIA)
  23. Etna
  24. Marsala
SARDINIA (SARDEGNA)

FIZZ FANTASTICO

Champagne may be the most famous fizz in the world, but Italy is just as important as France when it comes to producing wine with bubbles, and the Northeast and the Northwest have two famous sparklers. Right now, the wine that has taken the world by storm is Prosecco. The Glera grape, grown all the way from Vicenza to Trieste in the Northeast, is the basis of this bright, frothy, pear-scented party pop made by refermentation in tank, not bottle. Conegliano-Valdobbiadene is the classic area of production. The Northeast's other main sparkling area is Trentino, where some excellent dry wines are made by the traditional bottle method.

Italy's finest sparklers come from Franciacorta in the Northwest, near Brescia east of Milan. Using mostly Chardonnay and Pinot Noir, these traditional-method wines are always good, and, at their best, when they have been given several years of aging on their yeast lees before disgorging, they can rival top Champagne. Piedmont, southeast of Turin, boasts an entirely different style of fizz: the scented, grapey, relatively sweet and low-alcohol Asti and its less fizzy but delicious sibling, Moscato d'Asti. Wine snobs may not like them, but they're wonderfully refreshing when served ice cold on a warm summer's day.

Alpine slopes allow for wines of delicate crystalline purity, and, as we head south, their craggy heights are crucial in tempering the blazing southern sun.

Proximity to water is also vital, and Italy's long thin body means that many vines benefit from the cooling effects of the Adriatic and Tyrrhenian seas on the eastern and western flanks respectively. Inland lakes such as Lake Garda in the northeast create local climates that greatly influence wine styles. Then there are the rivers: from the Adige, tumbling out of the Dolomites in the northeast, to Piedmont's Tanaro creating the boundary between the Roero and Langhe hills, on to the Po bisecting northern and central Italy, to Tuscany's Arno and Lazio's Tiber. In some cases, these rivers moderate the climate, but with others, most notably the Po, they provide fertile valleys in which the vine really shouldn't be planted because it performs like an athlete on steroids.

Given the great climatic and topographical diversity, it is hardly surprising that Italy has such a wide range of native grape varieties, most of which are particularly suited to their local growing conditions. For instance, Nebbiolo, seems to flourish only in Piedmont and especially on the limestone rich soil of the Langhe hills; the white Moscato grape, although grown throughout the peninsula, excels in the white, chalky soil around Canelli in Piedmont's Monferrato hills.

Further east, around Verona, the white Garganega and red Corvina flourish in the Dolomite foothills, while in the hills along the Slovenian border, international varieties such as Pinot Grigio and Sauvignon do battle with natives like Tocai Friulano and Ribolla. On the eastern coast, the Montepulciano grape holds sway, but attempts to transport it across the Apennines to Tuscany have been thwarted by the cooler climate there. Sangiovese, however, produces meager wines on the eastern coast, but in Tuscany it rises to great heights. It is planted throughout the peninsula, as are Barbera and the white Trebbiano, the latter still being Italy's most widely planted white grape, although it is in decline in favor of Chardonnay. But while Barbera and Sangiovese can produce great wines in the right sites, Trebbiano is prized only for its resistance to disease and prodigious yields and is rapidly losing ground.

Moving south, we encounter varieties probably first brought to the peninsula by the Greeks three thousand years ago—Negroamaro, Uva di Troia, Aglianico,

The East of Sicily is dominated by the brooding volcano of Mount Etna, which is still active. Its lower slopes are clad with vineyards that thrive on the black volcanic soil, and, since 2000, it has become the most exciting wine area on the island.

Gaglioppo, and Greco di Tufo—all of which perform great in southern conditions. When northern grape varieties such as Sangiovese and Trebbiano are planted in the south, they ripen as early as August and, as a result, produce wines of ineffable neutrality, but the native southern grapes, being more accustomed to the hot summers, have a much longer growing season, which allows them time to develop interesting and complex perfumes and tastes, which shows in the resulting wines.

The islands, too, have their own varieties. In Sicily, Nero d'Avola is unrivaled, while in Sardinia, evidence of Aragon and Spanish domination in the Middle Ages is still to be found in the local grape varieties, such as the red Cannonau (Spain's Garnacha) and Carignano (Cariñena) and the white Vermentino (said to be a strain of Malvasia). Here, as elsewhere in Italy, the importance of matching these grape varieties with suitable terrain and climate cannot be underestimated.

WHAT DID THE ROMANS EVER DO FOR WINE?

What have the Romans ever done for us? Well, without them we might not have a Western European wine culture at all, and if we did, it probably wouldn't resemble what we have today because the Romans established most of the great vineyard regions of Spain, Germany, and, above all, France. If you enjoy Rioja, Mosel, or Bordeaux—thank the Romans and the thirst of their invading armies for planting the vineyards.

Rome got the idea of wine from the Greeks, but they set about modernizing vineyards and winemaking in a way we would still recognize. Luckily, Roman writers of every kind seemed to have an opinion to express about vineyards and wine. Horace, Virgil, Ovid, and Pliny were all mouthing off about wine, so we have a lot of source material, but Cato and a guy called Columella were the most useful writers—categorizing wine varieties according to quality, talking about preservatives (or lack of them), (natural wine fans, take note), cellar cleanliness, storage temperatures, aging methods (ability to age was highly prized in Roman wine), and the economics of making wine, running a vineyard, and conducting successful wine trading. The Romans also had some less charming habits. They were even more eager than the Greeks to add resin to their wine. They would add powdered marble and potters' earth to "invigorate" the wine. Then they'd dilute it with seawater. No, I haven't tried that.

Northwest Italy

RED GRAPES
There are several distinctive varieties, including Barbera, Dolcetto, and the famous Nebbiolo of Barolo and Barbaresco. Grignolino has a dedicated following, and Freisa is returning to favor.

WHITE GRAPES
Moscato is most widely known, but Cortese and Arneis are more fashionable. Erbaluce is declining as Chardonnay increases.

CLIMATE
The continental climate has long cold winters, slightly moderated by the influence of rivers. Summers are warm, while falls are plagued by fog.

SOIL
Subsoil is generally calcareous marl with some areas of glacial moraine. Topsoil is clay, sand, and gravel and can be very fertile.

GEOGRAPHY
Nearly half of Piedmont is mountainous with vineyards frequently planted on high, steep slopes and terraces carefully angled to take best advantage of exposure.

NORTHWEST ITALY HAS ALL THE NATURAL ATTRIBUTES necessary to produce good and even great wine. Mountains—the Alps to the north and west, the Apennines to the south—form a protective semicircle and act as a natural border between Piedmont (its name is derived from the fact that it lies at the foot of the mountains) and the coastal region of Liguria to the south. Rivers, such as the Po, Tanaro, and Bormida, water the lush, low-lying valleys that produce some of Italy's best fruit, while hills, such as the Langhe and Monferrato, and the Alpine foothills of Lombardy provide the vine with ideal growing conditions.

The Po, Italy's longest river, rises in the Alps near the French border before cutting a swathe through the plains of Piedmont, Lombardy, and the Veneto and is bordered to the north by an outcrop of limestone and dolomite (calcium magnesium carbonate), which forms the foothills of Lombardy's Alps. These extend into the Veneto, hosting the Classico zones of Valpolicella and Soave, but in Lombardy are largely responsible for the wines of Franciacorta. While the Alps act as a protective helmet for Italy's head, the Apennines—curving eastward along the southern border of Piedmont before turning south—act as the top of her spine.

Italy has few landlocked regions, yet in the northwest of the country only Liguria has contact with the sea. This nearness to the water gives this slight, crescent-shape region a more moderate climate than Piedmont, Lombardy, or the mountainous Aosta to the north. Inland, winters are bitterly cold, summers long and hot, and falls generally fine until thick fogs descend for days on end in early October. The prospects for a fine vintage are greatly increased if the fogs hold off or are counterbalanced by sunny afternoons.

PIEDMONT

In Piedmont, Italy's largest region, the Langhe and Monferrato hills (together accounting for more than 90 percent of the region's wine production) are often wreathed in thick swirls of fog. Known as *nebbia* in Italian, the fog has given its name to one of Piedmont's—indeed Italy's—greatest grape varieties: Nebbiolo. This fickle variety, the sole component of Barolo and Barbaresco, ripens late, and it is often struggling to reach maturity when the fogs cover the valleys and the lower slopes, hence its name. Other Piedmont neighbors include Gattinara, Ghemme, and Carema. Nebbiolo delle Langhe is a light, tasty interpretation of the grape. When Nebbiolo wins the battle, the results are splendid; when the fog wins, the growers are left with an insipid, raw, and rasping red wine that leaves tasters grimacing and wondering what all the fuss is about. But the producers have made so much progress this century that even Nebbiolo's legendary tannins now seem milder.

But as I said above, Piedmont has more weapons in its armory than just the noble Nebbiolo. Other red grapes, such as Barbera and Dolcetto, produce greater volumes of wine. Barbera is a prodigious variety that appears to flourish wherever it is planted, and it ripens easily to produce a rich, black-fruited wine that is high in acid and mercifully low in tannin. Dolcetto can taste raw but at its best is a vibrant, purple-red wine, packed with plummy fruit and

MAIN DOC AND DOCG
WINE AREAS

— AOSTA
— PIEMONT (PIEDMONT (PIEMONTE))
1. Gattinara DOCG
2. Barbera d'Asti DOCG
3. Roero DOCG
4. Barbera d'Alba, Dolcetto d'Alba
5. Asti DOCG, Moscato d'Asti DOCG
6. Gavi, Cortese di Gavi DOCG
7. Barbaresco DOCG
8. Barolo DOCG
9. Dogliani, Dolcetto di Dogliani DOCG
— LOMBARDY (LOMBARDIA)
10. Franciacorta DOCG
11. Valtellina, Valtellina Superiore DOCG
— LIGURIA
12. Cinque Terre

MORE THAN 985 FEET
MORE THAN 1,970 FEET

spice—unsophisticated, undemanding, and marvelously gluggable. There is also a clutch of scented, floral, fun-loving red grapes led by Freisa and Brachetto. Although noted for its red wines, Piedmont also produces large volumes of white, primarily from the Moscato grape grown in the Monferrato hills. Its heavenly scent, all elderflowers and white peaches, is found in the best sparkling Asti and Moscato d'Asti, and this makes it a perfect antidote to the Langhe's brooding reds. Less reliable, but delicately scented with a fruit that veers between pears and white peaches, are still wines from the Arneis and Favorita varieties. Gavi is a very dry, lemony white, while Erbaluce di Caluso has more stuffing to it.

OTHER REGIONS

The remainder of Northwest Italy's wines are dwarfed by the colossus of Piedmont. Liguria's wine, which accounts for just 0.15 percent of Italian production, is consumed mainly by the locals and summer tourists. But the potential for quality in Liguria is good—warm, coastal mountain slopes that are tempered by a strong maritime influence. The overriding sensation I've got from good examples of wines such as Ormeasco, Rossese, Pigato, Cinque Terre, and Vermentino is of the fat, round, ripe body so often missing in Italian wines, allied to some fascinating flavors.

Aosta is a high, cool alpine valley, where ripening the grape is by no means easy. I've had good, herb-scented Gamays and Nebbiolos, some really good Moscatos, and some exceptional unusual reds and whites from local grapes where you can taste the rocky mountain chill.

In terms of area and output, only Lombardy can even attempt to challenge Piedmont. Unfortunately, much of what is produced in the prolific zone of Oltrepò Pavese, in the southwest of Lombardy, is merely sound but uninspiring wine and is in any case soaked up by Milan, Italy's industrial center and the nearest large city. But Franciacorta, between the cities of Breganze and Brescia, is increasingly admired for its excellent sparkling wines that regularly match Champagne in quality, while in the north, Valtellina, the sole significant outpost of Nebbiolo outside of Piedmont, is making a quality comeback after decades in the doldrums.

Barolo and Barbaresco

RED GRAPES
Nebbiolo rules supreme in both Barolo and Barbaresco, but it needs careful siting. Less well sited vineyards are planted with Dolcetto and Barbera, which are more accommodating.

CLIMATE
The continental climate is tempered by air currents flowing along the Tanaro Valley, bringing slightly cooler summer temperatures and allowing formation of autumnal fog, which causes Nebbiolo's slow ripening.

SOIL
The soil is generally fertile with calcareous bluish-gray marl in the west, and an iron-rich sand and limestone conglomerate in the east.

GEOGRAPHY
Most vineyards here face south-west to southeast on steep to very steep hills. The Barolo vineyards, at about 820 to 1,475 feet, are higher than those of Barbaresco, which lie at between 655 and 1,150 feet.

I USED TO THINK THAT BURGUNDY was the most difficult wine to understand until I visited Barolo and Barbaresco. Before that, and despite the urging of friendly Italophiles, I had failed to find the magic they purported to divine in a glass of Barolo. All I found was a hard, tannic wine, its fruit eviscerated by long aging in large, old oak casks. Throughout the 1980s and '90s, I searched many times for the complexity and greatness said to reside in the Nebbiolo grape. More often than not, though, I ended up with my teeth and gums suffering from the full-frontal assault of tannin and acidity. But things have changed. When the great 1997s were released, I finally began to get the message, and my eventual conversion came with the stunning 2010s and elegant 2011s, austerity mixed with fruit and scent. At last they made sense to me.

As the wines improved, the differences between producers became more marked. Previously, the stylistic variations had been masked by tannin and oxidation. Now I began to find that the new approach in the vineyards brought lower yields with better ripeness and riper tannins. In the cellar, the extraction of better tannins meant less aging in barrel and more in bottle, which in turn ensured greater freshness, releasing the many beautiful notes Nebbiolo is capable of sounding.

In the early 1990s, I visited the town of Alba for the first time. First stop was Barolo. Alba lies on the banks of the Tanaro River, and the first slopes of the Langhe hills rise up from the narrow plain just south of the town. The road out of Alba is straight, but once you reach the small town of Gallo d'Alba it begins to twist and climb. It then splits into three, heading off toward Serralunga d'Alba, Castiglione Falletto, and Monforte d'Alba, or La Morra and Barolo. Being a moderate soul, I took the middle road and began climbing toward Castiglione Falletto. I got a sore neck and almost drove into the ditch several times as I tried to get my bearings and distinguish the south- and southwest-facing slopes. Those vineyards with the finest exposure are planted with Nebbiolo. Those with an easterly or southeast aspect are planted with Dolcetto and Barbera or with white grapes such as Chardonnay.

As the road evens out, you get a spectacular view of the whole of Barolo. To the west are the vineyards of La Morra and Barolo (the commune itself), while to the east are those of Castiglione Falletto and Serralunga d'Alba. Snow-capped mountains loom behind the hilltop town of La Morra, and the lighter, whiter chalky soil of the vineyards seems to reflect the snow.

The soil in the western part of Barolo is a Tortonian calcareous marl, while in the east, there is Helvetian marl with higher levels of lime and iron. Because of Nebbiolo's sensitivity to soil, the wines from the former tend to be lighter and more fragrant than the powerful, tannic wines that characterize Serralunga. The spur running through Castiglione Falletto to the southerly vineyards in Monforte d'Alba produces wines that combine the power of Serralunga with some of the grace of La Morra and Barolo. The Barbaresco region is much more compact, just to the east of Alba, Italy's white truffle capital. The soil is mostly Tortonian calcareous marl, and, at about 1,800 acres, the vineyards are fairly crammed in.

Barolo's roughly 5,075 acres are split between some 1,200 growers. Such fragmentation results in as many different approaches to winemaking as there are plots of land, producing a confusing picture. Old-timers remember when Nebbiolo, the last grape to be harvested in the Langhe, would be left in its fermentation vat, in contact with its skins, until after Christmas. The resulting wines were so tough that they needed aging in large *botti* (casks) for anything up to ten years before the tannins had softened enough for the wine to be bottled. But, by that time, the wine would have oxidized.

In the 1960s, younger producers such as Renato Ratti, Aldo Conterno, and Angelo Gaja from Barbaresco traveled to France and saw a different approach to winemaking. Fresher and softer wines were the aim. Some proposed little contact with the skins and even less with oak; others suggested substituting small oak *barriques* for large *botti*; others simply said reduce yields and clean up your act in the cellar. Top producers split into traditionalist and modernist camps. But the complexity of the zones and of Nebbiolo itself and the approach of different growers

Traditionally, Barolo has been aged in large, old wooden casks, or botti, *but in recent years more of the aging period has taken place in small oak casks or even in bottle.*

BAROLO'S VINEYARDS

Arguably Italy's greatest wine, Barolo is named after a village southwest of Alba in the Langhe, from the Nebbiolo grape grown in steep vineyards. The best wines come from sites (*bricci*) near the top of those hills. Having gone to excesses of austerity in the post–World War II period, Barolo in the 1990s almost threatened to go too far in the other direction, its subtle floral/wild fruit aromas being drowned all too often under expensive French oak *barriques* and compromised by excessively enthusiastic attempts to extract more depth and flavor from the grapes than they possessed.

Thankfully, in the twenty-first century, producers are finding their way back to the more traditional "tar and roses" beauty of the grape, respecting its talent for expressing site perfectly, while balancing out the prominent tannins and acidity. The clay soil of Verduno, La Morra, and Barolo villages tend to give more accessible, softer, perfumed wines, while Monforte, Castiglione Falletto, and Serralunga wines have more structure, minerality, and deep-seated power. The mention of a "subzone" (vineyard) on a Barolo label signifies that 85 percent of the fruit should come from that one site. Minimum aging is thirty-eight months from November 1 of the harvest year, of which eighteen months must be in wood. Leading vineyards: Bricco delle Viole, Brunate, Bussia Soprana, Cannubi, Cerequio, Conca dell'Annunziata, Francia, Ginestra, Monprivato, Monvigliero, Rocche dell'Annunziata, Rocche di Castiglione, Santo Stefano di Perno, La Serra, Vigna Rionda, and Villero.

defy such a simplistic solution. In Barbaresco, with lower vineyards, a warmer mesoclimate, and an earlier harvest, the wines were less polarizing in style, requiring less wood and bottle aging and consequently providing a perfect launching pad for Angelo Gaja's determinedly "international" approach to extracting maximum flavor and aging in small, new oak barrels.

However, debate has been healthy. Not only are the wines much better than they were twenty or thirty years ago, but the growers have established themselves as a great force in the region. In the past, merchants would buy wines from numerous growers and blend them together to make a wine of a house style. Improvements in the vineyard and cellar have led to a new emphasis on the wines of individual communes and, within these communes, single vineyards. Specific terms, such as *bricco* (hilltop), *sorì* (slope), and *vigna* (vineyard), now appear on labels. With a grape such as Nebbiolo, the importance of provenance cannot be overstated, which takes us back to Burgundy again. There, the Pinot Noir responds to the minutest change in its growing conditions, and the vineyards of Burgundy's heartland—the Côte d'Or—is about as minutely mapped and classified as any vineyard in the world. Nebbiolo's extreme sensitivity to growing conditions means this trend in Barolo can only increase. The move to single-vineyard wine is less evident in Barbaresco, but Gaja and Giacosa have long bottled examples, and the excellent growers' cooperative was labeling single plot wines separately as long ago as the 1980s.

Northeast Italy

RED GRAPES
The most significant local varieties are Vernatsch (Schiava), Lagrein, Teroldego, and Marzemino. Cabernet Sauvignon is making ground as are Cabernet Franc, Merlot, and Pinot Noir.

WHITE GRAPES
Although native Traminer and Nosiola remain locally important, Chardonnay and Pinot Grigio continue their relentless march. Müller-Thurgau, Sauvignon Blanc, and Moscato also produce wines of good quality.

CLIMATE
The north has a continental alpine climate with great temperature fluctuations. Summers can be very hot, especially on the valley floor. Trentino is less extreme although slightly warmer overall.

SOIL
The soil of subregions varies, but generally it is infertile, light, and well-draining. The subsoil is limestone with alluvial deposits of gravel, sand, or clay.

GEOGRAPHY
The mountainous terrain means that most vineyards are found in river valleys, where they are often planted on steep terraces.

SOAVE, VALPOLICELLA, PINOT GRIGIO. Each of these wines, virtually synonymous with Italian wine as a whole, is produced in northeast Italy—yet this is perhaps the least Italian of any part of the country. To the north and east are Austria and Slovenia, and both have contributed to the diversity of culture, peoples, food, and wine that exists in the Northeast. The region has been at the crossroads of Europe since at least Roman times. Merchants, scholars, and soldiers coming from the north or east would pass through this part of the country on their way to Rome, Florence, or Milan, as would the great traders of Venice, the city that controlled much of the world's commerce in the fourteenth and fifteenth centuries. Later on, Napoléon's armies were here, and until 1919 both Friuli-Venezia Giulia and the Alto Adige were part of the Austro-Hungarian Empire. Each of these visitors left a wine legacy that we are still enjoying today. The French grape varieties, Cabernet Sauvignon, Merlot, and Chardonnay, owe their presence to the fact that they were brought from France in the wake of the Napoleonic invasion more than two centuries ago.

Trentino-Alto Adige is tucked protectively into the high Alps and the Dolomites. Moving out of the mountains eastward, the far Northeast is protected from cool north winds by the Julian pre-Alps to the north. From the hills just outside Gorizia, the snow-capped peaks of this protective barrier can be seen standing guard on the border with Austria. In the east, the hills were once bisected by the southern reaches of the Iron Curtain, while to the south lies the Adriatic, its gentle waters providing a moderating influence on the continental climate that would otherwise prevail here.

Moving southwest on to the plains, the soil becomes more fertile and the vines more productive and the wines increasingly insipid. This trend continues and reaches its lowest point in the fertile plain of the Piave Valley, which produces a great deal of the bulk wine used to pad out the commercial Veneto blends of the Veronese merchants to the west but also a fair amount of the light, refreshing mealtime reds glugged and forgotten in the cafés and restaurants of Venice.

THE VENETO

It's pretty likely that one of your first experiences of Italian wine was a bottle of Veneto wine. It could have been Soave, Bardolino, Valpolicella, Bianco, Rosso, Merlot, Tocai del Veneto, or even a Pinot Grigio, Chardonnay, or Cabernet. The Veneto churns out a huge volume of wines, from Lake Garda in the west to the Piave Valley in the east, from the Alpine foothills in the north to the dull flatlands of the Po Valley to the south. Quality varies from anonymous whites and weedy reds to a few outstanding wines produced in the Valpolicella and Soave Classico zones in the hills that flank Verona.

Although, by and large, greater Italian reds are found in Tuscany and Piedmont, no other region makes such a range of styles at such a decent average of level of quality and charges relatively so little for them. Names such as Valpolicella and Soave are world famous, and in the 1960s they soon helped forge Italian wine's cheap-and-cheerful image. Despite this image, the Classico vineyards of both

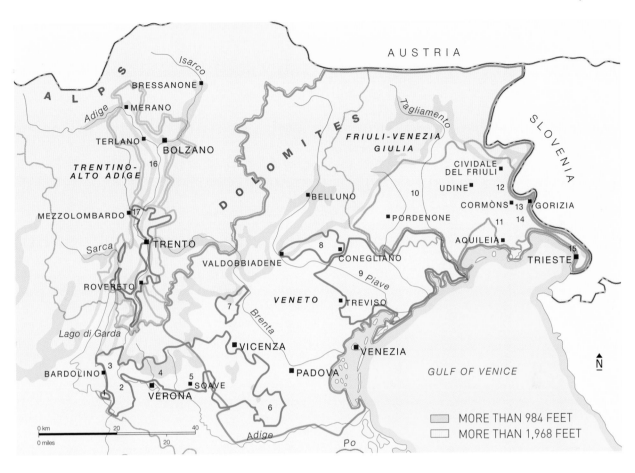

MAIN DOC AND DOCG WINE AREAS

— Prosecco

— VENETO

1. Lugana

2. Bianco di Custoza, Custoza

3. Bardolino, Bardolino Superiore DOCG

4. Valpolicella, Recioto/ Amarone della Valpolicella DOCG

5. Soave, Soave Superiore DOCG, Recioto di Soave DOCG

6. Colli Euganei, Colli Euganei Fiori d'Arancio DOCG

7. Breganze

8. Prosecco di Conegliano-Valdobbiadene e Colli Asolani DOCG

9. Lison-Pramaggiore, Lison DOCG

— FRIULI-VENEZIA GIULIA

10. Friuli Grave

11. Friuli Aquileia

12. Friuli Colli Orientali, Picolit DOCG

13. Collio, Collio Goriziano

14. Friuli Isonzo

15. Carso

— Valdadige

— ALTO ADIGE/SUDTIROLER

16. Lago di Caldaro, Caldaro/ Kalterersee

— TRENTINO

17. Teroldego Rotaliano

zones, up in the Alpine foothills, remain the finest in the region. But both Classico zones should be distinguished from the wines of the plains, which can use only the straight Valpolicella and Soave names. In Soave Classico, the Garganega grape is king. Traditionally supplemented with Trebbiano di Soave to add perfume, it may now be blended with Chardonnay or Sauvignon, but most top producers stick to Garganega. The steep slopes of the Valpolicella Classico zone, the climate of which is tempered by its

proximity to Lake Garda, are ideally suited to the Corvina and Corvinone grapes. The best wines have marvelous depth and intensity. Traditionally, such concentration has been achieved by refermenting the young wines on the skins of the dried grapes used in the production of Amarone and Recioto. These refermented wines, known as *ripasso*, have better alcohol and weight than the younger wines. The great wines of Valpolicella, however, are the dry Amarone and sweet Recioto (page 124).

To the west of Valpolicella, across the Adige, the glacial shores of Lake Garda are carpeted with vines making the light red Bardolino and the white Bianco di Custoza, which can be a surprisingly characterful blend of Garganega, Tocai, Trebbiano, and Cortese grapes. East of Valpolicella, again in the Alpine foothills, is the Breganze DOC producing a range of reds and whites. But, more important, around Conegliano, the Glera grape makes soft, creamy Prosecco fizz that charms the tired palates of Venice and increasingly the rest of the world as well. The success of Prosecco now means Glera grapes are grown from Vicenza right across to Trieste. South of Vicenza, the volcanic hills are home to the Colli Berici and Colli Euganei DOCs, where a wide range of varietals is used to make wines that have, at their best, more intensity than Breganze achieves. In the far eastern Veneto, hills give way to the broader plains of the Piave Valley and then the Lison-Pramaggiore zone, which produce large quantities of Cabernet, Merlot, Tocai, and Pinot Grigio.

TRENTINO-ALTO ADIGE

But before we head to the east and Friuli-Venezia Giulia, let's go back up the high river valley of the Adige, where vineyards nestle beneath the steep peaks of the Dolomites and southern Alps or cling improbably to scraps of land halfway up the giddy slopes. Trentino and Alto Adige are two regions with different histories and personalities. Trentino runs from Lake Garda north to the Dolomites above the town of Trento. Its historic links are with northern Italy, in particular the ancient republic of Venice, and before that the Etruscans. The boundary between the two is very precise, as the Adige Valley closes in like a pincer at Salorno, the high mountain walls warning off intruders from the south. North of here, most of the inhabitants don't use the title Alto Adige—they call their homeland Süd-Tirol (South Tyrol), because until 1919, when it was traded to Italy as part of the spoils of World War I, Süd-Tirol belonged to the Austro-Hungarian

RECIOTO AND AMARONE

This is your chance to taste the kind of wine the ancient Greeks drank. Dried grape wines were once produced all over the Mediterranean, their advantages being that they were lusciously sweet in an age when sweetness was rare and that they kept much better than other wines. Nowadays, such wines survive only patchily.

The Recioto and Amarone wines of Soave and Valpolicella in the Veneto region are among these survivors. You make them by picking ripe, healthy grapes and hanging them to dry under the rafters over the winter. They shrivel almost to raisins, and that's when you crush and ferment them. They make just about the thickest, stickiest must imaginable, and they turn into sweet, rich wine. If you want to know what Recioto della Valpolicella tastes like, imagine a cross between vintage Port and a classy northern Rhône Syrah, mixed with raisins, honey, and bitter cherries; Recioto di Soave is stuffed with citrus peel and raisiny flavors, bound together with acidity. Sometimes a winemaker will take things further and ferment a Recioto della Valpolicella to dryness; what you get is Amarone, which has the same cherries, raisins and honey of its sweet cousin but with a pronounced bitter cherry dryness. At its best, it's one of the great reds of the world. You can drink it young, but it really needs ten years to show its brilliance.

Italy's most famous dried-grape wines, Amarone and Recioto. Leading producer Masi uses trays to dry and shrivel the grapes in their winery before turning them into Amarone.

Empire, and to this day it is bilingual, with a strong inclination toward all things German.

The Alto Adige wine tradition is strongly Germanic. The most widely planted red grape is the Schiava or Vernatsch. This makes a soft, mild, light red more Germanic than Italian that can be delightful from a good grower. White grapes, such as Riesling, Sylvaner, Müller-Thurgau, and Traminer—named after the local town Tramin (or Termeno)—abound. There is also the French Pinot family, red and white, plus Chardonnay, Cabernet, and the excellent local Lagrein. Slopes of between 820 and 3,280 feet are festooned with vines relishing warm days and chilly nights. The snow-dusted Dolomites may make you think that these high vineyards must practice extreme cool-climate grape growing but it's relentlessly sunny, and the regional capital, Bolzano, is often the hottest place in the whole country. Yes, hotter than Sicily.

Trentino is, in general, a little warmer and lower and more of the vineyards are on flat valley soil, giving less exhilarating wines. Even so, Trentino seems well suited to international varieties such as Chardonnay, Pinot Bianco, and Merlot as well as its local Marzemino and Teroldego grapes. Apart from a few gorgeous sweet wines from the Nosiola grape, the only area of activity in which Trentino has made as much of its potential as it should is in sparkling wines, which are some of the best in Italy. Certainly conditions are ideal, both in the vineyard and for the winemaker, during those long cold winters when the wines can slowly evolve.

FRIULI-VENEZIA GIULIA

Tucked into the northeastern corner of the country, stretching from the plains of the eastern Veneto to the borders with Austria and Slovenia, Friuli is a relative newcomer to united Italy because it was, until 1919, part of the Austro-Hungarian Empire. Perhaps because of this, the locals take a view of themselves as hard-working, constant northerners who are different from their more fickle, flighty neighbors elsewhere in Italy.

There is a certain truth in this as far as making wine goes. Friuli white wines have become a byword for modernity and consistency. Thanks to its Austro-Hungarian legacy and its proximity to Eastern Europe, Friuli has a wide range of both imported and native grape varieties. Additionally, it has some outstanding vineyard sites, mainly in the Collio and Colli Orientali hills.

Friuli's northern borders are defined by the Julian and Carnic pre-Alps, which make up more than 40 percent of the total land area. These inhospitable peaks hold no prospects for the vine, though, as well as forming a stunning backdrop to the vineyards, they do trap the Bora, the cool wind, that blows off the Gulf of Trieste. The Bora blows from the south across the rest of Friuli, comprised largely of the Venetian Plain and the gentle hills along the Slovenian border, which are home to the Collio Goriziano and Colli Orientali zones. The cool Tramontana wind that blows off the mountains from the north also moderates the climate making the region ideal for quality white wine.

The numerous cultural influences to which Friuli has been subjected over the centuries have resulted in a multitude of primarily white grape varieties of German, French, Italian, and Eastern European origins. Riesling and Traminer perform well, as do Pinot Grigio, Pinot Bianco, Chardonnay, and Sauvignon Blanc, which have had no problem in adapting. The native Ribolla Gialla grape is currently enjoying something of a revival, with its waxy nature and tangy acidity, while the Tocai Friulano can produce some of the most interesting of Friuli's dry whites. Other natives include Picolit and Verduzzo, both highly regarded locally for the quality of their sweet wines, but their erratic quality means we rarely see them off their home patch.

Of the reds, Refosco dal Peduncolo Rosso can, at its best, be as much of a mouthful to drink as it is to pronounce, while Schioppettino produces lighter wines. Neither, however, produces wines of the stature of the whites, and they remain largely local pleasures.

The two hillier regions are Collio Orientali and plain Collio (or Collio Goriziano), both hugging the modern-day border with Slovenia, and, indeed, the vineyards on both sides of the border have historically been thought of as interchangeable. In the 1960s, these areas began to produce fresh, modern whites when most Italian whites bore more of a resemblance to a glass of tired Sherry. These wines were unoaked and not frankly particularly vivid in flavor but revolutionary for Italy at the time—and expensive. Many other parts of Italy now produce modern whites as good as or better than those of Friuli, and it is interesting to note that, in response, Friuli is now a center of experimentation for the natural and the orange wine movements.

As you move on to the plains, quality and price both descend, and the differences between the zones become far less pronounced. Isonzo still has a little of the intensity of the hillsides, but as we head westward through Aquileia and Latisana, the soil becomes more productive and yields—of both reds and whites—continue to rise, although the gravelly soil of Friuli Grave, around the city of Udine, produces some pleasantly drinkable reds, led by the Merlots and Cabernets.

Central Italy

RED GRAPES
Sangiovese is widely grown across Central Italy, but there are many other local specialities. Emilia-Romagna has numerous Lambrusco varieties, the Marche and Abruzzo have Montepulciano, Umbria has Sagrantino, and Lazio has Cesanese.

WHITE GRAPES
High-yielding Trebbiano is the dominant variety, from Emilia-Romagna to Abruzzo, but Verdicchio is the most important grape in Marche, and Grechetto adds character to the wine in Umbria.

CLIMATE
This is strongly influenced by the Apennine mountain range, which runs down the spine of Italy.

SOIL
The soil is incredibly varied, as you might expect in a region that starts north of Florence and ends near Naples. Much of Chianti Classico and Montalcino is rocky and infertile. Limestone clay is common.

GEOGRAPHY
Because much of central Italy straddles the high Apennine Mountains, altitude often plays a more significant part than aspect. Tuscany has vineyards rising up to 1,970 feet and the best wines of Marche and Abruzzo come from the hills, although both east and west coasts have low-lying vineyards.

THE DISPARATE COLLECTION OF REGIONS lumped together as central Italy separates the sub-Alpine landscapes of the north from the ancient hills and plains of the southern part of the country. Bisected by the Apennine mountains, central Italy begins on the southern bank of the Po River and stretches to an imaginary line, running from the Gargano Massif to the Gulf of Gaeta, which separates Lazio from Campania and Molise from Puglia. In short, northern Italy is a kind of sub-alpine world linked to France, Austria, and other wine cultures to the North. Italy's south is an area influenced by North Africa, by the hot southern Mediterranean, and by traditions hardly touched by the new wave of wine. Naples is its northern stronghold. What is in between? Well, a gigantic chunk of Italian culture. Rome is no great wine city, but you can't avoid it. Further north, Tuscany with its great cities offers a serious wine culture bang in the middle of Italy.

EMILIA-ROMAGNA

The lush, fertile plains of the Po Valley are among the most intensively farmed land in Italy. Most of this is orchard, but the land around Modena, Reggio nell'Emilia, and Bologna is carpeted with Lambrusco vines. Most commercial Lambrusco is prickly and sweet, but the real thing is a frothing, purple drink with high acidity and usually a touch of sweetness that perfectly complements the rich cooking of Emilia. There are also good still wines. With a fair amount of Sangiovese and Barbera, the white Albana di Romagna is pretty highly regarded, and grapes such as Trebbiano, Malvasia, Chardonnay, and Sauvignon Blanc provide a lot of fairly decent white to go with the antipasti.

MARCHE

The wines of the Marche are a pretty interesting lot because of two excellent grape varieties: the white Verdicchio and the red Montepulciano. Verdicchio dei Castelli Jesi and the richer Verdicchio di Matelica are two seriously good whites. While Sangiovese and Trebbiano are still prevalent, Verdicchio has had to overcome the reputation it acquired when it was bought more for its amphora-shape bottles than for the intrinsic merit of the wine. Rosso Conero, at its best, shows the generosity that the Montepulciano grape can lend to wines.

UMBRIA

Over the border in Umbria, Orvieto boasts a more diverse blend, which improves proportionally as the percentage of grapes such as Grechetto, Chardonnay, and Sauvignon Blanc increases. Nearly all of Umbria consists of hills or mountains, ensuring that the vine has many a felicitous spot in which to flourish. The higher altitude of the "green heart of Italy" compensates for the land-locked nature of the region, which would normally render it too hot for viticulture. Grechetto is the most characterful native white variety,

MAIN DOC AND DOCG WINE AREAS

— EMILIA-ROMAGNA
1. Lambrusco
2. Albana di Romagna (Romagna Alba) DOCG

— TUSCANY (TOSCANA)
3. Carmignano DOCG, Barco Reale di Carmignano
4. Chianti DOCG
5. Chianti Classico DOCG
6. Vernaccia di San Gimignano DOCG, San Gimignano
7. Bolgheri
8. Morellino di Scansano DOCG
9. Brunello di Montalcino DOCG, Rosso di Montalcino, Sant' Antimo
10. Vino Nobile di Montepulciano DOCG, Rosso di Montepulciano

— UMBRIA
11. Montefalco, Montefalco Sagrantino DOCG
12. Orvieto

— MARCHE
13. Verdicchio dei Castelli di Jesi, Verdicchio dei Castelli di Jesi Riserva DOCG
14. Conero DOCG, Rosso Conero
15. Verdicchio di Matelica, Verdicchio di Matelica Riserva DOCG
16. Rosso Piceno

— ABRUZZO

— LAZIO
17. Est! Est!! Est!!! di Montefiascone
18. Frascati, Frascati Superiore DOCG
19. Cesanese del Piglio DOCG

— MOLISE
20. Biferno

MORE THAN 985 FEET
MORE THAN 1,970 FEET

producing wines of good depth and breadth. Its red counterpart, Sagrantino, is one of Italy's great red grape varieties, but it is found only around the town of Montefalco, where the Montefalco Sagrantino DOCG is located. It produces deep-colored, tannic wines of great intensity and length. Umbria's other noted red is the Sangiovese-based Torgiano.

LAZIO

You would hope that the Romans' home town region would pulsate with wonderful wines, perhaps honoring a heritage of thousands of years. Well, it doesn't work out like that. They do drink a lot of wine in Rome, but the local stuff is mostly mild, and soft white from the surrounding hills. Frascati is the most famous, using Trebbiano and Malvasia grapes, and Est! Est!! Est!!! further north has

some kind of reputation—apart from the exclamation marks. The flatlands do produce some wine, some pretty good, usually from international varieties and usually sold under the IGT Lazio designation, although the Cesanese grape is local and at least different.

ABRUZZO AND MOLISE

The reegions of Abruzzo and Molise haven't yet hit the high spots, but their reds from the Montepulciano grape have the potential to do so. Unfortunately, the dominant white grape is the workhouse Trebbiano, so until more interesting varieties are planted, the white wines are strictly for drinking there but not here. Paradoxically, one of Italy's legendary whites is the Valentini Trebbiano d'Abruzzo. I wish there were more producers like Valentini.

Tuscany

RED GRAPES
The chief grape of Tuscany is the Sangiovese, also known as Brunello, Prugnolo Gentile, and Sangioveto. Canaiolo Nero and Mammolo are other local varieties nowadays joined by Cabernet Sauvignon and Merlot.

WHITE GRAPES
Vernaccia produces the best white wine, but high-yielding Trebbiano is much more common. International varieties are led by Chardonnay, Pinot Bianco, Sauvignon Blanc, and increasingly Viognier.

CLIMATE
The temperate climate of the central hills is in complete contrast to the river basins, which trap summer heat and damp, and the drier, hotter coastal regions. Hail can be a threat to fruiting vines.

SOIL
Soil is generally calcareous, with tufa and some sandy clay. The flaky marl called galestro *is highly desirable and features in Montalcino and the Chianti Classico and Rufina zones. Near Pitigliano, soil is volcanic.*

GEOGRAPHY
The best vineyards are carefully sited on slopes and steep hills, often interspersed with olive groves and woodland.

THE LANDSCAPE OF MODERN TUSCANY still looks remarkably like it did in Renaissance paintings. You know the kind of thing—cypresses, rounded green hills, old farmhouses with carved stone doorways and cool, dark interiors, the brilliance of the sun, the vast blue distances. It is a place where civilization seems unimaginably old and intensely alive.

To the west of Tuscany is the Mediterranean sea, in which basks the island of Elba with its echoes of Napoléon. To the east lie the Apennines, arching around to the north; while to the south there's Lazio, Rome, and the Mezzogiorno. The land lies flat near the coast, as if to let the Mediterranean climate as far inland as possible, but most of Tuscany is hilly. Not necessarily seriously hilly, although you'll find white grapes cultivated up to 2,300 feet and reds up to 1,800 feet. The hills are essential for viticulture because summers can be long and hot, and hills that rise high enough to temper the heat or catch a cooling breeze can make all the difference between a baked, flat white wine and one with perfume and fruit.

For reds, the slopes provide the concentration of heat that the sun-loving Sangiovese grape needs to ripen. Tuscany's vineyards were replanted, largely between 1965 and 1975, but it was with quantity instead of quality in mind. High-yielding clones of Sangiovese from Romagna to the north and a rash of dull, thin white Trebbiano sprang like disease from the hillside slopes. Copious quantities of simple, gluggable red were produced, and that seemed to be where the market lay. Today, it couldn't be more different. A remarkable sense of seriousness and endeavor pervades the wineries and the vineyards. New estates brimful of pride and determination appear with every new vintage, and the work done on the quality of the grapes, epitomized by the Chianti Classico 2000 movement that set out to provide the best clones and plant them in the best sites, is everywhere apparent.

SANGIOVESE AND OTHER GRAPES

Tuscany's main grape is Sangiovese. The wines are mainly 100 percent Sangiovese, but they can be blended with many other varieties, both red and white. Consistency, however, is not its strong point, and it needs low yields to produce grapes of quality. It is the ready availability of sun-drenched slopes that makes Sangiovese the most popular planting in Tuscany. The further north you go, the lower down the slopes you find the best Sangiovese: as low as 165 to 655 feet in northerly Carmignano, and in the south, in Montepulciano, from 820 feet up to 1,800 feet. Other grape varieties, mostly white but also Pinot Noir, may be planted at higher altitudes where it gets too cold for Sangiovese. Tuscan whites are mainly from the Trebbiano, in whole or in part.

VINO NOBILE DI MONTEPULCIANO

Montepulciano (from the Latin *Mons Politianus*) is situated 40 minutes' drive east of Montalcino in the province of Siena and is the most inland of Tuscany's classic zones. It has the most continental climate, and its vineyards are at a generally higher altitude than those of its rivals. Like Montalcino, it is a zone

VIN SANTO

When you step from the blazing sun into the cool of a Tuscan farmhouse, this is what, according to tradition, you should be offered. Literally, "holy wine," vin santo is made by everyone with some spare Trebbiano or Malvasia grapes and room under the rafters in which to dry them on straw mats. The grapes are left to shrivel before crushing, usually between November and March (the longer they are left, the more concentrated the sugars will be and the sweeter the wine). After fermentation, the wine is aged in small sealed barrels for at least three years and sometimes for more than ten.

that runs on Sangiovese—here called Prugnolo Gentile. Montepulciano wine was a papal favorite as far back as the fourteenth century, and much of its production used to be controlled by the local nobility—hence the name Vino Nobile di Montepulciano. But by the 1980s there was precious little "Noble" about the wine. But, led by the producer Avignonesi and with the granting of DOCG status, there has been a gradual but continual improvement in the wine, and, from the best producers, this is a red with just a little more richness and less aggression than most of the top Brunellos and Chianti Classicos. Fewer producers here have a quality track record, but the signs are very encouraging, and the feeling is that Vino Nobile di Montepulciano is finally coming back into its own in the early years of the twenty-first century. As in Montalcino nearby, the introduction of the Rosso di Montepulciano DOC as essentially a second wine has given producers the chance of improving the selection for the grander Vino Nobile wine.

BOLGHERI

In 1978, a six-year-old Cabernet Sauvignon wine called Sassicaia won an astonishing victory over an assortment of illustrious Bordeaux Grands Crus in a tasting organized by *Decanter* magazine. It put Bolgheri on the map. Before that, no one would have dreamed that a Cabernet, let alone a great one, could conceivably hail from central Italy, nor that a high-quality wine of any kind could be produced from the once-malarial, low-lying Tuscan coast known as the northern Maremma or Costa degli Etruschi.

Bolgheri itself is an insignificant parish, or *frazione*, of the commune of Castagneto Carducci, a zone named after a pretty hilltop town a couple of miles to the south. That the region's prototype wine, Sassicaia, comes from an estate situated near Bolgheri is no doubt the reason for the honor of DOC being bestowed on the *frazione*

instead of the commune. Bolgheri DOC wines can come from anywhere in the commune of Castagneto, except the part nearest the sea, west of the Via Aurelia. But the influence of Sassicaia and Bolgheri extends much further, spreading along the coast northward to Montescudaio, in the province of Pisa, and south to Suvereto-Val di Cornia in Livorno.

In terms of a history, this wine zone hadn't really got one, until the 1968 Sassicaia burst on the scene. But things moved rapidly, with an emphasis on luxurious interpretations of the red Bordeaux grape varieties, led by Cabernet Sauvignon and Merlot. After Sassicaia, the next to take the plunge in the early 1980s was Lodovico Antinori (brother of Piero, and cousin of Niccolò Incisa of Sassicaia), planting Cabernet Sauvignon, Cabernet Franc, Merlot, and Sauvignon Blanc at his Ornellaia estate. His brother Piero followed suit at Tenuta Belvedere with a Cabernet/Merlot blend, Guado al Tasso. A few years ago another big name, Angelo Gaja, from Piedmont, also bought an estate in Bolgheri—Ca' Marcanda. In all, there's a very glitzy feel now to this formerly woe-begone coastal stretch. Sassicaia now has its own estate DOC (the only one in Italy), and the region's wines are, in general, rich, ripe, and veering toward the jetset of international Cabernets and Merlots in style, with just an occasional nod toward Sangiovese. Its whites, such as Vermentino or Sauvignon Blanc, are usually good.

SUPER-TUSCANS

In the early 1970s Tignanello and Sassicaia were the first so-called Super Tuscan wines, and wineries piled onto the bandwagon faster than you could count. The idea was to thwart the more restrictive aspects of Italian wine law by producing wines that flaunted their supposedly lowly *vino da tavola* status—and their extremely high prices. Tignanello comes from the Chianti Classico zone but is nearly all Sangiovese; Sassicaia, from Bolgheri near the coast, is a blend of Cabernet Sauvignon and Cabernet Franc. Both are aged in small oak barrels, a move that, to its detractors, smacked of distinctly un-Italian activity. The wines that followed were either entirely Sangiovese or from both Cabernets and/or Merlot and often a blend of all of them. The idea spread out of Tuscany to Piedmont and elsewhere in Italy. But with the passing of the Goria Law in 1992, the option of a *vino da tavola* tag disappeared.

Super Tuscan wines must now, if they want to display a vintage or provenance on the label, come under the wing of either the IGT or DOC laws. Sassicaia, ever the first, became DOC (as Bolgheri Sassicaia) with the 1994 vintage.

Chianti

RED GRAPES
The most important grape is Sangiovese. Canaiolo Nero and Colorino are also sometimes used in Chianti as well as increasing amounts of Cabernet and Merlot.

WHITE GRAPES
Trebbiano is widely planted but rapidly decreasing in importance. Chardonnay and Sauvignon Blanc are becoming more fashionable in varietal wines.

CLIMATE
The central hills of the Chianti Classico zone are cooler and more temperate than the coast.

SOIL
Stony calcareous soil is varied by parcels of limestone, sand, clay, and schist. In the heart of Chianti Classico, the shaly clay known as galestro gives wine with notably good body.

GEOGRAPHY
The region is characterized by sloping vineyard plots among woods and groves of olives. Altitude plays a key role in determining the style and quality of Chianti produced.

CHIANTI AS A PLACE SEDUCED ME from the first second. I alighted from the train at Florence station, marveled at the city, and then, within a few hours, headed off south into the hills of what I now know were the northern reaches of Chianti Classico. But the wine? Well, my first mouthful of gushing, prickly sour red-fruited wine on that trip—from an unmarked bottle in some farmer's field by the side of a silent road—was a revelation. The vast majority of Chianti wine that I drank until at least the mid-1990s tottered between dull and disgraceful. The change in quality and attitude at the end of the twentieth century and the start of the new millennium was nothing short of remarkable.

Chianti first came to prominence around the beginning of the thirteenth century. At the time, Florence was the banking capital of the world. Its bankers—the Medici and Frescobaldi families, among others—funded the warlike campaigns of most of the rulers of medieval Europe and became rich in the process. This wealth spilled out of the city into the countryside, where the great villas and estates that now lure tourists to these verdant hills in summer developed into agricultural properties. Because of the rocky soil, only the olive tree and the vine flourished, yet the latter's products were greatly appreciated in affluent Florentine society.

This wealthy market provided the impetus to the development of Chianti as a quality wine zone. By the beginning of the fifteenth century, Chianti's name was already established, and, as has happened the world over when a certain area attains fame, others tried to pass off their usually inferior products as the real thing. This led, in 1716, to the grand duke of Tuscany mapping out the borders of the zone in an attempt to prevent fraud. While delimiting the area, the grand duke also pushed the borders north from their original area toward Greve and Panzano. Such elasticity, however, did little to stanch the flow of ersatz Chianti that increased toward the end of the nineteenth century, when Chianti enjoyed a boom thanks to the shortage of wine created by phylloxera. By this time, virtually every Tuscan red wine, no matter what its provenance or history—and some, like those from Rufina, Carmignano, and Montepulciano, had histories every bit as noble—was being sold as Chianti. Many then argued that some legal definition was required to protect the name of Chianti, but this was generally ignored in the rush for sales. It was only several decades later, during the slump that inevitably followed the boom, that people began to think along these lines. This resulted in the Dalmasso Commission, whose report in 1932 led to new boundaries being established.

CHIANTI CLASSICO

The original zone was doubled in size to take in the lower-lying, clay-clogged hills closer to Florence and was renamed Chianti Classico. This new name distinguished it from the new Chianti zones created by appending to the name a broad geographical designation. In most cases, this was simply a matter of mopping up all the vineyards in a particular province, such as Florence or Siena, not already covered by another zone. It is an idiotic basis upon which to define a wine, although, having said that, virtually every vine in the great Bordeaux region of France can claim at very least, the Bordeaux appellation. Even so, it was confirmed by the DOC laws of 1967, reaffirmed when the DOCG was introduced in 1984, and remains in practice to this day. Given that DOCG is supposed to highlight superior quality in Italy, it hardly builds confidence in the category when even the most basic, mass-produced red from the decidely broad area of Chianti is given the DOCG certificate. Chianti Classico made a major commitment to improvement, particularly with an initiative called Chianti Classico 2000, which greatly improved the vineyards and helped Classico gain a separate DOCG in 1996. (This is not a subzone of the separate Chianti DOCG, whose seven zones are Colli Aretini, Colli Fiorentini, Colline Pisane, Colli Senesi, Montalbano, Montespertoli, and Rufina.) Many of Italy's finest reds are from the Classico region, as well as a smaller number from the other zones, but a lot of poor wine still comes out as Classico, and the standard of basic Chianti is rarely better than decent.

By extending the name of Chianti over vast tracts of Tuscany, from the green rolling hills of central Classico to the arid Sienese slopes, from the cool reaches of Rufina to the low-lying vineyards of the Colline Pisane, the Italian authorities have succeeded not only in confusing the adventurous wine drinker but also in robbing the growers of their individual identities.

You could say, given the diversity of soil, altitude, climate, and, to a lesser extent, varietal composition, that there are as many different styles of wine. Even within Classico, altitude varies between 490 and 1,800 feet, resulting in great temperature variations. The vineyards in the central

The historic estate of Badia a Coltibuono sits high up in the forests and hills near Gaiole in Chianti.

Classico hills are higher and cooler than those on the coast, one factor that gives finer, more perfumed wines. Proximity to forests, valleys, or rivers throws another complicating variable into the equation. The vineyards on the western flank of Classico, for instance, produce fuller wines than do their neighbors several miles nearer to the central part of the zone largely because of the warmth generated by the Val d'Elsa. In the Rufina zone, on the other hand, the cool breeze funneled down the Sieve Valley from the Apennines sets this tiny area apart, creating a unique mesoclimate and a distinctive style of wine.

But through all the variations in climate, soil, and altitude within the Chianti zone, there is one constant factor: the Sangiovese grape. This grape forms the mainstay of Chianti, being used on its own in some of the best wines, or blended with native varieties such as Canaiolo and Colorino, or international ones like Merlot and Cabernet, in others. In lesser wines, white grapes, such as Trebbiano and Malvasia, still occasionally find their way into the blend, remnants of the lean times in Tuscany, when they were used to boost production and render the wine lighter and ready for drinking sooner. As vineyards are replanted, however, the production of white grapes dwindles, and what's left is usually made into white wine.

WHAT A FIASCO

It's no longer an adolescent rite of passage, but it was when I was growing up. A nerve-wracking date in some dingy trattoria, plates of spaghetti with ragù, which you gamely tried to eat with a fork, and a straw-colored bottle (*fiasco* in Italian) of a pretty raw Italian red called Chianti. You could then take the bottle home and use it to hold candles. In fact, Chianti has a long history going back to the twelfth century, but their glass was always pretty delicate, so they were first covered in straw in the fifteenth century to protect them, and then given straw handles so that they could be easily carried. The first "Chianti" exports—then called red Florence—came over to England in flasks, but they weren't a success—perhaps because they were stored upright in chests, and the wine was topped with olive oil. The fragile glass neck was then stuffed with rags to stop the mixture from spilling.

Brunello di Montalcino

RED GRAPES
Brunello is another name for the Sangiovese of Chianti. Some producers have also made experimental plantings of Merlot and Cabernet for use in alternative wines.

WHITE GRAPES
Moscato Bianco is grown to produce Moscadello di Montalcino. Chardonnay and Sauvignon Blanc are also planted.

CLIMATE
The temperate hill climate benefits from the influence of the Tyrrhenian Sea, while nearby Mount Amiata offers protection from storms.

SOIL
The best vineyards are on the prized galestro or shaly clay.

GEOGRAPHY
The longest-lived wines come from the relatively cooler, higher vineyards found on the four major slopes that dominate Montalcino. Further plantings have recently been made on lower-lying terrain.

LEAVING BEHIND THE WOODED HILLS of Chianti and the ancient towers of Siena, and heading south toward Rome, I could be forgiven for thinking that I have seen the last of Tuscany's vines. The hills of the wide Val d'Orcia are parched brown, the heavy, clay soil proving more suitable to the cereals swaying in the southerly breeze than to the vine. The horizon is open, with only few gentle hills occasionally providing relief from an otherwise unbroken vista.

Then, just past Buonconvento, I turn to my right, and, as the road winds uphill, clay gives way to rocky *galestro*, vines replace wheat, and, at and altitude of about 1,9700 feet, I arrive in Montalcino, the town famed for its Brunello, Italy's longest-lived and, some would say, greatest wine. This town lives on and for wine. On the main street is a wonderful bar, the Fiaschetteria, serving any number of Brunellos by the glass as well as a wide selection of other wines. Some of the old-style Brunellos would positively benefit from a day or two open on the bar.

The renown enjoyed by Brunello is relatively recent. Indeed, it was only in the 1960s that whispers reached the outside world of wines of incredible longevity from the cellars of one producer in Montalcino called Biondi-Santi. The legendary 1891, tasted by few but lauded by all, put first Biondi-Santi and then Montalcino on the map. A legend was created, and the prices of Biondi-Santi wines climbed higher than Mount Olympus. Some producers able to sell their wines at half the price (still double what the better bottles of Chianti fetched) were happy to let Biondi-Santi set the pace. Others, eager to jump on the bandwagon, planted vineyards, increasing the area under vine from fewer than 250 acres in 1968 (soon after the Biondi-Santi-drafted DOC regulations came into force) to just under 4,950 acres today.

Despite this growth, the legend lives on, but there is no doubt that Montalcino is a zone with a great vocation for viticulture. Rising from a sea of clay, it is ringed by a protective wall of valleys—the Ombrone to the west, the Orcia to the south and east—and mountains, with the forbidding face of Mount Amiata standing guard on Montalcino's southern flank. These protect the vineyards from nasty weather and help make the Brunello zone the most arid of all Tuscany's wine areas, with only about 20 inches of rainfall a year. But cooling breezes blowing off the sea, a luxury neither Chianti nor Montepulciano enjoy, provide some relief.

The dry, hot climate brings the grapes to maturity more quickly than in the Chianti or Montepulciano zones. There are years when producers in Montalcino have their grapes safely in the fermenting vats, while their colleagues further in Tuscany are still struggling to complete picking their harvest amid the onset of fall rains. In overly hot years, however, the wines of Montalcino can be brutish in character and lacking any of the gentler tones found in the best Chiantis. Hot and dry are not always best in Montalcino.

Perhaps because of their stature, Montalcino wines have traditionally aged in large old oak barrels for a protracted period in order to temper their ferocious tannins. This has now largely been replaced by the use of small oak *barriques*, but because many of these wines proved to be losing some of their "Brunello" personality, there is once more a move back toward using large oak casks for at least some of the aging. A compulsory wood-aging period of four years was inserted into the DOC law in 1966, reduced in 1998 to two years in oak before release, followed by a minimum of four months in bottle. Even so, the total aging period before release remains four years.

This lengthy period may have been fine a generation or so ago when tastes were different, but in today's market it all too often results in the wines' freshness perishing under the onslaught of wood. True, Biondi-Santi's great old wines (made as recently as 1964 and 1975) were able to withstand the maximum of wood aging, and their high acidity also enabled them to age well in bottle. There are those today who reckon that even two years is too long in wood in a light vintage and that the total of four in wood and in bottle is absurd. Why shouldn't the consumer take responsibility for bottle aging the wines, they demand, as in the case of Bordeaux? Relaxing regulations would more closely reflect the already widely diverging styles of Brunello, although traditionalists already feel they've moved far enough.

STYLES OF BRUNELLO

Brunello's original claim to greatness was based on the wine's longevity (and an inflated price), and the so-called classic style—as exemplified by Biondi-Santi—is still made by producers in the center of the zone where the soil is *galestro*-rich and the vineyards are relatively high, at between 1,310 and 1,640 feet above sea level.

On more recently established estates in the northwest and northeast of the zone, producers such as Castiglion del Bosco, Caparzo, and Altesino have planted vineyards on clay soil not previously cultivated with vines. Although these wines are good, they often need to be given polish by adding a little something from vineyards around Sant' Angelo in Colle in the south or from the *galestro*-rich ones around Montosoli.

This diversity of wine styles in Brunello illustrates the limitless number of masks the old trouper Sangiovese has at its disposal. As part of the myth-management process, Montalcino producers, led by Biondi-Santi, propagated the theory that their particular subvariety of Sangiovese, called Brunello, was distinctive from and superior to those found elsewhere in Tuscany. But independent research showed that there were numerous clones of Sangiovese in Montalcino vineyards, so the growers adopted a new position, claiming that Brunello was a local name for the Tuscan grape, stemming from the fact that, in the hot, arid Montalcino summers, the grapes often acquired a brownish hue at ripening, hence Brunello, or "little brown one."

Moves by California growers to cash in on Montalcino's success by labeling their wines "Brunello" have since forced the Italian growers to renounce Brunello as a grape name, and today it is officially viewed by them as just a wine.

However that may be, the sole use of Sangiovese for their wines did make the producers of Montalcino unique in Tuscany. But now that others in Chianti and beyond are adopting the same approach and improving the quality of their raw materials, the Montalcino producers are having to fight to retain their preeminent position.

Realizing that selling their wines at high prices brings with it a certain responsibility with regard to quality, they set up a "junior" DOC called Rosso di Montalcino as far back as 1984, followed in 1996 by a much broader and more inclusive DOC called Sant' Antimo. These "junior" DOCs have proved particularly successful not only in maintaining the generally high standard of quality but also in giving a modern and more attractive range of red wines to widen the choice in Tuscany. Of course, if you can sell the wine younger, you get your money earlier, which should partly satisfy those hankering for an earlier release date for their wine.

SANGIOVESE

Sangiovese, the most widely planted grape variety in Italy, reaches its greatest heights in central Tuscany, especially in Montalcino, whose Brunello wine is supposed to be 100 percent varietal. This grape has a wide range of subvarieties, plus a growing number of "improved" clones. Much care is taken when replanting the vineyards, whether in Chianti Classico, Brunello di Montalcino, Vino Nobile di Montepulciano, or elsewhere. Styles of Sangiovese wines range from pale, lively, and cherryish, to vivacious midrange Chiantis, to excellent Riservas and top Tuscan blends; the dense red fruit often has a sweet-sour streak, a whiff of herbs, and the scratch of raw earth.

Emilia-Romagna's still reds are usually from Sangiovese, and most of the red wines of the Marche contain varying amounts of the grape. It is also important in Umbria, where it may be blended with the local star Sagrantino. Lazio and Campania can grow good Sangiovese, too. However, all too often outside Tuscany, Sangiovese is used as a filler for other more characterful local grape varieties. (Its blending with the rich, mouth-filling Montepulciano in the Marche is an obvious example.)

Southern Italy

RED GRAPES
Local grapes, such as Negroamaro, Primitivo, Uva di Troia, Gaglioppo, and Aglianico still feature.

WHITE GRAPES
Native varieties include Greco di Tufo, Fiano, Falanghina, and Greco di Bianco.

CLIMATE
The plains can be bakingly hot and arid, but in the Apennines the climate is almost alpine.

SOIL
The soil varies from calcareous, alluvial, and volcanic to clay, sand, and marl.

GEOGRAPHY
Altitude is important in determining vineyard sites and methods of vine training.

SOUTHERN ITALY IS THE SPIRITUAL HOME of Italian wine. The vine's first foothold on the peninsula was said to have been in the south, where it thrived as never before in any Mediterranean habitat. Indeed, such was its affinity for the hills and plains of southern Italy—whether the lower slopes of Mount Vulture in Basilicata, Puglia's Salento plains, or Calabria's Cirò—that the Greeks called their new colony Oenotria, or "Land of Vines."

An eerie sense of history pervades southern wines, both in the vineyard and in the cellar. The vines tend to be trained low in the freestanding *alberello*, or bush, system, a configuration said to have been imported by the Greeks, and the generous and exotic flavors of figs and spices found in grapes such as Negroamaro, Gaglioppo, and Aglianico evoke the vine's Mediterranean origins to a much greater extent than the cool, northern Italian wine flavors ever can, reflecting a tangible sense of an unbroken tradition stretching back three thousand years and beyond.

Phoenicians, Greeks, Romans, Normans, and Bourbons have all been seduced by the Mezzogiorno, Italy's south. It is a land of incomparable light, unbearable heat, unencumbered plenty, immovable indolence, and unbelievable corruption, a land blessed by the gods with opportunites squandered by man.

To people from the north—whether from Italy or Europe—it is a foreign land, full of scents of musk and sensuality. The industriousness that pervades northern European culture is lacking here, and life under the searing sun is taken at a more relaxed pace. Such a languid approach is often confused with lassitude, yet it is, along with a diet of fresh vegetables and pasta, responsible for giving modern southern Italians the longest life expectancy of any Europeans.

Unfortunately, this lackadaisical, if healthy, approach to living has meant that the southern vineyards were easy prey to focused, aggressive northerners. Historically, the Bourbon royal family, based in Naples, had supported local quality wines, but Italy's unification in 1861 saw northern merchants, intent on sourcing dark, ripe reds to bolster their pale northern brews, invade the south, and many ancient, heady, exotic wines disappeared into blending vats in Verona, Florence, and Alba. In addition, the traditional, low-yielding, bush-trained vines were often replaced over the century following unification by high-yielding, wire-trellised ones, and the great southern grapes were ripped up and replaced by the unsuitable Trebbiano and Sangiovese from further north, which ripened too quickly in the south, never developing much flavor in the process.

In the 1980s and '90s, the European Union embarked on one of its periodic attempts to reduce wine production by initiating a scheme to finance the uprooting of vineyards. This was supposed to reduce the amount of high-yielding vines that did nothing but pump diluted swill into the wine lake. Who were they kidding? Certainly not the majority of local peasant farmers who enthusiastically ripped out those difficult, low-yielding ancient bush vines on the hillsides that gave such backache whenever they had to be pruned or picked. But a fair number of growers resisted the lure of EU cash, and they, with today's modern winemaking technology, are now in a prime position to capitalize on the superior nature of their raw materials. Indeed, the rich inheritance of native

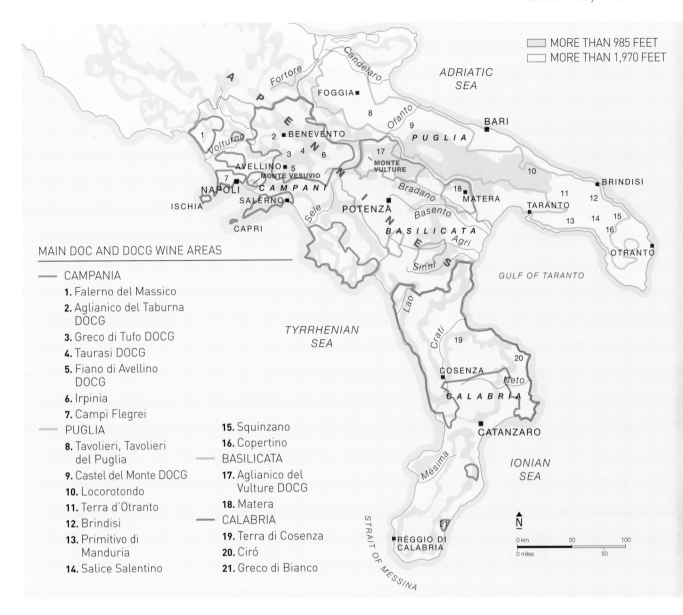

MORE THAN 985 FEET
MORE THAN 1,970 FEET

ADRIATIC SEA

FOGGIA

BENEVENTO

BARI

PUGLIA

AVELLINO

MONTE VESUVIO

MONTE VULTURE

BRINDISI

NAPOLI

CAMPANIA

SALERNO

MATERA

TARANTO

ISCHIA

POTENZA

OTRANTO

CAPRI

BASILICATA

GULF OF TARANTO

TYRRHENIAN SEA

COSENZA

CALABRIA

CATANZARO

IONIAN SEA

STRAIT OF MESSINA

RÉGGIO DI CALABRIA

N

0 km   50   100
0 miles   50

Fortore, Candelaro, Volturno, Ofanto, Bradano, Basento, Sele, Agri, Sinni, Lao, Crati, Neto, Mésima

MAIN DOC AND DOCG WINE AREAS

— CAMPANIA
  1. Falerno del Massico
  2. Aglianico del Taburna DOCG
  3. Greco di Tufo DOCG
  4. Taurasi DOCG
  5. Fiano di Avellino DOCG
  6. Irpinia
  7. Campi Flegrei
— PUGLIA
  8. Tavolieri, Tavolieri del Puglia
  9. Castel del Monte DOCG
  10. Locorotondo
  11. Terra d'Otranto
  12. Brindisi
  13. Primitivo di Manduria
  14. Salice Salentino
  15. Squinzano
  16. Copertino
— BASILICATA
  17. Aglianico del Vulture DOCG
  18. Matera
— CALABRIA
  19. Terra di Cosenza
  20. Ciró
  21. Greco di Bianco

grape varieties is now the South's greatest strength: few other wine regions grow such a range of individual varieties—including Aglianico, Falanghina, Fiano, Gaglioppo, Greco di Tufo, Mantonico, Montepulciano, Moscato, Negroamaro, Piedirosso, Primitivo, and Uva di Troia. These varieties, as the Greeks observed, are ideally suited to the varied terrain and climate of the South.

Altitude, topographical features, and proximity to the sea can all exert profound moderating influences on latitude and result in mesoclimates considerably cooler than one might predict in such a southern environment. On the slopes of Basilicata's Mount Vulture, for instance, Aglianico vines planted at 1,640 to 1,970 feet above sea level are, in late October, among the last in all Italy to be harvested. Such a long growing season results in wines which, with their fascinatingly complex flavors, belie their southern origins. In Campania's Apennine foothills, altitude similarly influences Taurasi (also made from Aglianico) and whites such as Greco di Tufo, Fiano, and Falanghina.

In other areas, however, it is proximity to the sea and its effect on the climate that tips the scales in favor of quality wine production. In Calabria's Cirò zone, for instance, cool breezes blowing off the Ionian Sea refresh the low-lying Gaglioppo vines, extending their growing season and resulting in the wonderful flavors of licorice, figs, and cumin found in the best wines.

Similarly in Puglia, on the flat Salento peninsula that comprises the heel of Italy's boot, the winds blowing between the Adriatic and Ionian seas alleviate what would otherwise be desert conditions and produce the ideal climate for strapping reds—Salice Salentino, Copertino, and Brindisi, among others—which can be some of Italy's most satisfying wines.

WINE REGIONS

Puglia is the South's most important wine region. Stretching almost 250 miles into the Adriatic, this mostly flat landscape produces some 15 percent of all Italian wine. Much of this bulk comes from northern Puglia, where high-trained Montepulciano, Sangiovese, and Trebbiano vines in the San Severo zone account for about 30 percent of Puglia's total DOC production. In central Puglia, the Uva di Troia grape forms the base for the Castel del Monte, Rosso Barletta, and Rosso Canosa DOCs, all of which have yet to realize their full potential. Quality remains patchy, yet occasionally I sample a really sumptuous mouthful, so, as I've been saying for a few years now, the promise for the future is great.

Further south, in the Salento peninsula itself, the bush-trained Negroamaro grape reigns supreme.

BACK TO THE FUTURE

Normally, when we talk of ancient Rome and ancient Greece and long to experience something of their lives, we have to make do with ruined temples, archaeological digs, mosaics, sculptures, gold plate, and coins. All wonderful, but not really alive. There's one way in which we can experience in live form something of these ancient times—a significant number of the grape varieties that the Greeks brought to Italy, which the Romans cultivated, are still here, producing crops every year that make wine for us to drink. Almost all of these varieties are in the far south of Italy, which has suffered until this century from antediluvian winemaking and an almost defunct wine culture. But a new wave of modernists has started to treasure these ancient vines and is now producing thrilling wines from them. Greco di Tufo—that name gives you a clue as to its Greek origins—is thought to be one of the varieties classified by Roman writer Pliny. Fiano could be another, as could the red Piedirosso—and they're all grown in Campania near Mount Vesuvius, giving excellent results. Aglianico is the star grape of Basilicata. It's a very ancient variety. Did it come from Greece? Did it make the famous Roman wine Falernian? Are the ancient Gaglioppo and Magliocco varieties indigenous, or are they Greek? The origins of Sicily's Nerello Mascalese, which creeps up the volcanic slopes of Mount Etna, are shrouded in mystery. But they're all ancient, and they're all now being turned into wines, red and white, that are thrillingly different in texture and flavor from those from better-known, modern varieties.

Because Negroamaro produces, as its name suggests, wines that are dark and bitter, Malvasia Nera is used to soften its rough edges and make the wines more supple and aromatic. This successful partnership works well in DOCs such as Salice Salentino, Copertino, Squinzano, Leverano, and Brindisi, where flavors of game, chocolate, and prunes are all wrapped up in a velvety texture and brushed with herb scent. Thanks to this partnership and some inspired winemaking, this once backward part of Puglia is now, along with the best areas of Sicily, the South's standard-bearer for quality wines.

In theory, this accolade should go to Aglianico del Vulture, Basilicata's best known DOC. The Aglianico grape is one of Italy's finest red varieties, and the long growing season in the hills south of Melfi provides it with an ideal stage on which to perform. But while the script is a classic, the performance tends to be amateurish. The young wines often have a thrillingly vibrant flavor, but, by the time they are bottled, they have become dull and flaccid. Only producers such as D'Angelo and Paternoster, plus relative newcomers like Basilico and Cantina del Notaio, score the odd hit.

Calabria forms the toe of the Italian boot, kicking out into the Ionian and Tyrrhenian seas and missing Sicily only by the two miles that are the Straits of Messina. With the exception of its 485-mile coastline, the whole region is wild and mountainous. Although such a terrain should provide many ideal vineyard sites—and in Greek times Calabria was noted for its high quality wines—little quality wine is produced here today other than by Librandi of Cirò on the Ionian side and Odoardi of Cosenza on the Tyrrhenian.

More than 90 percent of Calabria's DOC wine comes from the Cirò zone on the Ionian coast. The reds from the Gaglioppo grape tend to have less color and more tannin than those from Puglia's Negroamaro but display a similar broad range of exotic flavors. In recent years, the great advance here has been the introduction of temperature control in winemaking, resulting in wines with fresher, more defined flavors. The white wines of Cirò, made from an undistinguished member of the Greco family of grapes, have benefited to an even greater extent, although they are less distinctive than their red counterparts.

To the north of Calabria is Campania, bordered to the east by Basilicata and northern Puglia, to the north by Lazio and to the west by the Tyrrhenian Sea. Campania is better known for the beautiful Bay of Naples and Mount Vesuvius than for the intrinsic quality of its wines, but in the Apennine foothills, which slope gently from the inland mountainous peaks to the flat shoreline, there exists great potential that today is rapidly being turned into a reality. The grapes—reds such as Aglianico

The flat Salento peninsula in Puglia forms the heel of Italy and is now one of the most exciting parts of southern Italy for quality wines.

and Piedirosso and whites such as Fiano, Greco, and Falanghina—are in place, and the cool hills of northern and central Campania provide ideal conditions for them to flourish. For most of the past four decades, the venerable Mastroberardino was the only decent producer in Campania, creating the reputation of the Taurasi DOCG and the Aglicanico grape, but today we are witnessing an explosion of good to outstanding producers in Campania making some exciting wines, led by Feudi di San Gregorio and including Antonio Caggiano, De Conciliis, Galardi, Montevetrano, Terredora, Cantina del Taburno, and Villa Matilde. Even one of the ancient Romans' star wines, Falernian, has been revived as the Falerno del Massico DOC, and the wines look promising.

Sardinia

RED GRAPES
Cannonau, Monica, and Carignano are the most important traditional varieties.

WHITE GRAPES
Vermentino in Gallura produces the best wine, but Nuragus accounts for one-third of vineyard plantings. Other significant varieties are Torbato, Vernaccia di Oristano, and Malvasia Sarda.

CLIMATE
Sardinia has ample sunshine. The south and west are exposed to hot winds from Africa. Drought can be a problem away from the influence of the mountains.

SOIL
Most of Sardinia consists of granite and volcanic rock. The remainder includes calcareous deposits, alluvial sand, gravel, and clay.

GEOGRAPHY
The better wines come from the hills, but many new vineyards are in regions that are flat and dry.

CONSIDERING THAT IT IS the second largest island in the Mediterranean, Sardinia remains relatively unknown to outsiders. It is also remarkable, given its strategic importance, that while often subjected to long periods of foreign domination, the island was rarely conquered. The feeling of strangeness often experienced by visitors is enhanced by the local use of the Sardu dialect—an amalgam of Catalan, Spanish, Italian, and Arabic on a Latin foundation.

Sardinia's wines are considerably less well known than the rugged coastline, golden beaches, and azure seas of the beautiful Costa Smeralda peninsula in the far north of the island, and few tourists venture into the wild, mountainous interior where people scrape a living by tending their goats and sheep. These mountains, hills, and plateaus would be well-suited to quality winemaking, but most of Sardinia's vineyards are planted by growers who choose the easy option of planting on the Campidano plain between Cagliari and Oristano and on the flatlands near Alghero.

Certainly, the wines don't conform to a typical Italian wine style, but that's not surprising because Sardinia has undergone considerable periods of foreign domination, not least by the Aragonese, who arrived, along with grape varieties and their wine styles, in the fourteenth century. Sardinia was transferred to the

Vineyards belonging to Argiolas near Cagliari. Argiolas is the star producer on the island, leading the way in making lighter, modern table wines instead of the strapping reds and dark alcoholic fortifieds of previously.

Piedmontese House of Savoy in 1718, thus becoming a part of the future Italy, but by this time, the Spanish grape varieties and wine styles were well established.

GRAPE VARIETIES AND WINE STYLES

The strong sense of separation from the rest of Italy is reflected in the grapes grown on the island. Although several varieties are indigenous, some of the most important ones come from Spain, fostered by the Aragonese who arrived on the island in the fourteenth century. The best known varieties are Cannonau (Garnacha) and Carignano (Cariñena) and confirmed the popular wisdom that a hot maritime climate is best suited to big strong apéritif and dessert wines and strapping, hot climate reds. Here, Sardinia has one of its few points in common with Sicily.

For a period there was an effort to modernize on behalf of the island's cooperatives, which account for 60 percent of Sardinia's production. This resulted in large quantities of high-yield anonymous whites, but things have now balanced out, and a number of fresh, dry fruity whites are being made from such grapes as Nuragus and Vermentino, the best of the latter coming from the stony soil of inland Gallura.

Putting new trends aside, the most distinctive wines continue to be those traditional oddities for which Sardinia was once best known. Vernaccia di Oristano develops a light film of flor yeast in cask, similar to that found in Sherry production, which prevents spoilage while imparting a distinctive spiced and nutty character. The history of this wine dates back at least to the sixteenth century, when it was widely appreciated throughout Italy, and it can come either fortified or not. Nasco, made from the grape of the same name, is another rare delight that can also be fortified and comes in dry, medium-dry or sweet styles.

Malvasia di Bosa, too, can be vinified in different ways; it depends on the winemaker. It may be a sweet or dry apéritif or else a fortified wine. Sometimes, like Vernaccia di Oristano, a film of flor yeast might be allowed to develop in cask for added flavor and complexity. Malvasia di Cagliari can likewise be made sweet or fortified but is generally considered best as a delicate dry apéritif. Carignano del Sulcis is a tasty red from the southwest. The red Cannonau is usually made into a dry table wine, but it can make a glorious, sweet, mouth-filling dessert wine of real quality, the best known example of which is Sella & Mosca's Anghelu Ruju. Apart from these fascinating specialities, most wine from the island is fairly run-of-the-mill, but because most of the island's treasures rarely get exported, there's enough to work on.

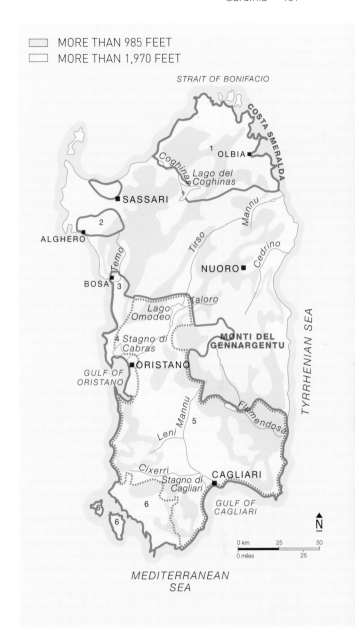

MORE THAN 985 FEET
MORE THAN 1,970 FEET

MAIN DOC AND DOCG WINE AREAS

— Cannonau di Sardegna, Monica di Sardegna, Moscato di Sardegna, and Vermentino di Sardegna DOCs cover the whole island
1. Vermentino di Gallura DOCG
2. Alghero
3. Malvasia di Bosa
4. Vernaccia di Oristano
5. Giro di Cagliari, Malvasia di Cagliari, Moscato di Cagliari, Monica di Cagliari, Nasco di Cagliari, Nuragas di Cagliari
6. Carignano del Sulcis

Sicily

RED GRAPES
The best red variety is Nero d'Avola (Calabrese), followed by Nerello. Others are Frappato di Vittoria and Perricone (Pignatello).

WHITE GRAPES
Forty percent of Sicily's vineyards are planted with Catarratto Bianco. Trebbiano Toscano is also widespread. Inzolia and Carricante thrive, but Grecanico is declining and Zibibbo is often grown as a table grape.

CLIMATE
Rainfall is scarce throughout much of the island, and the south is particularly arid. The north and east are cooler and less prone to drought.

SOIL
Near Etna, soil naturally is volcanic. Elsewhere, it ranges from chalky clay to limestone.

GEOGRAPHY

The best vineyards are found on the cooler slopes in the north and east. The most extensive vineyard area in Italy is on the plain and low hills surrounding Trapani.

WHEN I THINK OF SICILY, I am transported back to the haunting ancient Greek temple and theater at Segesta, near Alcamo, or I can see again the inspiring medieval mosaics in Monreale Cathedral above Palermo. My first ever job offer was as a baritone with Opera Massima in Palermo. They don't know how lucky they are that I turned to wine. But, unfortunately, ask anyone what they associate with this beautiful island, which has lovely beaches and remarkable art and architecture, and nine of ten people will probably mention the Mafia. The traditions of winemaking on the island go back to antiquity and reached dizzy heights in the late eighteenth century, when the English first created Marsala. But as fortified wines became less fashionable, Sicily was sidetracked. Now its fortunes are looking up again with the advent of some of Italy's most individual table wines.

The north of Sicily is dominated by the tail end of the Apennines, which sweep down through the entire length of Italy. Here, it can be cool with good rainfall, but enough sun to ensure ideal conditions for grapes to ripen. The south consists mainly of arid, scrubby hills where irrigation is essential, and the east is dominated by the brooding presence of the volcano Mount Etna, so it is not surprising that much of the island's soil is volcanic. The south and east are less well-favored, lying in the path of hot winds blowing straight from North Africa. Paradoxically, the coolest vineyards, on the slopes of Etna, overlook Catania, one of the hottest cities in Italy. The heart of Sicily provides first-class conditions for vines with cool, high altitudes and mixed volcanic, clay, and limestone soil. In the west lies the greatest expanse of vineyards not only in Sicily but in all Italy. Here the hot, dry climate and generally arid conditions lead to highly concentrated wines ideal for Marsala.

Sicily's wine reputation was built on its dessert and fortified wines, and these still show great depth, style, and complexity. Best known until it declined in both popularity and quality was Marsala, once again achieving great heights after an overhaul of the rules governing its production. Try dismissing all thoughts of Marsala as a wine fit only for sauce in some local Italian restaurant, and taste a dry, or *vergine*, version. It will come as a revelation. Marsala comes in various styles and levels of sweetness and can be made from different grapes, including Grillo, Catarratto, Inzolia, and Damaschino. Grillo is thought to have migrated to Sicily in the nineteenth century, but the others have been around since early times.

The sweet tradition is further reflected in a fascinating range of luscious wines made from either Moscato or Malvasia. The most northerly of these comes from the Aeolian or Lipari Islands and is called Malvasia delle Lipari. It is naturally sweet with an exquisite bouquet. On the other side of Sicily, close to Tunisia, lies the sun-baked volcanic island of Pantelleria. Here, the rich, intense wine is made from dried and concentrated Moscato grapes known locally as Zibibbo. In between these two geographic extremes come the rare Moscato di Noto and Moscato di Siracusa.

Table wines have improved out of all proportion in the last generation to the extent that some of Italy's finest red wines are now made here. The best tend to be based on the native Nero d'Avola and the best whites on Inzolia.

In a region where 90 percent of the output comes from cooperatives, it is usually the private producers who achieve the best quality. It is refreshing to find that Sicilians remain largely faithful to their traditional vine types, although Cabernet, Merlot, and Chardonnay have all made inroads, and Syrah, reckoned by Sicilians to be the cousin of, if not derived from, Nero d'Avola, is fairly widely planted. The downside is that only a small percentage of Sicilian wine qualifies for DOC or IGT (in some cases by choice of the producers). One of the best that does is Cerasuolo di Vittoria from the southeast of Sicily, a deep cherry-colored red made mainly from Frappato and Nero d'Avola grapes and promoted to DOCG in 2005. Some of the better known DOCs include Bianco d'Alcamo, which can show real class, although it is too often watery and anonymous. Faro, further north, was undistinguished until the excellent Palari came on the scene, while both red and white Etna can be terrific in the hands of a dedicated producer like Benanti. Etna is Sicily's most fashionable wine region with ancient terraced vineyards, at up to 3,280 feet high, of old Nerello Mascalese producing pale, vaguely smoky reds likened by some to Pinot Noir. Carricante makes excellent whites.

The combination of numerous cooperatives, political corruption, and lack of quality meant that, until this century, the two wine names most widely known outside Sicily were Corvo from the state-owned Duca di Salaparuta—large volumes of adequate red and white plus some excellent special selections—and Regaleali from Tasca d'Almerita, capable of world-class wines. Sicily has emerged with a renewed spirit and firms such as Planeta, Donnafugata, and Abbazia Santa Anastasia have achieved deserved international recognition.

Modern-thinking wineries, using both international and local grape varieties are spreading all over the island, and the trend is toward quality not quantity. These vineyards in the center of the island belong to the excellent Tasca d'Almerita estate.

MAIN DOC AND DOCG WINE AREAS

— Sicilia DOC covers the whole island
······ **1.** Marsala
     2. Alcamo
     3. Contessa Entellina
     4. Contea di Sclafani
     5. Faro
     6. Etna
     7. Siracusa
     8. Noto
     9. Vittoria, Cerasuolo di Vittoria DOCG
     10. Malvasia delle Lipari
     11. Moscato di Pantelleria, Passito di Pantelleria

Spain

In the upper Ebro Valley, the Rioja vineyards stretch away past the hilltop town of Laguardia to the Sierra de Cantabria mountains, which form an impressive backdrop along the northern edge of the Rioja region.

The late 1990s provided a dramatic turnaround in the quality of Spain's long-neglected wines and also in the international perception of the many Spanish regions that had long been overshadowed by the indomitable duo of Jerez/Sherry and Rioja. A drastic modernization of winemaking technology finally allowed regions such as Priorat, Ribera del Duero, La Mancha, Rueda, and Toro to muscle into the limelight with potent fruit-driven wines with the impact and style to convert the modern consumer.

Spain is far hotter and drier than its more famous wine neighbor, France, so the variation in local climates is less, and the range of grapes that find conditions ideal is limited. It has taken her a long while to appreciate the need to search out mesoclimates influenced by altitude and by maritime cooling conditions. It also has taken her some time to realize that hot-climate grapes, such as Garnacha, Cariñena, Tempranillo, Verdejo, and Monastrell, can produce delicious flavors if approached with up-to-the-minute New World technology and attitudes.

The lush, hilly northwest is heavily influenced by cool, damp Atlantic conditions, and the fragrant whites and tangy, juicy reds are marvelously individual. Further south, along the Duero River, are some of Spain's most exciting reds and whites. Andalucía in the southwest doesn't have much to offer in terms of table wines, but the fortified wines of Jerez and Montilla-Moriles can be among the world's greatest. In the large area of the Levante, stretching between Alicante and Valencia and the vast plateau of La Mancha and Valdepeñas inland, to the south of Madrid, the enormous potential for low-priced, attractive wine is at last being realized as the giant wine companies modernize their wineries, their techniques, and their desire to please.

The northeast has traditionally been seen as the quality wine capital of Spain, with famous reds and whites from Rioja and Penedès and Cava sparklers. But here, too, the winds of change are blowing, and areas such as Navarra, Somontano, Campo de Borja, and Costers del Segre are making thrilling contributions to the new, exciting Spain. After a long wait in the shadows of nations such as Italy and France, the twenty-first century could finally be Spain's century.

The Wine Regions of Spain

THERE WAS A TIME IN THE 1980s when much of Spain's wine was desperately mediocre and we turned right around and headed east to Central Europe for wine bargains and to the New World for more exotic bottles. But in the 1990s, across the Iberian peninsula, new equipment, the replanting of vineyards with better varieties, as well as disease-free vines and the use of highly trained enologists, some from abroad, often from Australia, all helped jump-start Spanish winemaking.

Spain's rich treasure trove of native grapes—Tempranillo, under many local pseudonyms, and Albariño are the best known—and her assortment of unique wine styles (from Sherry to red Rioja and Priorat and Galicia's whites) are now being recognized worldwide. It's almost as though Spain's time has finally come at exactly the moment when her food and cooking have taken the world by storm. Spanish food needs Spanish wine.

Look at the varied landscape of the wine regions: the broad Duero valley, the rocky foothills of the cool Pyrenees, the hillside pastures of Galicia, the scorching, stony central plains of La Mancha, or the baked white plains of Jerez in Andalucía. It seems that, however much the landscape and climate alter, there are always vineyards—indeed, Spain has the world's largest acreage under vine. But it is not the world's largest wine producer. Spain long relied on very low-yielding, dry-farmed old vineyards. New plantings and the now legal drip irrigation have changed all that.

Spain's main geographical features are the huge plateau, or *meseta*, in its center and high mountains rising steeply from the coast around and across this plateau—the Pyrenees, the Cantabrian mountains, the Iberian range, and the sierras Nevada, Guadarrama, and Morena being the main ones. Not surprisingly, there are several climates in this large, diverse country, from cool uplands to coastal Mediterranean and Atlantic belts and, inland in the high *meseta*, arid semidesert with its extremes of temperature.

Variety is the key to Spain's wine regions, and starting in the northeast, important vineyard areas are found within Navarra, Aragón, and Catalonia. Nestling up to Navarra is La Rioja, with its world-famous wine from the upper Ebro Valley, and over to the east in Catalonia vineyards are divided between many small demarcated areas, such as Priorat, with its powerful reds.

The northwest is known as "green" Spain, because of its Atlantic climate and high rainfall. Perched above the Portuguese border are the rainy regions of Rías Baixas, producing some of Spain's most fragrant whites from

CLASSIFICATIONS

New European Union rules about wine classification are causing havoc because former appellations have been allowed to continue or adopt the new name, as they want:

» Basic, generic wine, formerly known as **Vino de Mesa** (table wine) may now be called simply **Vino** (wine) and may include grape varieties and vintage on the label. Most producers have switched to the new name.

» **Vino de la Tierra** or VT (country wine) with a geographical designation may now appear as **Indicación Geográfica Protegida** (IGP) or **Vino de Calidad**.

» **Denominación de Origen** (DO), the main classification for wines from demarcated regions, can now be called **Denominación de Origen Protegida** (DOP), but only recently created appellations are using this; the older ones, for now, are not.

» **Denominación de Origen Calificada** (DOCa) is a super-category. Only two regions (Rioja and Priorat) have been promoted.

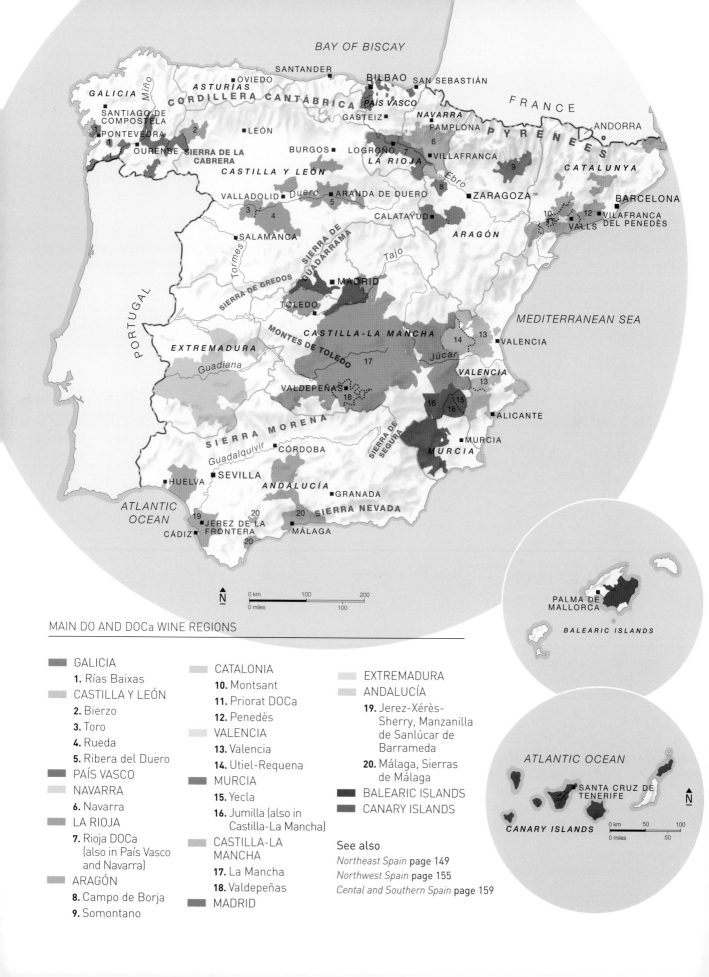

BAY OF BISCAY

SANTANDER
SANTIAGO DE COMPOSTELA
OVIEDO
BILBAO
SAN SEBASTIÁN
GALICIA
ASTURIAS
CORDILLERA CANTÁBRICA
PAÍS VASCO
FRANCE
PONTEVEDRA
Miño
GASTEIZ
NAVARRA
PAMPLONA
ANDORRA
OURENSE
SIERRA DE LA CABRERA
LEÓN
BURGOS
LOGROÑO
VILLAFRANCA
PYRENEES
CASTILLA Y LEÓN
LA RIOJA
CATALUNYA
VALLADOLID
Duero
ARANDA DE DUERO
Ebro
ZARAGOZA
BARCELONA
CALATAYUD
ARAGÓN
VALLS
VILAFRANCA DEL PENEDÉS
SALAMANCA
SIERRA DE GUADARRAMA
Tormes
SIERRA DE GREDOS
Tajo
MADRID
MEDITERRANEAN SEA
TOLEDO
Júcar
VALENCIA
EXTREMADURA
MONTES DE TOLEDO
CASTILLA-LA MANCHA
VALENCIA
Guadiana
VALDEPEÑAS
ALICANTE
SIERRA MORENA
SIERRA DE SEGURA
MURCIA
MURCIA
Guadalquivir
CÓRDOBA
HUELVA
SEVILLA
ANDALUCÍA
GRANADA
ATLANTIC OCEAN
SIERRA NEVADA
JEREZ DE LA FRONTERA
CÁDIZ
MÁLAGA

N
0 km 100 200
0 miles 100

PALMA DE MALLORCA
BALEARIC ISLANDS

ATLANTIC OCEAN
SANTA CRUZ DE TENERIFE
CANARY ISLANDS
N
0 km 50 100
0 miles 50

MAIN DO AND DOCa WINE REGIONS

GALICIA
1. Rías Baixas
CASTILLA Y LEÓN
2. Bierzo
3. Toro
4. Rueda
5. Ribera del Duero
PAÍS VASCO
NAVARRA
6. Navarra
LA RIOJA
7. Rioja DOCa (also in País Vasco and Navarra)
ARAGÓN
8. Campo de Borja
9. Somontano

CATALONIA
10. Montsant
11. Priorat DOCa
12. Penedès
VALENCIA
13. Valencia
14. Utiel-Requena
MURCIA
15. Yecla
16. Jumilla (also in Castilla-La Mancha)
CASTILLA-LA MANCHA
17. La Mancha
18. Valdepeñas
MADRID

EXTREMADURA
ANDALUCÍA
19. Jerez-Xérès-Sherry, Manzanilla de Sanlúcar de Barrameda
20. Málaga, Sierras de Málaga
BALEARIC ISLANDS
CANARY ISLANDS

See also
Northeast Spain page 149
Northwest Spain page 155
Cental and Southern Spain page 159

OUT IN THE ATLANTIC

Out in the Atlantic Ocean off the coast of Morocco, the Canary Islands have a treasure trove of pre-phylloxera vines, reputedly Europe's highest vineyards, and a total of ten DOs. Of course, I have fond memories of Canary wine. I used to call for a "cup of Canary" every night when I was playing Sir Toby Belch in Shakespeare's *Twelfth Night*. The only Canary wine of any repute used to come come from the gray volcanic sands of Lanzarote, but all over the islands plots of hundred-year-old vines are being revived, indigenous grape varieties are being rediscovered, and modern winemaking is producing some delicious reds and whites. Whites outnumber reds, but I have reveled in some truly irresistible reds from Tenerife. The La Palma DO and the sweet Malvasia from Lanzarote DO are also worth a try.

Volcanic soil and stone windbreaks protect the vines in winter on the island of Lanzarote.

Albariño, and Ribeiro, a pretty, hilly area with rapidly improving wines. On the north coast, the traditional wine of the Basque seaboard, Txakolí, is produced in three País Vasco DOs. In Castilla y León, through which the Duero River makes its way to Portugal (to become the Douro), is the harsh region of Toro, best for its red wines, and Rueda, producer of fresh whites. Just beyond is Ribera del Duero, literally, "the banks of the Douro," a high pine-strewn, undulating red wine region of world wide renown.

Down in central Spain, the land is as hot and baked as you will find anywhere in Europe. Castilla-La Mancha stretches out to form a huge, arid plateau of windmills and vines, alternately whipped by cold winters and scorched by impossibly hot summers. It is dry and mostly inhospitable, but more than half of Spain's vineyards are in this region. La Mancha encompasses the Valdepeñas DO, and they are increasingly known for highly drinkable red wines.

Over to the east are the regions of Valencia and Murcia, once known just for grapey Moscatels and blending wines but now showing real potential for reds. In particular, the local grape Monastrell (France's Mourvèdre) has been rediscovered and is shining in Jumilla, while Bobal is showing what it can do in Manchuela.

To the west, the sweet Málaga wines are, alas, becoming less and less important these days. Montilla-Moriles is another sunbaked area where white soil and Pedro Ximénez grapes create Sherry look-alikes. The real thing is produced further west in Jerez, where vast, gently sloping vineyards cover areas of chalky white *albariza* soil.

Finally, the wine produced on the vacation islands has really taken off with the emphasis on local grape varieties. Binissalem on the island of Mallorca is the main Balearic wine area, while the winemakers in the Canaries have recently gained DO status in numerous areas.

Tempranillo is Spain's best native red grape variety and goes by myriad names in different regions of the country. The wine can be deliciously fruity when young, but it also matures well, and its flavors blend easily with oak, as in Rioja.

Northeast Spain

RED GRAPES
Tempranillo, Garnacha Tinta, Cariñena, Monastrell, Moristel, and Graciano are the main ones. Cabernet Sauvignon and Merlot are also grown.

WHITE GRAPES
Macabeo (Viura), Garnacha Blanca, Xarel-lo, Parellada, Malvasía are the principal varieties, with some Chardonnay.

CLIMATE
This varies, from the damp northern Basque coastline to the pleasant moderate conditions of Rioja and the Catalan coastline, to the semiarid parts of southern Aragón and inland Catalonia.

SOIL
These are very varied, from the reddish-brown limestone of Navarra and Cariñena to the calcareous clay of parts of Rioja and Penedès chalk.

GEOGRAPHY
Vineyards are found on flat plateau land, coastal hills, and high inland terraces.

I MUST HAVE WANDERED THROUGH northeastern Spain more than most parts of Europe. I have traversed the Pyrenees—west to east, not just north to south—in and out of France and Spain, along tiny mountain roads, touching on Navarra and Huesca, but every time the broad, flat prairies of the Ebro Valley get too oppressive, I hightail it back to the hills. The northeast in general is endowed with widely differing conditions. You couldn't get much more different than the straggly dribs and drabs of vines that half-ripen in the damp, cool hills near San Sebastián and suck their moisture directly off the Bay of Biscay. Just south of these Basque vines the Cantabria Mountains soar, soaking up most of the rest of the moisture that rolls in from the Bay of Biscay. They act as vital protection for Rioja's and Navarra's vineyards, without which grapes such as Tempranillo and Garnacha would never ripen.

The Pyrenees, which act as the border with France, provide water for irrigation from the many rivers that hurtle out of the foothills before joining the Ebro and heading east for the Mediterranean. Without them, much of Aragón and western Catalonia would be almost desert. Indeed, it's surprising how close you get to the Mediterranean before the landscape relaxes and the hills become less jagged. It's a fairly narrow coastal strip from the French border down through Barcelona to the mouth of the Ebro below Tarragona, but the Catalans characteristically make use of every inch of land they've got.

PAÍS VASCO

Where better to start a tour around northeast Spain than in the country's tiniest DOs, those of Getariako Txakolina (Chacolí de Guetaria in Spanish), Bizkaiko Txakolina (Chacolí de Vizkaia), and Arabako Txakolina (Chacolí de Álava) in the Basque region. Here, on Spain's Cantabrian coast, the climate is exceedingly damp—about 63 inches of rain falls each year. It's also pretty cool, but that doesn't stop the locals farming a small number of vines of the local grape, Hondarribi Zuri, from which they make the traditional sharp, featherlight Basque white wine usually quaffed locally with fresh Atlantic seafood. A small amount of red wine is also made, from Hondarribi Beltza. In this damp region where fungal diseases quickly take hold, the vines are traditionally grown on overhead trellises.

The finest Basque vineyards lie in the south of the region in the Alava province. Not all Rioja vineyards are in the region of Rioja. Indeed, some of the best Rioja vineyards of all are in the Rioja Alavesa sub-region, which is in the Basque region (page 152).

NAVARRA

This large region used to be best known for its *rosado* wine from the Garnacha grape, but Navarra's progress over the past decade has been an example to the rest of Spain. New technology, plus better vineyard management on Navarra's soft, deep, fertile soil, has begun to coax excellent results out of traditional red Garnacha and, increasingly, Tempranillo, Merlot, and Cabernet Sauvignon.

BAY OF BISCAY

☐ MORE THAN 1,640 FEET
▨ MORE THAN 3,280 FEET

FRANCE

BILBÃO · SAN SEBASTIÁN
PAÍS VASCO
1
GASTEIZ · PAMPLONA
SIERRA DE
HARO · CANTABRIA · NAVARRA
CENICERO · OLITE 2
LOGROÑO 3 · Aragón
LA RIOJA · VILLAFRANCA
ALFARO

PYRENEES
ANDORRA
FIGUERES
HUESCA · BARBASTRO 4 · Segre · CATALUNYA · Ter · GIRONA
9
BORJA · Gállego · Cinca · 9 · LLEIDA · SANT SADURNÍ D'ANOIA
5 · ZARAGOZA · 9 · 8 · BARCELONA
CASTILLA Y LEÓN
Jalón · Huerva · Ebro · 10 · 11 · VILAFRANCA DEL PENEDÈS
CALATAYUD · 7 · CARIÑENA · 13 · VALLS
6 · 12 · FALSET · TARRAGONA
ARAGÓN · 14
CASTILLA-LA MANCHA
MEDITERRANEAN SEA
VALENCIA

0 km 50 100
0 miles 50

PALMA DE MALLORCA
BALEARIC ISLANDS
0 km 50 100
0 miles 50

MAIN DO AND DOCA WINE REGIONS

— PAÍS VASCO
1. Getariako Txakolina/ Chacolí de Getaria

— NAVARRA
2. Navarra

— LA RIOJA
3. Rioja DOCa (also in País Vasco and Navarra)

— ARAGÓN
4. Somontano
5. Campo de Borja
6. Calatayud
7. Cariñena

— CATALONIA
8. Alella

9. Costers del Segre
10. Conca de Barberà
11. Penedès
12. Priorat DOCa
13. Montsant
14. Terra Alta
— BALEARIC ISLANDS

The large Rioja region has more than four hundred producers, some traditional, some modernist, and some terroirists emphasizing single-vineyard wines. Such a ferment has brought with it plenty of buzz and investment, and stunning new winery buildings are springing up all over the region. This is the Bodegas Ysios winery at Laguardia.

The officially funded experimental winery Evena, at Olite, is one of the most important in Europe. Navarra has the potential to rival neighboring Rioja and, with a wider range of grape varieties, perhaps to outshine it.

LA RIOJA

The province of La Rioja has just one classified wine— Rioja—but in 1991 it was the first in Spain to be awarded the new super-category of DOCa, higher than DO. Rioja's three subregions—Rioja Alta, Rioja Alavesa, and Rioja Baja—span a segment of the upper Ebro Valley between Haro and Alfaro, with Rioja's capital Logroño marking its center point. I deal with Rioja in more detail on pages 152–153.

South of the Sierra de Cantabria, the climate feels more Mediterranean and Rioja is sunny enough to merit a high number of second homes for those who live in the large industrialized cities of Bilbao and San Sebastián north of the mountains. When you've experienced Bilbao rainfall, you'll see why.

ARAGÓN

The former kingdom of Aragón takes in a good part of the Spanish Pyrenees in the far north of Spain and reaches as far south as Valencia and Castilla-La Mancha. The long Ebro River runs southeast through the region, and the vineyards are situated around the edges of the wide, Ebro Valley. The main wine regions are in the southwest part of Aragón and are all primarily beefy red wine producers, using Garnacha grape above all. In what are pretty harsh, continental conditions of hot, dry summers and long, icy winters, along with a dry wind from the north, Garnacha can ripen superhumanly, though modern producers try to keep the wines to 14 percent alcohol or so. The wines used to be uninspiring stuff, but standards are rising. Although many wines are still pretty fearsome, there is a wave of utterly delightful, crunchy, fruity, unoaked Garnacha that make tremendous drinking. There are also plantings of Tempranillo, Mazuelo, Cabernet Sauvignon, and Merlot.

Calatayud DO, cut off from the Ebro Valley by several small mountain ranges, is the farthest west of these zones, and Cariñena and Campo de Borja are further north next to Navarra. There is one completely different Aragón DO. Somontano DO is up in the Pyrenean foothills (its name means "under the mountains"), and little mountain streams and high rainfall keep this area greener than those to the south. Here, international grapes such as Chardonnay, Pinot Noir, and Merlot mingle with traditional local varieties such as Moristel and Tempranillo.

CATALONIA

The thriving city of Barcelona and its hinterland has made Catalonia one of Spain's most prosperous regions, whose independence of spirit and strong cultural tradition is symbolized by the existence of an official second language, Catalan. The cluster of wine regions along the coastal belt show Catalonia, with its warm Mediterranean climate, to be an important part of Spain's wine story. Much of its wine prosperity is based on Cava, but Penedès, as well as being the heart of Cava production, is also well-known for good reds and whites.

Catalonia has a great deal of rugged mountain landscape: the Pyrenees dominate the north region, and mountains hem in the Mediterranean coast all the way south. The coastal zone, where many of the vineyards are situated, some even within sight of the glistening sea, enjoys a mild Mediterranean climate, but, as you travel inland toward Aragón, the climate becomes more continental, with hotter summers and colder winters.

The Penedès DO provides the widest variety of wine styles in this part of Spain partly because it has three very specific wine zones. Bajo Penedès is down toward the sea and and makes mostly beefy reds. Medio Penedès further inland is the heartland of the sparkling wine Cava industry and grows mainly white grapes. The cool conditions in Penedés Superior are good for fresh, modern whites. With such a wide range of growing conditions and the mighty city of Barcelona nearby to soak up its wines, you would have expected Penedès to be a quality leader for Spanish wine. But despite being the home of Miguel Torres, Spain's most innovative wine figure in the twentieth century and, despite—or perhaps because of—the success of the Cava

CAVA

Cava, the Spanish name for Champagne-method fizz, can legally be made in many parts of Spain, although in fact most wines come from Penedès in Catalonia. The standard of Cava has improved hugely in recent years— at least to foreign tastes. The Spanish used to revel in its slightly rooty, earthy flavors; now they are getting used to greater freshness and fruit. The grapes used— principally Parellada, Xarel-lo, and Macabeo—are not the world's best by a long way, and a dash of Chardonnay can perk up a blend to no end. The best-value, fruitiest Cavas are generally the youngest, with no more than the minimum nine months of aging and based on Parellada Those with more Xarel-lo are deeper, almost chewy, serious wine with bubbles.

sparkling wine industry, relatively few thrilling wines have emerged. In red wines, the focus has shifted further southwest to Priorat and Monsant.

Priorat, Monsant, and Terra Alta are relatively inaccessible inland areas in Catalonia's south. Rugged mountains form a backdrop to the small terraced vineyards cut into the steep hillsides and interspersed with almond and olive trees. Priorat has a special soil known as *llicorella*, which glints with mica particles; its heat-retaining qualities help create what can be monstrously powerful and alcoholic red wines. A group of new producers moved into the area around the village of Gratallops in the heart of Priorat in the 1980s, planted French varieties such as Cabernet Sauvignon alongside the native Garnacha and Cariñena, introduced modern winemaking techniques and new French oak barrels, and created a new style of Priorat that took the world by storm. As a result of these rare, expensive wines, Priorat has been promoted to DOCa (the only region other than Rioja to be awarded Spain's highest wine category). Monsant, its neighbor, makes excellent if lighter but still throaty reds and at lower prices. Terra Alta, literally "high land," had little contact with the rest of the country until the beginning of the twentieth century, and it shows. The southernmost Catalan DO, it is checkered with green vineyard oases nestling between the mountains.

Right up in the north of Catalonia the isolated Empordà DO hugs the border with France, squeezed in by the Mediterranean and the Pyrenees. The wines here are mostly reds from Garnacha and Cariñena and the whites come from Macabeo and Xarel-lo. Nevertheless, new international grape varieties, mainly Cabernet Sauvignon, Merlot, and Chardonnay, are creeping into the vineyards.

Just north of Barcelona is Alella DO, running from the coast inland to the foothills of the Cordillera Catalana. Down on the coast the vines are mainly Garnacha Blanca; in the new, higher vineyards you'll find Pansa Blanca (Xarel-lo) and a relatively good amount of decent Chardonnay. Conca de Barberà sits in a natural basin to the west of Penedès and produces good whites, especially Chardonnay. Further inland is the irrigated, semidesert of Costers del Segre, dominated by the futuristic Raimat winery, producer of good modern wines.

BALEARIC ISLANDS (ISLAS BALEARES)

Mallorca has two wine DOs—Binissalem DO, which lies north of Palma de Mallorca, and Pla i Llevant on the island's rolling central plateau. To the north, the Sierra de Alfabia shelters the vineyards from wet northerly winds. Hot summers, mild winters, and limestone in the light soil all add up to good conditions for vines, and the grapes

Priorat is hidden away on the steep schist slopes of rugged mountains. The red wines are powerful and long-lasting.

can become extremely ripe. In the nineteenth century, sweet Malvasía wine from Binissalem was popular; today, the native varieties Manto Negro and Callet make good, dry reds, while Moll (or Prensal) is used for light whites. Both reds and whites are marked more by rock and herb tastes rather than fruit.

Rioja

RED GRAPES
Tempranillo is the most important variety, followed by Garnacha Tinta and a little Mazuelo and Graciano. There is some experimental Cabernet Sauvignon.

WHITE GRAPES
Viura (Macabeo) is the main white grape. There are tiny amounts of Malvasía and Garnacha Blanca.

CLIMATE
The Sierra de Cantabria protects most of the vineyards from the Atlantic weather, and for the most part Rioja is sunny and temperate. Rioja Baja, to the southeast, has a Mediterranean climate and is hotter and more arid.

SOIL
Rioja Alavesa has yellow calcareous clay soil, as do parts of Rioja Alta. Rioja Alta and Rioja Baja are mainly alluvial silt, with ferruginous clay on the higher ground.

GEOGRAPHY
Vines are planted on relatively high ground in the Alavesa and Alta subregions, usually between about 1,310 and 2,625 feet. In the Baja, the ground slopes down to nearer to 985 feet, and the vines are planted on the flat, fertile valley floor.

I CAN REMEMBER the wonderful flavor of strawberry and black currant swathed in soft, buttery vanilla in the first Rioja reds I tasted. So soft, so enjoyable. Red wine wasn't supposed to be this irresistible, this easy to understand. In the days before the New World wine revolution taught us that it was okay to have fun with fine wine, Rioja was preparing the way. As such, it was effortlessly Spain's leading table wine. It's still the most famous, but despite being granted Spain's first supposedly superior DOC classification, the 1990s were a stressful time for the region, made worse by the introduction of irrigation in the late 1990s and seesawing prices. However, a majority of producers are now going back to basics—good fruit and gentle use of oak—and even many commercial Riojas are reassuringly reminiscent of the good old days when Rioja meant "red wine without tears."

Rioja was originally the name for the basin of land formed by the small Oja River that flows into the Tirón near Haro. The Tirón joins the Ebro River, and it is a chunk of the much larger Ebro Valley that Rioja has come to stand for—the part that lies about 60 miles south of the Atlantic and is bounded by mountains to north and south. The Rioja DOCa is divided into three subregions: Rioja Alavesa lies north of the Ebro in the province of Alava in País Vasco; Rioja Alta is in the west and lies entirely within the province of La Rioja; Rioja Baja lies to the east of Logroño, taking in land on both sides of the Ebro, as well as the Navarra and Burgos enclaves. Although Rioja is relatively close to the sea, the mountain ranges, especially the Sierra de Cantabria, protect its northern edge and shelter the vineyards from the cold Atlantic winds, and you can find yourself standing in warm sunshine among the vines, while in the distance, clouds gather threateningly over the mountaintops.

RED AND WHITE RIOJA

Much Rioja red is a blend from all three subregions and a blend of different grapes. Once, more than forty varieties were grown here, but today the rules allow just seven, with some experimental varieties, including Cabernet Sauvignon. Tempranillo accounts for more than 60 percent of all plantings; it is responsible for the graceful strawberry flavor of red Rioja and is well suited to long aging. Garnacha Tinta is added to flesh out the blend, and there may be a splash of Graciano, Mazuelo, or Maturano, too. The myriad combinations offered by the different subregions and varieties allow merchant *bodegas* to blend a unique house style. A little white Viura was traditionally added to help the acid balance and lighten the color. White Rioja is made largely from Viura.

The vines are densely planted and traditionally pruned in bush-shape *gobelet* style to protect them from the elements. However, many new vineyards are now trellised on wires. There can be few wine regions in the world that use so much oak. The casks (generally 225-liter *barricas*) are traditionally American oak, with its butter and vanilla flavors, and because the barrels were used again and again, there are probably no cellars in the world so piled high with wood as they are in Rioja, but French oak is increasingly being used, especially at the top level.

KNOW YOUR RIOJA WINE

Depending on the aging process, Rioja wine can fall into one of four categories, identified by different numbered back labels or seals:

* Joven wines: Young wines in their first or second year, which keep their primary freshness and fruitiness.

* Crianza wines: Wines that are at least in their third year, having spent a minimum of one year in casks. For white wines, the minimum cask aging period is six months.

* Reserva wines: Selected wines of the best vintages with an excellent potential that have been aged for a minimum of three years, with at least one year in casks. For white wines, the minimum aging period is two years, with at least six months in casks.

* Gran Reserva wines: Selected wines from exceptional vintages that have spent at least two years in oak casks and three years in the bottle. For white wines, the minimum aging period is four years, with at least one year in casks.

TO BLEND OR NOT

Decanter magazine recently held a tasting of top Rioja wines. Of the top ten, six came from single vineyards instead of from the more traditional blend across several vineyards. One was as small as one acre, and frankly three of the remaining wines were, in effect, single vineyard wines even if the labels didn't say so. None of the wines had the traditional quality words of "Reserva" or "Gran Reserva" anywhere on the labels. Just simple Rioja. If you'd said, "Where are the famous merchant names?" Well, they're not here—only the patrician López de Heredia featured in the list.

How things have changed. From time immemorial Rioja has been the home of brand-name wines. Of wines made in large cooperatives or mighty commercial cellars, blended, blended, and blended again to smooth away rough edges by relentless barrel aging and at the same time to smooth away the particular characteristics that any individual plot of vines might possess. The brand name was everything, and quality was measured by the length of time spent in the barrel (those Reserva and Gran Reserva designations). Well, it's changing.

The battle now is to allow both the village name and the vineyard name to be featured on the label. Remarkably for a great wine region, this isn't currently allowed. The other battle for the new wave of winemakers and grape growers is to be able to express the wine's personality regardless of rules about barrel aging. The most expensive wines are no longer venerable Gran Reservas but wines made by passionate iconoclasts devoted to small patches of vines, who just put their name and the simple term "Rioja" on the label.

Northwest Spain

RED GRAPES
There are many varieties of varying quality, but Galicia's best red is Mencía. In Castilla y León, Tempranillo (Tinto Fino), Garnacha Tinta (Alicante), and Mencía do well.

WHITE GRAPES
Albariño and Godello are Galicia's leading whites for quality wines. Rueda's Verdejo is the star of Castilla y León and has more character than most Spanish white varieties.

CLIMATE
It is very wet and cool on the coast in Galicia, and the climate becomes increasingly warm and dry as you travel inland past the mountains.

SOIL
The soil is varied, from the alluvial deposits found in Galicia's Rías Baixas and Ribeiro to Rueda's sandy and chalky soil, the ferruginous soil of Bierzo, and the stony land of Cigales.

GEOGRAPHY
Because of the reliance on river valleys for viticulture in both regions, the vineyards are characterized by terracing from the river level up the hillsides; they are also on plateaus in Castilla y León.

I SOMETIMES FEEL AS THOUGH I'm in Australia when I'm in the northwest of Spain. That's not as strange as it sounds. Australia has a precious narrow coastal strip where the rain falls and flowers bloom. But cross the Great Dividing Range and the blazing red hot heart of Australia stretches merciless and parched for thousands of miles. Spain isn't that bad, of course, but Galicia is so verdant, almost shimmering with lush plant life in the damp seaside air, that the speed with which you reach the austere, arid Spain of popular legend as you climb through the mountains is still something of a shock. From there across to the Mediterranean, in whatever direction you aim, you'll be in the hot, harsh heart of Spain.

The regions of Galicia and Castilla y León are different from each other. Galicia, with Cape Finisterre (Cabo Fisterra) at its extreme westerly point, is separated from the rest of the country by the Cantabrian mountains and this has helped to create a fierce spirit of independence in the region. Further inland, gentle hills start to appear and, as you approach Castilla y León, these grow more impressive and arid.

GALICIA

No wonder it's called green Spain. The rain in Spain doesn't fall mainly on the plain, as the winemakers of the La Mancha plain know only too well; here in Galicia, surrounded by the sea on two sides, it drenches the craggy coastline and rolling forested hills.

Galicia is strikingly beautiful, too. Its coastal landscape is cut through with low, wide fjordlike inlets known as *rías*. Dotted along the coast are tiny fishing communities huddled into rocky Atlantic coves, while further inland hilltop roads plunge through thick forests and deep river valleys, past dramatically impressive fortified castles. Galician winemaking has only recently become even a little sophisticated. The vineyards are scattered between grain fields and plots of kiwifruit, and modern viticultural practices have taken their time to catch on. In the past, visitors to the agricultural areas were more likely to notice the *hórreos*, strange stone granaries raised high on squat legs to repel hungry rats, than anything going on in the vineyard or winery.

But since the introduction of modern technology in the mid-1980s, Galicia has made some smashing discoveries. First came the realization that its Rías Baixas DO was capable of making whites that rank among the best in the country, thanks to the Albariño grape. Rías Baixas (literally, the "lower inlets") covers five zones near the coast around Pontevedra and Vigo. It's cool here because any potentially harsh temperatures are moderated by the Atlantic. This is one of Spain's wettest areas, and fungal diseases pose a constant threat. So the vines can be trained high on pergola systems, with branches pulled up onto granite posts to keep them well aired. This is how you may see the prized Albariño grapes growing, and they are used to make the acidic, aromatic whites that Rías Baixas is increasingly famed for. You'll also find the white grapes Loureiro and Caíño and the red grape Brancellao here, but it was for Albariño that Rías Baixas was awarded the DO in 1988.

MAIN DO WINE REGIONS

― GALICIA
  1. Rías Baixas
  2. Ribeiro
  3. Ribeira Sacra
  4. Monterrei
  5. Valdeorras

― CASTILLA Y LEÓN
  6. Bierzo
  7. Toro
  8. Rueda
  9. Cigales
  10. Arlanza
  11. Ribera del Duero

Inland from Rías Baixas, around Ribadavia, is the DO region of Ribeiro. Less rain falls here than on the coast, but it's still a lot more than in most parts of Spain. The word *ribeiro* means "riverbank" and that's exactly where the grapes grow here, in the alluvial soil of three river valleys of the Miño, Avía, and Arnoya, often on low terraces cut into the hillsides. Gentle winds blow from the Portuguese mountains, keeping the region relatively temperate, and flowers, especially carnations, grow alongside the vines, which have churned out cheap and cheerful wine for centuries. The quality has improved greatly, especially now that vineyards are being replanted with more aromatic whites, such as Treixadura and Torrontes, instead of the high-yielding Palomino, and fresher, juicier reds are being made from Garnacha.

Still less developed, but full of beguiling potential, are the two newest DO regions. Monterrei, right on the Portuguese border, is Galicia's driest region and is slowly modernizing. But it's in the Ribeira Sacra DO to the north, near Lugo, with its precipitous schist hillsides which are an Atlantic replica of Priorat, that some of

the finest reds (from Mencía grapes) in the whole of Galicia are made, along with good Godello. Valdeorras is the fifth Galician DO, and the farthest inland, about 95 miles from the coast. The Galician rain starts to dry up here, and temperatures are not moderated by the Atlantic. The summers can be blindingly hot, at up to 111 degrees Fahrenheit. Most of the vineyards lie in the valley of the Sil River, where about half the grapes are the heavy-cropper Alicante, a local name for Garnacha Tintorera (Alicante Bouschet). Mencía, one of Galicia's best grape varieties and a close relation of Cabernet Franc, is starting to produce exciting reds. Good whites are usually made from the aromatic Godello.

CASTILLA Y LEÓN

Castile, to give it its English name, was one of the original Spanish regions to unite against the Moors in the Middle Ages and thus became the northwest stronghold of the Catholics. It's sparsely populated and the historic towns with their castles, ancient fortifications, and royal residences contrast strongly with the wide, rolling terrain used for grain and the occasional grazing flock of sheep. The weather is much harsher than in Galicia, with hot summers and cold winters. The DO wine areas stretch west as far as Bierzo, on the Galician border, and east to Ribera del Duero in the provinces of Valladolid, Segovia, Burgos, and even Soria to the east.

Apart from Ribera del Duero, with its worldwide reputation (pages 156–57), there are five DO wine regions in Castile. Bierzo in the west is altogether suitable for

Vineyards and barley fields share the land near Pedrosa de Duero in the Ribera del Duero region.

winemaking, with plenty of sunshine but less rain than Galicia, and vine-friendly slate and granite-base soil. Since the 1990s, a growing band of new-wave producers has been making exciting reds from the Mencía grape, both in its light, crisp manifestation and as something much deeper, more concentrated, and ageworthy.

The Toro DO is a wild but thrilling area toward the Portuguese border along the Duero River. Pilgrims who took this route to Santiago de Compostela in Galicia used to stop in Toro and quench their thirst on the local wines. Since the late 1990s, it has become a fashionable hot spot as many of Spain's best wineries—as well as some French ones, too—open Toro subsidiaries to exploit some outstanding old vineyards. The best wine comes from the grape Tinta de Toro (alias Tempranillo), which makes powerful blockbuster reds, even with modern winemaking.

Rueda, with its sleepy little villages scattered across flat plains and low hills east of Toro, is the most famous Castile DO after Ribera del Duero and rightly so, for it now produces very good whites. Around the town of Rueda are

extensive medieval cellars. The Rioja *bodega* Marqués de Riscal has been making white wine here since the 1970s, concentrating on the local Verdejo grape and Sauvignon Blanc grown in sandy and chalky soil, with a dash of gravel in the best vineyards.

North of Rueda is Cigales, which follows the course of the Pisuerga River north from Valladolid. Cigales has long made pleasant *rosados*, although the most promising developments have all been in red wines from Tempranillo and Garnacha. Again as in Rueda, there are cellars running under the town of Cigales, with ventilators sticking up like small domes in the surrounding fields. South of Burgos, Arlanza is another Castilian DO, mainly for reds from Tempranillo.

RIBERA DEL DUERO

Ribera del Duero means "the banks of the Duero," the river best known as the Douro when it flows through Port country across the border in northern Portugal. The region lies in the heart of Castilla y León, about 120 miles north of Madrid, in the broad Duero Valley, which traverses the provinces of Burgos, Valladolid, and Soria. There are also some vines in the northern province of Segovia, making a total of more than 54,460 acres, more than half of which have been planted since 1995.

The area forms part of Spain's central plateau or *meseta*, so the vineyards are high, at between 2,300 and 2,790 feet. The altitude—pretty near the upper limits for viticulture—plays a large part in Ribera's success. Although the summer daytime temperatures are hot—it can soar to 104 degrees Fahrenheit—they drop dramatically at night, giving the grapes marvelous intensity and enhanced aromas. Add to this a perfect soil for viticulture (poor quality, yet easy to work) and you'll get vines that work hard to cram a great deal of concentrated flavor and high acidity levels into what little fruit they can produce. The continental climate is tempered by an Atlantic influence. Rainfall is moderate and mists from the nearby Duero River provide welcome humidity.

Ribera's rise to fame began in the mid-nineteenth century, when a *bodega* just south of Valbuena de Duero called Vega Sicilia planted vineyards with the red Bordeaux varieties (Cabernet Sauvignon, Merlot, and Malbec) as well as with more traditional white Albillo and Tinto Fino. Tinto Fino is said by proud locals to be their very own unique clone of Tempranillo, and it has clearly adapted to the rough conditions. For more than a century, Vega Sicilia was renowned as one of the best *bodegas* in Spain, and the prices of its powerful, complex red wines vied with those of a top Bordeaux—even the king of Spain had to stand in line to await his allocation—yet it remained the sole estate with any clout in Ribera.

Then, in the late 1970s, Alejandro Fernández set up a successful *bodega* making a red wine called Pesquera from Tinto Fino. This was followed by a rash of new quality producers during the 1980s, whose wines caught the attention of international critics, with subsequent rave reviews. In 1982, the region was awarded the DO for red wines made from at least 75 percent Tinto Fino. The number of *bodegas* has more than doubled since 2000 and the figure currently stands at 273. The most renowned Ribera vineyards are to the northwest of Peñafiel, where the Vega Sicilia and Pesquera *bodegas* are located. However, many of the remaining old vines and certainly many of the best sites are in the central Ribera around La Horra and Roa de Duero. Further east, the area near Aranda de Duero used to produce *rosados*, but it is rapidly becoming home to many of the most progressive producers. As so often in Spain, there is initial enthusiasm for heavy-handed oak use—a pity because the fruit here is some of the most focused and exciting in Spain.

NEW WAVE WINES

Traditionally, Spain wasn't a place you went to if you were after the new wave in wines. Everything seemed very staid and traditional there. Cellars were dark and quiet, age was revered, change not desirable, not welcomed. You could say the same about Spanish food. How things have changed. Not only is Spanish food and cooking regarded as some of the most exciting in Europe, there is a whole new wave of wine styles coming from the most unlikely places—the far, little visited remote Northwest. The reasons are that in a hot dry country such as Spain, the Northwest offers cooler, moister conditions, and in a country such Spain—which seems to be dominated by a small number of grape varieties—there was a treasure trove of exciting whites and reds just waiting to be discovered and nurtured in the forgotten Northwest. Albariño, Godello, and Treixadura among the whites and Brancellao, Garnacha Tintorera, and, above all, Mencía among the reds.

Albariño is one of Spain's most characterful white grape varieties. It can produce wines with fascinating flavors of apricot, peach, and grapefruit, refreshingly high acidity and highish alcohol.

Central and Southern Spain

RED GRAPES
*Tempranillo (sometimes locally
called Cencibel) is the best-quality
grape. Others include Monastrell,
Garnacha Tinta and Tintorera,
and Bobal. There is a little
experimental Cabernet Sauvignon
and Tempranillo in Montilla-
Moriles.*

WHITE GRAPES
*Airén is the dominant grape
in Castilla-La Mancha and
Merseguera in the Levante.
Palomino Fino is the classic
Sherry grape, while Pedro
Ximénez (PX) is grown
throughout Andalucía.*

CLIMATE
*The high central plain has a
continental, semiarid climate.
Further east in Levante it is
wetter and less extreme. Cooling
Atlantic breezes moderate the hot
summer in Andalucía.*

SOIL
*In central Spain, it is sandy clay
throughout but rich in limestone
in places. In the South, Jerez
has its famous white albariza
soil while Montilla-Moriles also
benefits from limestone soil.*

GEOGRAPHY
*On the high central plain, the
vines are planted in large plots.
The vineyards are more scattered
further southeast in the rolling
Levante hills. Condado's vineyards
start at about 80 feet above sea
level and the land rises to gentle
slopes in Jerez and Málaga, and
up to between 985 and 2,300 feet
in Montilla-Moriles.*

SPAIN'S VAST LANDLOCKED CENTRAL PLATEAU, Castilla-La Mancha, and
Murcia and Valencia to its east, contain the country's most important regions
for table wine. Even if this part of Spain does not produce the finest Spanish
wines, the sheer volume that comes from here is astonishing.

CASTILLA-LA MANCHA AND MADRID

The lonely Castilla-La Mancha plateau is relatively inhospitable at between
1,640 and 3,280 feet, with freezing cold winters and scorching summers. Apart
from some windmills and the odd castle, all you'll see are row after row of vines,
pruned with their canopy draped over the ground to retain as much moisture as
possible. La Mancha is Spain's largest DO, with more than 400,000 acres of vines
stretching north almost as far as Madrid.

Airén is the major white grape, and, with its thick skin and heavy leaf
canopy, it's ideally suited to the climate. New, higher-quality grape varieties,
new technology, and early picking mean that the wines are becoming lighter,
fresher, and faintly aromatic. Cencibel produces light and fruity or richer
red wines. To the south, where the central plain begins to descend toward
Andalucía, is the Valdepeñas DO. This small basin surrounded by sheltering
hills has excellent vineyard areas in its Los Llanos ("the plains") and Las
Aberturas ("the open spaces") subregions. There is increasing use of Cencibel
for quality reds, as well as Chardonnay and Cabernet Sauvignon.

Further north, the large Méntrida DO is traditionally home to dull, tannic
reds and heavy *rosados* mainly from Garnacha. But there are old vines here,
and hillside vineyards and a few producers are beginning to make better wines.
The Vinos de Madrid DO covers the vineyards around the southern edge of
the capital and produces some well-made reds from Cencibel and Cabernet
Sauvignon. East of Madrid, the Mondéjar DO is a mystery for now—no wines
of any quality have emerged from there yet. The Almansa DO is down in the
southeast, where the great La Mancha plain gives way to the Murcian plateau.
The wines are mainly dark reds, from Monastrell (Mourvèdre) and Garnacha
Tintorera, with some of the better ones, including Cencibel, in the blend.

Manchuela ("little Mancha") is a large area between La Mancha, Almansa, and
Utiel-Requena. Its scattered vineyards are on high, sloping clay-limestone soil
and show the region's potential for fine reds, particularly from the local Bobal
grape, often aided by Tempranillo. The addition of Cabernet Sauvignon, Syrah,
and even Petit Verdot and Touriga Nacional should make for some interesting
changes. Several of Castilla-La Mancha's best estates (Dominio de Valdepusa
and Dehesa del Carrizal in the Toledo mountains, and Finca Elez and Guijoso
in Albacete among others) lie entirely outside any DO boundaries, and a recent
law has created single-estate appellations (Vino de Pago DOs) for each of them.

VALENCIA AND MURCIA

Bordering Castilla-La Mancha to the east, this part of Spain is also known as
Levante. The scenery is a good deal more varied, if less dramatic—its green

Central and Southern Spain 159

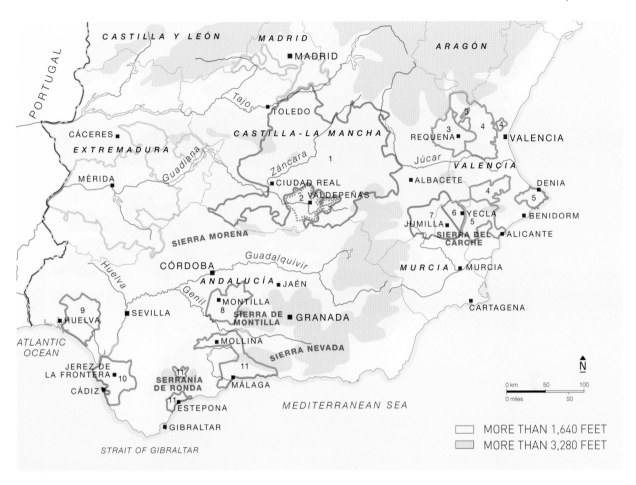

MAIN DO WINE REGIONS

— MADRID

— CASTILLA-LA MANCHA

  1. La Mancha

- - - **2.** Valdepeñas

— VALENCIA

  3. Utiel-Requena

4. Valencia

5. Alicante (also in Murcia)

— MURCIA

6. Yecla

7. Jumilla (also in Castilla-La Mancha)

— EXTREMADURA

— ANDALUCÍA

  8. Montilla-Moriles

  9. Condado de Huelva

10. Jerez-Xérès-Sherry, Manzanilla de Sanlúcar de Barrameda

11. Málaga, Sierras de Málaga

fertility is soothing after the desolate inland plain, as low mountains that cut off the *meseta* give way to the *huertas*, irrigated tiers of land covered in orchards and olive trees that form a giant stairway down to the coast.

There are six main wine districts. Valencia, with its pretty blue ceramic tiles covering the church roofs, is more famous for orange trees than for grapes. Even so, it has some modern *bodega*s, most producing dull whites, and some fair reds and *rosados*. Valencia's best known wine is a lusciously sweet fortified white made from Moscatel (the Spanish name for Muscat). It is not a sophisticated dessert wine, but good ones have an appealing crunchy, table-grape character. Driving west from Valencia is the promising region of Utiel-Requena, where the important Valencian *bodegas* have large holdings. The vines will probably be be Bobal, normally used for making *rosado*,

which can be some of Spain's best, and there are increasing amounts of decent reds from Tempranillo and Garnacha as well as French varieties.

Further south lie Alicante, Yecla, and Jumilla, forming a line of DOs marching progressively inland from the city of Alicante to the regional boundary. Monastrell, Tempranillo, and Cabernet Sauvignon produce good reds. Monastrell, a great grape variety when it goes by its adopted French name of Mourvèdre, has only recently begun to be mastered by winemakers in its native land. There is also some Garnacha here. Bullas is a quietly promising region and at the moment best known for *rosados* and promising reds. After the wind-whipped plain of Castilla-La Mancha and the sweaty tourist resorts of the Costa Blanca, it's as refreshing and relaxing a place as any to end up in.

SOUTHERN SPAIN

This is how everyone imagines Spain to be—golden beaches, whitewashed hilltop villages, and proud flamenco dancers, along with seven centuries of Moorish influence. This influence lives on in the food, customs, and architecture of the region. Being so far south, the climate is hot but not uncomfortably so because of the cooling sea breezes. Led by the famous sherries from Jerez (pages 162–63), the traditional style of wine is fortified, with the wine aged in a solera system. But a worldwide fashion for light, dry table wines means many winemakers are changing direction toward lighter wines.

The Sherry-style wines of Condado de Huelva and Montilla-Moriles were once world famous but are now just consumed locally. Across the Serranía de Ronda from Jerez is the Málaga DO, another region with a glorious past that has found itself now out of fashion. Its sweet butterscotch-and-nuts style of wine used to be among the most prized of southern Spain's "sack," more famous even than Sherry, but, at end of the nineteenth century, it became the first area in Spain to be attacked by the vine louse phylloxera. There is a huge range of wine styles with varying degrees of sweetness; PX is the main grape in traditional Málaga wine. Classic Málaga is aged in wood, but the Moscatel version is not and tends to be lighter, fresher, and more redolent of the Muscat grape itself.

The newer Sierras de Málaga DO covers still wines in the provinces of Málaga (at Ronda), Granada, and Almería. The rate of expansion is dizzying, and some of these high-altitude vineyards are making interesting reds that could be truly exciting with a few more years' practice.

The finest Sherry vineyards are located on finely grained albariza *chalk soil, which can appear almost white in summer but which absorbs the heavy winter and early spring rains to sustain the vines during the long summer drought.*

Sherry

WHITE GRAPES

Palomino is the classic Sherry grape. Palomino Fino is by far the better variety and is planted in most of the vineyards. There is also some Palomino de Jerez and Pedro Ximénez, with Moscatel grown for the sweet wines.

CLIMATE

The long, hot summers (at times 104 degrees Fahrenheit) are moderated by the influence of the Atlantic. The humidity near the coast is crucial to the development of flor and the production of Sherry. In the winter, there is heavy rainfall in the region.

SOIL

Chalky albariza soil with smaller amounts of clay and sand is the best type for Sherry grapes. The less good soil contains large amounts of clay, mud, or sand.

GEOGRAPHY

The vineyards lie mainly on bare, rolling hills, up to about 500 feet high, or else on flat land.

IF I VENTURE INTO SHERRY COUNTRY, I make sure I pack my sunglasses. It isn't that it's desperately hot. In August the temperature can reach 104 degrees Fahrenheit, yes, but gentle, cooling breezes from the Atlantic Ocean keep things comfortable. No, it's the effect of the sun glinting off the bleached land that dazzles me and makes me squint in pain. The vineyards of Jerez look as though someone has cut down all the trees, then took a big can of white paint and splashed it over the scenery before marking out the green vines against the bright canvas. This effect is caused by the special chalky soil of region, called *albariza*—literally, "snow white" (see below). It's one of the keys to the unique character of Sherry, the fortified wine that has spawned a thousand imitations, but which truly comes only from this corner of southwest Spain near Cádiz.

It surprises many who imagine southern Spain to be baked and arid to discover that Jerez has a relatively high rainfall—at 25 inches a year, much higher than, for example, Rioja in the northeast of Spain.

Palomino Fino, a heavy cropper even in poor conditions, now covers 95 percent of the Jerez vineyards. If you make table wine from these grapes (and many Sherry companies do), it's pretty dull, insipid stuff. But the neutral must, with its relatively low acidity, is perfect for undergoing the magical transformation that turns Jerez wine into Sherry.

The creation of Sherry calls for a clever performance by Mother Nature. Humidity from the nearby Atlantic encourages a yeast growth called flor to form on the surface of the new wine, although usually only when the wine has been made from the more acidic grapes and given a light fortification with *aguardiente* (grape spirit). At first, the flor looks like a sprinkling of powder, but it soon spreads and thickens to form a creamy protective layer, which prevents

ALBARIZA CHALK

The finest Sherry vineyards are located on *albariza* chalk soil, which contains between 60 and 80 percent chalk. This soil can appear almost as white as snow in summer and is high in calcium. It is finely grained and this even texture is important in the Jerez climate, where there are heavy rains in winter and early spring. March is the wettest month, but rains fall often during the winter, sweeping inland from the Atlantic. The deep *albariza* soil absorbs the rain like a sponge, which sustains the vines during the long summer drought. *Albariza* is also good for ripening grapes; the hot sun reflected off the bright white soil helps the maturing process. All this makes for contented, high-yielding vines.

Most of the *albariza* soil is found in two areas between Sanlúcar and Jerez, and the more outlying vineyards are mainly on poor, darker soil that contains less chalk; *barros rojos*, or clay soil, contain up to 30 percent chalk, and *arenas*, or sandy soil, has about 10 percent chalk. In an effort to improve quality, the proportion of vineyards on the *albariza* soil has grown from 50 percent in 1960 to more than 80 percent today.

oxidation and adds its own sour cream, bread dough character to the wine maturing in the cask. The bone-dry, pale straw Sherry that emerges from this process is *fino*.

Fino is made in large volumes at *bodegas* in the towns of Jerez de la Frontera and El Puerto de Santa María. At Sanlúcar de Barrameda, a coastal fishing port, the humidity means that the flor layer on the casked wine grows thicker and denser than elsewhere in Jerez. Sanlúcar produces a particular type of *fino* known as *manzanilla*—lighter and more delicate than *fino*—some tasters even find it salty. *Amontillado* is *fino* that has been allowed to mature and oxidize, developing a more rounded, nutty flavor and a chestnut brown color. *Oloroso* has had no protective layer of flor, so it develops a dark colour, marked oxidized flavors, and greater richness, but it is usually still bone dry.

So what does Sherry country look like? If you can stop squinting in the brightness, cast your eye over huge vistas of very gently sloping land with rows and rows of neatly pruned vines. They are nearly all Palomino Fino. Here and there a shimmering white building stands out on the soft brow of a hill. It will doubtless belong to a *bodega*—everything does here. You won't see much else, although further afield in the region, if you are there at the right time of year, you'll catch a glimpse of patches of bright yellow sunflowers. Today, as quality rises, volume decreases, with the better, chalkier soil being used more and more to provide better quality Palomino Fino grapes.

Sanlúcar and El Puerto de Santa María lie on lower, flatter land on the coast. Sanlúcar's vineyards are mostly on *albariza* soil, while Puerto's soil is less chalky. The grapes are not necessarily used in their hometown—they may be used by *bodegas* all over the region. But for a Sherry to qualify as a *manzanilla*, it must have been matured in Sanlúcar. The town's seafront, with its little fishing boats pulled up on the beach and traditional bars all serving the chilled Sherry straight from the cask, is one of the most delightful spots in the region. After experiencing this, drinking Sherry back at home is never the same again.

MAIN SHERRY STYLES

» **Fino and manzanilla** *Fino* Sherries derive their extraordinary, tangy, pungent flavors from flor. Young, newly fermented wines destined for these styles of Sherry are deliberately fortified very sparingly to just 15–15.5 percent alcohol before being put in barrels for their minimum of three years of maturation. The thin, soft, oatmeal-colored mush of flor grows on the surface of the wines, protecting them from the air (and thereby keeping them pale) and giving them a characteristic sharp tang. The addition of younger wine each year through the solera system feeds the flor, maintaining an even layer. *Manzanillas* are *fino*-style wines that have matured in the cool seaside conditions of Sanlúcar de Barrameda, where the flor grows thickest and the fine, salty tang is most accentuated.

ALL SHERRY IS MATURED IN A SOLERA SYSTEM

This is a stack of casks containing progressively older wines, which are continually refreshed by blending with younger wines creating greater complexity, so each time some of the older wine is drawn, the cask is topped off with the next oldest wine, and so on until the casks of youngest wine are topped off with new wine. The younger wine takes on the character of the older wines, while helping to keep them fresh, and this method also means there will always be a tiny amount of the original wine left in the solera—some soleras are more than one hundred years old. The barrels are usually in a stack, with the final blend at the bottom and the youngest wine at the top. A minute quantity of "vintage" Sherry will not have been through the solera system.

» **Amontillado** True *amontillados* are *fino* Sherries that have continued to age after the flor has died (after about five years) and so finish their aging in contact with air. These should be bone dry and taste of raisins and buttered Brazil nuts. Medium-sweet *amontillado* is dry Sherry sweetened with *mistela*, a blend of grape juice and alcohol.

» **Oloroso** This type of Sherry is strongly fortified after fermentation to deter the growth of flor. *Olorosos*, therefore, mature in barrel in contact with the air, which gradually darkens them while they remain dry, but develop rich, intense, nutty, and raisiny flavors.

» **Other styles** *Manzanilla pasada* is aged *manzanilla* with greater depth and nuttiness. *Palo cortado* is an unusual, deliciously nutty, dry style somewhere in between *amontillado* and *oloroso*. Sweet *oloroso* creams and pale creams are enriched mainly for the export market, and this is usually done by adding concentrated grape juice. Sweet, syrupy but frequently delicious varietal wines are made from sun-dried Pedro Ximénez (PX) or Moscatel grapes. A well-matured Pedro Ximénez sweet Sherry is about as thick and mouth-coating as it is possible for a wine to get.

» **New wave Sherries** There has been a definite attempt this century to revive Sherry's reputation as one of the world's great wines. There are now small releases each year of vintage-dated Sherries. Because Sherry has always relied on blending for its personality, these aren't always a success, but I've had blindingly good *palo cortados* and *olorosos* at between twenty and forty years old. Nonvintage age designations for blends start at twelve and fifteen years old but get exciting at VOS—Very Old Sherry—twenty years of minimum age; and VORS—Very Old Rare Sherry—for blends of more than thirty years of age. If you have ever tried fresh, dry Sherry in a Jerez or Sanlúcar bar, direct from the bodega, several companies have introduced a style called *en rama*, raw Sherry bottled without filtering and clarifying. It will stay fresh for only a few weeks, and its magic is in its first flush.

Sherry comes in a wide range of styles and colors: from left to right, Fino, Oloroso, Amontillado, and Pedro Ximénez.

Portugal

Portugal at its most traditional: terraced vineyards in the Douro Valley. For centuries, the steepness of the slopes meant that everything had to be done by hand. However, the terraces shown to the right of the picture are new ones, cut into the hillsides wide enough to accommodate a small tractor.

It isn't so long ago that I would have approached Portugal's table-wine world with exasperation at lost opportunities easily outweighing the pleasure I gained from its occasional triumphs. There seemed to be so much potential from its myriad native grape varieties, and yet the producers seemed supremely unconcerned about what we foreigners might like to drink. Well, that's half the story. She did have some wines that we liked to drink and which were always intended for export—the great fortified wines of Port and Madeira were invented by traders, largely from Great Britain. The medium-sweet, lightly sparkling rosado wines of Mateus and Lancers were created after World War II with the export market very much in mind. The rest of Portugal's wines, however, were mostly lapped up by the domestic market along with countries such as Brazil and Angola, which had strong Portuguese connections.

This has meant that only in the last generation have many wine producers begun to bring their methods and machinery to accepted modern standards. But it also meant that the rush to uproot old vine varieties and replace them with international favorites, such as Chardonnay and Cabernet, happened on only a small scale. For which we should give thanks because Portugal is a jewel house of ancient vine varieties. In a world of increased standardization, Portugal is a beacon of individuality. Portugal has been through several golden ages as a fortified wine producer. Its golden age as a table wine producer is only just beginning. As it is, Portugal, with the tempering influence of the Atlantic affecting all her coastal regions, already offers a fascinating array of wines. These range from the fiercely acidic yet fragrant Vinho Verdes of the Minho in the north to the majestic ports and succulent soft reds of the Douro Valley; past the rudely impressive reds of Bairrada and the potentially magnificent reds and whites of Dão; and on to the areas of the center and the south, where the transformation from simple bulk producer merely satisfying local thirsts to international player creating some of the most original and thrilling flavors in Europe has been astounding. In the low hills of Alenquer, in the broad acres of the Tejo inland from Lisbon, in the area around Setúbal to the east, and in the torrid plains of the Alentejo, good whites and great reds are beginning to appear, and frequently there isn't a Chardonnay or Cabernet Sauvignon vine in sight.

The Wine Regions of Portugal

IMAGINE TWO GLASSES OF WINE standing side by side. The first, a Vinho Verde, is almost water-white with a few lazy bubbles clinging to the side of the glass. It smells vaguely of citrus, and it makes you catch your breath with its acidic rasp. Then on to the second, a Port, with its deep impenetrable color. A heady aroma of superripe fruit wafts from the glass, and its rich flavors warm and soothe, conjuring images of a comfortable winter's evening by the fireside. It is hard to believe that the two wines, with at least ten degrees of alcohol separating them, come from the same country, let alone adjacent regions, but Vinho Verde and Port live cheek by jowl in the north of Portugal. It's not as if we're talking about a large area. Port and Vinho Verde cohabit in a country that is little more than 100 miles wide.

That's the beauty of Portugal. For such a small country, she has a strong regional feel, and the climate plays a vital role in this. With its prevailing westerly winds, the Atlantic Ocean exerts a strong influence on the coastal belt, but this diminishes sharply as you journey inland. As you travel across Portugal, the landscape, architecture, and traditions change dramatically, too. As mountains rise and subside, the temperate maritime climate with its lush vegetation gives way further south and east to more extreme temperatures and arid scrub. Sturdy gray granite houses built to withstand wind and rain become flimsy shelters painted white to reflect the burning sun.

This regional identity is reflected in the breadth of the wines. Two fortified wines, Port and Madeira, are world famous. Others, such as Setúbal and Carcavelos, popular in the nineteenth century, virtually gave in to the commercial pressures of the twentieth century. Apart from light, spritzy Vinho Verdes, the north also produces reds that are earning very different reputations for themselves. The Douro's best reds have a luscious, perfumed, soft-textured depth; Bairrada demands a sterner reaction to her aggressive but impressive wines; and Dão is now showing why it was so well regarded generations ago. Modern winemaking produces some attractive fresh whites. In the center and the south ripeness is the key, with healthy red grapes being turned into wines packed with ripe berry-fruit flavors.

Following examples set elsewhere in the world, the Portuguese have set out on a varietal path, but they focus on their own varieties, not on the well-known international ones such as Cabernet Sauvignon and Chardonnay. Varieties such as the deeply colored, scented Touriga Nacional, Trincadeira, Tinto Cão, and Castelão are unfamiliar names on the international circuit but making superb red wines in Portugal. Some native white grapes have also come to the fore. In Vinho Verde, there is the triumvirate of Alvarinho, Loureiro, and Trajadura. Then there's Bical, Fernão Pires, and in southern Portugal Arinto, a variety that hangs onto its crisp acidity in spite of the blazing sun.

WINE REGIONS

A journey around Portugal's wine regions can hardly ever be whistle-stop. From the Minho province that marks the border with Spain in the northwest to the Algarve in the south may be just under 400 miles as the crow flies, but there are more than thirty officially recognized wine regions in between, as well as a tier of Vinhos Regionais

CLASSIFICATIONS

Vinho is the lowest level, but it is commercially important because so much off-dry to medium-dry rosado is exported in this category. **Vinho Regional,** or **Indicação Geográfica Protegida** (IGP), is the next level, with laws and permitted varieties much freer than for DOC/DOP. There are currently fourteen IGPs. **Denominação de Origem Controlada/Protegida** (DOC/DOP) is the most strictly regulated; there are now thirty DOC/DOPs.

(VR), or regional wines, that cover most of the country. Almost everywhere you go in Portugal, apart from the highest mountain peaks where viticulture is simply not feasible, it seems that someone somewhere is making wine. The largest region is Vinho Verde, which covers the entire soggy northwest of the country. The Douro region itself, delimited both for Port and table wine, begins 50 miles or so upstream from Porto and extends east to the Spanish border. In the granite mountains to the south, Dão spreads over three river valleys with Beira Interior to the east. Bairrada, with its tannic red wines, occupies the flat coastal strip north of Coimbra.

Stretching along the rolling coastal hills to the south, Estremadura (known as the Oeste or "west") is a colorful region making bulk wines for the thirsty local market but also including two historic wines, Bucelas and Colares.

The Tagus or Tejo River, which flows into the Atlantic near Lisbon, marks the divide between the hilly north and the great plains of the south. The Setúbal peninsula southeast of Lisbon is one of the few Portuguese regions to embrace foreign grape varieties. East and south, the undulating Alentejo plain sweeps to the Spanish border with vineyards concentrated around the small whitewashed towns of Portalegre, Borba, Granja-Amareleja, Moura, Redondo, Reguengos, and Vidigueira, not forgetting Évora—the regional capital. Finally, the Algarve—warm and with a maritime climate but so far producing few fine wines.

The Portuguese are custodians of a number of volcanic Atlantic islands, which their early navigators were the first to discover. Vines were introduced to the Azores by Portuguese settlers in the fifteenth century, but the industry was all but wiped out by oidium and phylloxera in the nineteenth century. Madeira, about 680 miles southwest of Lisbon, has been home to a flourishing wine industry since it was first discovered in the fifteenth century. The island's subtropical climate and the manu-facturing process of heating the wine sets it apart from the rest of Portugal and indeed the world.

WINE REGIONS

1. Vinho Verde
2. Trás-os-Montes
3. Porto, Douro
4. Távora-Varosa
5. Bairrada
6. Dão, Lafões
7. Beira Interior
8. Lisboa
9. Tejo
10. Península de Setúbal
11. Alentejo
12. Algarve
13. Azores
14. Madeira

Northern Portugal

RED GRAPES
The best varieties are Touriga Nacional, Touriga Franca, Tinta Roriz, Jaén, and Tinta Cão, as well as Bairrada's Baga.

WHITE GRAPES
Alvarinho, Loureiro, Trajadura, Viosinho, and Gouveio are the main grapes.

CLIMATE
Near the coast are ample rainfall and a long warm ripening season. The inland Douro Valley has harsh winters and hot summers.

SOIL
The sandy clay of Bairrada gives way to granite with schist in the Douro and granite in Dão.

GEOGRAPHY
Mountainous inland with steeply terraced vineyards in the Douro. Flatter land on the narrow coastal strip.

IT'S ALL TOO EASY TO LOSE YOUR WAY in the backwaters of northern Portugal. But what seems like a rural idyll to the casual visitor can be more like grinding poverty when you actually live it. Northwest Portugal, alongside neighboring Galicia over the border in Spain, is one of the most densely populated parts of the Iberian Peninsula, and over the centuries, with successive generations staking their rightful claim, land holdings have diminished in size to such an extent that many can offer only the barest subsistence. Your land may measure less than a suburban backyard, but there will always be room for a vine to provide you with a splash of Vinho Verde.

WINE REGIONS

Vinho Verde is Portugal's famous "green wine," "green" simply meaning "young." For most people outside Portugal, Vinho Verde conjures up an image of a light, slightly sparkling, medium-dry white wine. But back in its homeland, it often means a dark, rasping, slightly fizzy red wine. Even the authentic Vinho Verde white will taste different. The hallmark of true Vinho Verde and the reason both the reds and whites go so well with the local salted cod, or *bacalão*, is its searing acidity. The Alvarinho grape growing along the Minho River in the extreme north produces a relatively full but delicate dry white wine. Further south in the Lima and Cavado valleys around Braga, the Loureiro grape makes a lighter, crisper style. Trajadura, often used alongside Loureiro, makes a slightly softer style of wine, while inland along the lower reaches and tributaries of the Douro River, the tangy Avesso grape ripens to produce fuller, riper flavors.

Mountain ranges separate the high, barren country of northeast Portugal—which deserves its name of Trás-os-Montes, or "behind the mountains"—from the heavily populated northwestern coast. The climatic extremes of this high, inland area make agriculture difficult. Wine is made from some of the same grapes as in the Douro Valley just to the south, but exciting wines are rare.

The Dão region around Viseu was given a new lease of life when Portugal joined the European Union in 1986. The potential is now being triumphantly realized. An increasing number of modern wines, especially from single estates, is holding onto Dão's traditional austerity but adding fascinating scents and mineral textures. Touriga Nacional is the best red grape variety for Dão, aided by Tinta Roriz, Jaén, and Alfrocheiro Preto. Dão is almost completely surrounded by wild, forbidding mountains. The mountains tend to protect this eyrie from the unpredictable onslaught of Atlantic storms, and summer months tend to be warm, leading to a dry summer harvest.

Like the Vinho Verde region, Bairrada is at the mercy of the Atlantic, with frequent sea mists and annual rainfall reaching 40 inches. The countryside is mainly flat and featureless, with tall pine and eucalyptus trees sheltering small plots of land planted with cereals, beans, and knotty old vines. Bairrada is unusual in Portugal in that it is very nearly a one-grape region, and Baga's small, dark berries produce fiercely tannic red wines.

Port and the Douro

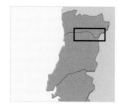

RED GRAPES
Up to eighty varieties are permitted, but Touriga Nacional, Touriga Franca, Tinto Roriz, and Tinta Cão have been identified as the four best varieties.

WHITE GRAPES
Varieties for white Port include Codega, Rabigato, Gouveio, and Viosinho.

CLIMATE
The humid Atlantic climate in Oporto is ideal for aging Port. Further east it is more arid.

SOIL
Port vines are planted only on schistous soil.

GEOGRAPHY
The Douro is famous for its steep terraces that follow the narrow river valleys.

AFTER THE TAGUS, THE DOURO is the most important river in Portugal (and its importance continues over the border into Spain, as the Duero). It is enormously important for its fortified wine, Port, and increasingly important for excellent table wines. The Douro Valley is a wild and beautiful part of Portugal, and the poverty of its natural resources has driven the inhabitants to ingenious extremes in order to wrest a living from what can only just be called soil. The vineyards here must be some of the most labor-intensive in the world. Until recently, in order to grow anything on these slopes of schistous rock, terraces had to be carved out of the hillsides, sometimes to support no more than a row or two of vines. Hillside profiles like step pyramids make you think that the Douro should be one of the wonders of the world. Indeed, UNESCO has made part of the Douro a World Heritage Site. Mechanization of the vineyards was impossible until a replanting program began in the early 1980s. Mechanical pruning, on the other hand, will always be impossible, except on the gentler slopes.

The Douro vineyards, where Port is made, are between 50 and 125 miles upstream from Porto. You will know when you reach the Port region. The hard gray granite gives way to flaky, silver-colored schist. The Douro DOC divides unofficially into three subregions. The most westerly one, Baixo Corgo, is centered on the town of Régua. Here, the climate is cooler and wetter than further upstream, and the wines here tend to be lighter and less substantial—ideal for young rubies and light tawnies that supply the insatiable French taste for cheap Port. Indeed, half of all Port comes from

Quinta do Côtto is one of many traditional Port producers now also making successful Douro red wines from their vineyards high above the Douro River.

PORT STYLES

» **Vintage** Finest of the Ports matured in bottle, made from grapes from the best vineyards. Vintage Port is not declared every year (usually there are three or four declarations per decade), and only during the second calendar year in cask if the shipper thinks the standard is high enough. It is bottled after two years and may be consumed soon afterward, as is not uncommon in America; at this stage it packs a punch. The British custom of aging for twenty years or more can yield exceptional mellowness. Vintage Port throws a thick sediment, so requires decanting.

» **Single quinta (Vintage)** A single-quinta Port comes from an individual estate; many shippers sell a vintage Port under a quinta name in years not declared as a vintage. It is quite possible for these "off vintage" Ports to equal or even surpass the vintage wines from the same house.

» **Aged tawny** Matured in cask for ten, twenty, thirty, or forty years before bottling, older tawnies have delicious nut and fig flavors. The age is stated on the label.

» **Colheita tawny** from a single vintage, matured in cask for at least seven years and usually for much longer—potentially the finest of the aged tawnies.

» **Late Bottled (Vintage) (LBV)** Port matured for four to six years in cask and vat, then usually filtered to avoid sediment forming in the bottle. Traditional unfiltered LBV has much more flavor and requires decanting; it can generally be aged for another five years or more.

» **Crusted** This is a blend of good Ports from two to three vintages, bottled without filtration after three to four years in cask. A deposit (crust) forms in the bottle and the wine should be decanted. A gentler, junior type of "vintage" flavor.

» **Reserve** (most can be categorized as Premium Ruby) has an average of three to five years to age. Some are full-bodied and tasty; others are marketing devices.

» **Ruby** The youngest red Port with only one to three years of age. Ruby Port should be bursting with young, almost peppery fruit, and there has been an improvement in quality of late, except at the cheapest level.

» **Tawny** Basic tawny is either an emaciated ruby or a blend of ruby and white Port and is usually best avoided.

» **Rosado** New category since 2008, usually very sweet, best served over ice or used in cocktails.

» **White** Only the best taste dry and nutty from wood aging; most are coarse and alcoholic and best with tonic water and a slice of lemon.

Hand-plunging the grapes in an open-top fermenter is done to extract as much color, flavor, and tannin from the skins as possible. This is at Quinta do Crasto in the Douro.

the Baixo Corgo. Pinhão is the heart of the Cima Corgo subregion. To most of us, the Cima Corgo around Pinhão is the epitome of Port country: steep schist slopes with vineyards facing north or south, east or west—there's no shortage of heat here. The shortage, instead, is of water. The lower slopes are more schistous and retain water well, as do the old, pre-phylloxera terraces, the ones with hand-built dry-stone walls that need constant maintenance. Irrigation is being discussed and, used properly, could improve quality. In the remote Douro Superior up toward the Spanish border, the climate is the most constant but also the harshest, and the climate in the Cima Corgo is better balanced with slightly more rainfall. The finest ports come from Cima Corgo, but some of the finest table wines are coming from way upriver in the Douro Superior. Even so, irrigation could definitely help improve the balance.

DOURO TABLE WINE

Demarcated for Port in the eighteenth century, the Douro Valley is now recognized as a source of increasingly good table wines. Made from the same varieties used for Port, many of these red table wines would be hard and unapproachable—probably not very far removed from the so-called "blackstrap" wines first exported from the Douro more than 300 years ago—if it were not for modern methods of viticulture and winemaking.

Ferreira's Barca Velha, made in the upper reaches of the Douro near the Spanish border, is the most famous example of what can be done, while properties downstream, such as Quinta do Côtto, Quinta do Crasto, Quinta de la Rosa, Quinta Vale Dona Maria, Quinta de Gaivosa, and Niepoort's Redoma have followed suit with supple wines that capture the portlike flavors of ripe Douro grapes, yet add a brilliant fragrance. Great Douro red is a relatively recent phenomenon, and during the next generation these wines will come to be regarded as some of Europe's greatest wines.

We shouldn't forget Douro whites—less thrilling than the reds, but there are a lot of white grapes in the Douro Valley, and the ones from cool sites are much better used for table wines than for Port.

Some properties make both table wines and Port with equal aplomb, deciding only at the last minute which grapes will go to which, and sometimes using the very best grapes for table wines. (There's an annual quota for Port production, which may not be exceeded.) Sometimes, however, it's the grapes with higher acidity and lower sugar content that are directed toward table wine, and these tend to come from the highest vineyards, where the grapes ripen later and make lighter wines less well rated for Port production. In some cases, grapes used for making good table wines today would, in the past, have simply been sent for distillation as being surplus to requirements.

Central and Southern Portugal

RED GRAPES
Castelão is found throughout the region, along with Tinta Miuda in Estremadura and Trincadeira in the Ribatejo and Alentejo. There are some Cabernet Sauvignon and Merlot in the Ribatejo and on the Setúbal Peninsula.

WHITE GRAPES
Arinto has the potential for good wines. Fernão Pires is widely planted in the Ribatejo, where there is also some Chardonnay. Roupeiro and Antão Vaz are the best white grapes in the Alentejo, and there is Muscat on the Setúbal Peninsula.

CLIMATE
The influence of the Atlantic is important in the west. Inland, the arid Alentejo can be very hot in summer.

SOIL
Estremadura has calcareous clay and limestone, Ribatejo has clay, sand, and fertile alluvial soil, and Alentejo has granite, limestone, and red clay.

GEOGRAPHY
The Ribatejo and Alentejo plains contrast with the hillier Torres Vedras, Alenquer, and Arruda areas.

THE MUDDY TEJO OR TAGUS RIVER flows southwest through central Portugal. Just north of the river the mountains subside, and as you drive south, the roads straighten, and the patchwork of poor, intensively farmed smallholdings of the north gives way to vast estates or *latifúndios*, some of which cover thousands of acres of low-lying plain.

WINE REGIONS

Lisboa is a strip of rolling countryside, stretching from Lisbon's populated hinterland along the wild and windy western Atlantic coast, and known colloquially as the Oeste (pronounced "wesht," a kind of drunken-sounding version of the word "west," which is what it means). Although the region produces more wine than any other in Portugal, there were few wines of any quality until recently. It has been divided into several wine DOPs but, apart from Alenquer, few are going to hit the headlines. Most of the wines emanate from a number of huge cooperatives that have benefited from significant investment since Portugal joined the European Union in 1986.

The picturesque towns and villages are considerably more memorable than most of the wines. Lush, high-yielding vineyards are predominantly planted with bland white grape varieties that used to produce large quantities for distillation but now find their way onto the local market as wine. Ripening can be difficult in this relatively cool maritime climate and red wines, made predominantly from the ubiquitous Castelão grape, often taste mean and thin. But there is hope for the region. A number of properties around Alenquer are making increasingly good red wines from grapes such as Touriga Nacional and Tinta Roriz as well as Cabernet, Merlot, and Syrah.

Two tiny enclaves in Lisboa are worth a special detour. The windswept, seaside vineyards of Colares, about only 20 miles west of the center of Lisbon, grow in the sandy soil on the clifftops, their roots anchored in the clay below. This sand protected the vines from the phylloxera louse that attacked vineyards throughout Europe in the nineteenth century. Consequently, the local Ramisco vine is one of the only European varieties never grafted onto phylloxera-resistant American rootstock. Cultivating vines in the sand is difficult and expensive today, and the region has been in slow decline for the last thirty years. Still, the few gnarled old vines that remain are a pilgrimage for incurable wine romantics who like to sample these strangely wild, tannic reds within sight and smell of the great ocean.

Inland, shielded from the damp, misty Tagus estuary by a low range of hills, the Bucelas region produces dry white wines from two grape varieties, the Arinto and the aptly named Esgana Cão, meaning "dog strangler." Both grapes, especially the latter, retain plenty of natural acidity in a relatively warm climate, producing crisp, dry white wines that became popular in Great Britain in the nineeth century under the title "Portuguese Hock." Mention that name to a Brussels legislator today, and it would send him into paroxysms. Carcavelos, a rich, raisiny, fortified wine with a nutty, portlike length, enjoyed a moment of glory in the eighteenth century, but it's hard to find any vineyards today. With the relentless expansion of Lisbon along the Tagus estuary, most of the Carcavelos vineyards have disappeared under roads and apartment buildings.

Journeying inland, the broad Tejo Valley serves the capital as a kitchen garden. Tejo has been subdivided into six smaller subregions—Tomar, Santarém, Chamusca, Almeirim, Cartaxo, and Coruche—but the whole of the Tejo has been raised to one DOC, with the designation "Tejo" also permitted for wines that fall into the Vinho Regional category (mostly those made from international grape varieties). Tejo wines reflect their soil. The fertile alluvial flood plain alongside the Tejo, known as the *leziria*, yields large volumes of light insubstantial red and white wine. However, the movement today is away from the river up to the heathland with less fertile soil and the result is far more substantial wines.

Two elegant suspension bridges span the Tejo linking the north bank of the river to the densely populated Setúbal Peninsula on the south. After a while, Lisbon's high suburbs finally subside, and you find yourself traveling through a forest of fragrant umbrella pines growing on the warm, sandy plain. The region around Setúbal is home to some of Portugal's most enterprising winemakers making wines from a wide variety of Portuguese and foreign grape varieties. The two leading companies are the internationally minded J P Vinhos (formerly known as João Pires and famous for its dry Muscat) and José Maria da Fonseca, who make a series of powerful reds as well as some superb Moscatel de Setúbal, luscious, grapey, and capable of aging for decades.

The large fishing port of Setúbal lends its name to the unctuous, raisiny fortified wine made mainly and sometimes completely from Muscat grapes from vineyards on the limestone hills behind the city. In recent years, this traditional sweet Muscat has been upstaged by other wines from the region, such as Quinta de Bacalhôa, a ripe, minty red made from a Bordeaux blend of Cabernet Sauvignon and Merlot. Chardonnay also seems to be well suited to the north-facing limestone soil of the Arrábida hills and the warm maritime climate. But foreign grape varieties still have some way to go before they oust native grapes, such as Castelão (still unofficially known as "Periquita"), which thrives on the broad, sandy plain around the walled town of Palmela.

What a change after the winding roads of northern Portugal! This is the Alentejo, with straight roads, few villages, and a giant, undulating plain. Golden wheatfields extend for almost as far as the eye can see, dotted by deep evergreen cork oak and olive trees that provide shade for small nomadic herds of sheep, goats, and black pigs. Green in spring, the landscape turns an ever deeper shade of ocher with summer temperatures that frequently soar above 104 degrees Fahrenheit and rainfall that barely reaches 24 inches a year. The open vista is broken by only the occasional dazzling whitewashed town or village and perhaps the jagged outline of a ruined castle on the crest of a low hill.

As we approach Évora, rows of vines stretch out before us. Until fairly recently, cork was the Alentejo's main connection with wine—cork oaks, stripped of their bark, are a common sight as you travel around—but this is now one of Portugal's fastest improving red wine regions. Alentejo is the name of the DOC as well as the province, and there are eight subregions: Borba, Évora, Granja-Amareleja, Moura, Portalegre, Redondo, Reguengos, and Vidigueira. The Vinho Regional wines from the entire province, stretching from the Tagus in the north to the Algarve in the south, use the name Alentejano.

The Portuguese used to deride the Alentejo as the land of bad bread and bad wine. Conventional wisdom dictated that climate was against it. It seemed healthy, fault-free wine was impossible when the summer temperatures were high enough to force the locals indoors out of the relentless sun. This wasn't helped in 1974 when the south was the most determined and aggressive part of Portugal in overthrowing the dictatorship. Having been a land primarily of absentee landlords—unlike the Douro, where relationships between landowner and worker were close and the revolution was a positively gentlemanly affair—the peasants and workers relished occupying the large estates. Unfortunately, they weren't interested in making them work, even on a cooperative basis. But now, with some gleaming stainless steel technology, the Alentejo has begun to prove that it can produce fine wines, especially reds from evenly ripened native grape varieties.

Among the red grapes, Trincadeira and Aragonez are the best performers, and both the white Arinto and scented Roupeiro manage to hang onto good, crisp natural acidity in spite of the heat. The best Alentejo vineyards are over to the east, not far from the Spanish border: Cartuxa near Évora; Quinta do Carmo and Quinta da Moura at Estremoz; Esporão near Reguengos; Cortes de Cima at Vidigueira; and Herdade do Mouchão at Sousel are just a few of the best properties.

The title "land of bad wine" should probably have passed to the Algarve, where the tourists that flock here each year are less than choosy about what they drink. The singer Cliff Richard has shown what can be done by planting vines and producing something pleasant that he calls Vida Nova ("New Life"), and top winemaker José Neiva is also in the region. The Lagoa cooperative makes an intriguing dry apéritif wine aged like *fino* Sherry under a veil of flor, but I still wait in vain for the Algarve to take off.

Madeira

RED GRAPES
Negramoll, also known as Tinta Negra Mole, is Madeira's most widely planted variety.

WHITE GRAPES
White grapes all planted in fairly small quantities: Sercial, Verdelho, Bual, and Malvasia.

CLIMATE
A warm, damp subtropical climate means that oidium and botrytis can be a problem. Rainfall varies from 118 inches inland to about one-third of that on the coast.

SOIL
The soil is volcanic. The pebbles of basalt have often weathered red.

GEOGRAPHY
The vineyards are planted on terraces up to 3,280 feet in the south of the island and lower down in the north.

IT'S DIFFICULT TO GET a really good look at Madeira. The early Portuguese navigators who saw a bank of black cloud billowing over the Atlantic thought that they had reached the end of the world and steered well clear. Approaching the island's airport today with a view of dark, cloud-covered mountains on one side and the ocean on the other, you could be forgiven for thinking the same.

There are two ways to appreciate Madeira when you have landed. First of all, clamber down to the rocky shore that passes for a beach and stare inland. Behind the subtropical shoreline with its decorative palms and exotic flowers, tiny shelf-like terraces stack up the mountainsides until they seem to be subsumed in the clouds. Then drive up one of the tortuous roads from the coast to Pico de Arieiro which, at 5,965 feet above sea level, is nearly the highest point on the island. On the way you pass through a belt of dank mist only to emerge in bright sunlight before the summit. From here, you can see volcanic peaks poking through the cloud, but on a clear day you might glimpse the ocean.

On the face of it, Madeira is an unlikely place to make wine. This humid, subtropical island 435 miles from the coast of North Africa has long, warm winters and torrid summers. But Madeira wine certainly has individuality, and there's no lack of finesse in a glass of venerable Malmsey. The answer is that the character of Madeira comes from the aging process.

Like so many of the best inventions, Madeira wine came about almost by accident. Soon after the island was discovered, it became an important supply point for ships en route for Africa and the east. Wine was one of many goods to be taken on board, and a generous drop of local brandy was added to prevent it from spoiling on its long voyage. The pitching and rolling across the tropics seemed to suit Madeira, and it often tasted better when it reached its destination than at the start of the journey. The taste caught on, and demand grew for *vinho da roda*, wine that had crossed the equator and back. As Great Britain and America emerged as important customers for Madeira in the nineteenth century, merchants looked for ways to simulate the long but costly tropical sea voyages that had proved so beneficial to the wine. They built *estufas*, store rooms with huge vats heated by fires to produce the maderized aromas and flavors to which the world had become accustomed.

But Madeira's economy has suffered from a catastrophic cycle of boom and bust. The boom began in the eighteenth century, when demand for Madeira began to outstrip supply. It lasted until the 1850s, when oidium (powdery mildew) reached the island and spread rapidly through the vineyards, encouraged by the warm, humid climate. Worse still, twenty years later phylloxera struck, destroying entire vineyards in its wake. Shippers left the island, and the wine trade never really recovered.

Bananas replaced vines as the island's most important crop, and the vineyards that remained were planted with disease-resistant hybrids that produced large amounts of dreary wine. In 1913, a number of shippers merged to form the Madeira Wine Association, precursor of the Madeira Wine Company that produces most Madeira today as well as controlling more than half the exports. Few of the shippers own any vineyards, and land is now too expensive to buy. Instead they buy their grapes from myriad tiny smallholdings perched on little terraces, or *poios*, carved out of the mountainsides; with approximately 1,600 growers owning only 1,235 acres of vines, the average vineyard holding is tiny, covering only about an acre and the largest single vineyard on the island is fewer than 10 acres. This is hardly conducive to good or progressive viticulture. Vineyards in the south are under pressure from building work, and many of the vineyards in the north, mainly planted with American hybrids, have been abandoned.

Along with vines, most farmers grow other crops, including bananas, avocados, lemons, and, especially in the east of the island, willow for baskets and other tourist items. The warm, damp climate means that the vines have to be trained off the ground to lessen the risk of fungal diseases, and this makes backbreaking work in the vineyards. Agriculture is only really possible on Madeira because of the high rainfall on the inland mountains. This water is diverted into a complex network of more than 1,240 miles of manmade channels called *levadas*, which ensure an even distribution to every tiny property.

NOBLE GRAPES

Most Madeira goes to the French and German market for cooking instead of for drinking. It is made from the versatile but dull local red *vinifera* grape, Negramoll. The pale, pinky-red wine is fortified with grape brandy and heated in an *estufa* to between 104 and 122 degrees Fahrenheit for a minimum of ninety days. The wines made in this heavy-handed manner often smell and taste coarse and stewed and are a poor imitation of the real thing.

The finest Madeiras, usually produced from one of four top-quality or "noble" grapes—Sercial, Verdelho, Bual, and Malvasia—are made without any *estufagem*, or artificial heating, at all. They age slowly on *canteiros*, or racks, under the eaves in lodges in the island's capital, Funchal. Warmed naturally by the sun, they gradually develop a unique pungency and intensity of flavor. Having been subject to this long, slow, controlled maturation, fine Madeira stands the test of time like no other wine.

Traditionally, different styles of Madeira have been distinguished from each other by the grapes from which the wines were made, and the styles range from dry to sweet. Of the four traditional noble grape varieties, Verdelho and Malvasia are the most planted, and there are smaller amounts of Sercial and Bual. However, all the noble grapes together comprise anywhere between 7 and 20 percent of the total—nobody knows the true figure.

Sercial likes the coolest vineyards and grows on the north side of the island and at the highest altitudes in the

The island is so mountainous that grapes and other crops are grown in myriad tiny smallholdings perched on little terraces carved out of the mountainsides.

south. With a lower accumulation of sugar it makes the driest wine with a distinctly sharp, acidic tang. Verdelho is also planted on the cool north coast but in slightly warmer locations, and it ripens more easily than Sercial, producing a wine that is softer and medium-dry. Bual is found growing on the warmer, steamy south side of the island, where it produces richer, medium-sweet wines. Finally, Malvasia (better known in English as Malmsey) grows in the warmest, low-altitude locations on the south coast, such as the spectacular vineyards at the foot of the island's highest cliff, Cabo Girão. The darkest and sweetest Madeira, a good Malmsey will be raisiny and smoky, still retaining a characteristic tang of acidity that prevents the wine from tasting cloying.

The productive American hybrid grapes that crept into the vineyards, following the destruction of the best vineyards by phylloxera, can no longer be used for bottled wine, and most Madeira now comes from Negramoll. A varietal Madeira wine must be made from at least 85 percent of the variety named on the label. A replanting program is underway to increase production of the four noble varieties that are in short supply, but for the moment most Madeira blends are labeled only with the terms *seco* (dry), *meio seco* (medium-dry), *meio doce* (medium-sweet), and *doce* (sweet or rich).

Germany

The heart and soul of German wine: an amphitheater of golden-leaved vines, a tranquil river, and a little village huddled on its banks. The sloping vines are those of the great Piesporter Goldtröpfchen vineyard in the Mosel Valley.

If ever there were a country whose vinous treasures need cosseting, whose ability to thrill depends upon an annual dance along a climatic knife-edge, it is Germany. No country's growers must take greater risks to create the brilliant wines upon which their reputation relies. No vineyard sites need to be more carefully chosen for maximum exposure to sun and minimum exposure to wind, frost, and rain. In no other country are the most famous vineyard names betrayed more shamefully by vineyards with no right to be associated with them.

Vineyards like those of the Mosel-Saar-Ruwer are pretty well as far north as you can go and still ripen any of the classic grapes. But the genius of the Riesling grape is that, if you allow it to ripen slowly through long, cool summers and are lucky enough to have a balmy fall, it is capable of a sublime balance between fruit acidity and fruit sweetness that is unique in the world—even at ridiculously low alcohol levels and scarily high levels of acid. Add a little noble rot and the result is even more remarkable.

Yet this is only possible on special sites. These should be as lovingly delineated and protected as are far less special sites elsewhere in Europe. Instead, such action was deemed elitist back in 1971, when Germany's current wine law was passed, while Germany's international reputation has been ruined by a misguided attempt at popularism in providing large amounts of innocuous, cheap wine. On the label there is no obvious difference between Piesporter Goldtröpfchen (right)—one of Europe's great natural vineyard sites—and Piesporter Michelsberg, a name covering any wine from numerous inferior villages in the area. Bernkastel is a great wine village with some superb sites, yet wine from the whole Middle Mosel can call itself Bereich Bernkastel. What began as an attempt to simplify and update traditional practice became one of the main reasons Germany's fine wine reputation became defiled in the late twentieth century. But there is hope. Various amendments to the Wine Law have helped. Efforts have been made, especially by the VDP—a group of two hundred top growers—to classify the best vineyard sites, and the best producers are regularly producing balanced, exciting dry wines from such sites as well as the more traditional sweeter, fruitier styles. While many of these wines are not of much interest to drinkers outside Germany, there is a notable minority of growers making exciting reds, mostly from Pinot Noir, which the Germans usually call Spätburgunder.

The Wine Regions of Germany

IN AN IDEAL WORLD, the names on this map of Germany would echo with romance for all wine lovers. "We're just popping to the Saar for the weekend," people would boast. "We'll fit in an afternoon on the Ruwer, and say hello to the Bernkasteler Doctor as well." Sounds absurd? It's how Europeans talk about Burgundy. You can see them driving along the main road through the Côte d'Or; they can't believe that they're seeing road signs to hallowed places they've only ever seen on wine labels. They should be doing that in Germany, whose great vineyards are equally precious and more visually thrilling. In fact, sightseeing is just as crucial to understanding German wine as it is to understanding what makes one Burgundy taste different from another. Winemaking is only possible in much of Germany when four elements come together: site, climate, soil, and grape. The greatest of these is site.

Nearly all the vineyards are in the southern half of the country. The best vines are often grown where no other crops will flourish: on slopes too steep for cattle or where the soil is too poor for wheat and other cereals. But steep slopes are good for vines. They offer shelter from the wind, particularly if they are crowned by woods or if there is a mountain range behind. Then again, they get stronger sunlight: on flat ground, the sun's rays strike at an angle; on steeply sloping land, they strike perpendicularly. That means fewer shadows and greater heat.

In order to maximize sunshine and warmth, the slopes in Germany must be south-, west-, or east-facing. East-facing slopes catch the morning sun; those facing west get the afternoon sun, and this can be useful if fog is common because it will usually have burned off by the afternoon. The best kind of slope of all is in a river valley, shutting out the wind, imprisoning the warmth.

Rivers are crucial to growing vines in Germany. The country has a lot of them, and nearly all the great vineyard areas are close to rivers and their tributaries: vines follow the progress of the Mosel and the Rhine, the Main and the Neckar, and (to a lesser extent) the Elbe, Saale, and Unstrut. An expanse of water has the effect of moderating extremes of temperature. It helps to ward off frosts, and it gives humidity in hot, dry summers. The

CLASSIFICATIONS

Germany's classification system is based on the ripeness of the grapes and therefore their potential alcohol level.

» **Deutscher Wein** (German wine) is the most basic term.
» **Landwein** (country wine) is a slightly more upmarket version, linked to nineteen regional areas). These must be Trocken (dry) or Halbtrocken (medium-dry).
» **QbA (Qualitätswein bestimmter Anbaugebiete)** is "quality" wine from one of thirteen designated regions, but the grapes don't have to be very ripe, and sugar can be added to the juice to increase the alcoholic content.
» **Prädikatswein** There are six levels of Prädikatswein (in ascending order of ripeness and generally sweetness): **Kabinett, Spätlese, Auslese, Beerenauslese, Eiswein, Trockenbeerenauslese (TBA).** "Prädikat" on the label usually indicates sweetness.

There are various terms for recognizing the best vineyard sites—Grosses Gewächs (or Great Growth, like the French Grand Cru) is one, but the mood of the modern German wine producer is to simplify rather than complicate the label.

"Bereich" is the term for a region or district dating from the 1971 German Wine Law. Bereichs tend to be large, and the use of a name, such as Bereich Bingen, without qualification was not an indication of quality. Used mainly for cheaper wines, the term has largely disappeared from use.

See also
Middle Mosel page 183
The Rhine Valley page 185

RIESLING

Riesling wines have a marvelous perfume and an ability to hold onto piercing acidity even at high ripeness levels as long as the ripening period has been warm and gradual rather than broiling and rushed. German Rieslings can vary from bone dry to medium to lusciously sweet. Styles range from crisp elegant Mosels to riper, fuller wines from the Rheingau and Nahe, with rounder, fatter examples from Pfalz and Baden in the south. The very sweet Trockenbeerenauslesen (TBA) wines are made from grapes affected by noble rot; for Eiswein (ice wine), also intensely sweet, the grapes are picked and pressed while frozen.

water surface reflects heat and light back onto the banks, particularly if they are steep.

Most wine areas are in the south of the country, but there is also an east–west division of climate, with the climate becoming more continental as you travel east. Sachsen, Saale-Unstrut, Württemberg, Franken, and parts of Baden are affected by this and have a risk of both early and late frosts. To the casual visitor, the climate may not appear to vary much from Bonn down to Basel. It's not really that far, after all. But in Germany grape growing is on the margin, and every half degree change in the climate counts. In the Pfalz, regarded as a relatively warm region, the mean annual temperature is 50 degrees Fahrenheit; in the Mosel, considered distinctly cool, it is 49.6 degrees Fahrenheit. Much of the time you'd hardly notice the difference. But the Pfalz also has an extra 138 hours of sunshine in the growing season, and produces wines that are rich and fat, whereas the wines of the Mosel are lean and delicate.

Soils in Germany are varied. Some are famous for giving character to the wine—Mosel slate, say—but grapes are grown on limestone, sandstone, marl, loess, and many other types. Generally, the valley floors have richer, alluvial soil and produce richer wines; the slopes, where the soil is poorer, produce more elegant wines.

Great German wines don't have to be Riesling—Silvaner, the Pinot family, and Scheurebe can all be first-class—but Riesling does have an uncanny ability to do well in Germany. It thrives on a wide range of soil, and its flavor reflects the character of the soil. It ripens late, so given a long, warm fall and a south-facing slope, it will go on gathering complexity until well into October. It is resistant to cold, and it can produce good wines at low levels of ripeness as well as when it is so overripe that the berries are shriveled and brown.

Mosel

RED GRAPES
There is a tiny amount of Spätburgunder.

WHITE GRAPES
All the great Mosel wines come from Riesling. Müller-Thurgau is the other important white grape but is on the decline.

CLIMATE
The Mosel is damp and cool, but there are sheltering hills, and dams along the river have improved the mesoclimates. The Saar and the Ruwer are cooler still.

SOIL
Different types of slate predominate in all areas apart from the Upper Mosel, which is largely limestone.

GEOGRAPHY
The Mosel has many south-, southeast-, and southwest-facing vineyards. The Saar flows north and has fewer ideal sites; the Ruwer's vineyards face mostly west-southwest. Vines are planted at between about 330 and 1,150 feet.

YOU KNOW THAT FEELING. You look out the window at blue skies in the morning. The trees are impossibly green, and the river below the town glitters in the sun. You throw on jeans and a T-shirt and hurry out. Seconds later you hurry in again. You want a sweater—or two. This is May in the Mosel, and it's cold. You leave the town and cross the river, and you take off one of the sweaters. You're in the vineyards now, on the lowest slopes where the river reflects all that early morning sun back onto the vines. It's dazzlingly bright. It's not warm precisely, but it's warmer, and you can see the town across the river, still in shadow. The vines around you are soaking up all the sun they can get. You scramble up the slopes, and at the top of the slope you're glad of that second sweater again. It's much cooler up here, and the wind whistles around your ears.

This chilliness is the essence of the Mosel. In the best stretch, the Middle Mosel, where the river has carved out sheltered, steep slopes that face south, southeast or southwest, Riesling has an immensely long ripening time: between 120 and 150 days, compared with 105 to 115 for Cabernet in Bordeaux. These warm spots are responsible for the fame of the entire river. Elsewhere and in inferior sites, vineyards are starting to fall out of cultivation: in 2015 there were about 21,185 acres of vineyards, a decrease of nearly 7,415 acres in a decade.

UPPER MOSEL

The Mosel River enters Germany from France (where it is called the Moselle), and for almost 25 miles it runs north along the border with Luxembourg. Here, in the Upper Mosel, the slopes are gentle and the river much narrower than it becomes later on, thus it is less able to throw the sun's warmth back onto the vines. The main stretch of the river from Trier north to Koblenz is wider than this first stretch. The slopes in the Upper Mosel are even a different color; composed of shelly limestone, sandstone, and red marl, they're softer and warmer in color than the harsh, dark gray slate that takes over further downstream. The Elbling has been the main grape here since Roman times; it makes dry, brisk, acidic wines that seldom manage higher quality than QbA and are a godsend to the Sekt industry.

SAAR AND RUWER

These two tributaries of the Mosel, flowing northward to join the larger river, on each side of the Roman city of Trier, are, generally speaking, cooler and less promising than much of the Mosel. It takes the hardy Riesling vine to withstand the cold winds that blow far more strongly here than along the Mosel, and it takes an old-fashioned mentality on the part of the grower to put up with the low yields—lower than just about anywhere on the Mosel. In a cool year, Riesling barely ripens here. But in long warm summers, when the sugar levels rise to meet the acidity, a Saar or Ruwer Riesling can be among the most exciting wines in Germany. But it will take its time. That acidity will need taming in bottle for several years before the wine gradually mellows and blossoms.

Riesling is increasing its share in both the Saar and the Ruwertal regions. Low yields and low levels of ripeness, plus high production costs, mean that only Riesling will fetch the high prices needed to keep at least some of the drafts out of the growers' rambling manor houses. In the Ruwertal, it is now 90 percent of the vineyards, and in the Saar it has risen to 78 percent. The less good vineyards, planted with inferior varieties, such as Müller-Thurgau and Elbling, are being grubbed up.

THE SAAR

Although they both flow in approximately the same direction and are not far apart, the two rivers produce wines of different character. The Saar can boast soil ranging from loam, quartzite, and volcanic to hard and soft slate—and it is even stonier than the soil of the Mosel. It is less sheltered and more open to the wind than the Middle Mosel; on a day when tourists are basking outside the bars of Bernkastel, a visitor will need a coat in the Saar. Here, where the Saar and the Ruwer (even more so), are not broad enough to have much tempering effect on the climate, the crucial questions of wine always come down to the weather. For a small area, the Saar has an astonishing roster of excellent vineyard sites.

THE RUWER

If the Saar is a backwater, the Ruwer is such a small area that you could overlook it completely. Like the Saar, this is Riesling country, and the wine similarly needs a good year for its style of piercing acidity to come into its own. But Ruwer wines, even when young, are less intimidating than those of its neighbor. In the Ruwer, the slate is often reddish in color and is more decomposed into a friable soil than the rocky splinters of the Middle Mosel; it contributes to some superb west- and southwest-facing vineyard sites.

MIDDLE MOSEL

Things change when you reach what is called the Mittel (or Middle) Mosel. This is where all the famous villages and vineyards are found, and on all the good sites Riesling is often the only vine planted. But over the Mosel area as a whole, Riesling covers only 61 percent of the vineyards, which shows that there is still a lot of second-rate land being used to produce high volumes of low-quality wine, usually on flat land that used to be fruit orchards and which is now thankfully beginning to revert to growing crops other than grapes. Red grapes don't ripen easily here; it's too cold, so you

MOSEL SLATE

The keys to the Middle Mosel are not just warmth and exposure; these enable the sun to ripen the grapes, but it is the soil that flavors them. The soil in the Middle Mosel is Devonian slate, dark and heat-absorbing, dry and instantly-draining, which decomposes into a thin topsoil that in the past was constantly replenished by the simple method of pulling chunks from the hillsides, breaking them up, and scattering the shards. Nowadays, this is too expensive, but because of slate's low pH it may be necessary to fertilize with lime every couple of years. Stand on these slopes and you'll feel them soft and flaky under your feet. The sun glints on the slate fragments and they slide as you move, bouncing down between the vines. Slate gives a particularly smoky taste to Riesling, a tang that, once tasted, is never forgotten. And when it rains, the rain pours straight through like water through a strainer. More absorbent soil would hold the water, and in so doing would be washed down the slope. (More absorbent soil would also mean more water in the grapes and more risk of rot; free-draining slate is one reason why growers in the Mosel can pick so late.)

Where the topsoil is thinnest, wines are more elegant; deeper soil make fuller wines. Ürzig gives spicy wine, particularly from its Würzgarten (spice garden) site and excels in dry years; so does Graach, where the slate is deep and rich in weathered claylike soil. Erden has lighter soil and prefers wet years; Wehlen's best vineyards are at the base of the slope, where it's 3.6 degrees Fahrenheit warmer than at the top. Bernkastel gives smoky wines, rich and concentrated. But rich is a relative term in the Mosel. It's a paradox of the Middle Mosel that such a forbidding-looking place yields such delicate wines —but they are wines with a shining core of steel.

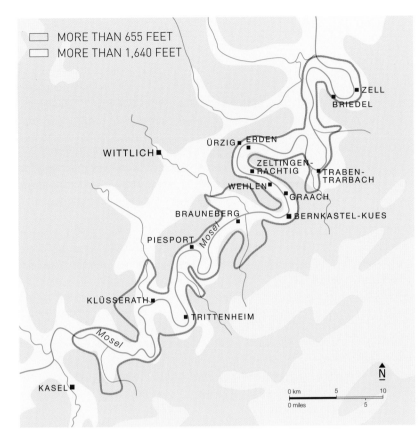

MORE THAN 655 FEET
MORE THAN 1,640 FEET

ZELL
BRIEDEL
ÜRZIG ERDEN
WITTLICH
ZELTINGEN-
RACHTIG
WEHLEN
TRABEN-
TRARBACH
GRAACH
BRAUNEBERG
BERNKASTEL-KUES
PIESPORT
Mosel
KLÜSSERATH
TRITTENHEIM
Mosel
KASEL

0 km   5   10
0 miles   5

N

WINE VILLAGES OF THE MIDDLE MOSEL

— Vineyard area

wonder why the scattered plantings of Pinot Noir and Dornfelder are there at all.

This coolness is recognized in law: Mosel wines require lower sugar readings at all Prädikat levels except Trockenbeerenauslese than do the wines of warmer regions such as the Rheingau. Yet the lightness and fragility of Mosel wines is deceptive, and even the fragile Kabinett level wines can last and improve for years.

The six Mosel Bereichs or subregions, going north, are Moseltor on the French border; Obermosel (Upper Mosel); Saar and Ruwertal, named after two tributaries; Bernkastel, the whole of the Middle Mosel; and Burg Cochem between Zell and Koblenz, covering the Lower Mosel (Untermosel). But village names are now more important than Bereich ones. Generally, the Upper Mosel is cooler and windier than the Middle Mosel, although increasingly exciting wines are being made at the best sites here. In the northerly Lower Mosel, the Hunsrück hills press in close to the river, leaving little room to live, never mind cultivate vines. Even so, there are some excellent sites here—steep, terraced slopes of sandy rocks even harder than the Devonian slate of the Middle Mosel. The villages of Winningen and Kobern-Gondorf would be better known were they closer to the clutch of famous villages further upstream.

TOP VILLAGES AND VINEYARDS

ALONG THE SAAR
» **Ayl:** Kupp
» **Kanzem:** Altenberg
» **Oberemmel:** Hütte
» **Ockfen:** Bockstein
» **Scharzhofberg**
» **Saarburg:** Rausch
» **Serrig Schloss Saarstein**
» **Wiltingen:** Braune Kupp, Braunfels, Gottesfuss

ALONG THE RUWER
» **Maximin Grünhäuser:** Abtsberg, Herrenberg
» **Eitelsbach:** Karthäuserhofberg
» **Kasel:** Kehrnagel, Nies'chen

ALONG THE MOSEL
» **Bernkastel:** Alte Badstube am Doctorberg, Doctor, Lay
» **Brauneberg:** Juffer, Juffer Sonnenuhr
» **Enkirch:** Batterieberg
» **Erden:** Prälat, Treppchen
» **Graach:** Domprobst, Himmelreich, Josephshöfer
» **Leiwen:** Laurentiuslay
» **Piesport:** Domherr, Goldtröpfchen
» **Trittenheim:** Apotheke, Felsenkopf, Leiterchen
» **Ürzig:** Würzgarten
» **Wehlen:** Sonnenuhr
» **Wintrich:** Ohligsberg
» **Wolf:** Goldgrube
» **Zeltingen:** Sonnenuhr

The Rhine Valley

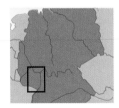

RED GRAPES
There are tiny amounts of Spätburgunder, Portugieser, and Dornfelder, except for in the Ahr, where Spätburgunder is the major grape.

WHITE GRAPES
Most of the wines are white and from Riesling. Müller-Thurgau, Silvaner, and Kerner are other varieties.

CLIMATE
The proximity of the Rhine and protection from forests and hills help moderate the climate in the northern part of the region. Further south, the Pfalz is Germany's sunniest and driest region.

SOIL
There is a wide range of soil, partly depending on the altitude.

GEOGRAPHY
Vines grow both on the plains and on slopes, where they are sheltered by the forests and hills. Many of the best sites are on river valley slopes.

THE RHINE (RHEIN) IS ONE OF THE MOST European of rivers. It rises in Switzerland and flows west along the northern border with Germany. At Basel, it turns north to form the border between France and Germany for some 106 miles before setting off through the heartland of Germany. But Rhine wine is universally understood as being German. If you wanted to understand the nature of German wine, you could do a great deal worse than take a trip up the river from Basel to Bonn.

In fact, to understand German wine at all you have to look at Germany's river systems; the rivers make viticulture an industry and not just a hobby in most of these cool-climate regions. Riesling can resist the cold better than most. The long falls enable it to go on ripening well into October. In spite of all this, the growing of fine grapes in the more northerly vineyards of Germany would be a matter of chance, of reliance on the vagaries of the climate, if the rivers were not there to even the odds a little. The rivers temper the extremes of climate. They keep frosts at bay and, by reflecting sunlight and warmth, give the vines on their banks an added advantage. In addition, over the millennia they have carved deep gorges from the rock through which they pass. Those steep banks, when planted with vines, catch all the available sunlight.

THE PFALZ

The Haardt mountains, which rise up to the west of the Pfalz vineyards and shelter them, are a northerly extension of the Vosges, which do the same protective job for the vineyards of Alsace in France. The Pfalz is divided into two Bereichs or subregions, the Mittelhaardt/Deutsche Weinstrasse north of Neustadt and the Südliche Weinstrasse to the south. Traditionally, the best wines come from the north.

The Südliche Weinstrasse has mostly flattish, easily worked vineyards and a large proportion of high-yielding grapes such as Müller-Thurgau and Kerner. But times have changed, and those quiet, rural villages in southern Pfalz are gaining a reputation for being among the most exciting regions in Germany. Yes, high-yielding vineyards are still there, but good growers are grafting over to higher quality clones and varieties. Generally, it is more fertile here than further north. Yields can be high, often too high, from the heavy, lime-rich soil. But many serious growers in the southern Pfalz are turning out top-quality dry whites, especially from Riesling, Weissburgunder, and Grauburgunder but also from Scheurebe, Chardonnay, and Sauvignon Blanc. Equally important, red wines have burst onto the scene, and red varieties now occupy more than one-third of the vineyards, especially in the south. Dornfelder is the leading variety, but you'll also find Pinot Noir, Cabernet, and even Sangiovese, more commonly found in Tuscany.

The Mittelhaardt/Deutsche Weinstrasse is where the grand old estates are based, especially in the villages of Ruppertsberg, Deidesheim, Wachenheim, and Forst. Riesling is the most common variety, and the wines are rich, spicy, and earthy, even though they are almost always dry.

MORE THAN 655 FEET
MORE THAN 1,640 FEET

0 km   10   20
0 miles 5   10

WINE REGIONS

Rheingau
Nahe
Rheinhessen
Pfalz

TOP VILLAGES AND VINEYARDS

NAHE
» **Bad Münster:** Felseneck
» **Dorsheim:** Burgberg, Goldloch
» **Kreuznach:** Brückes, Kahlenberg
» **Niederhausen:** Felsensteyer, Hermannsberg, Hermannshöhle
» **Norheim:** Dellchen, Kirschheck
» **Oberhausen:** Brücke
» **Schlossböckelheim:** Felsenberg, Königsfels, Kupfergrube,
» **Traisen:** Bastei, Rotenfels

PFALZ
» **Deidesheim:** Grainhübel, Hohenmorgen, Leinhöhle
» **Dürkheim:** Michelsberg
» **Forst:** Jesuitengarten
» **Ruppertsberg:** Reiterpfad
» **Ungstein:** Herrenberg, Weilberg
» **Wachenheim:** Gerümpel

RHEINGAU
» **Eltville:** Sonnenberg
» **Erbach:** Marcobrunn, Siegelsberg
» **Hattenheim:** Nussbrunnen, Wisselbrunnen
» **Geisenheim:** Kläuserweg
» **Kiedrich:** Gräfenberg, Wasseros
» **Oestrich:** Doosberg, Lenchen
» **Rauenthal:** Baiken, Gehrn
» **Rüdesheim:** Berg Schlossberg
» **Schloss Johannisberg**
» **Schloss Vollrads**
» **Steinberg**
» **Winkel:** Hasensprung

RHEINHESSEN
» **Bingen:** Scharlachberg
» **Nackenheim:** Rothenberg
» **Nierstein:** Glöck, Hipping, Ölberg, Orbel, Pettenthal
» **Oppenheim:** Herrenberg, Kreuz,
» **Wintrich:** Ohligsberg
» **Wolf:** Goldgrube

RHEINHESSEN

The Rheinhessen follows directly on northward from the Pfalz, covering a wide swathe of land between Worms, Mainz, and Bingen, all major cities on the banks of the Rhine. The vast majority of this undulating area used to be dismissed as the source of the sugar-water, high-yield, low-flavor grapes that went to make Liebfraumilch. This mild, thin, sweetish style of wine is now a busted flush, and numerous villages, anonymous until now, faced a decision: either make an effort to do decent stuff or rip up their vines. Luckily, a new generation of determined and talented winemakers has taken up the challenge. The most vibrant area is down toward Worms, an area called the Wonnegau, where every vintage brings more exciting Riesling, Silvaner, and Pinot Noir as well as numerous other varieties. All of this activity has overshadowed the traditional center of Rheinhessen excellence—the Rheinfront, a group of villages centered on Oppenheim, Nierstein, and Nackenheim. This area benefits from the fact that the land rises along this stretch of the river and provides beautifully positioned east- and southeast-facing slopes, with some limestone from Oppenheim southward but more importantly, a seam of red slate most evident in Nierstein and Nackenheim. The best growers produce marvelously rich, spicy—although often dry—Rieslings, but because of the damage done to the area's reputation by Niersteiner Gutes Domtal (mostly cheap garbage that had nothing to do with Nierstein), these wines are not as desirable as they should be. There are two other small areas of the Rheinhessen: Ingelheim, in the north, produces good Pinot Noir; and Bingen can offer some impressive spicy, smoky Rieslings.

NAHE

The wine can be similar to the Rheingau—rich, grapey, and complex—but also like the Mosel, too: slaty, floral, and delicate. It's also a loose-knit area. Its most famous and traditionally best wines come from just a few villages upstream of Bad Kreuznach, led by Slossbockelheim, Niederhausen, and Norheim. From these impressive, steep, south-angled riverbanks you get fireworks—wines packed with energy and personality, almost always from the Riesling grape. The most famous vineyards are truly spectacular. The Schlossböckelheimer Kupfergrube used to be a copper mine, and the improbably steep terraces were hacked out of the rock by local convict labor.

The vineyards on red-slate soil at Nackenheim on the west bank of the Rhine are some of the best in the whole Rhine Valley.

The remarkable Traiser Bastei vineyard is crouched among the scree on the bottom of Northern Europe's highest cliff. Between Bad Kreuznach and the Rhine at Bingen, vines are scattered all over the area to the west. Until recently, not much exciting wine came from this pleasant but unremarkable area. But there are some very special sites, and there is a new generation of wine producers determined to make their mark. The villages of Langenlonsheim, Dorsheim, and Münster-Sarsheim are particularly worth a look.

RHEINGAU

Until the recent emergence of fine dry wines from further south on the Rhine, the Rheingau region was always thought of as the producer of the finest wines. The Romans were here. So, later, were the Cistercians. So, later still, was Queen Victoria, although she stayed only for lunch. Thomas Jefferson came as well, but unlike Queen Victoria he didn't get a vineyard named after him. The reason they kept on coming was that great wine was being made, year after year, in the vineyards above and between a string of villages bordering one particular stretch of the Rhine—the great and historic Rheingau, covering more than 20 miles of consistently sun-soaked open slopes.

The Rheingau is all about slopes, and it is a land of Riesling, except at the far western end, where there is some good Silvaner and Assmanshausen makes some of Germany's most famous Spätburgunder reds. The answer to what makes the Rheingau special is very simple: solid rock. The Rhine flows more or less northward through southern Germany until suddenly, at Wiesbaden, it comes up against the Taunus Mountains. The river finds its route to the north blocked, so it swings westward and only 20 miles later, at Rüdesheim, is it able to turn north again. The heart of the Rheingau is here, along the stretch of the river that flows west, with the vines planted on the south-facing slopes of the Taunus overlooking the river and gazing across at Rheinhessen and the Nahe.

The Rheingau is fairly cool for viticulture, but the Taunus Mountains keep the north and east winds off the vineyards, and the Rhine, which is up to half a mile wide here, reflects the sun back onto the vines. The river also encourages the formation of mists, which, on warm fall days, foster the development of *Botrytis cinerea*—the noble rot that creates intensely sweet grapes to make superb sweet wines.

The botrytized wines come from the lower vineyards, and so paradoxically do Eisweins because of the presence of frost pockets in these low-lying areas. The lower slopes, too, yield the heaviest, richest wines; the upper slopes give more delicacy and elegance. Sweet Rheingau wines are thrilling, but the majority of the wines are now made dry or half-dry.

The Rheingau begins just east of Wiesbaden with the large village of Hochheim, which is not on the Rhine at all. Instead, it sits on the right bank of the Main River. It has lent an abbreviation of its name—"hock"—to the English language as a name for all Rhine wine. This is where Queen Victoria stopped for a picnic to watch the harvesters at work one fine day in 1850 and where a vineyard owner with a sharp eye for publicity asked if he could name a vineyard after her: the 12-acre Königin Victoriaberg.

The river curves past Wiesbaden and Mainz, and then it's a straight run westward past some of the most famous names in German wine. The great vineyards appear almost immediately, scattered here and there at different altitudes: some down by the river, such as the suntrap of Erbacher Marcobrunn, some in the middle such as Schloss Johannisberg, and some at 655 feet or higher, such as Rauenthaler Gehrn.

The Rheingau has been at the heart of German wine for two thousand years and consequently has some of Germany's most aristocratic grand estates: Schloss Johannisberg, Schloss Schönborn, Schloss Reinhartshausen, and others. But there are about one thousand vine-growing families in the Rheingau, and most of the modern drive for quality has been led by more bourgeois producers such as Georg Breuer, Peter Jakob Kühn, Johannishof, Josef Leitz, Franz Künstler, Robert Weil, Josef Spreitzer—and not a prince among them. It's high time the great estates take note because they have many of the best vineyards.

MITTELRHEIN AND AHR

From Bingen to Koblenz in the Mittelrhein, the Rhine is a tourist's delight—gorges, cliffs, delightful villages, and just enough vineyards to service all that thirst. A few vineyards around Boppard and Bacharach produce wonderful minerally Rieslings. The best vineyard sites are often tucked away in the side valleys, and the Sekt industry, with its need for light, lean wines, relies heavily on grapes from this region.

At Koblenz, the Mosel joins the Rhine, and after that there is only one more wine region to go before Bonn, where the Rhine vineyards stop. The tiny Ahr Valley, however, can surprise. Most of its wine is red or at least pink; it used to be mainly sweetish, but its Pinot Noirs (Spätburgunder) are increasingly popular and successful. There's also some good Riesling. North of Bonn the local drink is beer; the hop can ripen where even the hardy Riesling fears to tread.

Rest of Germany

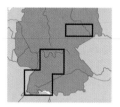

GERMANY HAS SEVERAL OTHER wine regions, some of minor importance, but two large ones, Franken and Baden-Württemberg, are now producing some of Germany's finest wines.

FRANKEN

Franken lies 50 miles east of the Rheingau and is centered on the Main River. The vineyards are scattered and include some of Germany's top vineyard sites: the Würzburger Stein, the Escherndorfer Lump, and the Julius-Echter-Berg. The soil is varied; there's a fair amount of marl and sandstone and some loam, gypsum, clay, limestone. But grape growing is pretty hardcore here because the climate is properly continental with cold winters and short, hot summers. Spring frosts can go down to –13 degrees Fahrenheit and kill vines, whereas fall is sometimes baking and long, making great sweet wines an occasional possibility. This is why Silvaner is the star grape here. Riesling is too late a ripener for the region's short growing season, except in the most favored sites of all. But Silvaner attains heights it reaches nowhere else. "Earthy" is the word usually used to describe it; it's minerally, too, low in acidity and high in extract. Made dry (and Franken's wines are always dry except when noble rot makes one of its rare visits), Silvaner is an ideal food wine.

BADEN-WÜRTTEMBERG

Baden and Württemberg make wines different from the rest of the country and different even from each other. They are both remarkably diffuse in terms of wine styles and grapes, yet here they are, yoked together into the state of Baden-Württemberg, and, while Baden's wines have for some years been trying to make an impact on foreign markets, the growers of Württemberg are only just beginning this process.

BADEN

It's easy to think of Baden as being a long, narrow strip of vineyards stretching for about 80 miles between the spa town of Baden-Baden down the Rhine Valley to Basel in Switzerland and looking west to Alsace in France. That's certainly the main part because 80 percent of its wines come from here and certainly most of the well-known ones. But wines labeled Baden also come from the Bereich Tauberfranken, tucked between the south of Franken and the north of Württemberg—belonging to Baden only because a political boundary says it does. Southwest of that, there's another chunk of Baden vineyards, this time wedged south of Hessische Bergstrasse and west of Württemberg. Then right down in the southeast, south of the Danube (Donau), there's a little enclave of Baden vines on the banks of Lake Constance (Bodensee) on the border with Switzerland.

Most of the Baden vineyards are tucked between the Rhine and the foothills of the Black Forest; they are effectively the mirror image of the Alsace vineyards just over the border, but the climate is marginally cooler and damper than that of Alsace.

In the south, down by Basel, the speciality of the Markgräflerland is the Gutedel grape (alias Chasselas), which makes a crisp, somewhat neutral wine. Increasingly, some good Pinot Noirs add some interest. It is not until near the beautiful medieval city of Freiburg that the typical full, dry style of Baden wine begins to emerge. It reaches its peak in the twin areas of Kaiserstuhl and Tuniberg. The Kaiserstuhl is the stump of a three million-year-old volcano partly covered with wind-blown loess, and its southern slopes, in particular the village of Ihringen, are Germany's warmest. This is the part of Germany where the Pinot family shines with a depth and weight frequently superior to the wines of Alsace across the river. Grauburgunder or Pinot Gris, Weissburgunder or Pinot Blanc, and Spätburgunder or Pinot Noir all ripen well here. The Tuniberg is a smaller hill than the Kaiserstuhl, at only about 997 feet high compared to the latter's 1,890 feet. Almost every inch of it is covered with vines, but the soil is limestone instead of volcanic, and it is slightly cooler and damper than its big brother.

Loess, as well as shelly limestone and gneiss, is the rule in the Bereich Breisgau as well, which runs up the Rhine Valley north of Freiburg, hugging the slopes of the Black Forest. This is becoming an exceptionally good area for Pinot Noirs.

The Bereich Ortenau opposite Strasbourg in France is home to some of Baden's best Rieslings, particularly on the granite hills east of Offenburg, where the Riesling (called Klingelberger locally) is dry and minerally. The vineyards die away abruptly at Baden-Baden. Southeast of Karlsruhe, at Pforzheim, they begin again; this is the Bereich Kraichgau, which runs north toward Heidelberg and another Bereich, Badische Bergstrasse. In the Bereich Tauberfranken, the wines are Franconian in character, sappy, and dry; they are made along the little Tauber River, which joins the Main River at Wertheim.

Finally, heading back south, the Seewein (or "lake wine") of the Bodensee is made almost entirely from Müller-Thurgau or Spätburgunder, the latter frequently made as a rosé. The broad lake modifies the cool climate, reflecting summer warmth back onto vines that, at up to 1,870 feet above sea level, are the highest north of the Alps.

There is an emphasis in Baden on organic viticulture, too, that tends to lower yields even further.

WÜRTTEMBERG

Nearly half the vineyards here are planted with red grapes, with Trollinger the leading variety. Sometimes red grapes may be mixed with white to make Schillerwein (allegedly named after the poet) and a Württemberg speciality. Württemberg is suited to making red wines. Its climate is more extreme than Baden's, with colder winters but sunnier summers, and red grapes ripen well. The pity is that most growers opt for the light, easy-drinking Trollinger instead of testing the limits with something more challenging such as Dornfelder or Spätburgunder (Pinot Noir). The soil tends to be marl and limestone; here, shelter and good exposure to the sun determine where the vine can be grown and where it can't. River valleys are the key to winemaking here, and Württemberg's vines go right from Franken in the north to Switzerland and the shores of the Bodensee.

HESSISCHE BERGSTRASSE

The Hessische Bergstrasse is a small, hilly region north of Heidelberg, with the old Roman road of Strada Montana—"mountain road"—running right through it. The Rhine, flowing north through a flat, fertile valley, is to the west of the region. To the east is the Odenwald. Logically, Hessische Bergstrasse is a northerly extension of Baden. There are two Bereichs in the region: Starkenburg, which encloses the 10-mile stretch of hillside that is the main part of Hessische Bergstrasse, and Umstadt, a more isolated area east of Darmstadt. The climate is pretty favorable for vines, with a mild, long growing season and more sunshine than the well-known wine area of Pfalz to the west. The soil is mostly light with a little loess

and granite. This suits Riesling, and it is given the best, warmest, most sheltered sites. The wines can reach Spätlese and Auslese level and even beyond, but they are usually on the delicate side.

SAALE-UNSTRUT AND SACHSEN

These are the two wine regions of former East Germany, and at reunification in 1990 some of the ancient vineyard land in Saale-Unstrut and Sachsen had lain fallow for decades. Much has now been replanted in the past few decades to give Saale-Unstrut about 1,815 acres of vineyards and Sachsen 1,235 acres. The Easterners learned quickly, and now there are some seriously good producers in both regions; look for Schloss Proschwitz and Klaus Zimmerling in Sachsen, and Lützkendorf in Saale-Unstrut. All make their wines dry.

The weather can be harsh. Summers are hot and sunny and bring plenty of extract to the wines to balance their decidedly high acidity; conversely, winters are long and cold. Saale-Unstrut is the most northerly wine region of Germany, and Sachsen, the most easterly, is not far behind; in Saale-Unstrut late frosts, hitting the vines roughly three years in every ten, cut the crop by 20 to 80 percent. In Sachsen, the cold is even harsher, and spring frosts, a threat until mid-May, can reduce the harvest by up to 90 percent. In both regions, then, it is only the most sunny and sheltered sites that have any chance of ripening grapes. In Saale-Unstrut, the main focus is on Freyburg, on the Unstrut, and in Sachsen it's the southern reaches of the Elbe around the city of Meissen. Saale-Unstrut's vines are planted on limestone and occasionally on sandstone; the wines are fruity, full-bodied, and generous even if they're backed up by fairly high acidity. Sachsen's are on granite subsoil and are sleeker and more racy.

In both regions, the best and warmest vineyard sites are planted with Riesling, although falls are really too early and cold for this late-ripening grape to show its best in this part of Germany. The early-ripening and reliable Müller-Thurgau is the main grape and gains some structure from the low yields. There's some good Silvaner in Saale-Unstrut, and both regions have small amounts of Weissburgunder, Traminer, and Gutedel. There are tiny plantings of red varieties (Portugieser, Spätburgunder, and Dornfelder), but nobody expects any great color or ripeness.

In Saale-Unstrut, the wines are usually vinified dry; Sachsen makes a softer, lighter style of wine that undoubtedly appeals to the tourists who gravitate to the region, and Spätlese and Auslese wines can be made in exceptionally warm years.

Switzerland

VERY LITTLE SWISS WINE seems to leave the country, and what does get out seems to be pretty expensive. That shouldn't surprise us. Everybody knows that Switzerland is an expensive country. The cost of manual labor is 20 to 30 percent more than in neighboring countries, and the cost of producing wine can be four times as high as in France because of the steepness of the slopes and the expense of maintaining the terraces. The vineyards are also small—the average holding is only around an acre or so.

But while the wine often has charm, while it may have individuality and go well with food, it's mostly not great wine. The most unusual wines are the Petite Arvines, Amignes, Humagnes, and Cornalins of the Valais, which can age in bottle for a good few years, but most Swiss wine is best drunk young, like most wine, in fact. The Valais is now also making some surprisingly good Syrah, which is usually better than the often muddy Pinot Noir, and the Vaud and Valais make light, bright Chasselas (known as Fendant in the Valais). Italian-speaking Switzerland makes good Merlot, and German-speaking Switzerland concentrates on Pinot Noir (or Blauburgunder), of which the best comes from the canton of Graubünden, and Müller-Thurgau.

Three-quarters of Switzerland's vineyards can be found in the French-speaking cantons of Valais, Vaud, Geneva, and Three Lakes; around 27,600 acres of the country's total of about 33,860 acres of vineyards are here, compared to about 7,050 acres in the German-speaking part in eastern Switzerland and only 2,730 acres in Ticino, the Italian-speaking part down near Lake Lugano. The vineyards tend to be squeezed around the edges of the country and in the corners, with only a few isolated patches in the more mountainous center and eastern section. Almost all Swiss vineyards depend on the beneficial influence of water for their existence. That water may be a river or a lake, and there are a lot of these. A large body of water moderates extremes of temperature and reflects the ample sunshine back onto the vines. Add protective mountain ranges—there are plenty of these—and some southerly winds, particularly the Foehn wind in the eastern part of the country that warms and dries the grapes, and this explains why some of Europe's highest vineyards can still regularly ripen their crops, particularly where the vines grow at altitudes of about 1,150 feet or more.

CLASSIFICATIONS

» Switzerland has federal and a plethora of cantonal regulations and uses four different languages. There are three different categories for wine.
» **Appellation d'origine contrôlée** These wines come from an individual canton or region within a canton. They may bear a place name, a combination of place and grape name, or a generic name (for example, Fendant). There are more than 650 appellations.
» **Vin de pays** These wines come from an area larger than a canton—for example, Chasselas Romand, for Chasselas from the Suisse Romande.
» **Vin de table** These wines are usually sold by the liter.

OTHER CANTONAL REGULATIONS

The cantons of Geneva and Valais also have Grand Cru and Premier Cru wines, which are more precisely delimited and have to meet stricter requirements. In the German-speaking cantons, there is a seal of quality—Winzer-Wy, or Vintner's wine—awarded by a tasting panel, and Ticino in Italian-speaking Switzerland labels its best Merlots with the VITI seal. The French-speaking cantons also have quality seals, called Terravin in the canton of Vaud and La Gerle in Neuchâtel.

CANTONS

- ░░ NEUCHÂTEL/THREE LAKES
- ██ VAUD
- ▓▓ GENÈVE
- ░░ VALAIS
- ▒▒ TICINO
- ██ GERMAN-SPEAKING SWITZERLAND

WINE REGIONS

Of all the Swiss wine cantons, the Valais is the most important, with around 12,295 acres of vines, and it also has the greatest variety of grapes. The Rhône River cuts its way between the Bernese Alps and the Valais, and in one startling, thrilling section, the river heads south-west from Sierre past Sion to Martigny for about 25 miles, providing a perfect southwest exposure for the steep slopes.

For a wine enthusiast, the train from Geneva through the Valais to the Simplon tunnel and into Italy has to be one of the greatest journeys in the world. Heading out along the idyllic north shore of Lake Geneva to Lausanne, the Vaud vineyards crowd in on the track. Turning east and south past Vevey and Montreux on to Yvorne and Martigny and the beginning of the Valais vineyards, the tranquil beauty of the lake is followed by the increasing grandeur of the mountains and the strips of vineyards creeping up into the warmer side valleys, whereas the valley floor is left to orchards. (The Swiss are fond of a fruit brandy to finish off a leisurely meal.) I don't know

anywhere else where the monoculture of the vine is more beautiful or more startling. Vines seem to climb vertically up the spectacular mountain faces; tiny villages perch on plateaus cut off from every other manifestation of life except their vines; and, even in the height of summer, the great mountain peaks glow with luminous snow as this Alpine suntrap bakes its perfectly exposed vines to a quite remarkable degree of ripeness. Some 85 percent of the Valais vineyards lie between Saillon and Leuk, on the right bank of the Rhône

This Rhône is the same river that produces massive, tannic Syrah reds a long way downstream in France. Here in the Valais, however, one-third of the wines are white, from Chasselas, Sylvaner, Marsanne, Pinot Gris, Arvine, Amigne, Muscat, Riesling, and a few others, including an increasing amount of Chardonnay. The reds are principally from Pinot Noir and Gamay—often blended into a Valais speciality, a Pinot-dominated wine called Dôle. Pinot Noir is sometimes bottled on its own, and there's also very good Syrah from these dry mountain suntraps as well as marvelous oddities such as Cornalin and Humagne. Talking of suntraps, this is a seriously dry area, and for hundreds of years locals have used little canals called *bisses* cut into the hillsides to carry snowmelt down into the vineyards, which, because the slopes can get as steep as 85 percent, are frequently terraced with an impressive Swiss neatness. Some of the vines here, such as Petite Arvine, are found nowhere else in Switzerland. They thrive in the Valais because this long gorge, with the Rhône flowing through the middle, is one of the sunniest parts of the country. Most of the vineyards are on the right bank, facing south and catching all the sun.

The Vaud, in terms of area under vine, comes next, with about 9,350 acres. More than 60 percent of the vines are Chasselas. When you look at the beautiful flowing slopes that roll down toward the banks of Lake Geneva, you do wonder whether a more exciting grape variety than Chasselas should be planted there. But the Vaud can make pretty good Chasselas, especially because this grape reflects the soil on which it is grown and changes in character according to whether it is planted on the scree of Chablais, the moraine of Lavaux and La Côte, or the puddingstone of Dézaley in Lavaux (Vaud's top village appellation), where the wine is more structured.

In the northern part of the Vaud, the vineyards of Côtes-de-l'Orbe, Bonvillars, and Vully are influenced by Lake Neuchâtel. La Côte, on the banks of Lake Geneva, is planted half with red (Gamay and Pinot Noir) and half with white grapes. Swiss red wines used to be low in acidity and high in yield, but steps are being taken to reverse that situation. Yields are lower than they were but, judging from the average quality, could come down still further. The vines are also being planted in cool sites so that the grapes gain more acidity. In the case of Chasselas, avoiding or limiting the malolactic fermentation, which changes the green apple-tasting malic acid in wine to the creamy tasting lactic acid, has improved quality. But the majority of Swiss wines still nearly always tend to be light in color and body. A few producers are experimenting with aging their reds in new oak, but the majority of the wines—even those from the warm Valais—just don't have the guts needed for this kind of treatment.

The tiny canton of Geneva has a ready market for wine and, despite its size, accounts for 10 percent of vineyard plantings in Switzerland. There are 3,545 acres of vines crammed between the western end of the lake and the French border. This is calm, rolling, fertile land, with most of the vineyards scattered amid fields of other crops. For a long time, white Chasselas and Müller-Thurgau dominated, but the move to red wine sees Gamay and Pinot Noir increasingly important, and even varieties such as Merlot and Cabernet Sauvignon are making an appearance. There's a lot of experimentation with whites, too, and you'll get a fair amount of Chardonnay, Pinot Gris, and others. After being a relatively complacent backwater for a long time, Geneva is beginning to buzz.

Viticulture in the Three Lakes region around the lakes of Neuchâtel, Bienne (Bieler See), and Morat is helped by the moderating influence of these large expanses of water. There are about 2,410 acres of vines. Pinot Noir accounts for just under half the plantings, and there is a special clone called Cortaillod. Chasselas is the next most important grape, growing on soil that is mostly limy, with alluvial soil lower down the slopes. The region is dry and sunny, although not as sunny and dry as the Valais.

Fribourg, with vineyards at Vully, has varying amounts of sandstone in the soil; again, the vineyards are lake-influenced. Jura has only recently rectified its record of being the only French-speaking canton with no vineyards at all by planting 17 acres. The canton of Bern is mainly German-speaking, but the vineyards are mostly in the French-speaking part, the Lac de Bienne. Here, they're happy to grow Chasselas (which they call Gutedel). The canton includes the vineyards of Lake Thun, looking relatively lonely all by themselves in the middle of Switzerland, but they don't do so badly. They're south-facing. The Pinot Noir and Riesling-Sylvaner vines grow up to about 1,970 feet, and Switzerland's favorite warm wind, the Foehn, keeps the chill off.

In the nineteen German-speaking wine cantons of eastern Switzerland, we're almost at the limit of vine cultivation, and the climate is cooler and often wetter. The average minimum annual temperature is 48 degrees Fahrenheit, which is as low as you can happily go for viticulture, and spring and fall frosts can be a problem. But vines are grown at up to about 1,970 feet in parts of Graubünden, and growers seek out sheltered south-facing sites and pray for the Foehn. The soil varies: there is chalky limestone in the Jura foothills; sandstone in the middle; and limestone, moraine, and schist elsewhere, with alluvial cones in parts of Graubünden. The best vineyards of Graubünden are on slate; effectively scree from the mountains above them. The cool climate doesn't stop them from growing red wine, mainly Pinot Noir. Whites are mostly Riesling-Sylvaner.

In the Italian-speaking canton of Ticino, the architecture is increasingly Italian the further south you go. Here, south of the Alps, the climate, too, is more influenced by the Mediterranean. That means a lot of sun and plenty of rain, and even the rain has an Italian temperament: it arrives in short, violent storms. The northern section of Sopraceneri still has a little of the old local varieties left, but Merlot is more important, as it is in the region south of Mount Ceneri, the Sottoceneri. Quality is increasingly good, with new methods of viticulture and up-to-date, even international winemaking being used effectively.

At about 3,610 feet, these vineyards at Visperterminen are the highest in mainland Europe. The steep terraces are angled toward the sun and produce surprisingly alcoholic wine from the Heida (Savagnin Blanc) grape.

Austria

I CAN'T THINK OF A EUROPEAN nation where the wine culture has changed so dramatically in recent years as it has in Austria. Austria still makes great sweet wines, but a new order based on world-class medium- and full-bodied dry whites and increasingly fine reds has emerged. Suddenly Austria seems sleek and positively New World in its ambition and innovativeness.

Ah, but is that the real Austria? Only partly. Spend a day out wine-tasting in the cellars of the Wachau, Burgenland, or Styria (Steiermark)—above all, Styria—and at every turn you'll be offered plattersful of sausage and ham and Speck and rye bread smeared with smoked lard (delicious, by the way) as your palate slowly learns to judge a wine through the smog of pork fat and pepper. Lunch will probably be in a *Buschenschenke*, a family-owned country inn, in which the food and the wine are all home-made.

WINE REGIONS

The Austrian vineyards, all located in the east of the country, have a climate influenced, in the main, by the warm, dry climate of the Pannonian plain to the east. Further west (take a look at the map), it's too mountainous and the climate too extreme.

In the northern part of Burgenland, the shallow Neusiedl lake makes great sweet wines possible; south Burgenland makes increasingly good reds; Lower Austria (Niederösterreich) makes the best Grüner Veltliner (an Austrian speciality) and Styria (Steiermark) makes high-acid but well-flavored wines that have achieved cult status in Austria. Vienna (Wien) has a wine region to itself and has become a jack-of-all-trades, with whole villages on the outskirts of the city apparently dedicated solely to serving wine to tourists in their *Heurigen,* or wine inns.

So favorable is the climate in eastern Austria that vineyards are scattered everywhere, rising up on south-facing slopes, while corn, pumpkin, or orchards occupy the lower ground. There is none of the feeling of battling against the elements that one gets in parts of Germany, and accordingly there is no skeleton of moderating

rivers to be found underlying the wine map. The Danube (Donau) runs east to west through Niederösterreich, but only in the Wachau, at the western end of the region, is the river genuinely necessary to viticulture. Here, the banks of the Danube rise into cliffs of rock and scrub, and the landscape is as beautiful and uncompromising as any in Germany's Mosel region. Some of Austria's finest dry whites come from these vineyards overlooking the river, just as her finest sweet whites come from the lush, low-lying, misty Neusiedlersee region in Burgenland. This is the other place where water plays a major part in Austrian wine—the large, shallow Neusiedl lake encourages the botrytis fungus to attack the grapes with a ferocity seen nowhere else in Europe. Consequently, it's possible to make great sweet wines here every year.

Most of the rest of vinous Austria is gently hilly or flattish. The hilliest region is Steiermark, down on the border with Slovenia, where the vines grow at between about 1,150 and 1,970 feet on the Alpine foothills, partly to avoid the frost in the valleys, partly to get more sun, and partly to benefit from the greater temperature fluctuations from day to night, which give acidity and finesse to the white grapes that dominate. Finding the right sheltered, south-facing site is the key here, and the best wines have elegance and taut balance combined with good levels of ripeness, but they can also taste exceedingly dry. Between 13 and 13.5 percent alcohol, without chaptalization, is not uncommon for the top wines. Even their botrytis-affected sweet wines keep a certain tautness and don't taste as rich and as fat as those of Burgenland.

Steiermark is divided into three regions: West, South, and Southeast (recently renamed as Vulkanland). The hills are lower here and the climate less extreme than elsewhere in Steiermark. Südsteiermark looks smallest on the map but has 55 percent of Steiermark's plantings of 10,482 acres of vines, mainly around Leibnitz and down to the Slovenian border. This is technically the warmest Austrian wine region, and the specialities are Chardonnay (here called Morillon), Sauvignon Blanc, and Gelber Muskateller. The wines can be excellent, but all are marked by their austere dryness, even the Muskateller. The vineyards in Weststeiermark are nearly all given over to a fearsome rosé called Schilcher, made from the Blauer Wildbacher grape, which is notable for its tooth-juddering acidity.

Vienna's vineyards are concentrated to the west of the city, although there are also some within the city limits. White wine is the thing here, especially from Grüner Veltliner, Riesling, Chardonnay, and Gemischter Satz. It's a short journey for the Viennese and for the tourist buses to the suburbs of Grinzing, Nussberg, Heiligenstadt, and Stammersdorf and their growers' *Heurigen*, or wine inns, with their vine-covered courtyards. Here, the pitchers of wine splash, and the accordionist plays late into the evening.

CLASSIFICATIONS

Wine categories are similar to those in Germany, but in practice the only ones frequently encountered are those defining the sweeter styles: Auslese, Beerenauslese, Ausbruch (a style only found around the town of Rust in the Burgenland), Trockenbeerenauslese (TBA), Eiswein, and Strohwein. The Wachau has its own ripeness scale for dry whites: Steinfeder wines are made for early drinking, Federspiel wines can last for three years or so, and the most powerful wines are known as Smaragd.

Over recent years, Austria has developed a geographical appellation system with stylistic constraints, called DAC. Because each DAC has different rules and restrictions, the system is hard to understand and often ignored even by producers, so you can imagine what the consumers think of it. Also, as in Germany, more producers are using the vineyard name on the label, not the village name.

MAIN WINE REGIONS

NIEDERÖSTERREICH
- Wachau
- Traisental DAC
- Kremstal DAC
- Kamptal DAC
- Weinviertel DAC
- Wagram
- Carnuntum
- Thermenregion

WIEN
- Wiener Gemischter Satz DAC

BURGENLAND
- Neusiedlersee DAC
- Leithaberg DAC
- Mittelburgenland DAC
- Eisenberg DAC

STEIERMARK
- Vulkanland Steiermark
- Südsteiermark
- Weststeiermark

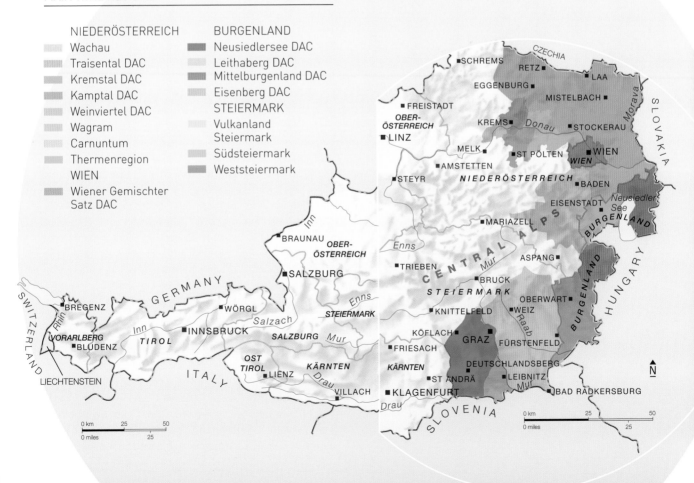

Along the Danube

RED GRAPES
*Zweigelt and Blauer Portugieser
are the most important red
grapes. There are small amounts
of Blauburgunder (Pinot Noir)
and St. Laurent.*

WHITE GRAPES
*Niederösterreich produces
Austria's best Grüner Veltliner,
and more than half the vineyards
are planted with it. There is
also great Riesling and good
Weissburgunder, Chardonnay,
and Welschriesling.*

CLIMATE
*The climate is generally dry,
but Niederösterreich is a large
area, and there is great variation.
Most parts are fairly warm; the
eastern Weinviertel can be cool
and damp.*

SOIL
*Gneis subsoil is common,
particularly in the Wachau.
Topsoil includes stony schist,
limestone, gravel, loess in
Krems, and occasionally loam.*

GEOGRAPHY
*Most Niederösterreich vineyards
are on plains or gently rolling
hills. In the Wachau, the Danube
Valley is the focus, with the banks
of the river getting steeper west
of Krems.*

NIEDERÖSTERREICH (Lower Austria), situated on the fertile Danube (Donau) plain, is one of the loveliest parts of Austria. It is a land of hills crowned with vast baroque monasteries and tunneled with troglodyte wine cellars, of terraced slopes and fertile fields, of picturesque villages and of course the broad Danube—calm, powerful, and, yes, blue. Well, on a good day, anyway.

The heart of the area is around the city of Krems, where four wine regions gather along the Danube's banks. In the west, on both sides of the river, is the Wachau, home of Austria's best Rieslings. Next comes Kremstal. Kamptal is centered on the Kamp River and the important wine town of Langenlois, while Wagram stretches away to the east along the Danube as far as Vienna. All these regions make dry whites.

The Wachau Rieslings both are and are not like German Rieslings. Coming from a relatively warm climate, the wines are dry, full of extract, and minerally instead of being flowery. They age well, although the Austrian taste is for young wine, so they seldom get the chance. The grapes grow in conditions as demanding as those of any German vineyard; about half the Wachau is terraced, and the vines have to work hard for their living on shallow, stony soil often only 20 inches deep. The summers are very dry, and the only concession the vine gets is irrigation, although not much; six days in any growing season is the maximum allowed.

The eastern end of the Wachau makes more opulent wines, but only where the soil is shallow and poor is Riesling planted, on slopes up to about 985 feet. On the flatter land and the sandy soil nearer the river, Grüner Veltliner is grown, and, in the right hands and providing yields are kept down to around about 3 tons per acre, the wines can be intense and powerful, with good structure and even the ability to age for a few years. There is Weissburgunder here, too, but Riesling gets the prime south-facing sites.

Growers say the terraces are three to five times more work than the flat vineyards, and the flatter vineyards, as mechanization increases, are getting cheaper to work. But the effort and expense of keeping these remarkable vineyards going are rewarded by an array of brilliant whites. Kremstal is less spectacular, but the wines are also seriously good. Niederösterreich generally is the home of Austria's best Grüner Veltliner (it's too warm in Burgenland and too cold elsewhere in the country), and Kremstal produces Grüner Veltliners as good as those of the Wachau, again providing the yields are kept low. The climatic influence is from the southeast—the great Pannonian plain stretches across into Hungary, where it is warm and dry—and Krems gets fewer than 20 inches of rain per year. The town of Krems is the wine capital here, and the town of Stein, next door, has some of Austria's best vineyard sites. Most famous is the Steiner Hund, steep and terraced and ideal for Riesling, followed by Pfaffenberg, Kögl, and Kremsleiten. Then there is the Krems Valley, winding down from the northwest; and to the east a great swathe of vineyards around Rohrendorf on loess soil.

Kamptal's fame rests mostly on the high-quality grapes led by exciting Grüner Veltliner as well as excellent Riesling, Chardonnay. Pinot Noir, St. Laurent, and a large chunk of Zweigelt coming from the great curve of south-

TOP VILLAGES AND VINEYARDS

» **Dürnstein:** Hollerin, Kellerberg
» **Kammern:** Lamm
» **Krems:** Kremsleiten
» **Langenlois:** Dechaut, Heiligenstein, Lamm
» **Loiben:** Loibenberg, Steinertal
» **Senftenberg:** Hochäcker
» **Spitz:** Hochrain, Rotestor, Singerriedel
» **Stein:** Hund, Kögl, Pfaffenberg
» **Strass:** Gaisberg
» **Viesslingen:** Bruck
» **Weissenkirchen:** Achleiten, Klaus
» **Wösendorf:** Kollmütz
» **Zöbing:** Heiligenstein

Niederösterreich's biggest region, the Weinviertel, can produce good reds, particularly on the granite soil around Retz near the Czech border, where there is less rain than in any other Austrian wine region. In the northeast of the Weinviertel, the climate is damper, and the vineyards here are a source of good Grüner Veltliner. In some of these villages, there are wonderfully pretty Kellergassen, tiny pedimented cellars built in a row into the hillside along narrow lanes running between high banks. Anyone on a wine tour of Austria really should try to get an invitation to one of these cellars if only to get a glimpse of a winemaking tradition that goes back centuries. At regular intervals along the lanes are front doors leading straight into the hillside, like a scene from a fairy tale. Inside, the cellars are deep and narrow, each one wide enough for only one row of barrels on each side and a pathway down the middle. As you go further into the hill, the temperature drops dramatically, and in these emerald- or scarlet-hooped black barrels is the entire harvest of one small-scale grower. Hopefully, he'll take some samples of wine for you to try. The wine will be cold and fresh, high in acidity, and with piercing fresh fruit.

facing vineyards that arches around the town—plus some good growers to make the most of it all.

Traisental's vineyards are along the valley of the Trais between St. Pölten and the Danube to the north. Wagram looks to the town and old monastery of Klosterneuburg as its capital; the monastery is the largest single vineyard owner in Austria, and the town is the home of Austria's first viticultural institute. Carnuntum lies southeast of Vienna and runs up to the Leitha Hills, which separate it from Burgenland. The climate here is warm and dry and, especially near the Burgenland border, fairly similar to that of Burgenland itself.

Thermenregion is a region of spas and hot springs. It's sunnier and drier here than in Vienna, but it is windy, and it's this wind that prevents much noble rot from settling on the grapes. So its wine capital, Gumpoldskirchen, developed its own speciality: semi-sweet wines made from a blend of two local grapes, Rotgipfler and Zierfandler. Zierfandler is planted on the higher slopes of the hills, where it develops plenty of acidity, and the Rotgipfler lower down. Red wines are the speciality in the south of Thermenregion, and the most successful ones come from Pinot Noir (Blauburgunder) and St. Laurent.

Most of the great vineyards of Northern Europe need a river valley to provide heat and protection from wind and frost. Here, in the Wachau region west of Krems, the Danube does its part by reflecting all that warmth back onto the vineyards.

Burgenland

RED GRAPES
Blaufränkisch and Zweigelt are the two main red varieties. There are smaller amounts of St. Laurent, Merlot, Pinot Noir, and Cabernet Sauvignon.

WHITE GRAPES
The Austrian speciality, Grüner Veltliner, has 23 percent of the vineyard area. Muskat-Ottonel and Neuburger, along with Welschriesling and Weissburgunder, are much used for Ausbruch and other sweet wines.

CLIMATE
This is the warmest and driest wine region in Austria. At Illmitz, just east of the lake in the heart of Neusiedlersee, the average annual temperature is 51.5 degrees Fahrenheit.

SOIL
The soil is varied, with sand around the Neusiedl lake and loam further away. There is limestone in the Leitha Hills and the Rosalien Hills to the west of the lake. Elsewhere there are gravel and deep loam.

GEOGRAPHY
The region is generally flat. The west of the lake is gently undulating, with good south- and southeast-facing slopes, and there are occasional ranges of hills in Mittelburgenland. In Eisenberg, the vineyards face east and southeast over the Hungarian plain.

FOR LOVERS OF LUSCIOUSLY SWEET botrytis-affected wine, this marshy, reedy corner of Austria around the Neusiedl lake (Neusiedlersee) on the border with Hungary is one of the most remarkable places on Earth. Nowhere else does *Botrytis cinerea* attack the grapes so reliably every year; nowhere else is it so easy to make great sweet wines and in such quantities. In Germany and France, growers watch their grapes anxiously for the first signs of the fungus that will shrivel and brown the grapes and impart its distinctive flavor to the wines. In the vineyards bordering Neusiedlersee, they seldom need to worry. This reliability has a produced a surge in quality in recent years because producers have focused on refining their techniques. Wines that were once safe and inexpensive and then fell out of favor after the Austrian wine scandal of 1985 are now world class, and (inevitably) they are also more expensive.

Burgenland has had a checkered history. Until 1921 it was part of Hungary, and it joined Austria just in time for the economic hardship of the 1920s and '30s. After the end of World War II, Burgenland was part of the Russian zone of occupation, and it was only when the Russians left in 1956 that the way was clear for investment in the vineyards. So while fine sweet wines have been made around the Neusiedl lake since the beginning of the seventeenth century, it is only in the last couple of decades that they have been made in such large quantities. The southern shores of the lake are still part of Hungary and form part of the Sopron wine region. But unlike the Austrian vineyards around the lake, these Hungarian vineyards are largely planted with red varieties, both Cabernets, Merlot, and Pinot Noir.

The eastern shore, a shallow expanse of warm water that imparts humidity to the area, has only a recent history of viticulture. This was a largely forgotten part of the country, given over to cattle farming until the late 1950s, when the local chamber of commerce suggested that the farmers plant bulk vines, such as Grüner Veltliner and Müller-Thurgau, for basic blending wine. Neither is remotely suited to this hot, humid, flat region, where grapes ripen early and can lack acidity unless care is taken in the winemaking process; it has only been with the planting of aromatic varieties, such as Traminer, and traditional Burgenland vines, such as Welschriesling and Weissburgunder, that fine wines have emerged.

The soil on both sides of the lake is sandy because the lake itself once covered an even larger area than its current size of 59 square miles. However, further away from the immediate lake area, the soil is loam, which tends not to heat up quite as fast, and there is limestone in the foothills to the west. The eastern side of the lake is warmer, and the grapes ripen here some two weeks earlier.

Burgenland is not all sweet wines. The Leithaberg DAC on higher ground west of the lake is producing serious, minerally reds. The region then extends in a knobbly strip southwest of the lake along the Hungarian border through the flat Mittelburgenland down to Südburgenland (where a tiny village called Eisenberg has given its name to the Eisenberg DAC covering Blaufränkisch wines from the whole of Südburgenland) and the border with Slovenia. The Mittelburgenland is red wine country. The majority of the grapes are red, and more than half of them are Blaufränkisch. Wines labeled Mittelburgenland DAC will be 100 percent Blaufränkisch, although some growers use Merlot or Cabernet Sauvignon to add backbone to the blend.

Eisenberg is an altogether quieter place and doesn't have a lot of vines, but it also makes some smashing Blaufränkisch reds. There are also scattered plantings of rarities, such as the American varieties Concord, Noah, and Otello, which were introduced after phylloxera. The wine, usually pink, is known as Uhudler, and I'm told it is an aphrodisiac. Who am I to argue?

SWEET WINES

The shallow Neusiedl lake (only 6 feet at its deepest) on the border with Hungary is in Austria's hottest region and is one of the most perfect mesoclimates in the world for the development of *Botrytis cinerea,* or noble rot. As fall draws in after the long, hot continental summer the falling temperatures cause night fogs and early morning mists over the warm waters of the lake and the surrounding vineyards, particularly those at Illmitz on the reedy, pancake-flat eastern shore, but also at Rust, a picturesque village on the western shore. Later in the morning, the bright autumnal sunshine burns off the fog and mists, and this alternation of humidity and sunshine provides ideal conditions for botrytis. The warmth and humidity in these low-lying areas near the lake mean that it is almost impossible for ripe grapes not to be infected with botrytis in late fall.

Further away from the lake there is less humidity, and botrytis infection occurs only occasionally, perhaps about twice a decade.

Alois Kracher burst on the scene in 1986 with his super-rich sweet wines from the reedy lowlands of Illmitz in Neusiedlersee. He rapidly became the stellar leader of the exciting new wave of Burgenland producers, self-confidently proclaiming that they made the best sweet wine in the world. He died in 2007, but his son Gerhard continues to make brilliant wine, and Neusiedlersee is now globally respected for the greatness of the sweet wines Alois Kracher first brought to our attention.

200

Central and Eastern Europe

CZECHIA AND SLOVAKIA

When Czechoslovakia was one nation, there was a relatively natural divide: Slovakia made the wine, the Czechs brewed the beer. Slovakia generally has better conditions for viticulture; indeed, on its eastern border with Hungary are some of the original villages for the famous sweet Hungarian wine, Tokaji (or Tokay in English). But the Czech vineyards of Moravia are pretty good. Nevertheless, if I had to choose the wines from either country that have given me most pleasure, they would be the violet-scented, damsony St. Laurent, the perfumed Irsay Oliver, and the crackly, peppery, celery stalk Grüner Veltliner—all from Slovakia.

After the division of the country into two in 1993, Slovakia found itself with two-thirds of the vineyards. Despite juicy St. Laurent and the occasional Frankovka, both countries are better suited to white wine production. There's huge potential for quality here: the latitude is virtually the same as that of Alsace, and many of the best wines have the same spicy fatness; most companies run on a refreshingly human scale; and Australian and French winemakers, there to advise, say that the winemaking equipment in several cellars is pretty good. Both countries enjoy a settled continental climate: warm and dry in the growing season, with cool, dry falls and little variation between regions, although Slovakia is slightly warmer.

CZECHIA

North of Prague, most of Bohemia's 1,235 acres of vineyards cluster round the Elbe (Labe) and its tributaries. These wines, seldom seen outside the region, resemble their Sachsen counterparts across the border in Germany, being dry with marked acidity—you see why most people drink the beer. Moving southeast, Moravia's 28,415 acres or so of vineyards are in the valleys of the Dyje, Svratka, and Morava rivers, which flow into the Danube (Dunaj). The grapes are mainly Grüner Veltliner, Müller-Thurgau, Welschriesling, Ryzlink Rynsky (Riesling), and Pinot Blanc for whites, and the spicy, plummy, St. Laurent and Lemberger (Blaufränkisch) for reds.

SLOVAKIA

Slovakia's 37,000 acres of vineyards are located mainly around the Váh, Nitra, and Hron tributaries of the Danube. Slovakia's most important producer is the state winery at Nitra, while Western investment is improving quality in the smaller wineries to the south and west, such as Gbelce and Hurbanovo near the Hungarian border at Komárno. The grape varieties grown here are virtually the same as the Czech ones, with the addition of some tasty Grüner Veltliners, the fruity Frankovka red, and the local Ezerjó and Leányka. In Tokaj, at Slovakia's eastern extreme, Furmint, Hárslevelü, and Muscat Ottonel can produce wines of similar character to the more famous Tokay wines of neighboring Hungary.

BLACK SEA STATES

I'm not sure the winemaking picture since the collapse of the Soviet Union is any clearer than it used to be. A few old certainties have been replaced by a swarm of uncertainties, and only a handful of these countries have so far done anything to improve the wine.

MOLDOVA

Winemaking is a major part of the Moldovan economy, and more than 7 percent of agricultural land is planted with vines, tended by more than 70,000 smallholders. The area planted to vines is shrinking, and many vineyards are in real need of replanting. That said, some 50,000 acres have been replanted since 2006, and international consultants have all reported on the great potential. The most important white grapes are Aligoté (used mainly for sparkling wine), Rkatsiteli, Sauvignon Blanc, Fetească Albă, Chardonnay, and Traminer. The leading reds are Merlot, Cabernet Sauvignon, Pinot Noir, and Saperavi, the great Georgian grape. Malbec and Syrah are now also being planted. It's easy to simplify talk of potential—Moldova has loads—but I've tasted the real thing: a 1967 Negru Purkar, a fabulous, dark, cedary, Saperavi-dominated red. All Moldova needs is some economic and political stability.

MAIN WINE REGIONS

- CZECHIA
- UKRAINE
- RUSSIA
- GEORGIA
- ARMENIA
- AZERBAIJAN
- TURKEY
- CYPRUS
- LEBANON
- ISRAEL

See also
More detailed map **page 203**

UKRAINE

Ukraine's wine reputation and capacity were dramatically affected by the Russian annexation of the Crimea in 2014—its best wine region. Even so, Odessa in the southwest still has 78,085 acres of vines and produces serious reds along the border with Moldova and on the Dnieper River, as well as quality sparkling wine. This is where future quality will come from.

RUSSIA

Since 2014, with the annexation of the Crimea, Russia has three main vineyard regions, all in areas where the presence of a mass of water tempers the effect of the icy winters. Crimea has specialized in dessert and fortified wines—often superb—for almost two hundred years, although sparklers and dry wines are also made. Krasnodar on the Black Sea makes still and sparkling wines, and further north at Rostov, where the Don River runs into the sea of Azov, sparkling wines are made.

GEORGIA

More than eight thousand years of wine history make Georgia a front runner for the title of birthplace or cradle of wine. With its diverse climates (from subtropical to moderate continental), frost-free winters, and hugely diverse soil, the five wine regions produce a great diversity of styles. International and indigenous varieties abound, and the peppery, powerful red Saperavi could be a world-beater. Kakheti, which spans the southeastern foothills of the Caucasus Mountains in the east of Georgia, has 70 percent of the vineyards and is not only important for Western-style wines but is also the center of Quevri winemaking.

Quevri are large clay jars buried in the ground, and at vintage time the grapes are piled into the jars—stems and all—and left to ferment and macerate for months, sometimes years. The result is wild, tannic (for both whites and reds), and thrillingly unmodern. If ever any wine culture could claim to be making its wines with the same methods they employed thousands of years ago, Georgia's claim is the strongest.

Romania

ALTHOUGH SURROUNDED ON MOST flanks by people of Slavic origin, the proud brown eyes of the Romanian burn with a definite Latin fire. The capital, Bucharest, still has much of the ambience and architecture that earned it the soubriquet "Little Paris." It comes as no surprise, then, to learn that grapes have been grown in the country for more than six thousand years. Romania covers much the same latitudes as France, but its climate is different, being generally continental with hot summers and cold winters. The Black Sea exerts a moderating influence, while the Carpathian mountains act as a barrier to cooler weather systems from the north. In general, the northern regions of the country, especially Moldova and Transylvania, favor white wine production, while the best reds come from the south, from Muntenia and Dobrogea.

Romania has the fifth-largest area under vine—about 452,620 acres, half of which are *vinifera*—in Europe and benefits from mature, reasonably healthy vines of a wide range of familiar and unfamiliar grape varieties and some superbly sited vineyards.

The change from Communism to democracy hasn't been easy, and accession to the European Union in 2007 hasn't transformed the wine business here—yet. But modern winemaking, along with expertise from abroad and new equipment, is beginning to make a difference. International-backed ventures, such as Recas and Cramele Halewood, are a sign of a mini-revolution, but challenges remain as more than one-third of the vineyard plots are 2½ acres or fewer in size. Of equal importance have been the emergence and in some cases the reemergence of private estates and wineries, such as Davino, Prince Stirbey, Corcova, Avincis, and Crama Basilescu. The challenge will be for these two different types of producer to develop a common front. Romania has made great strides in the export market, but this has been primarily through being able to supply decent, attractive whites and reds at prices that few other countries can match. Basic Romanian Pinot Noir or Pinot Grigio is often excellent. However, it is increasingly clear that Romania has both the terroir and the grape varieties—international and indigenous—to compete at a

higher level. Big companies such as Recas are developing more high-end wines and are involved in the revival of potentially excellent vineyards areas, such as Minis near the Hungarian border, but the private estates, without recourse to high-volume, low-cost business, will have to lead the way if Romania is to return to the glory days of its nineteenth-century zenith.

Of the native grape varieties, herby, rustic Fetească Neagră and Negru de Dragasani are the best reds, producing deep-colored, robust wines that are full and fruity when young but which can age for decades. Babeașcă Neagră and Crimpiosa produce lighter wines, while Cadarca (the same as Hungary's Kadarka) is used for more basic glug in the west of the country.

For dry whites, the spicy, grapefruity Fetească Albă and Fetească Regală are the most interesting grapes, while the ubiquitous Riesling is always the inferior Riesling Italico, not Rhine Riesling. The best sweet wines usually come from Grasă and Tămîioasă (both Alba and Românesca)—Tămîioasă is the Romanian name for Muscat, and it is known as the frankincense grape due to its aroma—while Traminer, Chardonnay, Pinot Gris, and Tămîioasă Ottonel (Muscat Ottonel) are used for wines of all degrees of sweetness and quality.

Most successful of the international varieties are Cabernet Sauvignon, Pinot Noir, and Merlot for reds and Chardonnay and Pinot Gris for whites. An increasing number of vines that were thought to be other varieties are turning out to be Sauvignon Blanc, which means that both demand and price are increasing.

WINE REGIONS

The wine appellations fall within seven main wine regions: Moldovan Hills, in the northeast, is the biggest wine region, with some vines right up on the Moldovan border, and others bunched beneath the eastern slopes of the Carpathian mountains. Whites from Aligoté and Traminer can be good. Cotnari is a sweet, botrytis-affected white that at one time enjoyed the same prestige as Hungary's Tokay. In good years, sugar levels can reach 10 ounces per quart, and the wines, bursting with raisin, honey, and orange peel flavors, taste great and can last almost indefinitely.

Near the mountains, Nicorești is known for its Babească Neagră, and the Pinot Noir from Cotesti has a good reputation. A sweet wine known as the Pearl of Moldova used to be Romania's most famous wine.

Murfatlar, in the center of the Dobrogea region, has some 210 days of sunshine a year, and the vines are tempered by cool winds from the nearby Black Sea, permitting an extended growing season. Long, warm falls encourage the development of noble rot in the Tămîioăsa, Pinot Gris, and Chardonnay grapes, producing prized sweet wines. There is every reason to hope that this could become a really classic vineyard region for dry wines, too. Muntenia's main wine district, Dealul Mare, in the foothills of the Carpathian mountains, is one of the largest and most important regions, where the warm climate allows the production of good and not excessively tannic red wines. It is particularly known for Pinot Noir,

Cabernet Sauvignon, and Merlot, but many of the most interesting reds are from the local Fetească Neagră. There is a sporadically brilliant scented white wine made in Pietroasa to the east, whose vines thrive in the calcareous, stony soil, and whose Tămîioăsa grapes are often affected by botrytis.

Drăgășani, on the left bank of the Olt in Oltenia, is becoming a standard-bearer for the new wave of private estates and is particularly successful with local varieties—both red and white. The Cabernet Sauvignon from the Olt's opposite bank at Sambures is highly regarded. Transylvania's premium wine area is Târnave. The high altitude means a cool climate, so white grapes predominate, and Traminer makes particularly good wines at several levels of sweetness. In the west, Banat produces a large output of drinkable whites and everyday reds, but so far it has not excelled itself in either color.

Hungary

OF ALL EASTERN EUROPE'S NATIONS, Hungary's traditions were the proudest and most individual, and they died slowly under the Soviet system of state-run farms and wineries. In the 1960s, fine reds were still being released under the Bull's Blood or Egri Bikavér label. At the end of the 1960s, you could still find marvelous yet fiery golden whites, almost viscous lanolin in texture, with sparks of spicy perfume, heady, rich, yet totally dry. Historic white wines, such as Hárslevelű (meaning "linden leaf") from Debrő, an old wine region now part of Mátra, and Szürkebarát (Pinot Gris) and Kéknyelű from Badacsony, fell into a sleep through the 1970s and '80s. The 1990s saw a reawakening of Hungary's pride and energy, and the rebirth of Hungary as a great wine producer began again at breakneck speed.

GRAPES AND WINE REGIONS

Since then, the wine export boom has been led by international grape varieties—full of flavor and extremely cheap, in particular Chardonnay, Sauvignon Blanc, Pinot Gris, Cabernet, and Merlot—and the country enthusiastically welcomed the Antipodean "flying winemakers." But top Hungarian winemakers are determined to put New World principles into practice as well as to rediscover Hungary's great past; they are set to produce gorgeous wines from both international and indigenous varieties. The Tokaj region has already attracted multinational wealth and expertise. Other regions, well stocked with international grape varieties, plus a clutch of marvelous indigenous ones, are also ideally placed.

White plantings account for 70 percent of the vineyards, but red varieties are increasing. There are now more than 162,500 acres of vineyards split into six regions and twenty-two districts. More than half of the country's output—easy-drinking styles made from Olasz Rizling and Kékfrankos grapes—comes from the Great Plain (Alföld) east and southeast of Budapest between the Danube (Duna) and Tisza rivers, where the sandy soil is suitable for little else but viticulture.

In the west of Hungary, Lake Balaton, central Europe's largest freshwater lake, is at the center of the Balaton region. Along the lake's north shore are Badacsony and Balatonfüred-Csopak, two districts that produce some of Hungary's best whites. The vineyards benefit from well-drained soil—a mix of sand and volcanic rock—and heat from the sun's reflection off the enormous lake. Badacsony produces good to excellent Olasz Rizling (Welschriesling), Szürkebarát, and Traminer as well as its own local variety, the spicy but increasingly rare Kéknyelű. Balatonboglár on the lake's southern shore produces mainly whites from familiar varieties, such as Chardonnay, Sauvignon Blanc, Olasz Rizling, Rhine Riesling, and Traminer.

In the south, Duna is a large region on the Great Plain between the Danube and Tisza rivers. The Kunság district has one-third of Hungary's vines, but most are everyday whites for local consumption. West of Duna is the Pannon region. South of Pécs, down on the Croatian border, the Villány district, with its loam and limestone soil, favors excellent Cabernet Sauvignon and some Syrah. Just north of Villány, the warm Pécs district has Chardonnay and good Olasz Rizling and Cabernet, while the Szekszárd district nearer the Danube River has its own Bikavér (Bull's Blood).

North of Duna is the Upper Hungary region. The south-facing vineyards of Eger are famous for Egri Bikavér (Bull's Blood of Eger), once a hearty blend of Kadarka, Kékfrankos, Cabernet Sauvignon, Kékoportó, and Merlot. While vinous anemia may have diluted much of the current output, especially where Kadarka has been replaced with other varieties, good examples can still be found, particularly from winemakers such as Vilmos Thummerer. There are also interesting white wines. In the foothills of the Mátra mountains, the Nagyréde cooperative has a reputation for reds and rosés made from Kadarka, but the best wines have been whites made by visiting international winemakers. West of Budapest is the Upper Pannonia region. The speciality of the Mór district has long been a high-alcohol, somewhat rasping white from the Ezerjó grape (ezerjó means "a thousand good things"). To the north of Mór, along the Danube, Neszmély is best known for white wines, including Olasz Rizling, Chardonnay, Sauvignon, and Irsai Olivér.

If there is a vinous equivalent of the fall of the Berlin Wall it would be the revival of the great vineyards and wineries of Tokay after the end of Communism in Hungary. This was the ultimate wine for aging. In 1939 one Polish merchant had thousands of bottles dating from the seventeenth century. How the "new" Tokay deals with its legendary status will be fascinating.

TOKAY WINE

This legendary wine has been produced since the middle of the sixteenth century. Bottles of the precious nectar were kept by the bedside of the Russian czars, and popes were eager to drink it, too.

This rich, golden wine has a unique sweet and sour, sherrylike tang. It comes from twenty-eight villages in the Tokaj region near the Hungarian–Slovak border, with a particular favorite being Mád. The region is sheltered by the Carpathian mountains to the northeast, while warm winds off the Great Plains maintain a reasonably high temperature. Indeed, drought at vintage time can be a problem. Mists rising from the Bodrog River in fall encourage the onset of noble rot in the Furmint grapes, which make up around two-thirds of a typical Tokay, with the balance being the sugar-rich Hárslevelu and Muskotály (Muscat Ottonel).

The intensely sweet, nobly rotted grapes, known as *aszú*, spend about a week in a bucket, during which time an unctuous juice known as *eszencia* seeps out. This precious fluid is so rich in sugar that, even with special strains of yeasts, it can take years to ferment. It's so thick it's virtually impossible to drink—you almost have to chew it.

After the removal of the eszencia, the remaining grapes are mashed to a syrupy paste and then added to dry base wine. The sweetness of the wine is determined by the number of *puttonyos* (8-gallon tub) of paste added to each gönc (36-gallon barrel) of dry wine. Three, four, and five *puttonyos* wines are reasonably easy to find; six is made only in good years. The Aszú Eszencia available today is about an eight-*puttonyos* wine, while Szamorodni (literally, "as it comes") is a wine to which no *aszú* has been added and can come as either a sweet (*édes*) or dry (*száraz*) wine.

After the grape paste has steeped in the base wine for around a week, the wine is racked off to begin its long, slow fermentation in barrel. In addition, a florlike fungus can attack the wine, giving it further complexity. The resulting flavors—a perfumed cocktail of apricots, marzipan, blood oranges, smoke, spice, tea, and tobacco—do take some getting used to, but they are certainly unique in the world of wine, and Tokay clearly deserves a place among the world's great sweet wines.

Western Balkans

THE WESTERN BALKAN STATES—torn by civil war in the early 1990s and still troubled in many areas—are working hard to rebuild their wine industry and infrastructure. So far, Slovenia and Croatia are now well-established as independent nations and are beginning to realize their considerable potential as wine producers.

SLOVENIA

Wine has always been part of Slovenia's heritage. The country has three defined wine regions covering about 52,500 acres. The Littoral (or Primorska) region touches the Adriatic for a stretch of the coast around Koper and extends north along the Italian border. The most famous vineyards of this area straddle the artificial border with Friuli-Venezia Giulia around Dobrovo, Nova Gorica, and the area called Goriška Brda—or Collio Goriziano in Italian. Some people say the best vineyards of traditional Italian Collio are actually in Slovenia. Grapes such as Ribolla (Rebula), Tocai Friuliano (Tocay), and Picolit (Pikolit) highlight the shared culture between this region and neighboring Friuli-Venezia Giulia. Also grown are Malvasia, Muscat Blanc à Petit Grains, Chardonnay, Sauvignon Blanc, Pinots Blanc and Gris, Merlot, Cabernets Franc and Sauvignon, and Barbera. For Slovenians, the most noted red wine is Teran, grown around Sezana in the Kras district and in Slovenian Istria on the Adriatic.

Posavje is a small region south of Lubljana. Podravje, on the northeastern tip, is more important. Previously known for Lutomer Riesling, the area is still best for white wines, with some Laski Rizling, Sauvignon Blanc, Chardonnay, Pinot Gris, and Muscat. Pinot Noir can be good, too. At Maribor they say they have the world's oldest vine—four hundred years old and still giving a crop.

CROATIA

The Croatian vineyards can be split geographically into two distinct areas. Inland Croatia or Kontinentalna Hrvatska runs southeast along the Drava tributary as far as the

THE HOME OF ZINFANDEL

They only just got there in time. There were only ten vines left in this old guy's yard near Split on the Dalmatian coast when the Americans dashed in and implored him, "Don't rip them out. They're priceless. They're the original Zin." In fact, they were called Crljenak Castelanska, but that name's not going to sell. The American vine sleuths then discovered a couple more vines in a yard of an old lady near Split. These were called Tribidrag.

But why was everyone getting so excited? Well, the Californians had always claimed the Zinfandel grape as their own. But there weren't any indigenous vines in California—they were all imported. But from where? Zinfandel doesn't seem to be related to any of the French, Spanish, Portuguese, German, Italian . . . ah, hang on. Italian. Yes, way down in the south, there's a grape called Primitivo. It's the same as Zin and had come from Dalmatia ages ago. So the race was on to see if any of the original Zin was left in Dalmatia—and it was. Ten old vines in one yard and a couple more in another. How did it get to North America?

Dalmatia was part of the old Austro-Hungarian Empire, and imperial vine nurseries held every variety from across the empire. A guy called George Gibbs bought a selection, including original Zin, took the vines to New York, and sold them to whoever came up the path, including some frontiersmen from the new gold-rush state of California. It didn't take these bombasts long to decide that Zin had been Californian all along. Well, we know better.

Danube. Coastal Croatia consists of Istria and Kvarner, on the Adriatic coast south of Slovenia, and Dalmatia, the long sliver of coast and islands stretching along the Adriatic coast past Dubrovnik to the border with Montenegro.

Inland Croatia is mainly white wine country, growing Welschriesling (here known as Graşevina), Muscat Ottonel, and Pinot Blanc often on terraces. In the Slavonia and Danube region, the best wines are said to come from the slopes of Baranja, north of Osijek, known as "the Golden Hill" since Roman times. Illoc on the Danube makes good Traminer, and further west, Kutjevo makes soft, fleshy whites. Reds are now gaining ground.

The Istrian peninsula is closer to Venice than Zagreb, the capital. In architecture and lifestyle, it also feels more like northern Italy. The leading grape here, Malvasia, makes a delightfully fresh, easy-drinking white (although there is also an "orange" wine movement here that makes excellent Malvasia). On a mix of red and white soil, Chardonnay and Pinot Gris also thrive, and reds such as Merlot and the local Teran achieve excellent flavrs at low alcohol levels. If Istria's wines are mostly refreshingly modern, those of Dalmatia are not. Dalmatia, both on land and on its islands, possesses some of the most remarkable vineyard sites in Europe, many of them cut into cliffs and hillsides of dazzlingly white Dolomite limestone. Given very sunny conditions, this is a recipe for big, rich reds, especially when the main grape is the foursquare Plavac Mali. Most of the wines are powerful, many are positively rustic. The best known examples are Postuc and Dingač from the Peljesac peninsula. Other grapes include the scented red Babic, and several interesting whites—Zlahtina, Vugava, Posip, and Grk. But the most interesting story concerns a rare red variety called Tribidrag that turned out to be America's Zinfandel (see opposite page).

OTHER STATES

Serbia is the most successful of the other Balkan states, with the native red Prokupac proving to be a good variety. Bosnia-Herzogovina has never had a strong wine tradition, but Kosovo was a good producer of red wine, and both Macedonia and Montenegro can make beefy reds from Vranac. Even Albania could be ripe for a makeover—it's got a whole bunch of grapes no one's ever heard of.

Vineyards are tucked into the steep mountainsides all along the beautiful Dalmatian coast with its many islands. This is the island of Brac.

Bulgaria

I'VE HAD A LOVE-HATE RELATIONSHIP with Bulgarian wine ever since the early 1980s. Back then, there were some remarkable hefty, violent, scabrous reds. But there was fruit there, too, rip-roaring black currant, unlike the delicate, lacy perfume of old Bordeaux. The reds were infinitely preferable to the whites. Toward the end of the 1980s Bulgaria was the fourth biggest exporter of bottled wines in the world, but then Russia introduced anti-alcohol laws, and Bulgaria's grape harvest dropped by more than half in just five years. The post-Communist years in the 1990s were confusing, and, by the millennium, Bulgaria was very much yesterday's man as the offerings from Australia, California, and Chile filled the gap.

Although Bulgaria has been cultivating vines for three thousand years, its immediate past doesn't stretch back much further than the end of World War II. Between 1396 and 1878, Turkish Islamic domination brought winemaking to a commercial halt. Hillside plantings were established after the end of Turkish rule, but the Soviet decision that Bulgaria should be a massive modern vineyard triggered the planting of the fertile flatland vineyards that now mark out Bulgaria. Some canny bartering with American cola companies gained her the vast acreage of international grape varieties upon which she has made her export reputation.

GRAPES AND WINE REGIONS

The grape most readily associated with Bulgaria is Cabernet Sauvignon. The wines first appeared in the West in the early 1980s, and they were a revelation at that time—unassuming but tasty and affordable. Since their debut, the easy, ripe, plummy, well-priced Bulgarian offerings arguably have done as much as anything from Australia or California to establish the variety as the world's most famous red grape. Merlot is now more widely planted and can also be good, particularly from Stambolovo in the Thracian Lowlands. Gamza (the same grape as Hungary's Kadarka) is vigorously fruity when young, while the sturdy, plummy Mavrud produces wines of character. Pamid is the most widely planted native red

variety, but generally its wines are thin and lacking in character. Much better is Melnik, which is grown almost exclusively in the southwest in the Struma Valley region and produces a powerful, fruity red wine that takes to oak aging well. Native white varieties include Dimiat, with a fairly aromatic, soft-centered character, and Red Misket, a musky, grapey variety. Rkatsiteli is the most widely planted white. There are also large amounts of Muscat Ottonel, Chardonnay, Ugni Blanc, Aligoté, Riesling, and Sauvignon Blanc.

Bulgaria is divided into two main table wine areas: the Danubian Plain, the northern half of the country, and the Thracian Lowlands, the southern part. These divisions are too vast to make much sense, but as a generalization the north is cooler than the south. There are more than fifty quality appellations, but they don't seem to be accorded great importance. Even so, there are significantly different conditions throughout the country.

The Black Sea region in eastern Bulgaria enjoys a more moderate continental climate than the rest of the country with long warm fall days. White grapes do best here. Reds and whites are made in roughly equal amounts in the Danubian Plain, although the reds are the real gems. Here, Suhindol was the first Bulgarian area to become famous with its Cabernet Sauvignon. Ready to snatch the crown for Bulgaria's top wine were the Cabernet and Merlot from the foothills around Russe in the northeast of the region and from Svishtov near the Danube on the border with Romania. Cabernet Sauvignon is also important in the Thracian Lowlands, along with Merlot and Mavrud. Here, Plovdiv and nearby Assenovgrad produce good Cabernet, as well as impressive Mavrud. The hilly districts of Sliven, Oryahovitsa, and Stara Zagora, just south of the Balkan mountains, are also sources of good Cabernet Sauvignon. In the hilly regions of the south, Merlot from Stambolovo and Sakar can be excellent.

The Struma Valley on the border with Greece enjoys a continental climate modified by warm air rising from the Struma River. It has a distinctly Mediterranean feel, although the altitude prevents temperatures from rising too high for viticulture. This is the home of the very late-ripening Melnik, a variety that thrives on the clay and sand soil around Damianitza and Harsovo.

Greece

IN GREECE A NEW GENERATION OF winemakers and grape growers, many of them trained in France, California, or Australia, have looked in horror at the decay of a wine culture stretching back thousands of years and resolved to do something about it. Technological upgrading of wineries has been matched by the revival of old vineyards and the creation of new ones, especially in the cooler parts of the country. But above all, these modern Greeks have a vision of the flavors they want to achieve and a reassuring pride in Greece itself. Many of the newer estates, which could have just planted a swathe of Cabernet Sauvignon, Chardonnay, and other international varieties, have in fact covered the majority of their vineyards with native varieties, and the wines are modern but marvelously original, too. Established companies together with a new band of small, quality-minded producers are upping the quality stakes every vintage.

It is worth mentioning the relative coolness of a lot of Greek vineyards. Most tourists never venture far from the islands and the main cities that bake during the summer months. But the northern heights of Macedonia, the mountains of Zitsa, and to the west the hills of Nemea and the plateau of Mantinia in the Peloponnese—and even some of the higher vineyards on islands such as Samos—are sufficiently cool that grapes, particularly the local varieties, can struggle to ripen, and wines of wonderful personality and finesse are the result. Greece has many of the most original wine flavors in modern Europe, and they come from the cool vineyards.

GRAPES AND WINE REGIONS

Along the wine roads of Macedonia in northern Greece, the Xinomavro grape is responsible for the dark, spicy powerful Naousa wine and, when blended with Negoska, the softer, rounded Goumenissa. These are regularly some of Greece's most fascinating red wines. On the Chalkidiki peninsula, Tsantalis leases vineyards from the Mount Athos monastery and produces red wines that blend the native Limnio with Cabernet and Grenache. Evanghelos Gerovassiliou makes terrific Rhône-like reds

and a fine Condrieu-style sweet Viognier in the rolling hills near Epanomi.

Central Greece is dominated by the Savatiano grape, the base for retsina, which gets its particular character from Aleppo pine resin added during fermentation. Love it or loathe it, retsina when fresh and young is a wonderfully individual drink. Retsina sales are falling fast, both domestically and internationally, which is a shame because there is no other wine like it in the world, and this intentional resinating of the wine gives us some idea of what flavors the ancient Greeks liked in their wines. (They were very enthusiastic resinators, as were the Romans.) However, the Hatzimichalis estate northwest of Athens makes fine Cabernet Sauvignon, Chardonnay, and Robola.

The homeland of Robola, where it makes austerely stony whites, is the Ionian island of Cephalonia (famous for *Captain Corelli's Mandolin*)—all are good if a little pricy. Robola plays second fiddle to the Savatiano grape further east on the island of Evvoia.

The best wine of the Peloponnese is the dark, spicy Nemea, made from Agiorgitiko. Vineyards are found between 820 and 2,950 feet with the best ones on slopes below the plateau of Asprokambos. Further west, the florally, aromatic white Moschofilero produces Mantinia, one of Greece's most enjoyable whites. Elsewhere in the Peloponnese, good Patras dry whites are made from Roditis, Lagorthi, and Sidevitis vines as well as sweet Muscat Mavrodaphne. Monemvasia Malvasia is a sweet wine from the far south.

Among the islands, Santorini (Thira) produces the most exciting dry whites from wild, windswept Assyrtiko vines. The vineyard conditions are so extreme that the vines are coiled around in nests for their own protections. The sharply citrus, rasping, mineral flavors speak of a vine that suffered to ripen its crop. Santorini also makes a fascinating sweet Vinsanto. Samos makes some of the most delicious sweet Muscat found in the whole Mediterranean, and Crete, after generations of making large amounts of very dull wines, is harnessing her cooler northern vineyards and an array of local grapes, particularly Liatiko and Mantilari reds and Vilana and Dafni whites.

Eastern Mediterranean

TURKEY

During the twenty-first century Turkish wine has been on an upward curve despite Turkey being 99 percent Muslim. International varieties are now widely planted in the west and southwest, but the traditional varieties, particularly Öküzgözü and Boğazkere reds and Emir and Narince whites, are best grown in central Anatolia and the east and southeast—both areas of political fragility. Even so, grapes do still get out and are made into some of Turkey's most interesting wines. The introduction of curbs on the sale and promotion of wine by the Turkish government in 2013 made a difficult job even more difficult.

CYPRUS

Cyprus has been undergoing a wine revolution since the 1990s, when its wine business was based on bulk production of poor wine (much of it Sherry-style) made in industrial-type wineries far from the vineyards. Loss of bulk markets (for example, Russia), followed by accession to the European Union, forced Cypriots to relocate vineyards up into the cool mountains (they have some of the highest vineyards in Europe) and to relocate their wineries nearby, as well as concentrating on improving local varieties (the white Xynesteri and red Maratheftiko are promising) and introducing international varieties. The potential is considerable. Cyprus's traditions are best demonstrated by the rich, unctuous Commandaria sweet wine, whose production is documented as far back as 800 BC.

LEBANON

Lebanon's wine culture goes back at least to Phoenician times in the eighth century BC and probably further. In periods of peace, you can visit the ancient Temple of Bacchus at Baalbeck in the Bekaa Valley, as I managed to do just weeks before yet more strife closed the area once more to Westerners. Lebanon's modern wine history was greatly enhanced by the French presence between the world wars, but only the famous Château Musar carried the quality flag until the late twentieth century.

Early spring in the vineyards high up in the beautiful Bekaa Valley in Lebanon. These produce Lebanon's best grapes but are periodically threatened by military conflict.

Since then, there has been a rapid expansion of wineries in the Bekaa Valley, generally basing their wines on international varieties, particularly Cabernet Sauvignon and Syrah. This has led to developments in the northern Batroun hills near Tripoli as well as in the mountain valleys to the southeast.

ISRAEL

Israel has been making wine as long as anywhere in the Middle East, but a very long period of Islamic control in the region intervened. Winemaking slowly returned at the end of the nineteenth century, but wine from the contested Golan Heights transformed the view of Israel's potential in the 1980s. The big companies have greatly improved, and there has been a considerable expansion of smaller independent wineries in the twenty-first century. Cooler, higher conditions are being exploited, particularly in Galilee to the north and the Judean Hills west of Jerusalem, although there are vines as far south as the Negev Desert. The majority of wines are kosher but by no means all.

England and Wales

IT WOULDN'T BE THAT FAR OFF THE mark to say that England is the newest of the New World, new wave wine countries. Okay, wines were made here by the Romans, and they were supposed to be good in the Middle Ages, but they never prospered, and in 1921 Castel Coch in Wales turned its last crop of grapes into wine of a kind, and that was it—no more English or Welsh wine—until a few hardy eccentrics, retired army types, slowly began to get it moving again in the 1950s. Very slowly. Nobody really understood how to plant a vineyard properly, and nobody believed that any of the classic grape varieties would ripen, so a hodgepodge of mainly German crossbred varieties that didn't need much sun but didn't have much flavor either were planted. Until the 1990s, decent mouthfuls of English wine were few and far between.

But you could see a brighter future, and several relatively large companies—Three Choirs, Denbies, and Chapel Down—were laboriously building professional outfits, harvesting better grapes and making decent wines. Then began a trickle, which became a rivulet and then a torrent of sparkling wine. Suddenly England had found its wine vocation. It should have been obvious. The North and South Downs that run across southern England are part of the same great ring of chalk and limestone ridges that give Champagne and Chablis their wonderful, pale, vine-friendly soil. Typically, southern England has been about 1.8 degrees Fahrenheit cooler than Champagne during the growing season and very much at the northern extreme of viticulture, itself possible only due to the tempering influence of the Gulf Stream. But as Champagne has warmed up remorselessly, so too has England, and conditions in southern England are now pretty similar to what they were in Champagne twenty years ago. Septembers in Great Britain continue to warm, and temperature records for October are regularly broken. This has meant that Chardonnay and Pinot Noir can regularly ripen well enough for fizz and quite frequently for still wines, too. These grapes, along with Pinot Meunier, now account for about 60 percent of 5,000 acres of vines planted. Total plantings have grown almost 150 percent in the last ten years. The new England

and Wales aren't all sparkling wine—but nearly all the new plantings are Chardonnay and the Pinots.

While vines are planted as far north as Leeds and York and even a few further north into Scotland, most lie below a line drawn from the Wash to the Bristol Channel. The counties of Kent, East Sussex, West Sussex, and Hampshire are the most heavily planted.

The style of white wines varies more between wineries than between regions and depends on factors such as which varieties will ripen and what winemaking techniques are used. The best are delicate and aromatic, with flavors of apples, grapefruit, elderflower, and hints of smoke, with enough ripeness and depth to balance the crisp acidity. Wines from varieties such as Bacchus,

WORLD CLASS FIZZ

It's been happening since the 1990s. English sparkling wines have been winning best sparkling wine in the world competitions ever since Nyetimber from Sussex blew the cozy world of bubbles apart in 1998 with its Classic Cuvée 1993. You could say, How on Earth could this happen? Or you could say, Why did it take so long?

The old-fashioned view of English wine is that of a cottage industry made up of amateurs struggling with the mud and the drizzle. The modern view is of a country amazingly blessed with vast tracts of soil suitable for viticulture, much of it almost indistinguishable from the chalky slopes of Champagne and Chablis, a country taking full advantage of the vagaries of climate change to ripen Chardonnay and Pinot Noir to levels perfect for sparkling wine, a country that so far has refused to take the low road but realizes that the only route to success is to make sparkling wines that match or surpass Champagne in quality and to sell them at a high price. This is the present state of the English sparkling wine industry in Kent, Sussex, Surrey, Hampshire, and Dorset. As long as nature doesn't start hurling hurricanes too regularly in the direction of the English Channel, this will be the future, too.

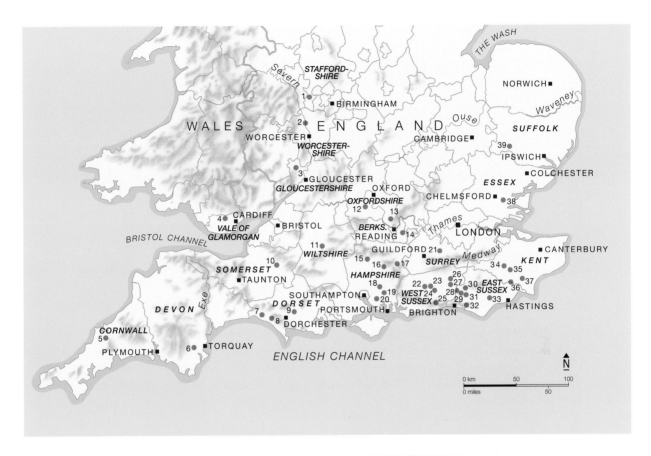

Huxelrebe, and Ortega can be drunk young. Bacchus, in particular, with its elderflower and hedge scent, makes what might be called quintessential English white. Clean, grapey fruit has replaced clumsiness in the better wines, with residual sweetness being retained from fermentation instead of being added later. Occasional excellent dessert wines are also made, either by botrytis infection or by freezing the juice.

Ripening red varieties can be a problem, but today, with better varieties and techniques, including the occasional use of top quality French and American oak *barriques*, results can be quite impressive. Although grown less widely than whites, red varieties are becoming more popular, with Regent, Rondo, Dornfelder, and Pinot Noir being the most widespread. But increasingly it all comes down to the sparklers. Typically, they hold onto a relatively high acidity, but usually this is expertly wrapped around with honey and hazelnut and brioche yeastiness, which are giving Champagne a run for its money. Which is why the Champagne house, Taittinger, established a vineyard in Kent in 2016, the same year that Champagne Pommery made an agreement to create a Hampshire cuvée. They won't be the last.

Regulations now require growers to submit their wines for testing before they can label them "English" or "Welsh."

SELECTED VINEYARDS

1. Halfpenny Green	**21.** Denbies
2. Astley	**22.** Stopham
3. Three Choirs	**23.** Nutbourne
4. Llanerch	**24.** Nyetimber
5. Camel Valley	**25.** Wiston
6. Sharpham	**26.** Bolney
7. Furleigh	**27.** Albourne Estate
8. Bride Valley	**28.** Court Garden
9. Langham	**29.** Ridgeview
10. Wraxall	**30.** Bluebell
11. A'Beckett's	**31.** Plumpton
12. Bothy	**32.** Breaky Bottom
13. Wyfold	**33.** Henners
14. Stanlake Park	**34.** Hush Heath
15. Coates & Seely	**35.** Biddenden
16. Hattingley Valley	**36.** Chapel Down
17. Jenkyn Place	**37.** Gusbourne
18. Exton Park	**38.** New Hall
19. Hambledon	**39.** Giffords Hall
20. Wickham	

North America

Mount Hood and the mighty Columbia River viewed from The Benches vineyard in the Horse Heaven Hills AVA. Vineyards on both sides of the river, Oregon on the south bank and Washington on the north bank, are highly prized.

The Judgment of Paris on May 26, 1976, proved to be a watershed in North America's winemaking history, the date with destiny the country had been heading toward since 1619, when Lord Delaware had tried to establish a vineyard of French wine grape varieties in Virginia. That day has had a more far-reaching effect on the world's perception of fine wine than any other in the modern era. Steven Spurrier, a young British wine merchant, held a tasting in Paris for the most finely tuned French palates of the day. Ostensibly a Bordeaux and Burgundy tasting, it also included a few Californian wines, which the French judges denigrated in pretty condescending terms.

Except that this was a blind tasting. The wines they were denigrating turned out to be French, some of the top names in Bordeaux and Burgundy. The wines they were praising as typical examples of great French wines . . . weren't. The top white was Chateau Montelena Chardonnay 1973 from California's Napa Valley, which trounced wines from vineyards in Burgundy planted a thousand years before. The top red was Stag's Leap 1973 Cabernet—only the second vintage of this Napa Valley wine—which beat the challenge of wines such as Bordeaux's Château Haut-Brion and Château Latour, which had the benefit of being rooted in hundreds of years of history. Until that moment, France had reigned supreme in the world of wine and had generally behaved as though its hallowed wines had a God-given right to be the best. No more.

The astonishing victory at the famous blind tasting gave Americans the confidence to believe that they could match the best of the Old World but on their own terms, and it inspired the other nations of the world that now produce world class wines—ranging from Australia and New Zealand to South Africa, Chile, and others—to do the same. With the exception of the bulk producers, there are winemakers in California, Oregon, Washington, Texas, Virginia, New York—and now Ontario and British Columbia in Canada, too—who take "the best" as their goal, the top wine as their role model, and buy the finest equipment to achieve their aim. Sometimes sheer ambition is their downfall. But more often their efforts sing with the excitement of a new industry turning the tables on old, revered institutions—and the whole world has cause to be grateful for that.

The Wine Regions of North America

THERE ARE NUMEROUS TALES about the cradle of winemaking being in the eastern Mediterranean, in Mesopotamia, Asia Minor, or Persia, and they make sense. Grapes grow well there and probably always did. More to the point, they've kept written records there for thousands of years for archaeologists and historians to discover.

But what about the Americas? Two twelfth- and thirteenth-century Norse sagas tell of Leif Erikson who established the colony of Vinland ("Wine Land") in northeast America, named after the wild vines that grew in profusion. Did he find bushes laden with grapes, and did he make these into wine? If so, surely the Native Americans had discovered the grape's ability to ferment centuries if not millennia before, just as the Mesopotamians had. There is evidence that fermented grape juice was offered to the gods of Native American tribes, such as the Seneca and Cayuga. How long had this been going on? Maybe for as long as in the courts of Cairo and Baghdad.

But since Europeans arrived in force in the sixteenth and seventeenth centuries, extensive records show a relentless determination to establish vineyards and wineries in almost every state of the Union. Also, the fact that American wines didn't break into the top league until the 1970s is evidence of the succession of natural and man-made obstacles that winemakers had to overcome. On the East Coast, the combination of a difficult climate and the presence of the indigenous vine-chomping phylloxera louse baffled generations of winemakers trying to make European-style wine from European grape varieties. In the center and the south of the country, climatic conditions defeated all but the hardiest pioneers. On the West Coast, a more promising start with European grape varieties was unceremoniously cut short by the invasion of phylloxera from the east.

To cap it all, Prohibition, the Great Depression, and then World War II meant that by the 1950s two generations had grown up with no experience of wine as anything other than a sweet, fortified beverage to be consumed for effect instead of flavor.

The picture began to change only in the late 1960s, when Robert Mondavi established his Napa Valley winery, filling a virtual quality vacuum. During the 1970s and '80s, winemaking spread to every suitable nook and cranny in California and the Pacific Northwest. The 1980s and '90s saw the Southwest and the Eastern Seaboard states at last conquer their difficult climate. Today's booming wine industry means there are almost nine thousand wineries across all fifty states, of which almost half are in California.

During the 1990s, the Canadians in Ontario and British Columbia threw out their mediocre wine traditions and struck out for the title of newest New World kid on the block, showing startling promise.

INDIGENOUS VINE SPECIES

Back in the seventeenth and eighteenth centuries, every European visitor who traveled along the East Coast commented on the vine that flourished from New England down to Florida. But all early efforts to make decent wine failed largely because the prevailing vine species, *Vitis*

U.S. CLASSIFICATIONS

The AVA (American Viticultural Area) system does not guarantee a quality standard but merely requires that at least 85 percent of grapes in a wine come from the specified AVA. A vineyard may be in more than one AVA. New AVAs are added every year. Currently there are 230 AVAs nationwide, from Arizona to Wisconsin, and 138 in California. AVAs come in all shapes and sizes, varying from the largest, Upper Mississippi Valley, which spans an area of 29,914 square miles, to the smallest, Cole Ranch in California, which covers a little less than one-quarter of a square mile.

MAIN WINE AREAS

■ MAIN U.S. VINEYARD AREAS
░ OTHER U.S. VINEYARD AREAS
▨ CANADA WINE AREAS

See also
California page 221
Sonoma and Napa page 225
South of the Bay and Central Coast
page 233
Pacific Northwest page 241
East Coast page 247
British Columbia page 253
Ontario page 255

labrusca, simply will not make pleasant-flavored wine. So generation upon generation of colonists imported European *Vitis vinifera* varieties, which were killed off by the cold winters and hot humid summers. But there was another hazard—the tiny phylloxera louse, indigenous to the northeast. Phylloxera could munch the roots of the hardy *Vitis labrusca* without weakening the vine, but *Vitis vinifera* had no natural tolerance to phylloxera, and every vineyard succumbed within a few years.

THE EASTERN SEABOARD

The whole pattern of vineyards in the northeast was established by these sets of circumstances. Wine still is made from *labrusca* grapes from New England down to the Carolinas and across to the Great Lakes, and some more neutral-flavored natural hybrids with phylloxera resistance did evolve. Others were bred specifically. When in the late nineteenth century the French were desperate for rootstocks and phylloxera-resistant plants for their

own devastated vineyards, a large number of so-called French hybrids were developed. These now dominate plantings in the eastern and central states, although classic *vinifera* varieties are at last succeeding on the East Coast and provide the bulk of the crop in such places as Virginia and Long Island, New York.

THE SOUTH AND CALIFORNIA

The southern United States is largely unsuitable for *vinifera* grapes because of the humid summers and insufficiently cold winters; the best known wine is from a non-*vinifera* vine called Scuppernong. But French and German immigrants did establish thriving wine businesses in Arkansas and Missouri, using a wide spectrum of grape varieties. From Mexico, in the early seventeenth century, *Vitis vinifera* grapes made their gradual progress north, Franciscan missionaries planting the first Californian vines in 1779. The 1849 Gold Rush drew the center of attention in California north from

Wine touring is an enjoyable way to discover more about wine. This is the rural Edna Valley in California's Central Coast region.

PHYLLOXERA

In the early nineteenth century, Europe seemed to be one massive vineyard. Thanks to explorers, colonists, and missionaries, *Vitis vinifera* had spread. It went to Latin America with the Spaniards, to South Africa with the French Huguenots, and to Australia with the British. Could anything halt its triumph? Yes, phylloxera could and did. *Phylloxera vastatrix* is an aphid that feeds on and destroys vinifera vine roots. It came to Europe from the east coast of North America in the 1860s and, by the end of the century, had destroyed all of Europe's vineyards and most of the rest of the world's, too. The solution, grafting *vinifera* onto American rootstocks—the phylloxera-resistant *Vitis riparia* being particularly favored—was exhausting work. Grafting every vine onto different rootstock depending on the local conditions is still necessary in most parts of the world. In California, in the 1990s a strain of phylloxera attacked the vines that had been grafted onto a semiresistant rootstock called AXR-1, and widespread replanting had to take place.

By the late nineteenth century, California had more than eight hundred wineries, growing more than three hundred different *vinifera* varieties. Phylloxera, two world wars, Prohibition, and the Great Depression doused the bright flame of Californian wine for almost a hundred years—until progress in the late twentieth century changed the face of North America's and the world's wine for good.

THE PACIFIC NORTHWEST

Further north, in Oregon, Washington, and Idaho, wine-makers set out to change the face of American wine as defined by the Californians. But the rekindling of fires in California sent sparks north. Although Washington had a wine industry of sorts based on hybrids and *labrusca* varieties, and there are references to nineteenth-century wineries in Oregon's Willamette Valley, for example, things really got moving only in 1966, when a couple of university professors in Washington making wine in their garage were noticed by a leading American wine critic. This coincided with the arrival of several "refugees" from the heart of California, who were prodding about in Oregon, trying to establish a vineyard for Pinot Noir. It wasn't until the 1970s that some Idaho fruit farmers decided to diversify into wine grapes. The wine industries of the Pacific Northwest are as recent as that.

Los Angeles to San Francisco and saw the establishment of the great vineyard regions of Sonoma and Napa, north of San Francisco, Livermore and Santa Clara to the east and south of the city, and the huge San Joaquin Valley in the interior.

CANADA

Far from being new to winemaking, Canada has been a producer since the nineteenth century, and in 1916 stole a march on the rest of North America by partly avoiding the Canadian Prohibition ban on alcohol. Grape growers negotiated an exemption from the Act, and by 1927, when their Prohibition ended, more than fifty wineries had a licence to operate. Wine is now produced in Ontario, Nova Scotia, and Québec, as well as tiny amounts in New Brunswick and Prince Edward Island, in the east, and large amounts in British Columbia in the far west.

Despite harsh winters, producers have moved away from the *labrusca* varieties that used to go into sweet "Port" and "Sherry" and can surprisingly make some decent examples and are having success with *vinifera* varieties from Chardonnay to Pinot Noir. Robust hybrids, such as Seyval Blanc, Vidal, Maréchal Foch, and Baco Noir, are still popular for their ability to withstand the alternate freezes and thaws of the Canadian spring, and winemakers have turned one major climatic factor to their advantage: the conditions that enable grapes to freeze on the vine occur every year here, and luscious, perfumed, sweet Icewine results. Quality is controlled by the Vintners Quality Alliance (VQA), set up in 1988 to do a similar job to the AVAs south of the border.

British Columbia's main wine region is the Okanagan Valley, which enjoys long hot days and scant rainfall in the growing season.

CLASSIFICATIONS

In countries with marginal climates, such as Canada, where the classic grape varieties will ripen only in the best mesoclimates, a proactive program such as the Vintners Quality Alliance, which lays down guidelines on geographical designations, minimum ripeness levels, and grape types, does make sense.

» Each potential VQA wine is subjected to a tasting panel. The judging takes place blind, and the award of a VQA medallion marks the best of the bunch. The VQA has a refreshingly high rate of rejection—around 20 percent.

» The majority of wines in the VQA program are made from *vinifera* grapes (although Icewine often uses hybrids, such as Vidal).

» Table wines labeled as originating from one of the Designated Viticultural Areas of Ontario— Lake Erie North Shore, Niagara Peninsula, and Prince Edward County—must be made from 100 percent *vinifera* grapes.

California

ON MY FIRST TRIP TO AMERICA, I never got anywhere near California. But as a student actor with a notable thirst, I did get to the very heart of Californian wine as it then was. Draining flagon after flagon of brews with such names as Hearty Burgundy or Mountain Chablis—neither in any way related to the famous wine areas of France—I got my first ever experience of good, cheap wine. Until then, cheap had invariably meant filthy. But that was in Europe. In California, the world's first inexpensive, juicy, beverage wines were widely available. Winemakers had harnessed the vast, sun-baked desert of her Central Valley (also called San Joaquin) and irrigated its parched soil with the limitless streams running off the Sierra Nevada mountains to produce these enjoyable wines in bulk. They were way ahead of their competitors, for this was when Australia was still stumbling out of a long period when beer and fortified wines were the national beverages and before Spain, southern France, and Eastern Europe had even grasped the concept that people might actually want a basic table wine to taste good.

That's one side of the Californian story, the side that has influenced the producers of basic wines across the world in the last thirty years, and that will eventually make bad wine at any price obsolete. But there's another, even more inspirational side to the story.

This begins in the 1970s, around the time of my second trip to the country, when I did get to California and I immersed myself, without realizing it, in the fine wine revolution that had been gathering pace since the 1960s. I didn't know it then, but the bottles I used to pick off the wine store shelves with names such as Mondavi, Heitz, Sterling, Freemark Abbey, and Schramsberg, were in the process of changing the face of the world of wine. These were the new wineries of the Napa Valley, north of San Francisco, which had thrown down the gauntlet to the classic French regions of Bordeaux, Burgundy, and Champagne.

Not only that, but they were trying to emulate these ancient wines not at their basic level but at the level of the greatest Grand Cru or De Luxe Cuvée they offered. They used the same grape varieties, the same methods of production as far as they could, and they bought equipment that only the very best French producers could afford. The wines they produced were stunning. They were

so clearly related to the great French models yet were so startlingly, thrillingly different. They set the tone for this other side to California that has been avidly pursued ever since in the cooler vineyards of the state.

There's the crux: cooler. The Central Valley is a broad, torrid, irrigated mass producer of grapes, making wines that never manage to achieve greatness because the climatic conditions here don't bring about exciting enough fruit. You need less sun, less heat, longer ripening seasons, and lower yields. Yet, if you look at the map, the Central Valley stretches from above Sacramento almost to Los Angeles, and that's exactly the same latitude covered by all the California vineyard regions that produce some of the world's most thrilling wine. The one factor they enjoy that the Central Valley doesn't, being tucked inland between the Coast Ranges and the Sierra Nevada, is that they're all near to the sea. Even that wouldn't be enough by itself. The California coastline, however, produces unique climatic conditions, and with the help of some cold Pacific currents (see box, page 222), the Coast Ranges and the Central Valley itself create every conceivable vineyard climate, often within the space of just a few miles.

More than 100 miles inland, the Central Valley is baked every day in summer by the blazing sun. The hot air rises and creates a vacuum. There's no replacement air available from the east because of the high Sierras, so it has to come from the west.

At the top of the valley, the San Joaquin River creates a gap as it flows westward into San Pablo Bay and out to sea through the mile-wide Golden Gate. As the Central Valley heats up, cold air and fog are sucked through the Golden Gate gap and over dips in the Coast Ranges. Most of the fog is drawn toward the Central Valley, but some sweeps over Carneros and heads up both the Napa and Sonoma valleys. All the way along the coast south to Santa Barbara and north to Mendocino, wherever a dip in the hills or a river valley creates a gap in the Coast Ranges, fogs and cold winds sweep in.

On the coast itself, it's too cold to ripen any grape. But as the fog and wind sweep inland, they gradually lose their force, and for every mile you travel up some of the valleys, the temperature can rise by as much as 1 degree Fahrenheit. Carneros, right down by San Pablo Bay is cool, yet Calistoga, 30 miles up the Napa Valley, is warm. There are climatic quirks in all the valleys, and there are

MAIN AVA WINE AREAS

— FAR NORTH
— NORTH COAST
  1. Anderson Valley
  2. Mendocino
  3. Clear Lake
— CENTRAL COAST
— INLAND VALLEYS/CENTRAL VALLEY
  4. Clarksburg
  5. Lodi
  6. Madera
— SIERRA FOOTHILLS
  7. North Yuba
  8. El Dorado
  9. California Shenandoah Valley
— SOUTHERN CALIFORNIA
  10. Malibu-Newton Canyon
  11. Cucamonga Valley
  12. Temecula

See also
Sonoma and Napa **page 225**
South of the Bay and Central Coast **page 233**

☐ MORE THAN 1,640 FEET
▨ MORE THAN 3,280 FEET

sites where altitude plays more of a part than fog and sea breezes, but this relationship between cool Pacific and warm interior is the most important influence on vineyard quality in California.

GRAPE VARIETIES

It is only recently that the relationship between different grape varieties and their suitability for the various Californian soil and climatic conditions has begun to be properly explored. Before the 1960s, the number of acres planted with bulk varieties dwarfed those growing top-quality grapes. Since then, with the birth of California's fine wine tradition, things have changed so dramatically that Chardonnay is the most widely planted variety of all, and Cabernet Sauvignon the most common red. But there is a danger here. Because Chardonnay and Cabernet Sauvignon—and more recently Merlot—fetch the best prices, they have often been planted in inappropriate places, where other varieties would have been much more suitable.

In the late 1980s, growers had the perfect chance to reevaluate what was planted in their vineyards. The phylloxera aphid (or, as some people believe, a mutation called Biotype B phylloxera) reappeared in California. This led to the uprooting and replanting of almost all the vineyards in the state. A great opportunity, one would have thought, to replace inefficient vineyards and unsuitable varieties with modern systems and ideal grape varieties. If this had happened, we would now be seeing a lot more Sangiovese, Mataró (Mourvèdre), Grenache, Marsanne, and Viognier.

But what we saw was a lot more Chardonnay, Cabernet Sauvignon, and Merlot as market forces rather than the relationship between terroir and variety lead the way. Only Syrah, of the warmer climate varieties, improved its standing. That's a pity, but even so some areas have proved themselves particularly suitable for certain varieties. Carneros is good for Pinot Noir and Chardonnay, as is the Santa Maria Valley, while Santa Ynez is good for Pinot Noir and Edna Valley for Chardonnay. Cabernet and Merlot have proved to work particularly well in mountainside vineyards in Napa and Sonoma, and Zinfandel pops up in the most surprising places in many different guises.

Indeed, in the years after 2000, much of California seemed to be heading in two different directions. Efforts to locate genuinely cooler conditions became ever more urgent as many producers accepted that global warming was beginning to affect the local vineyard conditions. The most impressive developments have been in the northern Californian coastal regions, particularly in Sonoma Coast, Fort Ross-Seaview, and around the Anderson Valley. However, commercial and critical pressures meant that many producers, especially those concentrating on Cabernet Sauvignon and the Bordeaux varieties in Napa Valley and to a lesser extent Sonoma County and Paso Robles began relentlessly to push the ripeness of their grapes, achieving alcohol levels of 15 and 16 percent and even more, with the resulting wines often tasting simply too rich and dense to provide much drinking pleasure—even though they would achieve high scores in wine tastings.

The 2010s have seen the return of restraint not only in Cabernet-based wines but also in Pinot Noir and Chardonnay. A movement toward lower alcohol wines called In Praise of Balance certainly had an important part to play, but it is also simply that the pendulum always swings, and now is the time for it to return toward the joys of balance, sensible ripeness, and drinkability.

THE CALIFORNIA CLIMATE

The cold summer water along the West Coast has a direct influence on the making of fine wine in coastal California. The cold ocean current running down the coast from Alaska wells up off Northern California partly as a result of the strong winds churning the water. The colder water below comes to the surface and meets the warmer surface air, creating massive fog banks. Meanwhile, on land, the morning sun heats the interior valleys, where the hot air rises and pulls the cooler air and the fogs inland through any gaps in the Coast Ranges to fill its space. The temperature falls and fogs roll in at night only to disperse again the next day with the midday heat. If it weren't for this cooling influence, the coastal areas would be too hot for fine wine grapes. The influence lessens as the breezes and fog banks travel inland. There is as much as an 18 degree Fahrenheit difference in temperature on a typical summer day between cool Carneros and warmer Calistoga 30 miles up the Napa Valley.

Vineyards above the fog line at Calistoga at the northern end of the Napa Valley. If it weren't for these cooling fogs that prolong the growing season, much of coastal California would be too hot for high-quality grape growing.

North Coast

RED GRAPES
Certain districts are associated with particular grape varieties, such as Dry Creek Valley Zinfandel, Napa Cabernet, and Carneros Pinot Noir. Merlot also features.

WHITE GRAPES
Chardonnay is most widely planted. Sauvignon Blanc shows regional variations in style. There are also Pinot Blanc, Gewürztraminer, and Riesling.

CLIMATE
The two-season climate of short, mild winters and long, dry, hot summers is dramatically influenced by summer fogs coming off the Pacific.

SOIL
An extraordinary variety of soil ranges from well-drained gravel and loam to infertile gravel and rock, volcanic ash with quartz, and sandy loam.

GEOGRAPHY
Hill slopes are favored for important vineyard sites, although much of the Napa Valley is flat.

THE NORTH COAST BASICALLY MEANS ANYTHING near to the sea north of San Francisco. California's two greatest wine regions—Sonoma and Napa—are both North Coast, but we cover those regions separately on pages 226 and 228. However, there are other less famous parts of the North Coast to cover. It's a good idea to start with Mendocino way up in Northern California because we're going to have to get used to the wild fluctuations in climate that afflict—or bless, depending on how you look at it—every single coastal wine region down to Santa Barbara. Up in Mendocino are some of California's hottest high-quality vineyards (I'm excluding the bulk-producing San Joaquin or Central Valley regions), best suited to grand, old-style, rip-roaring, throaty Zinfandel reds. But there are fog-draped, drizzly, chilly sites in Mendocino as well, which can just about coax Chardonnay and Pinot Noir to some kind of ripeness and that make the eyes of a winemaker from the windswept Champagne region of northern France well up with tears of homesickness.

MENDOCINO AND LAKE COUNTIES

The climatic variations found in Mendocino are all to do with those cold air currents rising up from the Pacific Ocean and their accompanying fogs. The Anderson Valley, the most dramatic of Mendocino's various vineyard areas, which slices northwest through the towering redwood forests, feels them right to the bone. Up on the ridges above the valley, way above the fog line at between 1,300 and 2,300 feet, are some great old Zinfandel vineyards, their

ZINFANDEL

Zinfandel has a wonderful reputation of being California's very own grape variety. Indigenous. Always grown here. Found by those frontiersmen of the Gold Rush in the 1840s and turned into the mighty, palate-bruising, ego-expanding red that can proudly proclaim its all-American heritage. Well, this is the creationist view. The trouble is, Zinfandel is a member of the *Vitis vinifera* species of vine, the European wine vine gang—and no such vines grew in California until Europeans brought them and planted them. So who brought the vines, and where did Zinfandel really come from? Well, the most glamorous suggestion is that the importer was Agoston Harazthy, a Hungarian adventurer who did bring in a pile of European vines—but not until 1862, well after the Gold Rush of the 1840s, and they'd been growing Zinfandel on New York's Long Island since the 1820s. Which is where various decidedly less glamorous figures than Harazthy got hold of it to fuel the Gold Rush miners' thirsts. McCoudray, Osborne, Smith, and Boggs are just four Californian producers who were making Zinfandel wine before Harazthy reached the West Coast. So what is Zinfandel? Ah. Well, it's not American at all. It's actually from Dalmatia in Croatia, and for that story you should see page 206.

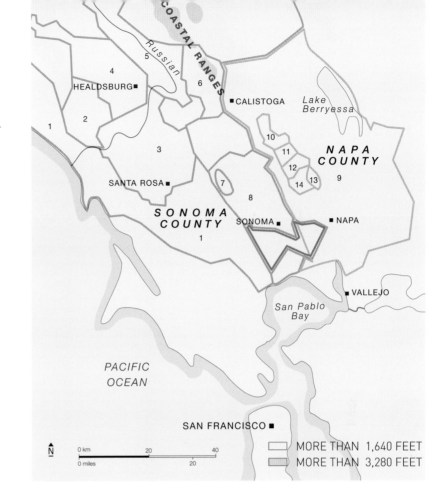

SONOMA AND NAPA MAIN AVA WINE AREAS

- — SONOMA
  - **1.** Sonoma Coast
  - **2.** Northern Sonoma
  - **3.** Russian River Valley
  - **4.** Dry Creek Valley
  - **5.** Alexander Valley
  - **6.** Knights Valley
  - **7.** Sonoma Mountain
  - **8.** Sonoma Valley
- — NAPA
  - **9.** Napa Valley
  - **10.** St. Helena
  - **11.** Rutherford
  - **12.** Oakville
  - **13.** Stags Leap District
  - **14.** Yountville
- — CARNEROS
  (in both Napa and Sonoma Counties)

origins dating back to the sites first planted by Italian immigrants back in the closing decade of the nineteenth century. With a surfeit of sun but cooled by their elevation, these mature vines give thrilling flavors. New plantings of Zinfandel, Pinot Noir, Syrah, and Merlot are also going on in the new AVA—known as Mendocino Ridge—for the scattering of vineyards in the west of the county sited at least 1,200 feet up.

Down in the valley, however, things are very different. Even the early pioneers in the 1970s planted cool-climate grapes, such as Gewürztraminer and Riesling, and there are still delightful examples being made, but all the recent action is to do with Pinot Noir and Chardonnay destined for sparkling wine that has proved to be some of California's best. Roederer Estate and Scharffenberger regularly make wine good enough to challenge Champagne.

But generally most of Mendocino just sits and sizzles in the heat. Whereas further south in California I talk endlessly about how gaps in the Coast Ranges allow maritime breezes into the interior to cool everything down, up in the north, in Mendocino, none of the little river valleys reaches far enough inland to make much difference because the Coast Range mountains here are 1,970 to 2,953 feet high. At that height, you are not going to get even a sniff of cooling breeze coming in from the

Pacific. Indeed, the main valley here runs north-south, carved out by the Russian River (although the Russian River Valley AVA wine region doesn't appear until further south, in Sonoma County), which has to head right down to Healdsburg before it can find a low enough gap in the Coast Ranges to force a way through to the sea. Up in Mendocino, we're at the river's source. The maritime influence affects things further downstream, but the whole upriver basin is simply left to bake.

The results are strong, ripe reds from the north around Ukiah—mainly from Cabernet Sauvignon and Zinfandel, but there are also encouraging results from Italian and Rhône varieties. Following the Russian River south, the beginnings of cooler conditions produce some fair whites down by Hopland. To the north of Ukiah, the Redwood Valley produces good whites and some excellent reds, while Potter Valley, further inland, is just enough warmer, but its elevation helps in providing cool nights. McDowell Valley, east of Hopland, is a high, sloping benchland that still has ancient plantings of Grenache and Syrah.

Further east is Lake County, where vineyards around Clear Lake, mostly at sites above 1,300 feet, experience scorching days with ice-cold nights and produce both red and white fruit of considerable intensity, but most of the grapes are used by wineries based elsewhere in California.

Sonoma

RED GRAPES
Zinfandel is successful in Dry Creek, and Pinot Noir is prized in Russian River, Carneros, and Sonoma Coast. Merlot and Cabernet Sauvignon are widely grown.

WHITE GRAPES
Chardonnay is the main variety, grown right through Sonoma County. There are patches of successful Viognier, Sauvignon Blanc, Chenin, and even some Italian varieties.

CLIMATE
The most important factor is the effect of the maritime fogs and breezes being drawn up the valleys from the Pacific Ocean over gaps in the coastal hills.

SOIL
Soil differs widely, depending on how close the vineyards are to the river. Valley floors can be gravelly—as in Dry Creek. Green Valley has sandy Goldridge soil or alluvial. Mountain slope soil is thin and rocky.

GEOGRAPHY
Hill slopes are favored for important vineyard sites, although much of Sonoma Valley is flat. The Russian River provides cool conditions, and Sonoma Coast/Fort Ross-Seaview vineyards are often perched high in the forest in sight of the Pacific.

IF MENDOCINO IS RELATIVELY SIMPLE to understand, Sonoma County, directly to the south, is the most complex but also the most intriguingly satisfying of the other main wine counties north of San Francisco. Again, the dominant factor is the cooling effect of sea fogs and breezes, both as they push inland through the Russian River Valley and as they flow off the northern slopes of San Pablo Bay at the southern end of the county—although obviously different soil, different elevations, and different exposures to the sun also count.

NORTH SONOMA

Coming south from Mendocino on Highway 101, the Alexander Valley opens out north of Cloverdale; it's warm here, and both Zinfandel and the Rhône varieties ripen easily. However, the valley doesn't really begin to show its form until you get south of Geyserville. The broad fertile swathes of gravelly loam encourage vines to run riot, but modern methods of pruning, trellising, and yield restraint now produce wonderfully soft-edged yet mightily flavored Cabernets that are a joy in youth and yet age with grace. Of slightly more concern are the swathes of high-yielding Chardonnay that carpet much of the southern section around Jimtown. One wonders who is going to buy it all. The small Knights Valley AVA, further east on the road to Calistoga in the Napa Valley, used to be very much a one-horse domaine—Beringer bottled a delicious fruity Cabernet from Knights Valley grapes—but apart from that the area was a vinous backwater. It isn't now. Much former pastureland is now strewn with vines, and the big players, such as Gallo, have significant plantings here. Chardonnay is much more important than it was. Encouragingly, there are some significant plantings on the low-yielding hillsides, led by the impressive Peter Michael Estate.

Dry Creek Valley was planted with Zinfandel by Italian immigrants during the 1870s, and Zinfandel, in the breezeless, baking northern half of the valley, still makes Dry Creek special and gives you a feeling that the old rural America is still hanging on in here. On both sides of the river are deposits of reddish rocky, gravelly soil, well-drained but able to retain the higher than average rainfall the valley receives. Cabernet is encroaching on these sites, but Zinfandel makes me want to shout for joy. On the valley floor, well-drained gravels produce surprisingly good Sauvignon Blanc and Chenin Blanc. At the cooler southern end of the valley, some fine Chardonnay, Sauvignon Blanc, and Chenin are grown.

RUSSIAN RIVER VALLEY

It's really only south of Healdsburg in the Russian River Valley AVA that Sonoma County changes from a warm environment with a few cooling influences to a cool environment with warm patches, especially in the areas affected by the river. Technically, it should be too cold for Zinfandel along this stretch of the Russian River, but some marvelous examples crop up, frequently in vineyards that also grow superb Pinot Noir. Don't ask me why, but you get the same paradox in Australia, where fine Shiraz and Riesling can grow in neighboring fields. But for Chardonnay and Pinot Noir the cooler reaches have become famous. Well-known brands, such as Sonoma-Cutrer, get much of their Chardonnay fruit here. The Chardonnays have tropical fruit flavors backed by healthy oak and really fill your mouth. Most are naturally high in acid, so winemakers generally put them through malolactic fermentation. Yet, thanks to a long growing season, they maintain their pinpoint fruit character without ever being flabby.

Russian River Valley has been seen as one of the premier areas for Pinot Noir in California for more than a generation. The typical Russian River style is based on either sweet black cherry fruit or on wild strawberry and a whiff of Coca Cola. Sounds strange, but it's not uncommon in good Pinot Noir. Does it work? Yes, it does, and so long as the wines retain their delightful lush texture, I'm pretty happy with what is yet another manifestation of Pinot Noir's increasing brilliance on the West Coast.

Most AVAs are politically motivated instead of being based on the special characteristics of vineyard land, but at the end of 2005 the Russian River Valley AVA formally changed to include all of Green Valley, all of Santa Rosa Plains, and a cool southerly section known as Sebastopol Hills, based on the fact that these areas were all affected by cool coastal fogs. Green Valley is a sub-AVA of Russian River south of Forestville and is even cooler—a prime site for Chardonnay, Pinot Noir, and sparkling wine. Interestingly, examples of Pinot Noir from here are darker in color than the rest of Russian River Valley, with more intense acidity and greater concentration. The sparkling wines, aided by these slow-ripening tasty grapes, are full and fleshy but age extremely well.

SONOMA COAST

The Sonoma Coast appellation is a mishmash that covers all of Russian River, along with parts of Sonoma Valley and Carneros. This boundary definition came about, as did several other AVAs in California, through political grandstanding and the desire of big producers such as Sonoma-Cutrer and Gallo to put "estate-bottled" on wines from a wide variety of Sonoma County vineyards. There are now efforts to define the really special areas of the Sonoma Coast. The Petaluma Gap, a windy area to the south, is coming up with a number of exciting cool wines, including thrilling Syrahs. Fort Ross-Seaview is an area north of the Russian River mouth—high, cool, and close to the sea—already proving superb for Pinot Noir, Chardonnay, and Syrah. Over the next few years, we are going to see some remarkable wines from the gullies, bluffs, creeks, and forest glades that make up the "real" Sonoma Coast region.

SONOMA VALLEY

The Sonoma Valley AVA stretches southward from Santa Rosa, taking in the lower slopes of the Mayacamas Mountains, and bordering the Carneros AVA down toward San Pablo Bay. The vineyards are cooled by the tail-end fogs and winds both from Russian River to the north and from San Pablo Bay to the south. Good Pinot Noir and Merlot grow in these cooler climates, and the valley has some of California's most famous Chardonnay vineyards. Zinfandel also performs well here from some very old vines; these versions are pure blackberry as opposed to the rich raspberry preserves and dates of Dry Creek Valley.

Conditions change dramatically when you climb above the fog line. On the west-facing slopes of the Mayacamas, the greater intensity of afternoon sunshine produces deep-fruited, dark-hearted Cabernets and Zinfandels. Sonoma Mountain is also above the fog line but has more vineyards angled east-to-northeast. Thrillingly fragrant and soft-hearted Cabernets and Zinfandels are produced as well as a famous Chardonnay at McCrea Vineyard southwest of Glen Ellen.

The coastal ridge just inland of the Pacific Ocean is one of the coolest spots in the Sonoma Coast AVA.

Napa

RED GRAPES
Cabernet Sauvignon is the dominant variety and has produced most of the wines, giving Napa its high reputation. Merlot and Zinfandel are also grown along with Syrah and Pinot Noir, mostly in Carneros.

WHITE GRAPES
Chardonnay is important but only in the south of the valley and especially in Carneros. There is a fair amount of Sauvignon Blanc, particularly on the valley floor, along with patches of Chenin and Grenache Blanc.

CLIMATE
The northern end of the valley is fairly hot because it is less affected by winds and fogs from San Pablo Bay. These cool the conditions rapidly as you head south through St. Helena, Rutherford, Oakville, and Yountville to Carneros. Mountain vineyards are often above the fog; the altitude keeps them cool.

SOIL
There are supposedly more soil types in Napa than in all of France. The valley floor is often heavy and clay-dominated, but alluvial fans at places such as Rutherford and Oakville provide well-drained, gravelly conditions. Carneros is based on clay. Mountain vineyards are usually thin and rocky, often volcanic.

GEOGRAPHY
Hill slopes are favored for important vineyard sites, but much of the Napa Valley is flat. Oakville and Rutherford are angled slightly to the northeast, Stag's Leap to the southwest.

THE NAPA VALLEY RUNS NORTHWEST to southeast for only about 30 miles, but the difference in conditions along this short distance is dramatic. Calistoga, at the head of the valley, has a daytime climate hot enough to ripen every known red variety and is saved from being a cauldron in which to bake the life out of its fruit only by the ice-cold air that drains down the high mountains, hemming it in on three sides. Yet down at the mouth of the valley is Carneros, chilled by fogs and gales, able to ripen its cool-climate Pinot Noir, Merlot, and Chardonnay only because of the brief bursts of sun that separate the morning fogs from the afternoon wind.

Throughout most of the valley, the climatic conditions govern what types of grape are grown and what wines excel, not the soil and its exposure to the sun. There are, in fact, more soil types in Napa, I'm told, than in the whole of France, and some committed growers are trying to match grape variety with soil conditions as they replant. But, with a few brilliant exceptions, such as the well-drained fans of soil around Rutherford and Oakville, much of the soil on the Napa Valley floor is heavy, clayish, overfertile, difficult to drain, and certainly unfit to make great wine. There's no shame in this because much of Bordeaux's great Médoc region cannot spawn a decent grape. The only shame is in pretending that this isn't so. The trouble is that the wines made from the good soil have been so good that every man and his dog wanted a piece of the action. When two Napa wines, a Chardonnay and a Cabernet Sauvignon, won the famous Judgment of Paris tasting in 1976 against Grand Cru white Burgundy and Premier Cru Bordeaux, Napa became a promised land—for those with ambition and money.

Vineyards were planted, and wineries sprang up like mushrooms after rain; a couple of dozen wineries at the end of the 1960s had become nearly 420 by 2015. Unfortunately, this traffic jam of growers and producers, many blending grapes and wines from sites all over the valley and outside it as well, led to a blurring of personality and a dilution of recognizable flavors. But a clutch of fine vintages at the end of the 1990s and into the 2000s and a greater maturity among winemakers who initially were slavishly following college textbook winemaking methods instead of allowing themselves and their grapes free rein led to an upturn in Napa quality and also great personal expression in the wines. This led in some cases to levels of ripeness too rich to be refreshing drinking, but the 2010s have seen a decline in the number of over-the-top Napa Cabs.

Wonderful conditions do exist in the Napa Valley, and there are more committed owners and gifted winemakers at work today than ever before, but as quality reaches an all-time high, the chief point of distress is that prices are at an all-time high, too. So let's see where they grow their fruit. We'll work from north to south. First, we'll stay in the valley floor, and then we'll look into the mountains, where some of the most exciting fruit is grown.

Calistoga at the head of the valley has a touch of the frontier town about it, with a more rough-hewn feel than the other wine towns and villages, and I always head here to try to dissolve some of the black Cabernet tannin off my teeth with drafts of local ale. But it has good vineyards, too. One or two

Fall in the vineyards in Howell Mountain AVA. In this northeastern corner of Napa Valley, there are many fine, high-altitude vineyards producing top-quality Cabernet Sauvignon, Zinfandel, and Merlot that manage to be sturdy but deliciously scented at the same time.

mesoclimates, such as Storybook Mountain to the north-west of Calistoga, produce startling Zinfandel; otherwise, the rocky outcrops and sandy loam produce good results with Cabernet and Merlot.

Just above St. Helena, the Napa Valley changes direction; instead of running east-southeast, it alters to something more like south-southeast and keeps this orientation more or less until Carneros. As it begins to broaden, vineyards stretch across the valley floor, but the best, such as Spottswoode and Grace Family, are still tucked into the base of the mountain slopes on either side.

The only time when there seems to be a general consensus about valley floor conditions being truly excellent over one great swathe rather than just in dribs and drabs is at Rutherford and Oakville. All the great original Cabernet Sauvignon vineyards were planted here, some of them more than a century ago, mostly on the so-called Rutherford Bench. Two alluvial fans spread out at

Rutherford and at Oakville, but Rutherford attached its name to the Bench first. They are well-drained in Napa terms although also heavy enough to hold moisture during summer, and they slope just perceptibly toward Highway 29, which is crucial for drainage. Whether these soils go beyond the road is one of those arguments to keep lawyers and pedants happy for generations. Suffice it to say that Napa Valley Cabernet made its reputation on fruit from these Rutherford and Oakville acres.

But was it just the soil? I think the soil gets heavier and more cloddish east of the road but fine Cabernets still turn up from sites not only east of the road, but east of the river, too. Nevertheless, the Rutherford Bench and Oakville vineyards do seem to have struck the right balance between water-holding and drainage, between vigor and restraint, for the climatic conditions of this particular part of the Napa Valley. Imprecise, sure. But there's more than a century of experience that says it's so. This imprecise but definable balance of elements affecting the grape is what the French would call terroir. It took them a while to work it out, too.

Oakville and Rutherford are separate AVAs, and while there are good examples of Chardonnay and Sauvignon Blanc made here, Cabernet is what both do best. Rutherford, further north, is slightly warmer and produces wines that feature black-cherry and black-olive fruit and a dusty, grainy, tannic flavoring known as Rutherford Dust. Oakville, being cooler, gets more hangtime in the vineyards, consequently producing wines that display a wider and more intriguing array of black fruits. These flavors, from estates such as Screaming Eagle, Opus One, and Harlan have created such a stir over the last decade. However, even within Oakville, two styles emerge. As the district runs the entire east-west width of the valley, wines vary according to where the grapes are grown.

The vineyards on the east side that receive the hotter afternoon sun (Dalla Valle) produce wines riper and softer in tannins than those from the west side. Wines from this cooler mesoclimate (Harlan, Far Niente) are tighter and not as sumptuous on release. These wines also show more herbaceousness and often a slight mintiness in the aroma, at least partly due to the effect of the prominent eucalyptus trees in the area.

When you drive south past the bluffs in the middle of the valley, just north of Yountville, you're driving past a barrier to the fog and wind that brings about a discernible dip in temperature to their south. Yountville is decidedly cooler than Oakville, and it gets even cooler down by the town of Napa. They do grow reds here—the Merlot is pretty good, and Napanook is a famous Cabernet vineyard—but the most impressive results are from Chardonnay. Even so, reds do flourish right to the bottom of the valley. Coombsville, by Napa City, and American Canyon, south

KING CAB

Romantics may try to claim Zinfandel as America's very own grape variety, but harder-headed wine people would be more likely to plump for King Cabernet Sauvignon. The grape variety grows everywhere there are enough rays of sunshine to ripen it. Its dark tasty wine has virtually become synonymous with a bottle of red wine throughout most of the country. Nowhere has it done a better job of colonizing and dominating red wine production than in California. If there's one place that has come to represent the best that Cabernet can achieve—in many people's eyes, worldwide—it is the small North Coast region of Napa Valley.

Cabernet Sauvignon was initially planted because it was the chief variety used by the great Bordeaux wines, and because these were the most famous wines in the world, Americans wanted to emulate them right from the start. Napa Valley's first Cabernet was planted in 1880, but the wines made at the Beaulieu Vineyard starting in 1936 gave California its first famous Cabernet. In the 1960s and 70s, led by producers such as Heitz and Mondavi, the belief grew that Napa could indeed rival Bordeaux in its red wines, especially if based on Cabernet Sauvignon. But the difference was that, whereas all the great Bordeaux reds are a blend of varieties, even if Cabernet Sauvignon is often the dominant component, Napa producers simply adored the dark, rich, heady flavors that Cabernet could produce by itself, and the variety now dominates many parts of Napa. Meritage is a term for blends mixing Bordeaux varieties, but Cabernet is usually sold in all its bumptious unblended glory simply as Cabernet Sauvignon.

of Napa City, can grow Merlots and Cabernets of lush texture but refreshing brightness.

The Mayacamas Range to the west is a collection of peaks where coyotes, rattlesnakes, and wild deer are as likely to impede your progress as people. But they do harbor some smashing vineyards, especially on Mount Veeder, Spring Mountain, and, further north, Diamond Mountain. We're talking primarily incisive, focused, powerful red wines from low-yielding volcanic soil at heights that can go past 1,970 feet.

Stags Leap District spreads out onto the valley floor toward Yountville, up the sides of several small hillocks about a mile away from the eastern mountains proper, and produces Cabernets rich and pinging with fruit yet that artfully balance tannin and acidity. Many of California's wine regions have acquired their fame through relentless marketing efforts. Stags Leap is famous because its wines taste better. Higher up the eastern mountains are Atlas Peak, Chiles Valley, Pope Valley, and above them all Howell Mountain, at the north end of the valley, whose vineyards have been famous since the nineteenth century and whose coppery red volcanic soil, exposed to the sun but cooled by its altitude of between 1,378 and 1,970 feet, regularly produces some of the sturdiest but most deliciously scented reds in Napa.

CARNEROS

Carneros extends across the southern end of the Sonoma and Napa regions; to its south is the San Pablo Bay, and over its border to the northeast is the city of Napa. It is one of the most important vineyard areas in California. In the search to make wines of a supposedly European delicacy and finesse, Carneros was singled out as long ago as 1938 by Californian wine wizard André Tchelistcheff, but the region had been growing vines for maybe a century before that, and California's first wine superhero, Agoston Harazthy, planted grapes here in the 1850s and '60s. The very un-California-ness attracted Tchelistcheff—small crops and small grapes struggling manfully to survive in difficult soil, with not enough rain, and with fog and wind a virtual certainty throughout the growing season. The Carneros wine region slithers across the southern end of Napa and Sonoma, the Mayacamas and Sonoma mountains splaying their feet into a series of rumpled hummocks that gradually subside into San Pablo Bay. There are more vineyards on the Sonoma side, but most producers are on the Napa side. Farmers have always known that this was difficult soil to grow anything on, and traditionally most of it was consigned to grazing. With the lowest annual rainfall in both Napa and Sonoma counties—usually about 22 inches—and a shallow, silty soil often only a couple of feet above impenetrable, dense clay, few people felt inclined to plant anything in the area.

When the search for a cool-climate vineyard began, they were converted. The Golden Gate gap at San Francisco is the only place where the Pacific Ocean actually breaches the Coast Ranges, forming the long-enclosed San Francisco Bay and San Pablo Bay. As the fogs and the winds are sucked inward by the baking heat of the inland valleys, the first land they come to is Carneros. Fogs blanket Carneros on summer nights. These clear by late morning to be replaced by bright sunshine, and then up comes the afternoon breeze, merely strong or positively howling, depending on the conditions that day. The net result of this combination of hot sun and clammy fog is a very long, cool ripening period from early March until well into October. The wind cools the vines, but its strength can also cause the vines' photosynthetic system to shut down temporarily, delaying ripening. This is almost too much for most grape varieties, but remember, even if the warmth of Carneros is not hugely different from somewhere like Chablis in Burgundy, we're at a latitude of 38 degrees north here; that's the equivalent of the toe of Italy in Europe. The intensity of sunshine, warm or not, is much greater in southern Italy than it is in northern France, and it's the same in Carneros. These conditions are ideal for zingy, crisp Chardonnays and tartly refreshing sparkling wines and, of course, expressive Pinot Noirs. While these Pinots were delicate wines at first, the introduction of new clones, plus careful canopy management to ensure riper fruit, has resulted in a bigger, meatier, and frankly much more exciting style. These new clones were planted only because of the devastation caused by the phylloxera infestation of the 1980s, which allowed producers to replace clones more suited to sparkling wine with more exciting ones developed to maximize ripeness, fruit quality, and perfume.

There is the occasional Cabernet and some fine Syrah emerging from Carneros as well, particularly from vines set back from the Bay, but the newest star is Merlot. Just as Pomerol is better suited for Merlot than Pauillac or St-Julien, so too does Carneros suit this variety. Two factors are at work: cooler temperatures and clay soil. Merlot likes both, and the examples from here, as opposed to those from the middle of the valley, have greater intensity and higher acidity. Black-cherry and black-currant flavors and soothing creamy textures dominate these wines instead of the simple raspberry or cranberry fruit and frequently rough unripe edges that characterize Merlot from the warmer reaches of the valley.

South of the Bay and Central Coast

RED GRAPES
Cabernet Sauvignon, Pinot Noir, and Zinfandel are widely planted, while the minor varieties include Petite Sirah, Grenache, Syrah, and Merlot.

WHITE GRAPES
Chardonnay and Sauvignon Blanc are ever-present, along with some Chenin Blanc, Viognier, Riesling, Pinot Blanc, and Gewürztraminer.

CLIMATE
This ranges from cool and foggy, when influenced by San Francisco and Monterey bays, to dry and very hot. Strong, incessant winds can also represent a threat to the vineyards. Rainfall is low.

SOIL
A wide variety of soil includes gravel, stones of considerable size, clay, and loam, with occasional granite and limestone outcrops. These can be mixed, even within single vineyards.

GEOGRAPHY
Elevation varies widely, which causes great differences in the influence of fog, wind, and sunshine.

THERE AREN'T MANY OF MY FAVORITE VINEYARDS that I can say I prefer to visit at night, but Ridge, high in the Santa Cruz Mountains, is one of them. Climb to the top of the rise above the tasting room on the night of a full moon. As the moon hangs heavy in the vast night sky, its cloak of silver stars spreadeagled across the purple blackness, the dark crags of the forested mountain peaks pierce the pale night light to the west. To the east, 1,970 feet below, lies the bustling city of San Jose, so far below that the brilliant city lights are just twinkling patterns on the valley floor. Away to the north, San Francisco Bay glows with a faint pewter sheen.

Ridge is the most famous of the wineries sprinkled sparsely around San Francisco Bay itself. There used to be many more, but as the Bay area's urban sprawl reaches further out, few wineries or vineyards have been able to resist the temptation of the easier profits to be gained by selling to housing developers. But that doesn't mean the companies have all gone out of business. They haven't. They've simply moved their vineyard interests further south. This North Central Coast region divides neatly into the old regions of Livermore, Santa Clara, and Santa Cruz, where wineries outnumber vineyards, and the great new tracts of land centered on Monterey County, where wineries are few and far between and indeed people aren't that common, but contract vineyards can stretch as far as the eye can see.

You have to use your imagination in the Livermore Valley to see it as one of the original great vineyard sites of California. Getting there, either from the north or the south, is a seemingly endless trek through industrial parks and housing subdivisions that don't let up until you're right in the vineyards themselves. But Livermore is a fine vineyard site, albeit one that has its back to the wall as the twenty-first century decides its land is more useful for houses and factories. There are still about 5,000 acres of vines, much of it owned by the Wente family, who are staunchly leading a fight against urbanization. It is relatively warm because hills to the west block off most of the chill Pacific winds, and the gravelly Médoc-like soil promises good results from grapes such as Cabernet Sauvignon. The reds are not that special, but white Bordeaux specialities—Semillon and Sauvignon Blanc—can be outstanding.

Santa Clara County's vines have been pushed relentlessly south by San Jose's suburbs, and it is really only around Gilroy that you get a sense of a wine culture still hanging on. Gilroy is the self-dubbed Garlic Capital of the World, and, boy, can you smell it. But good fruit is grown to the east of the town, and wineries pay good money for Pinot Noir, among others. If you turn west off 101 and head up through the Hecker Pass, you'll find remnants of the old farmgate Italian wineries that used to pepper Santa Clara and Santa Cruz counties, and you'll find scrubby patches of bush vines of varieties such as Grenache, which are at last beginning to be appreciated.

Santa Cruz County, along the Pacific Coast between San Jose and beyond the city of Santa Cruz, is important for its wineries as well as for its vineyards. The Santa Cruz Mountains AVA encompasses a huge area of 480,000 acres, some 60 miles as the crow flies, with just 1,300 acres of vines dotted through the forested hills and ridgetops that rear up above the ocean. Some of these vines—such as those belonging to Mount Eden, David Bruce, and of course Ridge—produce stunning wines, especially long-lived Chardonnay and Cabernet Sauvignon, but there are more than sixty wineries in the region, so much fruit is bought in from other areas. There is also some robust Pinot Noir. It is impossible to characterize the Santa Cruz conditions; the vineyards range in height from more than 2,600 feet high down to fog level, and their aspects can be east-, south-, north-, or west-facing. The only relatively consistent features are the soil, which is largely infertile, impoverished shale—keeping yields low and contributing to the startling flavors in many of the local wines—and the likelihood of an earthquake disturbing your slumbers. The latter is becuase the San Andreas Fault lies right alongside Ridge's winery.

Startling flavors were nearly the undoing of the other part of the North Central Coast—the vast, flat, fertile, dark-soiled acres of Monterey County. The "Monterey veggies" these unripe, green flavors were called. The Salinas Valley has every reason to proclaim itself the Salad Bowl of America, and most of its flat valley floor is given over to intensive vegetable and fruit cultivation. However, as long ago as 1935, experts were suggesting it would be a good area for vines, and, when vineyards in the Bay Area were squeezed by urban development in the late 1950s and '60s, big companies upped sticks and headed south to Salinas, planting like crazy as they came.

MORE THAN 1,640 FEET

MORE THAN 3,280 FEET

CENTRAL VALLEY
1. Lodi
2. Madera
CENTRAL COAST
3. San Francisco Bay
4. Livermore Valley
5. Santa Clara Valley
6. Santa Cruz Mountains
7. Monterey
8. Carmel Valley
9. Chalone
10. Santa Lucia Highlands
11. Arroyo Seco
12. Paso Robles

13. Edna Valley
14. Arroyo Grande Valley
15. Santa Maria Valley
16. Santa Ynez Valley
SOUTH COAST
17. Malibu-Newton Canyon
18. Cucamonga Valley
19. Temecula
20. San Pasqual Valley

Monterey County now has more than 40,000 acres. The only problem is they mostly planted the wrong grapes in the wrong places and in particular too many red varieties, such as Cabernet Sauvignon and Merlot, too near the sea. It's taken until now to gradually redress the balance toward Chardonnay, Pinot Noir, and one or two aromatic white varieties.

As we move further up the Salinas Valley, the winds become milder and warmer. At Gonzales, you can just about ripen white grapes, you can ripen most red grapes by Soledad and Greenfield, and by King City, with the wind dropping to a pleasant breeze, you can ripen anything, although so far nobody's been thrilled by the result. There is very little rainfall throughout the valley—an average of 10 inches a year—and, with the eternal sunshine, some growers claim that the valley has the longest ripening period in the world.

But where's the Salinas River? Right under your feet. The Salinas River is California's largest underground river and is fed by the Santa Lucia, Gavilan, and Diablo ranges. Given that the soil is mostly deep, free-draining silt and sandy loam, I can see why the early pioneers saw it as a paradise for the vine. But the vine is a greedy plant, and the early plantations suffered from massive over-irrigation, leading to vigorous vines pushing out forests of foliage—and producing grapes of a decidedly green vegetable flavor that made wines with an equally vegetal and unattractive taste.

Vineyard management is now far more advanced. The cooler areas, a little further inland, are left to white grape varieties, irrigation is properly controlled, and areas away from the valley floor have been developed for higher quality whites and reds. Indeed, all the really exciting wines so far have come from these sites. Facing north-east toward Gonzales and Soledad are the Santa Lucia Highlands slopes. Thanks to a few growers—mainly the irreverent Gary Pisoni—this AVA has become one of the state's most revered for Pinot Noir. Once again, it's the passion of the Pinot Noir enthusiasts that pushes back the limits in California, while the producers of the easier-to-grow, easier-to-sell Merlot and Cabernet will probably settle contentedly in the mainstream. The wines here share a meaty, spicy, muscular character that is attracting wineries from Sonoma, Napa, and Santa Barbara to buy this fruit. Carmel Valley and Arroyo Seco have some favored growing spots, and high up on the arid eastern slopes of the Gavilan range, the producers Chalone and Calera make world-class Pinot Noirs and a variety of whites in spendid limestone isolation. Limestone isn't easy to find in California but is at the heart of the greatest

Morning fog lifting from the Santa Lucia Mountains overlooking the Edna Valley.

sites in Burgundy—places where finesse usually wins over power. In the nineteenth century, a roving Frenchman called Curtis Tamm searched along the Californian coast for years for limestone soil to make sparkling wine. He finally found what he wanted on a parched wilderness 1,970 feet up in the Gavilan range below the Pinnacles peaks, the site of present-day Chalone. A dozen miles north, 2,200 feet up on the northeast-facing slopes of Mount Harlan, Josh Jensen established Calera in 1974 on limestone soil that he first had to clear of virgin scrub. Calera is still one of the highest and coldest vineyards in California.

This being California, neither winery manages to make wines of Burgundian delicacy, but what they do achieve is something more exhilarating—the savage, growling, unfathomable, dark beauty of the great red wines of Burgundy's Côte de Nuits. In land that deserves a desert rating for its aridity, the grape yields are tiny (as they have to be with Pinot Noir), the methods of winemaking are traditional to a fault, and, as is the case of their Burgundian role models, the Chalone and Calera Pinot Noirs are of an unpredictable yet brilliant magnificence.

If I have time when I head south, I take Highway 1 south from Santa Cruz, hugging the coastline, dipping and diving in and out of the cliff face and soaring up above the crashing ocean waves, and traversing Little Sur, Point Sur, and Big Sur. I bask in the glory of this wild Pacific coast but need to turn inland to reach Paso Robles, a good wine area with something of a Wild West quality about it. The bars are raw, the beers local and cold, the steaks the size of pineapples, and the winemakers don't get too strung up on delicacy.

Paso Robles is the high point in the Salinas Valley that runs northwest through Monterey County to the sea. Its hot, dry climate is the natural progression from foggy and cold at the seaward end to baking and arid at its head as the influence of Monterey Bay's chilly waters is finally dissipated under the burning sun. But the San Luis Obispo County line crunches across the map about 8 miles north of Paso Robles, so Paso Robles is lumped into the South Central Coast region.

Never mind that a 1,500-foot-high pass has to be traversed to get down to the sea level of San Luis Obispo. Nor that San Luis Obispo's reputation is for some of the coolest-climate fruit produced in the whole of California because the fog and sea breezes chill Edna Valley and Arroyo Grande so successfully that some of the most Burgundian-style Chardonnay in the state comes from Edna Valley and some of the most characterful Pinot Noir comes from Arroyo Grande.

There are several reasons that Paso Robles makes an increasing amount of red wine. It is divided from the Pacific to the west by the 2,950-foot Santa Lucia Range. Even the California fogs and sea winds can't get over these mountains.

To assist the last gasps of ocean breeze puffing up the valley from Monterey or along Highway 46 from the coast, you've got altitude. The vineyards are sited at heights between 590 and 985 feet, although the small, cool York Mountain area west of Paso Robles reaches 1,640 feet above sea level. Being protected from the maritime influence means that the temperature plummets at night. That's great for the flavor of the fruit, and fruit quality makes Paso Robles exciting. That and a willingness to break the stranglehold of Cabernet Sauvignon. Paso Robles does have a lot of Cabernet, more than one-third of its total plantings, and the wine has a joyous ripe quality and minimal tannic intrusion that makes for some of California's eminently approachable examples. Even so, I prefer the challenge laid down by such varieties as Petite Sirah, which at its best performs an unlikely pas de deux between hefty tannin and florally scented blackberry fruit.

The limestone soil to the west of Paso Robles is home to numerous old Zinfandel plantings, and both sides of the valley are becoming more interesting for their plantings of the now fashionable Rhône and Italian varieties. But it is the estates in these hills to the west that are creating most waves. That's where international investment is most obvious, and that's where trendy winemakers are eager to try growing the fruit. The creation of an estate, Tablas Creek, to grow Rhône varieties near Adelaida to the west of Paso Robles by the Perrin Brothers, who own the top estate of Château de Beaucastel in Châteauneuf-du-Pape in the southern Rhône, was a clear indication that things were getting exciting down here. Interestingly, it was their Rhône-style whites that shone first, not the reds, because the brothers discovered that a headstrong area such as the Paso Robles takes a few vintages to reveal how to grow the grapes and make the wine successfully.

EDNA VALLEY AND ARROYO GRANDE

On south into the real San Luis Obispo and the areas of Edna Valley and Arroyo Grande. Neither is big, neither is well known, but both are exceptional. Edna Valley's forte is Chardonnay. Led by Alban, Edna Valley has also proven to be exceptional for Syrah and Rhône varieties.

Sparkling wine used to be the strong point for Arroyo Grande. The Champagne company Deutz chose a coastal site for their California base. Now Chardonnay and Pinot Noir table wines dominate. Pinot Noir seems to do particularly well in the vineyards near the sea with their early February budbreak, early flowering, and a long, gentle ripening period.

The distance between the chilly coastal vineyards only just able to ripen Chardonnay and Pinot Noir, through the central section that produces superb ripe Pinot Noir and Chardonnay, to the top of the valley where Saucelito Canyon make magnificent, heady Zinfandels from a patch of vines planted in 1879 is just 10 miles. That Pacific Ocean effect again.

SANTA MARIA VALLEY

It's barely 10 miles south into Santa Barbara County and Santa Maria Valley, but we're in a very different kind of place. As I swoop into the wide valley, the dusty anonymous town of Santa Maria sprawls away to my right, and to the left, inland, it looks like yet another sub-*East of Eden* lettuce prairie spreading gloomily away to the distant hills. It may not look much, but the Santa Maria Valley is one of California's most important fine wine regions, in particular producing excellent Chardonnay as well as exciting Pinot Noir and Syrah.

Sea fogs play a part, yet again. Santa Maria must be one of the least pleasant of all wine towns to live in. It gets on average eighty-seven days a year of heavy fog, generally in the late summer-to-fall period. The late summer is particularly bad when deep, cold ocean currents well up, are carried landward as the summer progresses, and are pushed southward along the California coast. By August, these cold currents are icing up the shoreline as far south as Santa Barbara County. The wet off-shore winds are cooled down and head inland to meet warm inland air head on—*et voilà*, fog. Loads of it.

But remember we're a long way south here. The sun is incredibly powerful; glance up at the hilltops on both sides of the Santa Maria Valley, and they are scorched and windswept. So the fog may ooze in from the sea, but it is burned off by the sun. Yet as soon as that happens, cool ocean breezes take up the slack. So there's loads of sun, but it is always being tempered by the ocean.

The average summer temperature is only 75 degrees Fahrenheit, but the crucial thing is that the heat peak is at 1:30 p.m., after which up come those chilly ocean breezes that get to work sparing the grapes from the danger of roasting under a hot afternoon sun. Add to that an early budding and flowering in Santa Maria—and, because of the more southerly latitude, a long, reliable fall giving the grapes extra time to hang on the vine—along with the odd touch of noble rot, and you've got Chardonnay nirvana if it's handled properly.

Mostly it is. The soil here is a mix of sandy loam and marine limestone, which doesn't encourage foliage

vigor, and leads to yields that can be as little as two or three tons an acre—that's considered low for California. With average rainfall running at between just 12 and 15 inches a year, irrigation is essential, but so far it hasn't been abused.

Most of the vineyards lie mainly on a ledge to the north of the Santa Maria River, although there are a few excellent properties relatively close to Santa Maria township on the south side of the river. Chardonnay is the clear favorite here, but Pinot Noir can be spectacular (from Au Bon Climat and others), and the Bien Nacido ranch was one of the earliest sites in California to show superb results with the Rhône varieties Syrah and Viognier. A few miles further south, over the Solomon Hills, are considerable plantings in the Los Alamos Valley, an area without an AVA but with a good reputation for Chardonnay and for Pinot Noir.

SANTA YNEZ VALLEY

While the Santa Maria Valley goes from ultra-cool to, well, mild at best, the Santa Ynez Valley goes from equally cool to hot, so much so that it's hot enough for Cabernet Sauvignon, Merlot, and the Rhône varieties to ripen easily in the upstream vineyards. The whole feeling of the valley, only a short distance north of the city of Santa Barbara, couldn't be more different from that of Santa Maria. There are numerous small estates, fine homes, ancient trees, and paddocks sporting handsome stallions. It's wealthy country with more than a sprinkling of Hollywood and Los Angeles glamour about it, and this can't have hindered its entry into the limelight during the 1970s as the source of California's supposedly finest Pinot Noirs. Its prominence in the Hollywood movie *Sideways* can't exactly have hurt its cause either.

Those early Pinot Noirs were pretty weird, often managing to be rich and sour at the same time, but underlying the maverick winemaking was a core of exciting fruit, most of all from the Sanford & Benedict Vineyard west of Buellton. Located at between about 15 and 25 miles from the sea, this area is known as the Sta. Rita Hills—the vineyards are both north and south of these hills—and has been planted with Pinot Noir and Chardonnay by more than a dozen of the county's finest producers. A combination of north-facing slopes avoiding the direct strong afternoon sun, along with fog and sea breezes shrouding the vines, has convinced some that this may be the greatest site for Pinot Noir in the whole of California. How many "greatest sites" does that make, you may ask. I don't know, but the wonderful thing is that when it comes to Pinot Noir and excellence, so many people care.

Central and Southern California

I APOLOGIZE FOR ALLOWING the region that produces four of every five bottles of California's wine less than a full page to itself, but there's not a lot to say about most of the wine or the region. A minute proportion of the wine actually proclaims its provenance as California's Central Valley or, more correctly, the San Joaquin. Technically, there are two parts to the Central Valley—the San Joaquin Valley and the Sacramento River Valley—and there is a significant difference between the two because around Sacramento and pushing just a little south toward Lodi, the cool maritime breezes can still make their way up through the gap the Sacramento River has forged in the Coast Ranges. At Lodi, at Clarksburg below the daunting levees of the Sacramento River delta, and in parts of Solano County just above San Pablo Bay, interesting table wines are being produced, and a significant amount of fairly priced, good-quality red bears the Lodi name. However, the awesome vastness of the Central Valley starts south of Lodi, where a substantial amount of the country's vegetables and fruit are produced, as well as the massive majority of its wine. There are wineries that would dwarf oil refineries, producing more than many serious wine-producing nations. There is almost no moderating influence for the overpowering heat, and there's precious little rain. Few producers have made a name for quality wine, but there has been some high-quality fortified wine. Andrew Quady at Madera makes the best stuff—his imagination fired by a batch of Zinfandel grapes from Amador County in the Sierra Foothills in the early 1980s.

SIERRA FOOTHILLS

This is where the great Gold Rush began in 1848. Gold miners have massive thirsts, and, by the 1870s, there were more than one hundred wineries, largely in El Dorado and Amador counties. Some of the ancient Zinfandel vines still bear fruit, and, although more fashionable varieties have made their mark, dark, alcoholic, massively flavored Zinfandels are still what the Sierra Foothills do best. The vineyards can be as high as 2,950 feet around Placerville in El Dorado but will probably be just more than 985 feet in the main Amador area of the Shenandoah Valley and anywhere between 1,475 and 2,460 feet in Fiddletown. Differences between day and nighttime temperatures are similarly more extreme in the higher vineyards, helped by nighttime mountain breezes and the tail end of maritime breezes off San Francisco Bay. The resulting mix of tannin and intensity of fruit makes for some of California's most impressive and traditional wines.

SOUTHERN CALIFORNIA

South of Santa Barbara, the coast takes a long lurch eastward, and the effects of the ice-cold waters are largely lost. As you pass endless subdivisions of homes big and small, you'd think there was no room at all for vines, but somehow they've created a Malibu Coast AVA with fifty growers sharing 200 acres of vines. There are also vines at San Pasquale, way down by San Diego, but there is only one more vineyard region of significance along this coast—Temecula. Situated 24 miles inland to the southeast of Los Angeles, its high elevation—1,400 feet—gives it a welcome cool edge, and the mild Pacific breezes also help. Urban expansion is squeezing the vineyard areas, although local politicians and property developers regard vineyards as part of the lifestyle they are trying to promote. Disastrously, however, the area was hit by a deadly vine ailment called Pierce's disease, which has no known cure. While researchers race to find ways to combat the disease, producers have replaced many of their white varieties with more suitable reds, such as Syrah, Grenache, and Petite Sirah.

Amador County is a shrine to ancient Zinfandel vines.

Southern and Midwest States

NEW MEXICO LIKES TO CLAIM that it is the original wine state of what is now America. The conquistadors headed up from Mexico along the Rio Grande, and it makes sense that they'd have planted vines to rectify the extremely haphazard supply of sacramental wine from Spain. However, they'd have found it difficult. Rainfall is sparse—as little as 8 inches a year around Albuquerque—and the height of the Rio Grande Valley, rising to 6,560 feet at Santa Fe, not only makes for savage winter frosts but also extremely cold summer nights and consequently very acidic grapes.

Nowadays, all these factors are considered advantages when trying to grow grapes with good flavors. Irrigation water is now readily available, winter frosts can be countered by hilling up soil around the vines as protection, and, without the high-altitude cold, it would be too hot to grow decent *vinifera* grapes. Even so, this is still pretty much extreme winemaking. Wineries such as Anderson Valley produce remarkably good Cabernet Sauvignon, but that ability to ripen grapes in the relentless sun yet preserve high acids has, not surprisingly, led to some excellent fizz from producers such as Gruet. In the 1990s, the wine industry enjoyed a rebirth, and there are now about twenty boutique wineries.

The high altitude of the Rockies has also attracted winemakers to Colorado, where the vineyards, ranging from heights between 4,000 and 7,000 feet, are some of the highest in the world. Along the Grand Valley of the Colorado River, a clutch of wineries makes intense, relatively piercing *vinifera* wines for a chic and well-heeled vacation crowd. Syrah and Viognier are doing well here. Higher altitude vineyards in the West Elks AVA, along the North Fork of the Gunnison River, are showing promise for Riesling, Pinot Noir, Gewürztraminer, and Pinot Gris. High altitude is also what makes decent wine possible in Arizona. Most of the vineyards so far are in the southeast corner near Tucson. Plantings here go as high as 4,800 feet. Callaghan Vineyards at Elgin exploit the relentless sunshine tempered by mountain coolness and dramatic differences between day and night temperatures to produce not only memorable reds based on Zinfandel, Syrah, and the Bordeaux varieties but also thrilling white blends based on anything from Riesling to Viognier.

But the slumbering giant of southwest wine is Texas, which is now the fifth largest producer in the country. I've been tasting these wines since the boom-time days of the 1983 vintage, when even then the volume of production was doubling every year, but the trouble throughout the 1980s was that ambitious vineyard developments simply weren't matched by good winemaking skills, and most of the wines ranged from dreary to worse. Somehow you would expect Texans to be able to conquer all their problems simply through money, effort, and sheer self-belief. Perhaps, therefore, it is humbly reassuring to realize that establishing a wine culture is considerably more complicated than that. There do seem to be several areas that are suitable for viticulture. The Texas High Plains near Lubbock in northwest Texas, at around 4,000 feet above sea level, have dramatic shifts between day and nighttime temperatures, deep, fairly loose, limestone soil, low humidity, yet a reasonable amount of rainfall. The West Texas Mountains are surprisingly cool. The Texas Hill Country around Austin is indeed vaguely hilly, and there's a fair amount of decent limestone and sandy loam soil there as well as some cool mesoclimates. Scattered through these vast and isolated regions are more than 4,000 acres of vines, with more than 70 percent planted to Chardonnay, Cabernet Sauvignon, Merlot, Zinfandel, Colombard, and Pinot Noir. The growth of wineries has been spectacular, especially in the early twenty-first century, and there are now more than 350. Because the growth of wineries has outpaced the grapes available, about one-quarter of the wine made in Texas still comes from grapes grown outside the state.

In general, the southeastern states find it pretty difficult to grow decent grapes. But that doesn't mean that they haven't had a damn good try. Napoléon's soldiers planted Cabernet Sauvignon vines in Alabama when they were left at a loose end after the French defeat at the Battle of Waterloo. Mississippi, which kept Prohibition on the statute books until as recently as 1966, understandably hasn't been a hotbed of activity, and even in 2007 had only two wineries. But there is still a wine industry, and in several states they've made a virtue out of necessity by championing non-*vinifera* wine. Scuppernong isn't exactly a poetic title for a grape variety, but it is the leading member of the Muscadine varieties of *Vitis rotundifolia* that manage to survive the humidity and heat on the Gulf of Mexico and around to the southern

Atlantic seaboard. These are massive vines—a single wild Scuppernong vine can cover an acre, and the grapes, which can be 1 inch in diameter, have very thick skins and grow in loose clusters, so resisting the rot that is the scourge of tightly bunched *vinifera* grapes down here. The wine flavor is musky and distinctly fruity and was the basis for Virginia Dare, which was for some years after Prohibition the best-selling wine in the country. Down in the humid Gulf, a chilled glass of Scuppernong makes a really pleasant drink.

Even so, there are some *vinifera* plantings, and the wine and wine tourism industry is increasing almost everywhere. The magnificent Biltmore Estate in North Carolina has an 80-acre vineyard and, despite problems ranging from hurricanes to frost, even produces Champagne-method fizz. Swiss, German, and Italian immigrants planted vines in Arkansas in the nineteenth century, and, particularly around Altus in the state's northwest, vines still do well. Further north, Missouri has a rich tradition of grape and wine production and had the first AVA granted—for Augusta in 1980—although most of the state's wineries grow hybrids and *labrusca*, rather than *vinifera* grapes.

All the states bordering the Great Lakes in the north have some kind of wine industry, and there is a thriving business in creating hybrid vine types able to cope with the extreme cold winters. Even Minnesota and Wisconsin squeeze a few wines out of mainly hybrid vines. Indiana has a mix of hybrid and *vinifera* plantations struggling along, but Michigan and Ohio do better than that.

Michigan is the country's tenth biggest wine producer, and although a lot of the wine is from hybrid and *labrusca* vines, this is a state that exemplifies America's "can do" philosophy—remarkably tasty *vinifera* wines (mainly Pinot Blanc, Pinot Gris, and Gewürztraminer) coming from a clutch of wineries on the southeastern shores of Lake Michigan as well as some delicious Riesling from the Leelanau peninsula further north.

In the nineteenth century, Ohio used to grow more grapes than California, and, while those days are long gone, the conditions that prevail along the south shore of Lake Erie and on the offshore islands to the north of Sandusky, aided by the warm waters of this shallow lake, are good enough to produce some excellent Chardonnay and Riesling as well as those hybrids and *labruscas*.

Texas is an important wine-producing state. For grape growers, thunderstorms are capable of destroying entire crops in minutes.

Pacific Northwest

IT'S HARD TO IMAGINE TWO more totally different wine regions than those of Washington's Columbia River Valley and of Oregon's Willamette Valley. The Willamette Valley has a gentle, rural quality, with quietly prosperous families who run back generations tending the farm. It's more like New England than the state next door to California or more like one of the bucolic counties of Old England, such as Gloucestershire or Herefordshire.

The Columbia Valley is a desperate desert of a place—wild, empty, and far too savage for most people to settle in, however hardy they are. Through this inhospitable desperado's backyard runs the great Columbia River, and, here and there along its banks, are vast spreads of green gardens sprouting in the desert. Not people, not nice friendly communities, gabled barns, and paddock fences—just the raw bones of fields and crops against an eerie wilderness of bleached sagebrush ranges.

Yet both owe their existence to the same geographical phenomena. Both owe their rise from obscurity to international renown to a desire to prove that California and its particular styles of wine, based in the 1960s and '70s upon big, ripe, assertive flavors, weren't the only valid American styles and maybe weren't even the best.

What has been happening for millions of years in the Pacific Northwest is that the Oceanic plate has been crunching up against the Continental plate and sinking beneath it, at the same time depositing sedimentary layers on the Continental crust and pushing it upward. This uplift has pushed the Willamette area above sea level and created the Coast Range, which wards off just enough of the cold Pacific influences to make the Willamette Valley an ideal cool-climate area. Meanwhile, the Oceanic plate keeps on pressing inland, deeper and deeper below the Continental plate, until it melts. About 100 miles inland the molten basalt forces itself upward, creating the series of volcanic peaks known as the Cascades. This process is ongoing. The youth of the Cascades explains the majestic soaring beauty of the major peaks and the overall height of the range, often reaching 12,000 feet. Almost all the ocean influences—the breezes, fogs, and rain—get stopped by this mountain barrier. To its east is the virtual desert of the Columbia River basin—endless sunshine, almost no rain. All it took was human ingenuity to harness the Columbia's mighty flow for irrigation, and you had one of the world's great unnatural vineyards.

There's a lot more to the story than this—massive floods of lava sweeping across thousands of square miles of landscape at some 30 miles per hour; these enormous lava flows being buckled into ridges as the West Coast itself moves northward; vast glacial floods up to 985 feet deep scouring the landscape during the last ice age. If you want to get excited about geology and geography, the Pacific Northwest is the place to do it, and it explains the almost primeval desolation of so much of the land east of the Cascades.

THE FIRST VINEYARDS

The Willamette Valley has been settled since the first migrants arrived along the Oregon Trail, and parts of the Columbia, the Yakima, and Snake River valleys have been exploited agriculturally for the best part of a century, but none had been exploited for classic wine grapes. Western Oregon was reckoned to be too cool and damp for *vinifera* varieties. The Columbia Valley in eastern Washington was simply too far over the Cascades from any sizable market for anyone to take the gamble.

And yet, beginning in the 1960s and continuing through the 1970s, these two totally different wine regions grew and flourished together. Oregon's cool, wet Willamette Valley was sought out by Californians preferring cool-climate grapes, such as Pinot Noir, Riesling, and more recently Pinot Gris, and by refugees from the big, brash California way of living.

In Washington in the early 1960s, a group of university professors founded a little wine company (Associated Vintners) to produce homemade wine from some *vinifera* grapes they'd located in the Yakima Valley. Within a decade, the company—now renamed Columbia—was fashioning new vineyards out of the sagebrush along the Yakima and Columbia rivers, together with a big new operation based on a Yakima growers' cooperative called Chateau Ste. Michelle, owned and generously financed by U.S. Tobacco. Columbia and Chateau Ste. Michelle studied the figures for eastern Washington and saw a healthy bottom line based not on cheap bulk but on high-quality wine, grown in controlled conditions at a latitude similar to that of Bordeaux. With slower ripening fruit, and the combinations of long sunny days and chilly

nights giving higher acids than California yet ample sugar, Washington wine producers realized that perhaps they could approach the European ideal of a balanced wine more easily than their California colleagues, and they have based their business on this argument ever since.

The European card has worked for both states. Oregon's Eyrie Vineyards' 1975 Pinot Noir equaled Burgundy's greatest reds in a 1979 "Olympiad" held in Paris, and since then Pinot Noir has been Oregon's greatest achievement. Washington's first great success came with Riesling, but the market moved quickly on, and first Semillon and Sauvignon Blanc and now Chardonnay dominate white plantings. But the market moved again—to red—and now

Cabernet Sauvignon and Merlot with Syrah in hot pursuit are making the running. The red varieties have taken to Washington conditions with enthusiasm and give wines of a powerful, individual style.

IDAHO

Idaho's wine tradition goes back to the nineteenth century, when European immigrants brought winemaking ambitions with them. But Idaho was a keen prohibitionist state, and for most of the twentieth century the potato overruled the grape without too much difficulty. But there's something catching about the wine bug. Idaho now has 1,600 acres of vineyards and fifty wineries. Most of the plantings are near the cities of Nampa and Caldwell. Even so, if it weren't for fruit farms wanting to diversify, Idaho wouldn't seem a perfect spot for a wine industry. The Snake River allows some moderating maritime influence to flow up from the Columbia Valley, which is necessary because the vineyards are high. They enjoy hot bright summer days but intensely cold nights and are continually at risk from frost. There is some good sparkling wine, but then the best sparklers tend to come from not fully ripe grapes. Idaho is best known for whites, but there are now some good reds from classic Bordeaux and Rhône varieties.

Oregon

RED GRAPES
Pinot Noir rules in Oregon, especially in the Willamette Valley, with more than 50 percent of plantings. Syrah is the next planted variety.

WHITE GRAPES
Pinot Gris and Chardonnay are dominant, with Riesling a distant third.

CLIMATE
The lower Willamette Valley near Portland is cooler than the upper part, which in turn is cooler than Umpqua, itself cooler than Rogue Valley down on the Californian border. Frequent rainfall in the north declines in a similar sequence.

SOIL
In the Willamette Valley, particularly the "red" Dundee Hills, the soil is of volcanic origin and rich in iron. The Rogue Valley is more mixed with some granite.

GEOGRAPHY
Most vineyards are planted on slopes to avoid spring frosts and to make the most of summer sun, but the Rogue Valley also has plantings on the valley floor.

THERE WOULDN'T HAVE BEEN AN OREGON WINE INDUSTRY if it weren't for the bloody-mindedness of its pioneers. But by pioneers, I don't mean the settlers who followed the Oregon Trail west in the 1850s or the first wave of Californians who trekked north later on and began planting grapes just over the state line. No, I'm talking about the second wave of Californians, the 1960s wave, which has continued to this day and results in many of Oregon's wineries being owned by people who, for whatever reason, decided to head north.

Nowadays, there's good reason to forsake the easy life in California for the damp, cool Oregonian hills. Nearly fifty years of pioneering winemaking have finally proven that Oregon can make some remarkable wines unlike anything being produced in California. Back in the 1960s, a betting man wouldn't even have offered odds on such a dumb proposition. But a few people took the gamble all the same. Although California's astonishing growth didn't begin before 1966 at the earliest, when Robert Mondavi set up shop, the University of California at Davis already boasted the most important winemaking and vineyard management course in the nation. The aim of the course was then—and to some extent still is—to teach students how to raise huge crops of healthy grapes in warm climates and how to avoid foul-ups instead of encouraging them to strive for something difficult and unique.

But a few of the graduates didn't simply want to head off to warm fertile valleys and effortlessly produce copious amounts of adequate wines. Above all, they had visions based on two great European wine styles that California had never mastered: the stylish Rieslings of the Rhine and Mosel valleys in Germany and the classic Pinot Noir wines of Burgundy. One of the Davis professors is said to have told David Lett, a young student passionate about Pinot Noir, "You'll be frosted out in the spring and fall, rained on all summer, and you'll get athlete's foot up to your knees." Given that Oregon State University was warning that quality *vinifera* wine varieties would not ripen, you did have to be pretty pig-headed to grow them in Oregon. Richard Sommer of Hillcrest and David Lett of Eyrie were just that. In the early 1960s, Richard Sommer established a Riesling vineyard in the Umpqua Valley in southern Oregon, then in 1965 David Lett headed further north for cooler, more unpredictable weather—more like Burgundy, in fact. That's exactly what Lett wanted and exactly what he got.

PINOT NOIR RULES

The reputation of Oregon has been made on Pinot Noir. Lacking local expertise, many grape growers did turn to the University of California at Davis, and in general they got advice on methods of cultivation and ground preparation and choice of clones, especially in the case of Chardonnay, that might have suited California but that weren't relevant to the situation in Oregon. Big winery mentality simply didn't suit Oregon because, of all the American wine regions, Oregon is based on small family units. Five acres, ten acres, maybe twenty-five are typical; anything much bigger is rare. The total state plantings of more than 27,390 acres are still barely half those in California's Napa Valley.

PINOT NOIR ARRIVES IN OREGON

It was the search for "another Burgundy" that planted the seed for Oregon's newest fame and success. During the 1960s and '70s the California wine world, led by Cabernet and Merlot, was making wines of more tub-thumping intensity each vintage. A young winemaker called David Lett, who'd learned his art in the cool conditions of Switzerland and France's Alsace and Burgundy, couldn't stand it anymore. The few Pinot Noir producers in California were vinifying this delicate, scented grape as if it were a big, muscular Cabernet. Everyone told Lett he wouldn't be able to ripen Pinot Noir—or anything else—in Oregon (not enough sun and too much risk of harvest rain), and he realized that such capricious conditions were exactly what made Burgundy capable of producing wines of delicacy and fragrance.

It was this determination to produce another Burgundy that drove Oregon during its first forty years of Pinot-growing. Now both producers and growers have gone past this stage of pure emulation and have realized that Oregon has flavors and textures all its own—and not Burgundy lookalikes anymore. Cool subregions such as Eola–Amity Hills, Dundee Hills, Chehalem Mountains, and Ribbon Ridge are now making Pinot Noirs just as recognizably different from each other as the reds are of different villages in the heart of Burgundy.

The parallels with Burgundy don't end there. The sun often doesn't shine, and rain frequently falls before the grapes are ripe. In Oregon, as in Burgundy, mesoclimate is everything in the battle to ripen grapes. Uniquely, among the great red varieties, Pinot Noir needs cool spots instead of hot ones.

First, let's look at the Willamette Valley because almost all the best-known Oregon wines come from here. The long valley stretches from northwest of Portland to just below Eugene, with the Coast Ranges to the west and the Cascades to the east. The Coast Ranges allow through a fair amount of maritime influence. While the latitude may be similar to that of Bordeaux, the daytime summer temperatures are actually slightly warmer on average, but the nights here are considerably cooler.

A surprising number of subregions is already staking a quality claim and now have their own AVAs. Almost all of these are based on small ridges of hills running down the west side of the Willamette Valley, which afford protected south- and southeast-facing slopes. The Tualatin Valley has a group of good, primarily white vineyards in the north, and there are good vineyards almost within Portland's suburbs. Heading south, the east-west Chehalem Mountains, including Ribbon Ridge, grow some of Oregon's finest fruit; the Dundee Hills with their red volcanic soil are still the most heavily planted area, while the Eola-Amity Hills south of McMinnville have also produced top material.

The climate slowly warms as you head south, and so, although there are vineyards south of Eugene right down to the border with California, the real cool-climate action is between the Tualatin River and the Eola Hills. The Umpqua Valley, squeezed between the Coast Ranges and the Cascades, is warm enough to grow fair Cabernet Sauvignon alongside Pinot Noir. On the California border, the Rogue Valley sites, although higher than 1,000 feet, are still fairly warm and dry. The Illinois Valley, cooled by Pacific influences, can take even longer than the Willamette to ripen its fruit. The spectacular Columbia Gorge vineyards straddle the river east of Portland. In the northeast, past where the Columbia River turns north, there are now irrigated plantings of a similar character to the Walla Walla vineyards on the far bank of the river. Indeed, much of Walla Walla's best fruit is actually grown on its Oregon side. In the far east is the Snake River Valley AVA, most of which lies in Idaho.

Washington State

RED GRAPES
Cabernet Sauvignon and Merlot are the main grapes, followed some way behind by Syrah and Cabernet Franc.

WHITE GRAPES
Riesling was the first success in Washington but has now been overtaken by Chardonnay. Gaining in popularity are Sauvignon Blanc, Pinot Gris, and Viognier.

CLIMATE
There can be very dramatic contrasts between summer and winter temperatures. West of the Olympic Mountains is a maritime climate with high rainfall. East of the Cascades, the pattern is continental, and some areas are semidesert. Wahluke Slope has one of the driest, warmest climates in the state.

SOIL
Most of the Columbia Valley is basaltic sand with some loess and occasional river gravel. The Yakima Valley has sandy soil with low water retention, making irrigation essential.

GEOGRAPHY
Vineyards are few and far between. All plantings have been made on either low ridges, the south-facing slopes of hills, or near rivers. The most important factor is avoiding damaging winter cold, not excessive summer heat, and many vineyards are located on ridges and terraces with good air drainage.

IF YOU'RE AFTER THE MOST UNLIKELY, INHOSPITABLE vineyard site imaginable, explore the Columbia River Valley basin east of the towering Cascade Range in Washington. There are two vastly different landscapes in Washington. The part where people live, make money, support football teams, and go to the opera is cool and foggy, lies to the west of the Cascades, and is open to the influence of the northern Pacific Ocean that, in 1579, had Francis Drake reeling, beaten back by "the most vile, thick and stinking fogges." They're still there, around Puget Sound, Seattle, and the mouth of the Columbia River. But the coffee's better now.

But take Interstate 90 southeast out of Seattle, through the Snoqualmie Pass, and over the Cascades into the head of the Yakima Valley at Ellensburg. You'll feel you've moved to a completely different world of clear, dry mountain air, barren ridges, and uneasy civilization. Here you have a choice. Take Interstate 90 further east across the Columbia River, across Moses Lake way to Ritzville. You want moonscape? You've got it. Windswept sagebrush spreads out over the plain, and the vast sky threatens you with its emptiness. You find yourself nervously checking your fuel gauge every ten minutes. Then the plains flatten and spread, lifeless, inhospitable, useless. That's Eastern Washington.

But take the right turn just after Ellensburg and head south. Sure the mountain ridges are still as desolate and gaunt as you could want, but you'll suddenly see the Yakima Valley beneath you, a brilliant splash of dappled greens like a lush turf carpet laid on a sun-bleached earthen floor. However, someone wasn't too clever with the carpet shears; the neatly defined edges are erratically cut, the fertile greens come to razor-sharp edges, then nothing but parched bleached uplands, the hills like the vertebrae of some giant fossilized lizard. This is Eastern Washington, too. That spread of bright green is agro-industry at its most intense, the jagged edges marking out the limits of irrigation water rights. Without human resourcefulness, there'd be little more growing here than out in the empty vastness toward Ritzville and beyond.

Eastern Washington is desert. The curtain of volcanic peaks making up the Cascade Range runs north to south only 50 miles east of Seattle and continues to rise inexorably toward the Rocky Mountains of Idaho and Montana. Nothing much grows there except firs. But there's one vast bowl gouged out between the mountains and skirted by the mighty Columbia River as it hurls its mighty flow against the Cascades, turns unwillingly south until, aided by the extra volume of the Snake and Yakima rivers, its torrent forces its way back west and out to the ocean.

This is the Columbia River basin, all 23,000 square miles of it. Among the millions of empty acres lie most of Washington's 50,000 acres of vines. They're not here by chance but because the Cascade Range, rising to 11,975 feet, creates a virtual rain shadow to its east, guaranteeing minimal rainfall and maximum sunshine. However, not maximum heat. Columbia Valley can get incredibly hot, but all its vineyards are in mesoclimates that are warm at best. Yet being so far north—most vineyards are between 46 degrees and 47 degrees north—you can get up to two hours more sun daily than in California's Napa Valley. This is vital because photosynthesis, powered by sunlight, ripens grapes, not blasts of midday

Irrigation has changed the Yakima Valley from a drab, sun-parched expanse of land with poor soil into a major grower of vegetables, fruit, and now wine grapes. This is Red Willow Vineyard, one of the oldest in the state and a supplier of top-quality grapes to many wineries.

heat. Because this is a continental climate, temperatures plummet at night. So you get grapes full of sugar because of long, sun-filled days, yet chilly nights keep acids high, which is the perfect recipe for wine grapes.

One more thing—there's almost no rain. So you irrigate. The Columbia is America's second river in terms of volumes of water shifted. The Yakima and Snake rivers are two other significant performers. On the Columbia and Snake rivers, vineyards are either planted right on the banks to reduce the very real threat of winter and spring frosts or on low, south-facing ridges close to the water. Irrigation is simply a case of obtaining water rights.

Washington's wine industry used to be based on orchard fruits, *labrusca* vines, and a few vineyards of varieties such as Müller-Thurgau in the west near Seattle, in the area called Puget Sound. Several major wine concerns are still based there, including the two biggest, Chateau Ste. Michelle and Columbia. Pinot Gris and Pinot Noir are showing some promise here. But most of the vines are east of the Cascades in the Columbia Basin. Although the whole of Washington's acreage under vine is only about the same as the Napa Valley, the state has the second largest planting of classic *vinifera* varieties in America, after California, and new plantings

keep coming thick and fast. The overall AVA is Columbia Valley, which encompasses all the vineyards east of the Cascades. Many of Walla Walla's best grapes come from across the Oregon state line, but the wines are sold as Washington wines. Similarly, Columbia Gorge, east of Portland, is an AVA that includes both Washington and Oregon. Yakima Valley, including Red Mountain, Snipes Mountain, and Rattlesnake Hills, has about one-third of the state's plantings. Vineyards occupy the irrigated low ridges, especially on the south-facing Rattlesnake Hills. Horse Heaven Hills, Wahluke Slope, and Walla Walla are other top areas with large plantings.

Initially, Washington was seen as white-wine country because of its relatively cool climate, but long sunlight hours have started to produce superb Cabernets and Merlots as the vines mature, and the rare Lemberger (Blaufränkisch) makes excellent crunchy reds in the Yakima Valley. Reds now dominate, with Cabernet Sauvignon and Merlot between them accounting for one-third of the vines. Syrah is another red doing well here, and plantings are increasing fast. Both Riesling and Semillon positively shine, while Chardonnay flares brightly in places such as Woodward Canyon but is more often pleasant than exciting.

East Coast

THE EAST COAST IS WHERE the American wine industry started, but it took a long time to figure out how to make anything halfway decent. The region must have seemed a winemaker's paradise when the first settlers arrived to find fat, juicy grapes hanging off the trees at every turn in New England and Virginia. But, as early as 1606, Captain John Smith was complaining that, while they might be good to eat, these native varieties made horrendous wines. Numerous attempts were made to make drinkable wines, but nothing worked. The chief problem was the phylloxera aphid. It is endemic throughout North America, and so domestic varieties of vine evolved that could thrive even in soil seething with phylloxera. The imported European vines from the *Vitis vinifera* family had no such tolerance and immediately succumbed. The only legacy they left is that some of these doomed vines may have crossbred with native species. These resultant so-called hybrids gained an immunity to phylloxera's depredations and, at the same time, ameliorated the strange, sickly, sweet-scented yet sour-edge fruit of the local grape varieties, in particular those of *Vitis labrusca*.

Throughout the nineteenth and twentieth centuries, a reasonably thriving wine industry grew up on the East Coast, led by New York State. It was dominated by wine made from hybrids such as Concord. The wine wasn't good, but during the years of Prohibition, between 1920 and 1933, this reliance on Concord served the industry well. The grapes and their juice could be sold for eating or drinking just as they were. It wasn't until a few tentative moves in the 1960s, followed by a slow push first toward quality hybrids and then toward classic European *vinifera* grapes grafted onto American rootstocks, that things began to really hum. New York has been the leader in this movement, but a surprising number of other states has managed to produce attractive *vinifera* wines before the fading sunlight and icy air of Maine kill off the grape's chance of ripening in the north or the humid climes of South Carolina and Florida rot it on the vine to the south. New Hampshire grows just a few vines, and Massachusetts grows relatively more, with the best so far being those wines made from grapes grown on the island of Martha's Vineyard—proving that the sea's tempering influence does allow *vinifera* vines to survive at such a northern latitude.

Rhode Island claims a similar climate to Bordeaux, and certainly Sakonnet Vineyards has produced some pretty fair Chardonnay and fizz. Connecticut benefits from the mild influence of Long Island Sound. West Virginia also produces some wine up in her northeast corner, but the important wine-producing states after New York are Pennsylvania, Virginia, and Maryland.

Maryland's chief claim to fame is its oldest winery, Boordy Vineyards, founded in 1945, where Philip Wagner planted America's first French-American hybrids—just as resistant to the cold winters, the scorching summers, and phylloxera as the American versions but with a more European flavor. Black Ankle is now the leading winery. Pennsylvania divides its vineyards between the shores of Lake Erie in the northwest, where long but cool days suit some of the northern European varieties such as Riesling and Pinot Noir, and the southeast, in the Lancaster and Cumberland valleys, where winemakers are having particular success with Chardonnay.

Some winemakers say southeast Pennsylvania reminds them of Burgundy, but Virginia, which shares the same sweep of mountain slopes that run down to the west of Washington, DC, actually offers a more realistic comparison. This was where Captain Smith tried and failed to make wine from *vinifera* varieties in the seventeenth century and where Thomas Jefferson, a great admirer of Bordeaux wines, suffered the same fate in the eighteenth century on his estate at Monticello. Things got so bad that in 1960 Virginia grew only 16 acres of vines—and all for table grapes. Now there are some 3,500 acres of vines, 80 percent of which are *vinifera* varieties with Chardonnay leading the way. Virginia is perfectly placed not only for Washington, DC, but also for a thriving tourist trade. Luckily, Chardonnay has taken well to Virginia. But that hasn't stopped people experimenting not only with obvious choices such as Riesling, Merlot, or Cabernet Franc but also with such long shots as Viognier (now some of the best in the country) and Petit Manseng, Touriga Nacional, Nebbiolo, Petit Verdot, Tannat, and Barbera.

The warm climate still poses a constant threat. With the major exception of Shenandoah Valley to the west of the Blue Ridge Mountains, most of the vineyards are planted inland on the eastern slopes of the Blue Ridge Mountains, away from the tempering effects of Chesapeake Bay and with a latitude similar to that of southern Italy and southern Spain. The winemakers are saddled with all the classic problems of a continental climate—cold winters, spring frosts, tremendous heat, and possible excessive humidity, and summer rainfall. Even the soil is by no means perfect, consisting largely of fertile red clay and clay loam. But they do manage a considerable amount of success. By planting the vineyards at mostly between 1,100 and 1,500 feet up on slopes, the growers can provide drainage for excess water and good air circulation. This is vital to combat spring frosts and to reduce the incidence of grape rot when the humidity starts to climb. Wide spacing of vines and an open trellis canopy also help to circulate air and minimize rot. Some of the more cold-sensitive *vinifera* varieties find the winters too harsh in Virginia, but white wines from Viognier, Riesling, Sauvignon Blanc, and Chardonnay and reds from Cabernet (especially Cabernet Franc), Merlot, Nebbiolo, and even Petit Verdot point the way to Virginia, challenging New York for East Coast quality in the not too distant future.

MAIN AVA WINE AREAS

NEW YORK STATE
1. Lake Erie (also in Pennsylvania and Ohio)
2. Niagara Escarpment
3. Finger Lakes
4. Seneca Lake
5. Cayuga Lake
6. Hudson River Region
7. Long Island
8. North Fork of Long Island
9. The Hamptons, Long Island

VIRGINIA
10. Rocky Knob
11. North Fork of Roanoke
12. Monticello
13. Northern Neck George Washington Birthplace
14. Virginia's Eastern Shore
15. Shenandoah Valley (also in West Virginia)
16. Middleburg

MARYLAND
WEST VIRGINIA
OHIO
17. Ohio River Valley (also in Indiana, Kentucky, and West Virginia
PENNSYLVANIA
NEW JERSEY
CONNECTICUT AND RHODE ISLAND
MASSACHUSETTS

MORE THAN 1,640 FEET
MORE THAN 3,280 FEET

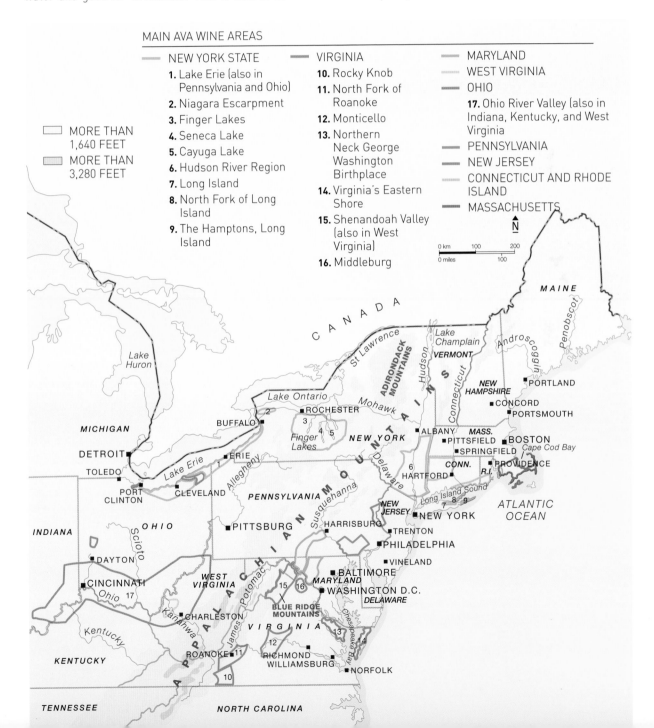

New York State

RED GRAPES
Native American and hybrid varieties dominate, with Concord at 75 percent of total plantings, but nearly 80 percent of this is used for juice, not for wine. Vinifera vines include Cabernet Sauvignon, Merlot, Cabernet Franc, and Pinot Noir.

WHITE GRAPES
Chardonnay leads, followed by Riesling, Gewürztraminer, and Sauvignon Blanc. Vinifera grapes now exceed all other varieties with the exception of Niagara, much of which goes into sweet fruit juice.

CLIMATE
The Finger Lakes have a short, humid growing season and severe winters. Long Island benefits from the moderating influence of water on three sides.

SOIL
The soil is varied. The Finger Lakes have calcareous shale, while Long Island is sandy with silt and loam and quick-draining vineyards.

GEOGRAPHY
Vineyards in the Finger Lakes and the Niagara Escarpment are on slopes to avoid frost. Long Island vineyards are on the flatlands near the seashore.

THERE'S ONE PART OF NEW YORK STATE where it's really easy to establish a vineyard, grow all the classic French wine varieties, bringing them to a juicy, mouthwatering ripeness, make the wine as modern and attractive as you want, and literally ship it to your target market between breakfast and lunch. Long Island. Just to the east of Manhattan. A balmy maritime climate, sun when you need it, soil that doesn't need much cultivation, sea breezes to ward off diseases, and the ability to grow not only the great Burgundy white grape Chardonnay but also Bordeaux's mighty red pair of Cabernet Sauvignon and Merlot almost as easily as if you were back home in France. What went wrong?

Well, a French guy called Fournier did briefly try Long Island in the seventeenth century. His vines failed because of the vine-destroying aphid phylloxera. That was the case right along the Eastern Seaboard. People kept trying, from New England to South Carolina—but not in Long Island, possibly the best site of all. In a funny way, with New York being such a cosmopolitan city and with its teeming hordes having such a Eurocentric view of food and drink, perhaps Long Island was simply too close to home to be taken seriously. The wines of Italy, France, and Spain were routinely preferred. Until in 1973, Alex and Louisa Hargrave uprooted a vegetable patch on Cutchogue, a couple of miles along the North Fork from Riverhead, and planted vines. They planted the French classics of Bordeaux and Burgundy. What should have been New York's most ancient major wine area is, in fact, its newest. That name "North Fork" is important. The Hamptons are in the South Fork, the parties, the beach palaces, the world of Gatsby and A-listers. The soil is heavier, spring frosts strike as late as May, winds are colder, ripening takes two to three weeks longer. There are some good vineyards, too, but the action is in the North Fork.

The Hargraves realized that the waters of Long Island Sound had a moderating effect on the North Fork, cooling the summer heat and warding off the worst of the northeast winter cold. They'd also found that the gently undulating farmland around Cutchogue—sitting on deep sand and gravel subsoil—was ideal for decent drainage and reasonable water retention. That's why their thoughts turned to Bordeaux and to the Médoc especially, which juts out into the Bay of Biscay on its tongue of low-lying land. They checked the growing season temperatures and found that, although the season starts a little later than in Bordeaux, slightly warmer summer temperatures bring both areas' grapes to ripen at much the same time, between mid-September and mid-October. The well-drained soil means that a slightly higher rainfall isn't that much of a problem and lessens the chance of late season rot.

But it hasn't been an easy ride. Fungicide sprays are crucial to control rot caused by the humidity despite the sea breezes. The soil is more fertile than those of Bordeaux's best properties, and pruning and trellising must be adapted accordingly. New York City has been slow to take Long Island's wines to its heart. I remember on an early trip trying to persuade the city's gastronomic glitterati of Long Island's brilliant potential. I might as well have been extolling the friendly nature of the great white shark to a group of scuba divers. But at last, the quality of Long Island Chardonnay, the fine Merlots, Cabernets, and occasionally Sauvignon Blancs and late-harvest Rieslings from more than 2,965 acres of vines, have become hot enough in the Big Apple that on a recent trip, every restaurant I ate in boasted at least one Long Island wine.

But other parts of the state have a longer grape-growing tradition and contribute the bulk of the volume that makes New York the third state for wine production, after California and Washington, with some 37,000 acres of vines. The Finger Lakes region is by far the most important in terms of exciting wines. It's an old area, too, getting its first vines in the 1820s—but its current reputation as a world-class producer of cool-climate whites such as Riesling is relatively recent. In upstate New York, the biggest problem is brutally cold winters with temperatures way below zero. Typically, the European wine vine, *Vitis vinifera*, can't cope with such seriously cold conditions, and this would explain why the majority of vines here are weather-hardy hybrids that are not great for quality wine. But there is a clutch of eleven glacial lakes—thin, deep, fingerlike—just south of Lake Ontario, that manage to hold enough summer heat over the winter to neutralize the worst of the weather along their banks and allow grapes such as Riesling to thrive. The three biggest lakes—Keuka, Seneca, and Cayuga— have the majority of the region's total 10,400 acres of vineyards. Initially, the region was seen as suitable for only native varieties and hybrids, but a visionary called Konstantin Frank believed that vines such as Riesling and Chardonnay could survive icy winters if grafted onto sufficiently hardy rootstocks. He eventually proved his

point (using rootstock from a convent in Québec) and there are now increasing numbers of delicate, delicious white wines being made on the shale-dominated soil. Riesling leads the way, from bone-dry to thrillingly sweet, and there's every reason to assert that New York's Finger Lakes region is now one of the leading producers of fine Riesling worldwide. Leading producers, such as Fox Run and Lamoreaux Landing, now make some delicate Pinot Noir, spicy Cabernet Franc, and juicy Merlot. Blaufränkish should work, too, but, in general, reds still struggle to ripen fully. The lower altitude and greater depth of Seneca and Cayuga lakes, allowing a slightly longer protection from frost, are regarded as the best sites, and they now have their own separate AVA designations.

The Lake Erie region, also known as Chautauqua, has 18,900 acres, yet few have heard of it because most of its vineyards grow Concord, which makes great grape juice but pretty duff wine. The Hudson River Valley, directly north of New York City, has the longest unbroken grape-growing tradition in the country. Yet, only recently have the 500 acres of vines begun producing good *vinifera* wines, including of some the state's best Chardonnay and Pinot Noir, as growers realized that the steep Palisades through which the Hudson flows south act as a conduit for warming maritime influences from the Atlantic Ocean. The state's newest wine area is the Niagara Escarpment up on the Canadian border, with 400 acres of vines dominated by native and hybrid vines but with some excellent Vidal ice wine.

It would be impossible to grow grapes this far north in New York were it not for the Finger Lakes, a group of deep glacial lakes named after their long, thin appearance.

Canada

TO BE TAKEN SERIOUSLY, any new country has to have a product that other people are not already doing better. Australia without Chardonnay or New Zealand without Sauvignon Blanc would have had a far greater struggle for recognition. For Canada, it wasn't the grape variety that mattered—it was the type of wine. One of the rarest, most difficult styles of wine to achieve in the world can be made every single year in Canada—sweet icewine—and all because of her terrible sub-Arctic winter weather. But if the numbing winter weather makes icewine possible, the rapid onset of winter and the late arrival of spring make life perennially difficult for anyone attempting to make any other kind of wine. For a long time, it was thought to be virtually impossible to ripen *vinifera* grapes satisfactorily in Canada and to prevent them from being killed during the worst of the cold spells.

In British Columbia and Ontario, these problems have to a large extent been solved, and there are exciting red and white wines. But icewine still remains Canada's trump card, and she is the world's largest producer of this style.

In the Okanagan Valley, the long, deep lakes are critical in moderating the worst extremes of hot and cold. This is Vaseux Lake.

However, there is another side to Canada's wine industry, too—the eastern seaboard. Here, they've had a wine industry going in fits and starts—but mostly fits—since, well, since one summer circa AD 1,000, when Leif Erikson, the Viking who discovered the Americas long before Christopher Columbus, settled in for a long, cold winter. The first chronicler of Leif's transatlantic adventure, Adam of Bremen, says Leif christened his landfall in northern Newfoundland Vinland because the vines he found yielded "the best of wine." It's horrifically cold in northern Newfoundland in winter, and any kind of wine would have tasted fantastic as they huddled together for warmth and watched the icefloes jostle and crunch. Anyway, the wine couldn't have been that good because as soon as spring came, they upped sticks and returned to Norway. That was it for Newfoundland wine.

But even though it isn't easy, there is a modern wine industry along the eastern seaboard in Québec and Nova Scotia. Most of Quebec's vines are about 50 miles southeast of Montreal, down near Lake Champlain and the U.S. border. There are pockets of slate and gravel that producers assidously seek out. Summers are short and humid, you may have snow until April, frost until May, and by October, the snow and frost are back again. Talking of frost—the winter temperatures can go as low as –22 degrees Fahrenheit. The vines split open at that temperature, so they have to cover them with soil after every harvest. There are, surprisingly, about 2,000 acres of vines, almost all being winter-hardy French and American hybrids.

Better known for its fishing fleets than its wines, Nova Scotia does have a fledgling wine industry, too. The vineyards are mostly in the Annapolis Valley, next to the relatively protected waters of the Bay of Fundy, although there are also some vines further north overlooking the Northumberland Strait, the warmest salt waters north of the Carolinas, across to Prince Edward Island—an area that calls itself the Sunshine Coast of Nova Scotia. All things are relative. Most of the 750 acres of vines are French hybrid, but there is a new trend for *vinifera* plantings (of Chardonnay and Pinot Noir) as well as L'Acadie Blanc, a local hybrid, and there's excellent sparkling wine. The Benjamin Bridge winery has shown that Nova Scotia can make world-class fizz. As in Québec, there really isn't enough heat, and some of the wineries have to blend imported grapes with their own produce. But one fascinating oddity is that they use *Vitis amurensis* varieties—Michurinetz and Severny—from the frozen wastes of the Amur River on the Chinese-Russian border—and, understandably, these hardy vines find it relatively balmy down in sunny Nova Scotia.

ICEWINE

Every winter, the temperatures in the vineyards of Ontario and British Columbia (from only the Okanagan and Similkameen valleys) drop way below freezing and frequently stay there for weeks if not months on end. If your grapes are still on the vine in late November and December, they freeze. This doesn't sound good. But if you gather these grapes, frozen (harvesting must take place at temperatures of 46 degrees Farhenheit), take them, still frozen, to the winery, and delicately press them—still frozen—you'll discover that the water that constitutes more than 80 percent of the grape juice has turned into ice crystals, and the sugar has separated out into a thick, gooey, sludgy syrup that is ridiculously sweet. Remove the ice from the syrup and you've got the basis for one of the most distinctive flavors in the wine world—the phenomenally rich icewine. Once or twice a decade, a few German vineyards attempt this wine style and sell their minute production at astronomical prices. In Canada, they can make it every year.

The first icewine was made by Hainle in British Columbia in 1973, and although British Columbia produces a small but growing amount, Ontario produces nearly thirteen times the amount. Things really took off in 1991 at the Vinexpo World Wine Show in France, when a 1989 Inniskillin icewine won the Grand Prix d'Honneur. Most icewine is made from Riesling and the hybrid Vidal, but there are red versions, too, from varieties such as Pinot Noir and Cabernet Franc.

British Columbia

RED GRAPES
Merlot is by far the most important variety. There are also Pinot Noir, Cabernet Sauvignon, Cabernet Franc, Syrah, and Gamay.

WHITE GRAPES
The quality whites are Pinot Gris and Chardonnay. There are smaller amounts of Gewürztraminer, Riesling, Sauvignon Blanc, Pinot Blanc, and Viognier.

CLIMATE
The Okanagan Valley receives scant rainfall during the short growing season, with its long hot days. Similkameen also has an arid climate and can be colder in winter than the Okanagan. The weather in the coastal regions is more variable, with very wet winters, large storms, and increased humidity.

SOIL
Soil in the Okanagan Valley varies from gravelly benchlands above the lake to sandier soil in the expanding areas that lie to the south of the lake. Drainage is good but combines with summer heat and low rainfall to make irrigation essential.

GEOGRAPHY
At this latitude, vineyards need to face south, although those actually sited on the lake slope more markedly east or west, toward the margins of the lake. Similkameen is a long narrow valley with steep mountainsides. The Fraser Valley is generally flat with rolling hillsides.

WHEN I DISCOVERED AN Okanagan Valley Syrah, I knew British Columbia was ready to join the ever lengthening line of serious New World producers. Not simply because Syrah is a smashing grape. Not only because many intelligent growers are realizing that Syrah, despite having been thought of as solely a warm-climate grape, can ripen in dry but cool areas better than Cabernet Sauvignon. New Zealand is proving this. Switzerland is proving this, for goodness sake. So why not Canada?

But there's more. Alex Nichol thought carefully when he established his vineyard on the east side of Okanagan Lake, looking out across to Summerland. He planted his vines at the base of a granite cliff, which, as the afternoon sun heats up, reflects blistering amounts of heat right down onto his vines and yet still manages to retain heat as the sun's glow fades away in the evening. By doing so, he was demonstrating the maturity that marks a new area on the up. Because he didn't just say—"Where has everyone else planted? I'll plant there, too." He started to seek out the nooks and crannies, the sheltered spots, the infertile soil that the grape vine flourishes in—all the things that will turn a marginal area into something special.

Marginal? Able to grow Syrah and yet marginal? Yes. Most areas of Okanagan won't be able to grow Syrah—although more sites, one or two down in the south near the U.S. border, are proving that they can. A few areas will find red wines in general pretty difficult to ripen, especially as things cool down, moving up toward Kelowna and beyond. Many growers, especially those who have come from a traditional farming background—after all, the Okanagan Valley is a paradise for growing fruit (you don't call of one your towns down by the lake Peachland for nothing)—found it difficult to accept the fundamental rule of producing decent, ripe wine grapes in a marginal area. The rule is you must keep the yield down or the fruit won't ripen and the wine will taste sour.

There's that "marginal" word again, and it is deserved. So let's look at some basics. Lake Okanagan runs pretty much north-south from Vernon in the north to Penticton in the south. Below Penticton, the area called South Okanagan continues down to the U.S. border, which cuts across Osoyoos Lake—Canada's warmest lake—on the 49th parallel. Well, if we look around the rest of the world to see which vineyards lie between 49 and 50.5 degrees north, as Okanagan's do, we don't get much of a choice. The Rheingau and Mittelrhein in Germany hover around 50 degrees north; the northernmost vineyards of Champagne in France are at about 49 degrees north. In Europe, few grapes ripen that far north, and Champagne is famous for sparkling wine precisely because its grapes are basically too acidic to make into palatable table wine. But there are some crucial reasons that Okanagan can ripen a decent array of grapes—both red and white—so far north.

The first of these is rain. Or lack of it. Northern Europe gets a lot of rain, which means two things—vigorous vines and large crops—especially when it rains near the harvest, which it usually does. And less sunshine. Well, think of it. The sky is full of rain-bearing clouds, so how are the sun's rays going to get through them and warm up the vines? The Okanagan Valley is lucky. In the north, the rainfall is only about 16 inches a year, but it is cooler, too, so

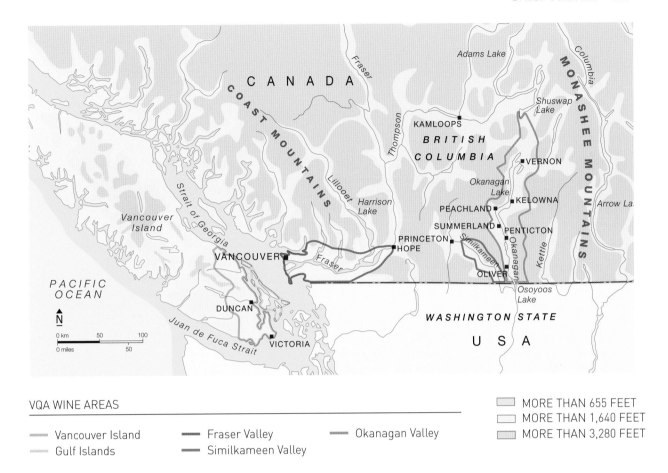

VQA WINE AREAS

▬▬ Vancouver Island   ▬▬ Fraser Valley   ▬▬ Okanagan Valley
▬▬ Gulf Islands   ▬▬ Similkameen Valley

▭ MORE THAN 655 FEET
▭ MORE THAN 1,640 FEET
▭ MORE THAN 3,280 FEET

once you get up to Kelowna and Vernon, the crisp, lighter wines are the most probable styles. But as you head south, down through Penticton to Okanagan Falls and Oliver and Osoyoos Lake, the rainfall drops right down to 6 inches a year. This little region is the only part of Canada officially designated as "desert," and irrigation is a must if vines are to survive and flourish. And think—only 6 inches of rain a year. That means clear skies and endless summer sunshine. Being so far north, they get about two hours more sunshine per day during high summer than the vineyards of California do. Not as hot, maybe, but it's sunshine, not heat, that builds up the sugar in those grapes. No wonder that a strip of land just southwest of Oliver in this southern stretch has been called the Golden Mile and that it is packed full of vineyards with Cabernet Sauvignon, Cabernet Franc, and Merlot, proving that you can ripen reds like these above the 49th parallel. They do taste special. Those very hot days are followed by very cool nights up here by the Columbia Mountains. High acids are the result, and this, combined with high sugar levels, makes for some very interesting wines.

Of course, there are a few problems. About every decade, an almighty winter freeze threatens to destroy your vines. Despite the torrid high summer conditions, winter closes in very fast here come mid-October. You can't let the grapes hang around for extra flavor, as you can in somewhere like New Zealand. If you're not intending to make icewine, those grapes have simply got to come off—ripe or not.

There are now more than 10,000 acres of vines in British Columbia, compared to just 1,000 acres in 1989, and the figure increases each year. More than 80 percent of the wine comes from the Okanagan, with most vineyards located south of Penticton. But there are a few other areas to note. West of Oliver lies the Similkameen Valley, described as high-desert cattle country with hot, dry summers and low humidity. This is proving to be exceptional grape country for everything from Riesling to Cabernet. There are already more than 700 acres of vines, and more vines continue to be planted as infrastructure and irrigation improve. Down in the Fraser Valley toward Vancouver, where it's cooler and wetter, there are more than 60 acres. More important, out on the heavily wooded lumber and leisure center of Vancouver Island, with a mild climate that is tempered by the sea, there are 432 acres of vines and a number of small vineyards and wineries that cater to an eager tourist trade. Finally, the Gulf Islands region with its mild climate, had, like the Okanagan and Fraser valleys, an established fruit and market gardening tradition in the nineteenth century and new vineyards are being planted on many of these small islands. There are currently 94 acres of vines.

Ontario

RED GRAPES
Pinot Noir seems most suited, but Cabernet Franc, Cabernet Sauvignon, Merlot, and even Syrah are on the increase.

WHITE GRAPES
Chardonnay leads, followed by Gewürztraminer, Pinot Blanc, and Riesling. The hybrid Vidal remains important, particularly for icewine.

CLIMATE
Ontario depends on the moderating effect of lakes for successful viticulture. Rainfall is moderate, and snow in December and January favors icewine production.

SOIL
The soil ranges from free-draining sandy loam, gravel, and sand to heavier soil with varying amounts of clay.

GEOGRAPHY
There is a mixture of flat and sloping vineyards. Those close to the shore of Lake Ontario and on the Niagara plain are basically flat. Those on the Niagara Bench reach up to about 600 feet in altitude, and the best sites are on the relatively steep, north-facing slopes.

THE LAKES THAT MAKE VITICULTURE POSSIBLE IN ONTARIO, by storing up the summer heat to release it slowly though the ferocious winter yet also providing breezes that help cool the fierce if short-lived summer sun. The 17,000 acres of vines are situated between 42 and 44 degrees north—the same latitude as southern France and Corsica, so we end up with summer temperatures higher than both Bordeaux and Burgundy—a crucial point because until the end of May, Ontario is appreciably cooler, and by September her temperature drops below that of Bordeaux once again. But in between, Niagara is hotter than Bordeaux in June, July, and August, and it's hotter than Burgundy right up to the middle of October, when there's a dramatic drop.

The heart of Ontario viticulture—and indeed the engine room for Canadian wine in general—is on the Niagara Peninsula, which has two-thirds of Ontario's *vinifera* plantings. The most important part of this is a narrow strip of land running for about 35 miles east from Hamilton to Niagara-on-the-Lake and comprising the southwestern shore of Lake Ontario, but there's also a stretch following the Niagara River south toward the Niagara Falls. This slim peninsula, bounded by the two Great Lakes—Ontario, one of the deepest, and Erie—is protected from the worst of the winter weather because of the heat those great bodies of water hold.

Running east–west just south of the Lake Ontario shoreline is the Niagara Escarpment—or the Niagara Bench, as wine people call it. This reaches up to about 575 to 600 feet in height. Vineyards here are cooler than those on the Plain, helped by the breezes circulating between the lake and the escarpment, but drainage is good on the slopes. It needs to be. There's a lot of fairly heavy clay loam soil mixed in with the sandy loam, and the continual air movement minimizes frost danger and helps to balance out loss of heat by eliminating the fungal diseases that bedevil humid areas at the end of the ripening season.

Two smaller wine regions are Lake Erie North Shore in the southwest corner of the province, where the shallow waters of Lake Erie moderate the climate, and Prince Edward County. This is the northernmost and the coolest area, on an outcrop of limestone near Kingston. It's cool here, and winters are sufficiently severe that they have to bury their vines to stop the cold from killing them, but this could prove itself to be one of the best sites for Chardonnay and Pinot Noir in all of North America.

Even the best hybrids are in retreat, except for Vidal, which due to its ability to produce startling icewines with the exotic flavors of mango, guava, and lychee—and yet keep the acid up—has earned itself its place. The first wave of *vinifera* plantings presumed that Ontario had to be white wine country— fair enough, and, of course, this was in the late 1980s to mid-'90s, when the world was mad for white. Early concentration on Riesling and Gewürztraminer was quickly superseded by the realization that you could grow the superstar Chardonnay here. But now the world wants red—and Ontario shows it can do that, too—from Cabernet Sauvignon, Cabernet Franc, Pinot Noir, and Zweigelt right up to that talisman of New Age, Syrah. And, of course, there's icewine. Where would Canada be without icewine?

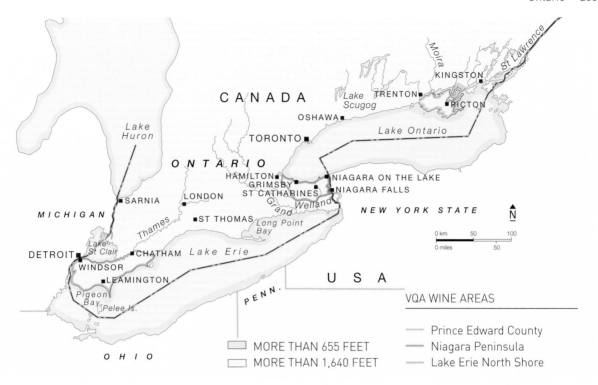

MORE THAN 655 FEET
MORE THAN 1,640 FEET

VQA WINE AREAS

Prince Edward County
Niagara Peninsula
Lake Erie North Shore

Vineyards on the gentle slopes above Lake Ontario (glimpsed in the distance) benefit from the moderating influence of the vast lake.

South America

GIVEN THAT THE EUROPEAN WINE vine *Vitis vinifera* arrived in the Americas through Mexico, spreading north and south with the missionaries and the conquistadors, it made relatively little impression on Central America, with only Mexico having any kind of wine culture. It made a considerable impression on South America, but until very recently the wine culture there seemed frozen in a premodern, pre-New World state. Then Chile, followed by Argentina, and then Uruguay and Brazil at last woke up, and now South America is rightly held up as one of the most exciting wine regions in the world.

The Andes and cooling breezes off the Pacific are the most important physical influences on viticulture. These maritime breezes help regulate excessive temperatures the length of the coast, from Baja California down to Chile's Central Valley. On the eastern side, vineyards in Uruguay and parts of southern Brazil are influenced by the problematic combination of warm, wet oceanic weather off the Atlantic and regular blasts from the cold Pampero wind that originates in the Argentine pampas.

URUGUAY

Unlike Chile and Argentina, Uruguay is small and has only about 22,500 acres of vines. Its wine culture was developed at the end of the nineteenth century mainly by Basque settlers. In Chile and Argentina, the Andes dominate the vineyards, but in ultra-flat Uruguay it's pretty hard even to find a hill. The unpredictable, rain-bearing Atlantic means that Uruguay is wet throughout the year. Some years the rain doesn't come at harvest time, and everyone rejoices. Of course, that's exactly what happens in Bordeaux. In the southern parts of San José and in Canelones, where 90 percent of Uruguay's vineyards are, it is almost all cold, damp clay. Not what's wanted in a wet climate. Gravel would be better. Well, on the sea shore, down at Rocha, like the Médoc, there's gravel aplenty, buffeted by the Atlantic winds, and just to the west Maldonado's granite hills promise much. These are Uruguay's two most exciting areas. Alternatively, head north—there's sandy soil on the Brazilian border

at Rivera and alluvial soil at Salto—both giving wines of encouraging quality—but with an annual rainfall of up to 63 inches, this isn't classic vineyard country. Then there's Tannat, an import from the Atlantic coast of France. It's much more of a brute of a grape, being thick-skinned, tannic, and requiring time in cask and bottle to soften and show delightful raspberry and blueberry fruit. But it can survive damp conditions, and it is different in a world increasingly looking for variety. It is often tempered by blending with a little Cabernet Franc. With wines such as this, Uruguay could emerge as a strong niche player among New World wine countries.

BRAZIL

Brazil is such a vast country that it seems to squeeze all the others in South America into margins of the continent, making you think there must be some ace places to plant vineyards. Well, there are, but they are few and far between because Brazil largely straddles the equator and the Tropic of Capricorn and is tropical,

MEXICO

Mexico should play a much more important role in this book because the whole Central and South American wine industry, as well as that of California, stems from the Spanish arriving in Mexico, planting imported Spanish vines, and establishing wineries. The oldest winery in the Americas was established here in the late sixteenth century, and is still going. But Mexicans have never taken to wine, and, although the country has 98,000 acres of vines more than 90 percent of the grapes are destined for brandy or just for eating. The few quality vineyards are mostly in the Baja California peninsula, just south of the U.S. border, where a number of east-west valleys draw cool winds and fog up from the Pacific Ocean. Two companies, Pedro Domecq and L. A. Cetto, dominate production and make some good reds from Petite Sirah, Nebbiolo, Tempranillo, and Zinfandel. On the other side of the country, in the Parras Valley, Casa Madero has had some success with Cabernet Sauvignon.

subtropical, or desert. In the world's largest tract of rain forest you'd expect it to be pretty hot and humid, which is exactly what most of it is. This doesn't stop there being a lot of vineyards—more than 200,000 acres, but only about 10 percent of these are for *vinifera* wine grapes.

Remarkably, there is a fascinating subtropical operation at Vale do São Francisco, only 9 degrees south, which in blistering conditions produces two crops a year of pretty tasty wine. The Moscato is particularly juicy. Otherwise you have to head way south to find decent stuff. The traditional area—the Rio Grande do Sul, centered on the mountain city of Bento Gonçalves—was settled by Italians in the 1840s. It's still pretty humid, but good wines are increasingly possible, and the need to pick early in wet conditions means that lowish-alcohol reds from grapes such as Merlot, Cabernet Franc, and Teroldego can be delightful, as can the Moscatos, many of which are made in the sweet sparkling style of Italy's Asti. There is clearly the drive to make riper, later-picked, and more heavily oaked "reserve" styles, and the best producers make a reasonable stab at these, but I believe that, in a world that increasingly wants lighter, fresher, reds, Rio Grande do Sul can provide them. Sparkling wine, dry or sweet, from Pinot Noir and Chardonnay or Moscato is always good and sometimes outstanding. The most promising areas for dry reds and whites are the high Planalto Catarinense vineyards north of Bento Gonçalves; with much drier conditions and good sunshine tempered by the altitude, they are well suited to grapes such as the Cabernets and Merlot. The dry and temperate vineyards of the Serra do Sudeste down near Uruguay, fairly high and influenced by the cold Atlantic, have shown impressive form with reds and whites. Further inland is the Campanha region; also promising, but less temperate, drier, and hotter, giving ripeness but less perfume and character than the grapes of the Sudeste.

OTHER COUNTRIES

Venezuela has vines, at around 10 degrees north, near Maracaibo; it can give three crops a year, and two is perfectly normal. There are discernible differences in flavor and quality between each harvest. I'm not sure how the Syrah and Petit Verdot vines feel about that. Bolivia has vines, too, including some of the highest in the world at up to 8,200 feet. I tried the wines this year after a long gap, and the improvement has been dramatic. Peru used to have a relatively important wine industry, but its vineyards have now slumped to about 27,180 acres, and most of the grapes are used for distilling Pisco, the local spirit, which can be dangerously delicious. Elsewhere, Ecuador makes good Chardonnay, and Colombia and Paraguay do produce some wine. I've also had Cuban Chardonnay.

MAIN WINE REGIONS

- VENEZUELA
- COLOMBIA
- ECUADOR
- PERU
- BOLIVIA
- CHILE
- ARGENTINA
- URUGUAY
  1. Colonia
  2. Canelones
  3. Maldonado
- BRAZIL
  4. Serra Gaúcha
  5. Planalto Catarinense
  6. Vale de São Francisco

See also
Chile page 259
Argentina page 265

Chile

DAWN IN CHILE'S CENTRAL VALLEY is spectacularly slow. The silhouette of the Andes appears like some giant frozen wave of water, swelling in color and shape as the sun struggles over the ridge. As more light filters through, the older but lower Coast Range comes into view to the west, and you realize you're caught in a lush, green trough between two immense walls of stone. Shielding your eyes from the brilliant light, there are fruit and vines as far as the eye can see. If wines were judged solely on the beauty of their vineyards, this country would be hard to beat.

Pedro de Valdivia, founder of the capital, Santiago, arrived in 1541, and in his day, before the region was shrouded in smog, it must have been a near perfect place in which to live. Cool winters and long dry summers make it climatically similar to California but with a more spectacular backdrop of snow-covered mountains. For the first three hundred years of its colonial life, the valley grew only País, an unremarkable black variety identical to Mission in California. Modern winemaking began as recently as the 1860s, when wealthy landowners around Santiago invited French winemakers, increasingly out of work after the phylloxera aphid had destroyed Europe's vineyards, and employed them to tend newly imported *Vitis vinifera* varieties, partly as an experiment in improving the quality of their own vineyards, partly as a status symbol. The timing is significant because cuttings had been taken out to Chile, particularly from Bordeaux's vineyards, just before the phylloxera arrived there. So far Chile has managed to stay phylloxera-free because of its geographical isolation, with the Atacama Desert, the Andes, and the Pacific Ocean all forming natural barriers against the pest. In fact, when Europe was ready to replant its vineyards, Chile supplied many of the scions to be grafted onto phylloxera-resistant American rootstock.

CLIMATE

The Andean range is one of the most influential forces affecting Chile's viticultural zones, which now extend from Copiapó, about 415 miles north of Santiago, with a couple of high Atacama outposts more than 11,000 miles north of Santiago, down to Malleco, 355 miles south of the capital, with a couple of brave outfits more than 200 miles further south at Osorno and Coihaique. From the singeing heat bouncing off the Elquí Valley, north in Coquimbo province, to the glacial chill slipping down from the Maipo Canyon, southeast of Santiago, every evening these mountains make their presence felt in every vineyard and wine.

Although vineyards extend for about 1,655 miles north to south, the most important climatic disparities are in the opposite direction, east to west across Chile's meager breadth. This is due to the presence of the Andean and also the Coast Range, which, together with the maritime climate, have a critical effect on temperature and rainfall in each vineyard area. The extent of this influence depends very much on where, east-to-west, the vineyards are located.

In the Central Valley, those vineyards on the east–facing slopes of the Coast Range are in a rain shadow and receive lower rainfall and warmer temperatures than vines situated closer to the Andes. Vineyards in

CLASSIFICATION

Chile has a fledgling Denominación de Origen (DO) system, which divides the country into five regions with further subdivisions. Atacama largely produces the grape spirit Pisco. Coquimbo includes the excellent wine areas of Limari, Elquí, and Choapa Valley. The three main table wine regions are Aconcagua, Central Valley, and the Southern Region. A recent move to create an east–west divide is encouraging. Andes is in the east, followed by Entre Cordilleras (between the mountains) and Costa (coastal).

the Andean foothills benefit from big variations between nighttime and daytime temperatures, with great downdrafts of cold night air producing high levels of grape acidity and a good concentration of fruit. From the Atacama Desert southward, river valleys provide routes for cold Pacific air to be sucked inland, crucially cooling the vineyards they pass and further tempering the heart of the inland Central Valley. Plentiful Andean runoff provides water for irrigation, young fertile soil makes grape growing child's play, and dry conditions help prevent most pests and diseases. Add to this the fact that this is the only country without phylloxera, and you realize that a struggling Chilean vine is an exception, not the rule. Chilean winemakers nowadays feel they could do with a few challenges in the vineyard because this would force change, which could lift Chilean wines to even greater recognition than they currently enjoy.

RED AND WHITE WINES

At their best, Chilean wines are packed with exhilarating, youthful fruit that almost kicks its way out of the bottle. País used to be the most widely planted variety, doing the same humdrum job of providing large amounts of cheap wine as Criolla in Argentina. But domestic wine drinking in Chile, especially at the bottom end, has slumped considerably, and now producers realize their future lies in exports— and at the top end of the quality range, too.

Costa
Entre Cordilleras
Andes

WINE REGIONS AND SUBREGIONS

— ATACAMA
  1. Copiapó
  2. Huasco Valley
— COQUIMBO
  3. Elquí Valley
  4. Limarí Valley
  5. Choapa Valley
— ACONCAGUA
  6. Aconcagua Valley
  7. Casablanca Valley

  8. San Antonio Valley
  9. Leyda Valley
— CENTRAL VALLEY
  10. Maipo Valley
  11. Cachapoal Valley (Rapel Valley)
  12. Colchagua Valley (Rapel Valley)
  13. Curicó Valley
  14. Lontué Valley
  15. Maule Valley

— SOUTH
  16. Itata Valley
  17. Bío-Bío Valley
  18. Malleco Valley
— AUSTRAL
  19. Cautín Valley
  20. Osorno Valley

CLIMATE

When the cool sea breezes from the icy Humboldt Current that flows northward along South America's west coast meet warmer coastal air, cool morning fogs and cold winds result. As each river valley cuts through the Coast Range of mountains, icy Pacific air is sucked up the valley, creating cool but sunny conditions that suit both red and white wines. These so-called Costa zones spread right down the Chilean coast, from Elquí in the arid north to Itata in the damp south. Superb Sauvignon Blanc, Chardonnay, Pinot Noir, and Syrah lead the way. Many of the river valleys then cross the warmer, more fertile Entre Cordilleras zone that contains the long north–south Central Valley before climbing into the Andes foothills—the Andean zone—where height also allows cool but sunny conditions to produce exciting reds and whites. Cold air comes into these eastern Central Valley vineyards at night from the Andes, whose towering peaks are snow-covered all year round. The combination of cool nights and hot days during the growing season prompts the vines to shut down at night, boosting grape acidity and enhancing their fruit intensity, color, and aroma.

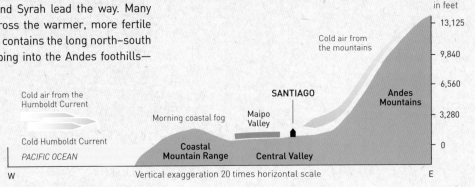

The grape leader is Cabernet Sauvignon. Cabernet Sauvignon from the Maipo Valley launched Chile's reputation in the nineteenth century, and the mixture of luscious ripe black fruit, low tannin, and often an intriguing whiff of eucalyptus that Maipo Cabernet possesses makes it Chile's most famous wine style. But it isn't just in Maipo. Cabernet is grown in the north in the Elquí and Limarí valleys, in the south at Bío Bío, and everywhere in between, even in ultra-cool Casablanca.

The new star in Chile's portfolio is Carménère, the best ones marrying lush black cherry fruit with an unexpected but delicious savoriness of capsicum, coffee beans, and soy sauce. Until the twenty-first century, it was routinely labeled as Merlot—much easier to pronounce and easier to sell. This would explain why Chilean Merlot was always some of the best in the world. Carménère was brought out to Chile in the mid-nineteenth century and is the great lost grape of Bordeaux. It used to play an important role in most of the top wines but was not replanted after the phylloxera scourge in the nineteenth century because it didn't give a regular crop and ripened after the other varieties. That's a problem in Bordeaux, where poor spring and fall weather is common, but it isn't a problem in Chile, where weather is consistently fine year by year. Sometimes you have to wait until May (that's November in the northern hemisphere) for Carménère to be ready but, because the sun is still shining, such a late harvest doesn't pose a huge risk.

We're now seeing a large number of wines labeled as Carménère, and most Chilean winemakers are taking its potential very seriously. They're also serious about Syrah/Shiraz—Aconcagua and Colchagua are producing excellent examples. Pinot Noir is beginning to shine, especially in Casablanca and the Leyda zone of San Antonio, while a reasonably wide selection of other red varieties, such as Malbec, Cabernet Franc, Petit Verdot, Zinfandel, and others, show that criticism of Chile as having a narrow range of wine styles is unfounded.

The white wine revolution has happened more recently with the discovery of cool climates, such as Casablanca, Limari, and Leyda, and the use of up-to-the-minute winemaking techniques. Chardonnay has lush fruit yet is satisfyingly savory, while Sauvignon Blanc from the cool coastal areas can be as tangy and lipsmacking as that of New Zealand. Also good are citrus Riesling, apple-packed Chenin Blanc, and Gewürztraminer, whose lychee-spiced personality has shone in Casablanca and, more recently, in the southern area around Mulchén. There's a lot of good, unfashionable Semillon, and ultra-fashionable Viognier has also been planted with mixed results so far.

Casa Lapostolle's Clos Apalta vineyard in the Colchagua Valley. The green vine leaves are the late-ripening Cabernet Sauvignon, the red ones are typical of Carménère (its name refers to the old French word for "red"), and the yellow ones Merlot.

WINE REGIONS

Chile's viticultural areas are often divided into the Irrigated Zone, fed by Andean riverwater, and the Unirrigated Zone. The latter involves areas to the west of the Coast Range and those in the wetter southern areas of Chillán and Bío Bío. This was fine in the old days when the only irrigation used was from the Andean rivers. But development of bore technology now means that irrigation is available to many areas where it would have been impractical to plant. Casablanca is the most obvious example, where today's highly successful vineyard cultivation would be impossible without water pumped from bore holes. But each year brings new examples especially because coastal regions can be very dry but are thrillingly cool and Chilean winemakers crave cool conditions.

First, let's look at the north. Right up in the Atacama region, virtually the only grapes grown are those used for distillation into the national spirit, Pisco. A Pisco Sour is an entirely irresistible drink after a long day researching the vineyards. But there are vines producing good wine in the Huasco Valley as well as one or two optimistic ventures even further north. South of Atacama in Coquimbo there are three river valleys, the Elquí, Limari, and Choapa, all of which are making a name for tangy, ripe reds and whites. Elquí's Syrah and Carménère are exciting but Limari, at 30 degrees south, leads the way with summer temperatures that rarely top 86 degrees Fahrenheit due to the icy Humboldt current just offshore. Most of the vineyards are only about 20 miles from the sea and get regular morning mists and afternoon breezes to keep the heat down. There are some ultra-cool vineyards only 7 miles from the Pacific. A series of superb Chardonnays and Sauvignons, backed up by very good Pinot Noir and Syrah, has cemented Limari's reputation. There's almost no rain, so reservoirs need to catch every drop as well as keep themselves supplied from bore holes, and, indeed, lack of water will be the limiting factor here.

We need to go south to about 60 miles north of Santiago for the next important area—Aconcagua. Its reputation was built by a single winery, Errázuriz, although there is now rapid expansion into its coolest zones nearer the coast. The Aconcagua Valley is the main pass over the

Andes into Argentina. Its prime activity has always been orchards and fruit, including table grapes, and frankly it should be too hot for wine grapes, except that around the town of Panquehue, the valley opens up out toward the sea and its wind. The mixture of downdrafts from the Andes and stiff breezes from the coast that seem to arrive on the dot of midday keeps things surprisingly cool. Errázuriz, having created its reputation with Cabernet, came out with Chile's first commercial Syrah in 1996 from vineyards at Panquehue. Cool vineyards near the mouth of the Aconcagua River are now giving even more exciting results.

Technically in the same region but vastly different in character are the Leyda Valley, forming part of the San Antonio zone, and the Casablanca Valley. Leyda, lying about 9 miles inland from the port of San Antonio, was first planted in 1997. A series of ridges, either wide open to the sea or protected by low bluffs, and a mixture of gravel and clay soil create conditions as ultra-cool as the coolest in Casablanca, especially in those vineyards within sight of the ocean. Exciting Sauvignon Blancs and Chardonnays and thrilling Pinot Noirs and Syrahs prove that the struggle to ripen the grapes is worth it.

The first Casablanca plantings were in 1982, but it wasn't until everyone saw the stunning intensity of these first white wines that a stampede for land occurred. There are around 14,825 acres—and there could be twice that if there was water, but the feeble Casablanca River doesn't rise in the Andes and so doesn't benefit from floods of snowmelt. Well, there could be water. So far there are one thousand wells feeding Casablanca, and water is the biggest cost in the valley. Yet because of the cool conditions, vines need only one-third of the water they need in the Central Valley between the Coast Range and the Andes. A lot of the land is still used for corn, which uses five times as much water as vines. Now, if the corn farmers could be persuaded . . .

Those cool conditions, well, they're a blessing and a curse. The Casablanca Valley is about 50 miles west of Santiago and between 12 miles and 22 miles from the coast. It is distinctly cooler at the coastal end partly because as early as 10 a.m. every morning in summer a breeze is being sucked up from the cold Pacific. The upper end of the valley can be warmer. I say can be because, although Cabernet and Carménère vines can ripen higher up on the slopes, the valley floor, where the sea breezes survive only right next to the river and where cold air from the east tumbles down every evening, is cool enough for snappy Sauvignon Blanc. Just 160 feet in height can make all the difference between a warm red and an ice-cool white, and it can make the difference between keeping your crop and losing it to frost. Spring

frosts are regular as clockwork, and in September and October, as the vine is budding and putting forth young shoots, the whole valley is on frost alert. Frosts in midsummer and before harvest aren't uncommon either. When you think that the Chardonnay harvest usually lasts from March 20 to April 30 and the reds might not be ripe until May, you can see why there are wind machines all over the valley to counteract frost.

Casablanca is very much the modern face of Chilean wine. If we head back through the mountains to Santiago, and in particular to the Maipo Valley just to the south, we get to the heart of traditional Chilean wine. The Maipo Valley is the core of old Chile, stretching from the Macul area, huddled between Santiago and the Andes, down through Puente Alto and Pirque, to Buin and Isla de Maipo, some 30 miles or so further south. It has been at the heart of Chilean wine ever since the mid-nineteenth century, when the wealthy of Santiago began to build French-style estates and vineyards as proof of their riches. They brought French experts and French grape varieties to Chile—above all from Bordeaux. Of these, Cabernet Sauvignon has adapted wonderfully to Maipo.

The vineyards are pushed right up to the edge of the Andes Cordillera, reaching almost 3,280 feet above sea level. Soil is poor—you hit gravel and rock at only 24 inches below the surface, and water is difficult to find especially because the city consumes more and more. Sometimes it's difficult to find the sun as well. Not because of clouds—rainfall is only 12 inches plus a year—but because of Santiago's smog and dust. The vintage is usually mid-April, and the flavors of the wines are astonishing, blending black-currant fruit, eucalyptus fragrance, and soft, silky tannins.

You will have barely left the southern suburbs when you arrive at the vineyards of Puente Alto just to the north of the Maipo River and Pirque just to the south. But we've already dropped around 985 feet in height—the vineyards of Puente Alto are between 2,100 feet and 2,230 feet—and we've drifted further away from the Andes, although one or two producers have crept back, looking for cool conditions and a lot of afternoon sunshine. Puente Alto has some of Chile's greatest Cabernet vineyards—used for Concha y Toro's Don Melchor, Viñedo Chadwick, and the Chilean-French blockbuster Almaviva. At Pirque, the Maipo River runs into a kind of gorge and then spreads out toward Buin. A clawlike extension of hills heading southeast provides some of Maipo's best conditions in a large west-facing horseshoe, and the marvelously seductive reds from here are picked ten days earlier than those further north.

There is one more important but less typical area of Maipo. To the west, where the Maipo River loops around

Pruning Chardonnay vines in the vineyard of William Fèvre in the Maipo Valley with the Andes beyond.

below an isolated mountain, is the Isla de Maipo—windy and fertile—and here Cabernet Sauvignon ripens four weeks later than at Puento Alto.

If we hit the Pan-American Highway and head south for a couple of hours, we get to Rapel and the areas of Cachapoal and Colchagua. The Cachapoal Valley and the more important Colchagua Valley make up the Rapel Valley region, which has 117,328 acres of vines.

Requínoa is huddled underneath the Andes, right to the east of the Cachapoal Valley. The proximity to the Andes brings extreme day-night differences of temperature. Add to this free-draining gravelly soil and a very low water table, and it makes for superb red wine conditions reminiscent of the Médoc in Bordeaux. A series of French and Bordeaux-financed properties in the area reinforces this impression, and there's a lot of Cabernet planted. Cachapoal's other important area is between Peumo and Las Cabras to the west, where exposure to the afternoon sun and gravelly clay produce exceptionally fresh but ripe reds.

Colchagua is directly south of Cachapoal, with some fairly serious mountains in between. Again, its strength is red wines. There are large plantings of Cabernet Sauvignon, Merlot, and Carménère but also Syrah, Zinfandel, and Sangiovese. Some of the best vines are planted on a steep, south-facing amphitheater called Apalta. Other exceptional vineyards are the hilltops planted by Luis Felipe Edwards at up to 3,300 feet. But most of the central Colchagua Valley is fertile and warm; reds are often good but not distinguished, and the whites are fairly soft. There is a new exciting area of Colchagua over toward the Pacific Ocean. Marchique is proving excellent for reds, as is Lolol for reds and whites. Paredones right down near the ocean is a new cool climate star for Pinot Noir and Sauvignon Blanc.

Further south is the Curicó Valley, another large wine region, with nearly 50,000 acres of vines. You would expect it to be getting colder as we head south. Well, not yet, it isn't, because the Coast Range rears up a good deal higher in Curicó between the vineyards and the sea, and you lose most of the effect of the cold breezes. The coolest part of Curicó is up the Teno Valley toward the Andes, but most of the vines are on the rich, fertile soil around the river Lontué. All the big companies have cellars or vineyards down here, but relatively few exciting wines appear.

At last, it does get cooler and wetter. The Maule Valley directly south of Curicó has 82,975 acres of vines. Here, Cabernet Sauvignon has overtaken the native País and is at its best in areas warm enough in the center and west of the Valley. Close to the Andes, rainfall can increase to 39 inches per year, and it does get cold. But Maule's real value is in its reservoir of old vines, especially Carignan, now being assiduously cherished for the first time. Out toward the ocean, at Cauquenes, there are some very good old, dry-farmed vines as well as some new plantings; the Californian giant Kendall-Jackson has planted vineyards here, attracted by reports of good Syrah, Mourvèdre, Cabernet Franc, and Carignan.

There are just a few more areas even further south. Itata is mostly given over to smallholdings of grapes such as Moscatel and País, but these grapes, along with Cinsaut, are now being converted into delicious wines. Bío Bío, more than 310 miles south of Santiago, with stony soil, more than 50 inches of rain a year, and Chile's coolest inland conditions, has produced good Gewürztraminer, Chardonnay, and Sauvignon Blanc, and Pinot Noir is promising. The Malleco Valley is Chile's southernmost appellation with a couple of acres of Chardonnay and Pinot Noir, although experimental vineyards have been planted even further south in Osorno and Coihaique.

Argentina

IN ARGENTINA, EVERYTHING SEEMS to come big. Distances, hailstones, steaks, even gin and tonics—all give the impression that you've arrived in the land of the giants. The wine industry used to be equally gargantuan, and it needed to be to service the Argentines' phenomenal thirst for their mealtime red. Well, consumption is now barely one-quarter of what it was only thirty-five years ago, and a lot of the vines that used to supply their grog have gone. But Argentina is still the sixth biggest producer of wine in the world and is now very much focused on export rather than the domestic palate. It wasn't until the 1990s that wine quality improved dramatically, and heavyweight investors from Europe and America began a whole range of vineyard and winery projects, especially in Mendoza, where 70 percent of the country's wine is made. The wine industry now seems to be emerging as one of the brightest stars in the global firmament.

GRAPE VARIETIES

Back in 1557, the Spanish started planting Criolla, the pink-skinned grape used to make huge quantities of deep-colored, oxidized white wine. Since then, the vine has spread out over a distance of 1,050 miles, from the Río Negro in the south up to the Calchaquí Valley, north of the far northern town of Salta. Of the 570,000 acres under vine, more than two-thirds are now planted with international varieties.

Of the European varieties, the intense black, licorice-lined Malbecs and ripe, spicy Syrahs show the most potential for red wines. But Italian immigration brought in varieties such as Sangiovese, Bonarda, and Barbera, and the Spaniards brought in Tempranillo, which are now showing how suited they are to Argentine conditions. Even so, Malbec is undoubtedly the grape best suited to the hot continental climate, producing wines packed with black currants, plums, and spice.

Of the white grapes, the highly aromatic Torrontés is the most widely planted quality variety and performs wonderfully in high-altitude Cafayate. Chardonnay predictably is beginning to produce seriously good, nutty, but full-bodied wines in the cooler areas, but Argentina, with the exception of those cooler areas such as Cafayate, Río Negro, and Tupungato, is still without question a red-wine country.

CLIMATE AND WINE REGIONS

The Andes form the most important physical influence on Argentine vineyards. This barrier removes all moisture from the Pacific winds, thus creating bone-dry conditions and 320 days of sunshine every year but also providing plentiful water for irrigation. A more negative role played by the mountains helps explain why nets are strung over many vines in the Mendoza region. High-altitude thunderstorms formed over the Andes regularly drop golfball-size hailstones just before the harvest, and this is more of a hazard than frost. Unlike Chile, Argentina does not have the natural barriers to protect it from phylloxera, which is now widespread in the country but which appears to cause little concern among winemakers. Most argue that poor soil and the use of flood irrigation keep the louse at bay. In general, soil is arid and stony with very little humus, creating stressful conditions for the vines.

Mendoza rightly dominates Argentine wine. The majestic Andes give everything to Mendoza, not only its weather, its water, its very soil, but also its heart. At dawn, they glow cherry pink above the city; by midday, they gleam white as models' teeth above the urban fug of the town, and, as the sun arcs west into the evening, the mountains are bleached of their form, the cotton clouds blending with the snow to create what seem like streams of molten silver flowing down the blue-gray mountainside. You can't get lost. East, south, west, and north—just look up to the Andes, and you'll know where you are.

Mendoza needs the mountains. Face them, and you are in a beautiful and spectacular wineland. Turn your back on them, and the vista in front of you is relentlessly flat. Find yourself on a spit of land where the irrigation channels don't go, and you're in a parched, scrubby desert. Which is exactly what Mendoza Province would be if the surging waters of four mighty rivers hadn't been tamed and their torrents of snow-melt channeled into irrigation systems, spreading out across the arid shrubland and creating hundreds of thousands of acres of horticulture. The broad Mendoza River valley, east of the city, has just a thin dribble of water trailing through; all the rest is nourishing crops. Yet even so, only 3 percent of Mendoza province is cultivated.

But that provides a substantial vineyard area—about 390,000 acres in all—with the bulk of it in a ring around the city of Mendoza. There are six main areas. North Mendoza is the least important, except for the fact that at Las Heras they've got Malbec vines going right back to

1861. Much more important is East Mendoza, except that it's very hot out there and these broad acres produce a lot of bulk wine.

Central Mendoza spreads out south of Mendoza city and along the Mendoza River. Many of the older vineyards have been grubbed up for urban development, but there are fine vineyards of old Malbec at Lunlunta and Maipú, and Barrancas is so stony it resembles France's Châteauneuf-du-Pape.

MAIN WINE REGIONS

NORTH (SALTA, CATAMARCA)
1. El Arenal
2. Molinos
3. Cafayate
4. Fiambalá

CUYO (LA RIOJA, SAN JUAN, MENDOZA)
5. Famatina
6. Tulum
7. Zonda
8. Pedernal
9. Maipú
10. Luján de Cuyo
11. Ugarteche
12. Valle de Uco
13. San Carlos
14. San Rafael

PATAGONIA (LA PAMPA, NEUQUÉN, RÍO NEGRO)
15. Alto Valle del Río Colorado
16. San Patricio del Chañar
17. Alto Valle del Río Negro

West of Maipú is Luján de Cuyo, the heart of Malbec in Mendoza. The area is higher than Maipú, going up to more than 3,480 feet above Las Compuertas, where the land visibly begins to rise toward the Andes. South of the Mendoza River, the areas of Perdriel and Agrelo have some of the best vineyards, particularly for reds. West toward the mountains and south right down to Ugarteche, there are numerous new plantings.

The Uco Valley, which lies over to the west, is much closer to the Andes and significantly higher in particular in Tupungato and Gualtallary. There's nothing under about 2,950 feet, and all of the major vineyard development is between about 3,280 feet and as much as 5,250 feet. The ripening season is much longer, often reaching well into April, and it's Argentina's top spot for Chardonnay. But reds such as Malbec, Merlot, and Pinot Noir are also excellent. Tens of millions of investment dollars from France, America, Holland, and elsewhere demonstrate that Tupungato and Gualtallary are Argentina's "coolest" areas in more ways than one.

It's a dull 80-mile drive southeast through lifeless shrub before you get to the most southern part of Mendoza—San Rafael. This region is irrigated by the Diamante and Atuel rivers, and the vines here are planted between about 1,475 feet and 2,625 feet high. That means that it is getting hotter, and wines such as Malbec and Barbera excel down here. But only if they survive to harvest. Hail is a perennial threat in Argentina, but it is at its worst in San Rafael. The hailstones here can weigh up to 1 pound, and they don't just destroy vineyards—they destroy cars, too. Nowadays, most of the vineyards are protected by hail nets. And the cars? Well, there's a thriving panel-beating industry in San Rafael.

MALBEC, A SUCCESS STORY

A lot of New World countries have seized upon a single grape variety to claim as their own: New Zealand chose Sauvignon Blanc, California chose Cabernet Sauvignon, and Argentina chose Malbec—a good choice. Malbec hadn't exactly distinguished itself in its homeland of France, being something of an also-ran in Bordeaux and the Loire and starring only in the fairly obscure area of Cahors. But in Argentina, Malbec found a glorious, riotous, rich, and scented style no one had suspected it of possessing. From the far north down to Patagonia in the south but above all in Mendoza, Malbec gives lush-texture, ripe, perfumed plummy wines easy to drink young but with enough tannin to age for years. A truly global crowd pleaser.

If you head south of Mendoza, well south, right down to Patagonia itself, you come to the small but highly promising Río Negro region. It doesn't look promising as you press your face against the window of the tiny plane that carries you south from San Rafael. Endless barren scrub is relieved only by minimal signs of human endeavor, and even these offer little reassurance. A settlement laid out near the Río Colorado is now nothing but rectangular scars scratched into the parched sandy soil. But then the greenery returns—the gash of fertility that marks the Río Negro. Yet again, you realize how most of Argentina would be mere desert if it weren't for irrigation. If you climb up to the ridge on the south bank of the Río Negro, you are looking at the beginning of Patagonia, the stone-strewn, inhospitable terrain in front of you that spreads south toward Cape Horn for approximately 1,555 miles. Turn back and look north toward the river, and you can see poplars swaying in the evening breeze, dark green fruit trees packed tight next to vineyards, and the odd cloud of dust as a rare car hurries along the unpaved roads. Below the ridge on the northern side of the valley is the reason for this verdancy—the Valle Alto irrigation channel that runs from the main town of Neuquén and waters all the plantations between the northern ridge and the Río Negro itself.

There are nearly 8,900 acres under vine in Patagonia. The Río Negro could very easily become Argentina's best white-wine region, with its long ripening seasons and cool conditions, giving grapes naturally high in acidity. But for now this is primarily red-wine country, and certainly Malbec is marvelously scented and deep in color. Several companies are successfully taming the upriver area west of Neuquén.

OTHER REGIONS

North of Mendoza, there are still substantial vineyards, but their wines are far less known than those of Mendoza itself. San Juan, 90 miles directly north of Mendoza, grows about 22 percent of the national grape crop mostly in hot dry conditions. The potential is much more exciting further south, especially in the cooler El Pedernal and Calingasta valleys down toward Mendoza, where there are vineyards planted as high up as about 4,920 feet. The Famatina Valley in La Rioja, around Chilecito, is hot and dry with mainly poor, sandy soil. Most grapes here are white and processed by the local co-op, which is luckily pretty competent, especially with Torrontés. Clearly this is an area that would better suit reds.

North of La Rioja, the high-altitude desert of Catamarca has some vineyards, including a new one at about 6,560 feet, but the real action is in Salta province,

The Andes mountains form a magnificent backdrop to the vineyards in Mendoza and have a dramatic effect on both climate and soil. This is Bodegas Salentein winery in the Uco Valley.

particularly in the mountain resort of Cafayate, sitting at about 5,575 feet in splendid isolation in the midst of what is virtually a desert. A new airport has made access easier, but I'd still recommend driving from the city of Salta to Cafayate through the Río de las Conchas Valley for some of the most breathtakingly beautiful mountain scenery you will ever encounter. Vineyards go well past 6,560 feet here—in fact, there are plantings at up to 10,200 feet north of Cafayate, although most are sited at around 5,575 feet. The speciality is a wonderfully scented version of Torrontés, although all whites are good, as is

the purple-hued Malbec. The height clearly cools things down, and although temperatures can rise to 100 degrees Fahrenheit in February, they generally drop back at night to between 54 and 59 degrees Fahrenheit. But Cafayate gets more than three hundred days of sun a year—so an important extra bonus for the grapes is a breeze that starts every day between 2 and 3 p.m. and blows until about 8 p.m., when the sun has already gone down.

Other minor but potentially exciting wine areas are La Pampa in the far south, Cordoba to its north, and Buenos Aires itself.

South Africa

THE MOST ENDURING MEMORY of my first arrival in the Cape is of a color. As I drove from the airport out to Somerset West then turned north toward Stellenbosch along the banks of the Eerste River, a great carpet of purply crimson vines stretched out on both sides of the road, glinting in the evening sun and casting a rosy glow onto the slopes of the Helderberg that reared up to the east. Captivating—yet that deep, dark red was nothing more than the color of an entire vineyard region suffering from viral infection. That crimson color meant diseased leaves that had lost their ability to trap sunlight for photosynthesis and to ripen the crop. This meant that many traditional Cape red wines displayed raw green acidity and bitter tannins, and since everyone was stuck with virused vines, producers defiantly labeled this unappealing character the Cape Red style. The virus is now a problem to be solved instead of being endured, and few modern Cape reds bear any resemblance to the old style.

There's another point worth mentioning. The beauty of the vine leaves is nothing compared to the beauty of the land itself. The mountains that rear up at this southern tip of Africa are some of the most uplifting and majestic in the world. Almost every vineyard is within sight of them, but in Stellenbosch and Paarl particularly they dominate your every thought, your every step, infusing you with calm and wonder—and, more mundanely, providing a rich variety of conditions in which to grow grapes.

But it wasn't until the 1990s, with Mandela released from prison, that the heady drugs of change and experimentation arrived in the Cape and we could begin to see how good South African wines might be. There is a mood of optimism and confidence. The changes being wrought in the vineyards are dramatic. And the wines? Transformed. Bursting with vibrant fruit, sensitively tempered by oak, and actually starting to speak of a sense of place. A Sauvignon Blanc from Constantia, a Riesling from Elgin, a Pinot Noir from Walker Bay, a Shiraz from Wellington, a Malbec from Paarl Mountain, a Pinotage from Simonsberg, and a bush-vine Chenin from the mountain slopes of Malmesbury. All special. All different from what the rest of the world might do with these varietals.

South Africa is the world's eighth-largest wine producer, although its position of only fourteenth in actual vineyard area shows you how high some of the vineyard yields are—as much as 10.5 tons per acre in the most irrigated regions, such as Olifants River and Orange River, although not all these dilute grapes will end up as wine. If you look at Stellenbosch or Paarl, the vines there can yield as little as 8 tons per acre, and other areas determined to improve quality—which means fundamentally reducing yields—include Robertson, Walker Bay, Elgin, Constantia, Durbanville, Swartland, Wellington, and Franschhoek.

If you try to persuade a grape grower in a producer cellar, as cooperatives are now called, to reduce his yields, you have to change his entire farmer's mindset that equates success with a big crop, and cooperatives do still play an important role. However, the drive for quality in the last generation is being led by a relatively new phenomenon in the Cape—a flood of new private producers. There are now about five hundred private wine cellars or wineries in the Cape, and more than half are small scale. They haven't just stuck to the traditional quality areas of Stellenbosch and Paarl; they have actively sought cooler and higher vineyard sites as well as breathing exciting new life into old areas, such as Constantia, Swartland, and Olifants River.

CLASSIFICATION

The Wine of Origin (WO) system divides wine-producing areas into regions, districts, wards, and single vineyards. Varietal, vintage-dated wines must be made from at least 85 percent of the named grape and vintage.

GRAPE VARIETIES

Around 80 percent of the annual crop ends up as table wine, and white accounts for about 55 percent of production. Chenin Blanc is still the leading variety at 18 percent, although it has been declining for years. Sauvignon Blanc and Chardonnay are the next most important white varieties. Cabernet Sauvignon and Shiraz are the most important red varieties, followed by Pinotage and Merlot. There has been a significant increase in Pinot Noir as the cooler areas back themselves to produce some of the New World's most stylish red Burgundy lookalikes. The swing toward classic, international varieties now includes small quantities of Viognier, Mourvèdre, Malbec, Nebbiolo, and Sangiovese. The Cape's favorable climate, and the worldwide interest in all things Rhôneish, has also put the spotlight on the likes of Grenache and old bush-vine plantings of Cinsaut.

WINE REGIONS

The first experimental grape plantings took place in Cape Town in 1655 in the gardens of the Dutch East India Company. Virtually the whole industry has since confined itself to the southwestern Cape area of South Africa from about 32 degrees to just over 34 degrees south because this is the only area that can at least partly boast a Mediterranean climate. There's good rainfall in the cold wet winters, and the long hot summers, which stretch from November to May, would be too hot for really fine wines were it not, on the west coast, for the chilly Benguela Current that surges up from the Antarctic and sends cooling breezes inland up the river valleys and the prevailing southeasterlies that cool down most parts east of Paarl.

MAIN WINE REGIONS

OLIFANTS RIVER
1. Lutzville Valley
2. Citrusdal Mountain
3. Citrusdal Valley

COASTAL REGION
4. Swartland
5. Darling
6. Tulbagh
7. Wellington
8. Paarl
9. Tygerberg
10. Franschhoek Valley
11. Stellenbosch
12. Cape Peninsula (includes Constantia Ward)

BREEDE RIVER VALLEY
13. Breedekloof
14. Worcester
15. Robertson

KLEIN KAROO
16. Calitzdorp
17. Langeberg-Garcia

CAPE SOUTH COAST
18. Elgin
19. Overberg
20. Walker Bay
21. Cape Agulhas
22. Swellendam
23. Plettenberg Bay

Increasingly, the best wines are from growers who have selected specific sites for specific varieties, some on the slopes of the mountain ranges in order to reduce temperatures even further. Grapes tend to ripen better there because, although there are numerous soil forms—Stellenbosch alone has twenty—they tend not to be overcropped like those on the alluvial very fertile, lower, and flatter sites. Growers who planted high up discovered that, because heat rises, the vines failed to go into dormancy during the winter, and that's if they avoided being devoured by the baboons who roam the peaks. So it's the midslopes that are now considered the most desirable, with deep, well drained soil and good aspects being seen as just as important as those cooling breezes.

Vineyards are moving further south; there are vines south of Elim, toward Cape Agulhas, Africa's most southerly point. The vines here are on decomposed granite outcrops, and the plentiful and pure spring water keeps them going through the long, dry summer months. The chief problem is high humidity from the southeasterlies encouraging rot, but wonderful Sauvignons and fine, taut reds are being made.

Traditionally the best table wines have come from vineyards influenced by the cooling breezes of False Bay. Earliest and most famous are the wines of Constantia, just south of Cape Town. Spectacular sweet wines were made here in the eighteenth and nineteenth centuries. In the mid-1980s, after a long gap, the tradition of Constantia dessert wine began to be revived, but the cool-climate, tangy, dry whites excite me most.

The vast majority of the top wines have always come from Paarl and Stellenbosch. Many still do, from vines beneath the towering peaks of the Helderberg, Stellenbosch, Simonsberg, and Drakensteinberg mountains. Many of the best-known wineries are in Simonsberg-Stellenbosch, the farthest from the cooling sea breezes of False Bay. Vineyards go up to about 1,575 feet, where mostly white varieties are planted. Deep red soil in the lower, more sheltered sites gives rich, structured reds, especially from Pinotage, Shiraz, and Cabernet. Many of these sites are relatively warm and have an annual rainfall of fewer than 40 inches, which is dry, but if your soil is right, it doesn't seem to be too much of a problem. In most of the major vineyard areas, the soil is decomposed granite mixed with clay, often sufficiently deep that the vines hardly need the subsoil and shale. The decomposed granite/clay soil in particular holds its water well, and although many vineyards are irrigated, you can dry-farm in these conditions—especially with old bush vines—and many producers do. Which makes sense. Some wine growers see the Rhône Valley in France as having similar conditions to much of the Cape. When you

drive through the Rhône, you see mile upon mile of dry-farmed bush vines clearly thriving in the arid conditions. Indeed, Stellenbosch is undergoing some soul-searching at the moment. It kind of wants to believe it's relatively cool, but most of it isn't, and hopefully the tremendous quality of the new Shiraz wines now appearing will dampen the cries of the would-be cool-climate brigade.

As if the scenery wasn't spectacular enough, if you really want to blow your mind, head for the Jonkershoek Valley and, further on, the new Banghoek Ward. Once through the low-lying land near Stellenbosch town, you come to towering mountains that press ever closer to the narrow, winding road. The vines are almost all near the valley mouth and scrambling up to about 1,150 feet on the steep but cool, south-facing slopes. The southeasterly winds tear down this valley, and steep peaks reduce the exposure to morning and evening sun, which would explain why initially Chardonnay was the chief grape. However, despite the conditions, the more exciting results are coming from Shiraz and Cabernet. Other new developments are at the northern end of the Helderberg in the Blaauwklippen Valley, where some new estates are already excelling. Just outside the Stellenbosch district, in the windswept Lourensford Valley, is Vergelegen, one of South Africa's top wineries.

Unlike Stellenbosch, Paarl has never claimed to be a cool area and receives only the tail end of the False Bay breezes plus some Atlantic winds from the west. Franschhoek is the most famous area, a long valley barricaded by mountains, but only a small part of the land is suitable for vines. Even so, there's still a wide variety of north-, south-, east-, and west-facing slopes to be exploited. Plantings so far go as high as about 1,380 feet, and the chief problem is to maximize the cooling effect of the southeasterly winds that sweep down the valley without having your vines bludgeoned out of existence. Simonsberg-Paarl, on the northern and eastern foothills of the Simonsberg, has clearly got something special because in a supposedly hot area Glen Carlou produces medal-winning Pinot Noir, while just across the valley on the south side of Paarl Mountain, Fairview's Rhône and Bordeaux varieties bake to perfection in the afternoon sun. Wellington Ward is hotter and well away from sea breezes. Its Chenin Blanc used to be a mainstay of Cape "Sherry," yet that's only half the story. There's a whole hillside of top-quality, iron-rich Glen Rosa soil producing excellent reds, and the east-facing slopes of the Groenberg have some of the coolest conditions in the Western Cape. The Voor Paardeberg Ward is west of Wellington with conditions fairly similar to the currently more fashionable Swartland.

One of the glories of South Africa's wine areas is that you are never out of sight of dramatic mountain ranges, as here in the Hex River Valley, Worcester, a warm, inland region.

With new areas opening up and small, quality-minded producers operating in regions previously dominated by cooperatives, competition is increasing. Those intent on finding the coolest spots have headed southeast through the mountains toward the Overberg District and Hermanus. As you drive up over the mountain pass into this bowl-shaped highland, the vegetation and the air change from warm to cool climate at a stroke. Famous for apples and pears, Elgin is increasingly producing exciting Sauvignon Blanc, Chardonnay, and Pinot Noir. It's very close to the southern coastline and often has protective cloud cover during summer for days on end as well as being one of South Africa's few wine areas that will probably enjoy some summer rain. Keep driving southeast and you'll come to Walker Bay and in particular the Hemel-en-Aarde Valley behind the cliffs at Hermanus. This is where Tim Hamilton-Russell planted in the 1970s, hoping to find South Africa's coolest conditions and re-create Burgundian Chardonnay and Pinot Noir. In a typically Burgundian way, the Hemel-en-Aarde Valley has already divided its small self into three districts—the Valley itself, the Upper Valley, and the Ridge—and there's no doubt results are different, especially for Pinot Noir, and increasingly exciting.

But these vineyard areas are no longer South Africa's coolest. There are the fascinating Elim vineyards in the extreme south, and on the west coast those sites cooled by fogs and breezes from the Benguela Current are also starting to shine, most notably Darling and its Groenekloof ward, whose Sauvignons are startlingly tart

and tasty. Durbanville Hills, its vineyards fighting a pitched battle against urban encroachment from Cape Town's suburbs, is another fine cool area. A couple of miles inland and the temperature warms up at every step. This is Swartland, and there are fine mountain slope sites at Piketberg, Riebeek, Porseleinberg, and Perdeberg, where old Chenin vines share the parched soil with Pinotage, Cinsaut, and Shiraz. There are also isolated patches of old bush vines that spring up when you least expect them to. As you head north to the Olifants River once again, cooperatives are battling to improve quality, while north of Lamberts Bay, at Bamboes Bay, yet another windy cool site produces tangy Sauvignon Blanc.

Inland areas, such as Worcester, Robertson, and the Klein Karoo, are among the warmest in the winelands, although Robertson does benefit from afternoon winds blowing up the Breede River from the Atlantic. Worcester produces the most wine of any region, much of it quaffable, easy-priced white, although some similarly undemanding reds are showing their worth. Robertson's limestone soil and good access to properly utilized irrigation have proved to be excellent for both whites and sparklers, and the move now is to see whether they can repeat their success with reds. Calitzdorp in the Klein Karoo lays claim to be the Port-style capital of South Africa; with the introduction of more Portuguese varieties and greater focus on the part of the producers, some real beauties are appearing. All three regions are known for other fortified wines as well, especially sweet Muscadels.

Australia

In the foreground, sheep graze as they have done for generations, and in the background, vineyards reach up from the Barossa Valley floor to the arid slopes above Tanunda.

Australia didn't have many advantages when it came to establishing a wine industry. There was no history of wine among the aboriginal people because there weren't any native vines. None of Australia's trading partners in Southeast Asia had ever had wine as part of their culture. It didn't seem propitious that the nation which decided to colonize the vast continent was Great Britain. Now, if the French, the Italians, or the Spanish . . .

We forget one thing. The British weren't much good at growing grapes at home, but they were the world's greatest connoisseurs when it came to appreciating the wine of other European countries, in particular the table wines of France and the fortified wines of Portugal and Spain. Because Australia was initially settled as a penal colony, the authorities were eager to establish a temperate wine-drinking culture instead of one based on the more savage rum. At the end of the eighteenth century, when New South Wales was gradually establishing itself, Europe was embroiled in war. The idea of a British Imperial vineyard not hostage to the recurrent political crises in Europe must have seemed enticing. Well, it almost did work out like that. For considerable portions of the nineteenth and twentieth centuries, Australia provided a steady stream of unchallenging—and mostly fortified—wines that were lapped up by Great Britain. But by the last quarter of the twentieth century, the country had embarked on a remarkable voyage of wine discovery that has placed her at the forefront of all that is best in the New Age of wine— despite having a vineyard area that is dwarfed by the major European nations.

This position has been achieved without Australia enjoying many of the perceived benefits of Europe's classic regions, most of which are poised on the cusp between not being able to and being able to ripen their fruit. Unlike Europe, the general rule in Australia is more than enough sunshine and not nearly enough rain. Traditionalists say you can't make great wine under such conditions, but Australia's winemakers have turned this to their advantage, using irrigation freely and highlighting the ripeness of the grapes in a succession of sun-filled, richly textured reds and whites. Despite the very different conditions, these may initially have been inspired by the best of Europe, but they have created such a forceful identity of their own that Europe now often attempts to ape the style of these down-under wonders. In the meantime, a better understanding of how to bring grapes to optimum ripeness—not over- or underripe but just so—has led to an explosion of cool-climate wine regions on the fringes of this parched continent.

The Wine Regions of Australia

WATER, WATER, WATER. That's the story of Australia. On this vast, parched continent, finding meager supplies of moisture is an ever-present priority and not just for grape growers. Yet Australians show amazing resourcefulness, and new vineyards spring up where no one had dreamed vines could flourish.

WESTERN AUSTRALIA

Western Australia is a vast state, virtual desert except for its southwestern coastal strip. Its wine industry was one of the first to be established in Australia in the sun-baked Swan Valley, but Perth's isolation kept it largely focused on supplying the local market. Nowadays, the most exciting wines come from the Margaret River and the Great Southern regions, where the continent's southwestern tip turns away from the Indian Ocean toward the cold depths of the Southern Ocean.

SOUTH AUSTRALIA

South Australia was the last of the major wine states to be established in the 1840s, but it more than made up for lost time. It dominates the Australian wine scene, growing the greatest tonnage of grapes, making the largest volume of wine and housing most of its biggest wine companies. The bulk of its grapes are grown in the impressively efficiently irrigated vineyards along the banks of the Murray River.

But South Australia has far more to offer than oceans of attractive, undemanding, gluggable wine. The single most important factor is that the phylloxera bug, which destroyed almost all the world's vines in the nineteenth century, never reached South Australia, so its vines, along with those of Chile, are planted on their own roots, not grafted. In the north, the verdant Clare Valley is an unexpected but excellent producer

of cool-climate table wines. Yet, as so often in Australia, local climates within an area provide a far broader range of styles than one would find in Europe—Clare Shiraz and Clare "Port" coexist with delicate Clare Riesling.

The Barossa Valley is South Australia's heartland, where most of the big companies are based. It is also home to some of the planet's oldest vines, and the blockbuster Shiraz and Grenache from these vines have made Barossa world-famous. Eden Valley, in the hills east of Barossa, has a spectrum of wine styles, but the crisp, steely Rieslings set it apart. Just south of Adelaide is McLaren Vale, the first wine area to be developed in South Australia. Despite incursions from the expanding city, the area is now a major producer of high-quality reds and whites. Population explosion has never been a problem at Padthaway and Coonawarra—hardly anyone lives in this damp, forlorn corner of the state—but this has allowed the development of superb vineyards making thrilling wines.

VICTORIA

Victoria's vineyards seem like they've been hurled into position with a shotgun. This is because they followed the Gold Rush, and when gold was exhausted odd vines were left all over the state. They can, however, produce some of the most exhilarating and distinctive Australian wines. Victoria was Australia's major wine producer for

CLASSIFICATION

The Label Integrity Program (LIP) guarantees all claims made on labels, and the Geographical Indications (GI) committee is busy clarifying zones (although vast, they are hardly ever seen on labels), regions, and subregions—albeit with plenty of lively, at times acrimonious, debate about where some regional borders should go. But interregional blending for commercial brands is still the order of the day.

most of the nineteenth century until phylloxera arrived. She has only recently reassumed her position as provider of some of the most startling Australian wines. Large amounts come from the Murray River area, but it's the stunning liqueur Muscats of Rutherglen and Glenrowan, the thrilling dark reds of Central Victoria, the urbane Yarra Valley and Mornington Peninsula reds and whites, and the lean, perfumed reds and whites that crop up in cool vineyard land right across the state that impress me most.

NEW SOUTH WALES

Colonial Australia began in New South Wales (in the Hunter Valley), as did the wine revolution that propelled Australia to the front of the world stage. However, the state is a major bulk producer along the Murrumbidgee River, and a clutch of new wine regions in the Central Ranges is grabbing headlines.

MAIN WINE ZONES AND REGIONS

— WESTERN AUSTRALIA
1. Swan District
2. Perth Hills
3. Peel
4. Geographe
5. Margaret River
6. Blackwood Valley
7. Manjimup
8. Pemberton
9. Great Southern

— SOUTH AUSTRALIA
10. Far North
11. The Peninsulas
12. Clare Valley
13. Barossa
14. Lower Murray
15. Fleurieu
16. Limestone Coast

— VICTORIA
17. Northwest Victoria
18. Central Victoria
19. Northeast Victoria
20. Western Victoria
21. Port Phillip
22. Gippsland

— TASMANIA
23. North Tasmania
24. South Tasmania

— AUSTRALIAN CAPITAL TERRITORY

— NEW SOUTH WALES
25. Western Plains
26. Northern Slopes
27. Northern Rivers
28. Hunter Valley
29. Central Ranges
30. Big Rivers
31. Southern New South Wales
32. South Coast

— QUEENSLAND
33. South Burnett
34. Darling Downs
35. Granite Belt

See also
South Australia page 277
Victoria page 283
New South Wales page 289
Western Australia page 293

South Australia

RED GRAPES
Shiraz and Cabernet Sauvignon predominate, but Merlot and Grenache are also important, as is Pinot Noir, especially in the cooler sites.

WHITE GRAPES
Chardonnay is by far the most important white variety, with Riesling, Sauvignon Blanc, and Semillon following behind. Viognier and Pinot Gris are also on the increase.

CLIMATE
This ranges from cool-climate areas, such as the Adelaide Hills and Coonawarra, to hot, dry areas such as Barossa.

SOIL
The soil is a mix of sandy loam, red loam, various clay, and fertile volcanic earth. Coonawarra has an area of terra rossa over a limestone subsoil.

GEOGRAPHY
This varies widely, from the flat vineyards of Coonawarra to vines on steep slopes in the Adelaide Hills, the Barossa Ranges, and parts of the Clare Valley.

THEY RECKON ADELAIDE'S DRINKING WATER is some of the worst in the civilized world. I do, too, but the beer is excellent, so, apart from brushing my teeth, I don't have a lot to do with it. However, throughout the state, water—or lack of it—is a hot topic. The only part of South Australia that has enough water is the southern tip, where Coonawarra almost drowns in the stuff. In the rest of the state every drop counts. Luckily, South Australia has one massive zillion-gallon water resource—the Murray River—which follows a tortuous route for nearly 1,615 miles between New South Wales and Victoria before arcing through South Australia and trickling out into the ocean at Lake Alexandrina. The exploitation of the Murray for irrigating hundreds of thousands of otherwise uncultivable barren acres was one of the great agro-industrial feats of the twentieth century.

WINE REGIONS

Vineyards were fairly quickly established in the northern reaches of the city, and the influx of German settlers to the Barossa Valley in the 1840s created a vineyard and winery community that has played a dominant role in Australian wine ever since and left it with some of the world's oldest vines.

But the first moves out of Adelaide were in fact to the south: to Morphett Vale, Reynella, McLaren Vale, and Langhorne Creek. Morphett Vale and most of Reynella have now largely disappeared under the creeping tide of urban sprawl, but McLaren Vale has largely been able to resist the developers and to enjoy a burgeoning number of vineyards and wineries both large and small.

The headwaters of the Murray River are numerous streams fed by the melting snowfields of the Great Dividing Range. Every year the river used to bulge and burst with the thaw. The waters flooded vast expanses of empty, arid land that gratefully lapped up the moisture—but to no avail because no one knew how to exploit this annual bounty. First at Renmark in South Australia and then at Mildura further upstream in northwest Victoria, two American irrigation engineers called Chaffey built pumping stations, dams, locks, and irrigation channels to harness the Murray River. As a result, market gardens and vineyards were planted where nothing but saltbush desert had existed before. This large-scale irrigation helped Australia transform the quality of budget wine worldwide, but long-term weather pattern changes have put the whole culture of irrigation farming in doubt as snowfalls evaporate, water flows dwindle along the Murray, and salinity in the soil increases.

It was near Adelaide that Australia's fine wine tradition began, when Max Schubert, Penfolds' chief winemaker, began work in 1951 on what was to become one of the greatest wines in the world—known first as Grange Hermitage, now as Grange. Schubert had returned from a trip to Europe's vineyards the year before, fired up most of all by the great red wines of Bordeaux's Médoc—a fine wine area with a lot of rain, barely enough sunshine, and a predominance of the Cabernet Sauvignon grape. The region produced wine that was aged in new French oak barrels and could mature for half a century. He was determined to make the same style of wine in South Australia—where there were tons of sunshine, hardly any rain, about one shopping basket full of Cabernet Sauvignon in the entire state, and not a new French oak barrel to be found. Until his visit to Bordeaux he had no idea that a red wine could hope to age for more than ten years at the outside.

No worries. Schubert had the vision and by pursuing it created what is Australia's greatest gift to the world of wine: the belief that everything is possible. He began with some Shiraz at Morphett Vale, south of Adelaide, and some at Magill in the foothills fringing Adelaide. They served him well for the first Grange. Later he added Kalimna, in the Barossa Valley, and when Morphett Vale was sold for housing he expanded into the Clare Valley. These

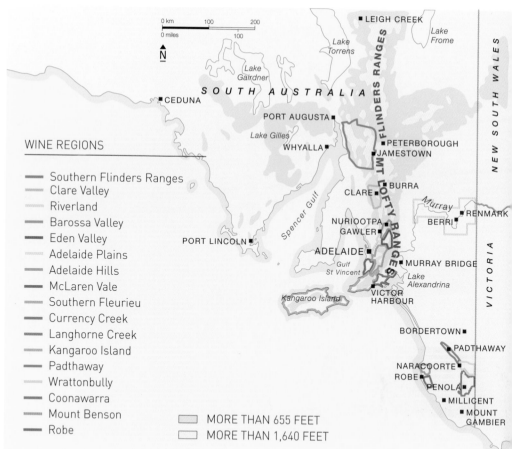

WINE REGIONS

— Southern Flinders Ranges
— Clare Valley
— Riverland
— Barossa Valley
— Eden Valley
— Adelaide Plains
— Adelaide Hills
— McLaren Vale
— Southern Fleurieu
— Currency Creek
— Langhorne Creek
— Kangaroo Island
— Padthaway
— Wrattonbully
— Coonawarra
— Mount Benson
— Robe

MORE THAN 655 FEET
MORE THAN 1,640 FEET

days, with Treasury Wines, Penfold's parent company, controlling a massive amount of South Australia's top vineyards, Coonawarra fruit joins McLaren Vale, Barossa, Clare, and indeed any fruit good enough. If the fruit is good enough, it will be considered for Grange, although recent vintages have been increasingly Barossa dominant.

The region directly south of Adelaide, with McLaren Vale at its center, is Fleurieu. Its success right up to the 1950s was based on its ability to produce fortified "ports" of high quality or strapping great red table wines. Generations of respectable British ladies supped happily on Tintara and Emu Burgundy, convinced they were imbibing for their health's sake. Perhaps they were. In fact, Fleurieu has proved a highly adaptable wine region. Although it is sunny and McLaren Vale and further north are genuinely hot, most of the vineyards benefit from afternoon sea breezes cooling down the vines. Langhorne Creek and Currency Creek on the eastern side of the Fleurieu Peninsula are positively cool, and Southern Fleurieu and Kangaroo Island are cooler still. Water is short in McLaren Vale, and the Cabernet, Shiraz, and even Grenache are rich and heady, but there are also surprisingly good Chardonnays and Sauvignons Blancs.

Just inland from McLaren Vale you reach the southern tip of the Adelaide Hills. These hills head north, skirting

Adelaide, to become part of the Mount Lofty Ranges, continuing up east of the Barossa Valley to Mount Pleasant, where they become the Eden Valley.

Just a 30-minute drive east of Adelaide is the small exciting wine region of Adelaide Hills. Here, the hills around Piccadilly are high, even slightly damp, and this subregion is now producing some exceptional cool-climate whites and exciting sparkling wines. Lenswood, a little to the north, can also produce gorgeous reds; and southward toward Mount Barker and Kuitpo, it's also warmer and lower, and lovely reds are the result.

Water dominates the cool far south of the state as well but in a different way. The Great Artesian Basin stretches across the area toward the sea. The water table is so high that most of the land is far too swampy for viticulture. But there is a series of limestone ridges in the southeast that offer wonderful conditions for vines, which explain the region's name—Limestone Coast. Coonawarra's exceptional qualities have been known about since the end of the nineteenth century, and it is now one of Australia's most desirable spots for vineyard land. Padthaway, 40 miles to the north of Coonawarra, is another fine region, and wherever limestone crops up, we are seeing vineyards being developed—right out to the coast at Robe and Mount Benson and around Naracoorte at Wrattonbully.

Barossa

RED GRAPES
Shiraz is the star red, dominating not only current plantings but new vineyards as well. Cabernet Sauvignon is also important, but the next most precious resource is hundreds of acres of old Grenache and a little ancient Mourvèdre (Mataró). There are also increasing quantities of Spanish, Italian, and Portuguese varieties.

WHITE GRAPES
Semillon and Chardonnay are the most important white varieties in the Barossa Valley, while Riesling still reigns supreme in the Eden Valley. There are also small amounts of Sauvignon Blanc and Viognier.

CLIMATE
The Barossa Valley is hot, with some drip irrigation used to counteract the arid summers. The Eden Valley and the Barossa Ranges are cooler with more rain, but it's winter rain when the vines are dormant, so irrigation is often necessary.

SOIL
Topsoil is varied, ranging from heavy loam with clay to light sand; some soil needs the addition of lime to counteract acidity. Subsoil is limestone, quartz-sand, clay, and red-brown loam.

GEOGRAPHY
Traditional valley-floor estates are best at big reds; estates in the higher Eden Valley are excellent for cool-climate styles.

JUST LISTEN TO THESE NAMES—Kaiser Stuhl, Siegersdorf, Bernkastel, Gnadenfrei—the names of wineries and vineyards in the Barossa. Listen to these names—Johann Gramp, Johann Henschke, Peter Lehmann, Leo Buring—the names of Barossa winemakers, ancient and modern. Add to these a delightful assembly of old Lutheran bluestone churches, bakeries offering streusel and kuchen, delicatessens with mettwurst and lacksschinken, and you know the Barossa is different. It's in a time warp from the early days when Lutheran settlers from German Silesia (now part of Poland) traveled halfway around the world to spread themselves across this valley just to the north of Adelaide, intent upon creating a new homeland.

Scratch the surface, however, and you find a different story. These days, Kaiser Stuhl and Leo Buring are mere brand names within the giant Treasury group. Many of Australia's largest-scale and most efficient wineries now cluster around the old settler towns of Nuriootpa, Tanunda, and Angaston. Today, more than half of all Australia's wine is made by these big Barossa-based companies. It was little short of a disaster for these ancient families in the late twentieth century when, one by one, the famous old Barossa wine concerns grew into national companies and two things dawned on the moneymen. First, the Barossa vineyards might produce good grapes, but their yields were low and their prices were high. Secondly, the reverse was true of the vast easily irrigated vineyards that were springing up along the banks of the Murray River. These might not produce exciting grapes, but they have high yields and low prices.

These large companies concluded that, if talented corporate winemakers could make perfectly good wines out of these inferior grapes, why use expensive local fruit? They showed a callous disregard for the welfare of the local Barossa growers, much of whose crop, during the 1980s, they were prepared to let shrivel, unpicked, on the vine. Beady-eyed financial ruthlessness pushed Barossa grape growing to the brink, and many ancient Barossa families cursed the men in suits who now ran the companies their forebears had created. But by the beginning of the new millennium, the pendulum had swung the growers' way. Enthusiasts worldwide realized that some of the oldest pre-phylloxera vines still alive survived in Barossa, many more than a century old. The incomparable flavors these centenarians offer has meant that boutique, high-quality wine production now flourishes in the Barossa. The big companies are still there and put these precious grapes to far better use than before, and now, when they try to browbeat a grower, the grower has somewhere better to turn.

The Barossa Valley was settled by a mixture of German and British pioneers in the 1840s and '50s. George Angas, a Scot, was one of South Australia's most important frontiersmen. To counteract the chronic shortage of labor to work his estate north of Adelaide, he paid for three shiploads of German Lutherans to emigrate from Silesia. They arrived in the Barossa Valley in 1842 and, although Anglo-Saxon families such as the Hill-Smiths of Yalumba have thrived since, settling at Angaston in 1849, it was the Germans—or Barossa Deutsch—who molded the valley. Vineyards and wine companies were established, which, by the beginning of twentieth century, already led South Australian production. With the abolition of interstate tariffs and the decimation of rival Victoria's vineyards

OLD VINES

You really have to go into the vineyard and get up close to understand the old fellas. They rear up out of the brown earth, muscle-bound, sinewy giants, tustling and wrestling in a bizarre embrace, as their ancient branches grow ever more entwined. Yet they are fragile. You can rock them with your hand, their roots barely holding them upright in the soil.

They are precious. These are the ancient vines of the Barossa, usually Shiraz, sometimes Grenache, many more than one hundred years old, some stretching back as far as 1847, when they were planted out from cuttings brought to Australia by the Silesian German immigrants who first populated the Barossa Valley. This was just before the phylloxera blight destroyed virtually every vine in France and caused almost all the vines of the world nowadays to be planted on non-wine vine rootstocks to combat the phylloxera, still ever present in the world's vineyards. But not here. The phylloxera pest never got to South Australia (although it destroyed Victoria, next door). So the ancient vines are on their own roots and provide direct bloodline back to . . . well, who knows how far back into antiquity, but it's certainly the Middle Ages, and it could be to the Romans and even back to the ancient Middle East. This sense of history is tangible when you visit the vineyards. It often, although not always, flows through the flavors the small crops of tasty grapes give their wine. Shiraz wines from these vines can be some of the grandest, darkest wines on Earth, but the best manage to balance richness of spice and fruit and wood, with a transparency on the palate that lets a little of their history shine through.

by phylloxera, South Australia fast assumed the dominant position in Australian wine, and the efficient Barossa companies were the natural leaders.

VINEYARDS

Vineyards were established in two main areas: the gently undulating valley floor, along the North Para River from Nuriootpa down to Lyndoch, and on the hills to the east. The valley floor is hot and dry; the soil veers from infertile yellow clay to deep red loam, suited to the production of dark intense red wines. The valley floor gets far less winter rain and almost none in summer. Not only that, subterranean water to the west of the North Para River is too salty to be of much use for irrigation. Consequently, most vineyards lie east of the river. But the dry land to the north and around Nuriootpa and Greenock can produce stunning reds from old, low-yielding vines. Further south, wineries such as St. Hallett, Rockford, and Charles Melton have built enviable reputations. This concentration on reds seemed to satisfy all parties until the 1970s, when there was a huge swing in public taste toward fresh, fruity, white wines—not at all what the Barossa was suited to with its gnarled old Shiraz and Grenache. It becomes blindingly obvious why big companies gave up using Barossa grapes and began developing huge, mechanized vineyards on the Murray River.

The Barossa Valley as a grape-growing region might have sunk without trace. But luckily a local hero—the late Peter Lehmann—was around to rescue one of Australia's greatest wine heritages. When the big companies broke their contracts with the grape growers and refused to buy their grapes, he set up a company with the sole aim of saving vineyards from the plow, and he bought every grape he was offered always simply on a handshake. His monument is the prosperous grape-growing community that now surrounds his winery.

EDEN VALLEY

Up in the hills it is different. Most vineyards are at between 1,300 and 1,640 feet, and greater height means much cooler conditions. This has made Eden Valley and the surrounding hills one of Australia's top white wine areas; the Rieslings with their steely attack and lime fragrance are often Australia's best. Led by the exceptional Henschke winery, Shiraz reds of tremendous focus and freshness are now widely praised. Big companies increasingly use Eden Valley fruit in their top wines, and it was significant that the French giant LVMH took over the trailblazing Mountadam. But the true glories still come from old family operations such as Henschke.

Coonawarra

RED GRAPES
Success with Cabernet Sauvignon makes this the predominant variety now, but there is a good deal of Shiraz and some Merlot.

WHITE GRAPES
Chardonnay is the most widely planted variety, but there are also Riesling and some good Sauvignon Blanc.

CLIMATE
These are the southernmost and, therefore, coolest of South Australian vineyards. The easily accessible water table gives high yields of good quality. Vintage can take place from early March to as late as May.

SOIL
An area of terra rossa (literally "red soil"), or crumbly red loam, covers the low ridges, with both black cracking clay and sandy soil over a clay base on lower ground.

GEOGRAPHY
It is flat here—uniformly so, and with its long growing season, high light intensity, and unique soil structure, it is ideal for vines.

UNLIKE MOST OF THE GREAT VINEYARD AREAS of the world, Coonawarra has no rivers. There are mountains to the east; there's sea to the west. But no rivers. There is a lot of water, however, falling in the mountains every winter. It seeps, inch by inch, just below the surface across the bleak swathe of bogland that makes up the southern tip of South Australia. Well, 600,000 years ago the area was underwater, with the shoreline marked by the Comaum Range east of Coonawarra. But two things happened. First, there was a reversal in the Earth's magnetic field, followed by a slow but continual upheaval in the land that has by now raised Coonawarra 200 feet above sea level. Secondly, about every 50,000 years, there has been an ice age and the seas have retreated. With each subsequent warm period, the seas have crept back to find the land sufficiently raised that a new beach is established, and a new ridge is built up of limestone over sandstone. There have been twelve ice ages in the last 600,000 years. There are twelve ridges between the Comaum Range and the sea—one for each ice age—running north to south, parallel to the shore.

Between each ridge the land is a sullen mix of sandy soil over a clay subsoil or black cracking clay. On the barely perceptible ridges, a thin sprinkling of fertile reddish soil sits above a tough limestone cap. Break through that cap and the limestone is damp and crumbly, and a yard or two further down, the pure mountain waters from the east seep slowly toward the sea. The limestone ridges topped with *terra rossa* soil provide perfectly drained sites for vines. The underground water provides one of the best natural resources for irrigation that any wine area in the world possesses—that is, if the vines need it; many of the older vines' roots tap directly into the water.

Coonawarra, 250 miles south of Adelaide, is surrounded by the chilly Southern Ocean. The winters are cold and damp. Springtime is squally and often frosty, too. Summer starts out mild but dry, yet in February and March there are often hot spells that can scorch and exhaust the vines; then the bore holes pump day and night, providing life-saving irrigation. As the grapes slowly ripen into April, the weather can break into sour, joyless early winter before the harvest is in and stay unfriendly and raw until the following spring.

Some of Australia's greatest red wines are made on this thin strip of land, where the climate makes vines struggle all year but the famous red soil and subsoil cosset and spoil them. Since its foundation in 1891, French-style reds, primarily from Shiraz and Cabernet, have dominated. In the 1960s, the world began to appreciate the relatively light yet intensely flavored qualities of Coonawarra reds, and by the 1990s this was some of the most desirable vineyard land in Australia. On both sides of the *terra rossa* ridges are heavy clay plains also planted with vines. Some decent white wine has been produced, but such damp cold soil cannot ripen Cabernet or Shiraz.

Of course, Coonawarra is only one ridge. There are other similarly good ones: St. Marys just to the west, Mount Benson on the coast, and various sites around Naracoorte to the north, in particular Wrattonbully, produce superb quality, as does Padthaway 40 miles north of Coonawarra. Also the regional title "Limestone Coast" is already achieving significant acceptance as a general description of the cool-climate wines of the whole area.

Clare Valley

RED GRAPES
The main plantings are Shiraz and Cabernet Sauvignon, with some Merlot, Malbec, and Grenache. There are tiny amounts of Mourvèdre, Sangiovese, and Tempranillo.

WHITE GRAPES
Riesling is the principal variety, with significant amounts of Chardonnay and Semillon plus some Sauvignon Blanc.

CLIMATE
The heat should lower acidity and send sugars soaring but instead produces light wines, especially Rieslings, with an unexpected natural acidity and delicacy.

SOIL
The main subsoil is of calcareous clay. In the north, there's a sandy loam topsoil; in the center, red loam; and in the south, red clay.

GEOGRAPHY
Vineyards are planted at 1,300 to 1,640 feet above sea level in the narrow valleys running from north to south and in the foothills to the west. Aspects vary, with twisting contours.

I'VE SEEN CLARE DESCRIBED as a frontier town and as the "hub of the north" in its early days. After the long trek up from Adelaide, nearly 80 miles away, Clare promises to offer the last relief before the endless parched plains that stretch away to the north. Since Clare's establishment in 1846, it's been a boom town several times. What is left now are a traditional, well-worn market town—still quietly prosperous long after those early frenzied years—and vines.

Clare was luckier than many areas in that there was a genuine effort made to plant only the better grape varieties—particularly Cabernet Sauvignon, Malbec, and Shiraz. But then, as elsewhere in Australia, these were largely supplanted by varieties planted for cheap fortified wine and brandy in the early twentieth century. However, the reestablishment of Clare Valley as a quality region during the 1950s and '60s saw the better red varieties dominate new plantings once again along with the white grapes Riesling and (more recently) Chardonnay.

The trick was to have planted the vines in the right place. The term "valley" isn't really an accurate description of this region. There are, in fact, three valley systems in Clare Valley, stretching both south and north more than 15 miles, with a watershed plateau in the middle at Penwortham. Incorporated into this are five subregions with differing soil at different heights above sea level—and differing mesoclimates, too. Confusing, especially because Clare seems to get about as much heat as, and even less rain in the growing season than, the impossibly hot Liqueur Muscat center of Rutherglen in Victoria. Well, it does, and it doesn't. Except in the valley floor, it would be impossible to establish vineyards without irrigation. Storage dams for winter rain are the most effective source of water. The tumbling landscape allows a wide variety of aspects to the sun, while nights are generally chilly, and breezes arise to cool the vines during the day.

There is some disagreement about these cooling breezes because they have a fair way to travel inland from the sea, 30 miles to the west and southwest. It seems that, by and large, they arise only in the late afternoon, cooling the vines in the evening and at night, but not affecting the most intense heat of the early afternoon. So ripening is not hindered, but acid levels in the fruit remain high. Some locals say it is the daily fade-out, at around 4 p.m., of the hot, northerly winds that is the crucial factor in cooling the vineyards, especially in the north-facing valleys above Penwortham. Altitude certainly seems to help. The excellent Enterprise and Petaluma vineyards, both giving outstanding Riesling, are more than 1,640 feet high, facing west over the town of Clare. The vineyards of the Skillogalee Valley, near Sevenhill, are not far short of 1,640 feet and are protected from the north. Their fruit flavors are particularly fine and focused.

Soil also plays a major role. Deep dark loam below Watervale produces ripe, fat reds and whites, yet the ridge of limestone north of Watervale provides white wines with an acid bite that such a warm climate should deny. In the Polish Hill River area, an acidic slaty soil seems to retard ripening by as much as two weeks, and the results are surprisingly delicate structured whites and reds. A paradoxical place, the Clare Valley? It certainly is. There are moves to divide Clare into subzones, and I can see why.

Victoria

RED GRAPES
Shiraz, Cabernet Sauvignon, Merlot, and Pinot Noir predominate.

WHITE GRAPES
The main quality variety is Chardonnay, followed by Riesling, Sauvignon Blanc, and Semillon, but there are also small amounts of Marsanne, Muscat Blanc à Petits Grains, and Muscadelle.

CLIMATE
Coastal areas have a maritime climate. The northeast of the state, producing fortified wines, is hot and dry.

SOIL
There is red loam in the north, quartz rose alluvial soil in the Goulburn Valley, crumbly black volcanic soil at Geelong.

GEOGRAPHY
Steep, sloping, north-facing vineyards in cool-climate areas allow extended ripening. Most of the interior is pretty flat and featureless.

ROLL UP, ROLL UP TO the great Victorian wine show! All human life is here, with its triumphs, its tragedies, its noblest qualities, and its greed. Especially greed. Swiss settlers were the first to make their mark with toil and honest endeavor. Later, gold fever hit Victoria, bringing speculators with a mighty yet indiscriminate thirst. Soon after came the first attempts to harness the Murray River and turn desert into orchards and vineyards. Then came phylloxera, the world's most feared vine predator, followed by the Great Bank Crash, bankruptcies, and ruin. The few remaining outposts of vines struggled for survival.

Then the new Victoria emerged. All the old vineyard areas have now been reestablished, and new ones have sprung into life, offering a wealth of styles more diverse than any in Australia, ranging from some of the richest, most succulent fortified wines in the world made at Glenrowan and Rutherglen in the torrid northeast down to damp, windy Drumborg in the southwest tip, where the grape struggles to ripen enough even for sparkling wine. The amounts produced of many of these remarkable wines are pitifully small, and, with few exceptions, the wineries are spread thinly across the state instead of being bunched together in comprehensible regional groups. But that just makes the effort to find them all the more rewarding.

FIRST PLANTINGS

First, let's have a quick look at the history. The vine arrived in 1834 from Tasmania of all places. Melbourne itself, at the north of Port Phillip Bay, proved ideally suited to vine growing, being not too hot, with an attractive maritime climate easing the grape toward ripeness. But the city's expansion was obviously always going to push out the vineyards, and the two areas that thrived were out of town at Geelong and the Yarra Valley.

Geelong is to the west of Port Phillip Bay and is challenging vineyard land. The best sites are on outcrops of deep, crumbly, black volcanic soil and are water-retentive but not prone to waterlogging. Although it isn't that wet, it's rarely that hot either, and the cold Antarctic gales haven't crossed any landmass to reduce their chilly force when they hit Geelong. The reason Geelong did well—by 1861, it was the most important vineyard area in the state—was largely due to the settlement of Swiss vignerons who knew how to coax good flavor out of cool surroundings. They did the same in the Yarra Valley (page 286).

The next wave of vineyards was established not because the land was thought suitable but because gold was discovered there in 1851. From all over the world, men flocked to the heartland of Victoria, their minds giddy with dreams of untold wealth from these extensive, easily dug lodes of precious metal. They were thirsty, too. Avoca established vineyards in 1848, Bendigo followed suit in 1855, Great Western in 1858, and Ballarat in 1859. Northeast Victoria already had vines near Rutherglen but was equally boosted by the madhouse prosperity brought by gold. Wine was scarce in the goldfields, and sellers could demand high prices—twenty times the price it would fetch in New South Wales, southern Victoria, or South Australia.

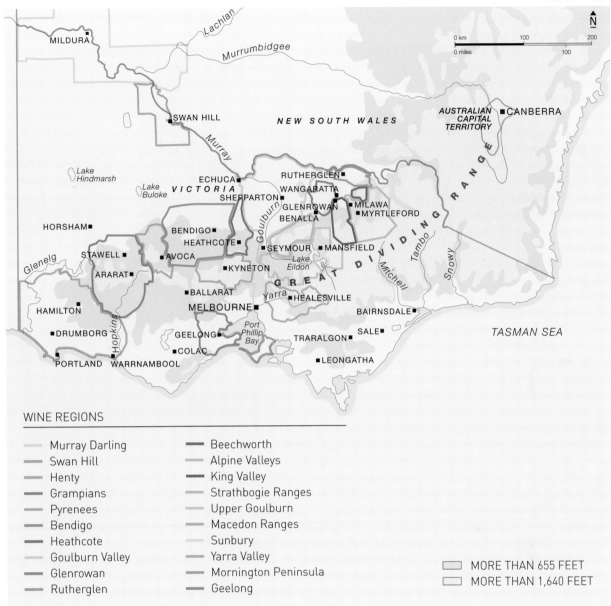

WINE REGIONS

- ▦ Murray Darling
- ▬ Swan Hill
- ▦ Henty
- ▬ Grampians
- ▬ Pyrenees
- ▬ Bendigo
- ▬ Heathcote
- ▦ Goulburn Valley
- ▬ Glenrowan
- ▦ Rutherglen
- ▬ Beechworth
- ▬ Alpine Valleys
- ▬ King Valley
- ▦ Strathbogie Ranges
- ▦ Upper Goulburn
- ▬ Macedon Ranges
- ▦ Sunbury
- ▬ Yarra Valley
- ▬ Mornington Peninsula
- ▬ Geelong

☐ MORE THAN 655 FEET
☐ MORE THAN 1,640 FEET

Eventually the Gold Rush died and with it most although not all of the vines. Bedraggled survivors lingered on at Ballarat and Great Western, Bendigo, Heathcote, and Rutherglen—the Goldfield Vineyards. But far worse was to come. Phylloxera arrived in Australia via Geelong in 1875. Geelong's vines were uprooted by government order, and so were those of Bendigo but to no avail. Phylloxera spread through most of Victoria, and by 1910 the state that was once the jewel in Australia's winemaking crown had seen her wine industry reduced to a withered rump centered on Northeast Victoria, the Murray vineyards (whose founders, the Chaffey brothers, were paupered by the combination of the Great Bank Crash of 1893 and the Murray River inexplicably drying up)—plus a few vines at Tahbilk in the Goulburn Valley and at Great Western.

WINE REGIONS

The rebirth of Victoria as a key wine region began with the reestablishment of vines at Geelong in 1966, but it really only began to take off in the 1980s. The result has been dramatic and triumphant.

Among the many wine areas to have enjoyed a resurgence, Geelong is no easier a place to grow vines in than it was 150 years ago, but it still manages to produce brilliantly focused, dark-hearted reds and attractive whites when the sun stays out long enough. The Mornington Peninsula is still windy, but any harsh winds are cooled and dampened during their journey across the waters of the bay. There are two main areas: the cooler, higher Red Hill, home to numerous small but high quality operations, and the lower, flatter, warmer areas

VICTORIA'S FORTIFIEDS

Until the 1950s and '60s, Australia's winemaking skills concentrated on fortified wines rather than lighter table wines. Now the pendulum has swung so far the other way that it is easy to forget that Australia still does make some fortifieds—and some are world class. There are delicious Port-style tawny wines that can age for decades—Para Port is released only when a century old. Refreshing, tangy fino- and amontillado-style wines are excellent, too, but best of all there are the fortified wines, or "stickies," from northeast Victoria. These are sweet dark wines from Brown Muscat and Muscadelle (now called Topaque) of almost shocking intensity. The grapes are left on the vines until they are shriveled and full of sweetness. The fermentation is stopped with a blast of alcohol, and the result is wine of sumptuous richness.

There are two main regions in Northeast Victoria noted for these wines: Glenrowan, where Baileys make fine sweet "stickies" as well as startling reds; and Rutherglen. Here, a host of winemakers young and old make a hodgepodge of styles but, above all, the magnificent "stickies" that leave your lips smeared and stained, your palate shocked and seduced, and your soul uplifted by their unashamed richness. These are some of the world's sweetest and most luscious fortified wines. At Milawa, Brown Brothers also make top-quality "stickies," often from Rutherglen fruit, but their more significant contribution has been the revival of King Valley as a top table-wine area and the establishment of Whitlands, at 2,600 feet, one of Australia's highest vineyards.

Northeast Victoria gets no cooling sea breezes, so grapes really do bake in the heat (though cold nights help preserve acid). Muscat and Topaque grapes often reach 20–22 percent potential alcohol as they shrivel in long

warm falls. When picked, they ooze richness, and the thick juice is barely fermented before being whacked with spirit to kill the yeasts. It's then left in barrels, virtually turning to molasses as it cooks under the winery eaves for anywhere between one year and one hundred. The best, from makers such as Chambers, Morris, Baileys, Campbell, and Stanton & Killeen, blend the bright floral grapiness of young Muscat with small amounts of thick and viscous ancient wines to give a "sticky" experience that is unique in the world of great sweet wines.

of Tuerong and Moorooduc just to the north. The wines, especially Chardonnay, Riesling, Pinot Noir, and Shiraz, are often lush in texture and magnificently piercing in fruit intensity. There was a time when Mornington Peninsula was regarded as something of a playground for the wealthy of Melbourne, with wine as a sideline. There's still some truth in that—it is a beautiful place with a long coastline only an hour's drive from a great city—but the emergence of a wave of excellent wines from both small and big producers means that the area is increasingly being seen as a true competitor to the Yarra Valley for Melbourne's affections. I'd recommend you go and sit in the evening sun at somewhere like Stonier, gazing out past the vineyards to the bright blue water at the mouth of Western Port Bay, and watch the sailboats gallantly dodging the white horses of white surf

breaking on the reef. Sip a little more Chardonnay. Then it makes sense.

There are further cool-climate vineyards whose fruit intensity is remarkable at Henty near Portland in the southwest and at Leongatha, southeast of Melbourne whose Bass Phillip Pinot Noirs have been among Australia's best for a generation. Sunbury and Macedon, barely further north of Melbourne than its airport, combine fine sparkling wine with stunning, lean, but concentrated reds and whites epitomized by Bindi's Pinot Noirs and Chardonnays and Craiglee's astonishing Shirazes, some of which have tasted good at one hundred years old. Bendigo is the next stop north, but neighboring Heathcote has turned most heads recently with joyfully dense, lush Shirazes mostly grown on incredibly ancient red Cambrian soil.

The central Goulburn Valley to the east is warm and principally famous for Chateau Tahbilk, whose ancient vines provide palate-crunching reds and heady but approachable whites. Next door, the Strathbogie Ranges grows small amounts of scented, focused reds and whites. Way to the east, the hills and valleys of the Victorian Alps—especially the King and Ovens valleys and the clifftop region of Beechworth—are providing yet more fascinating original Victorian flavors. Beechworth, in particular, has made world-class Chardonnay and Shiraz.

Scattered sparsely across the Central and Western Victoria zones are the remnants of the great goldfield vineyards. The soil is mostly poor, producing a low yield of fruit, and rainfall is generally meager. Although there is a considerable amount of sunshine, high altitudes—at places such as Ballarat, the Pyrenees, and much of the Grampians—moderate the heat and produce remarkable results from Shiraz, Cabernet Sauvignon, Chardonnay, and even Riesling. The Grampians region around Ararat is dotted with particularly fine performers, such as Mount Langi Ghiran and Best as well as Seppelt, who have been making sparkling wines in deep subterranean caves at Great Western since the nineteenth century. Their white fizz is good, but their sparkling Shiraz is ridiculously delicious foaming happy juice. You can't knock it if you haven't tried it. If you think you spot a fascinating streak of eucalyptus and mint in the reds around here, you're not wrong—they were commenting on its presence 150 years ago. Because you'll have to make your way through miles of daunting eucalyptus forests to find most of the vineyards, you can guess where that scent of eucalyptus comes from.

The Murray River marks Victoria's northern border. The majority of Victoria's wine comes from the vast, irrigated fields that fan out from the left-hand banks of the river. An increasing amount is made to a high standard. Lindemans' Karadoc, the biggest winery in Australia, processes much of the fruit, and the giant Mildara plant at Merbein, just north of the town of Mildura, does a similar job.

Mornington Peninsula is an exciting cool-climate region south of Melbourne, where vines have to share the beautiful landscape with wealthy weekenders from the city.

Yarra Valley

RED GRAPES
Pinot Noir is the leading red, with Cabernet Sauvignon and Merlot following some way behind. Shiraz is next, and there are tiny amounts of Sangiovese and other reds, including Tempranillo.

WHITE GRAPES
Chardonnay dominates and is the number one variety planted in the valley. Sauvignon Blanc is also important, and there are small amounts of Pinot Gris and other whites.

CLIMATE
The cool climate allows extended ripening. Wind and rain can interfere with flowering and fruit-set in December and January.

SOIL
There are two main types of soil: gray, sandy clay or clay loam and deep, fertile, red volcanic soil.

GEOGRAPHY
The angle of slope and height above sea level vary greatly, with vineyards planted at between 165 and 1,300 feet.

I CAN SEE IT NOW, 1837, AND William Ryrie breasting the hills above Healesville in the blazing afternoon sun. He'd trekked over mountain and prairie all the way down from Cooma in New South Wales. He must have been parched and exhausted. Spreading out below him was a lush valley with a glistening if sluggish river down the center. As the sweet air drifted up to him, he must have thought—yes, this'll do. Ryrie did settle in the Yarra Valley, and he laid the foundations for both its wine industry and its cattle-rearing business.

The first people to thank are the Swiss. Ryrie employed a Swiss assistant to prune the vines he planted and to help make the wine. In 1845, he managed to produce a Burgundy-like red and a Sauternes-like white. This sounds an improbable combination, but it may say something about the Yarra's climate that has been proven time and again in recent decades. The valley is not at all hot by Australian standards, providing rare suitable conditions for fussy Pinot Noir. The Swiss straightaway took a leading role in the Yarra Valley, and their winemaking expertise quickly created a reputation for delicacy and balance uncommon in Australia. But phylloxera and a series of financial and natural disasters put an end to all this. Not until the 1960s did vine leaves rustle once more in the valley breezes, and it was the 1980s before the big hitters of Australian wine remembered the valley's former reputation.

Since then, it has boomed and has shown an ability to produce virtually every type of classic cool-climate wine within its small boundaries. Marvelous traditional-method sparkling wines are made by Domaine Chandon, and superb Burgundian-style reds and whites are made by such outfits as Coldstream Hills, De Bortoli, Diamond Valley, Yarra Ridge, and Tarrawarra. Excellent Bordeaux styles also abound, particularly at Mount Mary, Oakridge, and Yarra Yering, which also excels in Rhône styles, as do De Bortoli, Jamsheed, and others, while wonderful sweet wines are made by producers such as Seville Estate and St. Huberts.

Yet none of these wines taste like their European role models. They are, in general, softer in texture, fuller of fruit, equally well-structured, but easy to appreciate at every stage of their lives. This is because the challenge of Yarra's cool conditions is attracting talented winemakers sensitive enough to want to work in harmony with nature instead of bludgeoning and straitjacketing her.

Certainly the Yarra Valley is cool—in Australian terms. Rainfall, while it can disrupt flowering in late spring, almost always stops around the end of December and, except for the odd welcome shower, doesn't usually return until fall, after the harvest. So you can let the fruit ripen gently on the vine, the prerequisite for delicate, perfumed wine. But all this depends on where your vineyards are. Up in the hills it is often too cold for vines, although the magnificent Hoddles Creek vineyard is high in the forest at 1,310 feet. The valley floor, a broad flood plain, has boggy soil that couldn't ripen grapes. Sites to the north of the valley ripen earlier than most to the south, and the area of Dixons Creek at around 650 feet in height has made a reputation for thrilling Shiraz and Viognier. Depending upon whether your sites face north or south and catch the full force of the sun or only part of it, crops at the same altitude can ripen two weeks apart.

Tasmania

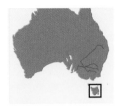

RED GRAPES
Pinot Noir is the most planted red variety, with some Cabernet Sauvignon and a little Merlot.

WHITE GRAPES
Chardonnay is the most popular white, followed by Riesling and Sauvignon Blanc, both of which do well in the cool climate. Pinot Gris and Gewürztraminer are also doing well.

CLIMATE
Tasmania has a moderate maritime climate with few extremes. Temperatures are lower and humidity higher than in most other Australian wine regions. Windbreaks on seaward slopes protect vines from sea winds.

SOIL
In the north, rich, moisture-retentive clay predominates, and in the south, peaty, alluvial soil.

GEOGRAPHY
Strong westerly winds off the Southern Ocean tend to restrict vineyards to the east-facing slopes.

VINEYARDS WERE ESTABLISHED in Tasmania in 1823, before either Victoria or South Australia, but they were short-lived and weren't revived until the 1950s. In 1974, the modern era of winemaking really began with Andrew Pirie's establishment of Pipers Brook on iron-rich but relatively exposed soil to the northeast of Launceston. The annual heat summation is generally similar to that of Burgundy's Côte de Nuits, but aggressive winds off the Bass Strait mean that only the best sites in Tasmania will really ripen grapes well. This would explain why the island is most successful at growing Riesling and grapes for sparkling wine base.

Ah, sparkling wine base. You hear that phrase again and again as you tramp the chilly vineyards of northern Tasmania. "What's that over there?" Pause. "Sparkling wine base." "And what's that?" Pause. "Er . . . sparkling wine base." Then you spot some lovely protected, steep, north-facing slope, and before you can ask, the grower is bubbling over with excitement—this little precious patch makes his top Chardonnay, Pinot Noir, or whatever. When you're up in the north of the island, you just have to stop dreaming about making the great Bordeaux and Burgundies of France and settle for making another French classic—Champagne with an Aussie accent. Tassie fizz from the north is superb. Although there are also a few fine Chardonnays and Pinot Noirs, the other wines from these exposed vineyards that thrill me most are the cool-climate stars Gewürztraminer, Pinot Gris, and Riesling, all wonderfully fresh, pinging with fruit, and irresistibly fragrant.

The Tamar River running north of Launceston is protected from the winds and warmed by the wide estuary. This, combined with lower rainfall, allows red grapes to ripen here reasonably well now and then. In the far south, both the Derwent River Valley and the Huon Valley seem to defy latitude by ripening grapes, if anything *better* than the north of the island. That is, unless the frosts get you. The Huon Valley is actually south of Hobart. Risky territory. Even so, sparkling wine, Riesling, and delicate Chardonnays perform best here.

The only places to ripen Cabernet and Pinot Noir satisfactorily, even excitingly, on a regular basis are on the east coast and on the Coal River to the south. Eastern vineyards near Bicheno, notably Freycinet, are squeezed behind a bluff that deflects coastal winds and allows the long sunshine hours to have maximum effect. Their Pinot Noirs are positively lush and exotic when placed against the usual Tasman offerings. The Coal River is in a rain shadow north of Hobart, and the long sunshine hours, balanced by cool nights, bring about full-colored, ripe-flavored reds and intense whites. Tolpuddle Vineyard has rapidly proven itself to be the equal of almost anywhere in Australia for its Chardonnay and Pinot Noir.

With their own Tasmanian Appellation of Origin program, the growers are determined to promote their regional individuality, but global warming is relentlessly changing their climate, and while their best bet for current fame remains as a world-class producer of sparkling wine grapes, in a warming world expect great red and white wines to challenge them not so far in the future.

New South Wales

RED GRAPES
Shiraz, Cabernet Sauvignon, and Merlot are widely planted. There is also a number of other reds, of which Pinot Noir is the most significant.

WHITE GRAPES
The main varieties are Semillon and Chardonnay, but Riesling and Traminer are also significant. In Riverina, there are also substantial plantings of Trebbiano, Muscat, Verdelho, and Colombard for everyday whites.

CLIMATE
It is hot even by Australian standards, particularly in the Hunter Valley and Riverina. Wet, humid falls encourage rot.

SOIL
Sandy and clay loam, along with some red-brown volcanic loam, granite, and alluvial soil predominate.

GEOGRAPHY
Vines are planted on the gently undulating valley floors (Cowra, Riverina, and Upper Hunter) or in the foothills of the Brokenback and Great Dividing Ranges (Lower Hunter Valley, Mudgee, Hilltops, and Orange).

NEW SOUTH WALES IS WHERE Australian wine started its journey. The very first vines to reach Australia sailed into Sydney Harbor with the First Fleet in 1788. They had been picked up in Rio de Janeiro and in the Cape of Good Hope on the long voyage out from England, and in no time the settlers had cleared some scrub by the harbor and planted vines. They weren't a great success—the humid atmosphere encouraged black spot disease, knocking out any grapes before they had a chance to ripen—but the scene had been set. All the main Australian settlements took a similar line, establishing vineyards at the same time as establishing a community. The reason usually given was to encourage sobriety. In a new, savage country where rough men became more savage and wild under the influence of fiery high-strength spirits, wine was seen as a moderating influence, a weapon against drunkenness and disorder. These attempts in New South Wales to promote a benevolent, rosy-cheeked, wine-sipping society didn't work out too well because there were very few places near Sydney suitable for vines.

Although a few vineyards did survive near Sydney until modern times—at Camden, Rooty Hill, and Smithfield—the story of wine in New South Wales is one of establishing vineyards well away from the main consumer marketplace, with quality acting as the magnet drawing the attention of Sydney.

The crucial factors in New South Wales are excessive heat from the relatively northerly latitude; the presence of the sea close by; and the Great Dividing Range of mountains that separates the humid, populated seaboard from the parched, empty interior. The Great Dividing Range provides cool vineyard sites in some of its high hill passes as well as the springs from which enough rivers flow inward to irrigate some of the largest agro-industrial vineyards in Australia. Proximity to the sea brings with it advantages and disadvantages: the priceless bounty of cooling breezes but also the seasonal curse of cyclonic cloudbursts, frequently around harvest time.

WINE REGIONS

The first real success came with the Hunter Valley, which is about 80 miles north of Sydney and just inland from the major industrial city of Newcastle. Vineyards were being planted there as early as the 1820s, but it wasn't until the 1860s that the areas now thought of as best—those around the mining town of Cessnock—were planted (page 290).

Mudgee and Cowra are two areas that owed most of their prosperity to their relationship with the Hunter Valley. Mudgee is to the west of the Hunter, and although it makes reds and whites of decent quality, its main strength has been as a source of fruit for Hunter wineries. Cowra, on the Lachlan River, a tributary of the mighty Murray, is best known for lush Chardonnay made famous by Rothbury, a leading Hunter player.

Riverina, in the new zone of Big Rivers, centered on the town of Griffith, way down in the scorched flatlands, is the most significant wine region in New South Wales in terms of the volume of wine it produces. It uses irrigation water from the Murrumbidgee, a tributary of the Murray, to produce well in excess of 110,000 tons of grapes from about 13,590 acres of featureless land. It adjoins the large Sunraysia area, which straddles the state of Victoria. One special product of Riverina is the remarkable botrytis-affected sweet Semillon that the De Bortoli winery pioneered and others have followed. The grapes are left to hang for up to two months after the normal harvest date, and the quality often matches that of a top Sauternes from Bordeaux.

Because you can't buy land freehold within the Australian Capital Territory (ACT), the vineyards have been developed just outside the ACT in New South Wales—mostly to the northeast near Lake George and to the north around Murrumbateman. The summer days are hot and dry and not tempered by sea breezes, yet the nights are cold. The fall, however, is cool and frequently wet. The soil and subsoil are not water-retentive, so irrigation is vital. Because of the cold night air moving north from the Australian Alps snowfields, sites have to be selected with care to avoid spring frosts that can occur as late as November. If this all sounds negative, I'd have to say, if Canberra weren't there, these vineyards probably wouldn't be there either, but wineries such as Lark Hill, Collector, Doonkuna Estate, and, above all, Clonakilla, have had success with Riesling, Chardonnay, and surprisingly with Cabernet Sauvignon and Shiraz.

Other developments in New South Wales have been more concerned with trying to locate high-quality, cool-climate sites, despite challenging climatic conditions. Tumbarumba in the Snowy Mountains, way down south near the border with Victoria, is producing some outstanding Sauvignon Blanc and Chardonnay, and Pinot Noir has great potential. It has red volcanic soil planted at over 2,500 feet, and granite soil in slightly warmer yet still cool sites at around 1,800 feet. Hilltops, further north, has the higher altitude and the well-drained soil to encourage a slow, regular ripening season with consequently intensified fruit flavors.

There are also successful vineyards around Orange, and although we're getting back into the spring frost problems that deterred settlers in the nineteenth century, the region has thrived. Bloodwood were the pioneers in the 1980s producing remarkable reds and whites, and many have followed, including ex-Rosemount whiz kid Philip Shaw, whose wines are the quintessence of cool.

Perhaps the most bizarre vineyard development is in the Hastings Valley near Port Macquarie, north of Newcastle. Here, one of Australia's hottest vineyard sites combines with the highest recorded rainfall—most of it during the ripening season—but somehow Cassegrain manages to make interesting wine.

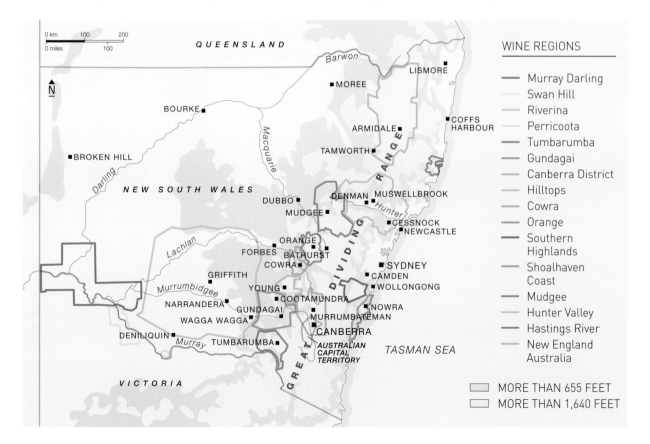

Hunter Valley

RED GRAPES

Mainly Shiraz and Cabernet Sauvignon are grown, with some Merlot, Pinot Noir, and Malbec. Tempranillo and Sangiovese are recent additions.

WHITE GRAPES

Chardonnay and Semillon are the most important grapes, but there are some decent Verdelho and Sauvignon Blanc. Pinot Gris is doing well.

CLIMATE

The Hunter Valley is warm, even hot, but the summer heat is tempered by cloudy skies. Fall is often wet. The Upper Hunter Valley needs irrigation.

SOIL

The rich, red volcanic loam and the alluvial soil near the Goulburn River are the best. The poor-draining, heavy clay subsoil is tough-going.

GEOGRAPHY

Vines are planted next to the Goulburn River in the Upper Hunter Valley. Lower Hunter vineyards are on the lower slopes of the Brokenback Range or on the valley floor.

I STILL HAVE VIVID MEMORIES of the first time I realized just how special the Hunter Valley could be. Some roaming wine gypsy I knew ended up in Sydney, and eventually he brought some wine back to London and decided to try it out on a group of us young whippersnappers. Tyrrell's Vat 47 1973. A Chardonnay—well, mostly Chardonnay, with a little Semillon, too, I shouldn't wonder. I can still see the astonishing Day-Glo, greeny-gold color, all fiery-eyed and demanding of attention, and the sensual viscous texture of the wine that swirled lazily round the glass like a courtesan interrupted during her siesta. And the flavor. I'd been brought up on French Chardonnay from Burgundy. I knew and understood the generally austere but fascinating if intellectual pleasure of those pale, oatmeal-, and mineral-scented whites from the east of France. Then there was my first mouthful of Vat 47. The explosion of peaches, honey, hazelnuts, woodsmoke, and lime sent stars bursting over my palate. In that single split second, I foresaw the greatness Australia could bring to Chardonnay and Chardonnay could bring to Australia.

Yet what I was tasting was not some classic wine style, carefully honed over the generations. This was only the third vintage of the Hunter Valley's very first varietal Chardonnay. Its brilliance was even more astounding because you shouldn't really be able to create exciting wine in the Hunter at all. Ask any modern vineyard consultant about establishing a vineyard there, and he'd say you must be crazy. You've got the heat and rain against you, and, except in a few charmed sites, the soil is against you, too. But, as Hunter winemakers have shown, if you're stubborn and obsessive—and, well, yes, slightly mad—you can produce wines of shocking individuality and quality.

UPPER AND LOWER HUNTER VALLEY

The Hunter Valley divides, in wine terms, into two parts as it snakes inland from Newcastle. The Upper Hunter is to the north around Denman. Its vineyards have to fight with powerful local coal-mining interests when they want to expand. Although initially planted in the nineteenth century, it achieved any prominence only in the 1980s. The area was heavily planted in the wine boom of the 1960s and '70s, mostly on rich, alluvial soil with irrigation enthusiastically applied. But the grape most often planted was the black Shiraz, whose reaction to such

QUEENSLAND

Queensland is almost too far north for successful viticulture but manages to use the height of the Granite Belt on the border with New South Wales effectively. South Burnett, northwest of Brisbane, is another important wine area. The wine industry—closely linked to tourism—is expanding fast. New areas showing promise include Darling Downs (around the town of Toowoomba) and Mount Tamborine in the Gold Coast hinterland. Alternative varieties, such as Verdelho and Fiano, are providing some inspiration.

fertile, high-yielding conditions was to produce limp, lifeless wine only halfway to red. White wines fare much better under these conditions, and fleshy Chardonnays and Semillons are commonplace.

Indeed, the drive southward from the Upper Hunter to the Lower Hunter exposes the contradictions of this area as a grape-growing center. You'll see more signposts to coal mines than vineyards. The black gold of coal or the white gold of Chardonnay? Until you descend into the heart of the Lower Hunter, the argument is still fierce. Even then the area is centered around Cessnock, a town more dominated by coal than wine for most of its existence, although now the grape has pretty well won the battle of vine versus mine. Spread out to the west and northwest are numerous vines, the healthiest-looking being those that run up to the slopes of the Brokenback Range, and odd volcanic "pimples"—ridges of weathered basalt typified by Lake's Folly and Evans Family vineyards. This red soil is fertile, well-drained, and deep, and it can produce good crops of high-quality red grapes.

The volcanic outcrops have marvelous soil, but vineyards still have to combat the heat and rain. Lake's Folly and Evans Family face south, away from the sun, and the best sites on the Brokenback slopes are those up as high as 1,300 feet at Mount Pleasant and set back on the slopes of Mount View, west of Cessnock. These escape the warm westerlies, get a little more rain, but have the slopes to drain freely, and often ripen up to two weeks later than the vines on the valley floor.

HUNTER VALLEY CLIMATE

Because the Hunter is relatively far to the north and close to the hotter inland zones, the climate does at first glance seem oppressive. Yet the quality of wine made here means that there must be some compensating factors. There are. Although Cessnock would appear statistically to get appreciably more heat than Montpellier in the broiling south of France, the warm spring and fall temperatures—which don't actually affect the grapes' ripening—distort the figures. Heat undeniably does build up fast until early afternoon, but because the Great Dividing Range dips to the north and west of Cessnock, the warm interior sucks cold air in up the Hunter Valley. Most summer afternoons, there's cloud cover over the Hunter, and, in any case, being closer to the equator than Montpellier means relatively shorter summer days. The humidity is also important in reducing vine stress.

But water is a problem in the Hunter. There's not enough when you want it and too much when you don't. The annual rainfall of 27 inches would be fine if it fell at the right time, but it tends to get dumped at the end of

HUNTER SEMILLON

I've just rediscovered the tasting note of my first ever Hunter Valley Semillon. It actually called itself Hunter Valley Burgundy, but it certainly wasn't made from the Chardonnay grape of France's Burgundy. It was made from Semillon because that's all they had in the lineup of white grapes in the Hunter Valley. It was a mere 9 percent alcohol. I'd never had a wine that looked, tasted, or smelled like it. In Europe, they didn't make wine the color of wheat that tasted like the grapes had been brushed in your armpit after an energetic game of beach volleyball. Then splashed with custard, squeezed with lime juice, and smeared over warm brown toast. It was a shocking flavor. No Burgundian would ever have wanted to make a wine like that. But that was the joy of it. No one in the world can make a wine like this, whether they want to or not, and I don't suppose the bravehearts of the Hunter Valley set out to make it either. It's just that the Hunter is a fair old hellhole of a place to grow grapes, and in some years getting a crop at all is regarded as a triumph.

The particular problem—of many—that afflicts the Hunter is late summer rain. Well, I don't really mean rain. Cyclones, more like, which are prone to roll down the coast from Queensland, and you simply dash out and harvest whatever grapes you can, even if they're only at 9 percent alcohol ripeness. Yet strangely this is where the Semillon's greatness lies. Traditionally, these wines tasted like battery acid when young—so what did you do? You kept them in the cellar and prayed a lot. It must work because these raw, thin Semillons, with no oak influence, undergo a most astonishing transformation over seven, ten, fifteen years into the remarkable bundle of flavors I described above. No one knows why. Unripe Semillon doesn't do that anywhere else in the world.

summer, often just before the Shiraz grapes are ripe. You also need good winter rains to fill the irrigation dams because borehole water here is far too saline, but winter droughts are frequent. When rain does arrive in January and February, cyclones come in off the Coral Sea and bang up against the Great Dividing Range, dumping their water on the vines. When they hit Queensland, Hunter winemakers know they've got only two or three days to harvest, regardless of ripeness, before the rains reach them. You can make great Semillon from underripe grapes, fair Chardonnay, and even passable Cabernet, but you just can't transform rain-bloated Shiraz into a classy red.

Western Australia

RED GRAPES
Shiraz and Cabernet Sauvignon are the main varieties, with much smaller plantings of Merlot, Pinot Noir, and Cabernet Franc.

WHITE GRAPES
Chardonnay, Sauvignon Blanc, Riesling, and Semillon are used for white wines. In addition, the Swan Valley grows Chenin Blanc, Muscadelle, and Verdelho.

CLIMATE
The coastal regions have a maritime climate. Regions further inland and to the north are hotter, drier, and more continental.

SOIL
Mainly brown or gray-brown alluvial topsoil, frequently fairly sandy with some gravel.

GEOGRAPHY
Vineyards are concentrated on the valley floors or gentle slopes along the coast, although there are some vines in more hilly areas along the Darling Ranges.

"WINES SHOULD BE RESPLENDENT with generosity; unless a wine can be diluted with an equal volume of water, it wasn't worth making in the first place." This wonderful remark was made by Jack Mann, the greatest of Western Australia's old-time winemakers. He made wines in the Swan Valley, the hottest serious vineyard area in Australia and one of the hottest in the world. He admitted he never picked his grapes until the sun-baked vine simply had nothing more to offer them, and I've tasted some of the old Houghton White Burgundy wines with which he made his reputation—deep, thick, viscous golden wines, oozing with overripeness.

WINE REGIONS

In the nineteenth century, the Swan Valley had more wineries than any other viticultural area of Australia. Western Australia never succumbed to phylloxera, so there was a boom in plantings during the 1890s as Victoria's vineyards fell to the rapacious aphid. As usual, the discovery of gold and the attendant influx of wealth-crazed, sun-parched prospectors in need of a bit of rest and recuperation didn't do any harm either. After World War I, numerous Yugoslavs took refuge in Perth, much as they did in New Zealand's North Island. They were doughty winemakers and loyal consumers of their competitors' wares and dominated the local wine scene which—until the late 1960s—was almost entirely centered on the hot Swan Valley. Indeed, these conditions sound ideal for fortified wines, but fortified wines in Australia belong to the past, so the Swan has done its best to moderate conditions with the usual modern tools of stainless steel, refrigeration, cleanliness, and better vineyard management. It also helps that three of its main white varieties can cope with heat—Chenin, Verdelho, and Semillon.

The wine industry in the Swan hit trouble in the 1950s. The vineyards were decaying, yields were falling, and in 1955 the government called in Professor Harold Olmo of the University of California at Davis to find the cause. He recommended planting vines around Mount Barker and Frankland, north of the port of Albany, sites now at the heart of the Great Southern. This was easier said than done. The Great Southern is a big area—the largest recognized agricultural area in Australia—with some fairly diverse conditions as well as a wild landscape of jarrah and red gum trees and scrub. Progress has been slow. Small vineyards established themselves east of Mount Barker beneath the rounded granite Porongurup Hills, west around Frankland and down near the coast, inland from Denmark and Albany.

Most of these are on gravelly sandy loam, although the soil may well be underpinned by impermeable clay subsoil, inhibiting drainage. The temperatures around Mount Barker and Frankland are fairly similar to those of the Médoc in Bordeaux—which is as cool as Western Australia gets—and this results in good, dark, but lean Cabernet styles and interestingly lovely lean Rieslings as well.

Porongurup vineyards are cooler because the slopes are planted up to 1,150 feet, and this can slow ripening by a good week, which serves to intensify

MORE THAN 655 FEET
MORE THAN 1,640 FEET

WINE REGIONS AND SUBREGIONS

— Swan District
 1. Swan Valley
— Perth Hills
— Peel
— Geographe
— Margaret River
— Blackwood Valley
— Manjimup
— Pemberton

— Great Southern
 2. Frankland River
 3. Mount Barker
 4. Porongurup
 5. Albany
 6. Denmark

the fruit of the Cabernets and Rieslings. Coastal vineyards between Albany and just west of Denmark benefit from cool days and warm nights, although some good vineyards near Denmark face north and are sheltered from the sea. The vines also get more rain, but this is a plus in a dry state because the extra usually falls outside the March–to–April harvest period. Piercing cool flavors are again the order of the day, with even some good Pinot Noir rearing its head near Albany and Denmark.

The twin regions of Pemberton and Manjimup are almost directly to the west of Frankland and just southeast of Margaret River. Pemberton is cooler and has fewer sunshine hours, more rainfall, and higher humidity. Manjimup has mostly gravelly soil. Pemberton has some gravel but also a lot of slow-ripening fertile loam. No clear picture has yet emerged about which varieties most suit which area. For now, Cabernet Sauvignon, Merlot, Pinot Noir, and Shiraz are the most important reds, while Chardonnay dominates the whites, followed by Sauvignon Blanc, and small amounts of Semillon and Verdelho.

More crowded, more inhabited, and more organized is the Margaret River region. Here, Southern Ocean influences meet those of the Indian Ocean, and the natural potential that results has already been exploited by brilliant winemakers and self-publicists alike. It is now Western Australia's most successful area (page 294).

Geographe is a diverse region covering the coastal plain near Bunbury and Capel, the dairy country around Harvey, the Ferguson Valley in the Bunbury hinterland, and the orchard and farmlands of Donnybrook between Bunbury and Bridgetown. The coastal strip from Capel to Harvey has a mix of sandy soil and fertile brown loam and

a climate tempered by the sea. Merlot, Chardonnay, and Verdelho do best here. The Ferguson Valley and the hills behind Harvey have vineyards between 850 and 1,000 feet above sea level, with a more moderate climate and about 10 percent more rainfall than those on the flat. The soil is granitic gravel over clay loam and retains water better than the alluvial sand nearer the coast. Shiraz, Merlot, Chardonnay, Semillon, and Sauvignon Blanc are good—there's even some Nebbiolo. Near Donnybrook, vineyards occupy the gentle slopes of the Darling Ranges, where fertile soil contains granite and ironstone gravel. This warm area is particularly good for Shiraz, Cabernet Sauvignon, Zinfandel, and Grenache.

The small Blackwood Valley region centered on Boyup Brook, Bridgetown, and Nannup has about fifty vineyards. For now, the standout wines are red, especially Shiraz and Cabernet Sauvignon. Chardonnay is the most widely planted white, with small amounts of Sauvignon Blanc and Semillon. North of Geographe, Peel has vineyards of almost talcum powderiness on the gray Tuart sand that runs almost up to Perth's southern suburbs. There've been vines here since 1857, and Peel Estate grows an eclectic range of wines.

Finally, the other small region is the Perth Hills that are, in effect, the Darling Range. These overlook Perth from 12 to 18 miles inland, and the wooded valleys have vineyards established at between 500 and 1,300 feet above sea level. Sea breezes blowing in across the range's western escarpment reduce daytime temperatures; by contrast, warm sea air stops the temperature from dropping too much at night. The hilly, irregular nature of the valleys creates widely differing mesoclimates that, at their coolest, ripen grapes two to three weeks later than those in the nearby Swan Valley flats. Soil is good, with a fair amount of gravelly loam, and rainfall is high—but almost all of it is in the winter. If you've got storage dams for spring and summer irrigation, that's no problem; but if you haven't, the gravelly soil will be too free-draining to raise a crop of grapes.

Margaret River

RED GRAPES
The main varieties are Cabernet Sauvignon, Shiraz, and Merlot.

WHITE GRAPES
There are substantial amounts of Semillon and Sauvignon Blanc, which are often blended together, and Chardonnay is a close second. There are also some Chenin Blanc and Verdelho.

CLIMATE
This is a maritime climate, with a coolish growing season and a mild, wet winter. Cold Antarctic currents flowing south of the land mass and westerly winds from the Indian Ocean cool this region and make it more temperate than Perth to the north. Sea breezes are good for preventing overheating but bad for drying out the soil, sometimes making irrigation necessary. In spring, the breezes may reach gale force, damaging early bud break.

SOIL
The topsoil tends to be sand or gravel, the subsoil often clay loam. The subsoil has the capacity to retain water, but irrigation is still often necessary.

GEOGRAPHY
Vines are planted on low, gentle slopes at around 130 feet above sea level.

THE MARGARET RIVER MIGHT NEVER have been discovered as a fine wine vineyard area had it not been for a clutch of beady-eyed local doctors. They saw a couple of reports in the mid-1960s by a Dr. John Gladstones that the Margaret River had unusually close climatic analogies with Bordeaux but with less spring frost, more reliable summer sunshine, and less risk of hail or excessive rain during ripening.

For some reason, Australian doctors right across the nation have never been able to resist such pronouncements. First Dr. Tom Cullity at Vasse Felix, then fellow doctors Bill Pannell at Moss Wood and Kevin Cullen of Cullen Wines planted vineyards that were to form the heart of the Margaret River region right from the start. Indeed, Margaret River went on to establish itself as a remarkably versatile if somewhat capricious cool-climate region that was good as any in Australia. But Bordeaux? Well, yes and no.

Dr. Gladstones was supposed to be doing research on lupins—the same as Cullity and Co. were supposed to be keeping the locals hale and hearty—but his good luck was that the legendary Jack Mann at Houghton vineyard in the Swan Valley let him use a spare couple of acres of land next to the winery cellars for his lupin experiments. Lupins are okay, but the ever-open cellar door at his neighbor's winery began to weave its magic on the doctor and distract him from his original research. The possibilities in Western Australia for fine wine, as yet barely touched upon by winemakers in the torrid Swan Valley, began to take up more and more of Dr. Gladstones's time.

A visiting Californian, Professor Olmo, had already suggested in 1956 that the far south of the state, near Mount Barker and Rocky Gully, would make a high-quality vineyard site. Gladstones thought the area on the southwest coast, about 80 miles further north, between Cape Leeuwin and Cape Naturaliste, would be warmer and more predictable in weather and more flexible in the varieties of grapes that could be grown. He felt the Great Southern Region, with its cool, southerly maritime influence, could indeed match Bordeaux's cooler regions but that the Margaret River, influenced by the Indian Ocean to the west, could match the warmer Bordeaux regions of Pomerol and St-Émilion. The added advantage for Margaret River was that it was an area free of the risk of frost and the rain at harvest time that so often spoiled things in Bordeaux. These thoughts galvanized the local winemaking doctors into action.

Yet there are problems, and the most intractable is wind. Sea breezes are crucial for cooling down vines in many areas of Australia, but these are gales we're talking about—especially in spring—when salt-laden winds power in off the Indian Ocean and can crucially affect the vine as it attempts to flower and set a crop. Given the fact that the winters are some of the mildest in Australia, vines are likely to wake up early, and the early-budding Chardonnay and Merlot often get into trouble.

Then there's the wildlife. Those lovely mysterious stands of tall Karri gums are home to legions of kangaroos. Delightful, shy little roos; how we Europeans wish they were less timid so that we could feed them lettuce from the palms of our hands. Try giving that sentimental nonsense to a grape grower in springtime when the little fellas have nipped out overnight and chewed all the emerging buds off his vines. Don't talk to him about how divine those lime green parrots are fluttering and cawing among the vines. They are rapacious pests that munch away at the grapes for nourishment and then, replete with his best Cabernet, chew through the vine branches for recreation. Don't mention silver-eyes either, sweet little migratory birds that find the netting protecting the vines really good for nesting in—and anyway they're tiny enough to wriggle through and devour the crop under the nets.

Such problems rarely occur in Europe or in traditional Australian wine districts. But where new vineyards are carved from virgin land there are bound to be upsets. In such thinly populated regions as Margaret River, the relatively small areas of vines and grapes make easy targets for hungry wildlife. Interestingly, the only effective defense against the yearly silver-eye invasion is a natural one: their favorite refueling food is the nectar of red gum blossom. When the gums flower on time, the silver-eyes relish this feast, but if flowering is late, they turn to the sugar-sweet grapes.

But it does all seem to be worth it. Although the region contributes only 3 percent of Australia's wine grapes, it commands more than 20 percent of the premium wine market. The quality of Margaret River fruit sings out loud and clear: from mighty, gum-scented Pinot Noirs to classic Cabernets and Chardonnays, from unnervingly French yet tantalizingly individual Semillons and Sauvignon Blancs to positively un-Australian Shiraz, Zinfandel, and even to vintage "Port."

VINEYARD AREAS

There were intermittent attempts in the nineteenth century to plant the area, but Drs. Cullity, Pannell, and Cullen really showed the way in the late 1960s and early '70s when they planted small vineyards in the locality of Wilyabrup, about 9 miles north of the township of Margaret River, an area that still boasts the most flagship estates in the region. However, some of the highest profile estates—Cape Mentelle, Leeuwin, Voyager, and Xanadu—are actually south of the Margaret River around Witchcliffe and Forest Grove. There has also been a lot of vineyard development around Karridale in the extreme south of the region. Here, summers are cooler than in the northern plots, although it also benefits from prolonged mild sunny weather into late fall. In the far north, around Yallingup, between Cape Clairault and Cape Naturaliste, are wineries such as Flametree, Clairault, Happs, and Marri Wood Park. In general, average temperatures rise as you move north, and leading estates south of the Margaret River definitely

produce wines of a cooler fruit flavor than those located to the north.

On the other side of the Bussell Highway, in the northeast, is the former potato-growing area of Jindong. Ex-potato fields are not famous for producing high-quality grapes, but these are good, and if they weren't muscling in on the Margaret River name, everyone would acknowledge the fact. Several big wine companies have taken advantage of its flat, largely fertile land, plentiful water, and moderate climate to plant large vineyards here.

CLIMATE AND SOIL

Soil in the region does differ, but most good vineyard sites in Margaret River are either located on gravel or sand over clay. These tend to drain well, which is fine as long as you've built plenty of dams to store your irrigation water. Of the area's annual 46 inches of rainfall, just 8 inches fall in the all-important growing season—between October and April—when the vines need it most. Efficient irrigation is vital. The intensity of the fruit and the acidic and tannin structure in the wines are the best rebuttal I can think of when people suggest that you can't make great wines using irrigation. With a few outstanding exceptions, such as the excellent Moss Wood, Cullen, and Leeuwin, you can't make great wines without it in the Margaret River region.

Magnificent red gums or marri trees skirt the vineyards at Cape Mentelle. They help protect the vines from the strong winds in spring and early summer.

New Zealand

The frontiers of wine are being pushed back all the time, but you can't push much further southward than these vineyards overlooking Lake Dunstan in the Central Otago region of South Island. Central Otago is the only New Zealand wine region to enjoy a continental rather than a maritime climate, and the ripening season is long and cool.

New Zealand used to be imprisoned by the tyranny of distance. These two little islands were as far removed from the wine culture of Europe as it was possible to be, and while a determination to transform their country's wines began to take hold in both Australia and California in the 1960s, New Zealand slumbered on, waking almost by chance with a shout and a gleeful leap when Cloudy Bay bounded into our consciousness with that very first Sauvignon Blanc vintage in 1985.

The dramatic transformation of New Zealand during the 1990s was nothing short of astonishing. From being thought of as a quaint, introverted nation at the far side of nowhere down toward the South Pole, New Zealand has become a vibrant, self-confident, exciting place to be. Yes, exciting. Has anyone but a sheep farmer ever called New Zealand exciting before? Has New Zealand ever been exciting before? I can't vouch for what the early European settlers thought two hundred years ago, but even the most venerable of my present-day New Zealand acquaintances are enjoying the current mood of excitement while remaining ever so slightly bemused by it all.

Since the 1990s, New Zealand has seemed increasingly blessed by its isolation in the vast Southern Oceans. In a polluted, noisy, angry world, New Zealand has some of the most pristine conditions on the planet to make wine, and in a warming world, most of New Zealand's great vineyard regions are blessed both by cool conditions and exceedingly long sunshine hours. If there is one country that should be able to face the twenty-first century and its challenges with confidence, it is New Zealand.

The Wine Regions of New Zealand

NEW ZEALAND'S WINE INDUSTRY seems to have started off well enough. A visiting Frenchman in 1840 enjoyed the local product—which he described as a "light white wine, very sparkling, and delicious to taste" (not bad praise from a Frenchman)—an early hint that light whites and sparklers were the styles most likely to succeed. During the nineteenth century, other good reports of vines and their wines surfaced from time to time, and there was a brief period in the 1890s when Hawkes Bay produced some supposedly good-quality wines, but districts were already starting to vote for local prohibition. Indeed, the whole country voted for prohibition in 1919, only for the result to be overturned by the narrowest of majorities, thanks to the votes of servicemen who were returning home from World War I.

Clearly New Zealand society had little regard for its wine industry, so how on Earth could it flourish? Not surprisingly, it didn't. Vine diseases such as oidium (powdery mildew) were already making life hell in the warmer, more humid wine areas, and the phylloxera aphid was laying waste to vineyards on all sides. Replanting, when it occurred, was either with the inferior *Vitis labrusca*—Albany Surprise was the most widely planted variety until the 1960s—or the marginally better French hybrids, and the production was mostly of thoroughly mediocre fortified wines. When a Royal Commission after World War II stated that a "considerable quantity of wine made in New Zealand would be classified as unfit for human consumption in other wine-producing countries," it was a reflection on how low the quality of New Zealand wine had sunk.

But now look at the way New Zealand society treated drinking; there were restrictions on every side. You couldn't drink on trains until 1968, in theaters until 1969, at airports until 1970, or at cabaret shows until 1971. It wasn't until 1976 that caterers were allowed to serve drink or that wineries themselves could sell a glass of wine. The first wine bar licence was granted in 1979, and, good grief, sports clubs couldn't sell drink until 1980! Although legislation against the "demon drink" gradually eased, a whiff of disapproval still lingered over the New Zealand wine industry well into the 1980s. But at last the past is being left far behind—a wine past with nothing of value to cherish, a prim colonial legacy with a long expired sell-by date.

If ever there was a wine nation that should look forward and not back, it is New Zealand. Having a past that you are ashamed of can be a marvelously liberating experience. There are no fusty old traditions that you have to try and drag into the modern world and no cobwebby wine styles stubbornly clung to by faithful consumers. In the 1960s, they decided to go for top advice. Not unreasonably, they looked to Germany as their model. The German influence had been important in teaching Australia how to make delicious, dry Riesling wines under difficult conditions. German wine was highly thought of at the time, and it seemed that a Southern Ocean Rheingau or Mosel was a feasible objective.

Unfortunately, Dr. Helmut Becker, their chosen adviser, was an expert on crossbred grape varieties, and instead of Riesling, he chose Müller-Thurgau. So the brave new dawn for New Zealand wine, which could have concentrated on creating a new Bernkasteler Doctor, instead set about creating a better Liebfraumilch. Well, they succeeded there. New Zealand Müller-Thurgau pretty quickly became the best in the world—and I wouldn't be surprised if it still is.

CLASSIFICATIONS

Labels guarantee geographic origin. The broadest designation is New Zealand, followed by North or South Island. Next come the designated wine regions, such as Marlborough and Hawkes Bay. Labels may also name specific localities and individual vineyards.

But the advice to go for light, Germanic white wines can be seen, in retrospect, to have been shortsighted. It is possible superficially to equate cool South Island regions such as Central Otago and Canterbury, maybe even parts of Marlborough, with some parts of Germany. But no grapes were planted in these South Island regions in the 1960s. Instead, all the plantings took place in the North Island, whose climate goes from pleasantly Burgundian in the south to subtropical in the north. Müller-Thurgau in these conditions won't create a drink fit for heroes.

New Zealand's social revolution was a tortuously slow affair, and long after Australian and Californian winemakers were touring the world, drinking up every wine experience they could learn from, New Zealanders were still poking about at home. It wasn't until the 1970s that visionaries such as John Buck of Te Mata or the Spence Brothers of Matua Valley began to establish vineyards, and when they did, it wasn't Müller-Thurgau they had in their sights—it was the classic grapes of Burgundy and Bordeaux.

It soon became clear that Chardonnay and Pinot Noir could ripen easily—indeed, that the North Island was mostly too hot for Pinot Noir. Buck was convinced that he could find ways to ripen Cabernet Sauvignon and Merlot in Hawkes Bay. The Spences hit lucky right away with Sauvignon Blanc. By 1973, the new era was finally ushered in with the planting of the first vines at Marlborough in South Island.

By the end of the 1980s, New Zealand was becoming known worldwide for the quality of its wines and in particular its Sauvignon Blanc and Chardonnay, although Riesling, Pinot Noir, Cabernet, and Merlot were also making their mark.

Despite the success of other varieties, it is the Sauvignon Blanc wines from those early Marlborough vines that have created a new classic wine style so thrillingly different that it has been the standard-bearer for New Zealand ever since. No New Zealand wine had ever tasted like those Sauvignon Blancs from the South Island. No previous wine had shocked, thrilled, offended, entranced the world before with such brash, unexpected flavors of gooseberries, passion fruit, and lime or crunchy green capsicum and asparagus spears. They catapulted New Zealand into the front rank of New World wine producers, and the gift she brought to the party was something that even California and Australia had been unable to achieve—an entirely new, brilliantly successful wine style that the rest of the world has been attempting to copy ever since. New Zealanders now often prefer to talk of their Chardonnays, Rieslings, Merlots, or Pinot Noirs, but the world is still thanking them for their Sauvignon Blanc.

North Island

RED GRAPES
Merlot is comfortably in the lead, with Pinot Noir second and Cabernet Sauvignon a distant third. Syrah is increasing.

WHITE GRAPES
Chardonnay rules, with Sauvignon Blanc in second place. Next come Pinot Gris, Gewürztraminer, Viognier, and Riesling.

CLIMATE
The North Island is generally warmer than the South Island, but overall the climate in both is maritime. Rainfall is plentiful and is often a problem during the ripening season, when it can lead to rot.

SOIL
Soil ranges from glacial and alluvial at Hawkes Bay, to loam and clay in the north, and friable gravelly silt around Martinborough.

GEOGRAPHY
Vineyard site selection is now carefully considered after a boom period when poor varieties were planted in many unsuitable places. Most vines are found on flatlands or gently rolling hills, where too high yields are controlled by skilled vine canopy management. Growing numbers of premium-focused vineyards are appearing on sun-drenched, north-facing slopes.

WHAT'S ALL THIS ABOUT NEW ZEALAND being a cool-climate wine region? Some parts are, to be sure, but some parts are as hot as Hades. It's more than 620 miles from Matakana north of Auckland to Central Otago in the far south. As for the farthest vineyards of the Northland, above Auckland, they're at about latitude 34 degrees south. In the northern hemisphere, 34 degrees north slices across the top of Tunisia and Algeria, so I think I'm going to leave most of this cool-climate chat until we get to the South Island.

If you want to suggest that New Zealand is a *wet*-climate wine region, I'll go for that. With the exception of the tiny Wairarapa area near Wellington, one of the driest places in New Zealand, which behaves as though it were a virtual extension of Marlborough on the other side of the Cook Strait, and perhaps Waiheke Island out in the bay, less than an hour's ferry ride from Auckland, the North Island is a wet place to grow grapes.

If you want to suggest that it is a wonderfully fertile landscape ideally suited to growing vines, I'll say, yes—fertile soil, a lot of sun, a lot of rain; you can grow vines the size of peach trees in no time at all. But don't expect a crop of decent grapes fit for making fine wine. The best wines come from small crops off vines grown in dry areas with infertile, impoverished, free-draining soil and just the right amount of sun. That's not too much of a problem in the South Island, but in the North, these conditions are few and far between. The story of how to find such sites—and if you can't, what to do instead—is very much the story of the North Island's wine industry.

Many producers actually started out in the nineteenth century by growing their grapes in greenhouses. That seems extreme and could explain why hardly any wineries grew to any size during the nineteenth century. But the early growers may not have been so dumb. Most of the vines in the North Island do suffer from the weather, particularly around Auckland, where most of the early plantings were located.

Although the latitudes should imply hot to very hot conditions, things aren't as simple as that. In Europe, the main maritime influences are the warm Gulf Stream and the warm Mediterranean. New Zealand is set alone among seas strongly influenced by the icy Antarctic currents. This would be okay if you were guaranteed a dry fall. But that's one thing you're not guaranteed in the North Island. The cyclonic depressions of the Pacific will probably move in from the east in the early fall. Some years you'll have picked your crop, some years you won't have. These cyclonic rainstorms are a particular problem over to the east in Gisborne and Hawkes Bay, which are otherwise well-protected from westerly rain. They nervously watch the sky as harvest approaches.

A lot of rain, a lot of sun—all you need is fertile soil for vines to grow like a jungle. Well, with a couple of exceptions in parts of Hawkes Bay and Wairarapa, North Island soil goes from fertile to supremely fertile, and that makes it very difficult indeed for quality-minded grape growers. Fertile soil rarely drains well, and they encourage large crops of grapes. Large crops take longer to ripen, and—you've got it—up roll those cyclonic depressions brimful of rain just when you're not ready.

WINE REGIONS

Nowhere are conditions more challenging than around Auckland. There are now very few plantings in Northland, where subtropical conditions make it difficult to ripen *vinifera* grapes before they rot on the vine. However, the Dalmatians who came to New Zealand to work the Kauri gumfields were good, old-fashioned thirsty Europeans, and many, having saved some money, migrated nearer to Auckland and set up as winemakers. Almost all the traditional wine companies in Northland, as well as several of the newer ones, were founded by families of Dalmatian origin.

The hot, humid weather and the mostly heavy clay soil didn't matter too much when the chief product was fortified sherries and ports. But the swing to fine table wine production has found most of the go-ahead Auckland area wineries sourcing the bulk of their grapes from elsewhere—Gisborne, Hawkes Bay, and Marlborough. Even so, there are some vineyards over by the airport to the south, relatively more at Henderson just to the north, and a good deal more further up the road at Huapai, Kumeu, and Matakana. There are some outstanding estate-grown wines from companies such as Kumeu River and Matua Valley, but most of Auckland's top wines are nonetheless made from bought-in grapes.

If we're looking for the region's most consistently exciting estate-grown wines, we may well have to look offshore, out into the Hauraki Gulf to Waiheke Island, a paradise of a place where you can sit on the bluffs above the bay and watch the ferries plying calmly between the island's tiny quays and the bustling port of Auckland. Vineyards were established here in 1978, but it was only in the 1990s that the tempo picked up and a swarm of hopefuls began to plant the island's slopes. They were tempted by the nagging New Zealand dream of producing great red wine from the Bordeaux varieties of Cabernet Sauvignon and Merlot. Both Goldwater Estate and Stonyridge were consistently creating deep dry reds with an uncanny Bordeaux-like structure and taste, but it was the 1993 vintage—so cold and mean in most of New Zealand, so deep and lush and intense on Waiheke Island—that persuaded doubters that this truly was an exceptional vineyard site. The remarkable thing is that Waiheke has such a warm dry climate within spitting distance of humid, rain-swept Auckland, but it does. There's very little summer rain, the soil is infertile and free-draining, and the surrounding seas create a balmy maritime climate. It's such a heavenly place to live. Who wouldn't give it a go?

The small Waikato region south of Auckland is one of the North Island's historic regions, but this relatively damp, humid spot is probably better suited to dairy farming. Although there are some large vineyards here, there are few wineries, and much of the crop is made into grape juice. Even so, the Rongopai winery has used the warm, clammy conditions to make some superb botrytis-affected sweet wines.

Heading east below the Bay of Plenty, there are several wineries but few vineyards, although there is a small vineyard on the pumice soil of Galatea to the south. But it is Gisborne, on Poverty Bay, that we are looking for. Most of the vineyards are sprawled across the Gisborne plains, where a deep bed of alluvial silt supplies fertile soil conditions. Chardonnay has still managed to produce high yields of decent to excellent fruit due to plenty of sunshine hours and protection from wet westerlies by the Huiarau Mountains. That protection counts for nothing, however, when cyclonic depressions form to the east in fall. Gisborne has unacceptably high rainfall in the vintage period of February to April, a fact that has deterred most growers from trying red grapes. However, state-of-the-art vineyard management, replacement of phylloxera-infected vines with better clones, and a move into the less fertile hillside sites are turning Gisborne's reputation around, and decent reds are starting to appear. For years, people have been talking of the area as New Zealand's Chardonnay capital; some of Auckland's top wineries make their best Chardonnays from selected Gisborne vineyards, and the soft, gentle, ripe quality of most recent releases shows that they may well be right. All they need now is to become more fashionable.

Hawkes Bay is way down the coast from Gisborne (page 302). But there is one more booming area in North Island—Wairarapa just northeast of Wellington. This is centered on the little town of Martinborough, although vineyards are now flourishing on the river terraces above Martinborough as well as further north toward Masterton. If the North Island's weak points are too much rain and excessively fertile soil, the Martinborough region has the answer. Surrounded by mountains to the southwest, west, and northeast, it is protected from both summer and fall rains. Although the land down by the river flats is heavy clay, a series of flat-topped river terraces to the northeast around Martinborough is shallow, gravelly silt over deep, free-draining, virtually pure gravel.

Add to this relatively cool and windy but rainless summers and falls and some drip irrigation, and you have positively Burgundian conditions for great Chardonnay and Pinot Noir. That, despite there being a reasonable amount of Sauvignon Blanc, plus a splash of Pinot Gris, Riesling, and a handful of other varieties, is increasingly exactly what you get.

Hawkes Bay

RED GRAPES
Merlot is by far the most widely planted red grape, ahead of Syrah and Cabernet Sauvignon.

WHITE GRAPES
Chardonnay is the most important white grape, with Sauvignon Blanc catching up fast. Pinot Gris is next.

CLIMATE
This is ideal for high-quality wine production. Regular sunshine ensures full ripening of the grapes, and there's optimum rainfall.

SOIL
Almost all the vineyards are planted on alluvial plains, but soil types still vary from well-drained gravel and sandy loam, to fertile, heavier silty loam.

GEOGRAPHY
The best vineyards are on free-draining soil of low fertility. Most Hawkes Bay plantings hitherto have been made on flat land, but nearby limestone hills may be found superior in the future.

"WELCOME TO SUNNY HAWKES BAY" the sign says, and they're not kidding. A while ago, I arrived here in March—straight from the heartland of Australia, where I'd been boiled and bullied by the merciless sun, day after day. I had wondered, well, as New Zealand is so much cooler than Australia, will I really need sunscreen in March? But I'd slapped some on anyway and gone off to my first meeting. By late morning I was uncomfortable. By lunchtime I was hurting. By evening my hands were so sore I could neither bear the sunlight on them nor soothe them with anything but cool water. Sunny Hawkes Bay? There should be a health warning.

But it's a serious point I'm making here. The sun may not feel hot, but it shines relentlessly at Hawkes Bay. New Zealand is known as the Land of the Long White Cloud, and you can see the clouds piling up near Gisborne to the north. You can watch them follow the coastline down toward Napier, yet a mile or two before the bay they head inland to hug the mountain range until, south of Havelock North and Te Mata, they return to the coast. More important, the ozone layer is presently extremely thin over the southern Pacific. I've been told that ultraviolet penetration around Hawkes Bay is higher than in any other populated area in the Southern hemisphere. It's generally reckoned this is a "good thing" when it comes to aiding photosynthesis, the development of pigment, and the physical maturing of the grapes. It is not a good thing for poor, pale Celtic skin like mine. But long before ozone layers were even discovered, Hawkes Bay's long sunshine hours, reasonable rainfall that usually fell at the right times, and large tracts of suitable land had made the area New Zealand's most exciting vineyard region. That was at the end of the nineteenth century. Various vineyards were established, mostly on good, infertile land and mostly with classic grape varieties, and by 1913 Hawkes Bay was producing one-third of New Zealand's wine. However, as elsewhere in New Zealand, phylloxera, prohibition, and lack of interest took their toll, vineyards were turned over to *Vitis labrusca* and hybrid varieties, and the heavy Heretaunga river flats were planted in preference to the low-yielding gravel beds. One man, Tom McDonald, kept the flame of Chardonnay and Cabernet Sauvignon flickering. But when John Buck visited Tom McDonald in the 1960s, Tom had pointed over to the Te Mata peak and said, "That's the best Cabernet land you'll get in Hawkes Bay—frost-free, facing north, and free-draining."

So John bought the old Te Mata property in 1974 and released a Cabernet in 1980 that sparked the revival of Hawkes Bay as a great vineyard area. Hawkes Bay could once again enter the contest for New Zealand's premier wine region. It's a battle that can't ever be decisively won, however, because other leading areas, such as Marlborough and Central Otago, produce such completely different styles, and tip-top areas, such as Nelson, Wairarapa, and Waiheke Island, are a fraction of its size and so don't bear comparison. Hawkes Bay's reputation relies increasingly on its ability to fully ripen the red Bordeaux varieties and Syrah—not easy in New Zealand—plus an impressive performance with the less challenging Chardonnay and Sauvignon Blanc. There is still significant planting on the heavy river flats, but Hawkes Bay's reputation depends on several different areas.

The warmest of these is Bay View and the Esk Valley. It is also the least planted so far. Nevertheless, conditions are excellent. The bay swoops inward north of Napier and presses up against the hills. It's warm; apricot trees are all around and budburst comes as much as two weeks ahead of the rest of the bay. The grapes can really fry on the terraces cut into the hillside, and red Bordeaux varieties romp to ripeness. The Esk Valley joins the sea just north of Bay View, and its well-protected, sandy alluvial soil over gravel enjoys daily sea breezes.

GRAVEL

The heart of the Hawkes Bay revival lies in the gravel beds left behind by various rivers flowing into the bay. Most important of these are the Tutaekuri and the Ngaruroro. It's worth driving along and across these rivers to gaze on some of the purest gravel beds you will probably ever see. Only the best parts of Margaux in Bordeaux get anywhere near them, and yet here they stretch, mile upon mile, westward up into the hills. Get out of the car and tramp through the vineyards next to Highway 50 and the Gimblett Road, and you're walking along the old Ngaruroro river-bed itself. Half the time there's no soil at all—just ashen gravel everywhere with an aquifer running beneath to provide as much irrigation as you could want.

In 2001, a group of thirty-four wineries and grape growers banded together to define their own appellation based on a 2,000-acre plot of this gravelly soil that produces some of Hawkes Bay's finest wines. Gimblett Gravels, as this area is now known, is claimed to be up to three degrees warmer than most other areas in the bay during the day in summer and fall. If you see "Gimblett Gravels" on a wine label, at least 95 percent of the grapes must be from there.

One Gimblett Gravels grower describes the area—which includes land along Gimblett Road, Highway 50, Fernhill, and Roy's Hill—as "the G-spot of Hawkes Bay." Land prices here increased fifteen-fold at the start of the twenty-first century, and there was an air of feverish activity as all the major players in New Zealand planted like mad to make sure of their share of what they rightly see as Kiwi red wine heaven. Gravel quarry owners were fought off in the courts, and now the Gimblett Gravels is pretty much wall to wall vines. Much of the land is virtually hydroponic, and nothing survives without irrigation. Indeed, the gravel can be so pure that nutrients sometimes have to be put back to avoid the wines turning out with all the right technical figures but tasting dull.

The thing about such free-draining soil is that it hands control back to the winemaker; crops can be regulated and vines trellised to maximize the sun. But the weather still

Warm gravelly soil alongside the Ngaruroro River in Hawkes Bay, helped by plentiful sunshine, makes this one of New Zealand's top wine areas.

comes into it. Normal weather patterns at Hawkes Bay are like Bordeaux in a good year, albeit with slightly lower maximum temperatures but a larger spread of sunny days and less rain. You can pretty much rely on a dry warm fall (although cyclones do sometimes deluge the vines at vintage time). The real cauldron is around Fernhill, where Cabernet and Syrah always ripen, and there's a tiny parcel of Zinfandel. As you head up the valley past Roy's Hill, you come first to the Bridge Pa triangle of red metal soil, which ripens reds nearly as well as the Gimblett Gravels, and then up the Ngaruroro Valley to Riverview, where the cooling influence of the mountains delays budding and ripening by a good week or more but means increasingly good conditions for Pinot Noir and Riesling.

The Tutaekuri River cuts its way through the hills north of the Ngaruroro, and much of its course is protected from maritime winds. The same gravelly conditions exist here and also in the Tukituki Valley to the southeast, right down near the beach at Te Awanga and in outcrops near Havelock North and the Te Mata peak. But the south side of the bay is typically shallow alluvial soil over impenetrable pug clay. This terrain is harder to control than pure gravel but restricts yields and can produce fine wines. Te Mata's best vineyards are either on tan-colored, gravelly terraces ("red metal") or loess over limestone and sandstone.

South Island

RED GRAPES
Pinot Noir is best suited to South Island's cool conditions and accounts for the lion's share of red plantings. Merlot and tiny amounts of Cabernet Sauvignon and Syrah are also grown.

WHITE GRAPES
Sauvignon Blanc covers nearly seven times the vineyard area of Chardonnay, in second place. Pinot Gris is a rising star.

CLIMATE
The climate is cool with abundant sunshine to help the ripening process. Fall rainfall is low, but wind and frosts can be troublesome.

SOIL
Soil types are variable. Alluvial gravel or alluvial silt loam over gravel subsoil is free-draining. In addition, there are areas of chalky, limestone-rich loam, and patches of loess.

GEOGRAPHY
Much of the vineyard land is flat and low-lying. Nelson is more hilly with some sunny, sheltered sites.

WINEMAKING IN THE SOUTH ISLAND is a lot older than you might think. It's true that when the large-scale producer Montana began planting in Marlborough in 1973, it was generally seen as the beginning of the modern industry there—the modern industry, yes, but of the centers of winemaking now spread across the island, Marlborough was the only place that hadn't had a proper wine industry before. Well, perhaps wine industry is stretching the point because none of the original wine producers survived very long.

But Nelson, to the northwest of Marlborough, was visited in 1843 by boatloads of Germans who, looking at the steep hills covered in virgin bush, thought the place looked too tough for them and sailed on to Australia. Standing on the low hills running down to the sparkling waters of Tasman Bay while a long white cloud hangs motionless in the warm sky, I find it inconceivable anyone could ever want to leave this paradise. Eventually, some kind of winemaking got going there in 1868 and continued fitfully until 1939.

The French landed at Akaroa, south of Canterbury, in 1840 and planted vines around their homes on the mountainous Banks Peninsula. But when they died, so did their vineyards. Further south, in Central Otago, was born that perennial fair-weather friend of the winemaker, a gold rush. It didn't spawn vineyards on the same scale as the Australian or Californian gold fevers, but a Frenchman called Jean Desiré Feraud was doing good business in 1870 selling his wine and liqueurs to speculators. Yet this waned as the luster of precious metal faded and the island reverted to sheep, cattle, and fruit.

Until 1973, that is. That's when Marlborough, now New Zealand's leading wine region, was born out of nothing. At the time Montana, New Zealand's biggest wine company (now called Brancott Estate), was looking to expand and wanted cheap, easy land. Land in Hawke's Bay was then about NZ$1,920 per acre whereas Marlborough was between NZ$240 and $480 per acre, depending on whether it was good for nothing but pasture or good for almost nothing but pasture.

Montana bought fourteen farms—3,954 acres—and before the locals had even woken up to what was happening, they had planted 964 acres of vines, mostly Müller-Thurgau. But they took a punt and planted 60 acres of Sauvignon Blanc—just a hunch after tasting an early New Zealand Sauvignon—and what a hunch. With Marlborough Sauvignon Blanc, New Zealand created a classic flavor that no one had ever dreamed of before and set a standard for tangy, incisive, mouthwatering dry wines that the rest of the world has been trying to copy ever since.

SOUTH ISLAND'S GROWTH SPURT

Startling changes in the South Island wine industry have happened over the last generation, not least in the development of new wine regions, such as Marlborough and Otago. Back in 1960, the total vineyard area for the whole of New Zealand was 960 acres. The South Island didn't have a single vine, and the most widely planted in the North Island was the *labrusca* variety Albany Surprise, followed by a clutch of hybrids, such as Baco 22A and Seibel 5455.

By 1975, when there was massive vineyard expansion in the North Island, with six times as much land under vine as there had been in 1960, the first South Island vines were only just being planted. The hybrids had increased their acreage in the North Island, but the German influence was evident with Müller-Thurgau being nationally the most widely planted variety and some 1,604 acres yielding fruit. Expansion continued at a breakneck pace, and, although North Island led the way, Marlborough on South Island was rapidly proving its worth. By 1982, New Zealand's total vineyard area stood at 14,580 acres; Auckland and Waikato still had the same area of vineyard as before, but the leaders now were Gisborne with vines planted on 4,749 acres, Hawkes Bay with 4,673 acres, and Marlborough with a remarkable 2,904 acres. Small areas, such as Nelson and Canterbury in South Island and Wairarapa in North Island, had now begun planting grapes, too.

The dramatic government-sponsored vinepull of the mid-1980s led to a sea change in the industry, and the significant growth since then has been entirely in high-quality areas. By 2016, the total area of New Zealand vineyards totalled more than 89,000 acres, with Marlborough being the largest and most important at 59,354 acres, followed way behind by Hawkes Bay covering 11,722 acres, and Otago, invisible in 1982, with 4,801 acres.

It's interesting to look at grape varieties, too. In 1970, the hybrid Baco 22A was the top variety. It is now officially extinct. There was no Sauvignon Blanc in New Zealand in 1970, but by 2002 it had overtaken Chardonnay and moved into the number-one slot. By 2016, it accounted for 58 percent of all New Zealand's plantings with 51,931 acres of vines, and 89 percent of these are in Marlborough. White grape varieties presently account for 78 percent of the total planting area. Pinot Noir is the second most planted grape, with 13,771 acres, mostly in Marlborough and Otago.

WINE REGIONS

Marlborough is the best known wine region in the South by far, but back in the South Island's early days, one of the first regions to stir was Nelson, 45 miles northwest of Marlborough. The tiny Victory Grape Wines vineyard at Stoke, a mile or so southwest of the city of Nelson, produced its first vintage in 1973, and in 1974 Hermann Seifried established what is Nelson's largest vineyard; numerous others have since been planted. Yet development has been relatively small scale. The Waimea Plains, on flat but well-drained land running across to Rabbit Island and Tasman Bay, could have become another Marlborough, except that land prices and start-up costs are significantly higher. Much of the development has been in the beautiful Upper Moutere hills, just a few miles further northwest. The soil is mostly clay loam but well-drained on these slopes, as they need to be, because Nelson is cooler than Marlborough and gets more concentrated periods of rain in fall. Yet overall it has more rain-free days and long hours of sunshine, with the west coast taking the brunt of the westerlies. Despite the grapes ripening a week later than in Marlborough and with the risk of rain during harvest time, some of the South Island's best Pinot Noir, Riesling, and Chardonnay come from here.

About three hours' drive to the south from Marlborough, Christchurch sits at the heart of the Canterbury region on the shores of Pegasus Bay. The local Lincoln University began grape trials in 1973, despite all the traditional indicators that said the area had to be too cold for grapes. There appears to be less heat here than in Champagne in France, hardly as much as on the Rhine in Germany and yet, and yet . . . One of my most vivid "road to Damascus" tasting experiences ever was the St. Helena Pinot Noir 1982, grown on an old potato field 20 minutes' drive north of Christchurch, and only its second vintage. Startling, intense, brimming with passionate fruit and heady perfume, it could have held its own with many Côte de Nuits Grands Crus.

From a standing start, Canterbury suddenly became New Zealand's promised land for Pinot Noir. But it's not as simple as that. Wairarapa on North Island and Central Otago way to the south would now breezily dismiss this claim, and Canterbury itself does have several different mesoclimates. The most regularly exciting Pinot Noirs and Chardonnays are now coming from Waipara, 25 miles north of Christchurch, where the Teviotdale range of hills protects the vines from the sea breezes and creates an average temperature between 3.6 and 5.4 degrees Fahrenheit warmer than to the south around Canterbury, while the Southern Alps keep off rains from the west.

Loess and gravel river terraces and their stressed low crops create a wine style that is lush and warm for Pinot Noir and Chardonnay and thrillingly lean for Riesling. It's difficult to say if the area is really warm enough for Bordeaux varieties, but I've had some marvelous, austere, yet satisfying examples off the stoniest vineyards, as the grapes creep to ripeness in the long dry falls, finally being harvested as late as May. Vines near Christchurch are battered by wind, none more so than Giesen's, which nonetheless manages to produce fabulously concentrated Rieslings, the wind's aggression being offset by low rainfall and reliably long, dry falls. To the south, French Farm is trying the Banks Peninsula again, but that's

Rippon Vineyards on the shores of Lake Wanaka, one of New Zealand's largest, in Central Otago. This large body of water helps protect the vines from frost.

long, slow ripening is what brings flavor intensity—just like northern Europe but without the harvest rains.

Even so, you do have to have a certain amount of heat for flavor intensity. Won't Central Otago, the world's most southerly wine region and stunningly beautiful, too, way down near Queenstown in the heart of New Zealand's skiing region, be too cold? When you fly into Queenstown's tiny airport, wobbling between mist-wreathed mountain peaks, you feel as though you're in Scotland, not New Zealand. On the ground the feeling remains—those raw, gaunt hillscapes are too Scottish for vines, surely. Well, on paper, yes. But this is the one continental climate among South Island's wine regions. It is New Zealand's only desert, with all that suggests about lack of rain and intensity of sunshine. After all, latitude 45 degree south lies on the same parallel as the heart of the northern Rhône Valley as well as Bordeaux in the northern hemisphere. There are hot spots here and there—on the shores of lakes, beneath sheer rock faces that reflect heat and retain it in the chilly summer nights—where heat readings rocket upward.

This far south the summer days are very long and the rainfall frequently the lowest in New Zealand. Fascinating fact: the Milford Sound 75 miles to the west is the second wettest place on Earth. That's New Zealand for you, with the Southern Alps shielding Central Otago from all that rain. Between December and February, the number of cloudless days with temperatures hour upon hour above 68 degrees Fahrenheit—and often peaking at above 86 degrees Fahrenheit—is exceptional. Equally important and a major factor in the remarkable intensity of Central Otago fruit are the fiercely cold nights. Hot days equal high ripeness; cold nights equal high acidity. Result: memorable fruit flavors in the wines.

Chardonnay, Pinot Gris, Riesling, and Sauvignon Blanc all give exciting results here, but the star is Pinot Noir. The leading subregion is the Bannockburn district at the south end of Lake Dunstan, a north-facing ridge riddled with abandoned gold mines and the driest area in New Zealand. Lowburn and Pisa Ranges to the west of the lake and the hotter Bendigo on the eastern shore are two more exciting areas. Alexandra, south of the lake and the most southerly subregion, was one of the first areas to be developed, while Gibbston, over toward the ski slopes of Queenstown, is the coolest area and in a warm year produces some of the most scented wines. Further north, Lake Wanaka makes exceptional Pinots in breathtakingly beautiful conditions. The Pinot Noirs from the whole region are now challenging those of Burgundy for their variety and style. Marlborough Sauvignon Blanc and Central Otago Pinot Noir—two world originals from one tiny island. Not bad.

nothing compared to what's happening along the Waitaki River, even further south, where several plantings are already yielding exciting results. A new north Canterbury area, around Pyramid Valley to the northwest of Waipara, is another new district that shows great promise with seriously limestony soil. The overriding influences allowing grapes to ripen are low rainfall and free-draining soil. Long, dry summer days lead to a dry, mild fall, letting grapes hang on the vine until May. But then

Marlborough

RED GRAPES
Pinot Noir is by far the most planted red grape variety, with most of it used in still table wine. Merlot is a minor player.

WHITE GRAPES
Sauvignon Blanc rules with about two-thirds of the region's total vineyard area. Chardonnay is next, with Pinot Gris and Riesling following well behind.

CLIMATE
The climate is cool, but sunshine is abundant. Rainfall is scarce between October and April, and frost and wind can cause problems.

SOIL
Soil varies from clay in the Southern Valleys to stony gravel in Awatere. Very stony districts are so well-drained that irrigation is essential.

GEOGRAPHY
Generally low and flat, but the Awatere Valley benefits from protected terraces allowing maximum exposure to the sun.

MARLBOROUGH IS ONE OF THE MOST significant wine regions in the whole world. What, little old Marlborough? Stuck on the northern tip of the South Island of tiny New Zealand? There wasn't a single vine growing there fifty years ago, and that's a big reason that it is so important to this New World of wine that we gratefully inhabit. Marlborough showed that you don't have to possess a track record to excel in the modern world of wine. You can do the whole thing from scratch with some secondhand milk vats and some dairy scientists to make sure the juice doesn't turn to vinegar. You can do it with grapes grown on land so poor even the sheep turn their noses up at it and in a climate that the local agricultural experts said, "Might do for apples but never grapes."

Marlborough. The most modern of modern wine regions. The most radical of radical wine regions. But, because of its astonishing success in creating an entirely new style of wine—the tingly, tangy Sauvignon Blanc, a style that a new generation of wine drinkers was crying out for—also the most commercial of wine regions. This is a commercial success based on quality, personality, and the willingness of the wine drinker to pay a significant price for significant pleasure.

The first plantings in 1973 were basically of whatever variety the growers could get hold of but dominated by Müller-Thurgau and Cabernet Sauvignon (not much sign of these two now). The small plantings of Sauvignon Blanc

MARLBOROUGH SAUVIGNON BLANC

I remember exactly when I first tasted Marlborough Sauvignon Blanc. It was on February 1, 1984, at 11 a.m. On the seventeenth floor of New Zealand House in London. Just inside the door. On the left, third wine along. That's when Montana 1983 was introducing itself to the world. Nobody's world of wine would ever be the same again. There had never before been such a wine that crackled and spat its flavors at you from the glass. A wine that took the whole concept of greenness and expanded it, stretched it, pummeled it, and gloriously reinterpreted it so that suddenly greenness wasn't raw and mean but exhilarating, mouthwatering, tongue-tingling stuff—and it got better.

Cloudy Bay made their first Sauvignon Blanc in 1985, and in 1986 it won the title of best Sauvignon Blanc in the world. From nothing. A wine tasting like nothing had ever tasted before from a vineyard that had never existed before. Yet within a year people were waiting in lines outside wine shops desperate to get an allocation of a bottle or two of this new nectar. These weren't the old wine drinkers who were lining up in the rain an hour before the shop opened. These were a new breed of enthusiasts, a classless breed dismissive of convention and tradition who had found a new wine hero. Marlborough Sauvignon Blanc. The truly radical grape. The grape variety wine snobs cannot bear. Yet all around the world, producers look enviously at Marlborough's success and try their best to craft a Sauvignon Blanc in the same style.

were almost serendipitous—the owner of Montana would have planted whatever arrived in the boxes. Luckily, a few of the vines were Sauvignon Blanc. The whole spectrum of grapes has since been planted there, but like any other great vineyard area, Marlborough is not all-purpose because then you'd have to trade memorable brilliance for overall reliability. Most of Marlborough can't do much with Cabernet Sauvignon, although Syrah is showing good form, and Merlot isn't bad. People thought the cool conditions were tailor-made for Pinot Noir, but it took until the 2003 vintage to work out the best ways to grow and vinify it, and the southern valleys are proving to be the best sites. Chardonnay, too, was expected to be uniformly brilliant. It isn't. Much of it ends up as fizz, but, that said, there are already some stunning luscious, buttery, intense Chardonnays.

Sauvignon Blanc was world-class virtually from its first vintage, and every year new examples appear. I love Marlborough Sauvignon Blanc. You may hate it. No problem. It's that kind of wine; it demands a reaction. It would be nice if Riesling one day demanded a reaction again because Marlborough makes superb Riesling, too, usually dry, occasionally lusciously sweet. But I suspect Pinot Gris will swoon from the applause first.

So where does all this flavor intensity come from? A long, slow ripening season is the key. Blenheim, the main town, often gets more sunshine hours than any other town in New Zealand. Over a ripening season, Marlborough gets about the same amount of heat as Burgundy and slightly less than Bordeaux. But the average daily temperature is lower than either as the sunny ripening season spreads into April or even into May, with cold nights helping to preserve acidity.

This is fine if you can guarantee a dry fall. Almost always, you can. Most of New Zealand's bad fall weather comes in from the Pacific in the east and is soaked up by the North Island. The southerlies get headed off by the Southern Alps, and the wet westerlies during the growing season are fended off by the mountains to the west. Rainfall from February to April is lower than in any other New Zealand wine region, while March is the driest month. Given that it is relatively cool, it is vital that the growers have the confidence to let their fruit hang, and the dry falls give them that (although a fall frost occasionally wreaks havoc). A lack of rain also allows growers to minimize antidisease programs, with substantial cost savings, but it also means irrigation is essential. The valley's north side has as much water as it needs from the Wairau River and its aquifers, which are some of the most plentiful in New Zealand. The south side is more barren, and water needs to be pumped from the north. There is a Southern Valleys irrigation program that has transformed the

grape-growing possibilities, and an increasing number of the best wines is coming from there instead of from the original rocky lands on the north side. This is particularly true for Pinot Noir, which seems to flourish on the clay-rich southern soil, but Sauvignon Blanc flourishes, too; this is because clay is a colder soil than gravel, and it can take a couple of weeks longer to ripen the crop, making it easier to pick fruit that has retained its mouthwatering green pepper and lime zest tanginess. Nevertheless, it needs less water because its soil is more fertile and water-retentive. The vineyards in the north are mostly shallow silt over virtual free-draining gravel. In some vineyards, you can't even see the soil for the stones. Add to this a drying northerly wind, and you need irrigation all right.

Although the central Wairau Valley is the heart of the wine region, a significant number of subregions has developed with genuine differences in their styles of wine. To the south there are river valleys joining the Wairau River, such as the Waihopai, Omaka, and Fairhall. All of these are now developed almost to their maximum. There is also a number of vineyards in the ridges above the valleys. Vineyards have been developed way upstream past Wairau Township. It's much more difficult to ripen grapes up there, and the risk of frost is sometimes severe. In warm years, you might get a bumper crop. In cool years, nothing. Vines have also been widely planted on the seaward side of the main town of Blenheim, particularly at Dillons Point and Rarangi, which is almost on the beach. Results have been surprisingly good.

If you drive southeast out of Blenheim on Highway 1, twisting and turning through the sun-bleached Wither Hills, you come to the Awatere Valley, another subregion of Marlborough. As the climate warms, Awatere becomes ever more important as the source for the pungent green perfumes and flavors so important in Sauvignon Blanc blends. Toward the sea, the land is intensely planted with vines, and exposure to chilly easterly and southerly winds means later bud burst, flowering, and harvest and also greater risk of rain and storms. But the results are tremendous—tingling with sharp, fresh, finely focused fruit. The Awatere Valley is also planted well inland, and the conditions become more extreme with big day-nighttime temperature variations, but the vines also produce stunning whites and some reds.

The search for fresh, crisp flavors continues. Blind River and Grasmere produce exciting flavors, as does Ward; the Ure Valley has blindingly white limestone soil, and the little upland valleys sneaking in from the coast right down to Kekerengu and maybe even further toward the whale-watching center of Kaikoura are being tried out to keep the great Marlborough adventure moving.

The Wairau Valley is the center of the wine industry in Marlborough, but producers have spread out into the outlying valleys in search of cooler conditions. As the climate warms, the Awatere Valley, seen here, becomes ever more important as a source for the pungent green perfumes and flavors so important in Sauvignon Blanc wines.

China

CHINA IS THE NEWEST OF THE NEW and the oldest of the old. There is archaeological evidence of Chinese grapes being fermented as long as eight thousand years ago, and there is sporadic evidence of it ever since, but it is only in the twenty-first century that a grape wine culture seems to finally be taking off.

I've been tasting the occasional Chinese wine literally for more than thirty years. In the old days, it was usually Great Wall (redolent of mothballs) and Dynasty (more recognizable as being derived from the grape). But as early as 1986, I was seeing exciting signs of change. I started tasting wines such as Cabernet Franc, Riesling, and Chardonnay, usually from the Shandong region southeast of Beijing. The Cabernet Franc was weedy but pleasant enough, while the unoaked and fairly low-alcohol Rieslings and Chardonnays were fresh, easy-going, relatively delicate. Shandong's vineyards were mostly on a peninsula jutting out into the Yellow Sea. This brought pleasant temperate conditions—which are in themselves rare in China, whose climate is mostly relatively extreme, and for the most part very continental, leading to hot summers but exceedingly icy cold winters. In other words, conditions quite unlike those of the typical European vineyard. So Shandong did look promising. The only trouble was that storms were fairly frequent in the summer, and in late summer, rains would always arrive before the black grapes had ripened. This would explain the weedy reds, but it also explained the fresh, attractive, low alcohol, early-picked whites. I remember telling anyone who would listen that light, fresh whites were the future for China. Well, they might have been if the Chinese had wanted them, but what they wanted was red. Red was the color of good luck. Red wine is good for your health. So red was what China would set out to make.

WINE REGIONS

In the early part of the twenty-first century, new wine regions began to pop up—in particular, Shanxi, southwest of Beijing, Ningxia further inland, and Xinjiang, way to the northwest up toward Kazakhstan. It all began to make sense the first time I tasted Grace Family Wines from Shanxi. Things gathered pace as other ambitious red wines became available. Silver Heights, Helan Mountain, and most famously Helan Qing Xue, whose 2009 Jia Bei Lan (Little Feet, named after the winemaker's daughter's footprints) won the *Decanter* World Wine Award for the Best Red Bordeaux Varietal costing more than $15. These wines and others were from Ningxia. This area on the east-facing gravel terraces and banks along the Huáng Hé (Yellow River) seems to be the region most probable to excel—at least in the near future, with considerable investment, international, local, and most importantly governmental. But a vast amount of money has also been invested in Shandong. The greater proportion of grapes is actually grown in the challenging conditions of Xinjiang in the northwest. Perhaps the area most promising in the long term might be in the high foothills of Yunnan and Sichuan in the far south, where vineyards at heights of between 5,250 and almost 9,850 feet are being developed by groups such as LVMH. The logistics are nightmarish, but the conditions—temperate, frost-free, with rainfall at all the right times—just might be the best in all of China.

WINES AND THE MARKET

With its massive population, burgeoning middle class, and taste for luxury, China has been an appealing prospective market for wine producers throughout the world. In 2005, China's tariffs on imported wines were reduced from 64 percent to 14 percent, widening the door for imported wines. Currently, wine from grapes accounts for only about 1.5 percent of alcohol consumed in China—but it is growing fast. Initially, interest was primarily in red wines, encouraged by the commonly used translation of wine as "red alcohol," with Bordeaux reds still perceived as the best; but there is also increasing enthusiasm for the great estates of Burgundy, Tuscany, and Napa. However, until relatively recently, most of the wine sold was used in gifting and banqueting; buyers did not need to like—or even taste—the wine. It was all sold on labeling. President Xi Jinping's anticorruption campaign has led to a change in consumer habits, and the wine market has

Xinjiang

Gansu

Ningxia

Shaanxi

Shanxi

Hebei

Tianjin

Shandong

Sichuan

Yunnan

been developing more in tune with the palates of consumers. Thus, there has been an increase in whites and entry-level wines, especially in the economically developed areas of the southeast of the country, with, for instance, Prosecco seeing a large rise in sales. It can't be long before we see a Chinese version.

Production has been stepped up to meet the increase in demand. China has vast vineyards—just under 2 million acres and counting—and is already the second largest grower of Cabernet Sauvignon in the world. Around 80 percent of wine consumed in China is produced domestically from local grapes often blended with a large proportion of cheap bulk wine imports and sold as "Chinese wine." There is, however, a growing number of wineries that are seeking to make genuine China-reared wines. The emphasis is on Cabernet Sauvignon, with plantings rocketing regardless of suitability of vineyards and climates. The best results of recent vintages range from drinkable wines that are recognizably Cabernet to some very good efforts indeed, but even the finest are nothing to strike fear into the hearts of Bordeaux First Growths just yet. That said, in 2009 Domaines Barons de Rothschild (DBR) Lafite famously partnered with CITIC, China's biggest state-owned investment company, to establish vineyards in China with the aim of producing a Chinese "Grand Cru" for domestic consumption. Progress is also hampered by the poor quality of planting material. Varieties such as Marselan show great promise using virus-free stock.

China currently has more than five hundred wineries. Many larger operations, international companies, and joint ventures, including DBR Lafite, have based themselves around the city of Penglai in the coastal province of Shandong. For wine tourism, this makes sense, and some of the extravagant "châteaux" buildings need to be seen to be believed. There is little doubt that the best red wine quality so far has come from further inland—parts of Hebei and Shanxi provinces but, above all, the Mount Helan region in Ningxia province. You still have to bury your vines in winter to counter the extreme cold, but the ripening season does seem compatible with the production of quality red wine grapes, being in fact a little bit cooler than modern-day Bordeaux. You can taste that Bordeaux effect in wines such as Silver Heights' The Summit and Helan Qing Xue's Jia Bei Lan. The Xinjiang area, which is considerably further inland, in the extreme northwest of China, is promising but extremely challenging. Not only is it in a predominantly Muslim area, which has been politically volatile in recent years, it is also a vast distance from potential markets. Even so, it is warm and very dry, but there is ample water runoff from the Tian Shan mountains. Xinjiang has a particularly dry late summer/fall spell during the critical ripening period. It also has hot summer days and very cool nights, which could slow the ripening process and extend hang time. However, this hampers attempts to grow late-ripening varieties, such as Cabernet Sauvignon and Carménère, particularly as winter descends swiftly on this area, with snow often arriving in October.

Dynasty, Changyu, and Great Wall are the major producers in China in terms of volume, controlling around half of grape wine production, but those top boutique wineries are making real quality inroads—Grace Vineyard in Shanxi province and Silver Heights, Helan Qingxue, Chateau Zhihui Yuanshi, and Helan Mountain in Ningxia province. China's first major sparkling wine joint venture has been set up in Ningxia with LVMH, with its white and rosé Chardonnay/Pinot Noir-based wines released in 2014 to general critical acclaim. Their first red was released in 2016. Called Ao Yun (Roaming Cloud), it came from Yunnan, so things really are beginning to move.

Asia

INDIA

India has a long winemaking history, but in spite of a population of 1.3 billion, wine consumption remains minuscule. Tales of the burgeoning Indian middle class abound—supposedly 250 million strong at the moment—but attempts to turn them into a mighty wine-drinking army are proving tough because India is the world's largest whiskey market. Importing wine into India involves all kinds of bureaucratic and logistical hurdles, and it doesn't help that some states ban alcohol altogether, and in others politicians take a very anti-alcohol stance. Most wine drinking takes place in the tourist-friendly and more cosmopolitan centers of Mumbai, New Delhi, Bangalore, and Goa—they account for 80 percent of the national consumption. About 75 percent of this total is produced in India.

India has a lot of vines, more than 275,000 acres. However, of these only 5,760 acres are for wine—a tiny percentage. These vineyards are concentrated in two states—Maharashtra and Karnataka (although Madhya Pradesh has about 57 acres and Tamil Nadu has just under 74 acres). Experts say that the most promising areas for vines are such sub-Himalayan regions as Kashmir, but given the political situation, vineyards probably won't be established there any time soon. Other areas, such as the borders with Nepal and Bhutan, might show promise, but for now the chief region is Nashik in Maharashtra, with about 2,720 acres. Pune is also significant with about 400 acres. Bangalore and southern Karnataka have 1,970 acres and northern Karnataka about 1,010 acres.

Most of the vineyards are planted at heights of between 650 and 1,000 feet. However, there are a few going up to 2,600 feet and gaining a little coolness from the extra height. But we're not talking European cool here, and in any case, the vines never become dormant and deliver two harvests a year—the monsoon crop is understandably less well-regarded. The most widely planted grape is the neutral bulk producer Thomson Seedless, which actually provided a fairly good base for one of the sparkling wines that briefly made a mark on the wider world—Chateau

MAIN WINE REGIONS

1. Madhya Pradesh
2. Maharashtra
3. Karnataka
4. Tamil Nadu

Indage (or Omar Khayyam, as it was labeled). Higher quality varieties are increasingly being planted, with Cabernet Sauvignon obviously taking a leading role, but white grapes, such as Chenin Blanc and Clairette, are showing some style.

Nashik is the most important vineyard region, with the highest number of wine companies, too. Sula Vineyards is the most successful, both in quality and in volume—controlling up to 70 percent of the domestic market. The other winery with an international reputation is Grover Vineyards from Bangalore, whose reputation has been greatly enhanced by employing the world-famous Michel Rolland from Bordeaux as their consultant in 1995. Fratelli, near Pune, has also made some waves, and there is some international investment—Moët & Chandon have begun producing an Indian Chandon sparkler at York

Winery in Nashik, and Alpine Wineries have 247 acres of vineyards near Mysore in Karnataka with a star Bordeaux wine consultant, Stéphane Derenoncourt. But you have to wonder whether really good wines will be possible from these vineyard sites.

INDONESIA

Bali is the only Indonesian wine-producing region, which makes sense given its popularity with Western tourists. The best grapes are grown at altitude, but this is a tropical island, and the heat means the vine never has a dormant period and is endlessly ripening its crops of not very tasty grapes. Hatten Wines is the main producer, and I've had some nice enough rosé.

JAPAN

It's not easy to grow wine grapes in Japan. The problem is too much rain. There are spring and fall monsoons, typhoons in summer, and icy winters. Land is either mountainous or flat and waterlogged; there's little gently sloping terrain, beloved of vine growers. But a trellising system called *tana-zukuri* spreads vines out along wires, so they can dry.

The major viticulture regions, Nagano and Yamanashi, are located near the center of the main island of Honshu, and producers face a number of climate challenges during the growing season. The trouble is the damp. Too much rain, too much humidity and relative warmth; the result of all these is a disease paradise, particularly for the rot- and mildew-prone classic European grape varieties. Potentially the best area for European varieties is on the northern island of Hokkaido. It's much cooler there—summer and winter, with some of the vines needing burying to protect them from the winter freeze—but it's also significantly drier, and some attractive whites, even including organic examples, are surfacing.

In Japan, 90 percent of the grapes grown are table grapes; very few are of the European wine grape species *Vitis vinifera*. Some wineries try to use table grapes or wine grape hybrids (which are easier to grow than *vinifera*), and wines made from Delaware, Kyoho, Ryugan, and Muscat Bailey A are common, but they can have that distinctive and generally unappealing "foxy" or chemical/epoxy character found in species other than *vinifera*.

Some vaguely interesting Japanese wine is made from Koshu, a pink-skinned, apparently *vinifera* grape, believed to have come to Japan from Europe many centuries ago, via the Silk Road. Koshu usually produces a clean, dry, light-bodied wine with a delicate citrus character that pairs well with sushi and sashimi. Good Koshu

producers include Grace, Château Mercian, Katsunuma Winery (good sparkling Koshu), Marufuji Rubaiyat, and Asagiri Wine Company. However, several wineries are making considerable efforts with red and white wine, often using mainstream *vinifera* varieties. Suntory in Yamanashi, Yamazaki Winery in Hokkaido, and some of the upper level Château Mercian wines, including a very tasty Private Reserve Chardonnay, are well worth a try.

SOUTH KOREA

South Korea is an increasingly enthusiastic wine-drinking nation, but the wine is almost all imported. With very cold winters and hot humid summers, *vinifera* vines find it pretty difficult to flourish. An occasional new winery does emerge, with a fanfare of French grape varieties and new French barrels, but the limited production is dominated by the large Doo San Company. Some wine is made from *Vitis amurensis*, the species of vine originating on the Amur River in Siberia and capable of withstanding extreme cold.

THAILAND

The very concept of growing wine grapes anywhere within Thailand's tropics calls for a suspension of disbelief, but Thailand, close to the equator, has fewer than eight major wineries, producing nearly a million bottles of wine a year. Being tropical, the vines don't go dormant, and you can get two or sometimes more crops a year, but any producer enthusiastic about quality limits the harvest to one a year. The first still wines appeared in 1995 from Chateau de Loei in northeastern Thailand, using Chenin Blanc and Syrah. Siam Winery, which had begun producing wine coolers in 1986, launched its Monsoon Valley label in 2003; the wines are now exported to more than fifteen countries. Siam had initially made a name for itself by making wines from "floating vineyards" in the Caho Phraya Deltea south of Bangkok. Entry-level red and white blends are made mainly from hybrid grapes, but premium range wines made from grapes such as Chenin Blanc, Colombard, and Shiraz grown at high elevation in the Pak Chong hills or in the Hua Hin Hills vineyard show potential.

VIETNAM

Because Vietnam was part of French Indo-China, the French predictably tried to make vineyards work there. But in this tropical country, with vines giving up to three harvests a year, they weren't a great success. Vineyards are in the cooler regions north of Ho Chi Minh City. Dalat Winery is the country's leading winery. For the record, Cambodia has a single winery, too.

Index